Beginner's Guide to Adobe Fresco

Enhancing your Images using the Digital Paint Brush

Jennifer Harder

Apress®

Beginner's Guide to Adobe Fresco: Enhancing your Images using the Digital Paint Brush

Jennifer Harder
Delta, BC, Canada

ISBN-13 (pbk): 979-8-8688-1556-0   ISBN-13 (electronic): 979-8-8688-1557-7
https://doi.org/10.1007/979-8-8688-1557-7

Copyright © 2025 by Jennifer Harder

This work is subject to copyright. All rights are reserved by the Publisher, whether the whole or part of the material is concerned, specifically the rights of translation, reprinting, reuse of illustrations, recitation, broadcasting, reproduction on microfilms or in any other physical way, and transmission or information storage and retrieval, electronic adaptation, computer software, or by similar or dissimilar methodology now known or hereafter developed.

Trademarked names, logos, and images may appear in this book. Rather than use a trademark symbol with every occurrence of a trademarked name, logo, or image we use the names, logos, and images only in an editorial fashion and to the benefit of the trademark owner, with no intention of infringement of the trademark.

The use in this publication of trade names, trademarks, service marks, and similar terms, even if they are not identified as such, is not to be taken as an expression of opinion as to whether or not they are subject to proprietary rights.

While the advice and information in this book are believed to be true and accurate at the date of publication, neither the authors nor the editors nor the publisher can accept any legal responsibility for any errors or omissions that may be made. The publisher makes no warranty, express or implied, with respect to the material contained herein.

> Managing Director, Apress Media LLC: Welmoed Spahr
> Acquisitions Editor: Spandana Chatterjee
> Editorial Assistant: Gryffin Winkler

Cover designed by eStudioCalamar

Distributed to the book trade worldwide by Springer Science+Business Media New York, 1 New York Plaza, New York, NY 10004. Phone 1-800-SPRINGER, fax (201) 348-4505, e-mail orders-ny@springer-sbm.com, or visit www.springeronline.com. Apress Media, LLC is a Delaware LLC and the sole member (owner) is Springer Science + Business Media Finance Inc (SSBM Finance Inc). SSBM Finance Inc is a **Delaware** corporation.

For information on translations, please e-mail booktranslations@springernature.com; for reprint, paperback, or audio rights, please e-mail bookpermissions@springernature.com.

Apress titles may be purchased in bulk for academic, corporate, or promotional use. eBook versions and licenses are also available for most titles. For more information, reference our Print and eBook Bulk Sales web page at http://www.apress.com/bulk-sales.

Any source code or other supplementary material referenced by the author in this book is available to readers on GitHub. For more detailed information, please visit https://www.apress.com/gp/services/source-code.

If disposing of this product, please recycle the paper

Table of Contents

About the Author ix

About the Technical Reviewer xi

Acknowledgments xiii

Introduction xv

Chapter 1: What Is Adobe Fresco? 1

    What Is Adobe Fresco? 1

    What Applications Should I Know to Be Able to Use Adobe Fresco to Its Full Potential? 2

        Photoshop 2

        Illustrator 3

        Creative Cloud Files and Libraries 4

        What Fresco Is and What It Is Not 5

    Resources, System Requirements, and Versions of Software Based on Device 5

        Mac and PC Options on the Desktop for Fresco 9

    Installing and Opening Adobe Fresco 9

        Taking the Interactive Tour and Reviewing the Learning Tutorials 11

        Exiting the Application 15

    Summary 16

Chapter 2: Starting a New Document in Fresco 17

    Starting a New Document in Fresco 18

        Working with Document Presets and Custom Size Options for Files That Are Recent, Saved, Digital, and Print 19

        Understand the Power Plan Dialog Box Message 28

        Opening a Current Document with Preserved Photoshop Layers 29

    Title Bar Menu: Commonly Required Actions, Upper Help, and Settings 32

TABLE OF CONTENTS

    Commonly Required Actions 33

    Saving Files 34

    Navigation: Zooming In and Out and Panning 34

    Undo and Redo 35

    Help Menu Options 35

    Settings Menu and Adjusting the Canvas on the Desktop 40

    App Settings 45

    Setting Full Screen 46

On the Desktop: Can I Use My Stylus, Pen Tablet, or Mouse? 47

Exiting File: Auto Save to the Cloud and File Format 48

Uploading Files onto the Creative Cloud 52

Project: Creating a New Blank File 55

Summary 57

Chapter 3: Exploring the Workspace of Fresco and Its Tools: Part 1 59

Using the Toolbar Panel 63

Brush Tools and Their Options 67

    Pixel Brushes 69

    Live Brushes 119

    Vector Brushes 127

    Eraser Brushes (Pixel and Vector) 141

    Smudge Brushes 151

    Painting Inside and Outside of a Boundary 158

    Touch Shortcuts for Various Brushes to Quickly Change the Brush Size 162

Project: Adding Custom Brushes to Fresco from Photoshop Through the CC Library 164

    Adding Other Brushes to the Library from Photoshop 164

Summary 188

Chapter 4: Exploring the Workspace of Fresco and Its Tools: Part 2 189

Move and Transform Tool 190

    Transform (Ctrl+T): Scale, Rotate, and Constraint Options 193

    Skew 199

iv

TABLE OF CONTENTS

 Distort 200

 Perspective 202

 Liquify 205

 Additional Grid and Future Settings 224

Selection Creation Tools and Their Options 227

 Lasso (L) 229

 Magic Wand (W) 240

 Paint Selection 243

 Rectangle Selection 245

 Ellipse Selection 246

 Polygon: Adding or Subtracting Sides from the Selection 248

 Key Commands Deselecting or Inverting an Active Selection 251

Fill (G) Paint Bucket Tool 251

Shape Tools 253

 Working with Default Shapes 254

 Tips on Using the Contextual Task Bar with Shapes 257

 Project: Learning to Import Shapes (SVG) from Photoshop 261

Text Tool and Its Properties 276

 Creating Vertical Type 284

 Note on Troubleshooting Missing Fonts 286

Eyedropper Tool (I): Single and Multiple Color Eyedropper 286

Altering the Color Chip (RGB, HSB) Solid and Multicolor Swatches 288

 Project: Add Some Colors from the Creative Cloud Library Using Photoshop or Illustrator 292

Overview of Place Tool for Graphics 297

Project: Practicing with Your Brushes and Selections on a Single Layer 298

Summary 313

Chapter 5: Working with Layers in Fresco and the Vertical Taskbar 315

Layer Panel 316

Layer Properties Panel 322

 Layer Blending Modes and Layer Opacity 323

Precision Tool 330

TABLE OF CONTENTS

Comments Tool 331

Adding and Editing Pixel and Vector Layers with Layer Actions and Icons 332

    More Layer Options and Actions 336

Reference Layer (Line Art, Selections, and Shapes) 353

Masking Different Kinds of Layers and Their Content Setting 357

    Editing the Mask and Reveal/Hide Layer Masking in the Contextual Task Bar 358

    Mask Enabled and Mask Linked 362

    Text Layer Masking 364

    Mask Properties: Mask Density 364

    Layer Mask Actions 366

Appearances 371

    Brightness/Contrast 372

    Hue/Saturation 375

    Color Balance 381

    Clipping Masks 386

    Adjustment Layer Masks 390

Project: Review Working with the Layers in a Fresco Document 394

    Review of Previous Layers 396

    Adding Additional Layers 399

Summary 423

Chapter 6: Working with Drawing Aids on the Canvas 425

Working with the Drawing Aids 426

    Ruler 426

    Circle 430

    Square 433

    Polygon 435

    Adjusting Settings, Hiding, and Showing 440

    Working with the Grid and Perspective in Precision Options 440

    Create a Perspective Grid 454

    Using Other Tools with the Perspective Grid 455

TABLE OF CONTENTS

Project 1: Creating a Geometric Tile Pattern and Using Drawing Aids 457

Project 2: Drawing Creatures with the Drawing Aids 470

Project 3: Drawing a Cityscape 481

Summary 497

Chapter 7: Importing Images and Editing 499

Placing and Importing Options 500

Color Profile and Color Mode Conversion Tips for Photoshop Users 507

Project: Steps to Adding Graphics to a Creative Cloud Library Using Photoshop 509

Other Importing Options 517

Project: Painting over an Image Layer and Overlaying a Pixel Layer to Edit
with Brushes and Layer Properties 526

Saving Your Files Review 538

How to Remove or Download Files from the Creative Cloud Desktop or Fresco Home
Page 538

Summary 543

Chapter 8: Basic Animation in Fresco 545

Creating a New Document for Animation 546

Creating GIF Animations with Motion Layers 552

Adding a Frame-by-Frame Layer Motion and Its Actions 554

Define an Animation Using a Motion Path and Path Actions 576

Adding Clipping Masks or Layer Masks to an Animation 609

Configuring Motion Settings 617

Play All and Pause Animation to Adjust the Frames 622

Publish and Export in Various Motion Formats 624

Motion Settings 626

Adjusting the Timing by Adding More Frames to Improve Motions 631

Timelapse Settings 633

Possible New Drawing and Animation Features That Are to Come 636

Animation Photoshop Tips 637

TABLE OF CONTENTS

Project Idea: Creating a Basic Animation 639

    Layer Motion Properties for Path Layers 646

    Fresco Final Thoughts on Basic Animation 656

Summary 657

Chapter 9: Exporting, Editing Files, and Using Them Later in Other Adobe Apps 659

Share: Publish and Export Settings 660

    Pattern Options 665

    Additional Share Options 671

What Is "Invite In"? 675

Downloading from the Creative Cloud Desktop 675

    Working in Photoshop with Your Fresco File 676

Recommended Exported File Formats to Use in Other Adobe Applications 679

    Animate 679

    InDesign 680

    Video Applications 681

    Adobe Dreamweaver and the Web 682

    Getting Additional Inspiration from Behance 682

Project: Saving an Exported File 683

Summary 683

Index 685

About the Author

Jennifer Harder has worked in the graphic design industry for over 20 years. She has a degree in graphic communications and has taught Acrobat and Adobe Creative Cloud courses at Langara College. She is also an author of several Apress books and related videos.

About the Technical Reviewer

Sultana Begum is a semiconductor product management expert and AI technology enthusiast with over 12+ years of experience at Intel and Accenture. She is a quantum computing enthusiast with a deep understanding of quantum mechanics and physics principles of Qubits. She is the lead author of the book *Competitive Semiconductor Product Management*. Sultana held critical roles in technical product marketing and hardware and software product management to gain broad and deep-rooted expertise in the semiconductor technology industry. With deep technical expertise and a keen eye for strategic thinking, her expertise spreads widely across semiconductor design development to define and execute a competitive product strategy, with hands-on experience in launching multiple software and hardware products.

Sultana holds both bachelor's and master's degrees in electronics, an MBA in product management, and Stanford LEAD Executive Management Education from Stanford University.

Acknowledgments

Because of their patience and advice, I would like to thank the following people, for without them I could never have written this book:

- My parents, for encouraging me to read large computer textbooks that would one day inspire me to write my own books and for their assistance in selecting photos for chapter projects
- My dad, for reviewing the first draft before I sent a proposal
- My friends and coworkers who encouraged me to write this book about creating digital art

I would also like to thank Spandana Chatterjee and Sowmya Thodur at Apress for showing me how to lay out a professional textbook and pointing out that even when you think you've written it all, there's still more to write. Also, thanks to the technical reviewer for providing encouraging comments and to the rest of the Apress team for being involved in the printing of this book and making my dream a reality again. I am truly grateful and blessed.

Introduction

Welcome to the book *Beginner's Guide to Adobe Fresco*. In this introductory guide, we will be exploring one of Adobe's newer Creative Cloud applications. Adobe Fresco is a unique drawing application that was added in 2019 to the suite of Adobe Creative Cloud. In this book's chapters, we will explore the application and its latest updates.

As a graphic artist, you may be familiar with using Adobe Photoshop and Illustrator but may not have had the opportunity to use this newer product. Fresco allows you to use a combination of vector and raster (pixelated) layers and brushes to create a digital painting effect to enhance your artistic designs or create a simple animation.

We will look at and create several projects throughout the book so that you can practice your skills.

If you are not familiar with Fresco, you may want to know what its practical applications are for your next design project. Chapters 1 through 6 of this book will explore when Fresco can be used as a stand-alone creative application while using its various tools, brush options, and panels. However, in Chapter 7, we will also look at how to import your current artwork, created with other Adobe applications like Photoshop, into Fresco to enhance the design. Later in Chapter 8, we will look at Fresco's basic animation options. Finally, in Chapter 9, we will look at export options so that you can use the final files for projects and share them with other Adobe applications outside of the Creative Cloud Desktop online file folder.

Readers will discover that Fresco is a great application to add to your "tool belt" of knowledge when your clients ask for that additional artistic brush effect to be applied to a project. Throughout the chapters, you will also see the various similarities between this application and Photoshop and Illustrator.

Note This book will focus on the application being used mainly on the Windows desktop, but there will be Adobe resource links in the book for those that are using other Mac iOS systems like the iPad and iPhone. Fresco is not currently available for the Mac desktop, which will be explained later in Chapter 1.

INTRODUCTION

However, if you would like to follow along in this book, make sure that before you begin, you have a subscription to the Adobe Creative Cloud. In my case, I have an Individual license, but you may have a Business, Student & Teacher, or some other plan. More details on these plans can be found here:

https://www.adobe.com/creativecloud/plans.html

Note Because Fresco for Windows desktop is not sold separately, once on the webpage to review which plans included Fresco, click the link such as "See all plans & pricing details." In my case, I am using Creative Cloud All Apps, but if you mostly work in Photoshop and not Illustrator, then you could just purchase the Photoshop option, and Fresco is included in the price.

Once you have paid for the application, you will then follow the instructions provided to download and install the application:

https://helpx.adobe.com/download-install/kb/creative-cloud-desktop-app-download.html

If you already have the Creative Cloud Desktop installed and available on your computer, you may have already installed several Adobe applications including Fresco. However, if you have not, it is important to read Chapter 1 so that you can learn more about installing Fresco and its supporting applications.

The project files for this book can be found at the following link:

Apress/A-Beginners-Guide-to-Adobe-Fresco

Let's now begin our creative journey.

CHAPTER 1

What Is Adobe Fresco?

In this chapter, we will look at what the Adobe Fresco application is and is not, when Adobe Fresco can be used by designers, and how to install the application from the Creative Cloud Desktop as well as what other applications can be used in conjunction with Fresco. You will also discover what resources are available to you, to learn more about the application. I will also refer to additional resources if you do or do not have the same platform as what is described in this book. Finally, we will then take a quick tour of the Fresco home page once you have opened the application and learn how to exit the application.

Note There are no projects in this chapter. However, subsequent chapters will have projects which can be found at the link provided in the introduction.

What Is Adobe Fresco?

As mentioned in the introduction, Adobe Fresco appeared as one of the Creative Cloud applications in 2019. It is considered a drawing and painting application that can be used to also create basic animations. While Photoshop and Illustrator can also be used to do many of the functions of Fresco with their brushes and painting effects, the purpose of Fresco is to focus more on the creative side of art rather than technical. This is not to say that artistic photos cannot be a part of Fresco. As we will see in later chapters, they can play an important role in the creation of your artwork. However, as you will see, using touch, stylus, or mouse, you can focus on emulating an artistic illustration style rather than fixating on other things that you would expect to focus on in Photoshop, like intensive color correction or working with filters. Where Fresco excels is in its ability to emulate different brush styles to make painterly-like effects.

CHAPTER 1 WHAT IS ADOBE FRESCO?

You can learn more about this from the following link:

https://helpx.adobe.com/fresco/using/what-is-adobe-fresco.html

What Applications Should I Know to Be Able to Use Adobe Fresco to Its Full Potential?

While Fresco can be a stand-alone program and is the main focus of this book, it is best suited to working with a few of the Adobe applications which I will mention here briefly and will then mention in various chapters as they apply to the work which will be done in Fresco. Refer to Figure 1-1.

New power for the paintbrush.

Figure 1-1. *Adobe Creative Cloud Fresco app icon*

Photoshop

Adobe Photoshop, as mentioned, is an application used for working with digital images and applying color correction or filter effects to improve or distort an image for artistic purposes. Many of the brushes that you will encounter in Fresco are also present in Photoshop. Other similar tools that you will encounter are for color adjustments to all or sections of art as well as warping and distortion that I will discuss more in Chapters 3, 4, and 5. Images and other assets can be created in Photoshop and then later imported into Fresco in various ways as you will see in upcoming chapters such as Chapters 6 and 7. So, if you already have experience with Photoshop, this is good so that you can compare the two workflows. As you will see in Fresco, however, many of the tools are simplified for this application, and so, a beginner artist may want to start in Fresco first to build up their creative skills and then tackle more advanced topics in Photoshop. Refer to Figure 1-2.

Figure 1-2. *Adobe Creative Cloud Photoshop app icon*

For more details on Photoshop, if you need to reference some tool for comparison, information can be found at the following link:

https://helpx.adobe.com/support/photoshop.html

After reading this book, if Photoshop is of interest to you, here are some books that I have written which you may want to consider:

- *Accurate Layer Selections Using Photoshop's Selection Tools*
- *Perspective Warps and Distorts with Adobe Tools: Volume 1*
- *A Beginner's Guide to Digital Image Repair in Photoshop: Volume 1*
- *A Beginner's Guide to Digital Image Repair in Photoshop: Volume 2*

Illustrator

Adobe Illustrator is a drawing illustration program that can be used to create artistic and technical drawings. Having prior knowledge of working with Illustrator can be an asset but is not a requirement to working with Fresco. However, if you do, as you progress through this book, you will discover that there are some related tools that Illustrator has that are very similar to the tools in Fresco, such as artistic brushes and tools for the purpose of distortion. Drawings that you create in Illustrator can also be imported into Fresco but only after a conversion using Photoshop. However, some features can be exported back to Illustrator afterward. I will discuss how to do this in Chapters 8 and 9. Refer to Figure 1-3.

Figure 1-3. *Adobe Creative Cloud Illustrator app*

For more details on Illustrator, if you need to reference some tool for comparison, information can be found at the following link:

https://helpx.adobe.com/support/illustrator.html

After reading this book, if Illustrator is of interest to you, here are some books that I have written which you may want to consider:

- *Perspective Warps and Distorts with Adobe Tools: Volume 2*
- *Creating Infographics with Adobe Illustrator: Volume 1*

CHAPTER 1   WHAT IS ADOBE FRESCO?

- *Creating Infographics with Adobe Illustrator: Volume 2*
- *Creating Infographics with Adobe Illustrator: Volume 3*

Additional books that I have written are available on the Apress and Springer Nature site as well.

Creative Cloud Files and Libraries

My files that you will be working with in Fresco, as well as your own files, will need to be stored in the Creative Cloud Desktop and Creative Cloud "Files" or "Your files" area as you will see in later chapters. These stored Fresco files will update as you work on them. However, some graphics and brushes that you created in applications, such as Photoshop, Illustrator, and other Adobe applications, can be stored and imported into Fresco using that application's Libraries panels as you create your personal libraries, which are collectively found in the "Your libraries" tab. We will look at this in more detail in later chapters, throughout the book. Refer to Figure 1-4.

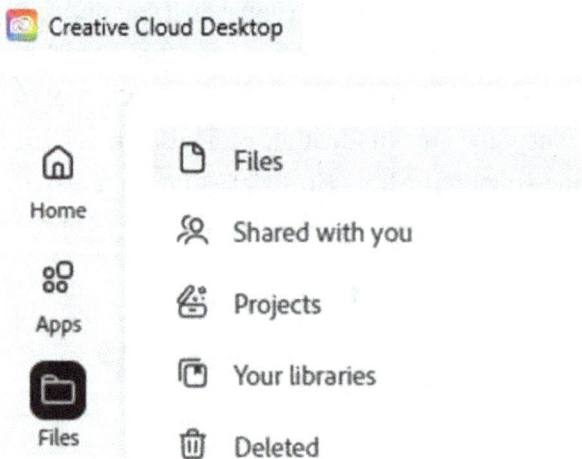

Figure 1-4. *Creative Cloud Desktop files area with the Files tab selected*

What Fresco Is and What It Is Not

While Fresco is an artistic application that can do a number of painterly things that can also be accomplished in Photoshop and Illustrator, it will in no way replace either application. Its focus is on creating artistic illustration and painterly effects and is not intended for professional color correction of photos or very detailed technical illustration. However, art from either of those Adobe applications can be enhanced with Fresco.

Resources, System Requirements, and Versions of Software Based on Device

After you have downloaded Creative Cloud from your desktop, open the application. Refer to Figure 1-5.

Figure 1-5. *Creative Cloud Desktop app shortcut and application header*

However, before you install Fresco, you can review the various applications that are part of your plan. You can view all these applications in the area under Apps ➤ All Apps, and in this case, if you are working on the desktop, set the platform to Desktop to narrow down your search as it may be found under the section called More apps from Adobe. Refer to Figure 1-6.

CHAPTER 1　WHAT IS ADOBE FRESCO?

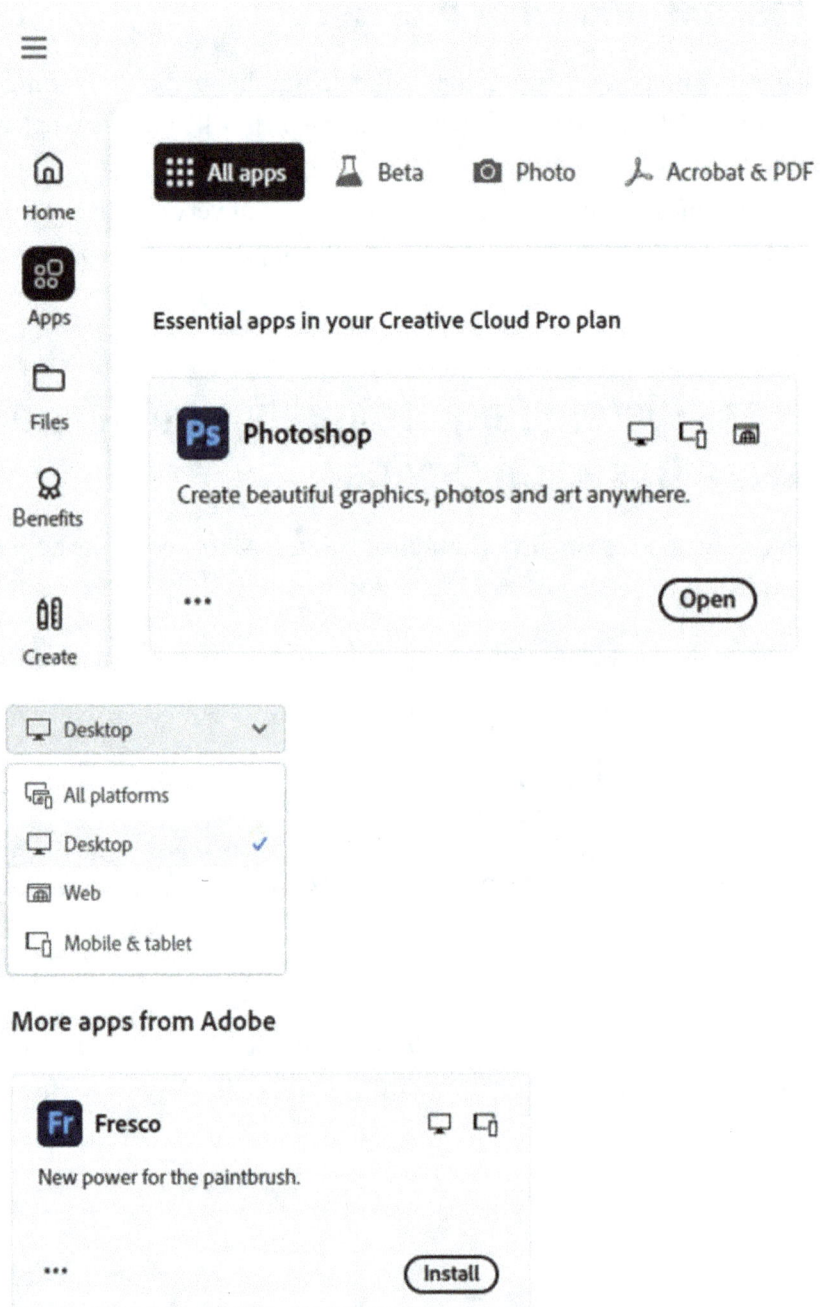

Figure 1-6. *Creative Cloud Desktop app in the All apps selection with platform Desktop selected and Fresco app option displayed ready to install*

CHAPTER 1   WHAT IS ADOBE FRESCO?

Most Fresco resources that I refer to in this book can be found at the following link through Adobe Help:

https://helpx.adobe.com/support/adobe-fresco.html

In your case, you may have already installed Photoshop and Illustrator. Once they are installed, the icon will change to an open button; you can then click the open button if you need to test that the application is working. File ➤ Exit in each application will allow you to close the applications if you do not plan to use them now. However, they are optional, and I will only be discussing them as they relate to Fresco. I recommend, for this book, installing them anyway so that you can follow along with any figures in this book. Refer to Figure 1-7.

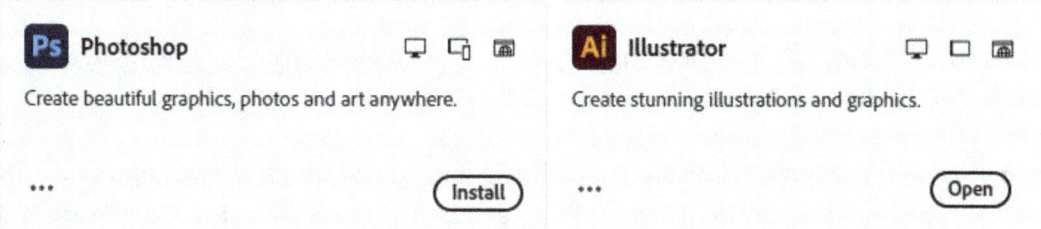

Figure 1-7. *Creative Cloud Desktop apps Adobe Photoshop and Adobe Illustrator*

Note   The desktop application's Camera Raw, Bridge, or Media Encoder may be downloaded as well, but they are not required for this book and will not be discussed in this book. Refer to Figure 1-8.

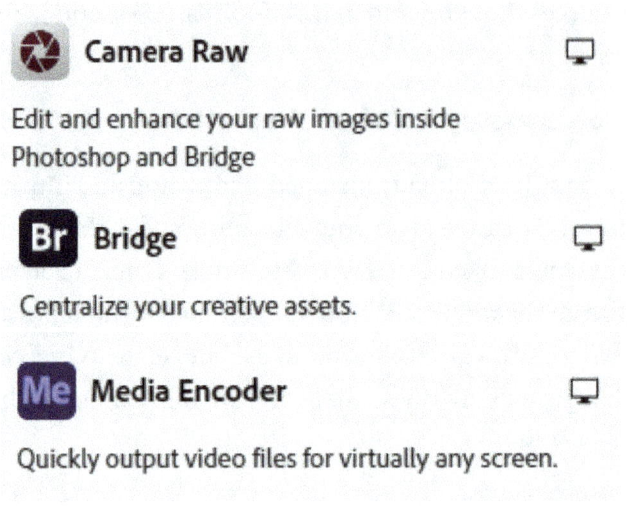

CHAPTER 1 WHAT IS ADOBE FRESCO?

Figure 1-8. *Creative Cloud Desktop apps Adobe Camera Raw, Adobe Bridge, and Adobe Media Encoder*

Other optional applications such as InDesign, Animate, Dreamweaver, and those for video will be briefly mentioned later in Chapter 4 and Chapter 9, but are not required for this book.

For system requirements for those applications, you can refer to the following link and search for the application in the list that you have installed or wish to install:

https://helpx.adobe.com/creative-cloud/system-requirements.html

As mentioned, if you have a Windows PC computer, you will also see in your "More apps from Adobe" area the application Fresco. However, if you have a Mac, this application may not be available, and the next section will explain some options for Fresco. Refer to Figure 1-9.

CHAPTER 1 WHAT IS ADOBE FRESCO?

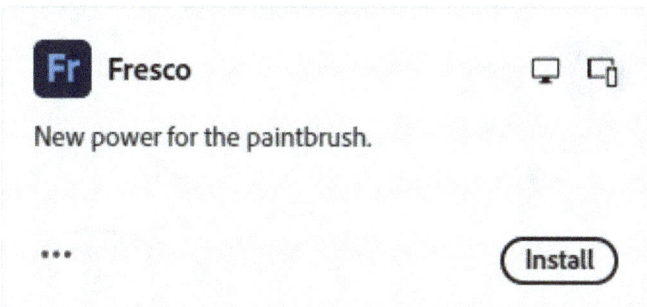

Figure 1-9. *Adobe Fresco app is installed from the Creative Cloud Desktop*

Mac and PC Options on the Desktop for Fresco

In this book, the focus is on using Fresco on the Windows desktop, as there is no desktop version available for the MacOS computer.

Before you install, you can review platform and system requirements here:

https://helpx.adobe.com/fresco/release-notes.html
https://helpx.adobe.com/fresco/system-requirements.html

The current version that I am using for this book is 5.5.5 on my Windows 11 computer.

Alternatively, for Mac users, Fresco is available for iPhone and iPad.

For more details on this, you can refer to the following links:

https://helpx.adobe.com/fresco/using/fresco-on-iphone.html
https://helpx.adobe.com/fresco/using/supported-features-ios-windows.html

Installing and Opening Adobe Fresco

Once you have installed applications like Photoshop, you can then install Fresco for the desktop as well. Once complete, the application button in the Creative Cloud Desktop will change to Open, and then, you can click the button to open the application. Refer to Figure 1-10.

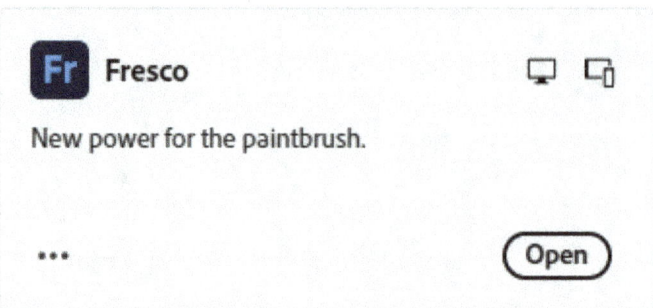

Figure 1-10. *The Adobe Fresco app is installed and can now be opened*

Note that the Adobe Creative Cloud Desktop will keep your applications up to date and will alert you if you need to update any application that is part of your subscription. This can be viewed under the Installed apps area, and you can click View updates at any time to check what the updates are. Currently, I am getting a message that All installed apps are up-to-date. Refer to Figure 1-11.

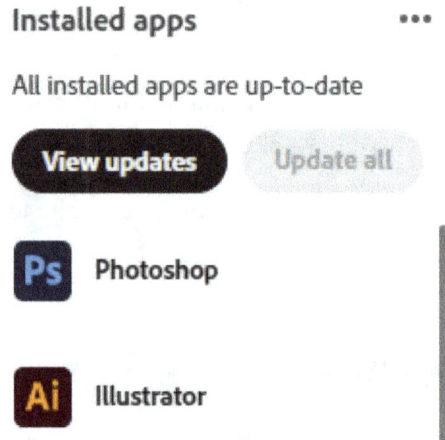

Figure 1-11. *Check for updates in the Creative Cloud Desktop and install when available*

CHAPTER 1   WHAT IS ADOBE FRESCO?

Taking the Interactive Tour and Reviewing the Learning Tutorials

Once Fresco is open, you will be presented with the Home page. From here, you can begin to Start a new document or view any Recent files you may have created that are stored in the Creative Cloud Desktop files area, as we will review in Chapter 2. Refer to Figure 1-12.

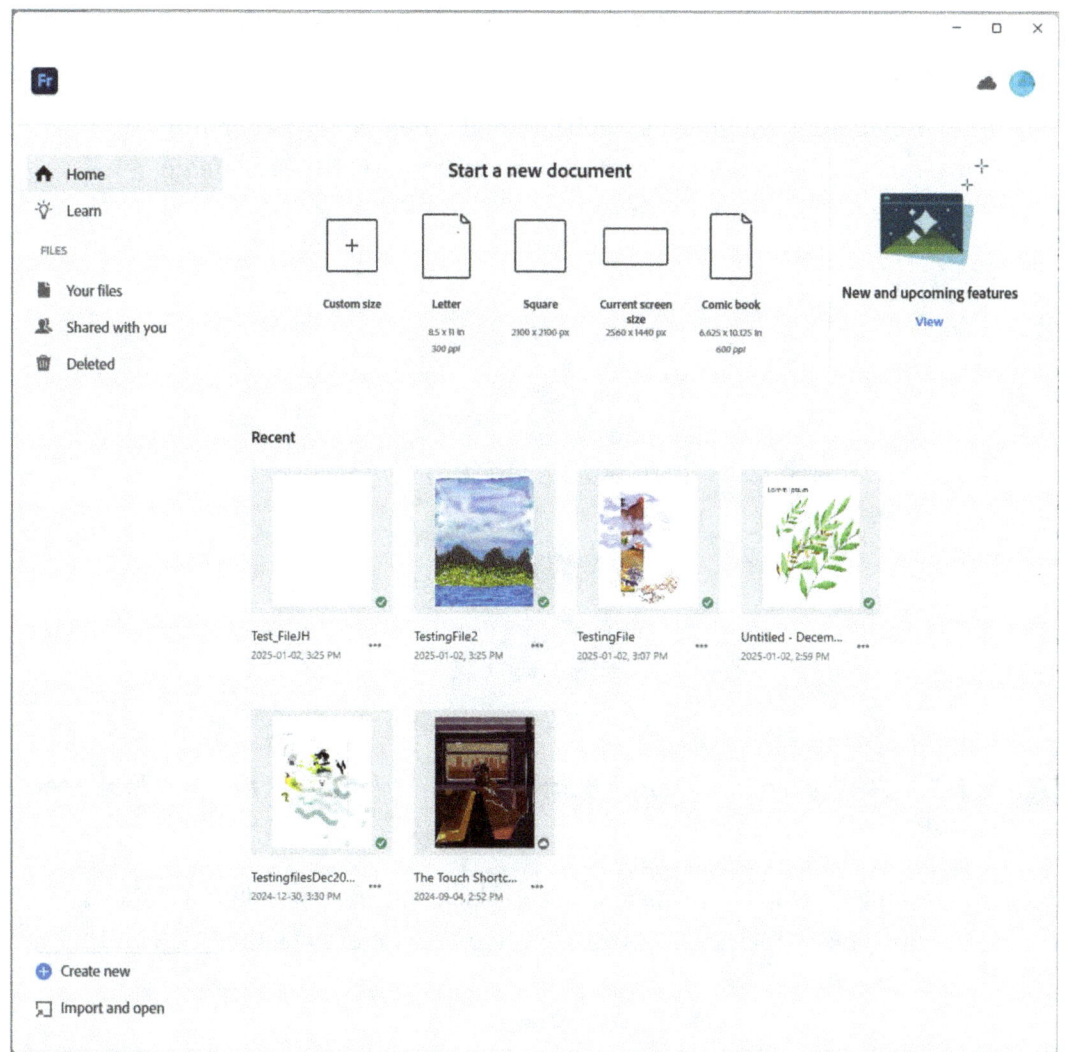

Figure 1-12. *Adobe Fresco Home page and its options*

11

Rather than going to the Creative Cloud Desktop, you can check from the File area in Fresco, by clicking the icons below the word Files on the left:

- Your files: Using the icons above the previews of the files, can be sorted by date modified, date created, name as well as in ascending or descending order, on the right are more icons refresh, create a new folder, or view as a list. Refer to Figure 1-13.

- Shared with you: Files that you are sharing if you are working with others. No files will show in this area if you are not sharing documents with others.

- Deleted: Any deleted files will be found in the Deleted folder and will remain in the Creative Cloud Desktop for at least 30 days. Refer to Figure 1-13 for icon reference.

Figure 1-13. *Review your currently active Creative Cloud files in the Adobe Fresco application*

In the lower left of the Home page, you can also create new documents or also import and open files which I will discuss in Chapter 2. Refer to Figures 1-12 and 1-14.

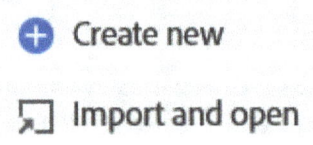

Figure 1-14. *Fresco options for creating a new document or importing and opening a current document*

CHAPTER 1 WHAT IS ADOBE FRESCO?

If you want to take an interactive type of tour as you work in the application, you can click the Learn button icon below the Home button, and this will present you with over 20 different Hands-on tutorials and Video tutorials to help you get started. Refer to Figure 1-15.

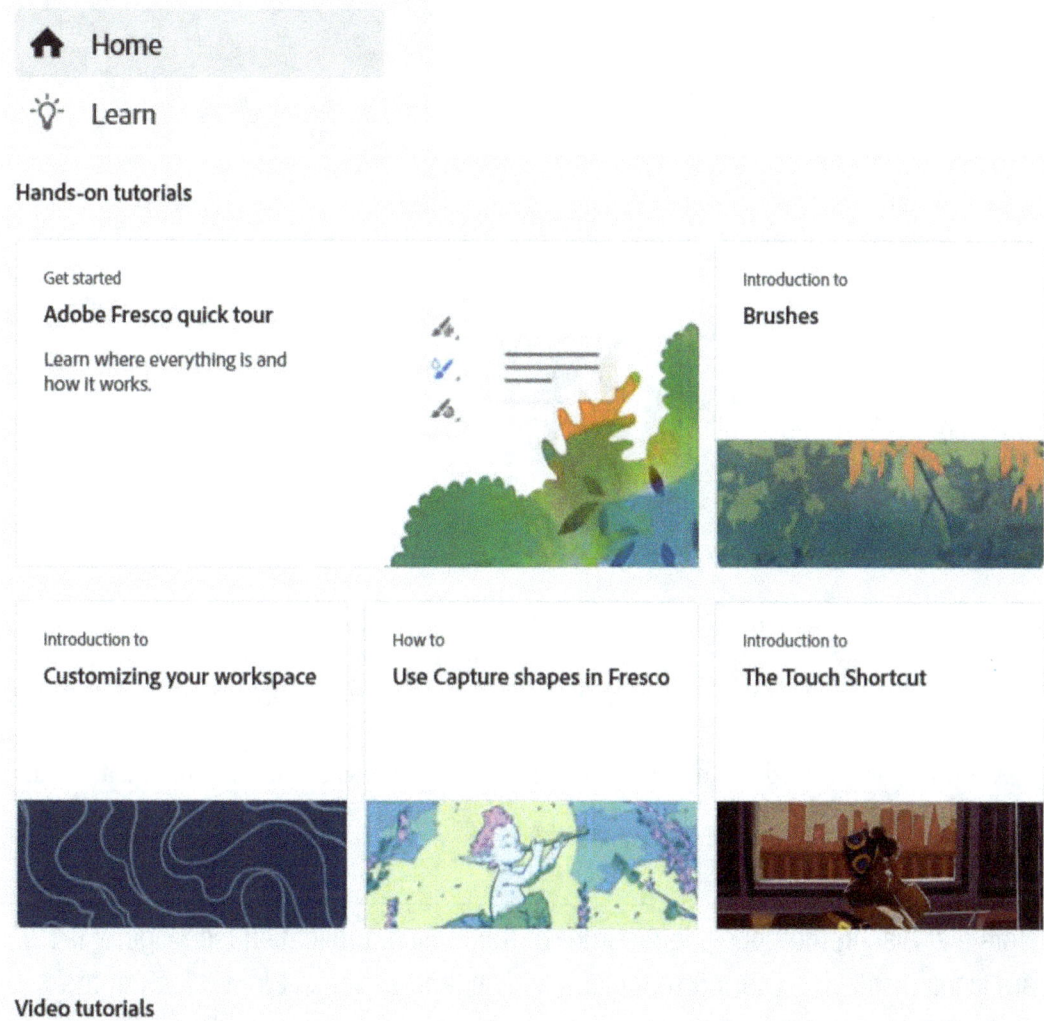

Figure 1-15. *From the Fresco Home page, you can click the Learn tab to find a variety of fun tutorials*

The first tutorial called Get started – Adobe Fresco quick tour is a good interactive tour you can view and will assist you as you go through this book. I recommend clicking and viewing all the tutorials as time permits.

13

CHAPTER 1 WHAT IS ADOBE FRESCO?

Clicking back to the Home page, on the right-hand side, you will see an area called New and upcoming features which I will discuss in more detail later in the book. For now, click this View link to check out the latest features. Refer to Figure 1-12 and Figure 1-16.

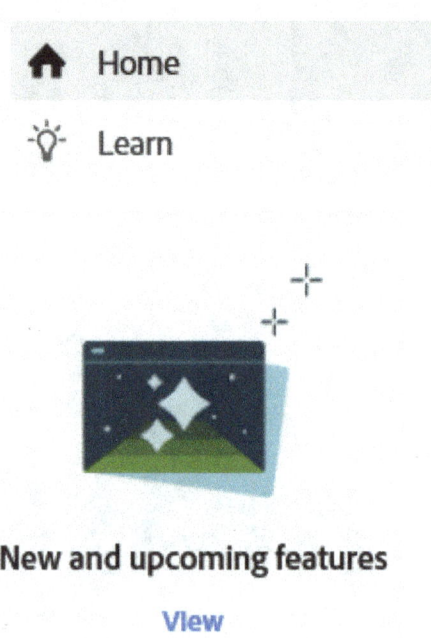

Figure 1-16. *Fresco Home page with options to view new and upcoming features*

Alternatively, as updates are introduced, you can review the following link as well:

https://helpx.adobe.com/fresco/using/whats-new.html

Note that also in the upper right corner of the Fresco application (see Figure 1-12) are icons displaying your current cloud activity and settings. We will look at the Fresco menu app settings in more detail in Chapter 2. If you open the dialog box, click the X in the upper right corner if you need to close it. Refer to Figure 1-17.

CHAPTER 1   WHAT IS ADOBE FRESCO?

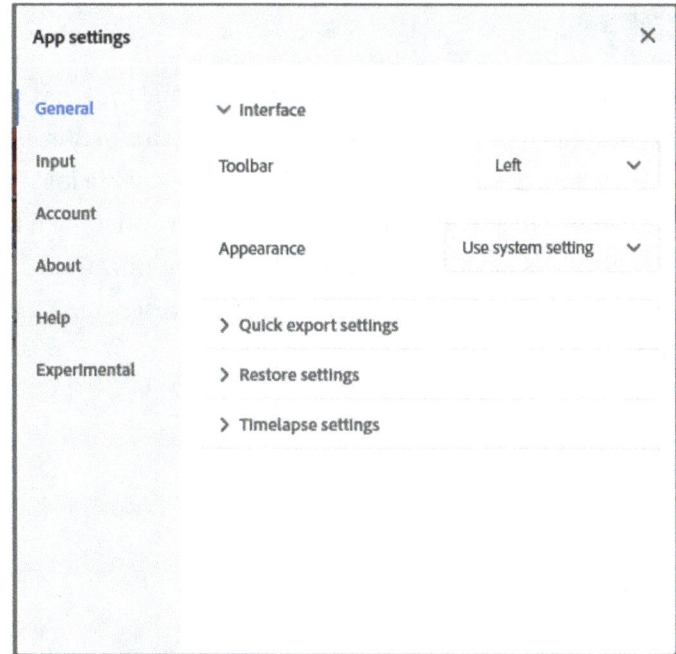

Figure 1-17. *From the Fresco Home tab, click the blue circle to check your application's settings icon dialog box*

Exiting the Application

Once you have completed reviewing this area of Fresco, you can keep the application open for the next chapter, or you can close it on your Window's computer by clicking the X in the upper right corner. Note that in Fresco, there is no File ➤ Exit option, so always use the X to close the application. Refer to Figure 1-18.

Figure 1-18. *Use the X in the upper right to close the Fresco application*

15

CHAPTER 1   WHAT IS ADOBE FRESCO?

Summary

In this chapter, we did a quick overview of what Adobe Fresco is and how it relates to other Adobe applications like Photoshop and Illustrator. We also looked at the importance of having the Creative Cloud Desktop available for viewing files. Then, we also reviewed how to install and open Adobe Fresco and looked at several of the help and learning resources available before exiting the application.

In the next chapter, we will again open Adobe Fresco and begin to create our first new document.

CHAPTER 2

Starting a New Document in Fresco

This chapter covers how to start creating a new document. While you do that, we will also be studying the layout and workspace of the Fresco application and what hardware you can use to digitally draw your artwork. You will learn how to save and navigate your document and then practice the steps on your own in the first project.

> **Note** The project files for this chapter can be found in the Chapter 2 folder. Refer to the link in the introduction.

This chapter does not require that you load the (.psd) file into your Creative Cloud folder until the end of the chapter. However, in future chapters, refer to the section in this chapter on uploading Fresco files onto the Creative Cloud so that you can work with them.

Make sure, as you did in Chapter 1, to open your Fresco application using the Creative Cloud Desktop. Refer to Figure 2-1.

CHAPTER 2 STARTING A NEW DOCUMENT IN FRESCO

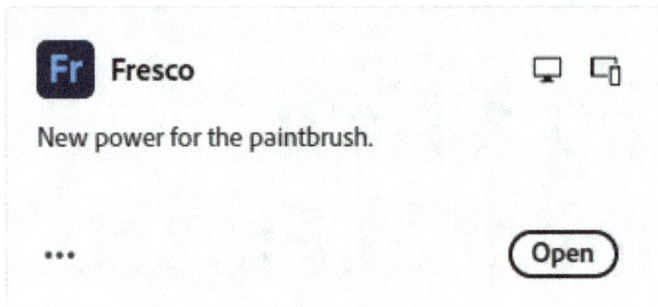

Figure 2-1. *Adobe Creative Cloud Fresco application*

For the remainder of the book, as noted in Chapter 1, we will be using the Windows desktop version of Fresco. Refer to the links in that chapter if you are working on a different platform, and note that the layout of the application will be slightly different.

Starting a New Document in Fresco

At this point, when using the application, you should be on the Home page. Refer to Figure 2-2.

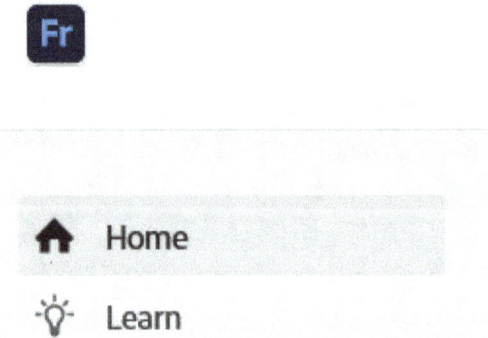

Figure 2-2. *Fresco Home page*

To create a new document, you can either click the icon in the lower left or in the upper center click one of the icons below the words "Start a new document" where several preset page sizes are listed. In this case, we will click Custom size (+) and look at the next dialog box. Refer to Figure 2-3.

18

CHAPTER 2 STARTING A NEW DOCUMENT IN FRESCO

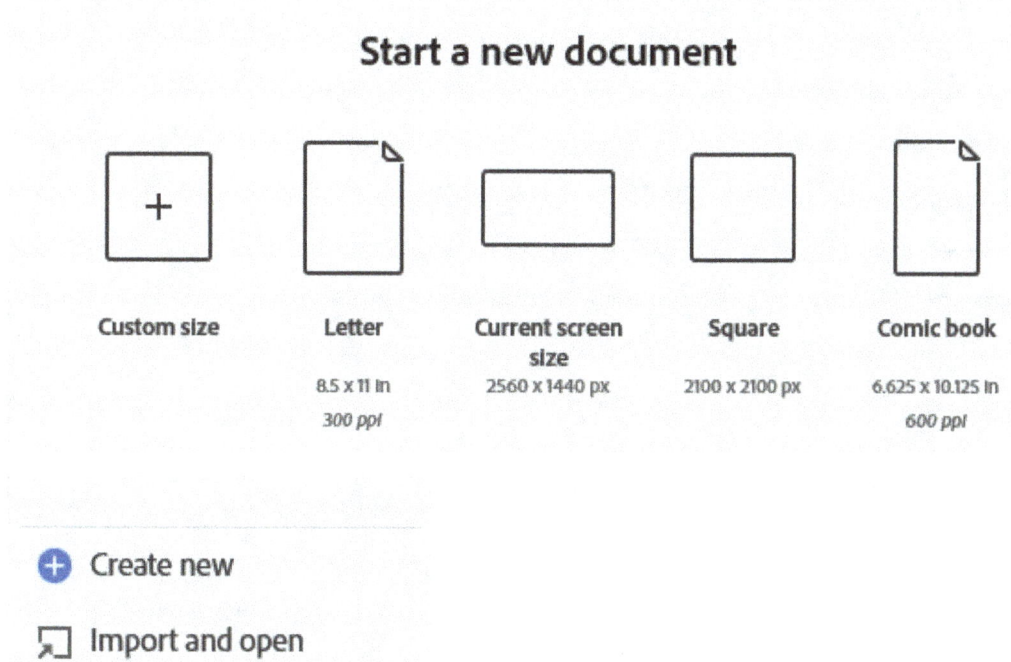

Figure 2-3. *Options for starting or opening a Fresco document from the Home page*

Working with Document Presets and Custom Size Options for Files That Are Recent, Saved, Digital, and Print

In the New document dialog box, you will be presented with various preset options, which you may already be familiar with when working with other applications like Photoshop or Illustrator. However, we will review them here now. Refer to Figure 2-4.

CHAPTER 2   STARTING A NEW DOCUMENT IN FRESCO

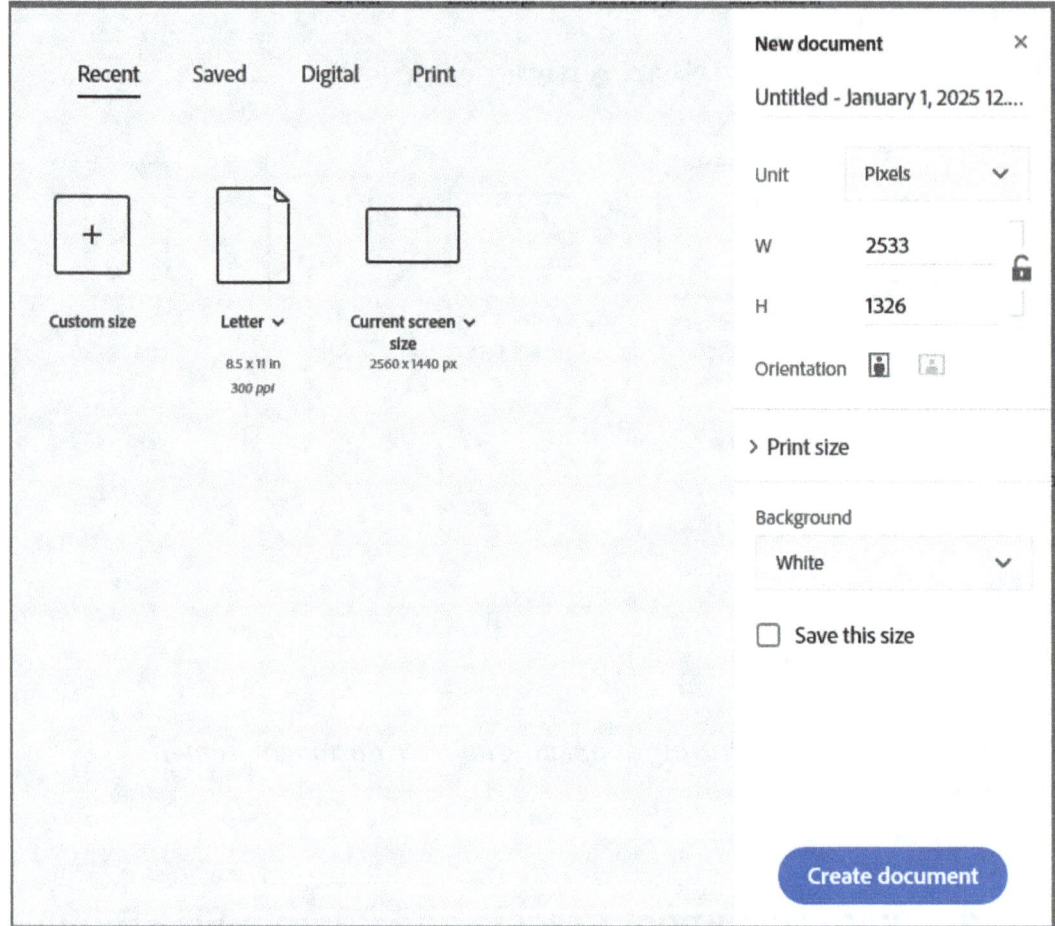

Figure 2-4. *New document dialog box with presets listed in the Recent tab*

The Recent tab refers to preset sizes that you have used lately. If you have not, several sized presets will be shown.

Saved: This tab refers to saved presets that you have created. If you have not, none will be shown. Presets can be saved when you create a custom size and choose the check box option of Save this size, on the right, which I will discuss shortly. Refer to Figure 2-5.

Figure 2-5. *New document dialog box with presets listed in the Saved tab*

Digital: This tab lists several preset sizes of documents for web or video animation. The drop-down arrow beside each allows you to create a new size from the format, or you can click and change from portrait to landscape or from landscape to portrait if the dimensions are rectangular. This changes the details on the right under the New document area. Clicking the preset will create the new document automatically which, for the moment, is not what we want to do. Refer to Figure 2-6.

CHAPTER 2   STARTING A NEW DOCUMENT IN FRESCO

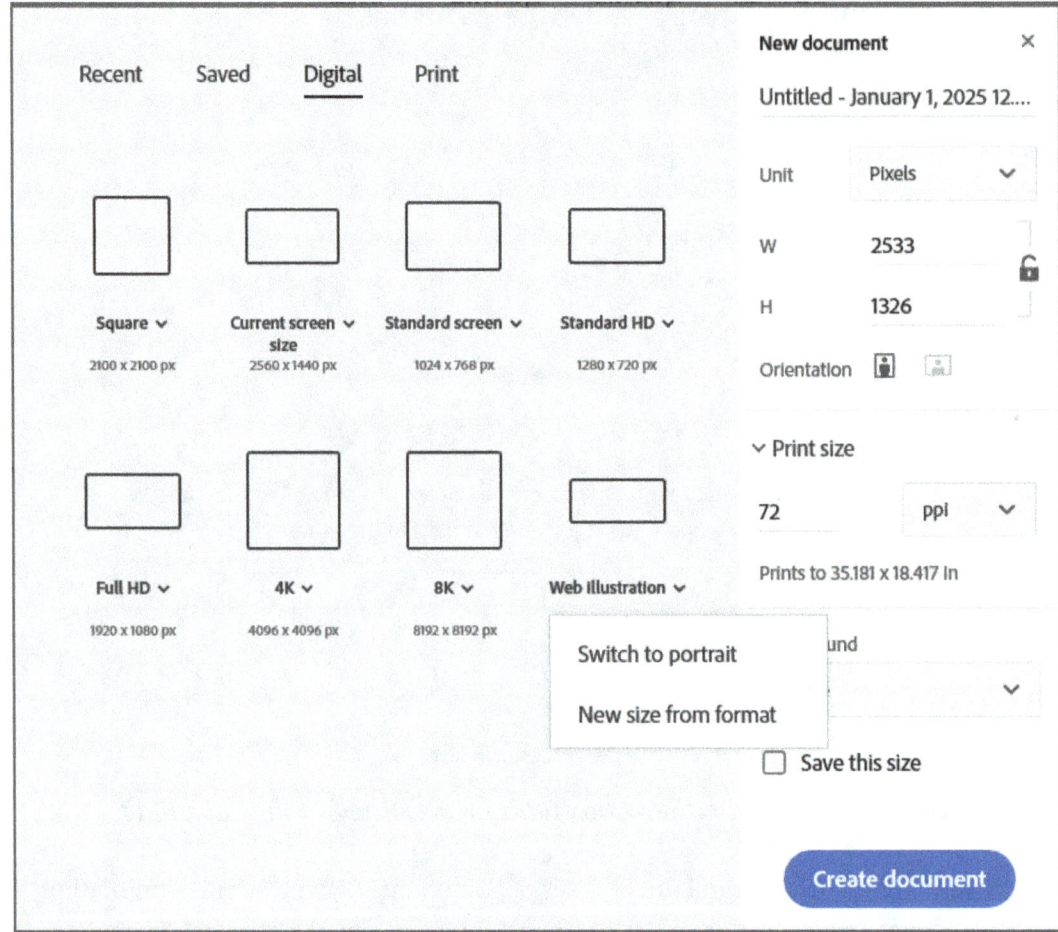

Figure 2-6. *New document dialog box with presets listed in the Digital tab*

Print: This tab lists several preset sizes of documents for print. The drop-down arrow beside each allows you to create a new size from the format, or you can click and change from portrait to landscape if rectangular. This changes the details on the right under the New document area. Clicking the preset will create the new document automatically which, for the moment, is not what we want to do. Refer to Figure 2-7.

CHAPTER 2   STARTING A NEW DOCUMENT IN FRESCO

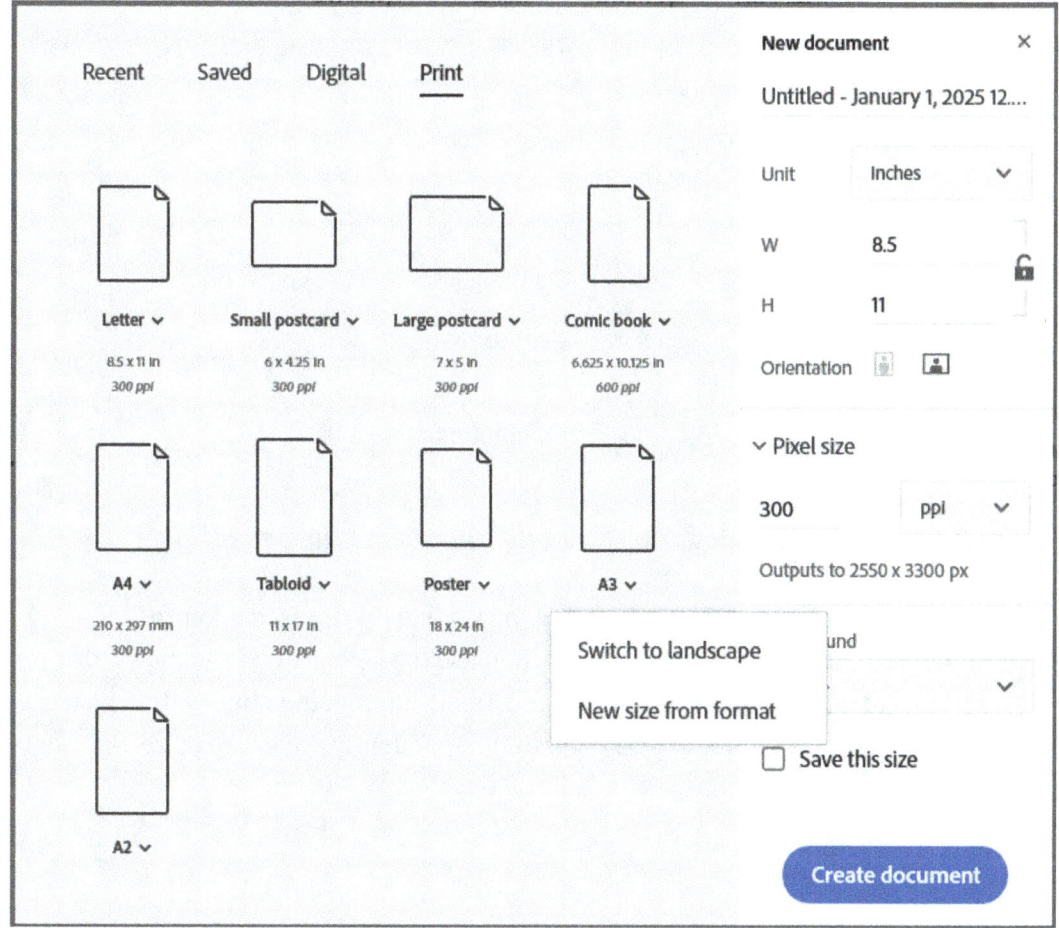

Figure 2-7. *New document dialog box with presets listed in the Print tab*

On the right-hand side, you can type in your custom size. In this case, you can first name your file. The file, if not named, will start with the word Untitled followed by today's date and time.

Next, choose a unit of measurement (pixels, inches, centimeters, millimeters). Often, if the artwork is for the Web, it will be in pixels, but if for print in inches. Refer to Figure 2-8.

CHAPTER 2　STARTING A NEW DOCUMENT IN FRESCO

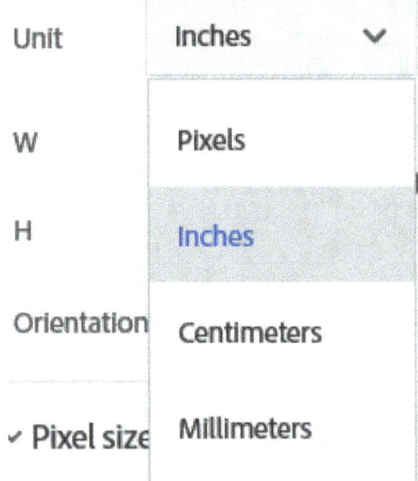

Figure 2-8. *New document dialog box with units of measurement*

Set width and height separately by using the keypad numbers to enter the dimensions. You can also lock the ratio and then use the keypad again so that both width and height scale to some common ratio dimension together, but by default, it is unlocked so that each number can be entered independently. Refer to Figure 2-9.

CHAPTER 2　STARTING A NEW DOCUMENT IN FRESCO

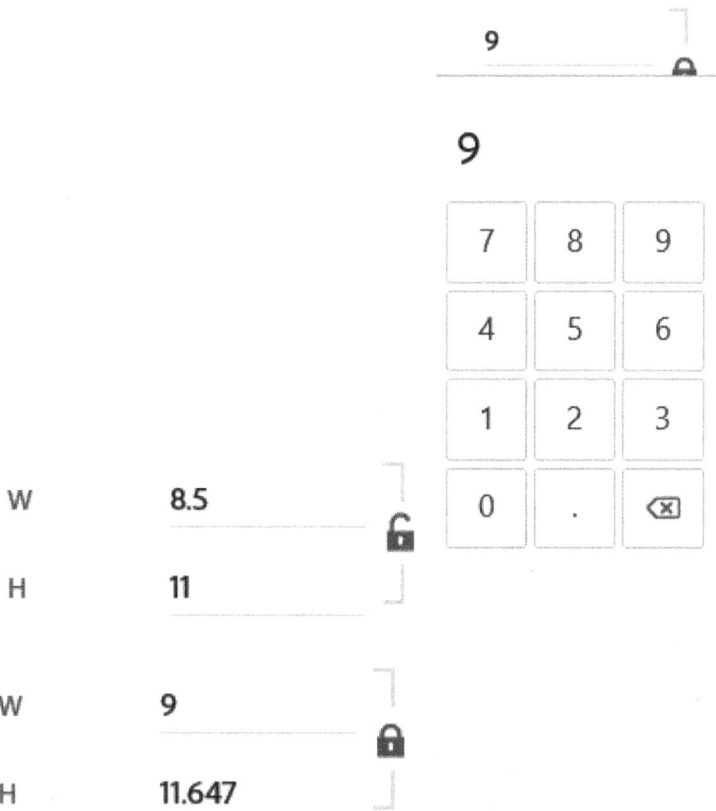

Figure 2-9. *New document dialog box with width and height settings to type numbers with keypad*

To alter the orientation, toggle between the portrait and landscape icons by clicking them. Refer to Figure 2-10.

Figure 2-10. *New document dialog box setting the orientation*

Set the pixel size number for either the unit ppi (pixels per inch) or ppcm (pixels per centimeter) This then describes what it outputs. Refer to Figure 2-11.

25

CHAPTER 2 STARTING A NEW DOCUMENT IN FRESCO

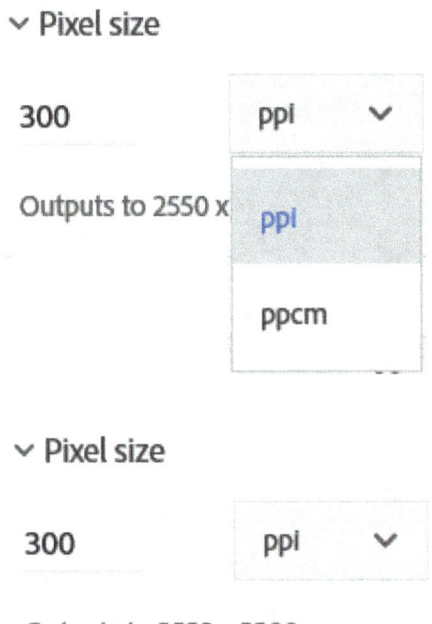

Figure 2-11. *New document dialog box setting the pixel size*

In my case, when I am working with a print document, I will set the resolution to 300 ppi which is considered high. However, when working with a digital image that I plan for the Web or an animation, I will set to the lower resolution pixel size of 72 ppi to keep the file size small or low. It is important to keep this in mind, depending on how you plan to use your artwork, and we will look at this again for animation in Chapter 8. For now, your print work should remain at 300 ppi in the Print tab. If you are in the Digital tab, the Pixel size tab will appear as Print size as seen in Figure 2-6.

The background can be white or transparent. By default, it is set to White. Refer to Figure 2-12.

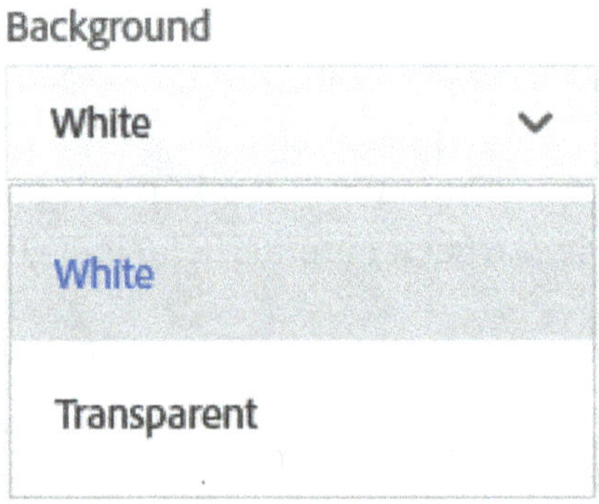

Figure 2-12. *New document dialog box setting the background color*

CHAPTER 2   STARTING A NEW DOCUMENT IN FRESCO

And then, you can also choose to save this size for a later preset. Click the name if you need to rename the preset. Click OK to commit or Cancel without changing the name. Refer to Figure 2-13.

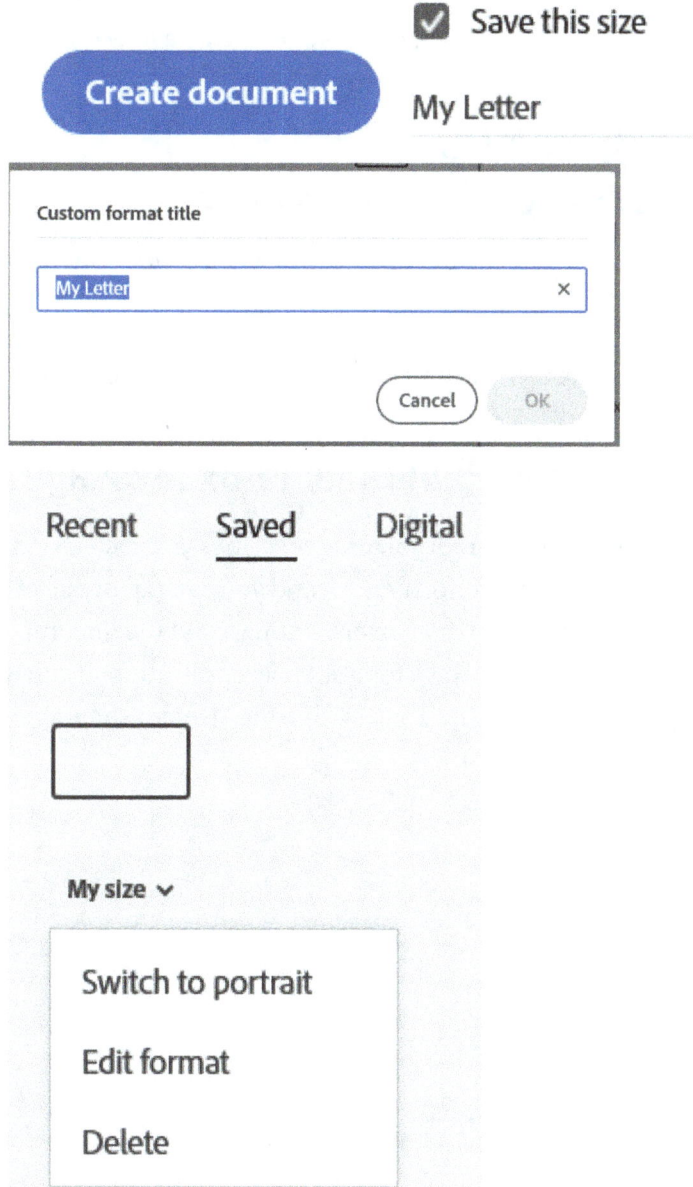

Figure 2-13. *New document dialog box options to save the custom preset for later uses and rename the file in the Custom format title dialog box*

27

CHAPTER 2   STARTING A NEW DOCUMENT IN FRESCO

Custom sizes can later be edited or deleted from the New document dialog box under the Saved tab if you click the arrow for that preset to reveal the options. Refer to Figure 2-13.

When done, you can choose to click Create a document or to cancel and click the X icon in the upper right to close the dialog box and not create a new document. Refer to Figure 2-14.

Figure 2-14. *New document dialog box; click the Create document button or New document X*

In this case, choose some settings and click the Create document button.

Understand the Power Plan Dialog Box Message

Upon the new document being created, you may see a message called Change your power plan. Fresco runs on "High performance," and you can tap or click OK to change to continue or click Cancel and keep the current settings, and the document will open. This setting relates to the graphic settings for a specific application. If you do not want to see this message again, you can alternatively enable the "Do not show again" check box and then click OK. Refer to Figure 2-15.

CHAPTER 2   STARTING A NEW DOCUMENT IN FRESCO

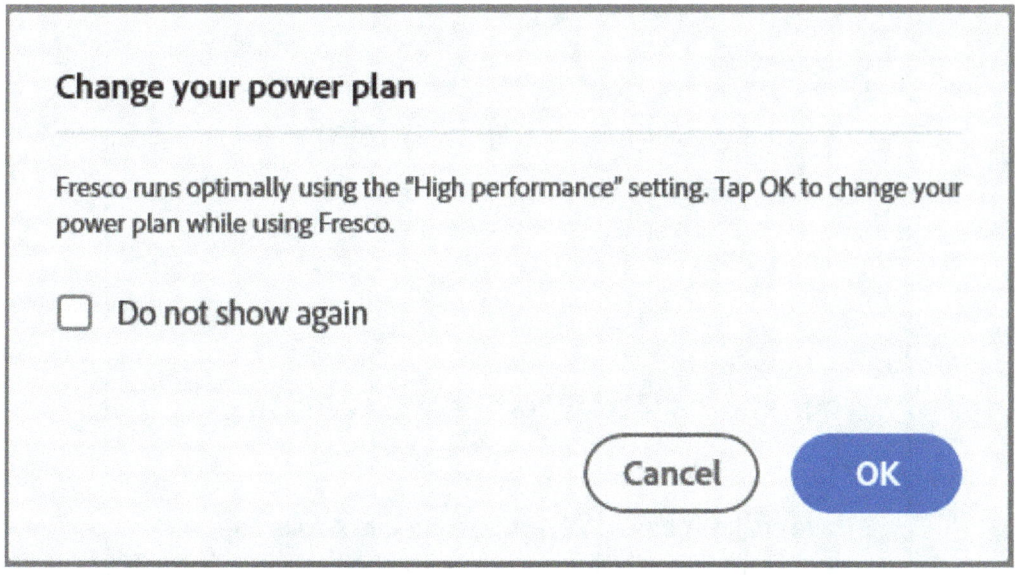

Figure 2-15. *Power plan info message in Fresco*

You can keep this document open or click the Title bar upper left back Home (Ctrl+Shift+H) arrow to auto save the file and then open another new document. I will talk about saving and auto saving later in this chapter when we further explore the Title bar menu. Refer to Figure 2-16.

Figure 2-16. *Exiting the new document*

Opening a Current Document with Preserved Photoshop Layers

Another message you may see later on in edited documents that you open, if you have also opened them earlier in Photoshop, is the warning message that your Photoshop layers have been preserved. Refer to Figure 2-17.

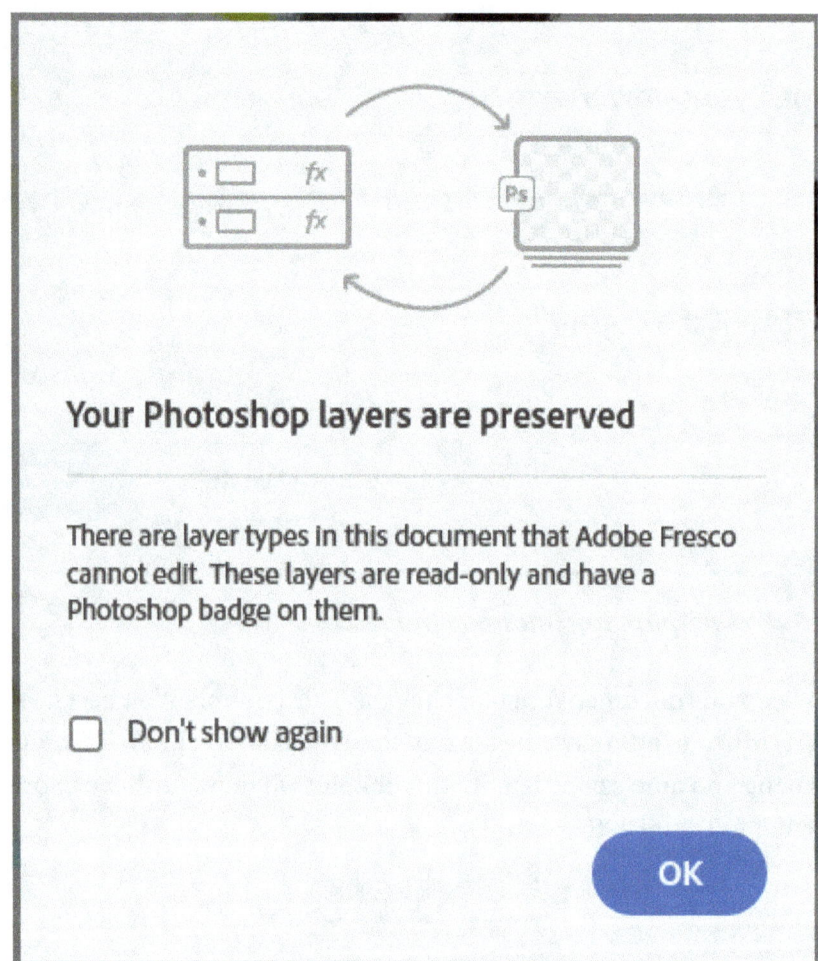

Figure 2-17. *Fresco info message about Photoshop layers in the application which are set to read-only*

This refers to layers from that application that will be set to Read-only and cannot be edited in Fresco with a Photoshop Badge; we will talk more about layers in Chapter 5. If you see this warning, click OK, leaving the "Don't show again" check box unchecked to continue to work in the document in Fresco.

The file you just created can be reopened in the Recent area because it is stored in the files of the Creative Cloud Desktop. Refer to Figure 2-18.

CHAPTER 2   STARTING A NEW DOCUMENT IN FRESCO

Figure 2-18. *Recent blank Fresco document thumbnail as seen from the Home page*

Stay in the blank document for now to review the application's workspace layout. Refer to Figure 2-19.

CHAPTER 2 STARTING A NEW DOCUMENT IN FRESCO

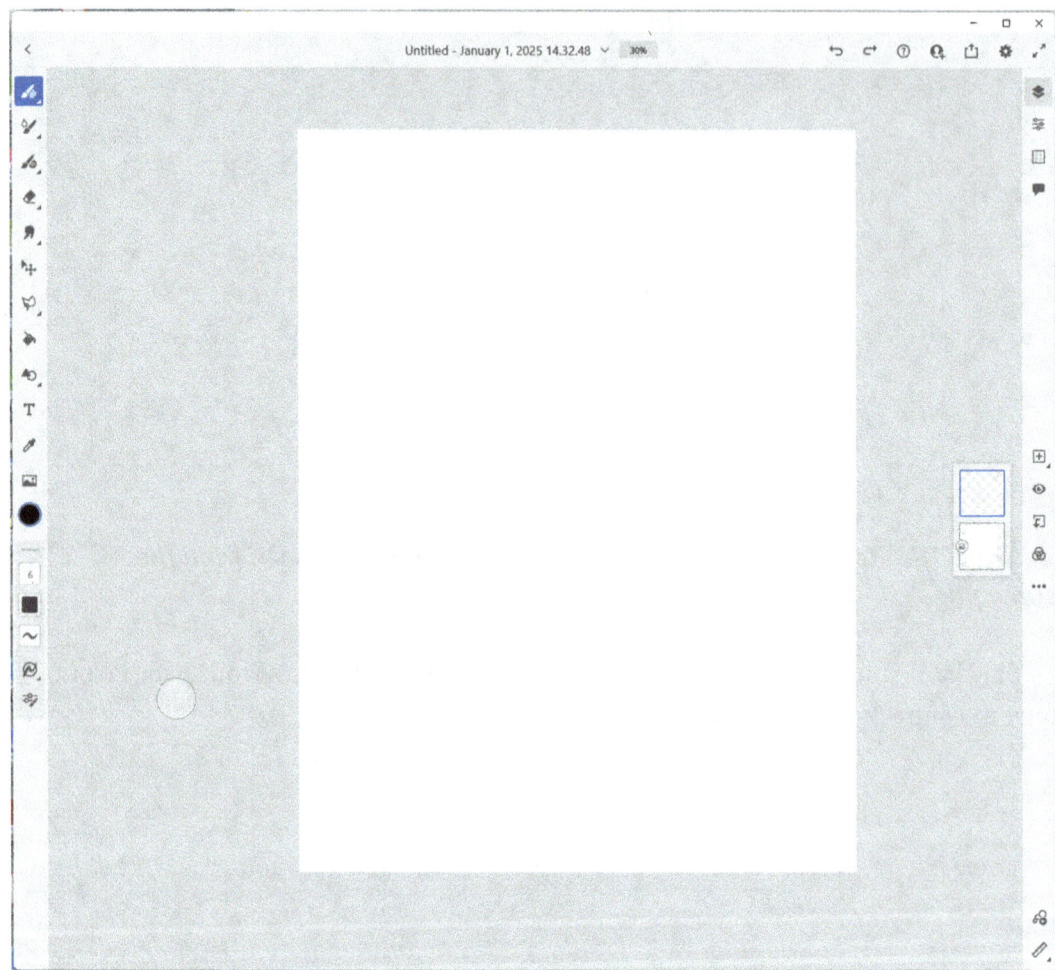

Figure 2-19. *Fresco workspace layout for a blank document*

Title Bar Menu: Commonly Required Actions, Upper Help, and Settings

Though you may not access the title bar continuously, it is important, before you begin, to use the application to familiarize yourself with the icons in this area before you begin to use the application. Refer to Figure 2-20.

CHAPTER 2   STARTING A NEW DOCUMENT IN FRESCO

Untitled - January 1, 2025 14.32.48   41%

Figure 2-20. Information and icons found in the Title bar

Commonly Required Actions

Moving from left to right, you can edit the name of your document at any time using the drop-down menu if you did not give it the correct name when you first created the document by clicking the name. Refer to Figure 2-21.

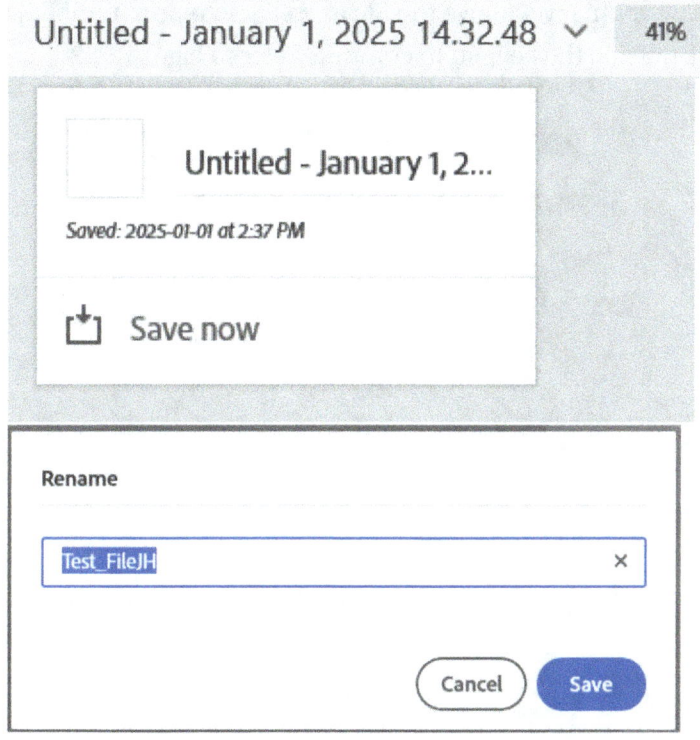

Figure 2-21. Title bar menu rename your file

Then, click Save to commit.

CHAPTER 2   STARTING A NEW DOCUMENT IN FRESCO

Saving Files

After editing the document, you can save right away. The current saved time is displayed. If at any time you need to save the document as you work, click Save now. Notice that an unsaved document will have an asterisk (*) beside the title.

Navigation: Zooming In and Out and Panning

While you work in your canvas, you can zoom in and out, as you would in applications like Photoshop, using the keyboard shortcuts Ctrl++ to zoom in and Ctrl+- to zoom out. You can also set the zoom level above the file as well and type a number in, using the keypad, and click outside the keypad to commit. Refer to Figure 2-22.

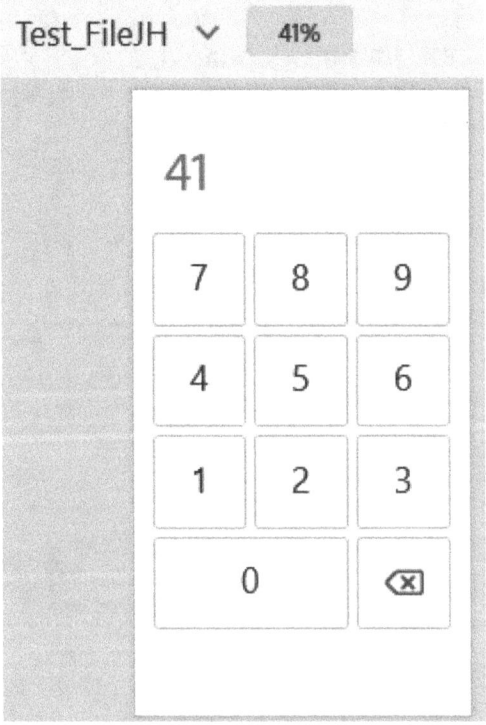

Figure 2-22. *Title bar menu zoom settings*

In the case of locating the Hand tool, when you want to pan or move without altering the artwork, hold down the spacebar key as you drag with the mouse. Shortly, we will look at the Help menu keyboard shortcuts to familiarize you with any settings or navigation actions that are unfamiliar with to you as you work.

CHAPTER 2 STARTING A NEW DOCUMENT IN FRESCO

Undo and Redo

The next set of icons are Undo (Ctrl+Z) and Redo (Ctrl+Shift+Z) icons, which we will use later as we work on a project in Chapter 3 and throughout the book. Refer to Figure 2-23.

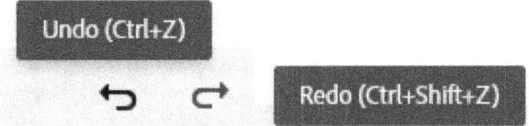

Figure 2-23. *Title bar menu Undo and Redo icons*

Help Menu Options

This Help icon appears as a circle with a question mark within it. Refer to Figure 2-24.

35

CHAPTER 2   STARTING A NEW DOCUMENT IN FRESCO

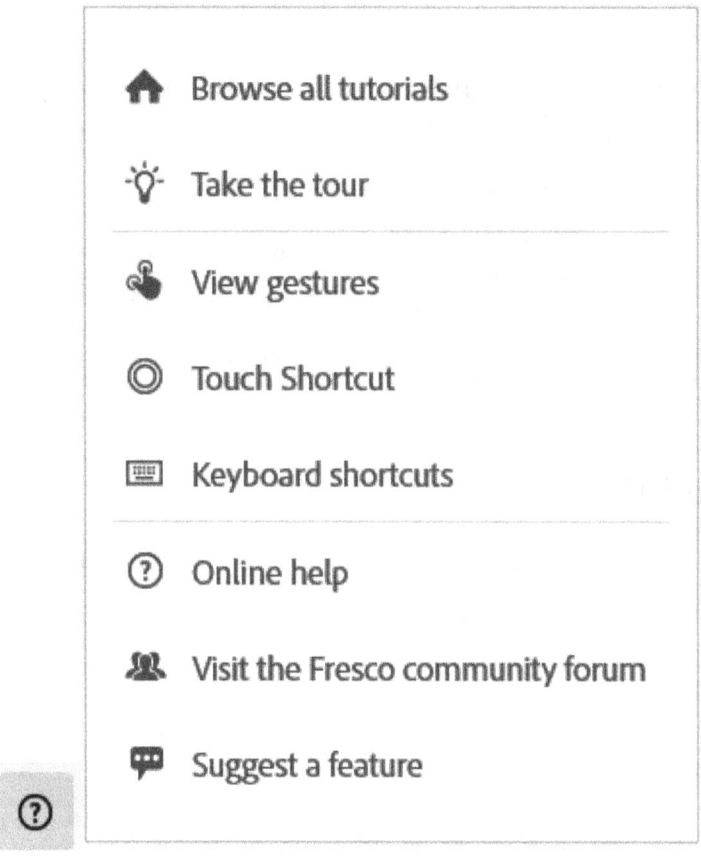

Figure 2-24. *Title bar menu with help menu options listed*

Using the help drop-down list menu, you can access other Helps which include

- Browse All Tutorials or Take a Tour: These options were mentioned in Chapter 1 (refer to that chapter for more information).

- View Gestures: These diagrams can be helpful if you are working with a touch screen and not on the desktop with a mouse as I am doing. Scroll through them to familiarize yourself with them. Click the X in the upper right to close this dialog box. Refer to Figure 2-25.

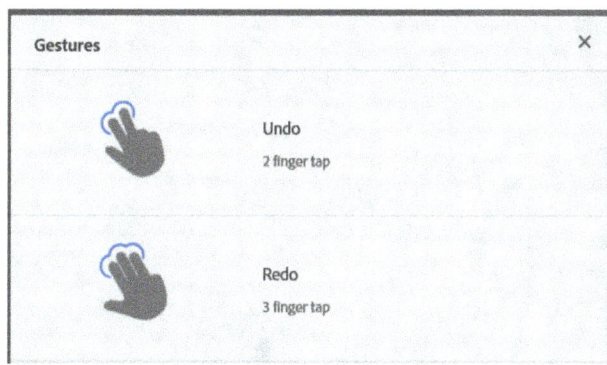

Figure 2-25. *Help menu Gestures info box*

- Touch Shortcut Map: This can be used to show how to make touch shortcuts if you are using a touch screen and not a mouse. However, the mouse, when used correctly with the primary dot (circle) and secondary ring, can emulate many of these behaviors as well, as you will discover in Chapter 3. Scroll through the list to familiarize yourself with them, and then click the X in the upper right to close the dialog box. Refer to Figure 2-26.

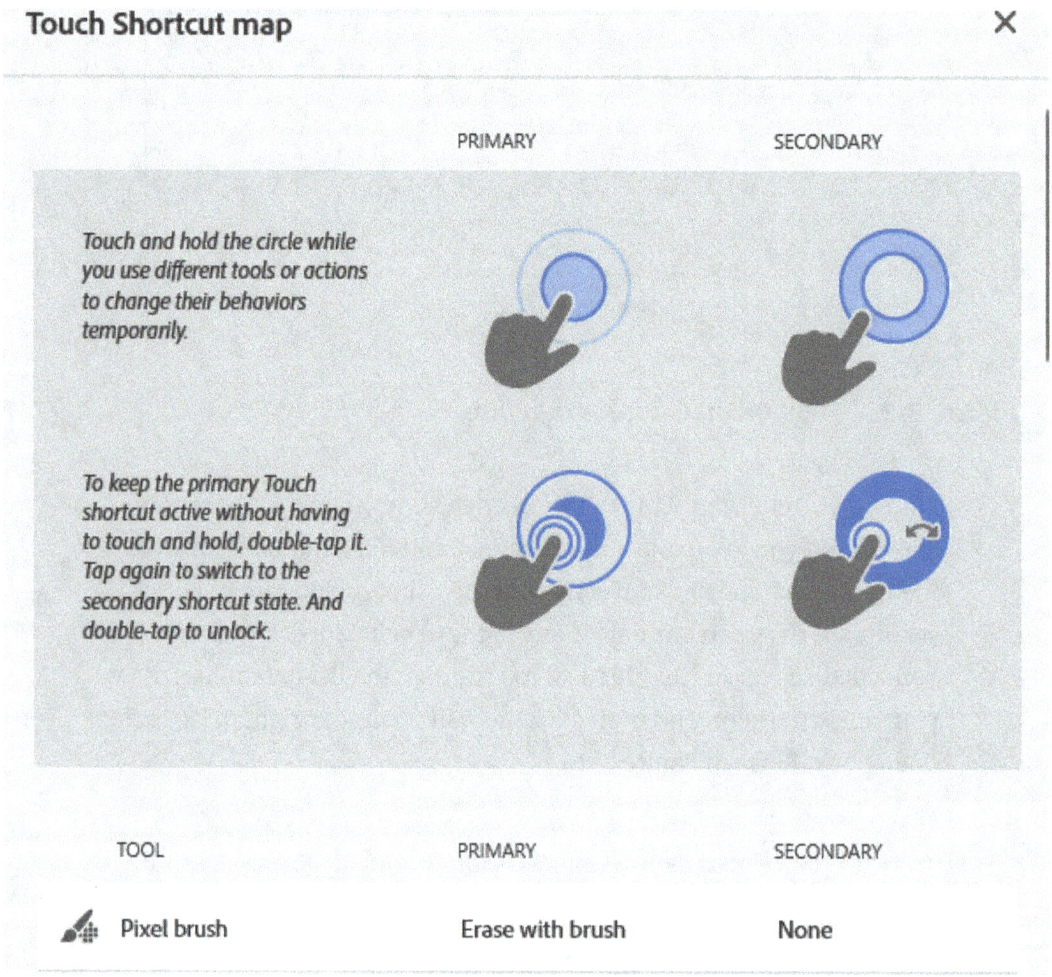

CHAPTER 2 STARTING A NEW DOCUMENT IN FRESCO

Figure 2-26. Help menu showing the Touch Shortcut map info box

---

Note that the Primary touch shortcut circle and ring will be found to the left of your canvas as you work. Currently, it is inactive as we are not actively using it, but it can be activated by double-clicking it and then double-clicking to deactivate. Refer to Figure 2-27.

CHAPTER 2 STARTING A NEW DOCUMENT IN FRESCO

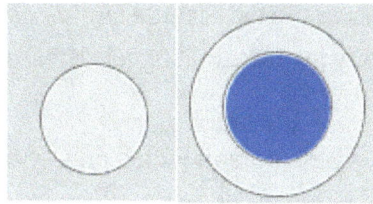

Figure 2-27. *Primary touch shortcut circle inactive and then ring (secondary) inactive and inner circle (primary) activated*

- Keyboard shortcuts are also listed for control of various tools. You can also find a list of this information at this link as well:

    https://helpx.adobe.com/fresco/using/keyboard-shortcuts.html

Scroll through the list to familiarize yourself with them, and then, click the X in the upper right to close the dialog box.

Refer to Figure 2-28.

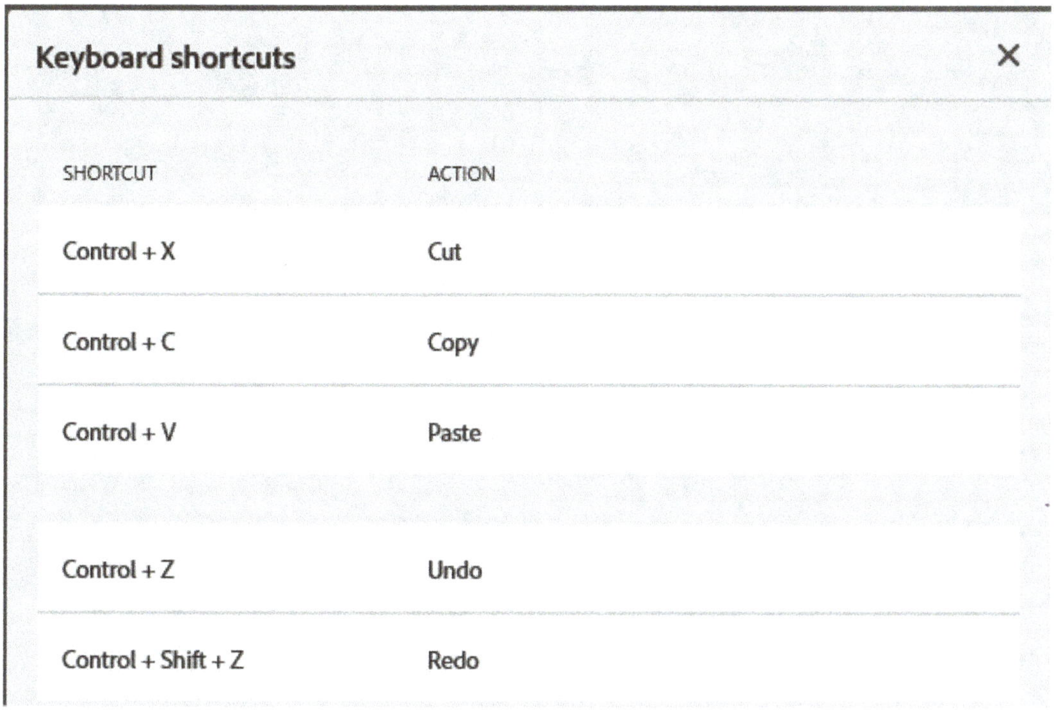

Keyboard shortcuts	
SHORTCUT	ACTION
Control + X	Cut
Control + C	Copy
Control + V	Paste
Control + Z	Undo
Control + Shift + Z	Redo

Figure 2-28. *Help menu Keyboard shortcuts info box*

- Other Help resources in the list include Online help, Visit the Fresco community forum, and Suggest a feature. Refer to Figure 2-24.

The next icon, which looks like a person with a plus symbol, is "Invite In" which I will mention in Chapter 9. Refer to Figure 2-29.

Figure 2-29. *Title bar menu icons Invite In and Share icons*

The Share icon with the arrow pointing upward is a list of export options and will be discussed in Chapters 8 and 9. Refer to Figure 2-29.

Settings Menu and Adjusting the Canvas on the Desktop

The Settings menu is found under the gear icon. Refer to Figure 2-30.

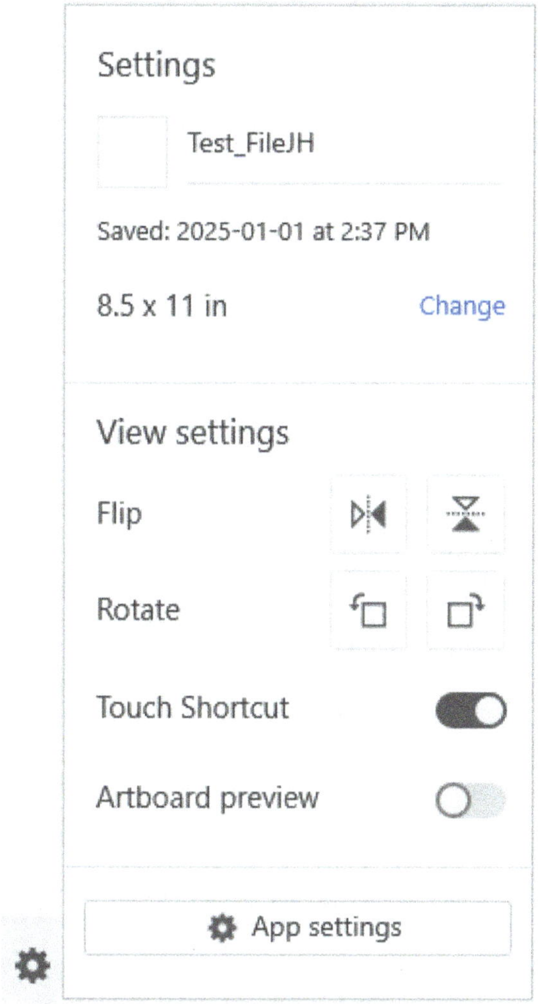

CHAPTER 2 STARTING A NEW DOCUMENT IN FRESCO

Figure 2-30. *Title bar menu Settings icon and list of options*

From here, you can adjust such settings as title of document (rename) by clicking the name to change, as you did earlier.

The document's dimensions and scale can be altered by clicking the word Change. Refer to Figure 2-30 then to Figure 2-31.

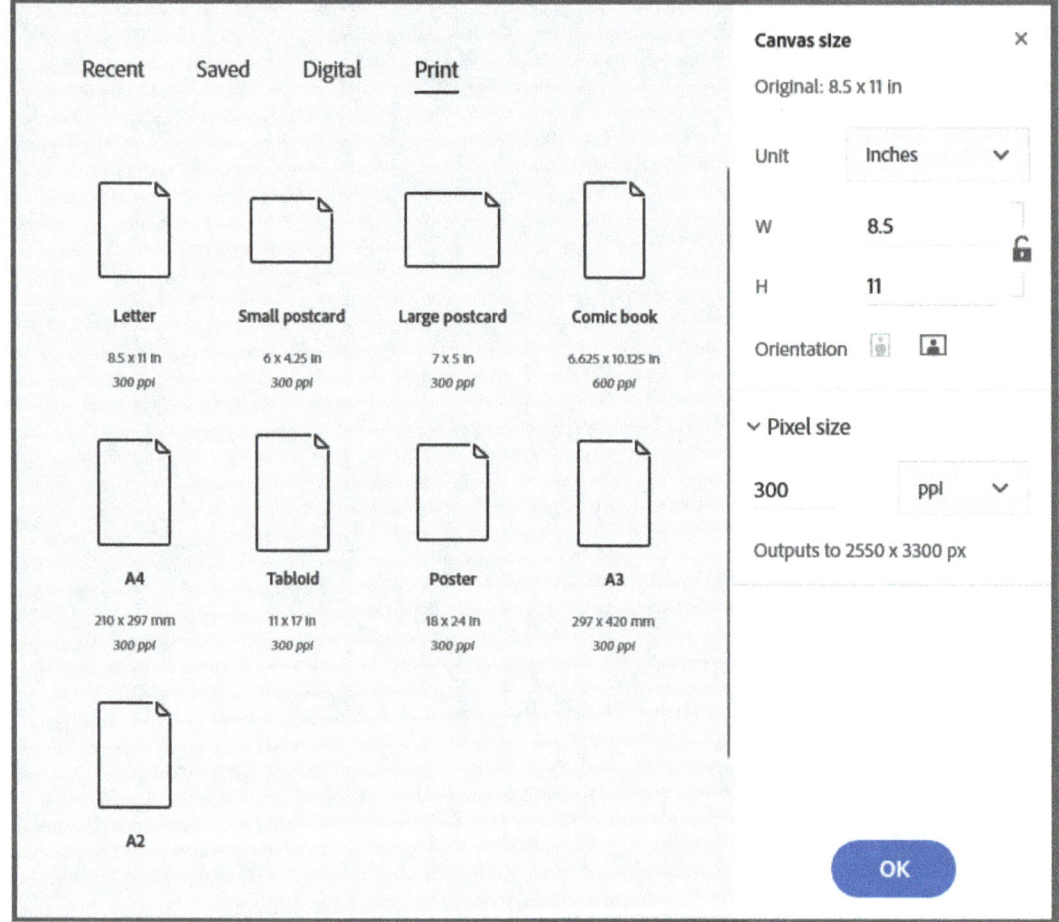

Figure 2-31. *Change Canvas size dialog box and its options for a quick update*

Then, change your settings in the dialog box and click OK. Refer to Figure 2-31. Note that you may be sent to the Transform workspace area at this point. If so, for now, just click the Done button in the upper right corner to commit any size change. We will review this area in more detail in Chapter 4. Refer to Figure 2-32.

CHAPTER 2 STARTING A NEW DOCUMENT IN FRESCO

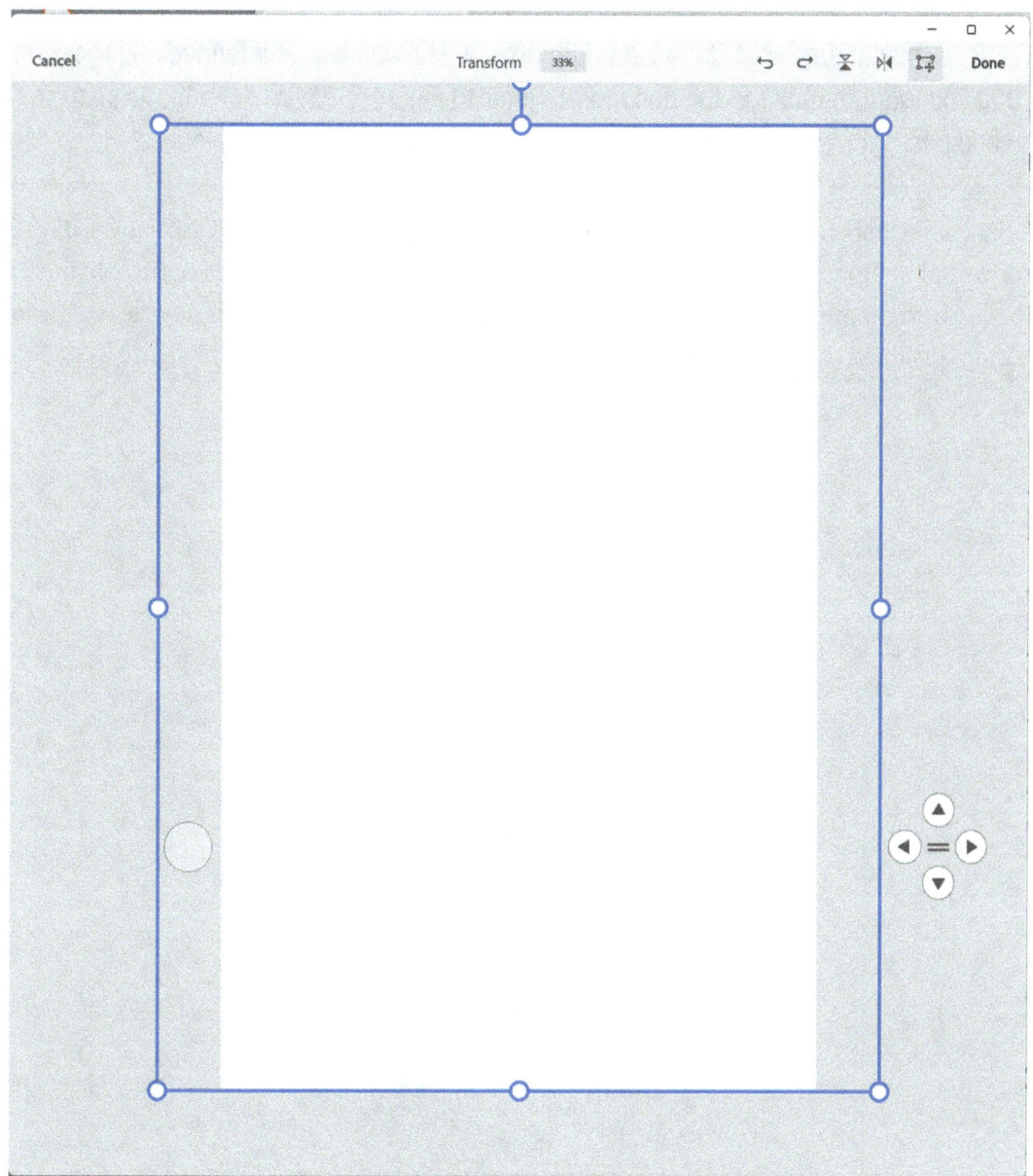

Figure 2-32. *Fresco's Transform workspace area*

CHAPTER 2   STARTING A NEW DOCUMENT IN FRESCO

Note   You can use your Undo icon right now, if this was not an intended change that you want to make to the document. Refer to Figure 2-23. While in the Transform workspace, you also have the option of clicking Cancel as well; see Figure 2-32.

View settings can also be adjusted for better viewing on the screen of the canvas. Flip horizontal or flip vertical, or rotate counterclockwise or clockwise. Enable or disable the Touch Shortcut preview, and enable or disable the Artboard preview. For now, leave these settings disabled except for the Touch Shortcut so that it is visible. Refer to Figure 2-33.

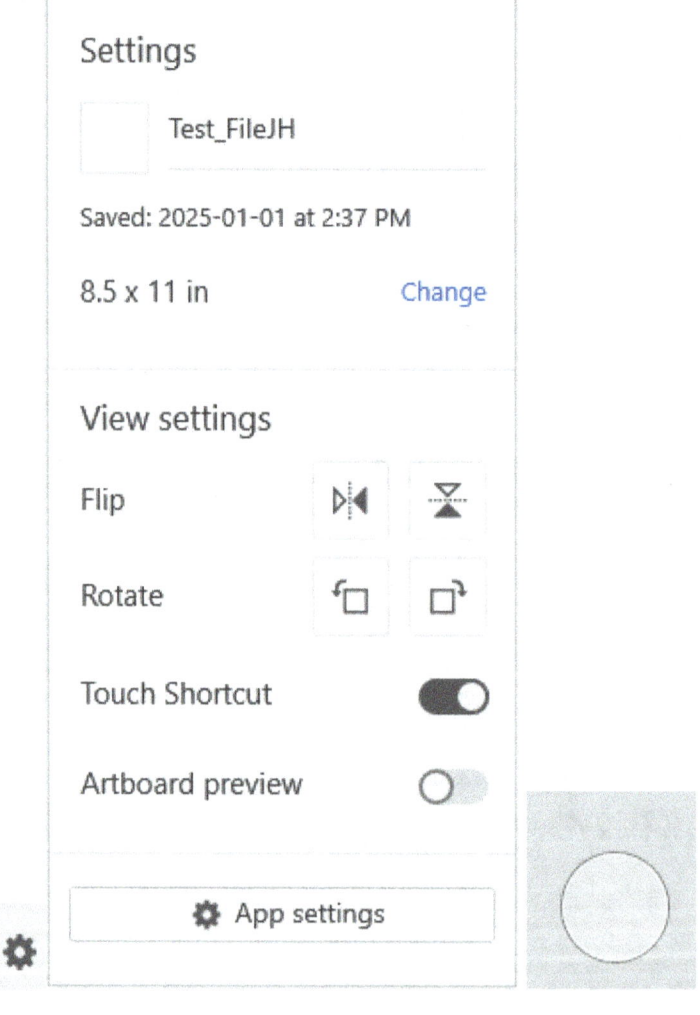

Figure 2-33. *Title bar menu Settings icon and list of options with Touch Shortcut visible*

44

App Settings

Within the settings menu is the App settings button. These are the preferences for the application. While I will not be going into details on each tab, I will just give you a general overview of each. Refer to Figure 2-33 and Figure 2-34.

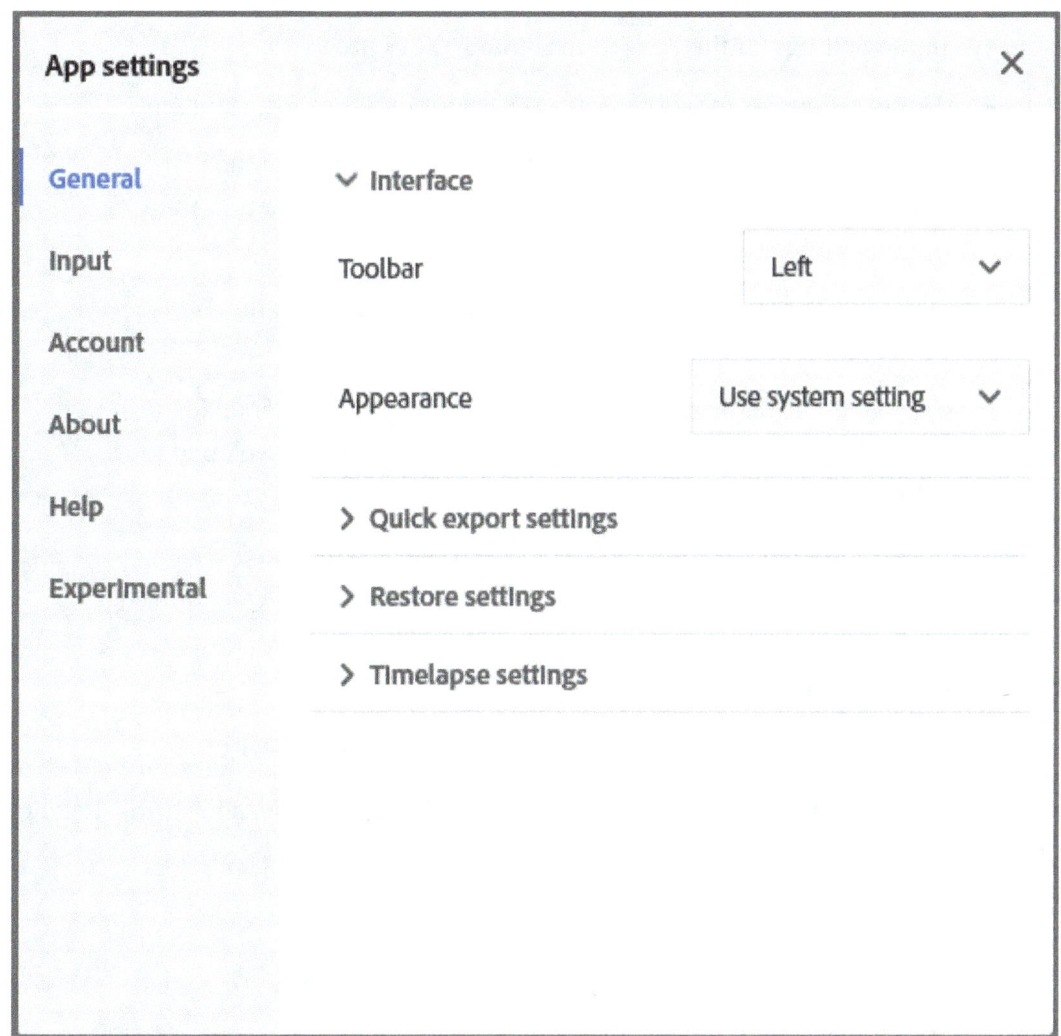

Figure 2-34. *App settings dialog box*

CHAPTER 2　STARTING A NEW DOCUMENT IN FRESCO

In the App settings dialog box are the following tabs which you can review:

- General: The following settings in this section are for the Interface ➤ Toolbar and Appearance. Quick export settings for file format settings. Restore settings reset learning content if it has changed. Time-lapse settings are for video.

- Input: Settings for the Pen, Touch, and Brushes previews.

- Account: Settings for your account, Subscription, and local storage.

- About: Settings for Adobe Fresco, notes on what is new in the application, view what is coming in Adobe Fresco, Follow and share options, and Legal details.

- Help: Options for learning and support as seen earlier in the Help menu.

- Experimental: Settings will be listed here if new experimental features are added. Currently, there are none as they are being developed in Adobe design lab.

We will return to some of these app settings throughout the book.
To exit this area, click the X in the upper right corner. Refer to Figure 2-34.

Setting Full Screen

The last icon allows you to click the diagonal arrows for a full screen view (Shift +F) if you want to view your artwork larger on the screen or click again to reset and shrink. Refer to Figure 2-35.

Figure 2-35. *Full screen view toggle icon*

On the Desktop: Can I Use My Stylus, Pen Tablet, or Mouse?

For those of you who are not using touch screen devices such as a tablet, I am showing how much of the painting and artistry in this book can be created using a mouse or if you have a pen stylus and tablet connected to your computer via a USB. If you have used a stylus in Photoshop or Illustrator that you used for drawing, it should be fairly similar in Fresco. It is good for drawing more delicate brush strokes or when you need to add a signature, and you can erase with it as well rather than selecting another tool. However, I will use my mouse first to make sure I am set to the brush tool and then start using the pen. While you work with the pen stylus, keep Fresco app at full screen or fully expanded so that you do not draw in another application outside of Fresco by mistake. In the case of using pen stylus, I am experimenting with my Wacom Intuos pen and touch small pen tablet. However, you may want to do some online research into newer versions and other brands. When I am not using it, I disconnect it from my computer. Refer to Figure 2-36.

Figure 2-36. *Illustration of using a pen stylus to create a signature in my document*

In this book, it is optional to use a pen stylus, and you may prefer to continue to practice with the mouse. We will start to look more at drawing with various tools in Chapter 3.

Exiting File: Auto Save to the Cloud and File Format

Exiting the file will cause it to auto save, and, as mentioned earlier, you can click the left pointing arrow in the Title bar to exit the file at any time. Refer to Figure 2-37.

Figure 2-37. *Using the Title bar to exit the file*

There is no message that comes up asking if you want to save your changes. It is just saved directly to the cloud and can be viewed in the Recent area when you open the file or under your "Files" in the Creative Cloud Desktop. Refer to Figure 2-38.

CHAPTER 2   STARTING A NEW DOCUMENT IN FRESCO

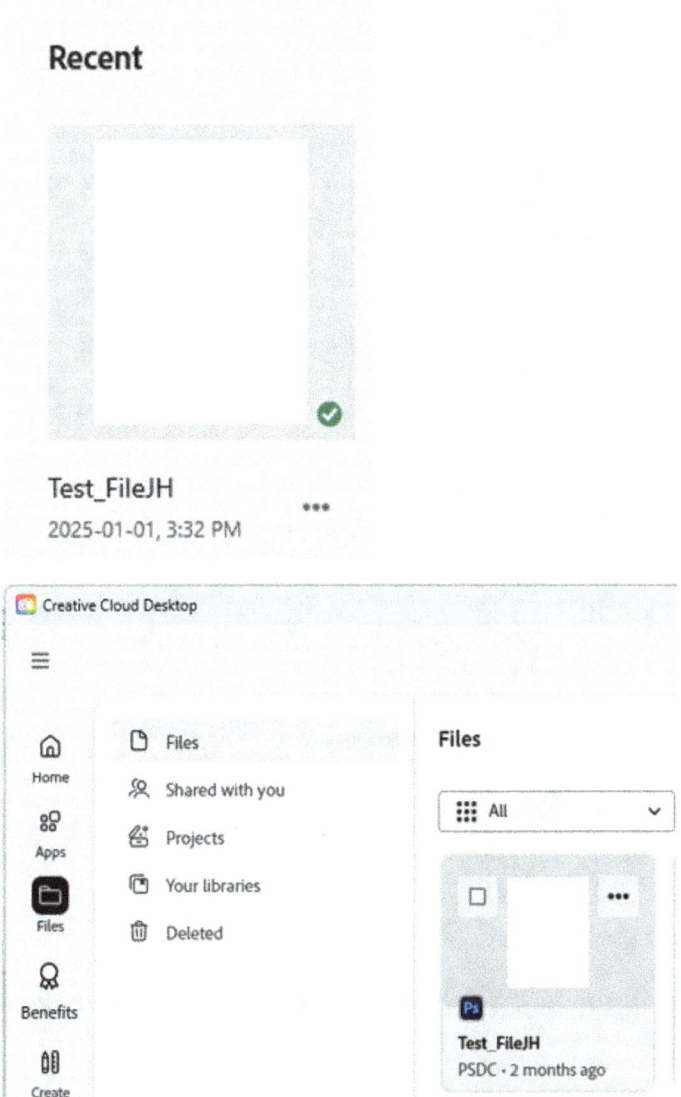

Figure 2-38. *Viewing the document on the Fresco home page and in the Creative Cloud Desktop*

Likewise, they can also be viewed in Photoshop under the Your files selection. However, for now, we will not open this file in Photoshop. Refer to Figure 2-39.

CHAPTER 2 STARTING A NEW DOCUMENT IN FRESCO

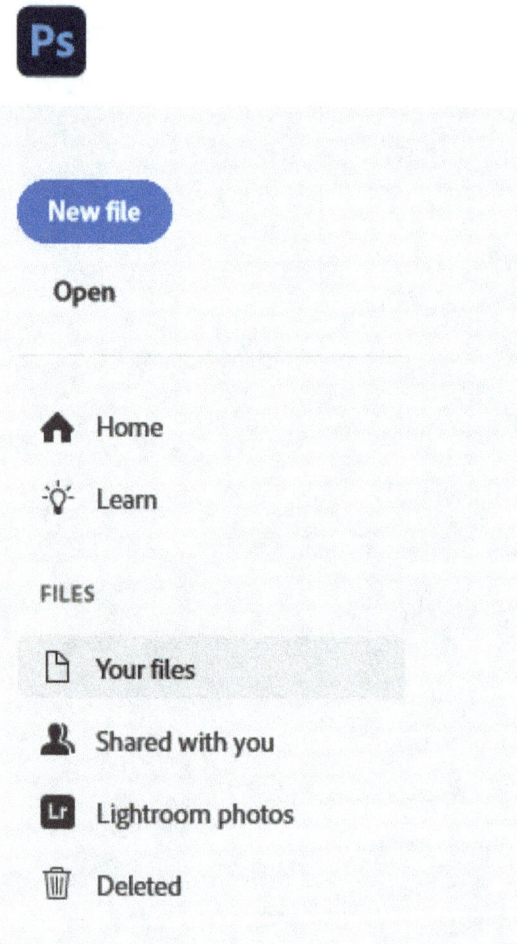

Figure 2-39. *Location in Photoshop where you can view your Creative Cloud Fresco documents*

The files are stored as .PSDC files or Photoshop Document Cloud. When selected, they can be deleted from the Creative Cloud Desktop when you click that file's ellipsis (…) and choose that option from the list. It will go into the Deleted folder. However, a file can be deleted directly from Fresco if you select the ellipsis (…) beside each file on the Home page Recent or under Your files. We will talk about this again in more detail in Chapter 7. Refer to Figure 2-40.

CHAPTER 2 STARTING A NEW DOCUMENT IN FRESCO

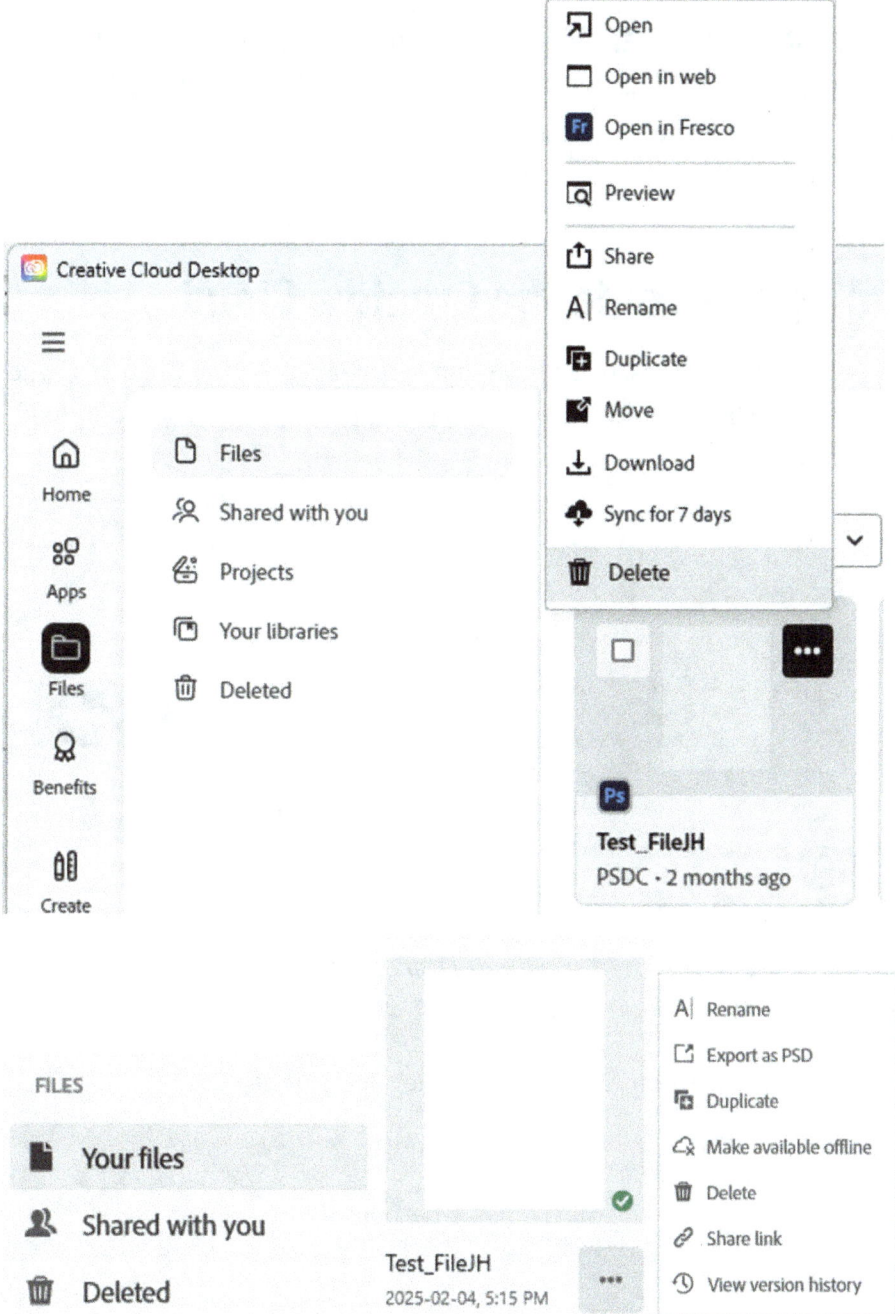

Figure 2-40. *Use Adobe Creative Cloud Desktop (above) or Fresco (below) to do tasks from the menu such as downloading or deleting a Fresco file*

51

CHAPTER 2 STARTING A NEW DOCUMENT IN FRESCO

Note From the same Creative Cloud Desktop menu, the file can be downloaded to the desktop as a (.psd) file which can be further edited in Photoshop. Refer to Chapters 7, 8 and 9 for more information.

Uploading Files onto the Creative Cloud

Likewise, project files for Fresco can be added or uploaded via the Creative Cloud Desktop when you click the plus Add icon on the upper right and choose Upload from the list. Refer to Figure 2-41.

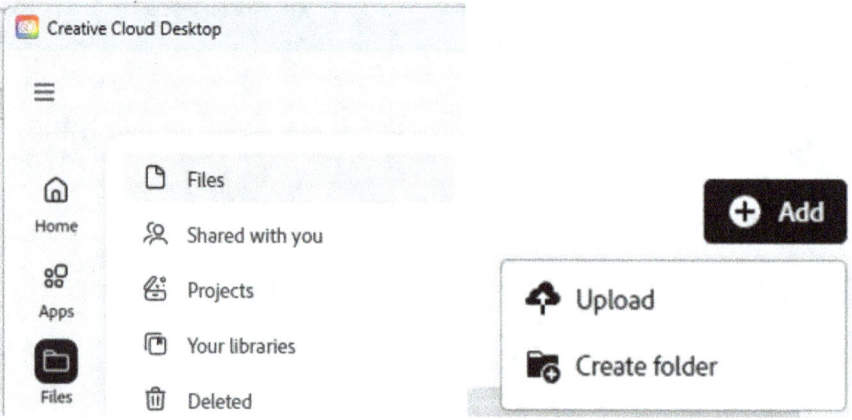

Figure 2-41. *Use Adobe Creative Cloud Desktop to upload files that you want to open later in Fresco*

Locate the file, select it, and click Open. Refer to Figure 2-42.

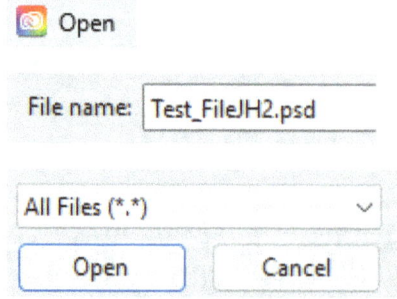

Figure 2-42. *Use the Open dialog box to locate and Open button to upload a file*

52

CHAPTER 2 STARTING A NEW DOCUMENT IN FRESCO

Note that if you get a warning letting you know that the file is going to be converted to a Creative Cloud document, click Continue. Refer to Figure 2-43.

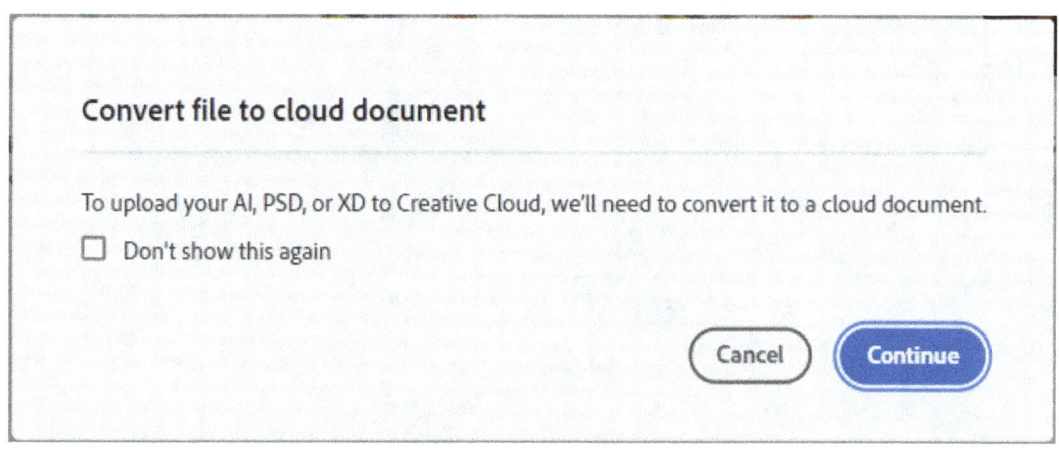

Figure 2-43. *Creative Cloud Desktop info box alerting you that the file will be converted to a cloud document*

This may take a few seconds, and then, the file will be added to the Your files area for both the Creative Cloud Desktop and be updated in Fresco. Likewise, if there are any Photoshop layers, they will be preserved. Refer to Figure 2-44.

53

CHAPTER 2 STARTING A NEW DOCUMENT IN FRESCO

Figure 2-44. *Example of a file added to Creative Cloud*

Alternatively, while working in Fresco, you can go to the Home menu, and in the lower left, choose the Import and open icon. Locate the file on your computer, and click Open. The file options that you can import, in this case, are .psd and .psb. Both are Photoshop document formats. Refer to Figure 2-45.

CHAPTER 2　STARTING A NEW DOCUMENT IN FRESCO

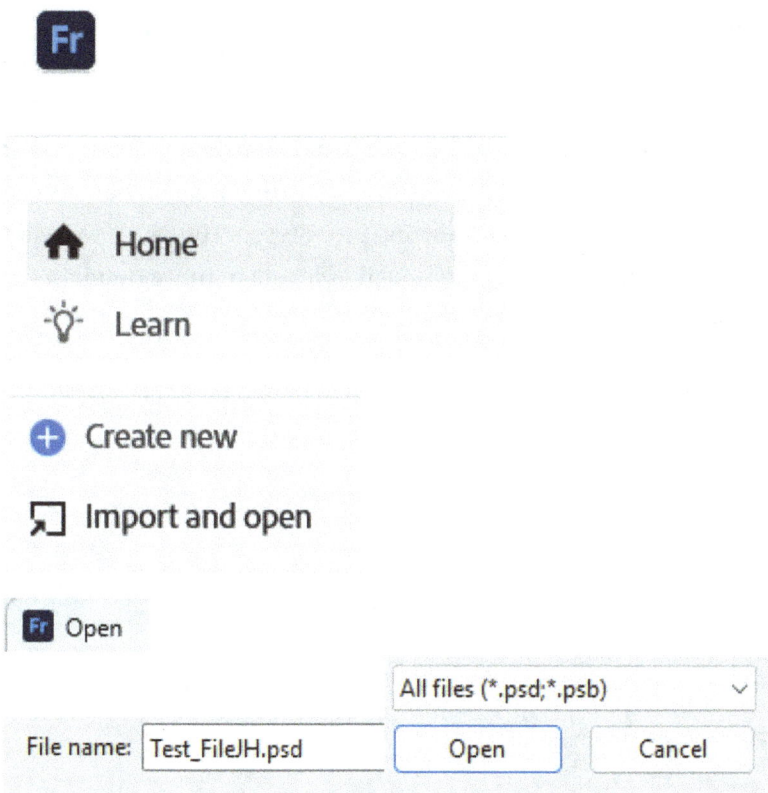

Figure 2-45. *Open and import to the Creative Cloud Desktop directly from the Fresco Home page using the Import and open button icon and the Open dialog box*

Project: Creating a New Blank File

At this point, practice creating a blank Fresco file as in the steps provided earlier in this chapter. Use a standard preset or create a custom preset and save the document.

Likewise, you can also practice opening my blank **Test_FileJH.psd** file and try uploading to the Creative Cloud Desktop using one of the methods suggested from Creative Cloud, or Import and open it in Fresco. Then, exit and close the file.

Once you have done this, you can continue to work in Fresco for the next chapter or close the application at any time.

Important Photoshop user note: If you plan at this point to practice importing a Photoshop (.psd) file that contains Photoshop layers which are preserved, be aware that attempting to change the size of the document using the Fresco Settings change link to

CHAPTER 2　STARTING A NEW DOCUMENT IN FRESCO

adjust the canvas size may not get you the exact result you anticipate. When you click OK to confirm the change, you will get a warning message saying that those layers will be flattened. Fresco cannot edit them. They are read-only and must be flattened to change the canvas size. To avoid flattening the layers, if this is not your intent, click the Go back button and leave your document at the current file size. It may be best to alter the size of your Photoshop document prior to importing into Fresco. However, we will look at other image import options later in Chapter 7 as well as layers in more detail in Chapter 5. Refer to Figure 2-46.

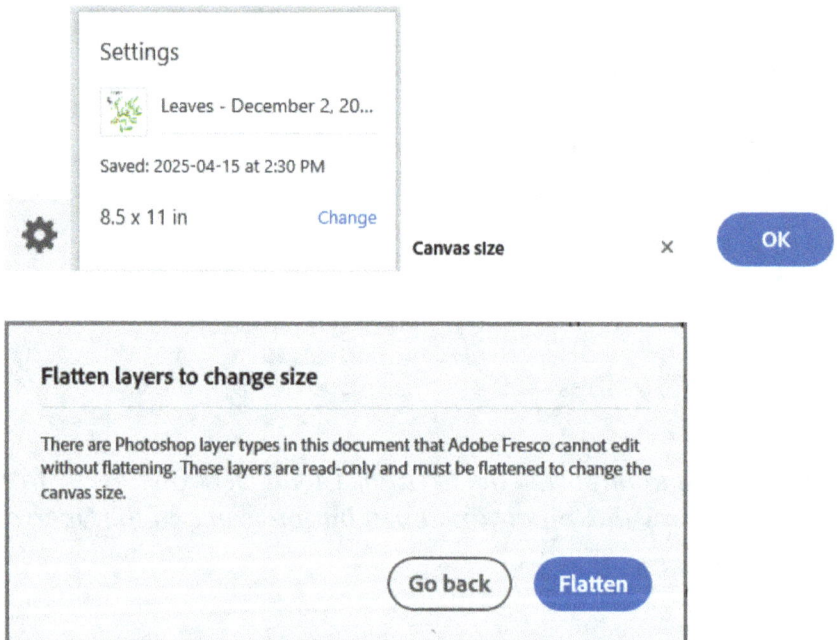

Figure 2-46. *The Fresco Settings panel and Canvas size dialog box may produce an additional warning when Photoshop layers are present*

Summary

In this chapter, we looked at how to create a new Fresco document as well as reviewed some of the actions, resources, and help and app settings within the application found in the Title bar. We looked at how to navigate and set various view settings. Then, we auto saved the file. Then, we looked at how Fresco files can be quickly deleted, downloaded, imported, and opened.

In the next chapter, we will start to look at some of the tools within the Fresco workspace and review how they are similar to other Adobe applications.

CHAPTER 3

Exploring the Workspace of Fresco and Its Tools: Part 1

Continuing from the previous chapter, we will now explore and work with various tools from the Tools bar panel within the document. Some of these tools may already be familiar to you if you have used the applications of Photoshop and Illustrator. As well as while doing a project, you will discover how to create custom brush assets in Photoshop that can be added, via the Creative Cloud Library panel, to Fresco to enhance your artwork.

Note The project files for this chapter can be found in the Chapter 3 folder. Refer to the link in the introduction.

Before we begin this discussion, I want to note how Fresco's strength is to focus on brushes and creating painterly effects. In reality, there are many brush options available to artists. Refer to Figure 3-1.

CHAPTER 3 EXPLORING THE WORKSPACE OF FRESCO AND ITS TOOLS: PART 1

Figure 3-1. *Image of real-world artist tools for painting on a canvas that includes a palette, brushes, and paint*

However, if you are an artist that, besides painting, also enjoys working with other types of media like chalk, pastels, charcoal, pencils, or markers on paper to create drawings and sketches, then I think you will appreciate Fresco's ability to emulate these kinds of media which we will see as we progress through this chapter and others. Refer to Figure 3-2.

CHAPTER 3   EXPLORING THE WORKSPACE OF FRESCO AND ITS TOOLS: PART 1

Figure 3-2. *An image of various media materials that an artist might use to create artwork*

The benefit of Fresco is you don't have to start from a hand-drawn artwork to begin painting or drawing; you can start being creative right away. Having said that, starting at the end of this chapter and later in Chapter 4, we will look at how to work with a project as well as import files that you can enhance in Fresco.

For Photoshop users, if you are not familiar with how to scan your drawings, I recommend you read my book *Accurate Layer Selections Using Photoshop's Selection Tools* mentioned in Chapter 1. However, scanning is not required for this book as I have supplied all images in their digital form. For this chapter, let's just focus on the Fresco tools.

CHAPTER 3   EXPLORING THE WORKSPACE OF FRESCO AND ITS TOOLS: PART 1

As you did in Chapter 1, open the Fresco application to begin. Refer to Figure 3-3.

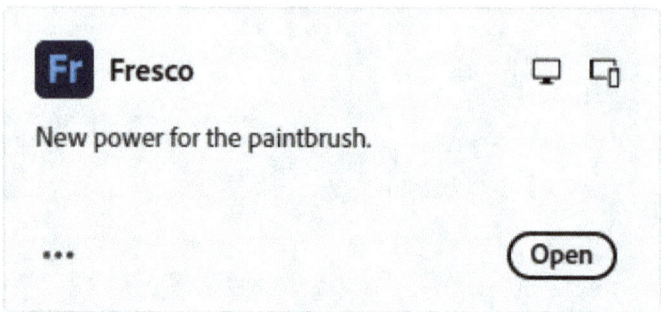

Figure 3-3. *Creative Cloud Desktop setting to open Fresco*

From the Home page, you can then create a new document for practice or open the recent blank document you created in the previous chapter. Refer to Figure 3-4.

Figure 3-4. *A recent blank document that was created in Fresco*

CHAPTER 3　EXPLORING THE WORKSPACE OF FRESCO AND ITS TOOLS: PART 1

Using the Toolbar Panel

The Toolbar panel, along with the disabled Touch shortcut and blank canvas, will appear in the workspace. Refer to Figure 3-5.

Figure 3-5. *Fresco toolbar, the Touch shortcut circle (disabled), and a blank canvas*

The Toolbar panel is generally found on the left side of the application unless you have set it in the Settings ➤ App settings ➤ General ➤ Interface ➤ Toolbar on the right-hand side. Refer to Figure 3-6.

63

CHAPTER 3   EXPLORING THE WORKSPACE OF FRESCO AND ITS TOOLS: PART 1

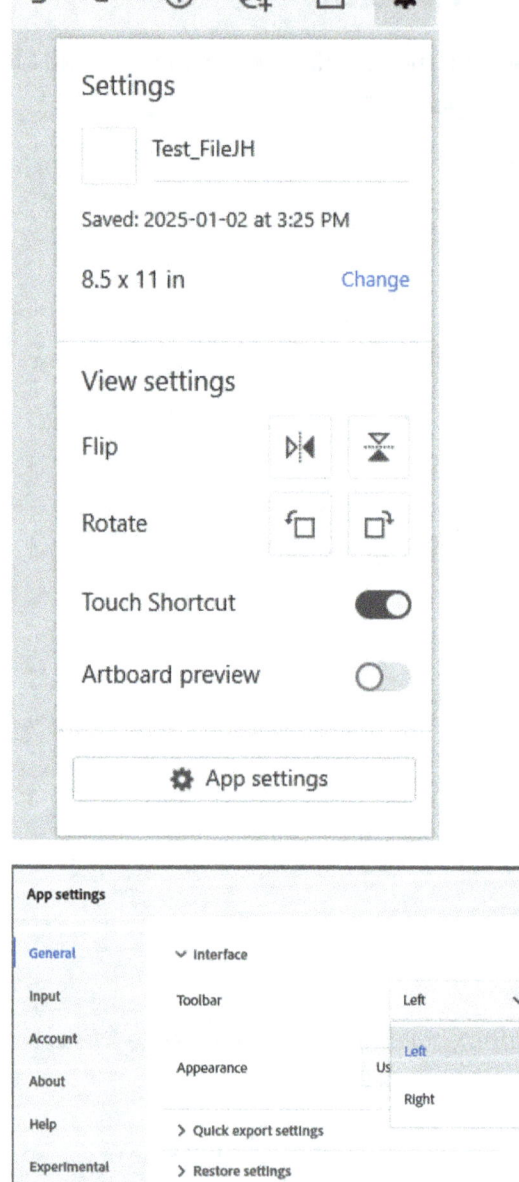

Figure 3-6. *Setting menu and App settings dialog box*

CHAPTER 3   EXPLORING THE WORKSPACE OF FRESCO AND ITS TOOLS: PART 1

Leave it on the default left for this book; use the X on the dialog box to exit this setting area.

Like Photoshop and Illustrator, the Toolbar panel is a great way to access all of your important tools while you work within the workspace of Fresco. Refer to Figure 3-7.

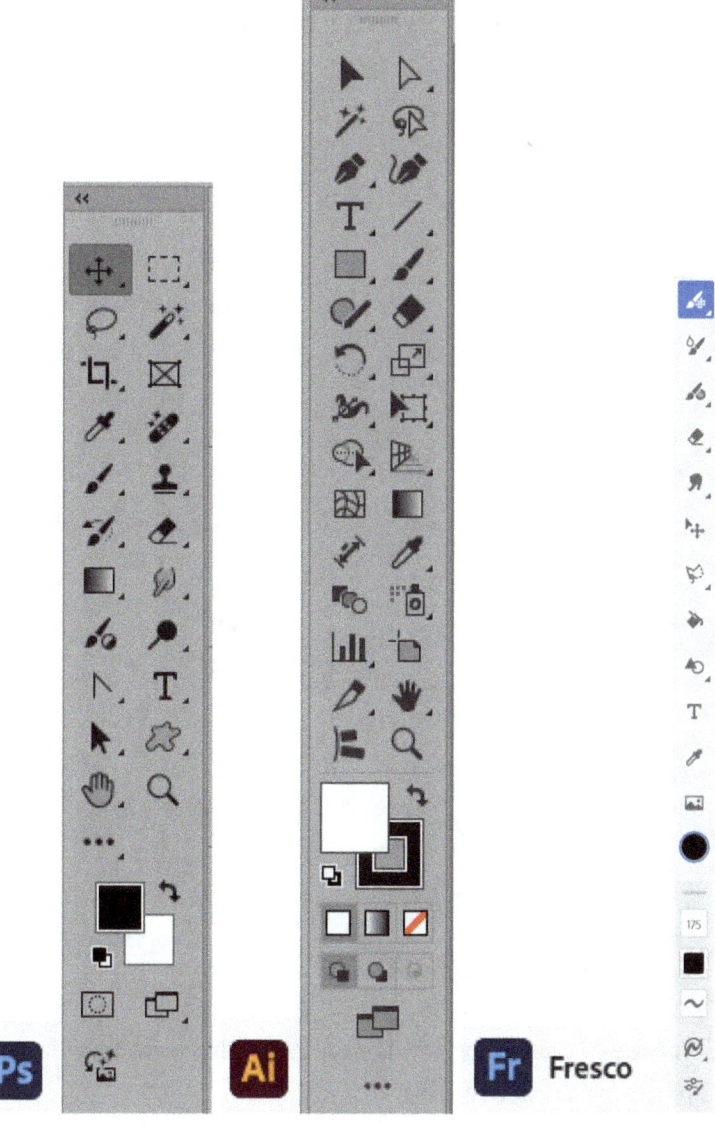

Figure 3-7. *Comparison of Photoshop Toolbar, Illustrator Toolbar, and Fresco Toolbar*

CHAPTER 3　EXPLORING THE WORKSPACE OF FRESCO AND ITS TOOLS: PART 1

In this example, as you work in Fresco, you will notice on the right-hand side of your workspace to the left of the Vertical Taskbar that a layer is added to the Layer panel as you experiment with various brush tools. I will talk about this more in Chapter 5 as to what each layer kind is used for. But when you start a new document, you will generally see a background layer and then a pixel or vector layer will appear as different brushes or tools are used. For now, our focus is just on how to use the brush tools. Refer to Figure 3-8.

Figure 3-8. *The Taskbar and active layers*

You can continue to work on your blank document from Chapter 2 or create a new blank document again to practice with.

CHAPTER 3   EXPLORING THE WORKSPACE OF FRESCO AND ITS TOOLS: PART 1

Brush Tools and Their Options

Within the column of the Toolbar panel, starting from the top, you will find five main kinds of "brushes." They are called Pixel brushes (P), Live brushes (H), Vector brushes (V), Eraser brushes (E), and Smudge which is brushlike. Like brushes in reality, you can use them to emulate a variety of painterly effects to add an artist's flare to your painting. Refer to Figure 3-9.

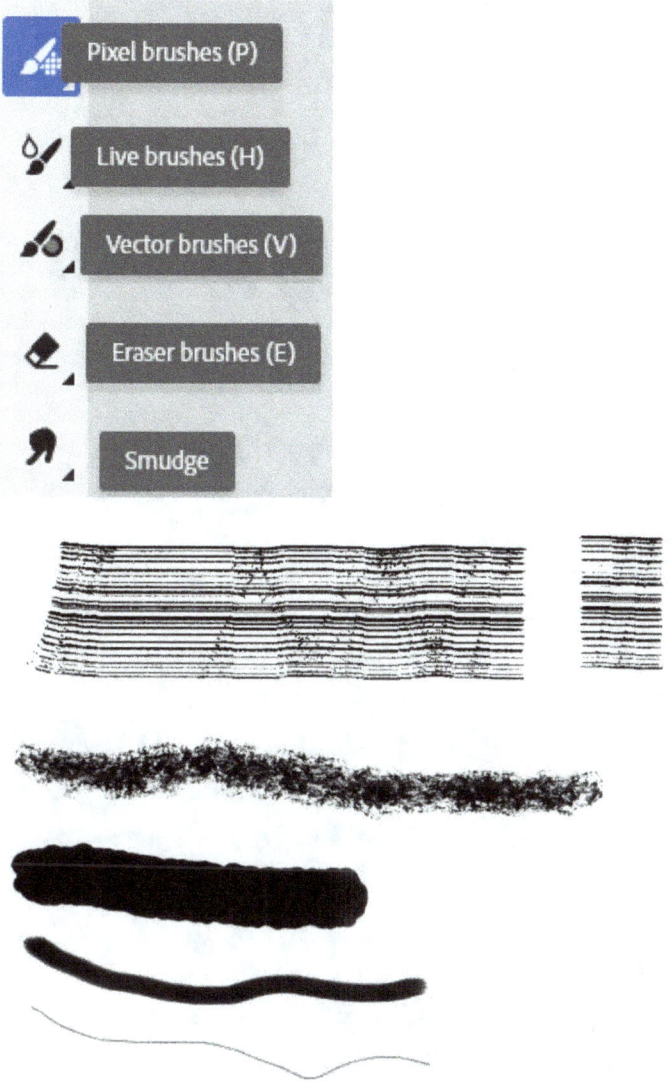

Figure 3-9. *Fresco Toolbar five main kinds of brushes and some examples of a few brush strokes*

However, brushes in Fresco, unlike brushes in the real-world, have some consistency in how they react on the canvas when they lay down color. Brushes in reality rely on the amount of paint applied to them, their change in condition, holding of the brush, pressure, and the roughness of the canvas. Thankfully, the Fresco designers have built some unpredictability and emulation of natural behavior into these brushes as you will discover. Here are some kinds of real-world brushes Fresco tries to mimic. Refer to Figures 3-10, 3-11, and 3-12.

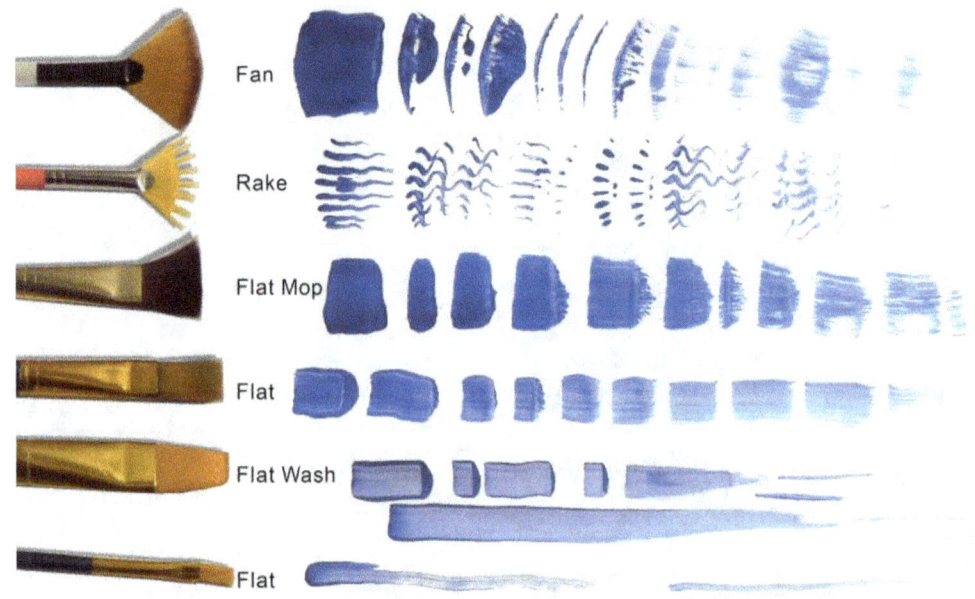

Figure 3-10. Real examples of Fan, Rake, and Flat brushes with paint applied to a canvas

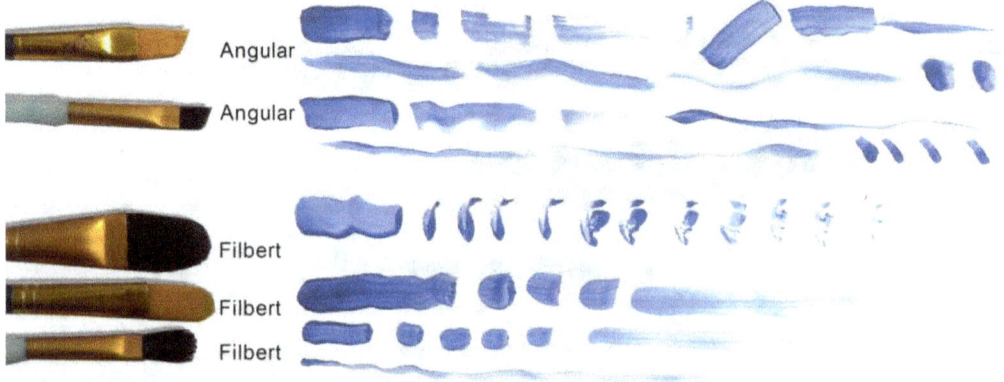

Figure 3-11. Real examples of Angular and Filbert brushes with paint applied to a canvas

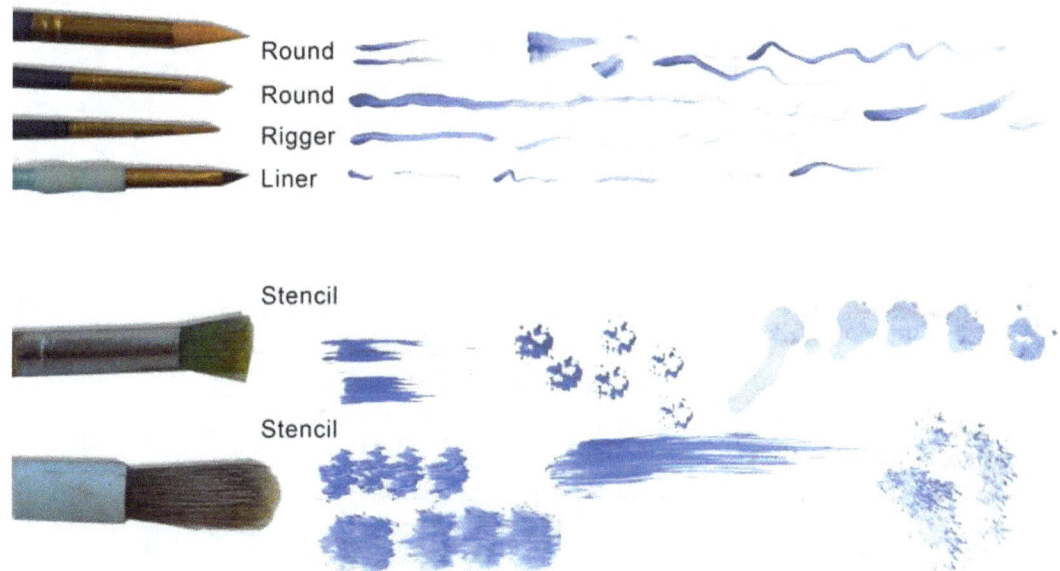

Figure 3-12. *Real examples of Round, Rigger, Liner, and Stencil brushes with paint applied to a canvas*

I will now discuss each kind of Fresco brush in more detail.

Pixel Brushes

Pixel brushes operate very similarly to the ones found in the application Photoshop in that you can use them to paint on your canvas or layer and cover them with a colorful dot pixel display. To access your Pixel brushes, you need to hold down the mouse on the tool for a second so that the menu can pop out and display all the brush kinds. Then, click the right pointing arrow to view the brushes within the category. Refer to Figure 3-13.

CHAPTER 3   EXPLORING THE WORKSPACE OF FRESCO AND ITS TOOLS: PART 1

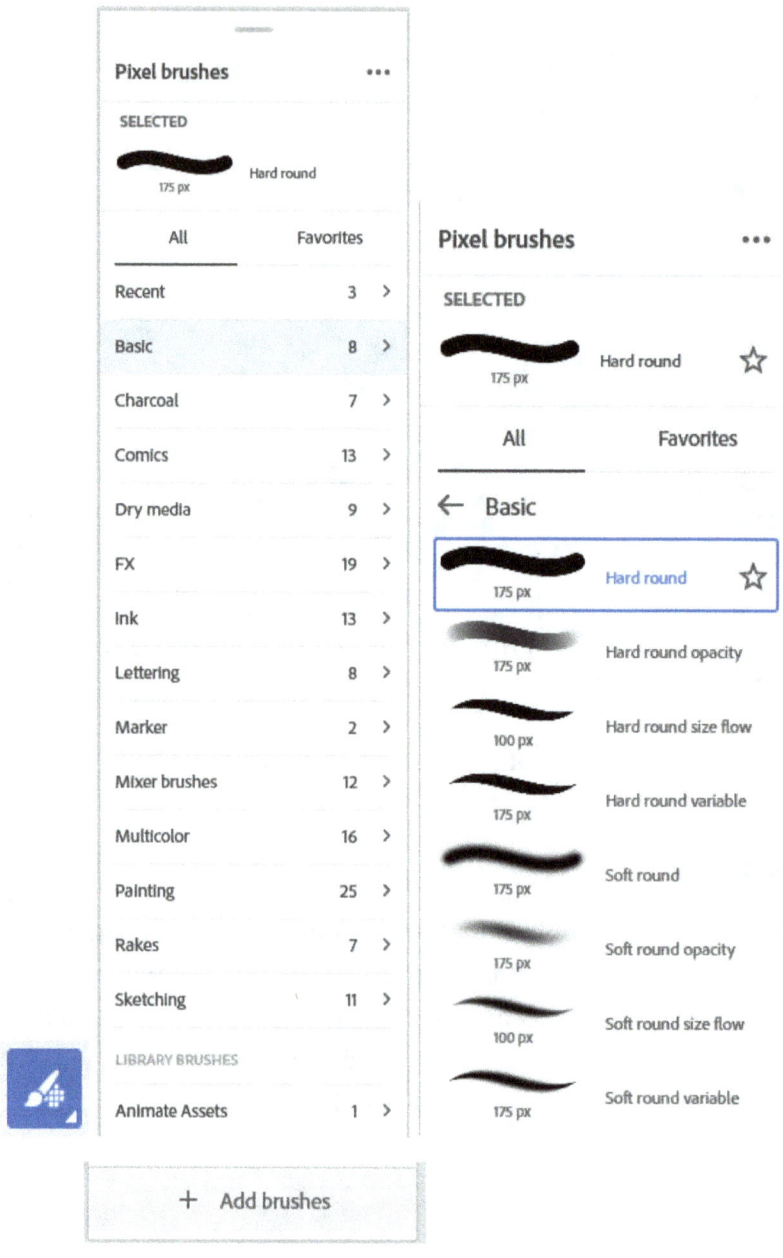

Figure 3-13. *Pixel brush icon with category list and with basic brush subcategory selected*

The Recent or current selected brush will appear at the top of the list. However, there are many brush styles that you can choose from. These can be filtered by All brushes or your Favorites. Click the left pointing arrow if you find yourself in the Recent tab and want to exit this area. Refer to Figure 3-14.

CHAPTER 3　EXPLORING THE WORKSPACE OF FRESCO AND ITS TOOLS: PART 1

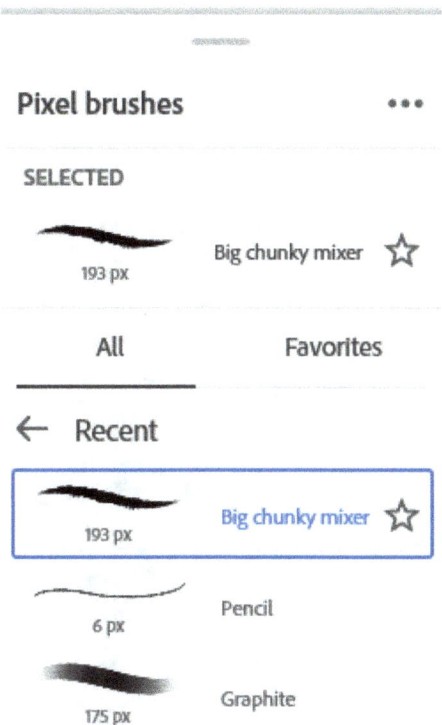

Figure 3-14. *Pixel brush Recent subcategory list*

While in the All tab, as noted, all the Recent brushes will be at the top of the list. However, for each, you can click the right pointing arrow to reveal brushes from these categories. Then, select a brush of your choice and begin to paint on the canvas. Refer to Figure 3-15.

CHAPTER 3 EXPLORING THE WORKSPACE OF FRESCO AND ITS TOOLS: PART 1

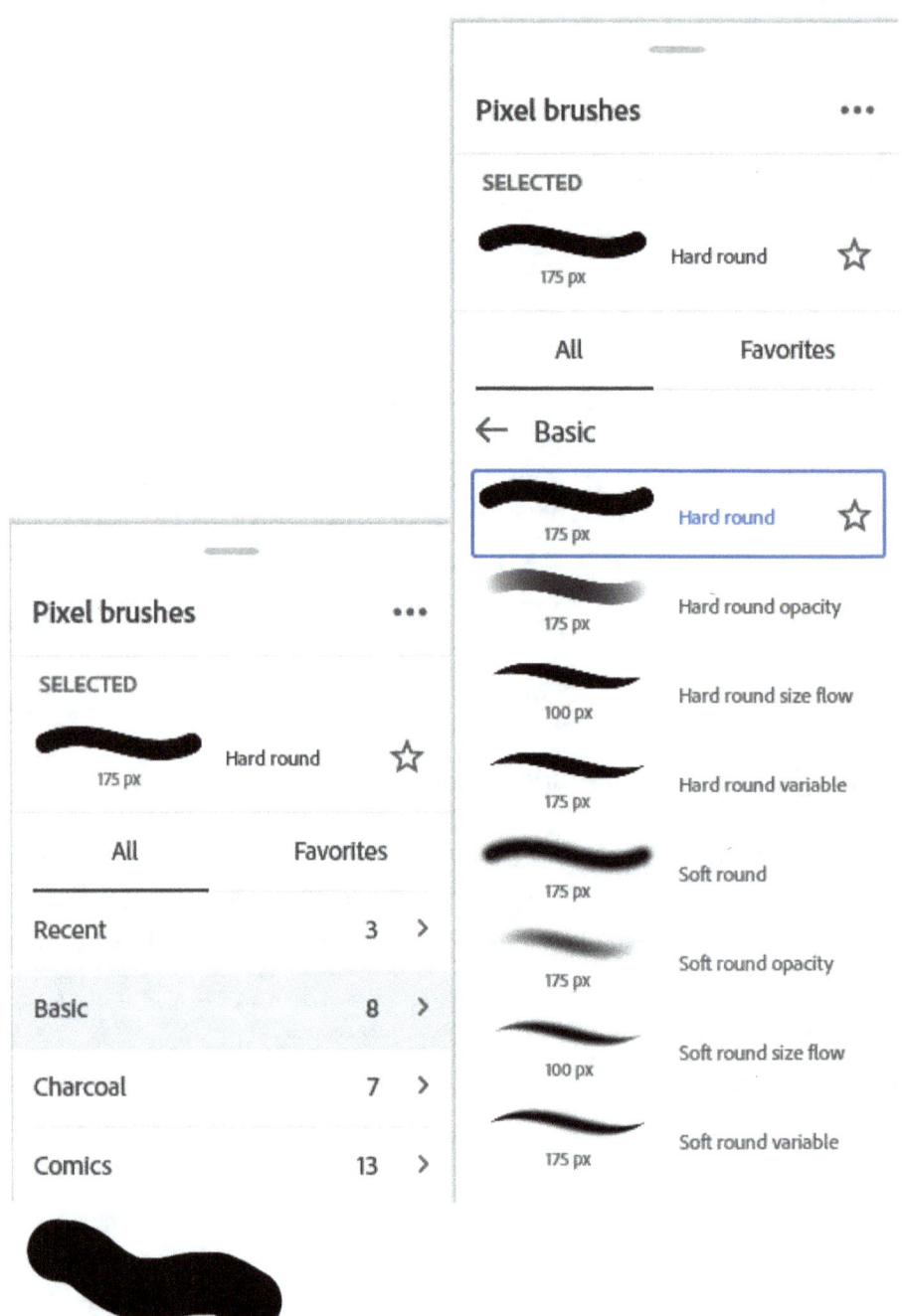

Figure 3-15. *Pixel brushes, Basic category selected, and Basic Hard round brush selected from the list and painted on canvas*

Tip If by accident as you work with a brush, you click on it and select the Hide button by mistake and need to retrieve that brush again, you can get it back by clicking the upper right ellipsis (…). Manage pixel brushes in the tool's menu, and then, use the dialog box to search and show all brushes again, and click Done to commit the change and exit. Refer to Figure 3-16.

Chapter 3 Exploring the Workspace of Fresco and Its Tools: Part 1

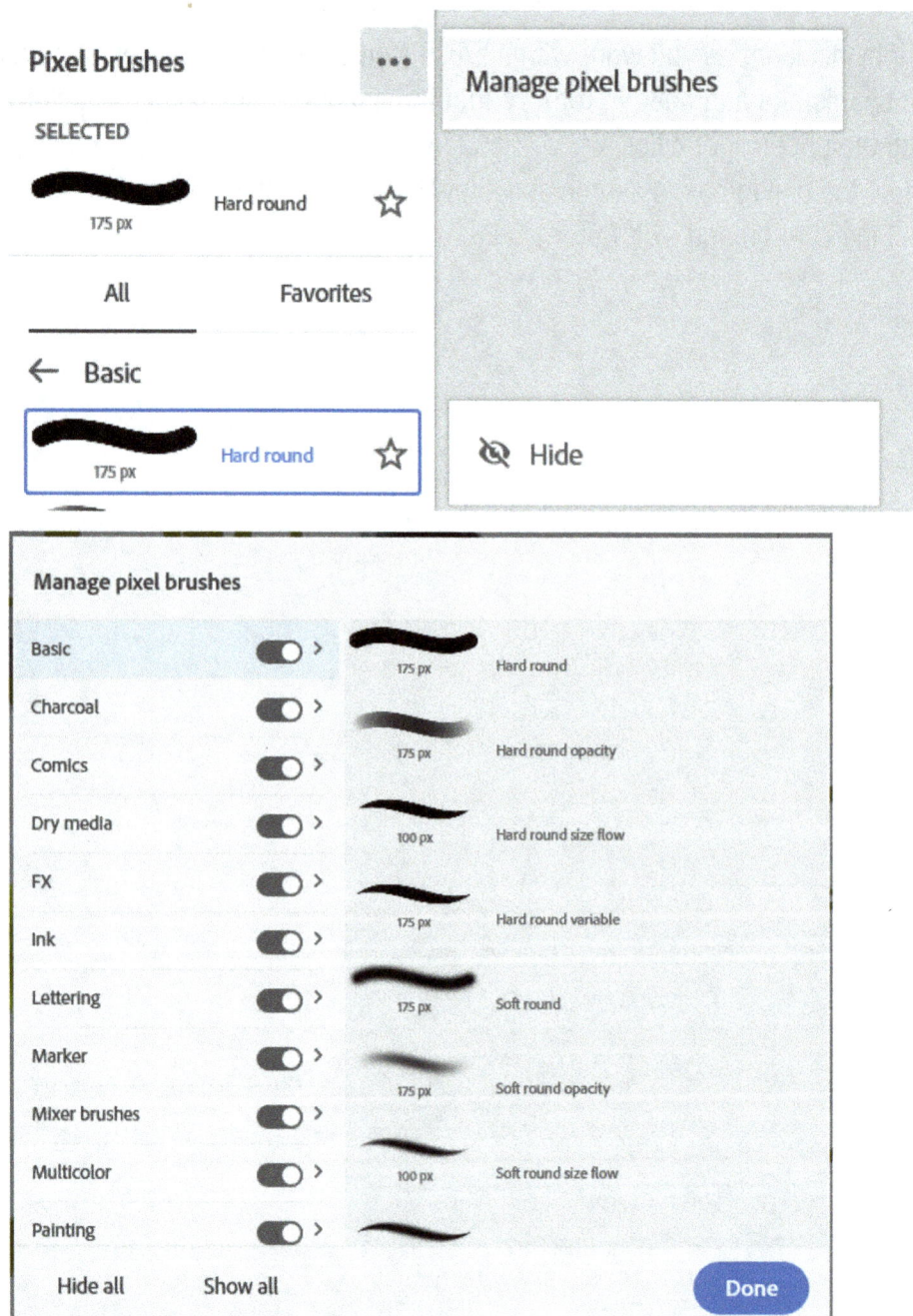

Figure 3-16. *When Pixel brushes from a list become hidden, use Manage pixel brushes icon and dialog box to reveal again*

This is the same for every kind of brush in this chapter, except for erasers.

CHAPTER 3   EXPLORING THE WORKSPACE OF FRESCO AND ITS TOOLS: PART 1

Tip   If while you work with the brushes you need to see a preview of the shapes of the brush, go to Settings ➤ App settings, and in the dialog box, under the Input ➤ Brushes ➤ Brush preview, choose the option of Brush stamp. Alternatively, it can be set to Off or Crosshairs. Refer to Figure 3-17.

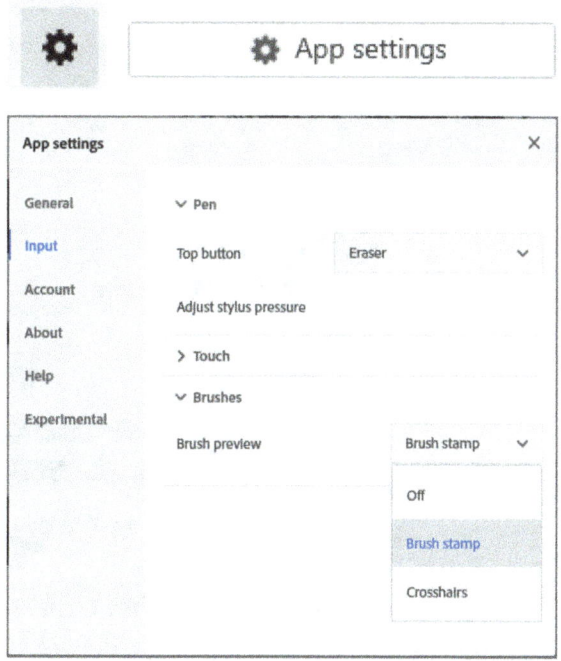

Figure 3-17. *Adjust the brush settings using the App settings icon and dialog box*

This will give you a better preview of your brush head as you work. Close the dialog box using the upper right corner X.

Returning to the Brushes menu, the kinds of brushes you can choose are in the following categories:

- Basic: Default standard brushes that can be used to create lines that are either clean or feathered and blurred around the edges. A Hard round or Soft round is often good for this kind of work. It can have a pointed or dull edge. The angled, pointed edge is much more apparent when using a stylus rather than a mouse. Refer to Figure 3-18.

75

CHAPTER 3   EXPLORING THE WORKSPACE OF FRESCO AND ITS TOOLS: PART 1

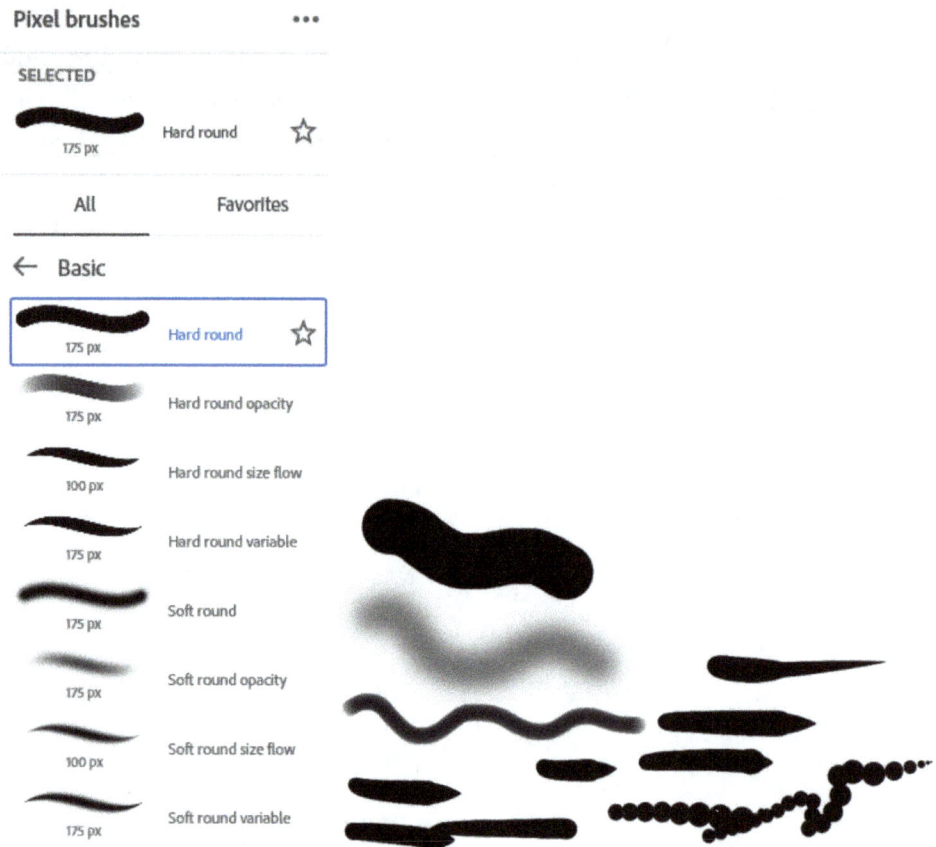

Figure 3-18. *Pixel brush, category Basic, and various brush strokes painted on the canvas*

- Charcoal: Emulates the look of chalk and charcoal stick, or with a vine pencil, the lines appear rough, giving a more natural effect. These are ideal for creating sketches of figures. Refer to Figure 3-19.

CHAPTER 3 EXPLORING THE WORKSPACE OF FRESCO AND ITS TOOLS: PART 1

Figure 3-19. *Real examples of charcoal or black crayon. Pixel brush, category Charcoal, and various brush strokes painted on the canvas*

- Comics: Emulates different patterning that appear in a comic or how a comic book artist might draw with their ink pen to create black and white artwork. There are a variety of styles to choose from that give us cross hatch and halftone styles. Refer to Figure 3-20.

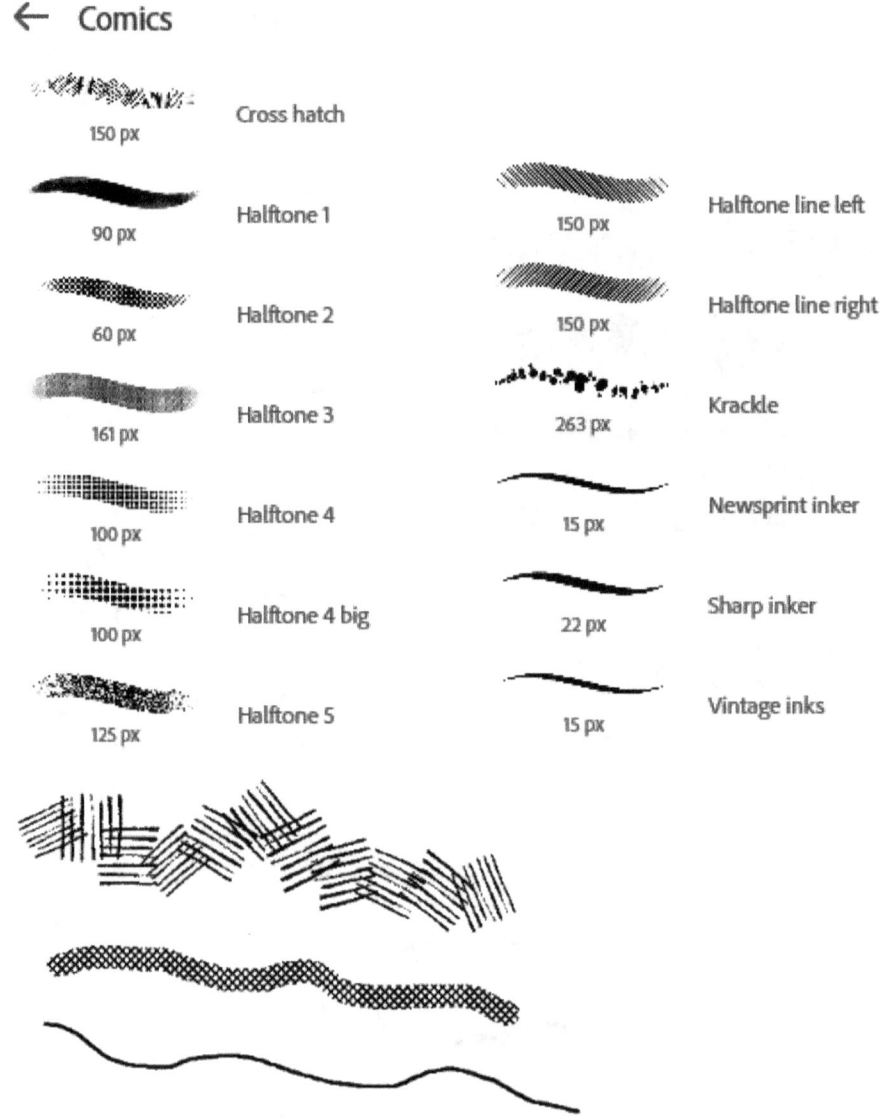

Figure 3-20. *Pixel brush, category Comics, and various brush strokes painted on the canvas*

- Dry Media: Emulates how you would work with a dry brush and paint over a canvas. Or you might use charcoal, chalk, pencil, pastel, and graphite, and the painting can appear very rough and but also bristlelike as the digital paint moves over the canvas. Refer to Figure 3-21 and Figure 3-22.

CHAPTER 3　EXPLORING THE WORKSPACE OF FRESCO AND ITS TOOLS: PART 1

Figure 3-21. *An example of some pastel artwork and some pastel crayons and holder*

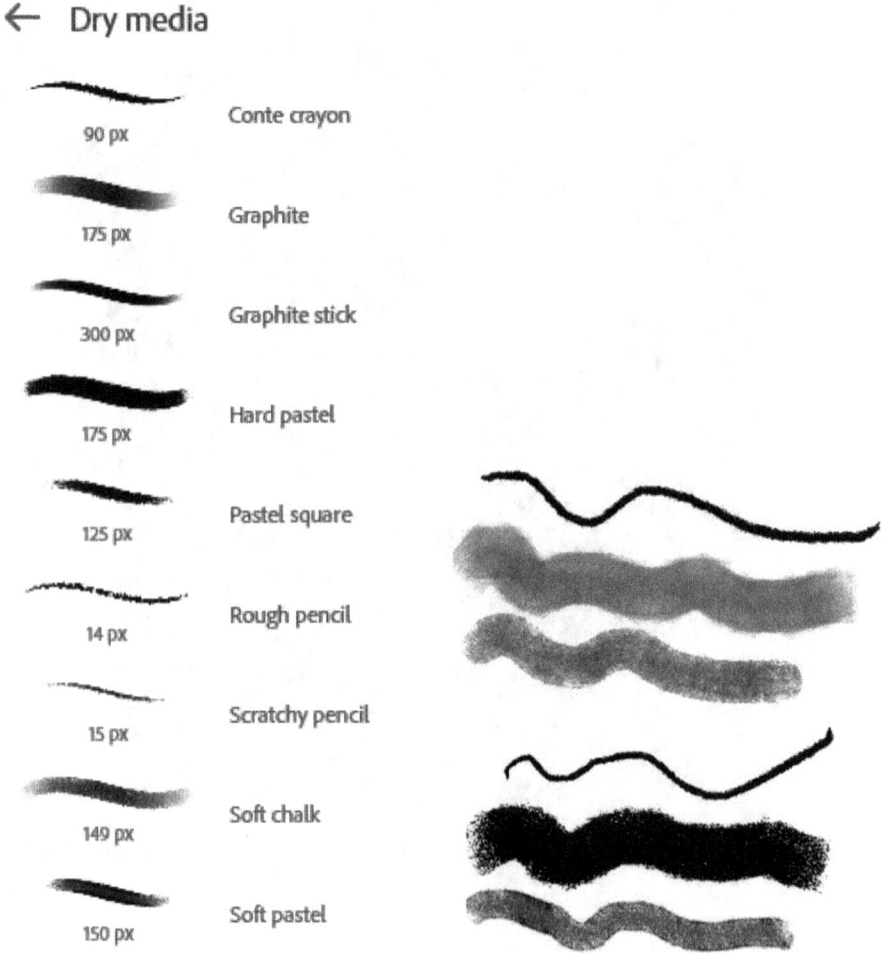

Figure 3-22. *Pixel brush, category Dry media, and various brush strokes painted on the canvas*

- FX: Similar to the Comics brushes, these brushes can be used to create effects like clouds, dust, foliage, ink spatters, leaves, ink stains, lines of leaves or stars, smoke, sponging, and other kinds of spatters. In the real world, spatters and imperfections are also created with stencil brushes or older brushes whose bristles have overtime become damaged. Refer to Figures 3-12, 3-23, and 3-24.

CHAPTER 3 EXPLORING THE WORKSPACE OF FRESCO AND ITS TOOLS: PART 1

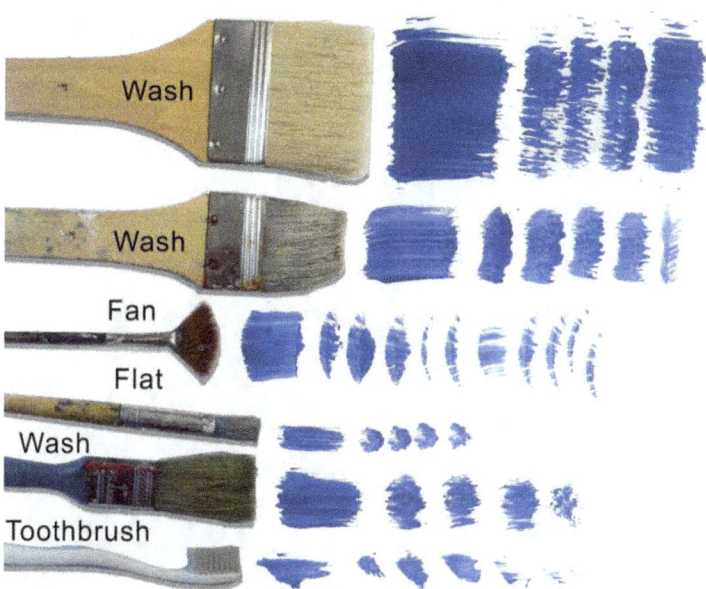

Figure 3-23. *Example of older brushes used to create effects on the canvas*

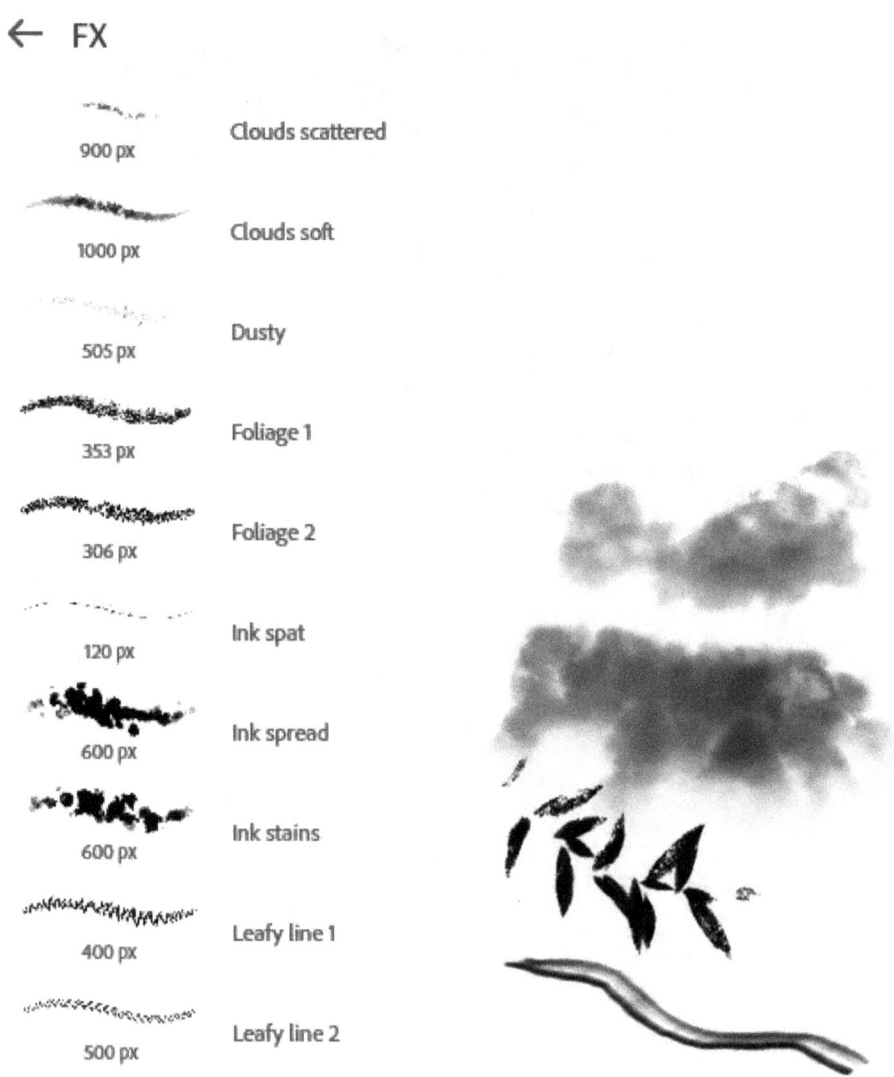

Figure 3-24. *Pixel brush, category FX, and various brush strokes painted on the canvas*

- Ink: Emulates how you would work with an ink pen tip. When drawing, the lines can be clean and smooth which resembles calligraphy and a steady hand but can also be slightly jagged or jittery and spotty which may add more interest or texture to your art. Refer to Figure 3-25 and Figure 3-26.

CHAPTER 3   EXPLORING THE WORKSPACE OF FRESCO AND ITS TOOLS: PART 1

Figure 3-25. *Real pen used to create ink strokes*

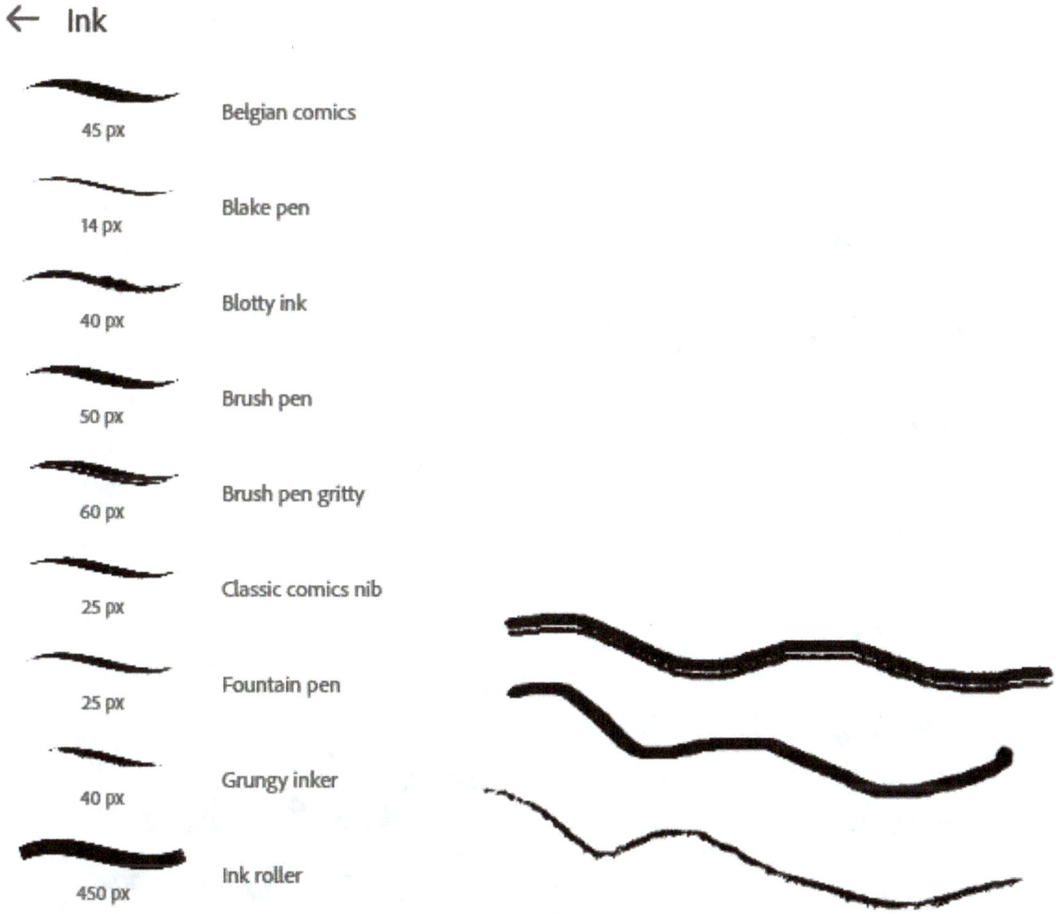

← Ink

- 45 px — Belgian comics
- 14 px — Blake pen
- 40 px — Blotty ink
- 50 px — Brush pen
- 60 px — Brush pen gritty
- 25 px — Classic comics nib
- 25 px — Fountain pen
- 40 px — Grungy inker
- 450 px — Ink roller

Figure 3-26. *Pixel brush, category Ink, and various brush strokes painted on the canvas*

- Lettering: Similar to the Ink options, this can be used to draw custom calligraphy letters or for comics or for your personal signature. The brush can be very thin or thick and chunky. Refer to Figure 3-27 and Figure 3-28.

83

CHAPTER 3   EXPLORING THE WORKSPACE OF FRESCO AND ITS TOOLS: PART 1

Figure 3-27. *Real pen used for lettering*

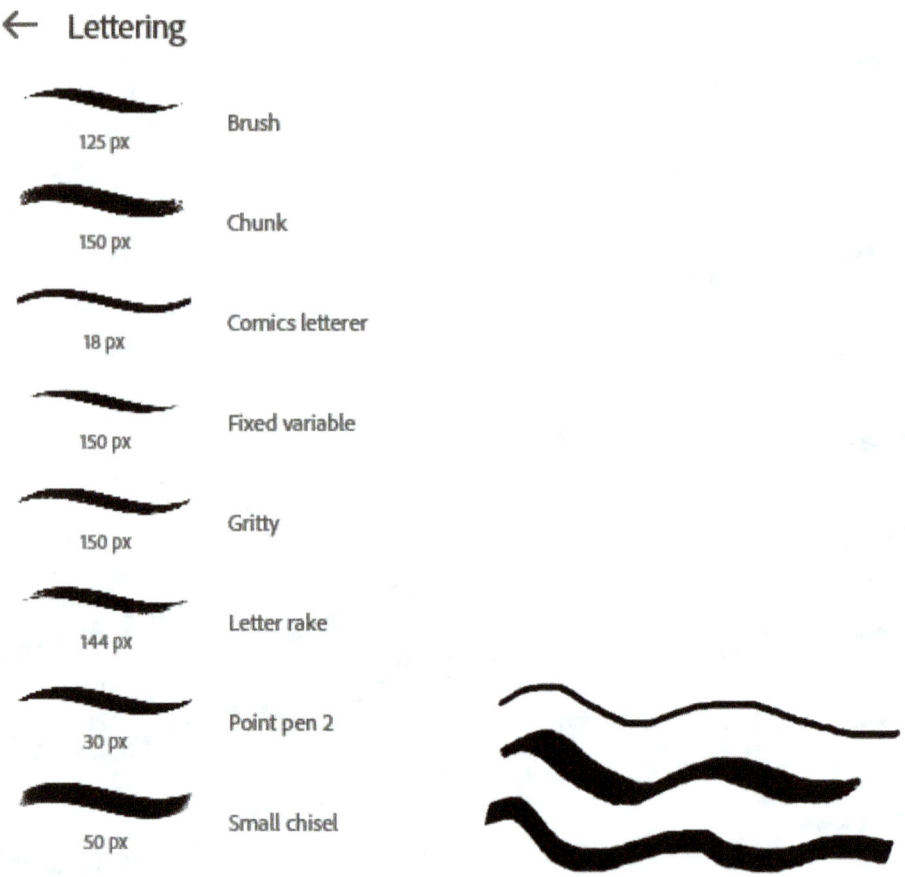

Figure 3-28. *Pixel brush, category Lettering, and various brush strokes painted on the canvas*

- Marker: Similar to ink and lettering, this brush emulates how ink would flow out of a thick marker pen while drawing, for a bold or chiseled effect. Refer to Figure 3-29.

84

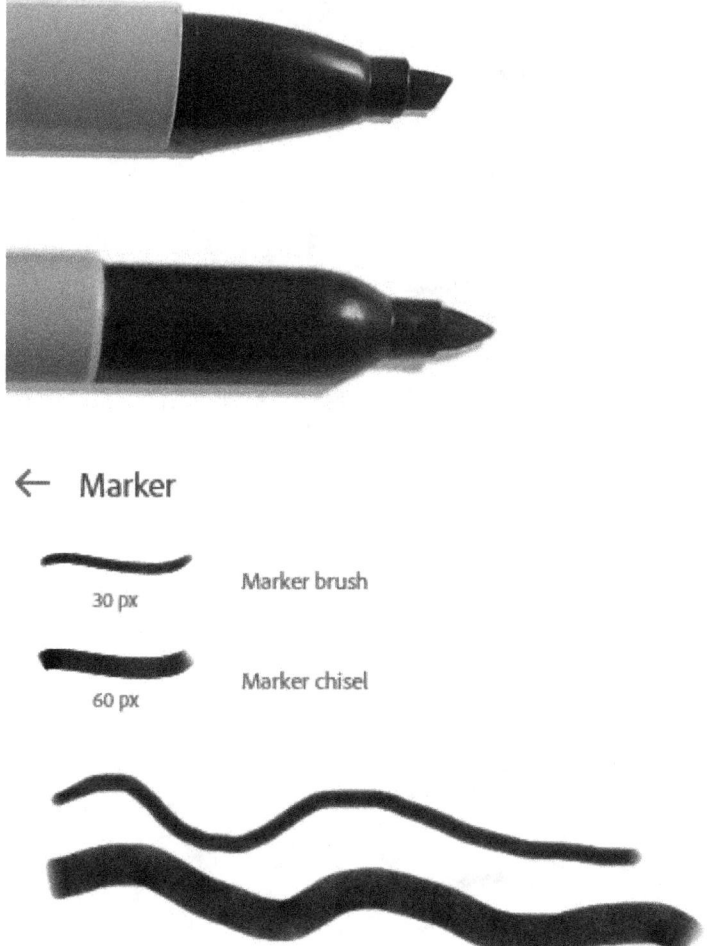

Figure 3-29. *Real markers and Pixel brush, category Marker, and various brush strokes painted on the canvas*

- Mixer Brushes: These are special brushes for the blending of two or more colors as you would with pastels or paint with a brush. Color changing will be explained shortly when I describe the brush properties or settings. The brush can be thick and chunky to create texture and a wisp-like pattern but also thin with a dull or pointed end. As with other brushes, the angle of the brush is more obvious when you use a stylus rather than a mouse. Refer to Figure 3-30.

CHAPTER 3   EXPLORING THE WORKSPACE OF FRESCO AND ITS TOOLS: PART 1

Figure 3-30.   *Pixel brush, category Mixer brushes, and various brush strokes painted on the canvas*

- Multicolor: These are a variety of graphically colorful brushes which can be used to lay down colorful patterns of paint which appear almost like ribbons or a repeating stamp. Refer to Figure 3-31 and Figure 3-32.

Figure 3-31. *Real examples of paint being rolled on the canvas*

CHAPTER 3   EXPLORING THE WORKSPACE OF FRESCO AND ITS TOOLS: PART 1

Figure 3-32. *Pixel brush, category Multicolor, and various brush strokes painted on the canvas*

- Painting: These brushes are used to emulate a variety of brush effects. Paint brushes often come in a variety of bristle shapes and sizes when we buy them in the store. These can include flat heads, angled heads, or even a brush that has older damaged bristles. Wet, dry, impressionist, and acrylic painting effects can also be emulated. As seen in the earlier Figures 3-10, 3-11, 3-12, and 3-23 in the real world, here, they are now emulated in Fresco. There is a large selection of brushes in this category, so experimentation is important. Refer to Figure 3-33.

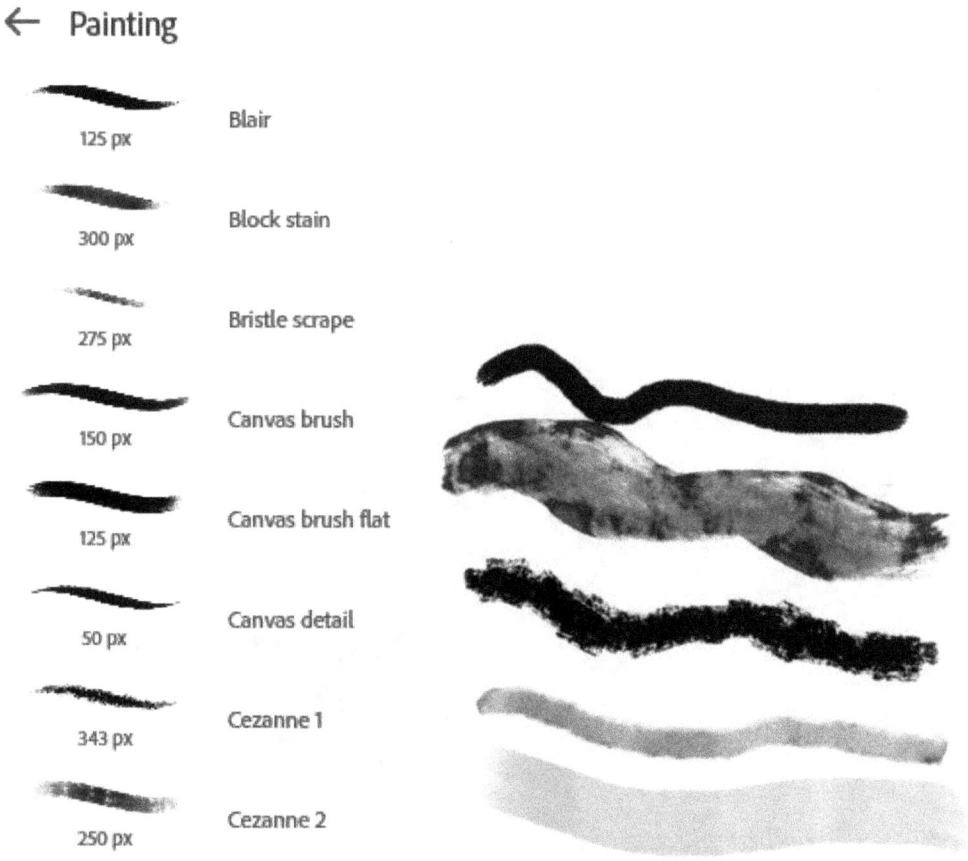

Figure 3-33. *Pixel brush, category Painting, and various brush strokes painted on the canvas*

- Rakes: This category emulates a special kind of painting brush known as rake which creates line effect similar to dragging a rake across a canvas. Refer to Figures 3-10 and 3-23 for real-world examples of rakes and fans. When painting in the real world, you would need several rake brushes in various sizes and imperfections to create this effect, but with Fresco, the options are all packed into one category for you, which is great for the budget and storage. Refer to Figure 3-34.

CHAPTER 3 EXPLORING THE WORKSPACE OF FRESCO AND ITS TOOLS: PART 1

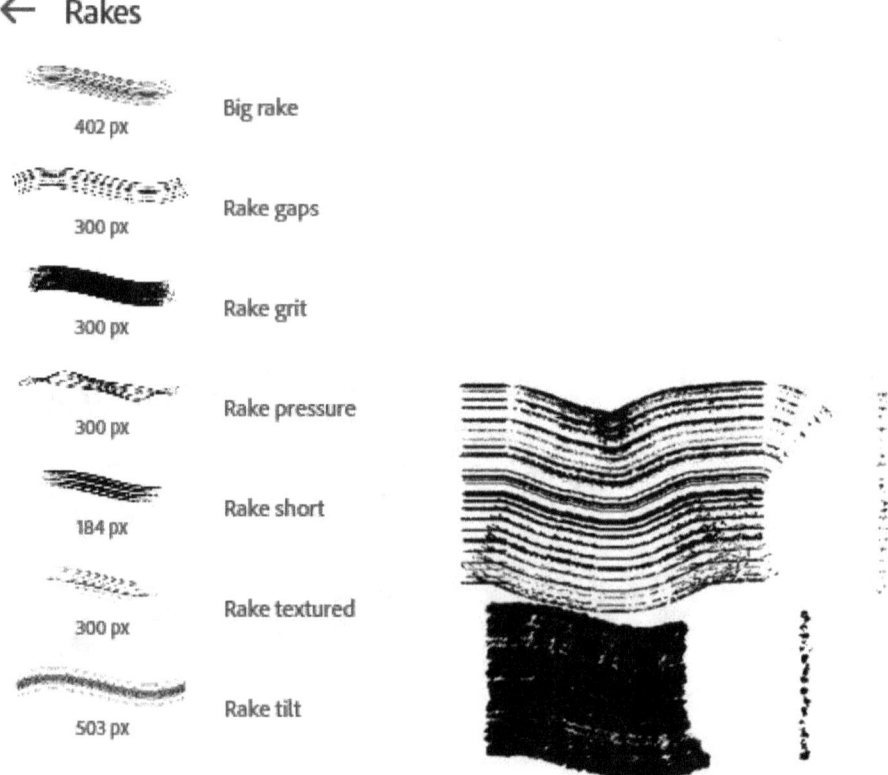

Figure 3-34. *Pixel brush, category Rakes, and various brush strokes painted on the canvas*

- Sketching: Emulates the sketching style with the pencil, pen, vine, and graphite. Much like the Charcoal style in roughness but has a thinner line which can be dull or pointy at the tip end. Sketching in the real world often requires pencils of various lead thicknesses that are both hard and soft to get a desired effect and need to be sharpened occasionally to maintain that effect. But in Fresco, they are all found here and never become dull ended until you decide they should be, plus you can change their color at any time to create pencil crayons as you will see later in the chapter. Refer to Figure 3-35 and Figure 3-36.

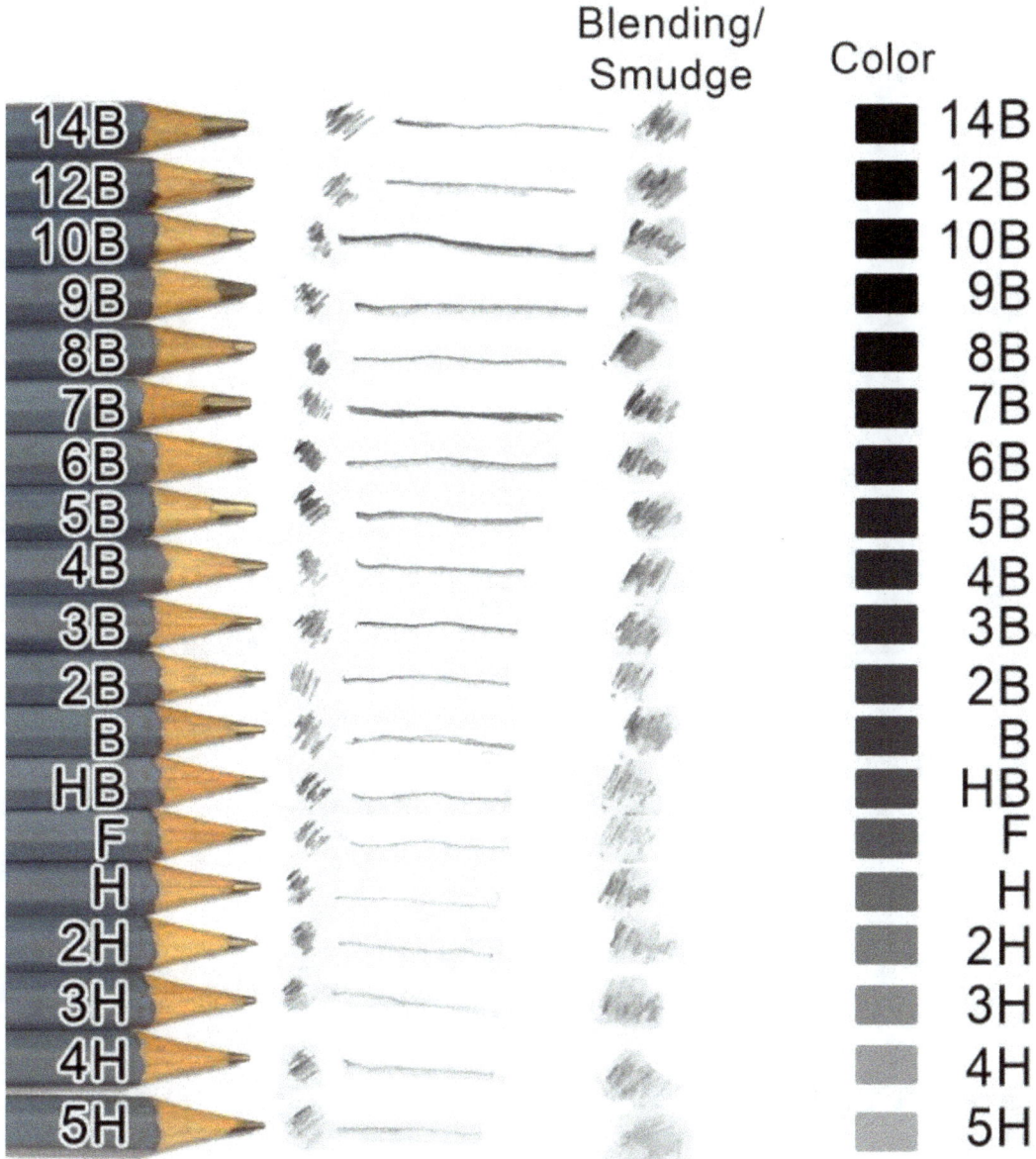

Figure 3-35. *Real examples of sketching pencils of various degrees of hardness from 14B to 5H for blending and smudging and color when accurate pressure is applied*

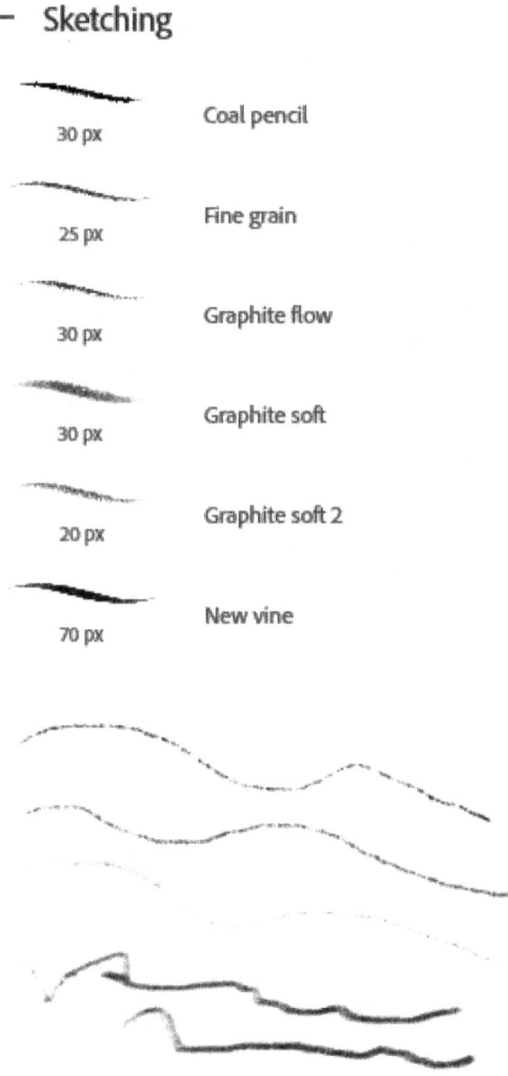

Figure 3-36. *Pixel brush, category Sketching, and various brush strokes painted on the canvas*

- Library Brushes: These are brushes that were created in another application such as Photoshop and added via the Libraries panel through that application. Photoshop, as mentioned, does a great job of creating a variety of brushes. However, it can be a bit more of a technical process than just selecting the brushes from the list you see in Fresco. Being able to use the brushes that you are familiar with in Photoshop is great, and you can import most of your favorite brushes using a library as I will explain in this chapter, after we have reviewed all the various brush kinds. Refer to Figure 3-37.

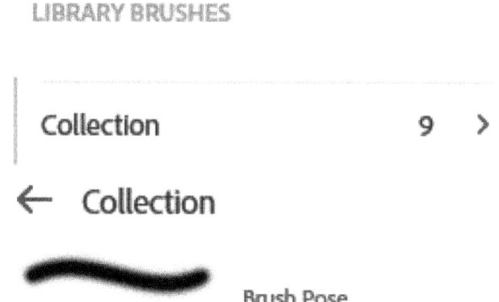

Figure 3-37. Pixel brush, category Library, selected from a library called Collection, and a brush stroke from that library painted on the canvas

Add Brush Feature

At the end of the list, you can now add additional brushes where you can discover new brushes directly from Fresco or import from files on your computer that you created either in the file formats of (.tpl) or (.abr). Refer to Figure 3-38.

CHAPTER 3   EXPLORING THE WORKSPACE OF FRESCO AND ITS TOOLS: PART 1

Figure 3-38. *Use the Pixel brushes list Add brushes button to import and discover more brushes to add*

CHAPTER 3   EXPLORING THE WORKSPACE OF FRESCO AND ITS TOOLS: PART 1

Later, I will mention a few other ways that new brushes can be created and added as well as using Photoshop or Capture when we start the project.

Pixel Brush Properties, Settings, and Changing Colors

Now, after using the default brushes and color of black, you may want to customize those settings. In the real world, we would use a paint palette of premixed colors and clean or switch the brush before trying a new paint. However, in Fresco, the lower area of the Toolbar contains the color chip and various settings for each brush. Refer to Figure 3-39 and Figure 3-40.

Figure 3-39. *Artist's painting pallet for organizing color*

CHAPTER 3   EXPLORING THE WORKSPACE OF FRESCO AND ITS TOOLS: PART 1

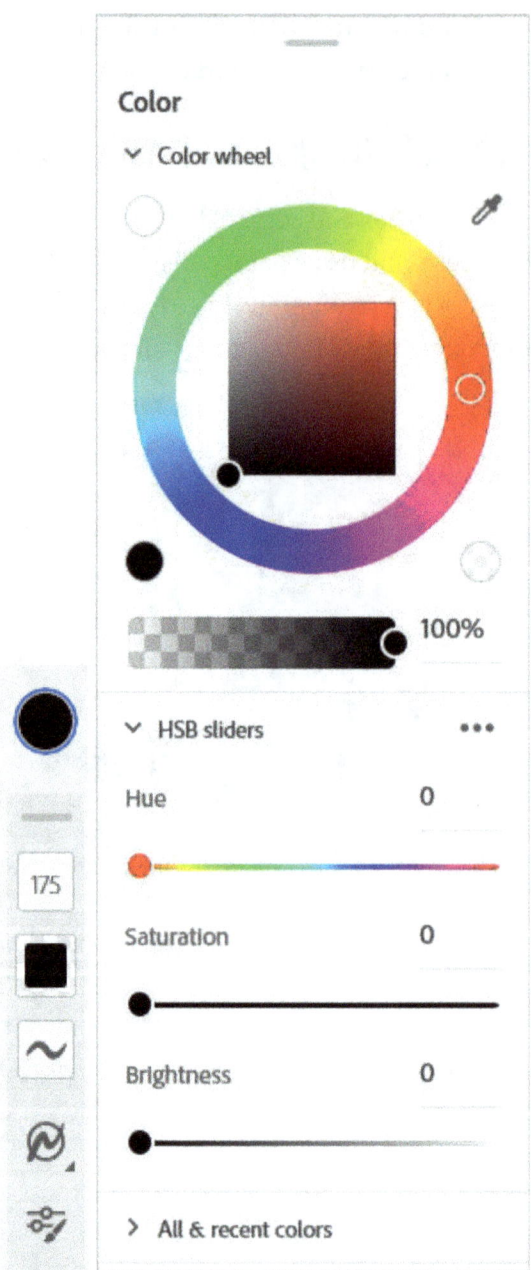

Figure 3-40. *Fresco Toolbar color chip and settings for Color wheel, sliders, and all or recent selected colors*

CHAPTER 3   EXPLORING THE WORKSPACE OF FRESCO AND ITS TOOLS: PART 1

To change colors of your brush in the Toolbar panel, you can click the circle color chip to reveal the color wheel and panel. This area may change for different brushes, but it will allow you to do such things as adjust colors by dragging with your cursor to a new color on the square or surrounding wheel. Alternatively, use the eyedropper to click on a color somewhere on the canvas and acquire that color directly from your art. You can also use your default color spots surrounding the wheel to return to white, black, or no color. Refer to Figure 3-41.

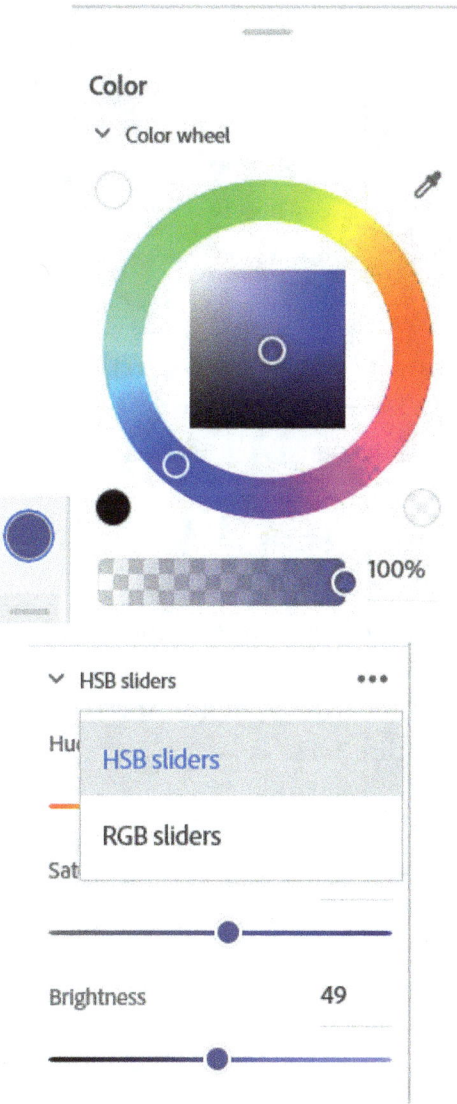

Figure 3-41. *Color wheel setting alerted from the color chip, opacity, and slider options*

Below the wheel, you can change the opacity of the selected color from 0% to 100% and then work with HSB (Hue 0–360, Saturation 0–100, Brightness 0–100) sliders or RGB (Red, Green, Blue) sliders which each range from 0 to 255. Note there is no CMYK slider option. In this book, I am using HSB. Refer to Figure 3-41.

You can also see your recently used colors under the Recents tab or use the All tab to review colors that came from other Creative Cloud libraries used in applications like Photoshop and Illustrator. Refer to Figure 3-42.

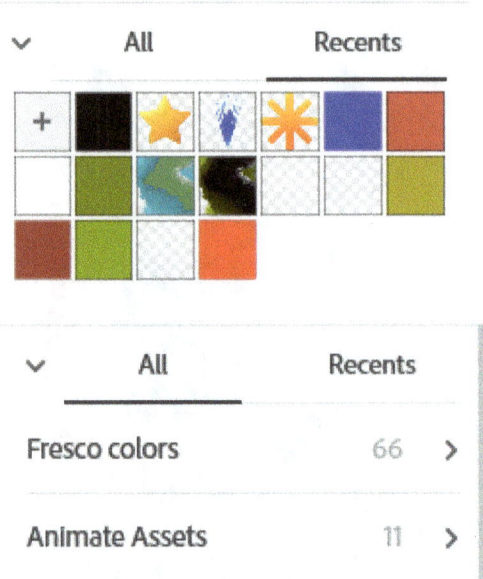

Figure 3-42. Color chip All and Recents tabs and their options

Under Fresco colors, click the right pointing arrow (Figure 3-42) to see more options of colors to review. Refer to Figure 3-43.

CHAPTER 3   EXPLORING THE WORKSPACE OF FRESCO AND ITS TOOLS: PART 1

Figure 3-43. *Additional Fresco Swatches, Multicolor Swatches, and Themes you can find in the color chip Fresco colors list*

I will review how to collect swatches from Photoshop libraries later in Chapter 4.

Note that depending on the brush chosen, multicolor or pattern options may appear. We will look at the multicolor later in Chapter 4. Refer to Figure 3-44.

Figure 3-44. *Example of a color chip multicolor swatch*

You can then, below the color chip, set other brush properties and settings for each brush. Refer to Figure 3-45.

Figure 3-45. *In Toolbar below the color chip are more brush settings*

These settings include the following:

- Brush Size (1–3500) Pixels: Click to reveal the panel, and then drag on the slider up (increase) or down (decrease) to change the size. Note that the size range can vary from brush to brush, and some may have a lesser or greater size range than others when selected. Refer to Figure 3-46.

CHAPTER 3 EXPLORING THE WORKSPACE OF FRESCO AND ITS TOOLS: PART 1

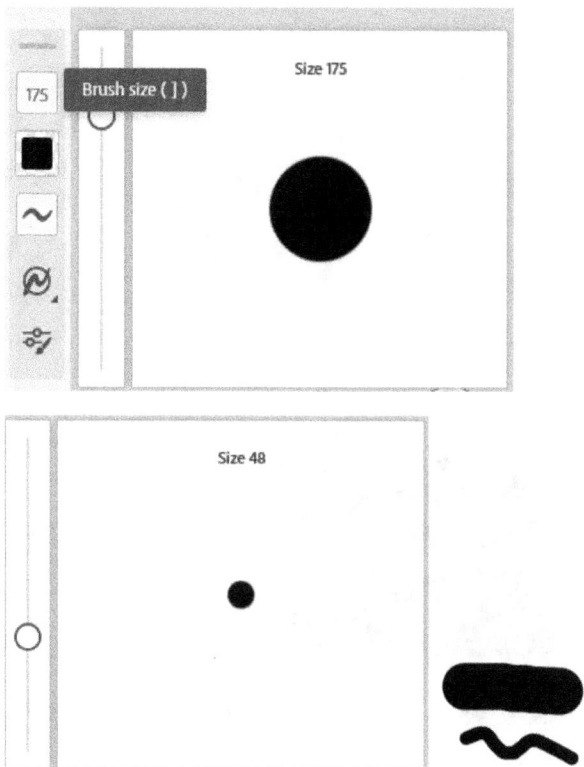

Figure 3-46. *Toolbar setting the Brush size and painting on the canvas*

- Brush Flow (1–100%): Click to reveal the panel, and then drag on the slider up (increase) or down (decrease) to change the amount of flow as a lower flow (27) will create a blurry edge. Refer to Figure 3-47.

CHAPTER 3 EXPLORING THE WORKSPACE OF FRESCO AND ITS TOOLS: PART 1

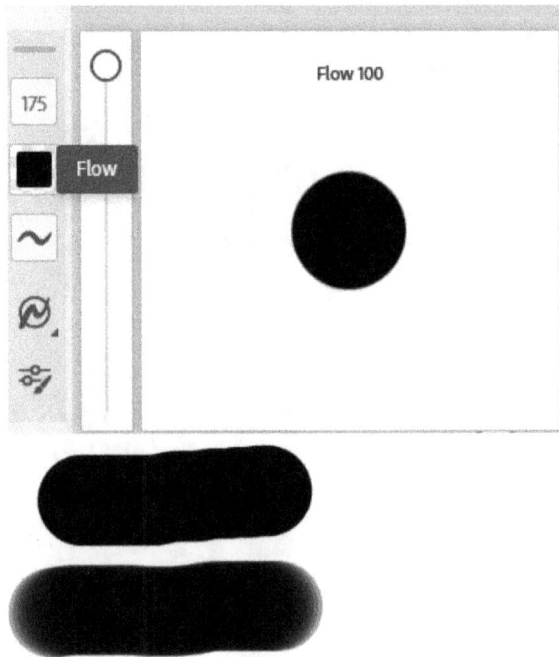

Figure 3-47. *Toolbar setting the brush Flow and painting on the canvas*

- Smoothing (0–100%): This setting can work in conjunction with size and flow; smoothing can give a sharper angle (1) or rounder curve (100) as you paint and move the brush stamp. Refer to Figure 3-48.

CHAPTER 3　EXPLORING THE WORKSPACE OF FRESCO AND ITS TOOLS: PART 1

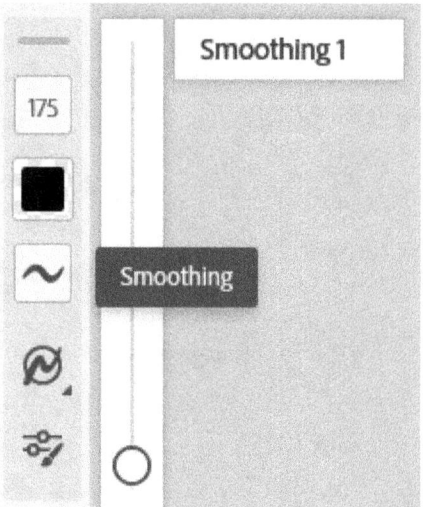

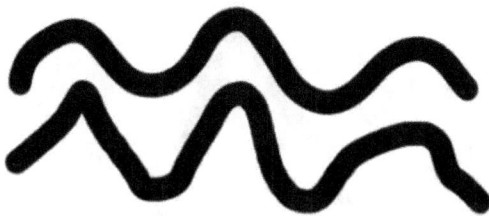

Figure 3-48. *Toolbar setting the brush Smoothing and painting on the canvas*

- Painting Inside Settings: The icon toggles off and on; by default, it is off and will be discussed later in the chapter in more detail. Refer to Figure 3-49.

CHAPTER 3   EXPLORING THE WORKSPACE OF FRESCO AND ITS TOOLS: PART 1

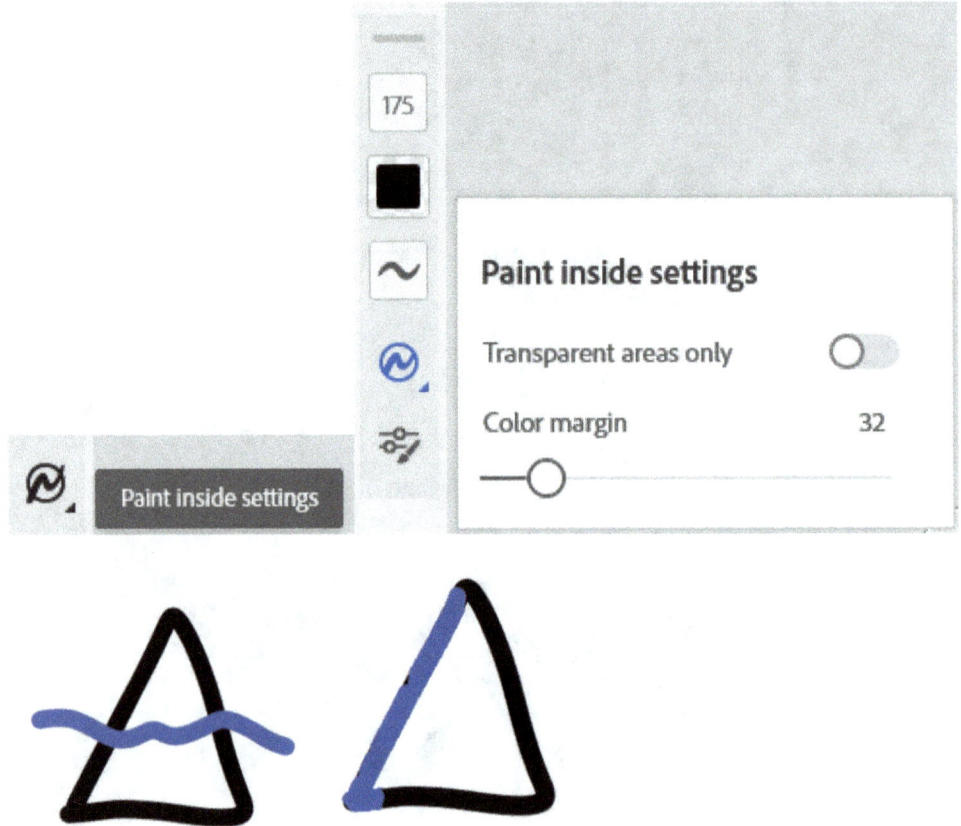

Figure 3-49. *Toolbar setting the Paint inside settings, enabling, and painting on the canvas with different colors*

- Brush Settings: Different brushes will have their own unique settings depending on the category chosen. Refer to Figure 3-50.

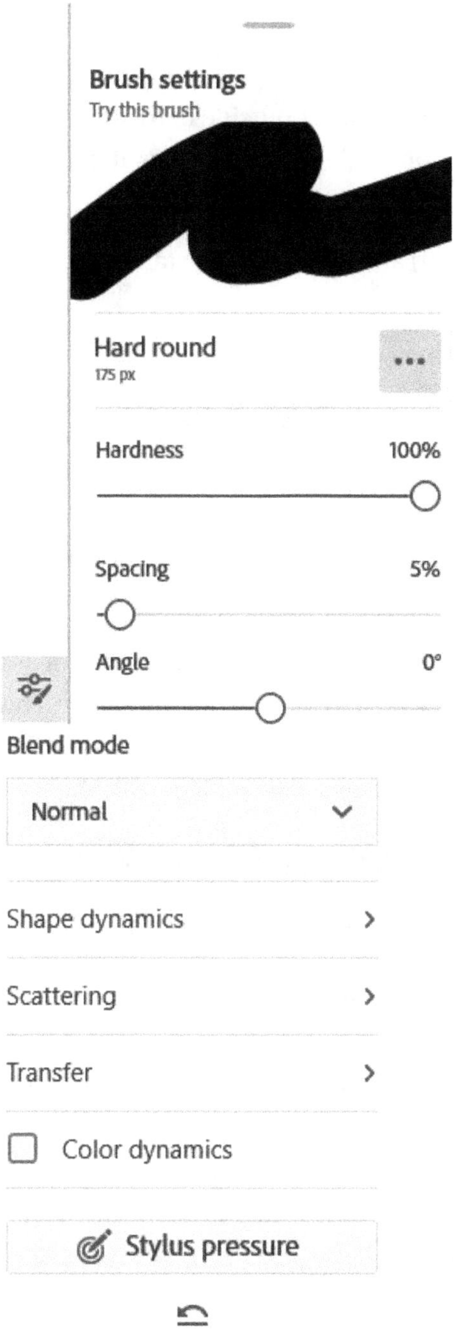

CHAPTER 3   EXPLORING THE WORKSPACE OF FRESCO AND ITS TOOLS: PART 1

Figure 3-50. Pixel brush examining the following settings from the list

- They include the following settings but are not available in all brushes:

- Brush Size: This is set earlier outside of the Brush settings panel. Refer to that section earlier in the chapter. Refer to Figure 3-50.

- Hardness (0–100%): By dragging the slider, it creates a hard (100) or blurry soft edge (0) around the brush stamp area. Refer to Figure 3-50 and Figure 3-51.

Figure 3-51. *Adjustment to brush hardness and then painting on the canvas*

- Spacing (0–200%): By dragging the slider, you can alter how the color is laid down; spacings higher than 5% will create a bumpiness or scattering rather than a solid line. Try a setting of 141% to see the difference. Refer to Figure 3-50 and Figure 3-52.

Figure 3-52. *Adjustment to brush spacing and then painting on the canvas*

- Angle (−180°, 0°, 180°): By dragging the slider, you can change the angle of the head of the brush. This is more obvious when using a stylus than with a mouse for some non-round brushes or when spacing and other dynamics such as shape are altered which we will look at next. Refer to Figure 3-53.

CHAPTER 3   EXPLORING THE WORKSPACE OF FRESCO AND ITS TOOLS: PART 1

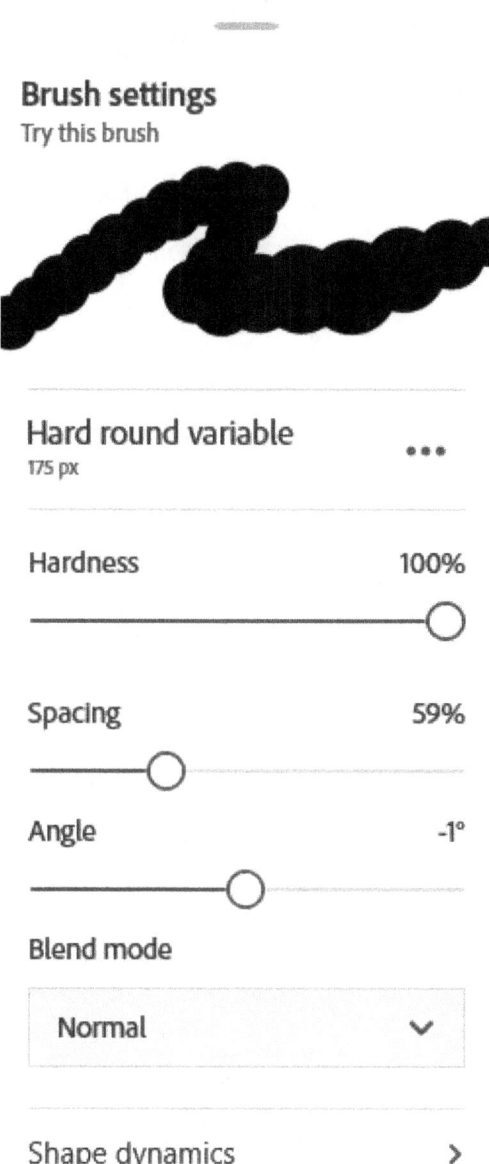

Figure 3-53. Adjustment made in the Brush settings panel to the Angle of a round brush head

- Shape Dynamics: When spacing is adjusted, settings can control such settings as the randomness of size and spacing of the brush head as you paint. The settings include Size jitter (0–100%), Control (Pen pressure, Pen Tilt, True Tilt, Fade, None (default)), Minimum

107

diameter (0-100%), Angle jitter (0-100%), and Control (Pen pressure, Pen Tilt, Fade, Direction, None (default)). The setting of Fade allows additional steps (1-9999). Flip X jitter and Flip Y jitter can also be enabled.

When not working with a stylus or pen, leave the Control menu at None. Refer to Figure 3-54.

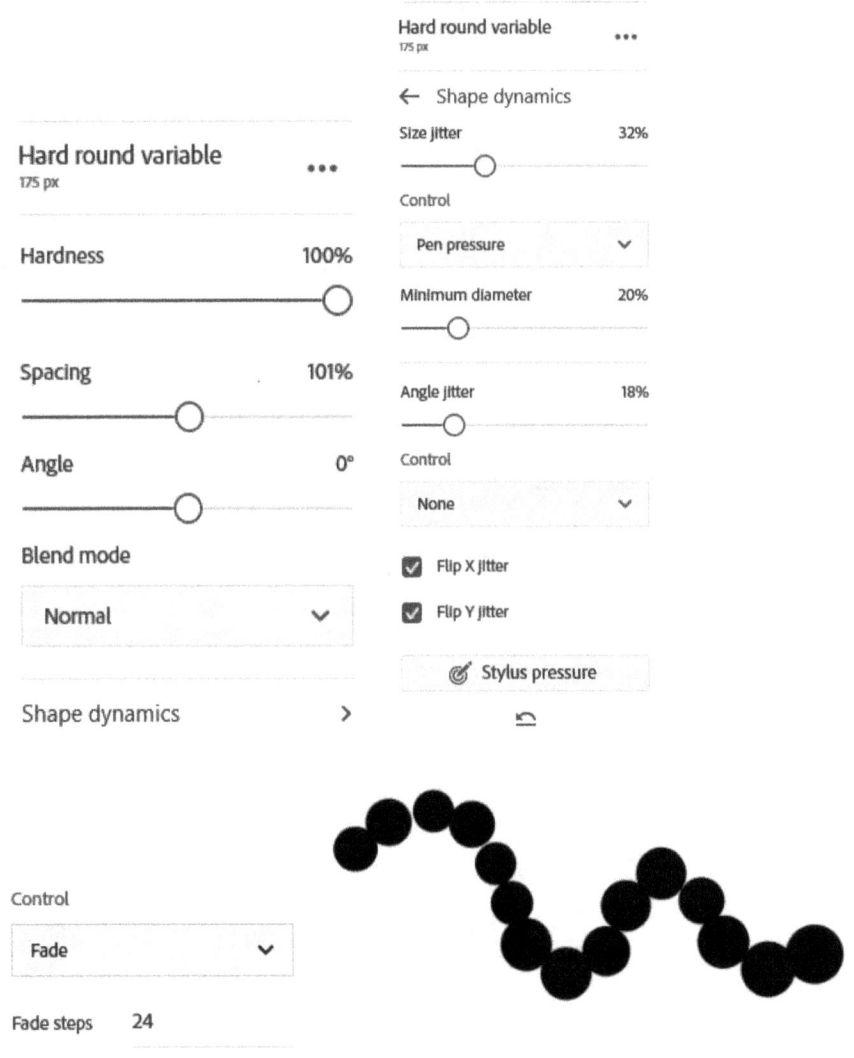

Figure 3-54. *Adjustment made in the Brush settings panel to the Shape dynamics of a round brush head*

- Pressure Dynamics: Size (−100%, 0%, 100%) and Flow (−100%, 0%, 100%). These are available for Marker brushes, but not all brushes. Prior to using pressure with a stylus pen, you can move the sliders to control size and flow and then press more firmly or lightly as you work. The setting works in conjunction with the Velocity dynamics. Refer to Figure 3-55.

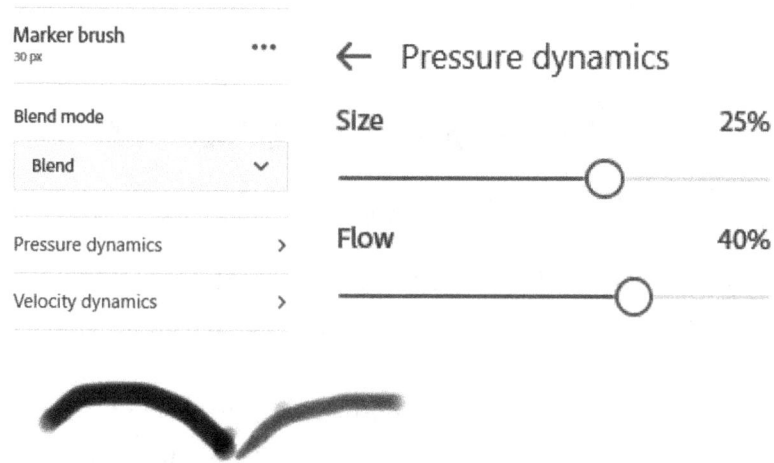

Figure 3-55. *Setting the brush settings for a Marker brush for Pressure dynamics and painting on the canvas*

- Velocity Dynamics: Size (−100%, 0%, 100%) and Flow (−100%, 0%, 100%). These are available for Markers brushes, but not all brushes. Prior to using pressure with a stylus pen, you can move the sliders to control size and flow or speed of the color and then press more firmly or lightly as you work. The settings work in conjunction with the Pressure dynamics. Refer to Figure 3-56.

CHAPTER 3   EXPLORING THE WORKSPACE OF FRESCO AND ITS TOOLS: PART 1

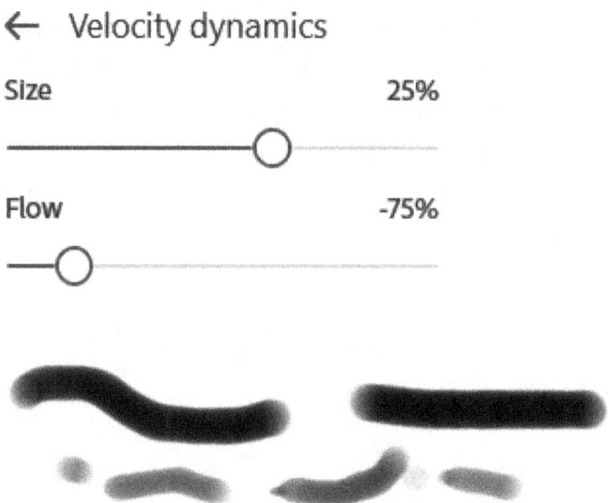

Figure 3-56. *Setting the brush settings for a Marker brush for Velocity dynamics and painting on the canvas*

- Scattering: In, for example, a basic brush, this setting controls the height spacing of the brush and can be used in conjunction with the earlier Spacing settings. The Scattering settings you can control if you click the right arrow are Both axes (enabled to control both X and Y), Scatter (0–1000%), Control (Pen pressure, Pen Tilt, Fade, None (default)), Stamp count (1–16; decreases or increases the stamp amount), Count jitter (0–100%), and Control (Pen pressure, Pen Tilt, Fade, None (default)). A setting of Fade will allow for additional steps. Refer to Figure 3-57.

CHAPTER 3   EXPLORING THE WORKSPACE OF FRESCO AND ITS TOOLS: PART 1

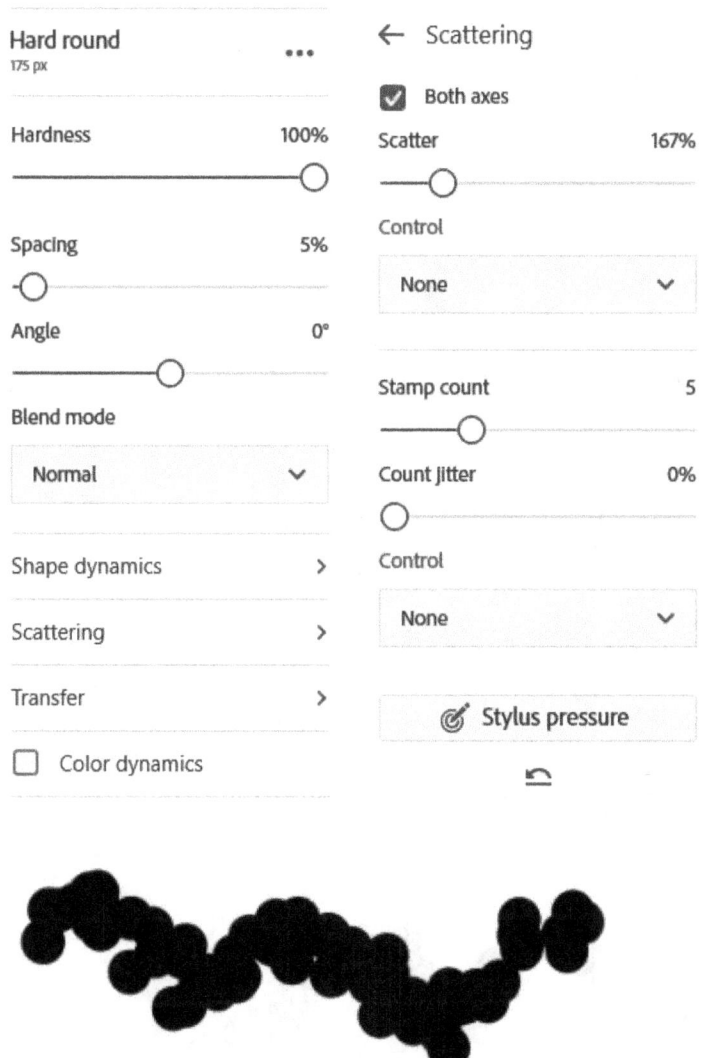

Figure 3-57. *Setting the brush settings for Scattering and painting on the canvas*

- Transfer: Found below Scattering in the settings, this can affect the opacity and flow of the brush as you work, creating varying degrees of shading. It is often more apparent if the Spacing setting is first adjusted. You can control such settings as Opacity jitter (0–100%), Control (Pen pressure, Pen Tilt, Fade, None (default)), Opacity Jitter Minimum (0–100%), Flow jitter (0–100%), Control (Pen pressure, Pen Tilt, Fade, None (default)), and the Flow Jitter Minimum settings (0–100%). Note that other brushes besides Basic when selected may have less transfer options. Refer to Figure 3-58.

111

Figure 3-58. *Setting the brush settings for a Basic brush for Transfer dynamics and painting on the canvas*

- Mixing: This setting is available for Mixer brushes when working with various color paints. The settings include slider for Wet (0–100%), Load (1–100%), and Mix (0–100%). Reload color toggle by default is disabled. The settings are best viewed when you change the brush color with the color chip. Refer to Figure 3-59.

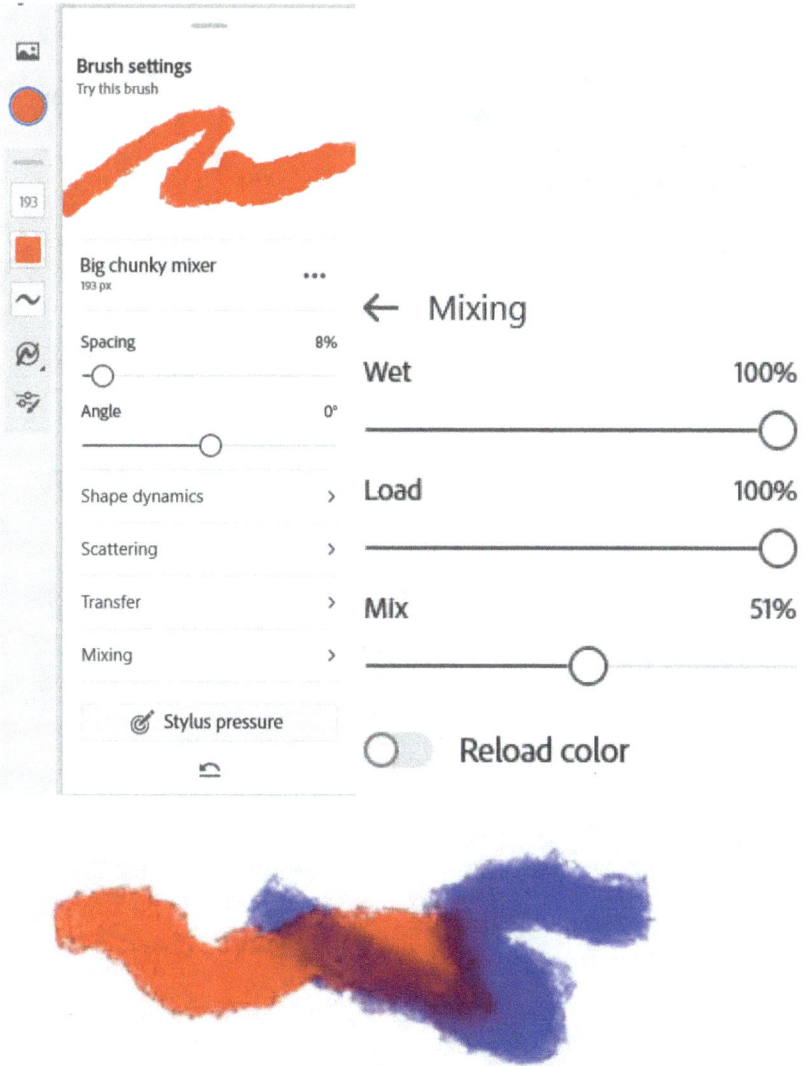

Figure 3-59. *Setting the brush settings for a Mixer brush for Mixing and painting on the canvas*

- Color Dynamics: When, for example, a Basic brush with a color paint has this setting enabled, you can control the following settings using the slider: Hue jitter (0–100%), Saturation jitter (0–100%), Brightness jitter (0–100%), and Purity jitter (−100%, 0%, 100%). Apply per tip can be enabled or disabled as well if you want a broader range of colors as you paint and can be adjusted with the earlier Spacing or Scattering settings. Refer to Figure 3-60.

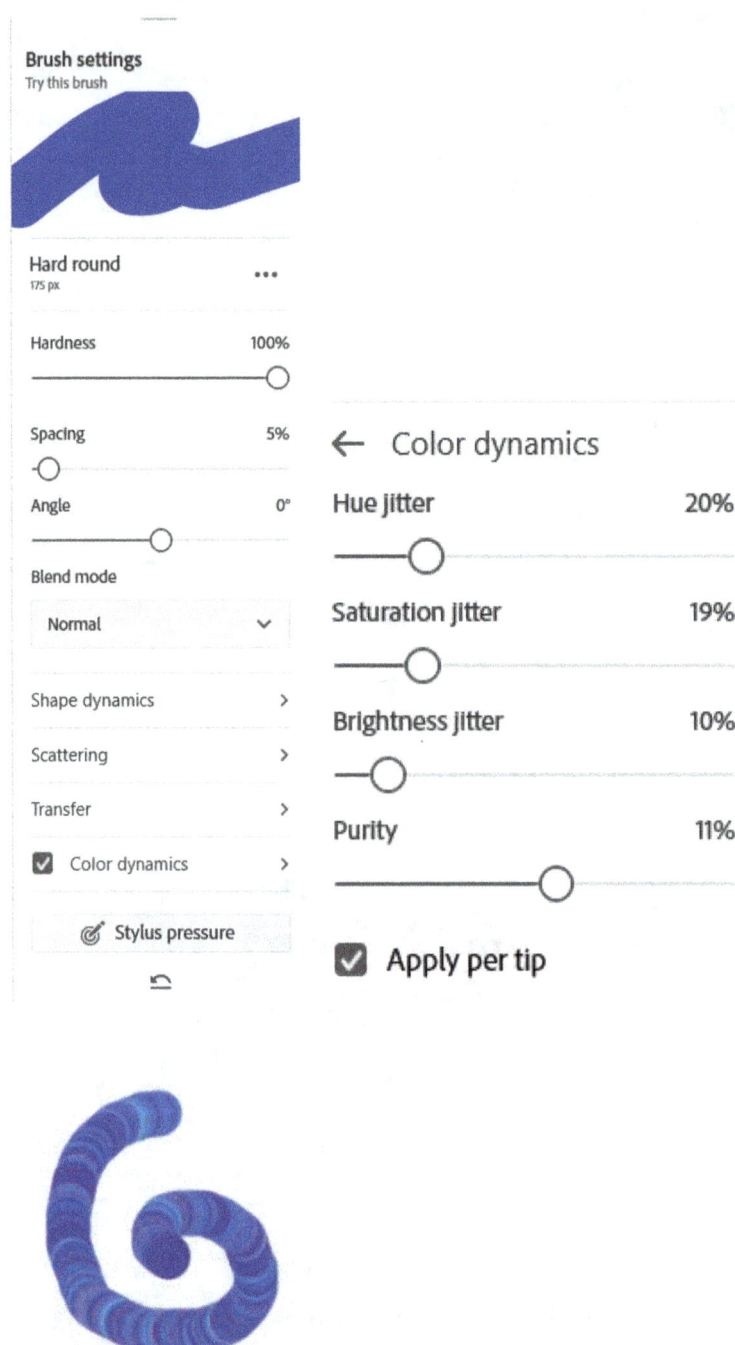

Figure 3-60. *Setting the brush settings for a Basic brush for Color dynamics and painting on the canvas*

- Blend Modes: When painting, you can select the following settings from the drop-down list: Normal (default), Dissolve, Behind, Clear, Darken, Multiply, Color burn, Linear burn, Darker color, Lighten, Screen, Color dodge, Linear dodge, Lighter color, Overlay, Soft light, Hard light, Vivid light, Linear light, Pin light, Hard mix, Difference, Exclusion, Subtract, Divide, Hue, Saturation, Color, and Luminosity.

  These options, when selected from the list, can cause color changes to areas where one painted brush stroke passes over another painted brush stroke as you work. In the real world, this is very similar to using color changer markers where passing a second ink over the first alters the color. Refer to Figure 3-61.

Chapter 3 Exploring the Workspace of Fresco and Its Tools: Part 1

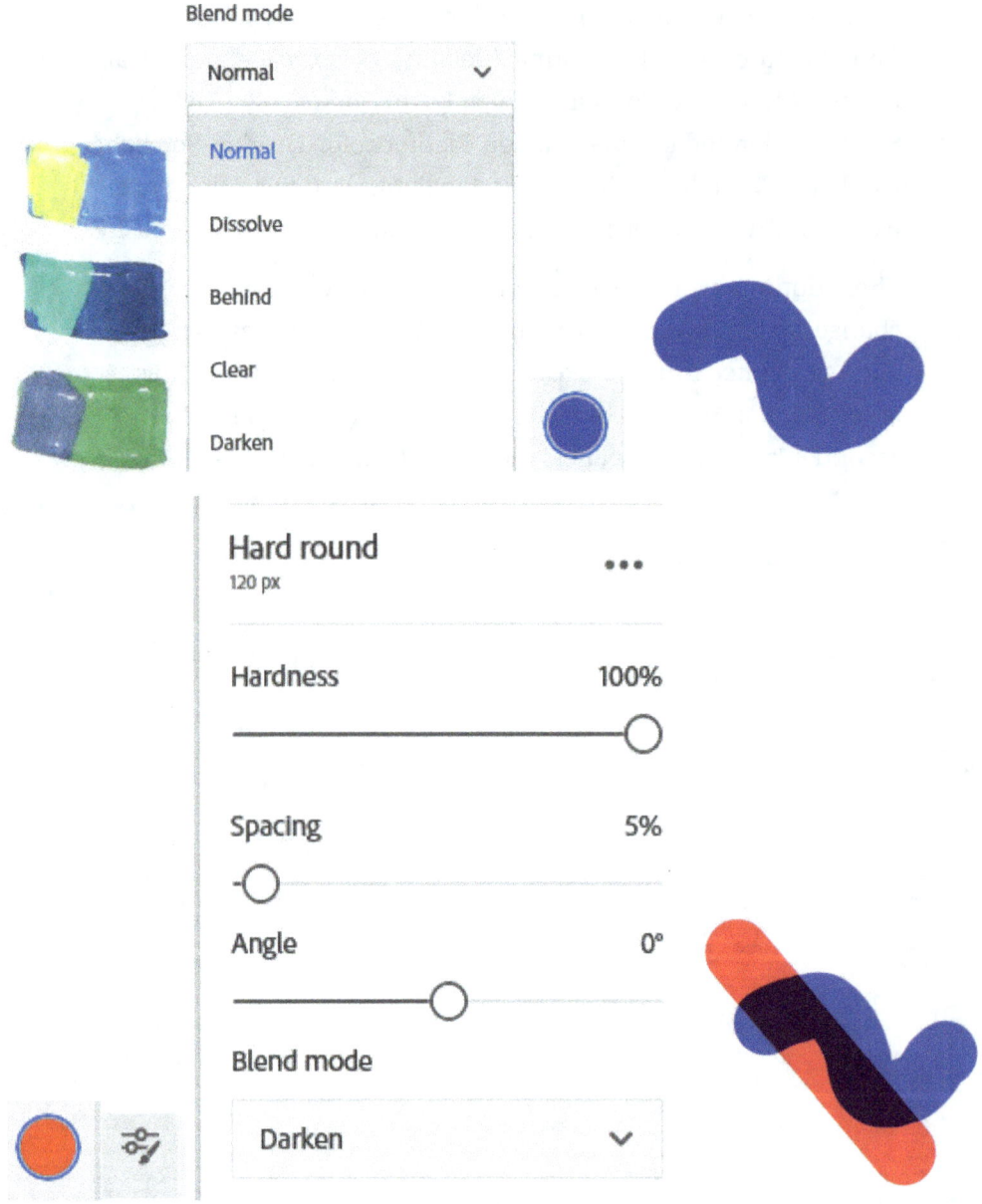

Figure 3-61. *Example of color change pens. Fresco current color chip and Pixel brush setting for Blend mode and painting on the canvas*

Note that in the brush, Blend mode settings is slightly different than the layer properties of blend modes which we will look at in Chapter 5. If you need more details on blend modes and how they work with paint brushes similarly in Photoshop, you can refer to the following link for reference:

https://helpx.adobe.com/photoshop/using/blending-modes.html

- Stylus Pressure: This button is found near the bottom of the Brush settings panel, which brings up a dialog box. Optionally, you can alter and reset if you are using a stylus. Refer to Figure 3-62.

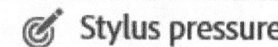

Figure 3-62. *Stylus pressure button*

- In the dialog box, the pressures can go from light to heavy or you can adjust the point on the graph or trash a selected pressure point on the graph. Use the test area or reset to find your ideal stylus pressure. You can also save your new altered pressure settings by clicking Done. Click Cancel to exit without saving changes. You can also access this area under Settings ➤ App settings ➤ Input ➤ Adjust Stylus Pressure. Refer to Figure 3-63.

CHAPTER 3   EXPLORING THE WORKSPACE OF FRESCO AND ITS TOOLS: PART 1

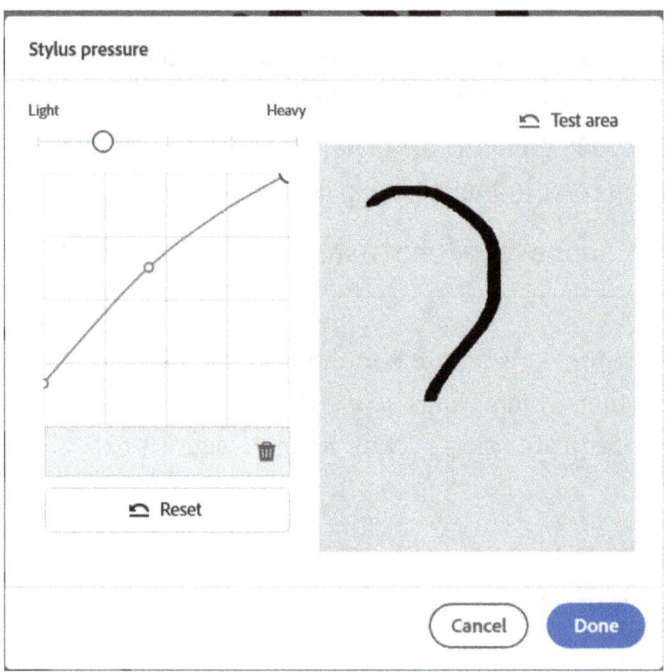

Figure 3-63. *Stylus pressure dialog box with Test area*

- The lower back pointing arrow in the Brush settings panel will allow you to reset all the settings of the current brush back to default. Refer to Figure 3-64. However, you will need to use the color chip to reset a color if it was altered due to a previous brush choice.

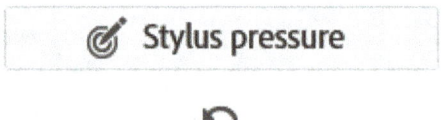

Figure 3-64. *Reset Brush settings in Brushes panel*

Remember, if while working on your brushes they become hidden from the list, you can restore them by clicking the ellipsis (…) and choosing Manage pixel brushes; then select that section in the dialog box, and you can restore all or the selected brushes that you want to unhide. In this book, I want them all to be visible. Refer to Figures 3-16 and 3-65.

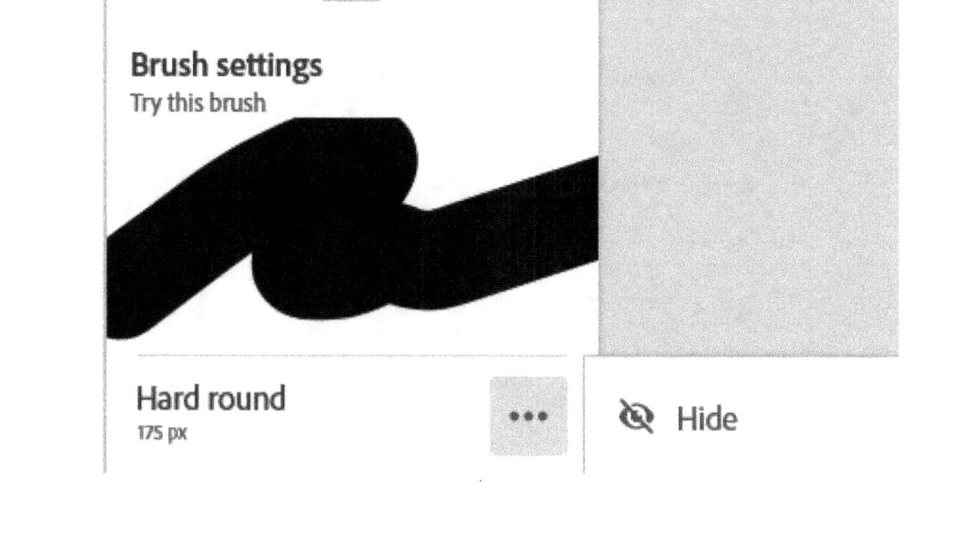

Figure 3-65. *When you hide a specific brush you can, under Pixel brushes, access the Manage pixel brushes dialog box to restore settings*

More details on these brushes can be found here:

https://helpx.adobe.com/fresco/using/pixel-brushes.html
https://helpx.adobe.com/fresco/using/mixer-brushes.html
https://helpx.adobe.com/fresco/using/pressure-curve.html

Live Brushes

These brushes allow you to emulate more accurately two different painting styles, Watercolor and Oil. Refer to Figure 3-66.

CHAPTER 3   EXPLORING THE WORKSPACE OF FRESCO AND ITS TOOLS: PART 1

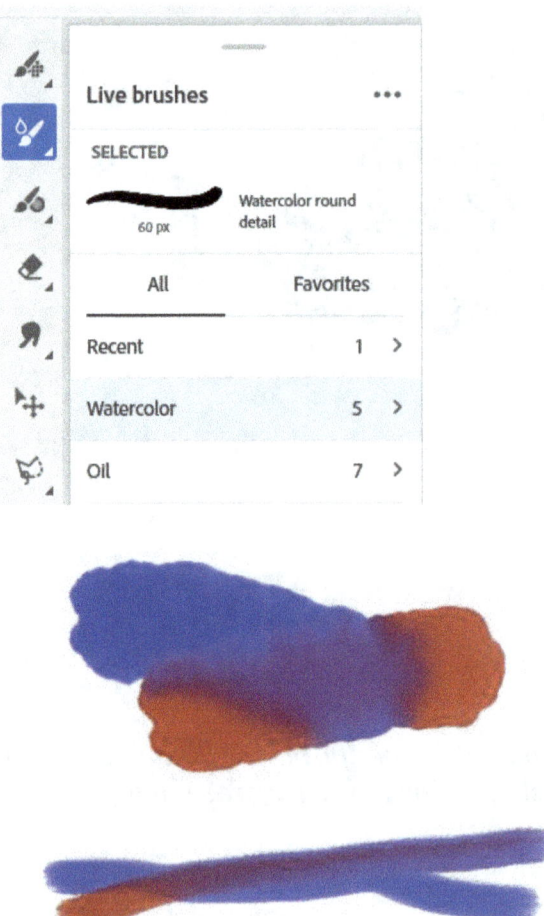

Figure 3-66. *Live brushes categories of Watercolor (top) and Oil (lower) and painting on the canvas with paints*

Recent brushes are displayed first, and you can filter between All or your Favorites.

- Watercolor: Can be rounded soft with spattering or fading to emulate how watercolor paints would be transferred. Since water is trying to be emulated, the paints spread and bleed into each other similarly to how they would as one paint color is applied over the other. Refer to Figure 3-67.

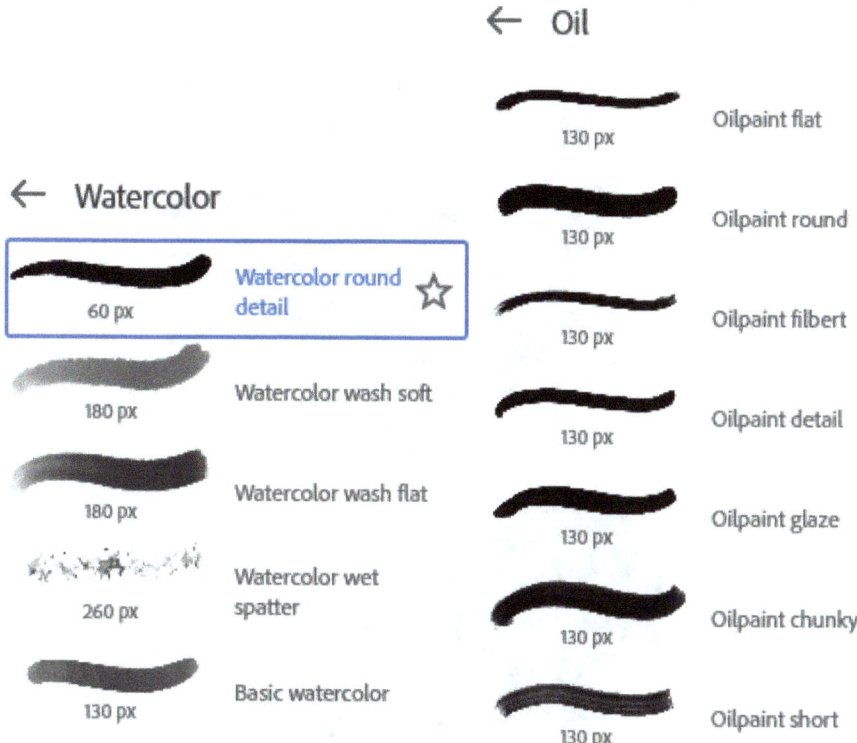

Figure 3-67. *Live brushes for Watercolor and Oil brush examples*

- Oil: Thick strokes that resemble how oil paint is transferred to the canvas using various brush heads. Unlike watercolor, there is not as much bleeding but still some blending as the new paint passes over the other. We can see this similar blending even in the real world when mixing or painting with acrylics. Refer to Figure 3-67 and Figure 3-68.

Figure 3-68. *Real example of mixing with a painter's paint knife and painted on the canvas*

Note that new brushes currently cannot be added from the Creative Cloud Library or imported to Live brushes.

Live Brush Properties, Settings, and Changing Colors

Like Pixel brushes, you can change the color using the color chip's color wheel, and for more details, you can refer to the earlier section, "Pixel Brush Properties, Settings, and Changing Colors."

Most of the main Live brush properties settings are the same as Pixel brushes so you can refer to that section for more details of definitions. However, I will point out a few key differences. Refer to Figure 3-69.

CHAPTER 3   EXPLORING THE WORKSPACE OF FRESCO AND ITS TOOLS: PART 1

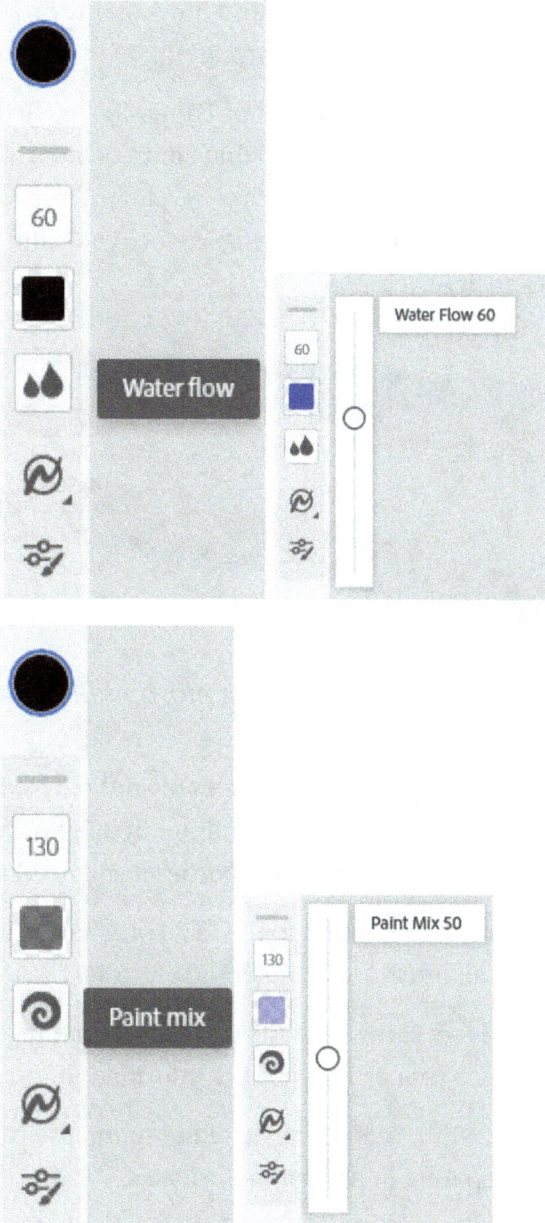

Figure 3-69. *Settings for Live brushes adjusted in the Toolbar*

Additional brush settings for these brushes include

- Brush Size (3–1024) Pixels: Refer to Pixel brush properties for more information. Note that based on the brush chosen, this range can be greater or lesser for a specific brush.

- Brush Flow (1–100%): How much paint flows off the brush. Refer to Pixel brush properties for more information.

- Water Flow (0–100%) for Watercolor or Paint Mix for Oil (0–100%): This is a second paint flow dynamic that controls how the paint reacts or mixes with other paints and the canvas. Click on the tool, and then use the slider to adjust the settings before you paint. Refer to Figures 3-69 and 3-70.

Figure 3-70. *Adjusting Water flow and Paint mix and then painting on the canvas*

- Painting Inside Settings: The icon toggles off and on; by default, it is off and will be discussed later in the chapter in more detail. For now, refer to Figure 3-49 in Pixel brush properties if you need an example.

- Brush settings which are similar to the Pixel brushes include but are not available for all brush kinds. Refer to Figure 3-71.

- Brush Size: This is set earlier outside of the Brush settings panel. Refer to Pixel brush properties for more information.

- Angle (−180°, 0°, 180°): Sets the angle of the stamp or brush head which is more apparent in non-round brushes.

- Spacing (0–200%): Only for watercolor, sets the spacing on each brush making them closer or further apart. Refer to Pixel brush properties for more details.

- Scatter (0–200%): Only for watercolor, sets the scattering of brush stamp. Refer to Pixel brush properties for more details.

- Quality: Only available for oil paints, using the list, you can set a setting of Good, Better, or Best.

- Canvas Texture: Only available for oil paints, set a setting from the list of either Canvas or None.

- Shape Dynamics: Only for watercolor. Use the sliders to alter the shape of the brush. This can control settings such as Size Jitter (0-100%), Angle Jitter (0-100%), and Control (Pen pressure, Pen Tilt, Fade, Direction, None (default)). Fade can have additional steps (1-9999). Refer to Pixel brush properties for more details.

- Pressure Dynamics: Use the slider to control Size (−100%, 0%, 100%) and Flow (−100%, 0%, 100%). Refer to Pixel brush properties for more details.

- Velocity Dynamics: Use the slider to adjust Size (−100%, 0%, 100%) and Flow (−100%, 0%, 100%). Refer to Pixel brush properties for more details.

- Reload color toggle is only for oil paint and is on by default. This can affect how colors that are brushed over with another color mix and blend.

CHAPTER 3   EXPLORING THE WORKSPACE OF FRESCO AND ITS TOOLS: PART 1

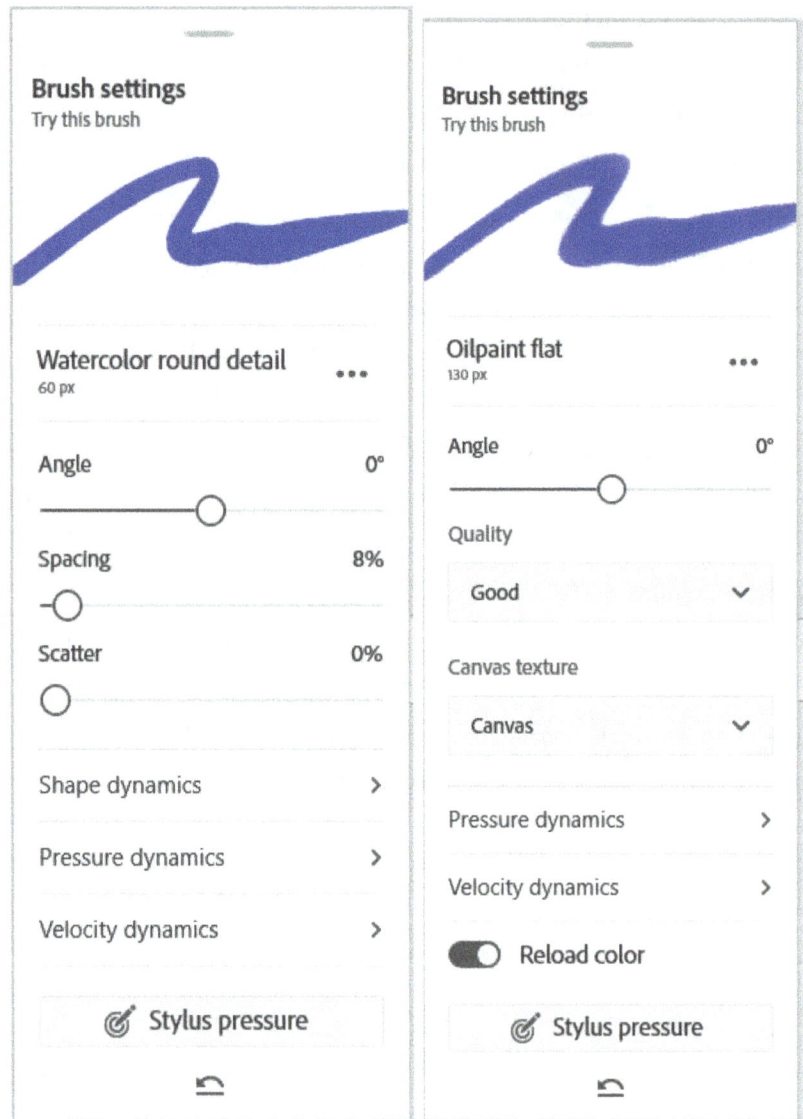

Figure 3-71. *Main Brush settings for Live brushes of Watercolor and Oil*

- Stylus Pressure: Create a custom Stylus pressure if you are using a stylus; these settings can also be reset in the dialog box. The pressures can go from light to heavy, or you can adjust the point on the graph. Refer to Pixel brushes if you need more details. Refer to Figure 3-63 and 3-71.

CHAPTER 3 EXPLORING THE WORKSPACE OF FRESCO AND ITS TOOLS: PART 1

- Use the lower back pointing arrow reset icon in the panel to reset the brushes' current settings. Refer to Figure 3-71.

Tip   If, while working on your brushes they become hidden from the list, you can restore them by clicking the ellipsis (…) and choosing Manage live brushes; then select that section in the dialog box and you can restore all or the selected brushes that you want to unhide. In this book, I want them all to be visible. Refer to Figures 3-16 and 3-72.

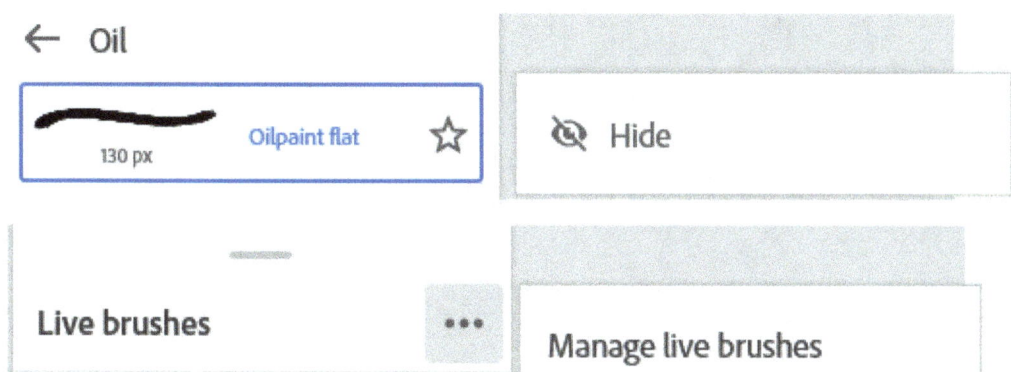

Figure 3-72. *When a brush is hidden, use the ellipsis to go to the Manage live brushes dialog box and restore hidden brushes*

More details on these live brushes can be found here:

`https://helpx.adobe.com/fresco/using/live-brushes.html`

Vector Brushes

These brushes act very similar to the brushes that you would find in Adobe Illustrator. Once they are painted with on a vector layer, they can later be scaled and transformed without loss of quality. Refer to Figure 3-73.

CHAPTER 3 EXPLORING THE WORKSPACE OF FRESCO AND ITS TOOLS: PART 1

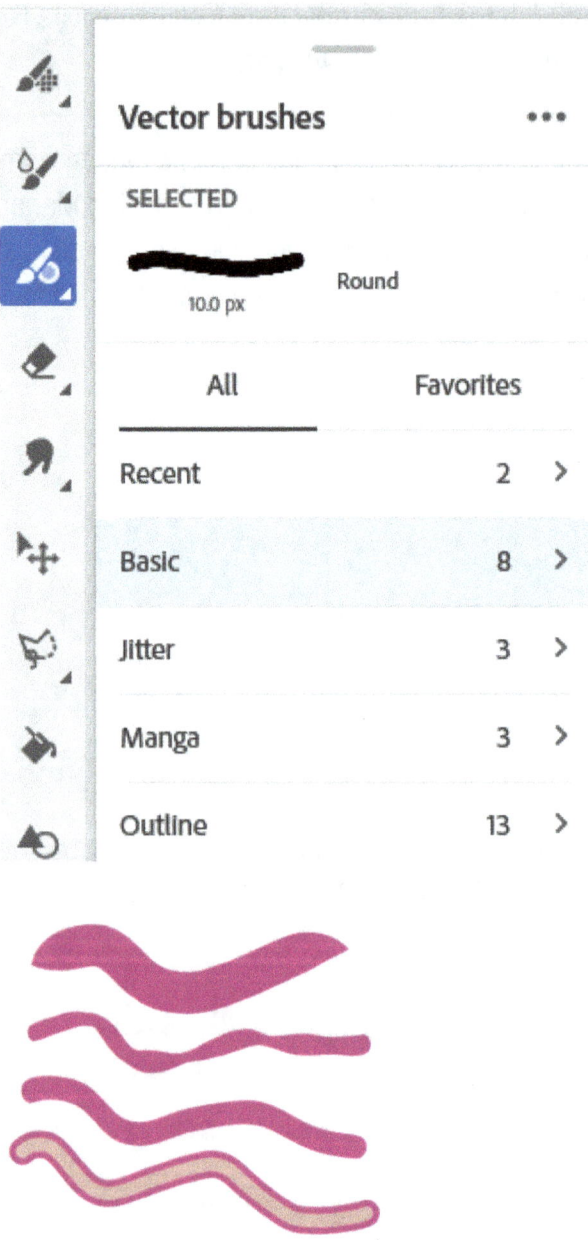

Figure 3-73. *Toolbar Vector brushes and their categories and then painted on the canvas*

There are four style categories available: Basic, Jitter, Manga, and Outline. Recent brushes are displayed first, and you can filter between All or your Favorites.

- Basic: Similar in design to basic Pixel brushes, you can use these to create thin and thick lines with blunt or tapered edges. Refer to Figure 3-74.

Figure 3-74. *Vector brushes Basic category*

- Jitter: Gives the appearance of an ink line that was created with an unsteady hand from light to heavy extreme. Refer to Figure 3-75.

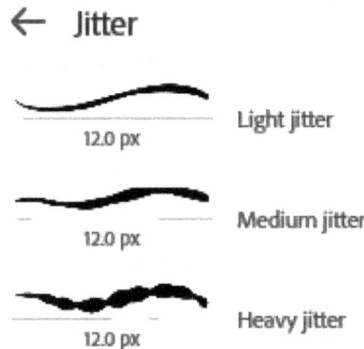

Figure 3-75. *Vector brushes Jitter category*

- Manga: Thin pen drawing line that may be used by artists in manga or comic book artwork. Refer to Figure 3-76.

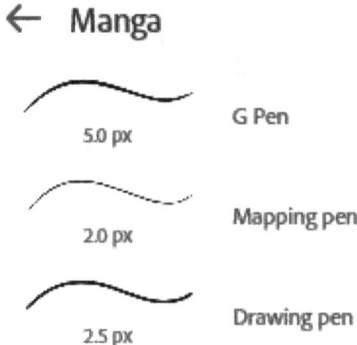

Figure 3-76. *Vector brushes Manga category*

- Outline: As in Illustrator, you would add an outline to a shape. As you paint, the outline is applied; it can be with jitter appearance or have a chiseled, blunt, or tapered edge. In the Vector brush properties and settings section, I will show you how to change the outline color using the color chip. Refer to Figure 3-77.

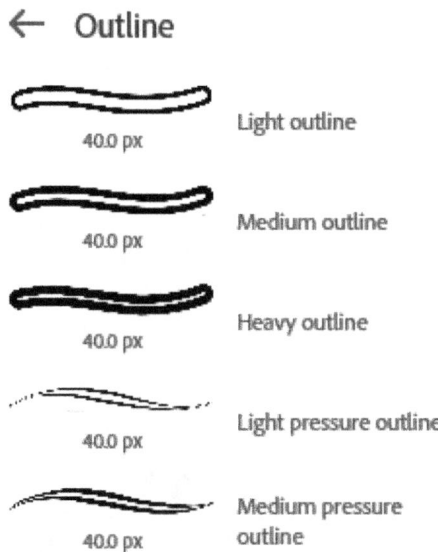

Figure 3-77. *Vector brushes Outline category*

Note that new brushes currently cannot be added from a Creative Cloud Library or imported here. However, in future versions of Fresco that option may become available.

Vector Brush Properties, Settings, and Changing Colors

Like Pixel brushes, you can change the color using the color chip color wheel, and for more details, you can refer to that earlier section on Pixel brush properties. For most Vector brushes, the primary stroke color chip controls the Fill color. However, with an Outline brush the difference is, it can be painted with two colors, one for outline (stroke) Primary and it has a Secondary Color chip (Fill) that you can select and change using the color wheel. Refer to Figure 3-78.

CHAPTER 3   EXPLORING THE WORKSPACE OF FRESCO AND ITS TOOLS: PART 1

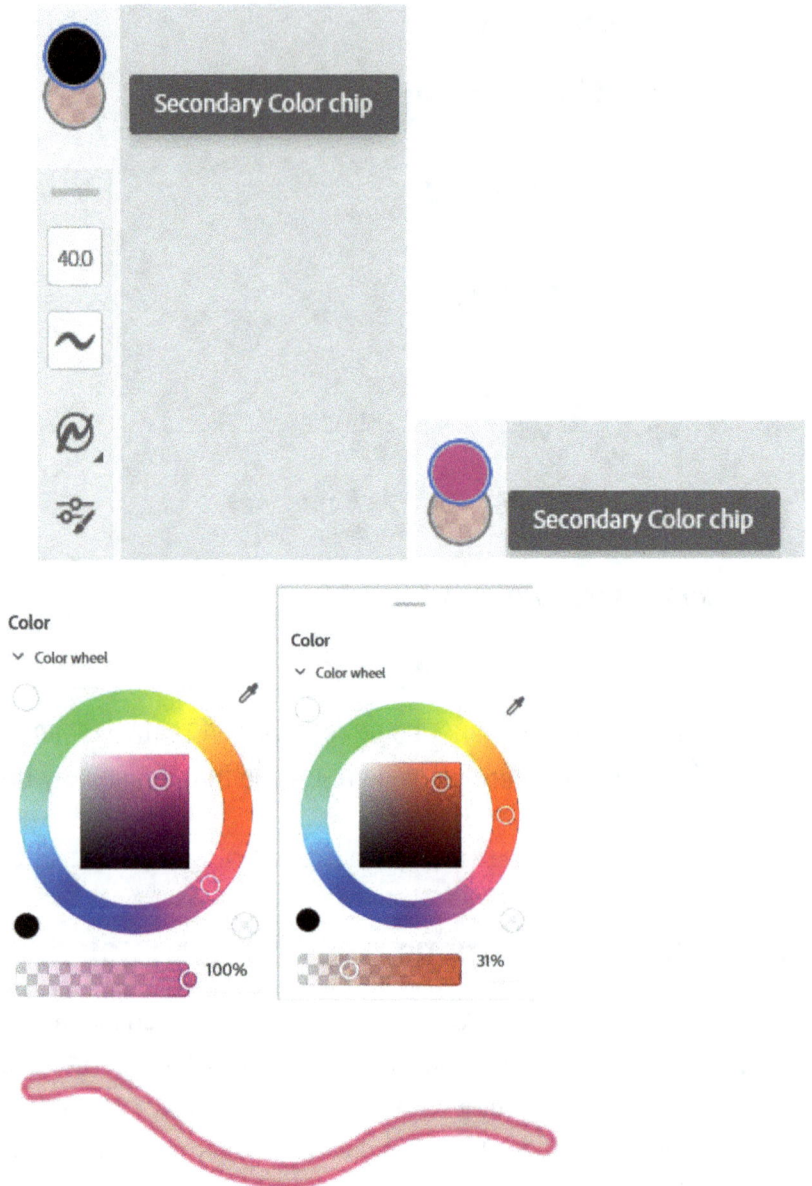

Figure 3-78. *Vector brush for outline; use your secondary chip and color wheel when altering the color fill while the primary color chip controls the stroke*

Additional brush settings for these brushes include

- Brush Size (0.5–500) Pixels: See Pixel brush properties for more details. Note that depending on the brush selected, the size range can vary.

CHAPTER 3   EXPLORING THE WORKSPACE OF FRESCO AND ITS TOOLS: PART 1

- Smoothing (0–100): Smooth out the angles of the brush stroke as you paint. See Pixel brush properties for more details. Refer to Figure 3-79.

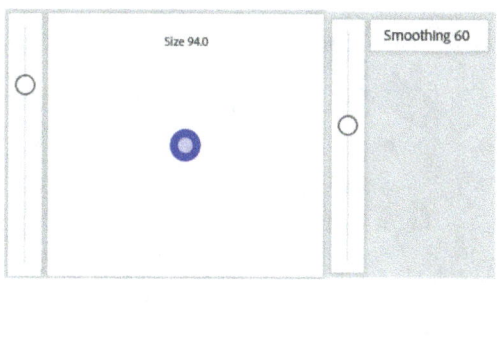

Figure 3-79. *Vector brushes set the Size and Smoothing before painting on the canvas*

- Painting Inside Setting: This icon toggles off and on; by default, it is off and will be discussed later in the chapter in more detail. However, using the settings with a Vector brush affects how paint flows behind or in front of another brush stroke. Refer to Figure 3-78 and Figure 3-79 for examples.

- Brush settings for the Vector brush are similar to the Pixel brushes include the following but are not available for all Vector brushes kinds:

    - Brush Size: This is set earlier outside of the Brush settings panel. See Pixel brush properties for more details.

    - Roundness (5–100%): Sets the roundness of the brush stamp or brush head; by default, it is 100% for a completely round brush.

133

- Angle (0–180°): Compared to Pixel brushes, the setting is more limited. The angle is more apparent when the roundness setting is altered. Refer to Figure 3-80.

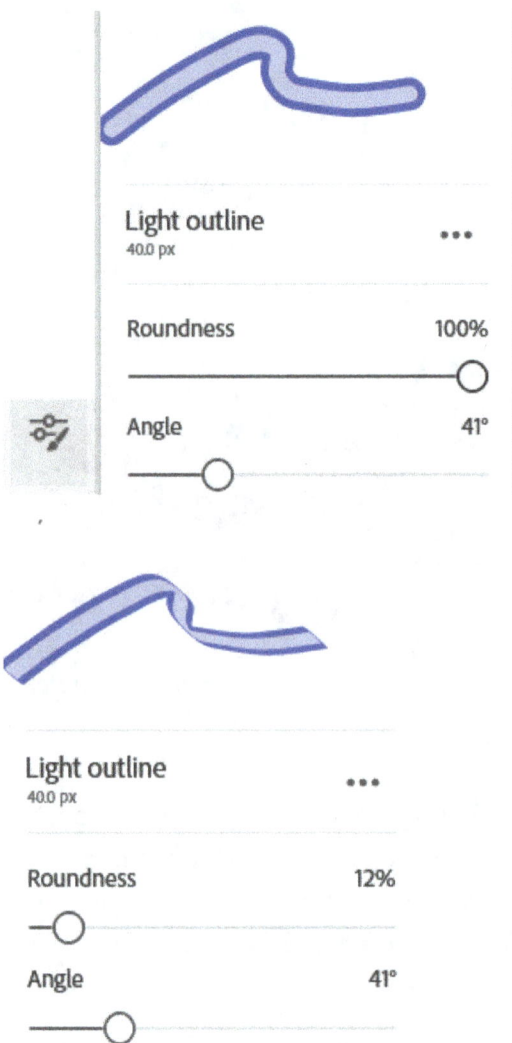

Figure 3-80. *Vector brush settings altered for Roundness and Angle*

- Taper Mode: Choose an option from the list of either Length or Velocity. This will alter the beginning and end of the brush Taper. Refer to Figure 3-81.

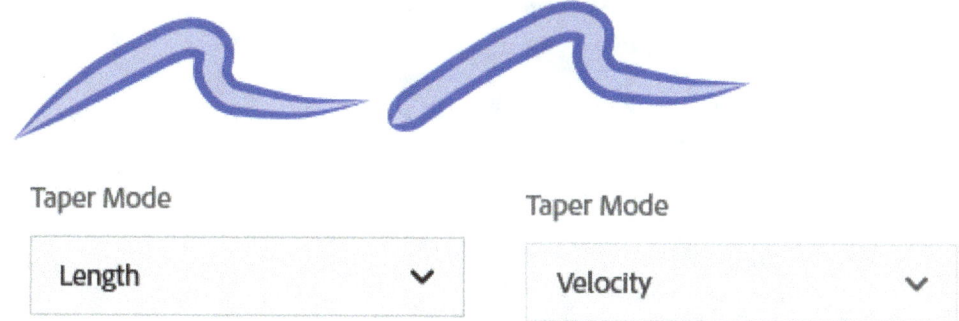

Figure 3-81. Vector brush settings altered for Taper Mode

- Begin Taper (0–100%): Set the amount of taper to start using the slider.
- End Taper (0–100%): Set the amount of taper to end using the slider. Refer to Figure 3-82.

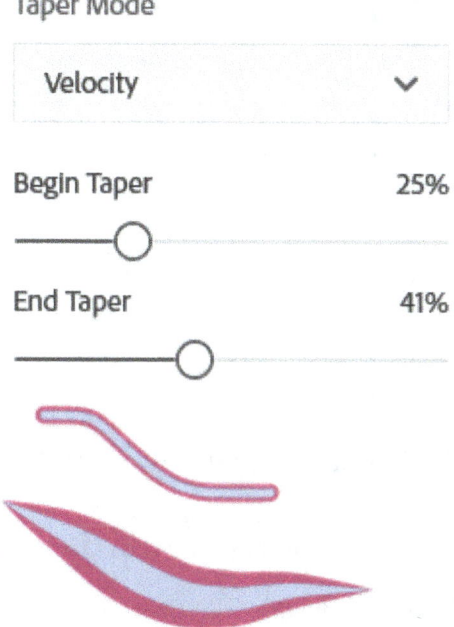

Figure 3-82. Vector brush settings altered for beginning and ending of taper

- Pressure Dynamics: Enable and use the slider to adjust the Size (−100%, 0%, 100%). Refer to Figure 3-83.

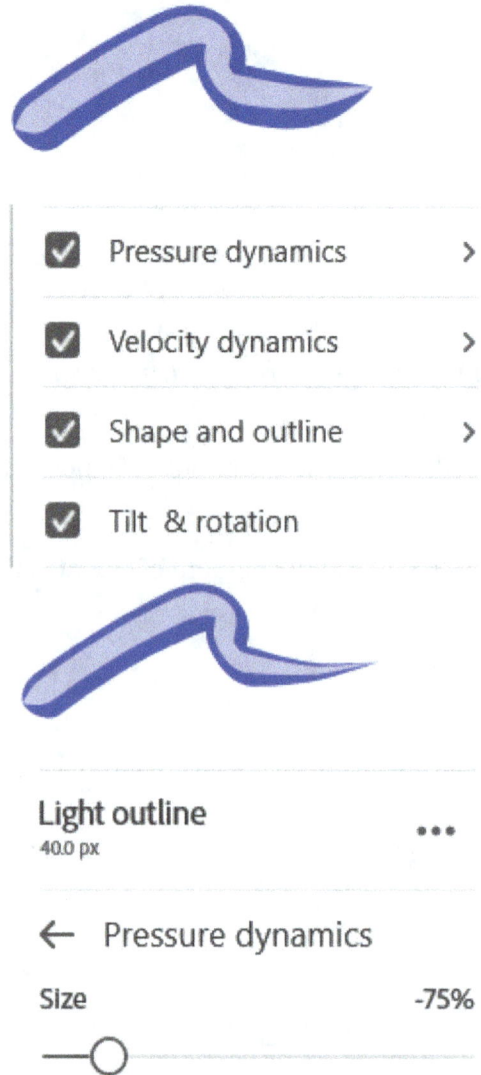

Figure 3-83. *Vector brush settings adjusting the Pressure dynamics*

- Velocity Dynamics: Enable and use the slider to adjust the Size (−100%, 0%, 100%). Refer to Figure 3-84.

CHAPTER 3　EXPLORING THE WORKSPACE OF FRESCO AND ITS TOOLS: PART 1

Figure 3-84. Vector brush settings adjusting the Velocity dynamics

- Shape and Outline: Enable and adjust the following settings: Jitter (enabled; set with sliders), Size jitter (0–100%), Jitter distance (1–100%), and Outline (enabled; set with the slider Outline thickness 5–95%). Refer to Figure 3-85.

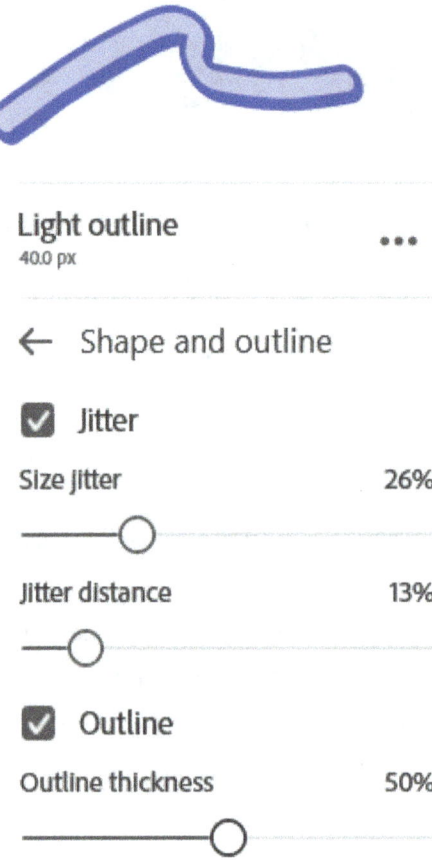

Figure 3-85. Vector brush settings adjusting the Size jitter and Outline thickness

- Tilt and Rotation: No additional settings; when enabled, this alters the tilt and rotation of the stroke. Refer to Figure 3-86.

Figure 3-86. Vector brush settings adjusting the tilt and rotation

- Stylus Pressure Button: Sets custom Stylus pressure if you are using a stylus; these settings can also be reset in the dialog box. The pressures can go from light to heavy, or you can adjust the point on the graph. More details can be found under Pixel brush properties on the dialog box. Refer to Figure 3-63 and Figure 3-87.

CHAPTER 3   EXPLORING THE WORKSPACE OF FRESCO AND ITS TOOLS: PART 1

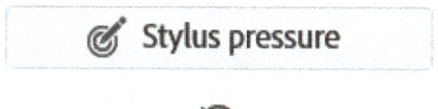

Figure 3-87. For the Vector brush, set the Stylus pressure and reset brush settings

- In the Brush settings panel, you can also use the backward pointing arrow if you need to reset your brush settings. Refer to Figure 3-87.

Tip If while working on your brushes they become hidden from the list, you can restore them by clicking the ellipsis (…) and choosing Manage vector brushes; then select that section in the dialog box, and you can restore all or the selected brushes that you want to unhide. In this book, I want them all to be visible. Refer to Figures 3-16 and 3-88.

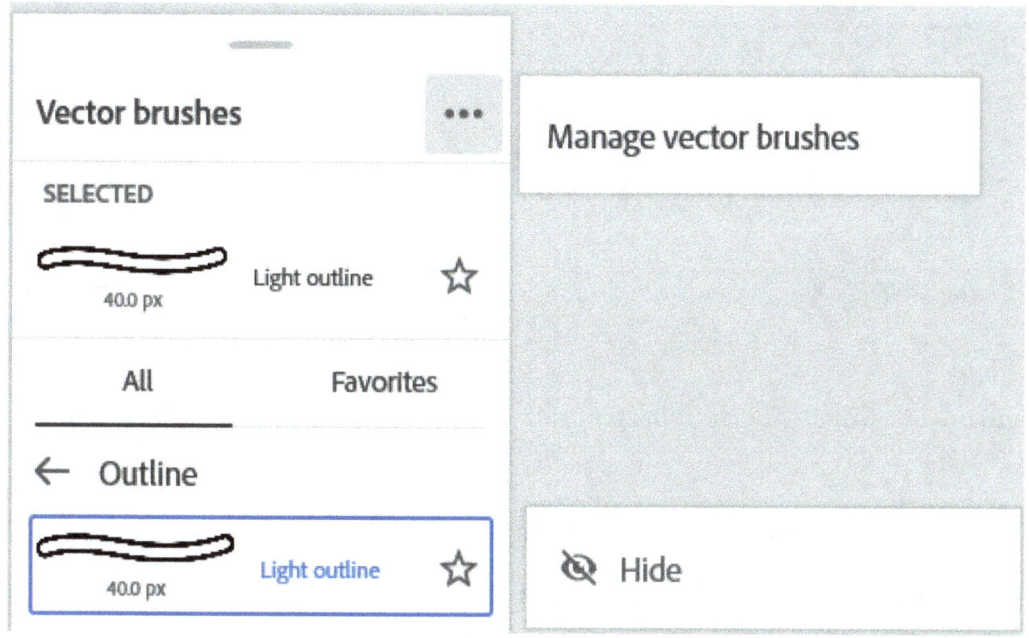

Figure 3-88. When Vector brushes become hidden, you can restore them by accessing the Manage vector brushes dialog box

Tip Consult your Help ➤ Touch Shortcut map for details on how to trim lines very quickly by double-clicking the Touch shortcut circle. The inner circle can be used for the task of erasing which we will look at next, but if the outer secondary ring is selected, it can be used to trim a selection of the line by drawing over it quickly. Once to trim and three times to remove the vector stroke. Refer to Figure 3-89.

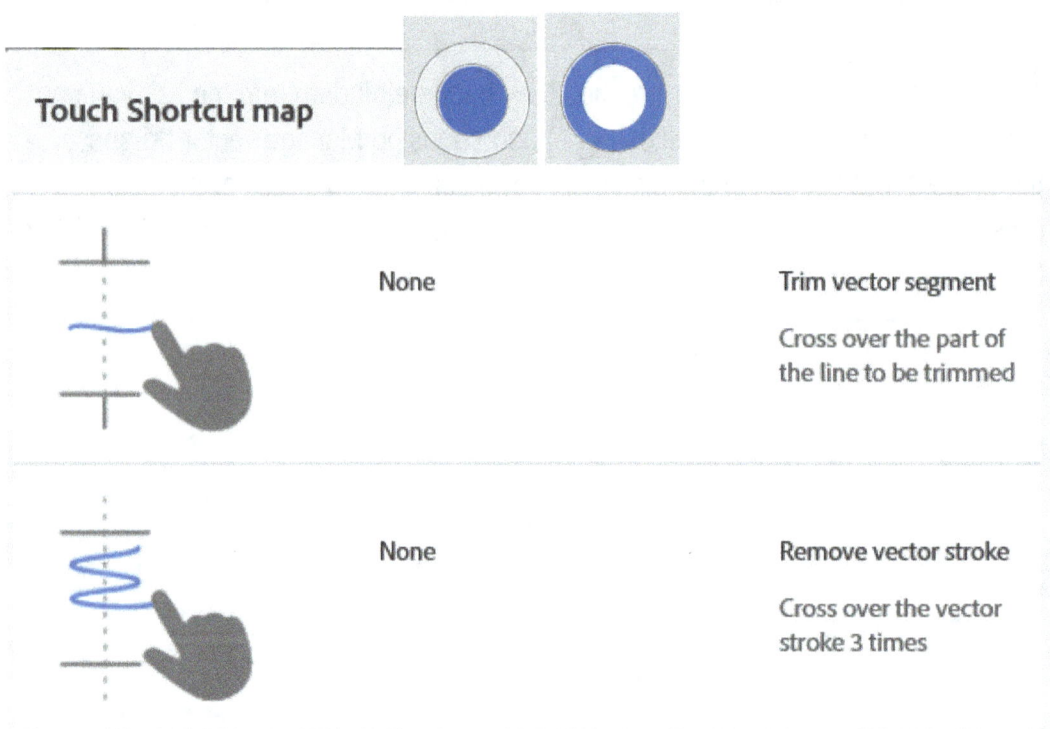

Figure 3-89. *Touch Shortcut map options when using the primary circle and secondary ring*

More details on this kind of Vector Brush can be found here:

https://helpx.adobe.com/fresco/using/vector-brushes.html

Eraser Brushes (Pixel and Vector)

Eraser brushes can be both pixel and vector and are changed, based on what kind of previous brush you have selected. They can erase Live brush strokes as well. These brushes are similar to how you would use a brush in either Photoshop or Illustrator, using the respective eraser tool. In reality, we use erasers for many art projects whether it be to remove the lines of a pencil, charcoal, or another media we do not want to see or fade. Refer to Figure 3-90 and Figure 3-91.

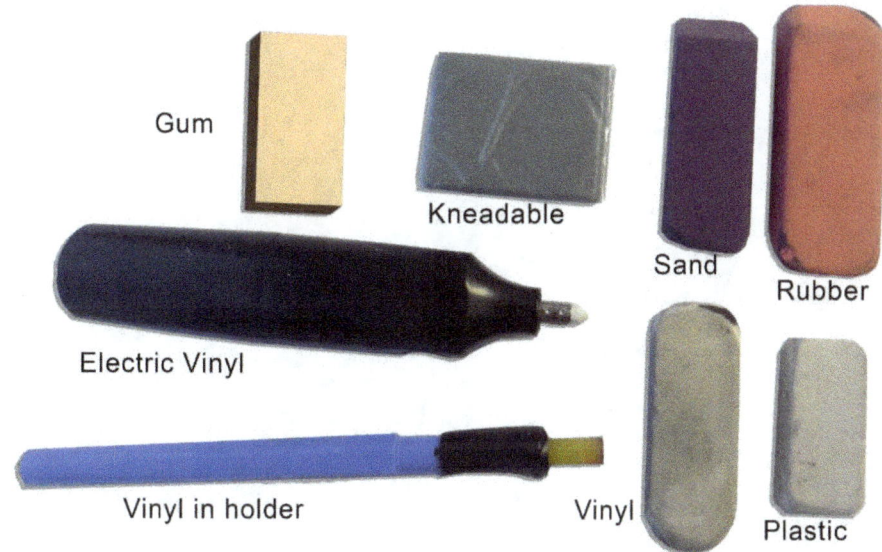

Figure 3-90. *Example of erasers that artists use*

CHAPTER 3　EXPLORING THE WORKSPACE OF FRESCO AND ITS TOOLS: PART 1

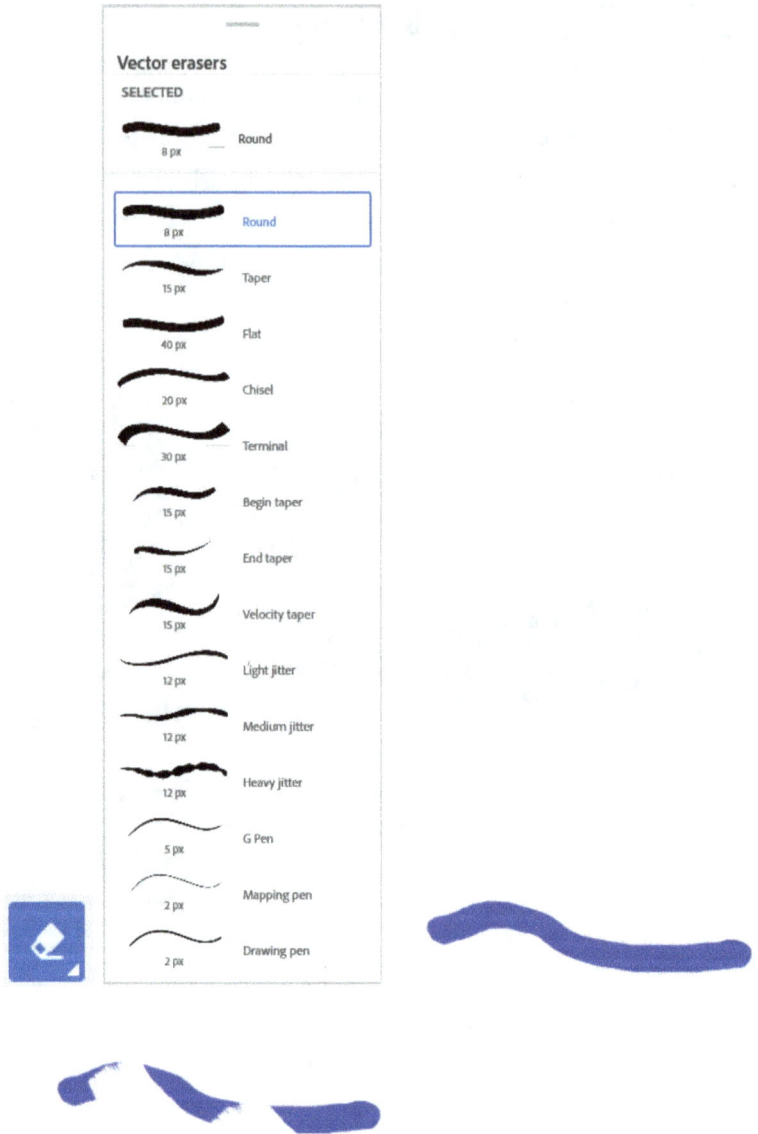

***Figure* 3-91.** *Toolbar Fresco Vector eraser brushes and apply an eraser to a painted area*

However, with these kinds of brushes, there are no styles or categories, and Creative Cloud Library Brushes cannot be directly accessed from this menu or additional brushes imported.

CHAPTER 3 EXPLORING THE WORKSPACE OF FRESCO AND ITS TOOLS: PART 1

To access a current brush beyond the list while working with another current brush like Pixel, do the following to turn it into an eraser: you can double-click the center Touch shortcut circle to enable this function, and then, you have more options of primary and secondary tasks as mentioned earlier. Refer to Figure 3-89 and 3-92.

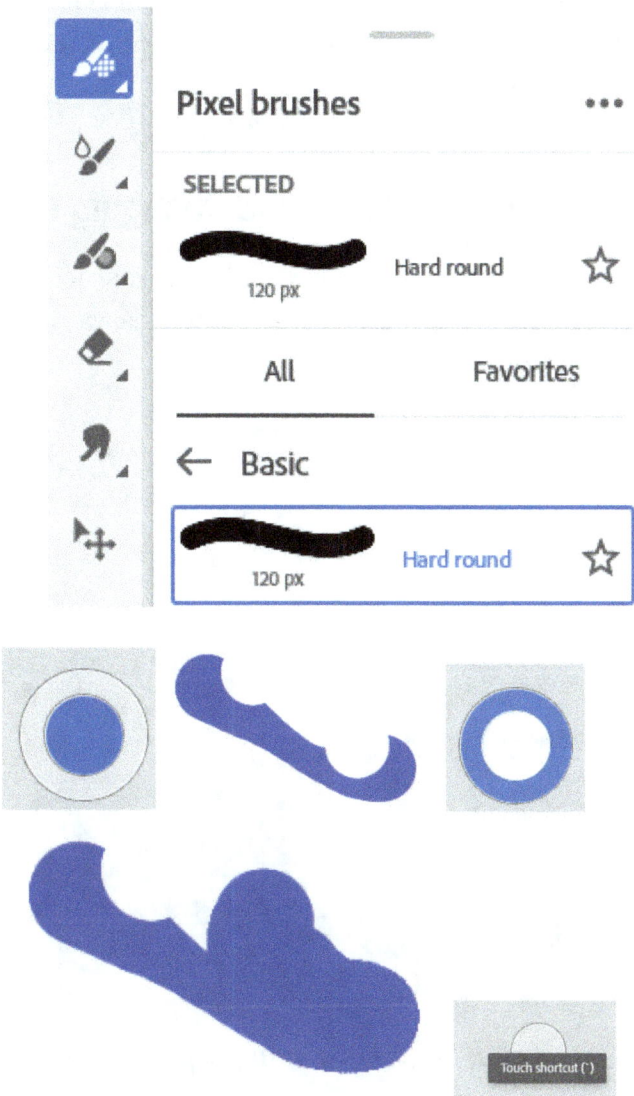

Figure 3-92. *Use a Pixel brush to erase on the canvas when you activate the primary Touch shortcut circle or secondary ring to paint pixels and then deactivate the Touch shortcut later*

143

CHAPTER 3　EXPLORING THE WORKSPACE OF FRESCO AND ITS TOOLS: PART 1

The primary circle can erase, while the outer secondary ring can be used for painting in Pixel brushes and trimming for Vector brush. For Live brushes with the primary circle set, a clear color will paint or become like a "dry brush" for oilpaint or "pure water" for watercolor which results in a kind of smear. This erase feature can also be used for Smudge brushes which will be reviewed shortly. Consult your Help ➤ Touch Shortcut map for more details on this. Double-click the Touch shortcut again to turn it back into a paint brush. Refer to Figure 3-92.

Then, return to the Eraser tool; refer to Figure 3-91.

Eraser Brush Properties, Settings, and Changing Colors

For the Eraser brush, though the color chip and color wheel are accessible, they are not required as you use this tool as you would an eraser in the real world to remove pixels, not add more. Refer to Figure 3-93.

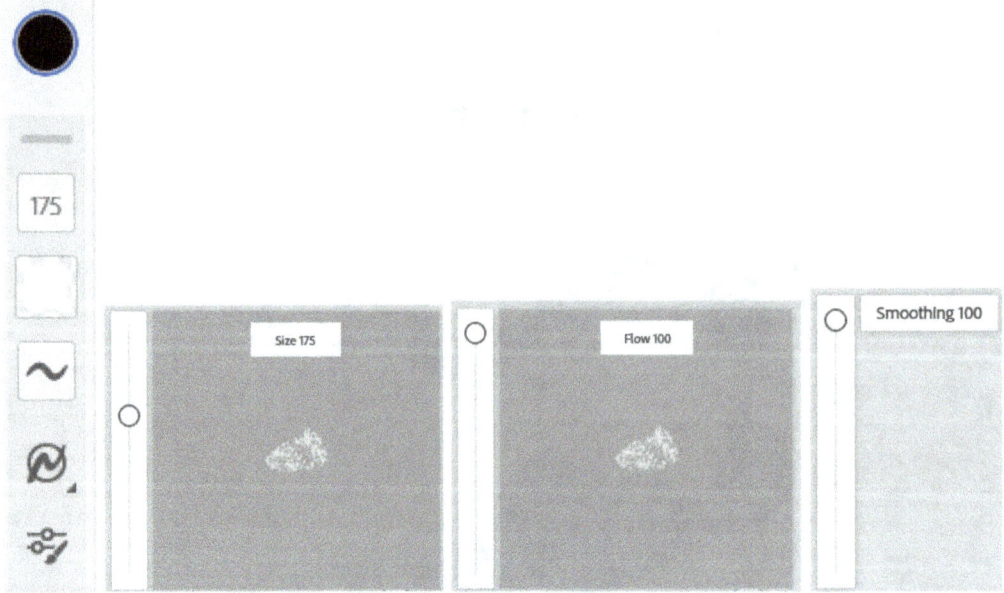

Figure 3-93. *Adjust the Size, Flow, and Smoothing for the Eraser brush*

CHAPTER 3 EXPLORING THE WORKSPACE OF FRESCO AND ITS TOOLS: PART 1

Below the color chip are additional brush settings for these brushes. Refer to Figure 3-93. They are the same as the ones found for Pixel and Vector brushes, and they include

- Brush Size (1–1024) Pixels: Refer to Pixel brush properties for more information. Note that the size range may vary depending on which brush is selected from the list or if you are painting with a Vector brush.

- Brush Flow (1–100%): Controls the amount of erasing. Refer to Pixel brush properties for more information. Not available for Vector brushes.

- Smoothing (0–100%): Controls how smooth the erasing is. A lower setting will be more angular, while higher settings are more rounded.

- Painting Inside Settings: This icon can be toggled off and on; by default, it is off and will be discussed later in the chapter in more detail. With this brush, you would be erasing rather than painting. Refer to Figure 3-94.

Figure 3-94. *Paint inside settings tested for the Eraser brush*

- Brush settings which are the similar to the Pixel or Vector brushes include the following but are not for all brushes. Refer to Figure 3-95.

145

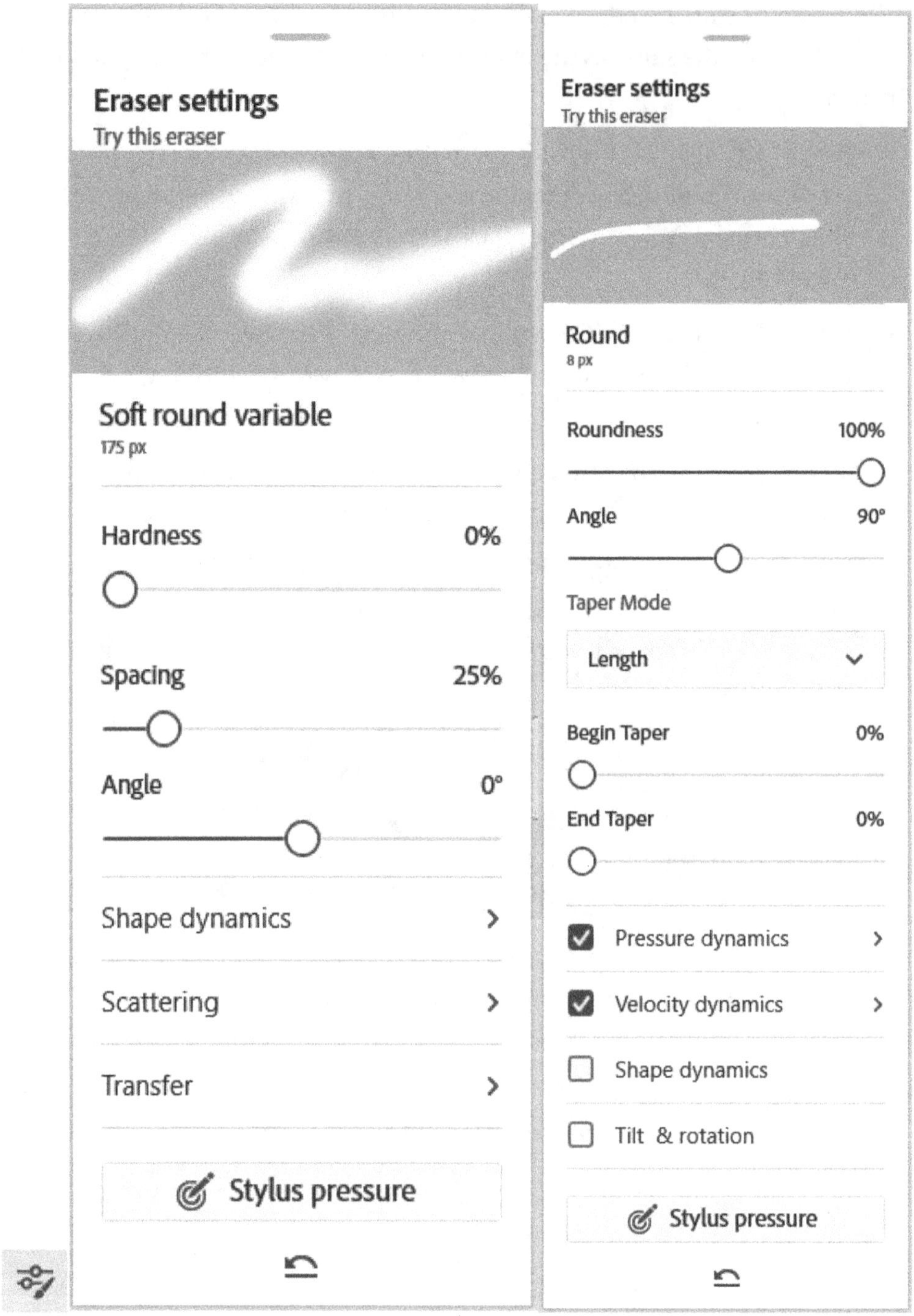

Figure 3-95. Eraser settings for the Pixel and Vector eraser

- Brush Size: This is set earlier outside of the brush properties settings panel. Refer to Pixel or Vector brushes for more details.

- Hardness (0–100%) (Pixel): The hardness or softness of the edge of the eraser stamp.

- Spacing (0–200%) (Pixel): Sets the spacing of the eraser stamp. Higher spacing moves the stamp farther apart.

- Roundness (5–100%) (Vector): Sets the roundness of the brush.

- Angle (−180°, 0°, 180°): The angle of the non-round brush head. Note that angle options may be different if you are using a Vector brush (0–180°). Using a stylus may allow you to add angles better with certain brushes. Refer to Figure 3-95.

- Taper Mode (Vector): Set the Taper mode from the list of Length or Velocity. Then, set the Begin and End Taper using the sliders. Refer to Vector brush settings for more details. Refer to Figure 3-95.

- Shape Dynamics (Pixel): Use the right pointing arrow to access the following. This can control such settings as Size jitter (0–100%), Control (Pen pressure, Pen Tilt, Fade, None (default)), Minimum diameter (0–100%), Angle jitter (0–100%), and Control (Pen pressure, Pen Tilt, Fade, Direction, None (default)). Fade will allow for additional steps. Flip X Jitter and Flip Y Jitter can also be enabled. Refer to Pixel brush properties setting for more details.

- Shape Dynamics (Vector): The following settings are controlled: Jitter: Size jitter (0–100%), Jitter distance (1–100%), and Outline: Outline thickness (5–95%). Refer to the Vector brush properties settings section for more details. Refer to Figure 3-96.

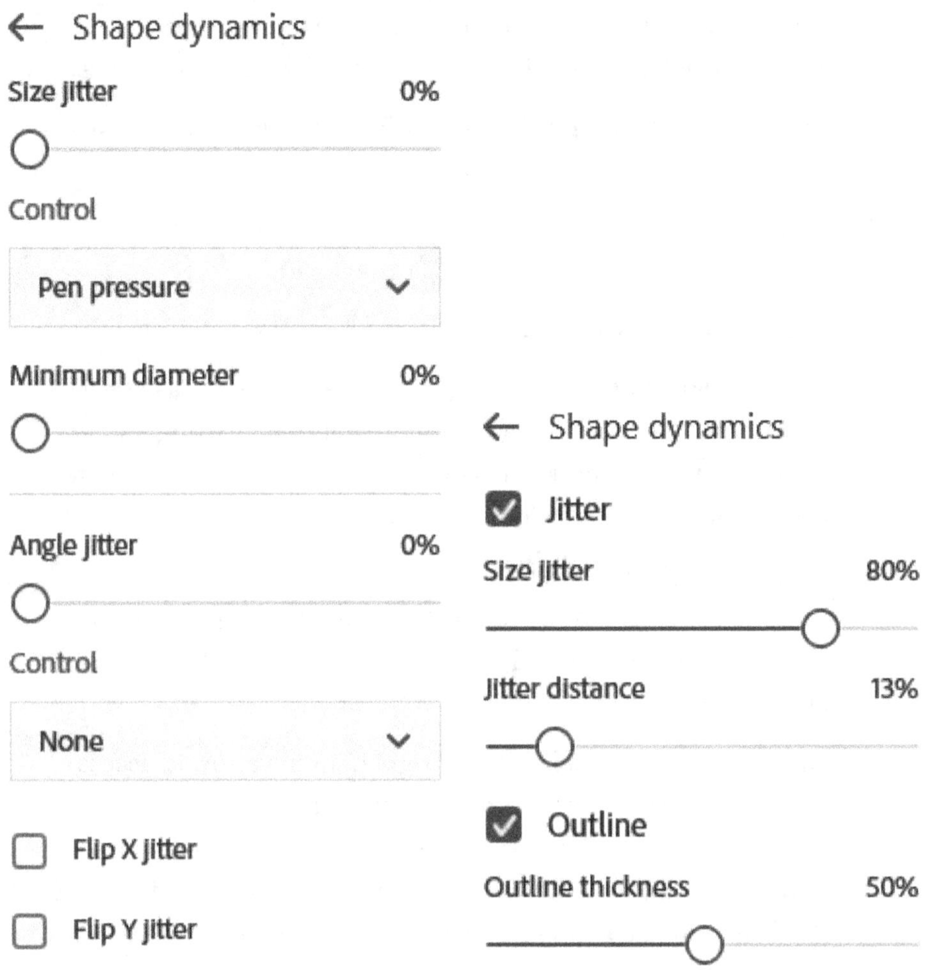

Figure 3-96. Eraser Shape dynamics settings for Pixel and Vector brushes

- Scattering (Pixel): Use the right pointing arrow (see Figure 3-95) to access the settings of Both axes (enable/disable), Scatter (0–1000%), Control (Pen pressure, Pen Tilt, Fade, None (default)), Stamp count (1–16), Count jitter (0–100%), and Control (Pen pressure, Pen Tilt, fade, None (default)). Refer to Pixel brush properties settings for more details and refer to Figure 3-97.

CHAPTER 3   EXPLORING THE WORKSPACE OF FRESCO AND ITS TOOLS: PART 1

Figure 3-97. *Eraser Scattering settings for Pixel brushes*

- Transfer (Pixel): Use the right pointing arrow to access the settings of Opacity jitter (0–100%), Control (Pen pressure, Pen Tilt, Fade, None (default)), Opacity Jitter Minimum (0–100%), Flow jitter (0–100%), Control (Pen pressure, Pen Tilt, Fade, None (default)), and Flow Jitter Minimum (0–100%). Refer to Figure 3-98.

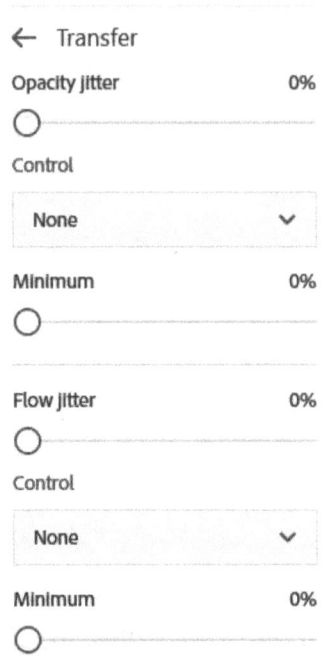

Figure 3-98. *Eraser Transfer settings for Pixel brushes*

- Other settings for Vector Eraser brushes include Pressure dynamics (Size: -100%, 0%, 100%), Velocity dynamics (Size: −100%, 0%, 100%), and Tilt and rotation check box. You can learn more about this under the Vector brush properties settings section. Refer to Figure 3-95 for image reference when Vector brush is selected.

- Stylus Pressure Button: To set custom stylus pressure if you are using a stylus. These settings can also be reset in the dialog box. The pressures can go from light to heavy, or you can adjust the point on the graph. Refer to Pixel brush properties settings for more details and to Figures 3-63 and 3-99.

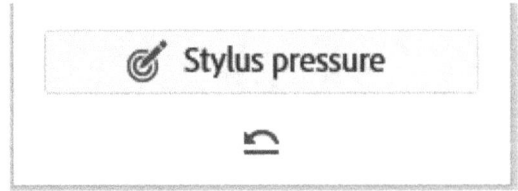

Figure 3-99. *Eraser brush list button Stylus pressure*

- You can also reset all Eraser brush settings using the backward pointing arrow. Refer to Figure 3-99.

For more information on using erasers, you can refer to the following link:

https://helpx.adobe.com/fresco/using/erasers.html

Smudge Brushes

This type of brush is similar to using the Pixel brushes earlier but adding a more smudged or blurred effect. Smudging in the real world is often done with paper sticks (blending stumps) known to smear or smudge the charcoal of a pencil. Refer to Figure 3-100 and Figure 3-101.

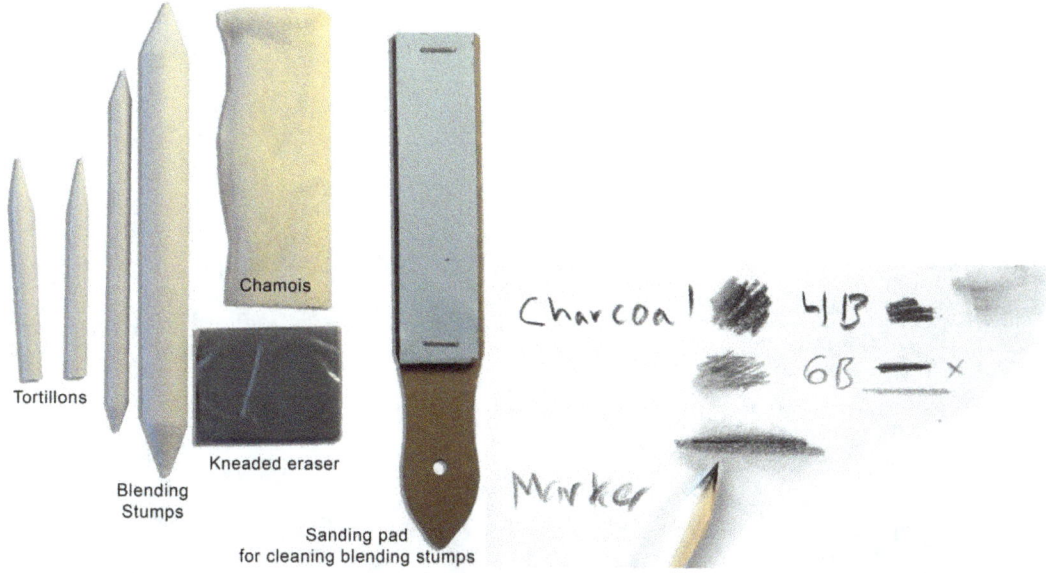

Figure 3-100. *In the real world, various tools like tortillons and blending stumps are used to smudge pencil and charcoal strokes*

CHAPTER 3   EXPLORING THE WORKSPACE OF FRESCO AND ITS TOOLS: PART 1

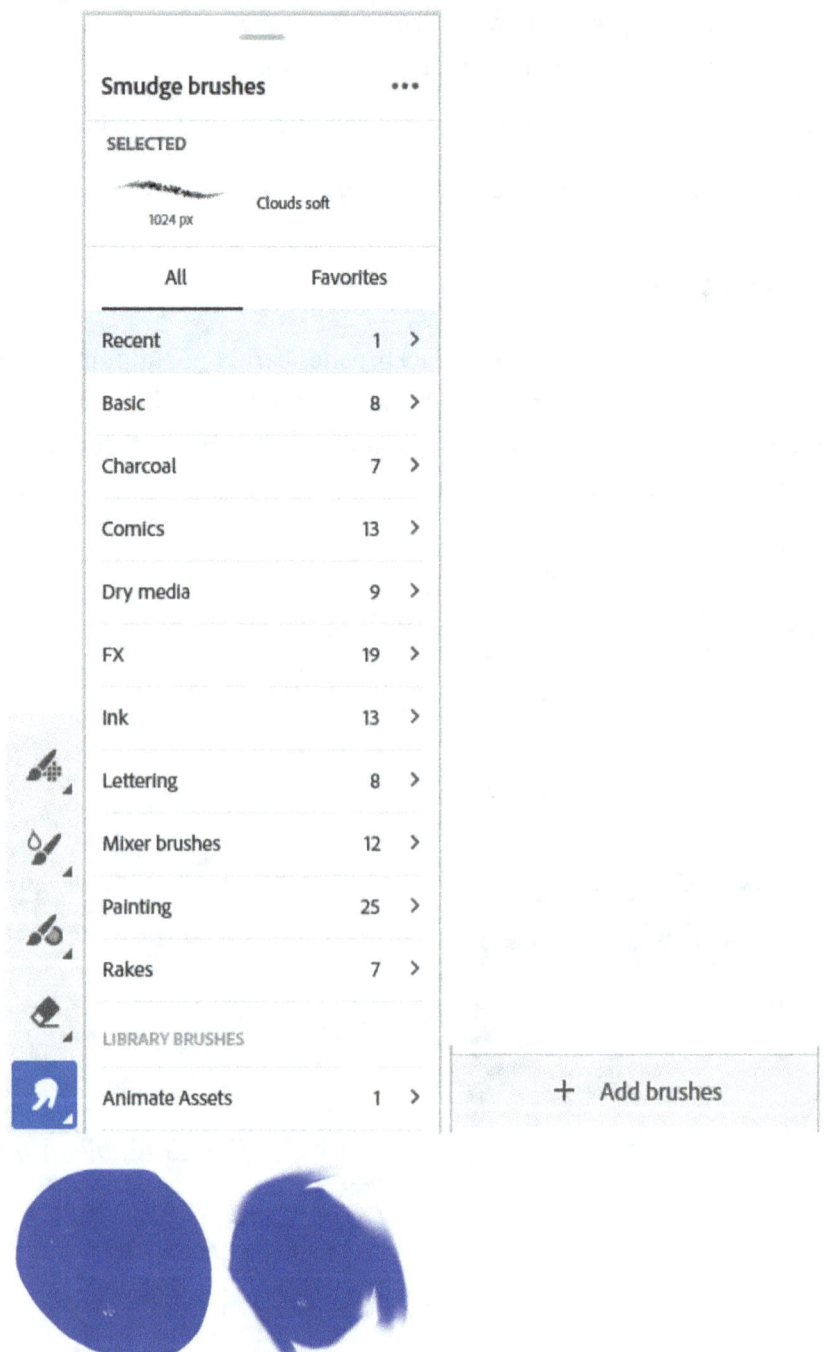

Figure 3-101. *Toolbar with available Smudge brushes and options for Pixel brushes*

In Photoshop, this action is done with the Smudge and Blur tools. Refer to Figure 3-102.

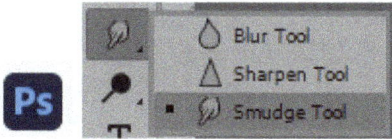

Figure 3-102. *Photoshop Toolbar panel with Blur and Smudge tools*

Note that in Fresco, not all Pixel brush categories will be available in the Smudge brushes, but you can always return to those brushes at any time to compare. Refer to the Pixel brush definitions if you need to review the styles. However, note that Multicolor, Marker, and Sketching and Vector brushes are excluded from the list to be used for smudging. However, you will still have access to your Library Brushes, and you can add and discover or import additional brushes as well. Refer to Figure 3-101.

Smudge Brush Properties, Settings, and Changing Colors

Like Pixel brushes, you can change the color using the color chip color wheel. However, this color will not affect the smear as you are just altering the original painted pixels and not adding more colors. Refer to Figure 3-103.

CHAPTER 3   EXPLORING THE WORKSPACE OF FRESCO AND ITS TOOLS: PART 1

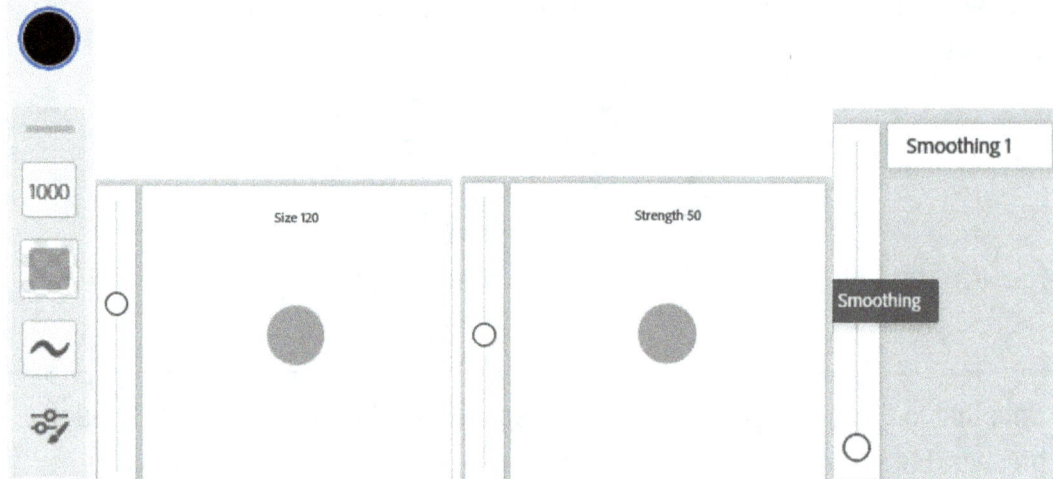

Figure 3-103. *Smudge brush settings of Size, Strength, and Smoothing*

Additional brush settings for these Smudge brushes include

- Brush Size (1–1024) Pixels: Use the slider to adjust the size of the smudge. Note that the size range may vary depending on which brush is chosen.

- Brush Flow Strength (1–100%): Use the slider to control the strength of the smudge.

- Smoothing (0–100%): Use the slider to control how angled or smooth the smudge is. The default is 1.

- Brush settings which are similar to the Pixel brushes, and they include but are not available for all brush kinds. Refer to Figure 3-104.

CHAPTER 3 EXPLORING THE WORKSPACE OF FRESCO AND ITS TOOLS: PART 1

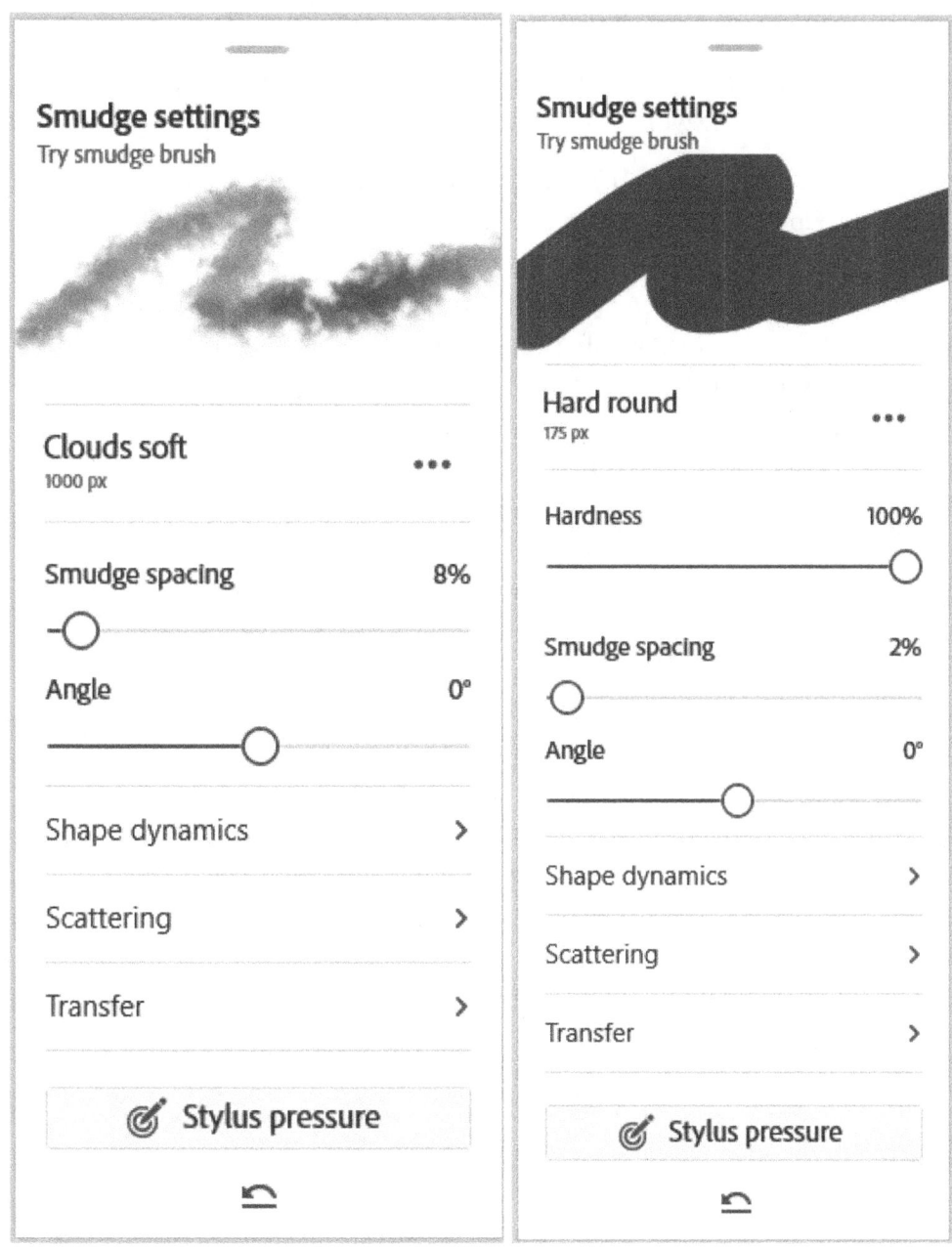

Figure 3-104. Smudge Brush settings panel

- Brush Size: This is set earlier outside of the Brush settings panel.

- Hardness (0–100%): Slider sets the softness or hardness of the smudge.

155

CHAPTER 3 EXPLORING THE WORKSPACE OF FRESCO AND ITS TOOLS: PART 1

- Smudge Spacing (0–200%): Slider sets the spacing of the smudge.
- Angle (−180°, 0°, 180°): Slider sets the angle of the smudge and is more visible with non-round brushes.
- Shape Dynamics: Use the right pointing arrow to access the following. This area can control such settings as Size jitter (0–100%), Control (Pen pressure, Pen Tilt, Fade, None (default)), Minimum diameter (0–100%), Angle jitter (0–100%), Control (Pen pressure, Pen Tilt, Fade, Direction, None (default)), and Flip X jitter and Flip Y jitter check boxes. A setting of Fade can also include steps (1–9999). More details can be found in the Pixel brush properties settings section. Refer to Figure 3-105.

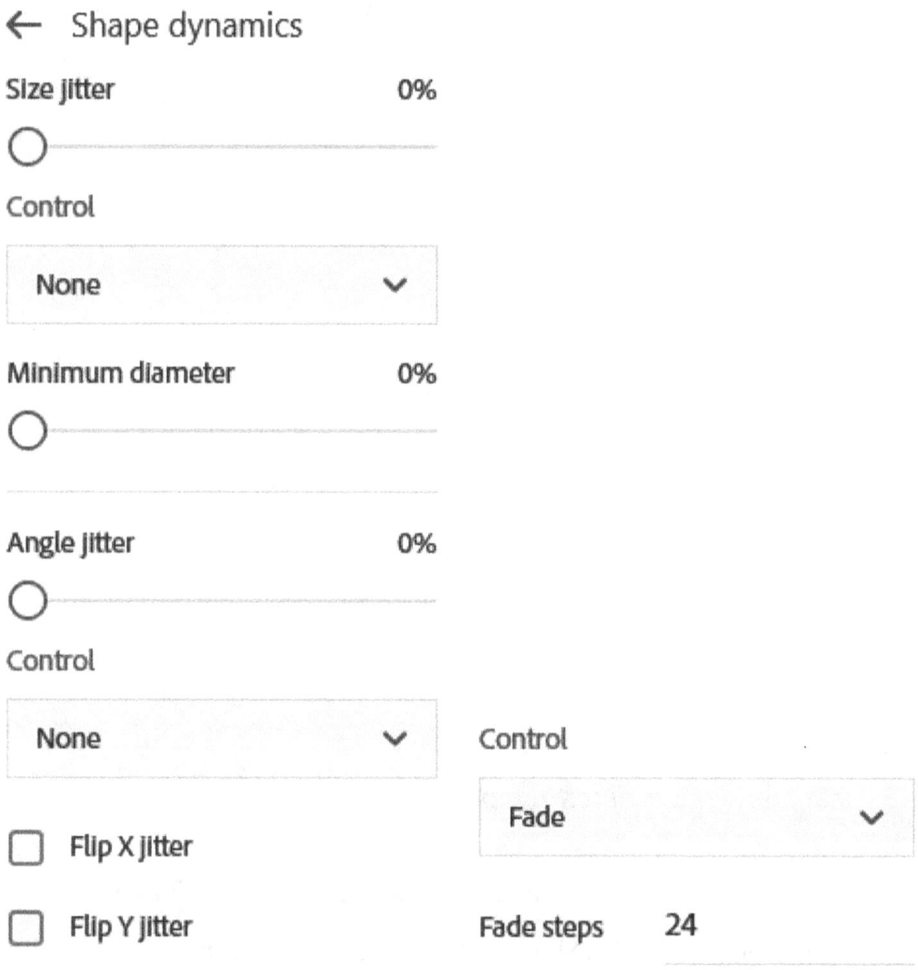

Figure 3-105. Smudge brush settings for Shape dynamics

- Scattering: Use the right pointing arrow to access the following. This can control such settings as Both axes check box, Scatter (0–1000%), Control (Pen pressure, Pen Tilt, Fade, None (default)), Stamp count (1–16), Count jitter (0–100%), and Control (Pen pressure, Pen Tilt, Fade, None (default)). More details can be found in the Pixel brush properties settings section. Refer to Figure 3-106.

Figure 3-106. Smudge brush settings for Scattering

- Transfer: Use the right pointing arrow to access the following. This can control such settings as Strength jitter (0–100%), Control (Pen pressure, Pen Tilt, Fade, None (default)), and Minimum (0–100%). Refer to Figure 3-107.

CHAPTER 3　EXPLORING THE WORKSPACE OF FRESCO AND ITS TOOLS: PART 1

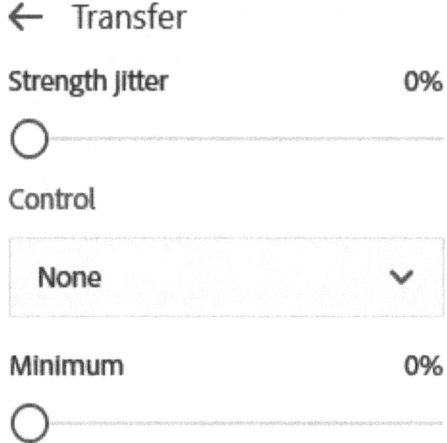

Figure 3-107. *Smudge brush settings for Transfer*

- Stylus Pressure Button: Create a custom stylus pressure if you are using a stylus. These settings can also be reset in the dialog box. The pressures can go from light to heavy, or you can adjust the point on the graph. Refer to Figures 3-63 and 3-108.

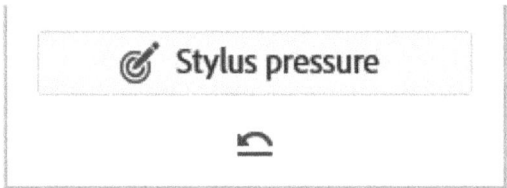

Figure 3-108. *Smudge brush panel Stylus pressure setting button*

- The left pointing arrow at the bottom of the panel allows you to reset the brushes' properties. Refer to Figure 3-108.

More information on the Smudge tool can be found at the following link:

https://helpx.adobe.com/fresco/using/smudge-tool.html

Painting Inside and Outside of a Boundary

One setting that is common to the Pixel, Live, Vector, and Eraser brushes is the option of Paint inside settings which can be toggled on and off. Refer to Figure 3-109.

CHAPTER 3   EXPLORING THE WORKSPACE OF FRESCO AND ITS TOOLS: PART 1

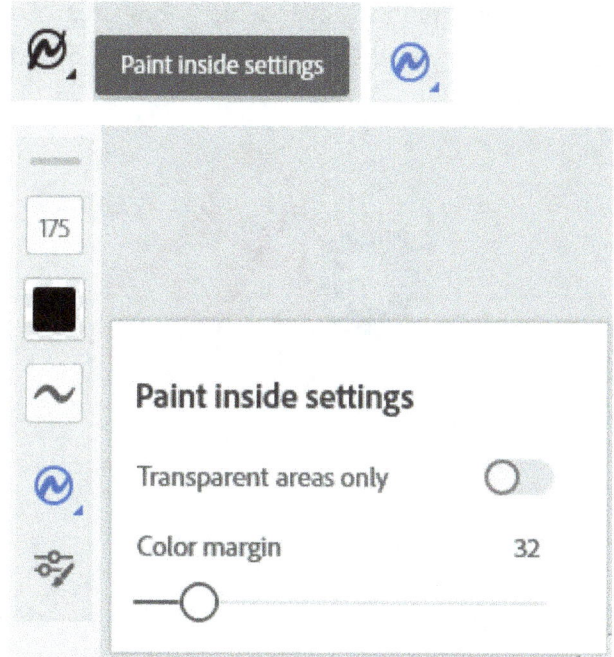

Figure 3-109. *Toolbar Paint inside settings button and the settings panel*

Currently, the default is the off settings or black icon which allows you to paint or erase anywhere on the current selected layer as required. Refer to Figure 3-109 and Figure 3-110.

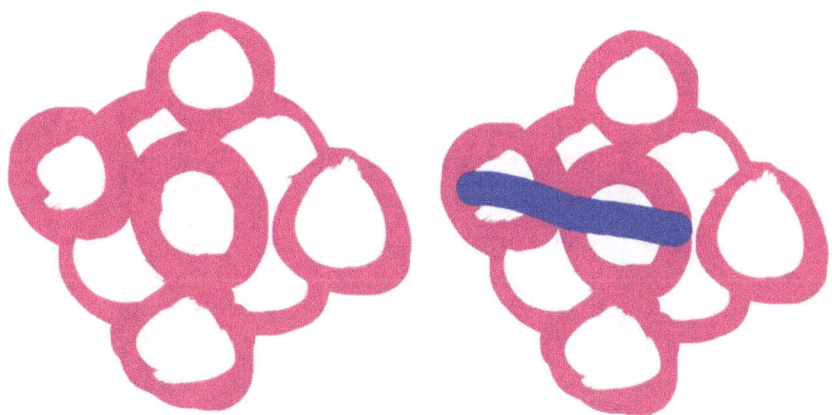

Figure 3-110. *Painting with the Paint inside settings off*

However, if you want to avoid painting over an area that already contains paint or inside of an unpainted area, then you should click to activate this button so that it shows as blue. Refer to Figure 3-111.

Figure 3-111. *Painting with the Paint inside settings on*

This will allow you, with any brush, to paint in a tight location. Currently, in this example, I was able to also paint inside the magenta area but not over the edge into the white transparent area.

However, you may instead want to paint in the transparent area. Click in the corner of this tool button to activate and view the settings. Refer to Figure 3-112.

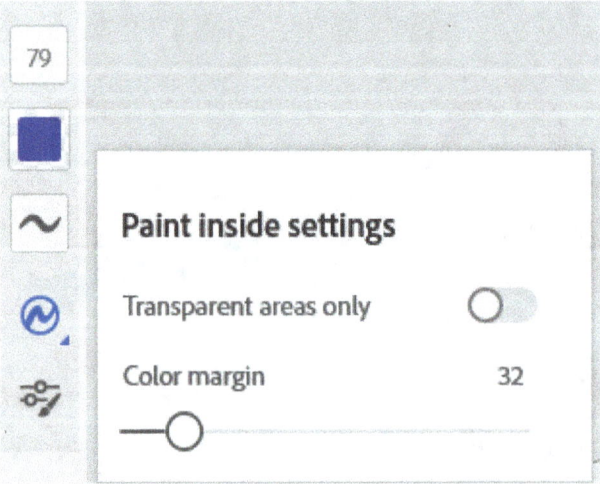

Figure 3-112. *Paint inside settings on and viewing the settings in the panel*

CHAPTER 3   EXPLORING THE WORKSPACE OF FRESCO AND ITS TOOLS: PART 1

You will see, because I left the setting of Transparent area off and left the Color margin at the default of 32, my result was painting in the inside of the painted area. For a more accurate selection, you could toggle the "Transparent areas only" on and adjust the color margin range slider (0–255) to make the boundaries closer with a higher setting (231) or slightly separate with a lower setting (8). Refer to Figure 3-113.

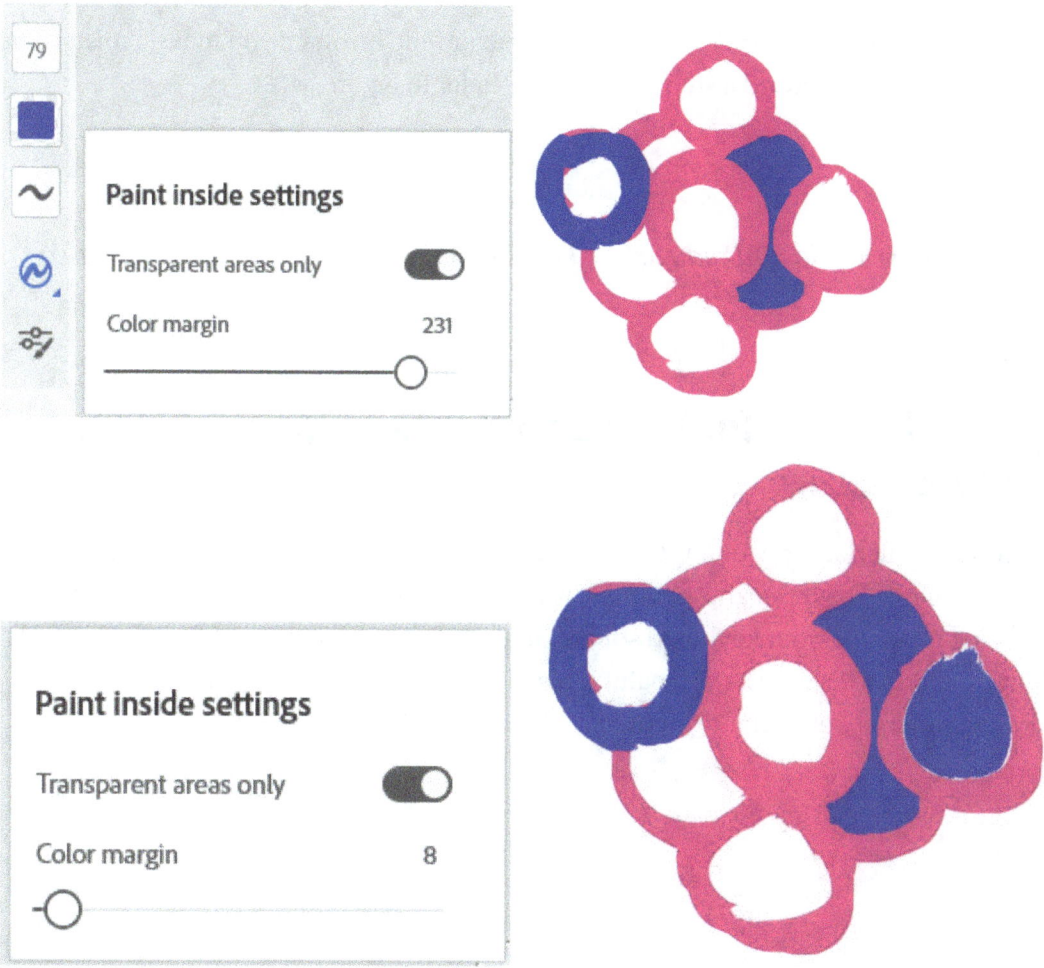

Figure 3-113. *By adjusting the Paint inside settings in various ways to get better result*

If you no longer want to use those settings, click the settings icon off back to black. However, your current settings will be retained while working on the project should you need to activate the setting again. Note however that if you paint the exact color

161

using the Paint inside settings, a distinct separation will not occur for that color even if Transparent areas only is disabled. Later, in Chapter 4, we will look at other ways to create selections to restrict painting.

Refer to this link if you need more information on Paint inside boundaries:

https://helpx.adobe.com/fresco/using/paint-inside-boundaries.html

As you practice, remember to use your undo or redo arrows if you make a mistake or want to go back or forward a step as you paint. Refer to Figure 3-114.

Figure 3-114. *Undo and redo arrow keys found in the upper right of the Fresco interface*

Touch Shortcuts for Various Brushes to Quickly Change the Brush Size

As we saw earlier, several touch shortcuts are available for the brush and can be found in the Help menu. However, another quick way to increase the size of your brush while you are using it is to use your keyboard square brackets left [to decrease the brush size and right] to increase the size as you paint. This information can be found in the Keyboard shortcuts area as well. Refer to Figure 3-115.

CHAPTER 3 EXPLORING THE WORKSPACE OF FRESCO AND ITS TOOLS: PART 1

Keyboard shortcuts	
]	Brush size increase
[	Brush size decrease

Figure 3-115. *You will know that the keyboard shortcut is working when you observe the brush size in the Toolbar*

Make sure to observe your brush size settings area in the Toolbar panel to see that the size change is taking place.

Next, I will present a few additional details for working with brushes in the form of a project.

CHAPTER 3   EXPLORING THE WORKSPACE OF FRESCO AND ITS TOOLS: PART 1

Project: Adding Custom Brushes to Fresco from Photoshop Through the CC Library

If you have already created a library using Photoshop, if they are active, some of the brushes that you added as assets will be available to you. However, if you have not, I will present here a brief overview of how that is accomplished so that you can use these brushes in Fresco. Refer to Figure 3-116.

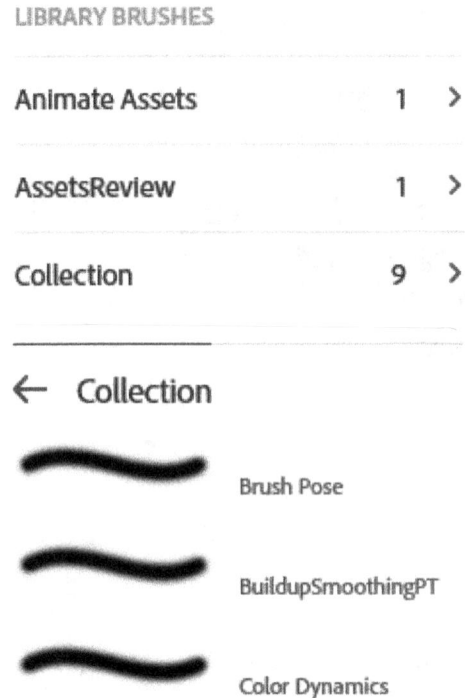

Figure 3-116.   *Pixel Library Brushes and one of the libraries selected*

Adding Other Brushes to the Library from Photoshop

It's important to note here that certain kinds of brushes, if you want to use them, must be created using alternate settings in Photoshop, such as Mixer-like brushes or any type of brush from Photoshop. You need to experiment with your brush settings. Then, first, save your brush in the Brushes folder as a file before it can be dragged into a CC Library and be available to Fresco.

CHAPTER 3   EXPLORING THE WORKSPACE OF FRESCO AND ITS TOOLS: PART 1

More details on Mixer brushes can be found here:

https://helpx.adobe.com/fresco/using/mixer-brushes.html

Let's review the step of custom brush creation in Photoshop now.

Steps of Brush Creation in Photoshop

To begin, open Photoshop to create a brush. Refer to Figure 3-117.

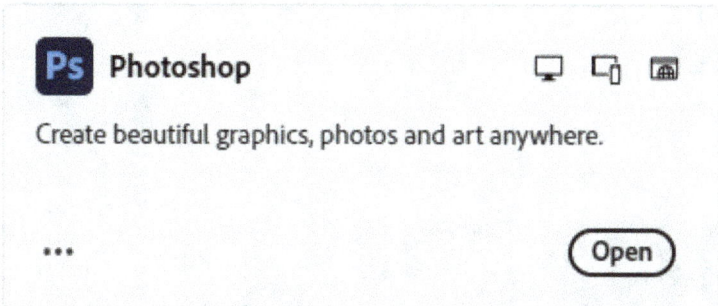

Figure 3-117. *Using Creative Cloud Desktop to open Photoshop*

You need to create a new file or open an existing file so that you can access the appropriate panels.

For practice, from the Home page, click New file, and from the Document menu, choose the tab of Print, and the document preset of **Letter 8.5x11 in @ 300ppi**. Make sure the color mode is RGB. Now, click Create, and a new blank document will appear. Refer to Figure 3-118 and Figure 3-119.

CHAPTER 3 EXPLORING THE WORKSPACE OF FRESCO AND ITS TOOLS: PART 1

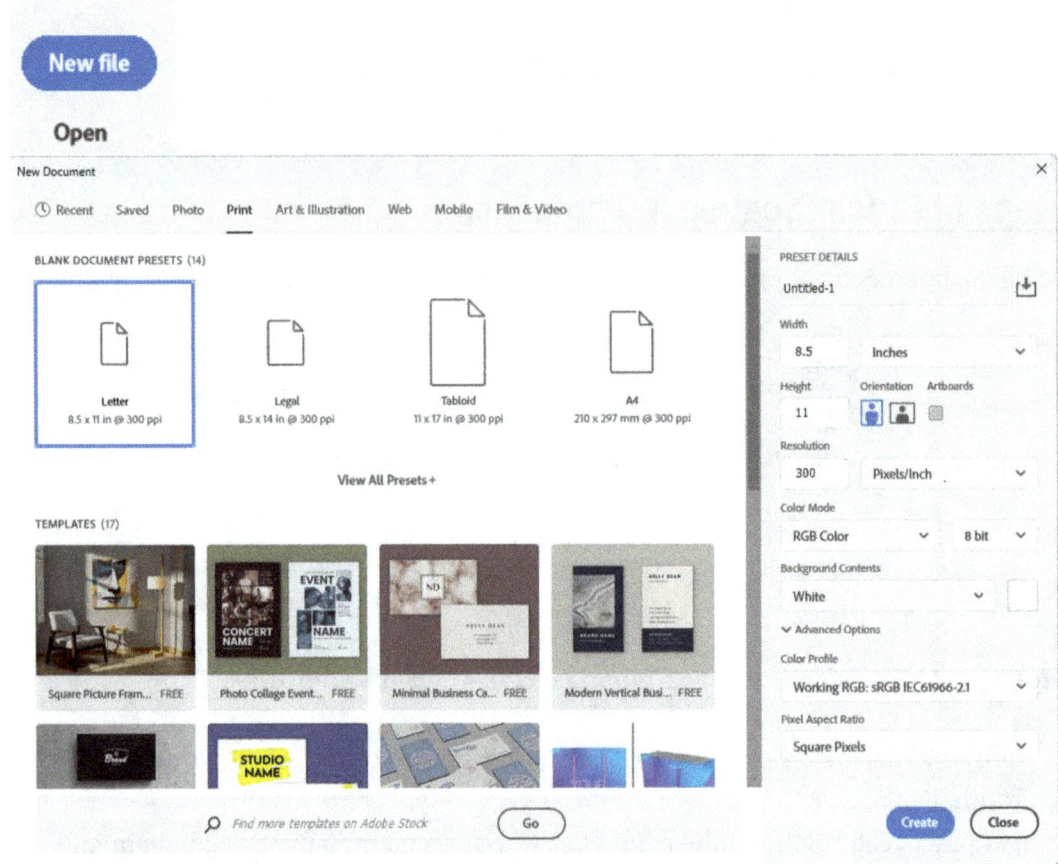

Figure 3-118. *Photoshop New file Button and New Document dialog box with the Print tab selected*

CHAPTER 3 EXPLORING THE WORKSPACE OF FRESCO AND ITS TOOLS: PART 1

Figure 3-119. *The Photoshop application opens to a blank page and current workspace*

Because this lesson is about Fresco and not Photoshop, I will focus on the core information and not go into any major details about the layout and workspace. Currently, I am working in the Window ➤ Workspace ➤ Essentials (Default) if you want to follow along with me.

The next step is to select your Brush Tool from the Toolbar panel. You can then review your Options bar above, with the Brushes and Brush settings panels available. Refer to Figure 3-120 and Figure 3-121.

CHAPTER 3   EXPLORING THE WORKSPACE OF FRESCO AND ITS TOOLS: PART 1

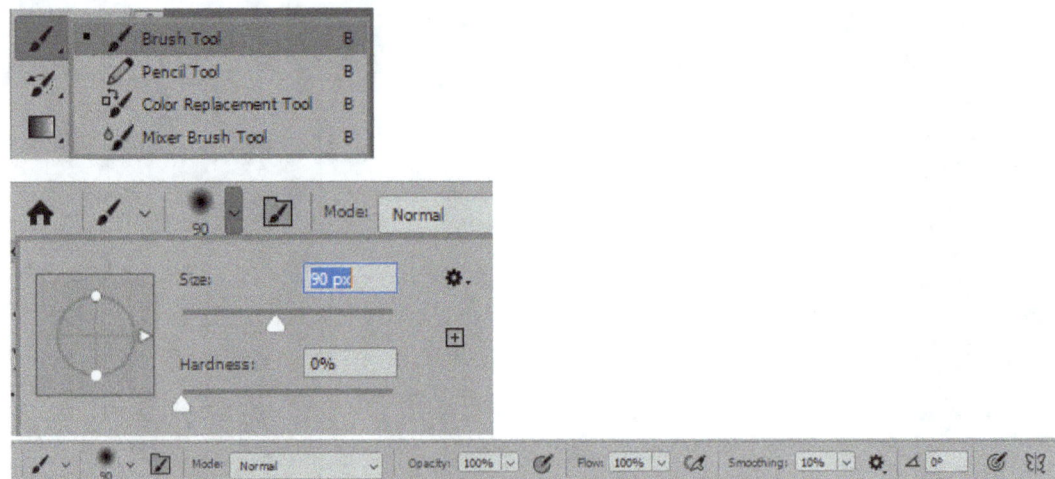

Figure 3-120. *Photoshop Brush Tool and settings in the Options bar panel*

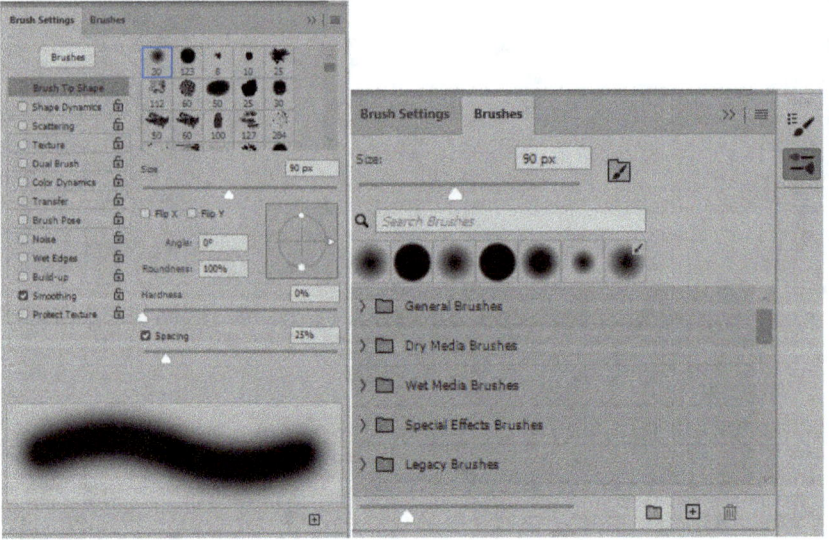

Figure 3-121. *Photoshop Brush Settings panel and Brushes panel*

If you cannot see those panels, locate them under Window ➤ Brush Settings and Brushes, and they will appear on the right-hand side with icons you can click to reveal the panels. Refer to Figure 3-122.

168

CHAPTER 3 EXPLORING THE WORKSPACE OF FRESCO AND ITS TOOLS: PART 1

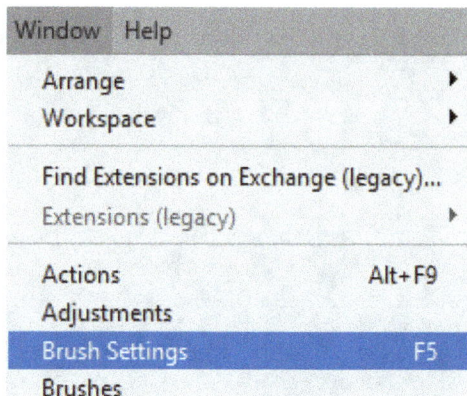

Figure 3-122. *Photoshop Window menu for accessing the panels*

Note There are two ways you can create a brush. First, I will present the simple way using a round brush and then, later, from an image defined as brush.

Creating a Round Brush

If you don't know where to start with a brush, I recommend selecting the Brushes panel, and in the General Brushes folder, select either a Soft or Hard Round as your brush to start creating a custom setting. The brush can be any size you like, but larger brushes 90 px and higher will reveal more details as you test. Refer to Figure 3-123.

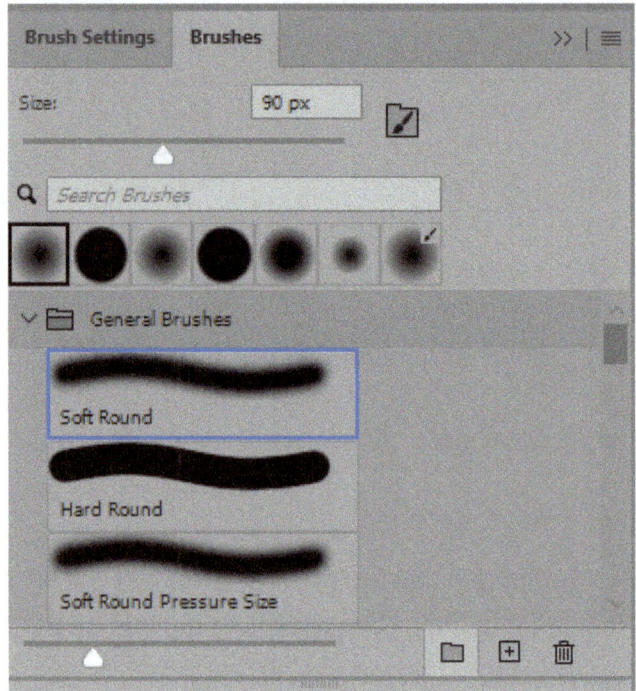

Figure 3-123. *Brushes panel selection of the folder General Brushes and Soft Round or Hard Round*

Using the Brush Settings panel, begin to experiment with various settings while viewing the preview area below in the panel as you work. You can turn various settings on and off to create your brush using the check boxes. Refer to Figure 3-124.

Click each tab; some will have more settings than others, and some of these, now that you are working in Fresco, may already be familiar to you. The tabs include Brush Tip Shape, Shape Dynamics, Scattering, Texture, Dual Brush, Color Dynamics, Transfer, Brush Pose, Noise, Wet Edges, Build-up, Smoothing, and Protect Texture. Refer to Figure 3-124.

Here is an example of how the settings might look like when you return to the Brush Tip Shape tab. Refer to Figure 3-124.

CHAPTER 3 EXPLORING THE WORKSPACE OF FRESCO AND ITS TOOLS: PART 1

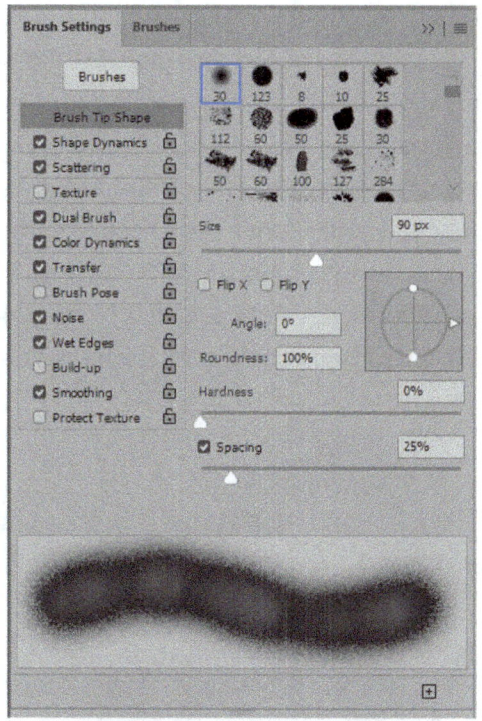

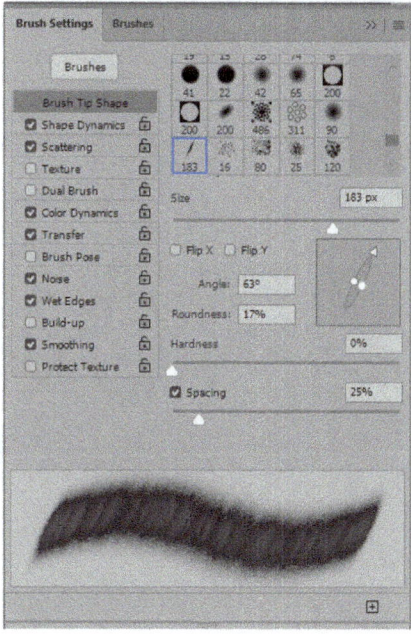

Figure 3-124. *Brush Settings panel with alterations*

CHAPTER 3   EXPLORING THE WORKSPACE OF FRESCO AND ITS TOOLS: PART 1

In the Brush Tip Shape tab, for a more angled calligraphic brush, you can change the Roundness from 0% to 100% as well as adjust the Angle (−180°, 0°, 180°). In this case, for a round head, I left the Size at 90 px, Angle at 0°, and Roundness at 100%. In both cases, I left the Hardness at 0% and Spacing at 25%. Refer to Figure 3-124.

After you have made your changes, test it in Photoshop on the white background canvas. It does not matter what color paint you use. But if you need to set the default to black, press the D key so that black becomes the foreground color. However, for brushes that have Color Dynamics, you may want to use another color for testing. In that case, select a test color from the Swatches panel, such as RGB red, and paint again on the canvas. Refer to Figure 3-125.

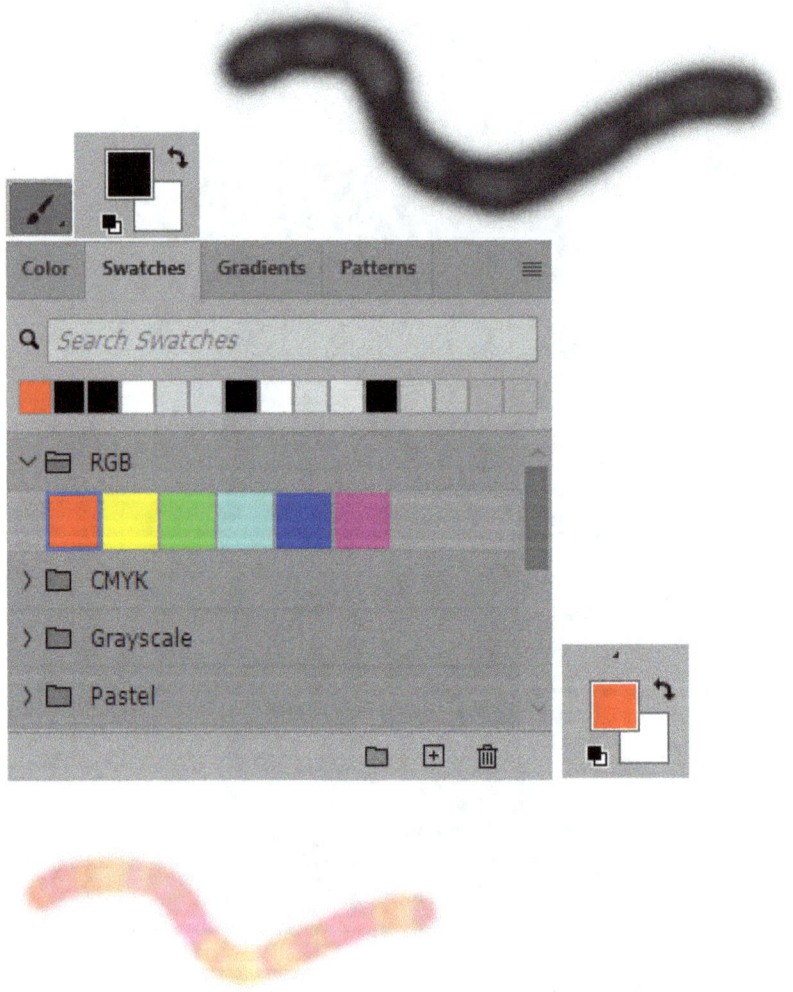

Figure 3-125. *Use your brush tool Toolbar foreground and background color and Swatches panel to test and alter colors*

CHAPTER 3 EXPLORING THE WORKSPACE OF FRESCO AND ITS TOOLS: PART 1

In the Brush Settings panel, once you have created the brush you like, you can then save it by clicking the Create new brush button in the lower right. Refer to Figure 3-126.

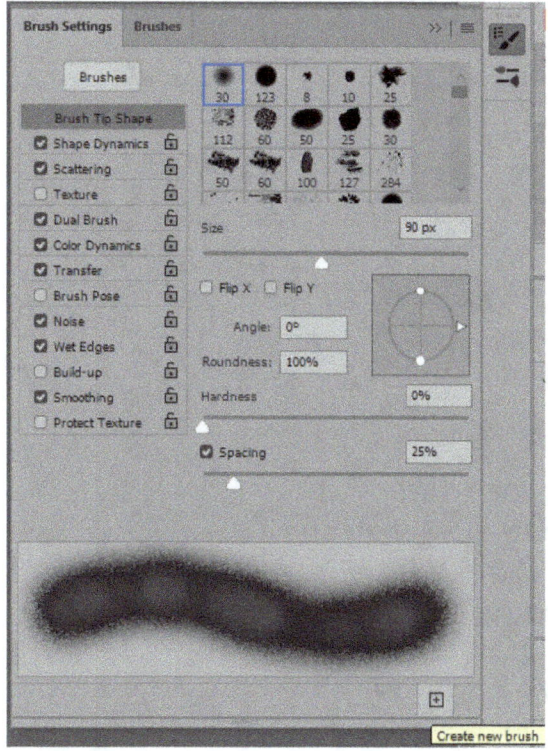

Figure 3-126. *Brush Settings panel; click the Create new brush button to add it to your collection*

In the dialog box, name your new brush. You can choose to make sure that you "Capture Brush Size in Preset", Include Tool Settings, and Include the Color as well if you want that red color to be part of the brush. Click OK. Refer to Figure 3-127.

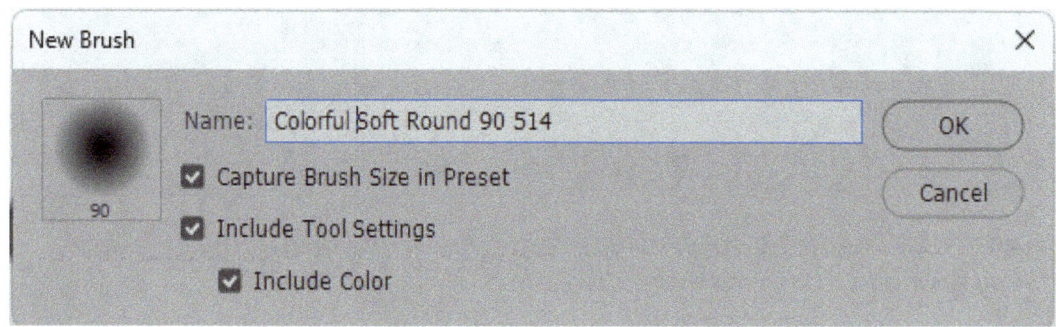

Figure 3-127. *New Brush dialog box*

173

CHAPTER 3   EXPLORING THE WORKSPACE OF FRESCO AND ITS TOOLS: PART 1

This adds your brush to the Brushes panel, and then you can create a folder group, name it, and (click OK) to drag the brush into it for storage, and you can use it in Photoshop any time when you select it. Refer to Figure 3-128.

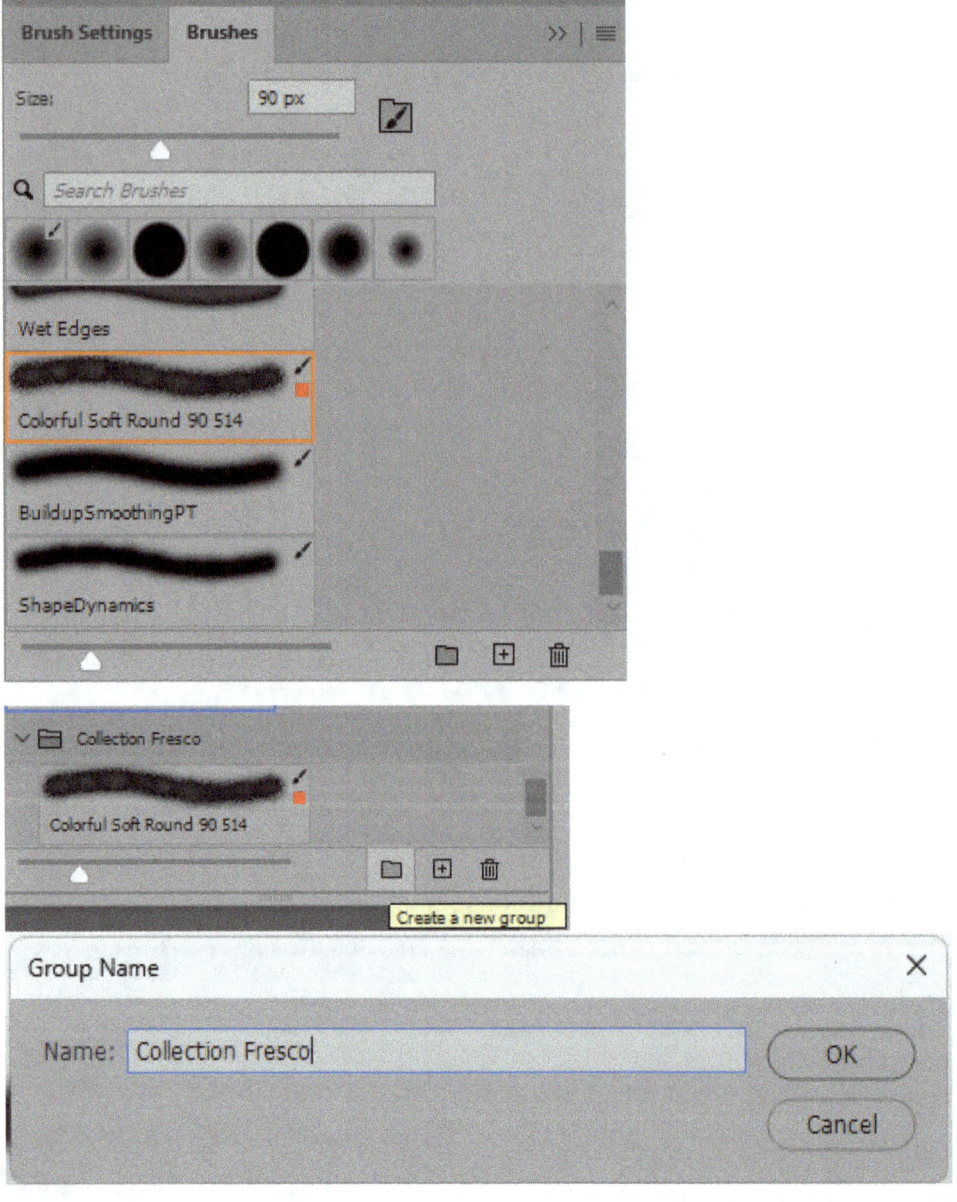

Figure 3-128. *Adding a brush to the Brushes panel and then adding to a new group folder and the Group Name dialog box*

CHAPTER 3   EXPLORING THE WORKSPACE OF FRESCO AND ITS TOOLS: PART 1

Creating a Shape Brush

To Create a shape brush, is another way to create a unique brush for Fresco, this time start with creating a pattern on your canvas. If you are not familiar with painting in Photoshop, you could start with one of your legacy brushes found under the Brushes menu Legacy Brushes folder if you cannot locate them. In this case, I was using was from the Assorted Brushes sub-folder, I selected Circle 1 brush, and I stamped several times on my canvas to create a pattern. I recommend using a clean white background when doing brush creation to avoid unwanted parts added to the brush. The brush in this case should be initially painted with black but can have variations of gray as well, as this will add a blur or fade as you paint. Refer to Figure 3-129.

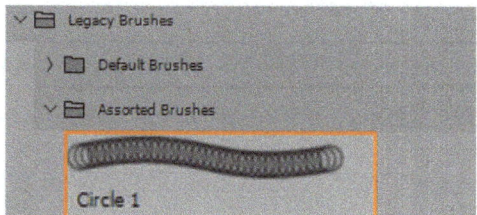

Figure 3-129. *Brushes panel locating a legacy brush and creating a new brush shape on the canvas*

Then, with the Rectangular Marquee selection tool found in the Toolbar and its Options bar panel, I will draw or drag a tight selection around the shape I created. Refer to Figure 3-130.

CHAPTER 3　EXPLORING THE WORKSPACE OF FRESCO AND ITS TOOLS: PART 1

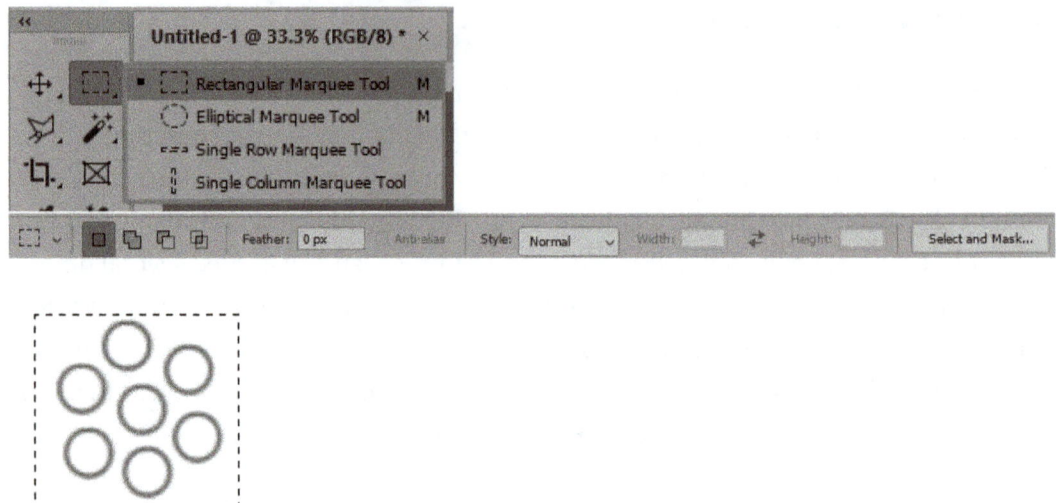

Figure 3-130. *Use the Toolbar Rectangular Marquee Tool and its Options panel to draw a clean selection around the brush*

Now, in the main Menu, go to Edit ➤ Define Brush Preset. Name your brush in the Brush Name panel and click OK. Refer to Figure 3-131.

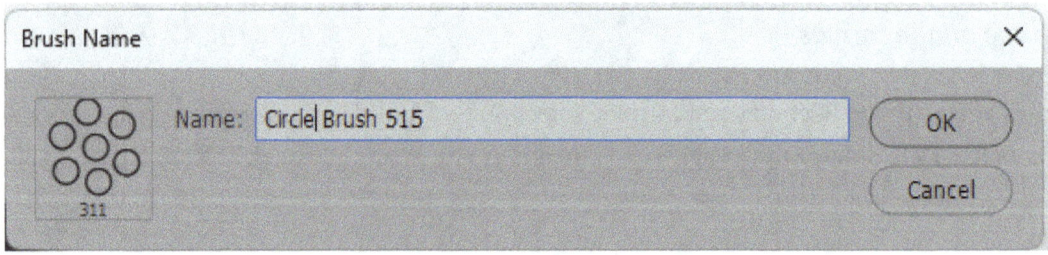

Figure 3-131. *Brush Name dialog box*

This brush will also be added to the Brushes panel, and you can test it on the background. Just make sure to Select ➤ Deselect (Ctrl/CMD+D) your previous selection first before you test. Refer to Figure 3-132.

CHAPTER 3 EXPLORING THE WORKSPACE OF FRESCO AND ITS TOOLS: PART 1

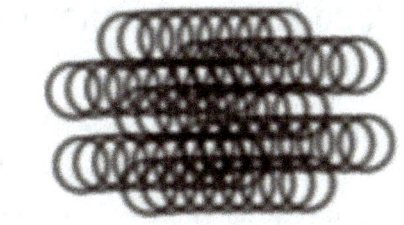

Figure 3-132. *Paint with the brush tool with your new brush*

In the Brushes folder, select the brush, and you can drag this brush to the Brushes folder group you just created as well. Refer to Figure 3-133.

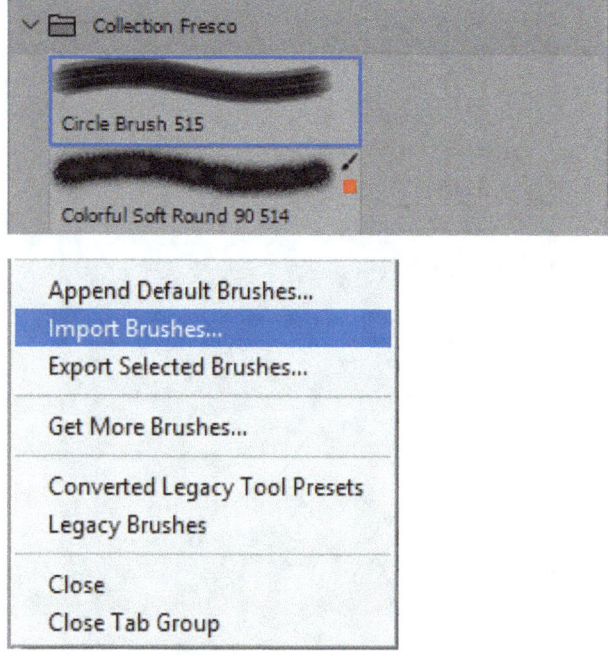

Figure 3-133. *In the Brushes panel, place the brush in a group folder, or use the menu to import some more brushes*

Continue to build more brushes if you like. You can find my files in the **Fresco Brushes.abr** file if you need to import them into Photoshop using the Brushes panel's menu.

177

CHAPTER 3   EXPLORING THE WORKSPACE OF FRESCO AND ITS TOOLS: PART 1

Steps of Creative Cloud Library Creation in Photoshop

The next step is to create a Creative Cloud or (CC) Library so that you can use the brush or brushes in other Adobe applications, in this case Fresco. Make sure that your Libraries panel in Photoshop is visible. If other libraries have already been created, it will show Recent and All libraries that you can click and access. Refer to Figure 3-134.

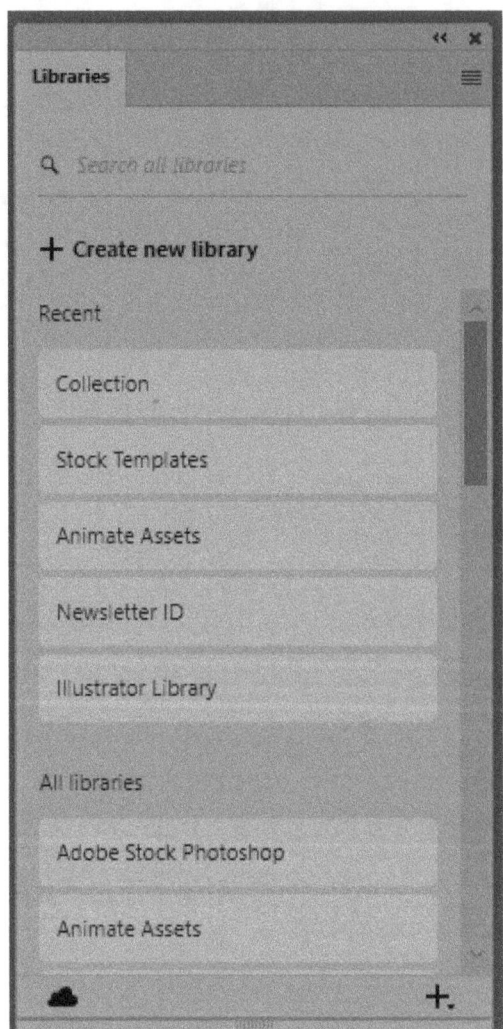

Figure 3-134. Libraries panel viewing some recent libraries

If you do not already have a library of brushes in the Libraries panel, you will want to start by clicking the "Create new library" button. Then, name the library and click Create. Refer to Figure 3-134 and Figure 3-135.

CHAPTER 3   EXPLORING THE WORKSPACE OF FRESCO AND ITS TOOLS: PART 1

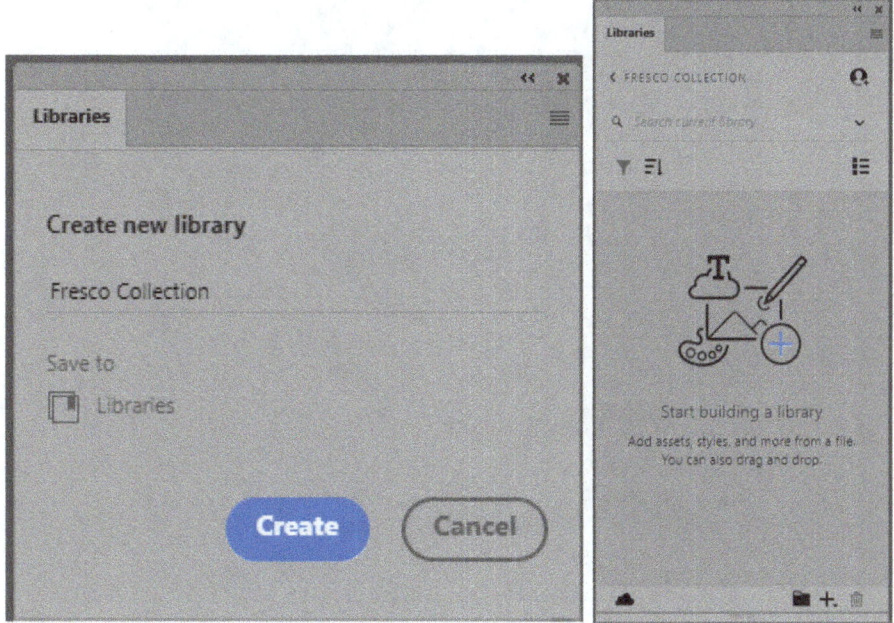

Figure 3-135. *Adding a new library to the Libraries panel and getting it ready to add assets to*

You will then begin to fill it with assets which could include color swatches, shapes, graphics, and brushes. Later, in Chapter 4, we will look at how to add shapes and colors and in Chapter 7 graphics.

Adding Brush to Library

Now, select the brush or brushes in the Brushes panel that you want to add to your CC Library, and then, drag it into the Libraries panel. This adds them to your library. Refer to Figure 3-136.

CHAPTER 3　EXPLORING THE WORKSPACE OF FRESCO AND ITS TOOLS: PART 1

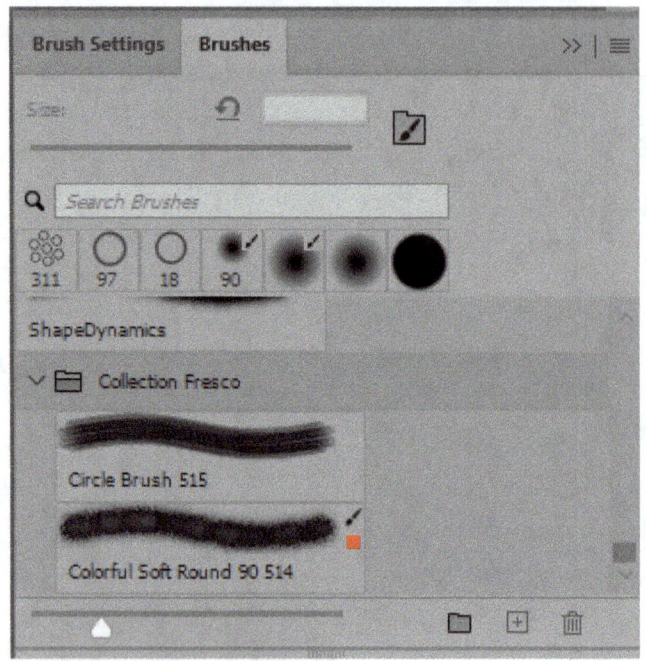

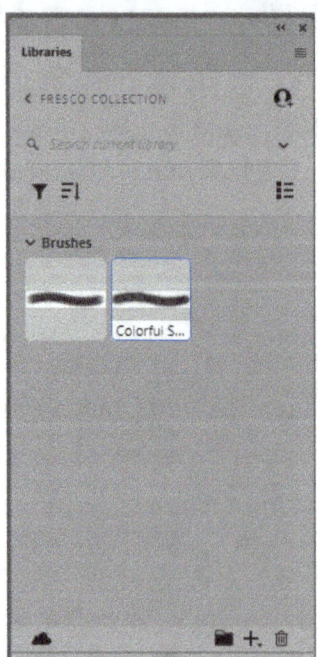

Figure 3-136. *Dragging brushes from the Brushes panel to the Libraries panel*

You can then leave Photoshop open and return to Fresco.

Viewing Your Brushes in Fresco

When you open a document in Fresco, the Libraries automatically update since they are connected to the Creative Cloud Desktop. Select a Pixel brush tool, and then look in the Library Brushes section of the menu, and locate the library you just created or another library you made earlier. In most cases, that brush will be available for you to select and then use on your canvas. Refer to Figure 3-137.

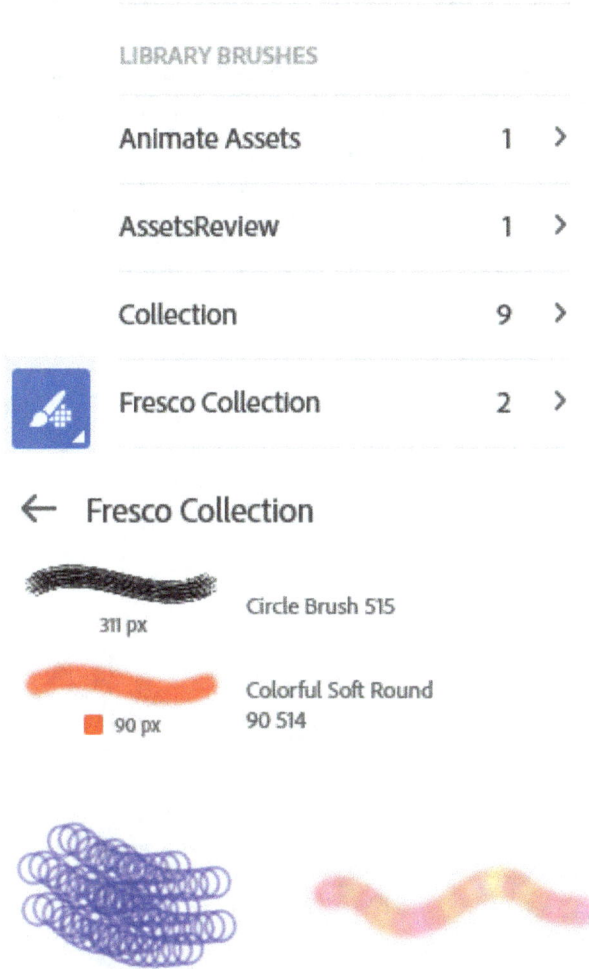

Figure 3-137. *Pixel brush selected and Library Brushes accessed and then painted onto the canvas*

Brush Import Limitation

Be aware that not all brushes that you create in Photoshop with the Brush Settings panel will import if those settings do not match the ones in Fresco, and you may see a warning in the panel if that is the case. Refer to Figure 3-138.

1 Unsupported brushes

Figure 3-138. *Warning message about an unsupported brush that was created*

For example, in Photoshop, if a brush contains Texture or Protect Texture settings, that brush can be added to the Cloud Library and will be available to share with another Photoshop user, but not in Fresco. Refer to Figure 3-139.

CHAPTER 3 EXPLORING THE WORKSPACE OF FRESCO AND ITS TOOLS: PART 1

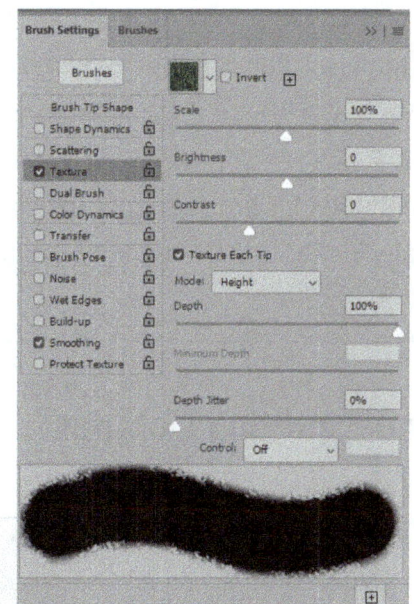

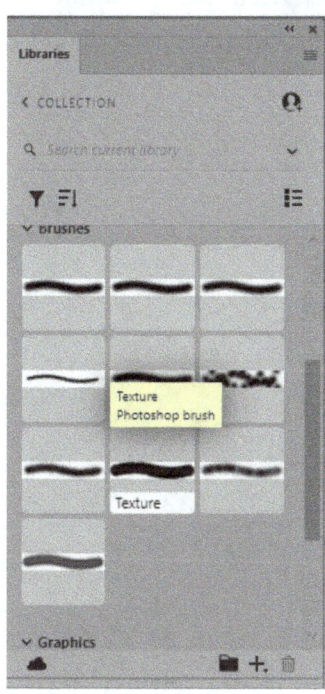

Figure 3-139. *Photoshop brush was created with Texture settings in the Brush Settings panel and added to the Libraries panel*

This is due to the fact that the Texture is tied to a pattern in Photoshop and that option is not currently available in Fresco. So, avoid using those check box settings when creating your brush if it is to be used in Fresco.

Note that currently, Vector brushes from the Illustrator Library will not be imported and any Vector brushes created and added to a library will be excluded from Fresco.

Importing and Exporting Libraries

Coming back to Photoshop, if you would like to test my brushes in Photoshop and Fresco found in the Projects folder. You can import these files through the Libraries panel by choosing Import library using the panel's menu and selecting and locating that library's (.cclibs or .cclibc) file formats in the folder. Click OK and click Import. See the file called **Collection.cclibs** and **Fresco Collection.cclibs**. Click OK to any additional info messages that appear. Refer to Figure 3-140.

CHAPTER 3   EXPLORING THE WORKSPACE OF FRESCO AND ITS TOOLS: PART 1

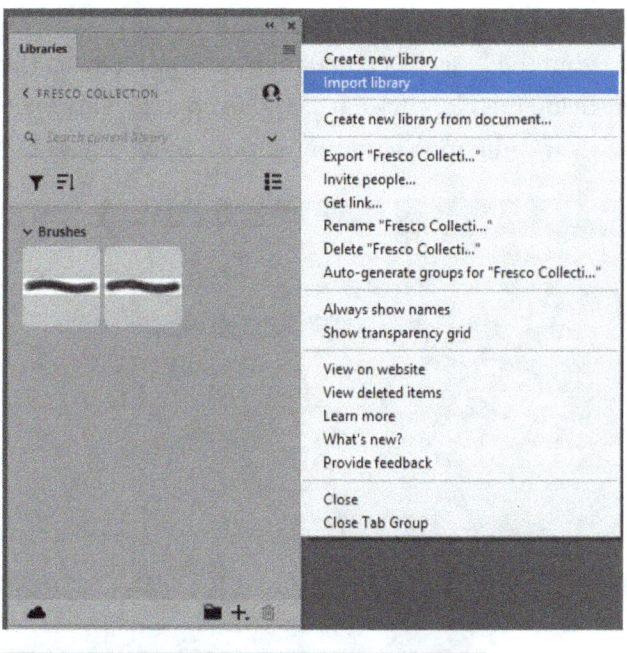

Figure 3-140. *In Photoshop, use the Libraries panel to import another library file*

CHAPTER 3   EXPLORING THE WORKSPACE OF FRESCO AND ITS TOOLS: PART 1

If you need to export a copy of your library off the Creative Cloud, select the library in the panel, and then, from the Libraries panel menu, choose Export (library name), locate the Select folder for saving the file, click Save, and export the file as a (.cclibs) or (.cclibc) file format. Click OK to any info messages that appear. Refer to Figure 3-141.

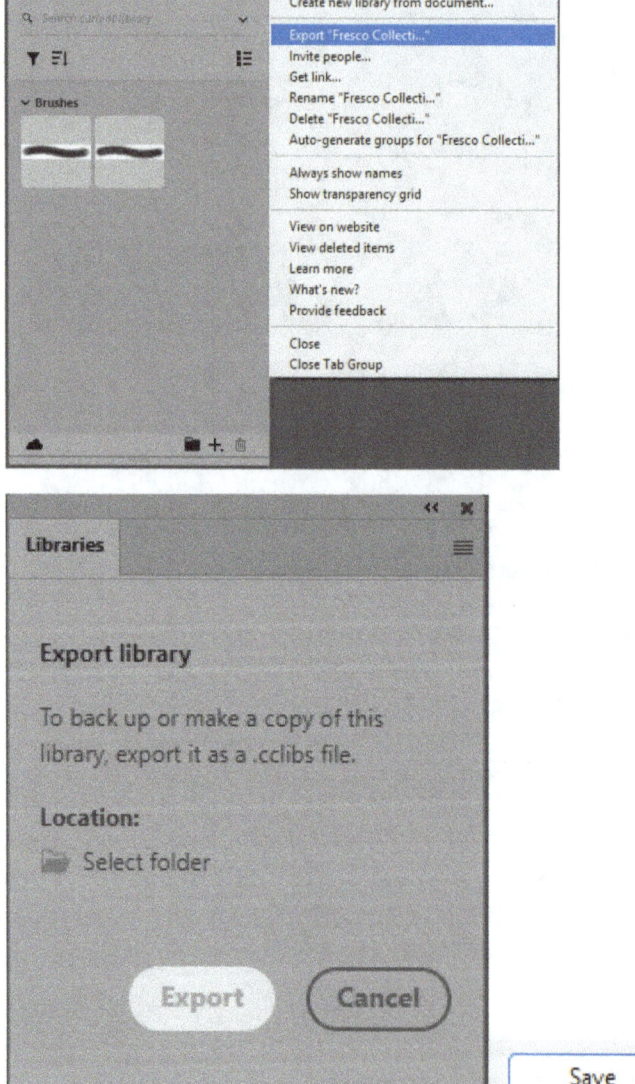

Figure 3-141. *In Photoshop, use the Libraries panel to export a library file*

CHAPTER 3 EXPLORING THE WORKSPACE OF FRESCO AND ITS TOOLS: PART 1

More details on creating Creative Cloud Libraries can be found here:

https://helpx.adobe.com/photoshop/using/cc-libraries-in-photoshop.html
https://helpx.adobe.com/fresco/using/fresco-creative-cloud-libraries.html

Note Use your Creative Cloud Desktop Files ➤ Your libraries as seen in Chapter 1 and 2 if you need to delete a library. Refer to Figure 3-142.

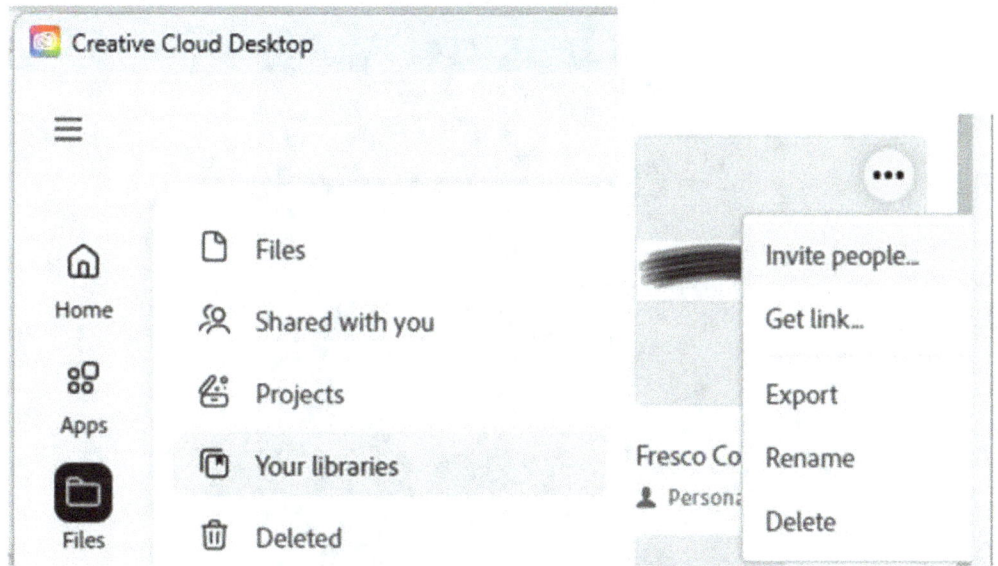

Figure 3-142. *Creative Cloud Desktop Files ➤ Your libraries tab to delete a library*

Tips on Capture Ribbon Brushes

A second kind of brush is the Capture ribbon brush. This kind of Pixel brush can only be created using a Capture app which you can learn more about here:

https://helpx.adobe.com/fresco/using/ribbon-brushes.html

While Photoshop's Libraries on the desktop also have access to the Capture app, it cannot create this kind of brush using its version of Capture. The Photoshop's version of Capture can, however, be used to create shapes which can be added to the Fresco library, which we will look at later in Chapter 4. Refer to Figure 3-143.

CHAPTER 3   EXPLORING THE WORKSPACE OF FRESCO AND ITS TOOLS: PART 1

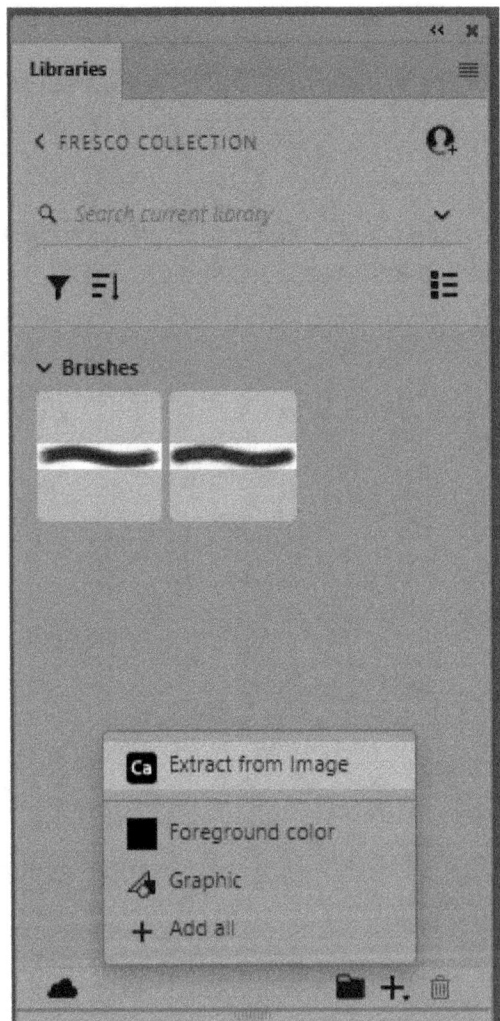

Figure 3-143. Photoshop Libraries panel with menu open

In Photoshop, make sure to File ➤ Save any documents you may have open if you need to return to them later. For now, remain in Fresco as we look at the next set of tools.

Summary

In this chapter, we reviewed the five brush kinds found in the Fresco Toolbar panel along with their properties and settings and then ended with a project to create custom brushes in Photoshop that could later be added to the Creative Cloud Library and used in Fresco. In the next chapter, we will continue to explore the Toolbar panel and look at the rest of the tools.

CHAPTER 4

Exploring the Workspace of Fresco and Its Tools: Part 2

Continuing from the previous chapter, we will now explore and work with various Transform, Selection, Shape, Text, and Coloring tools from the Toolbar panel. You can continue to work within your open blank practice document from Chapter 3. Some of these tools may already be familiar to you if you have used the applications of Photoshop and Illustrator. As well, you will discover how to add assets of shapes and colors from Photoshop via the Creative Cloud Library panel to enhance your artwork. You will then complete the chapter by working with a project using the skills you learned in this chapter and the previous chapter.

Note The project files for this chapter can be found in the Chapter 4 folder. Refer to the link in the introduction.

Continue at this point in Fresco to work with a new blank document or open the one you created in Chapter 3. Later in the chapter you will from the Home page Import and Open some files using that button as seen in previous chapters.

CHAPTER 4   EXPLORING THE WORKSPACE OF FRESCO AND ITS TOOLS: PART 2

Move and Transform Tool

The Move and Transform tool on the Toolbar has several sub-tools that are similar to the Photoshop and Illustrator tools for the purpose of moving and transforming items on various layers. They are Transform, Skew, Distort, Perspective, and Liquify. While the tools are enabled, you are within the Transform workspace. Refer to Figure 4-1.

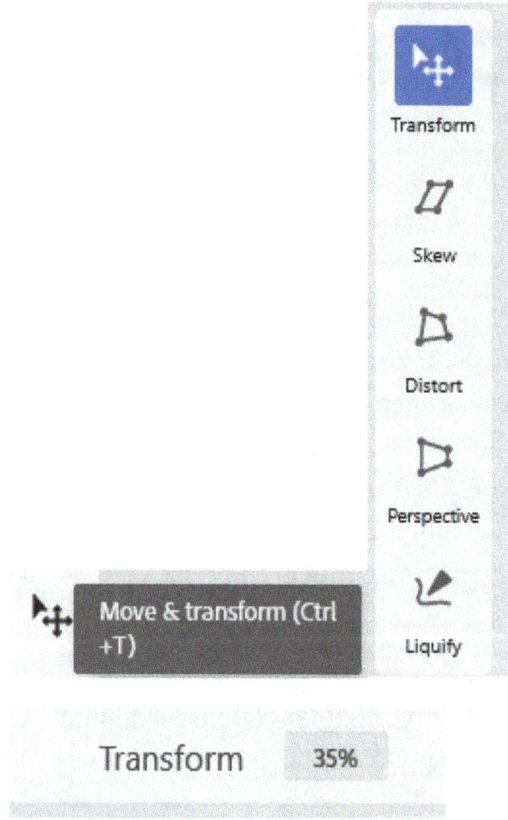

Figure 4-1. *Fresco Toolbar Move and Transform tool with its sub-tools displayed while in the Transform workspace*

Note that for the Move tool (V) in Photoshop, actual Transform options are found under the Edit ➤ Transform menu area. Also, you can access these options in the Options bar panel, and Liquify options are found in the Filter menu. Refer to Figure 4-2.

190

CHAPTER 4   EXPLORING THE WORKSPACE OF FRESCO AND ITS TOOLS: PART 2

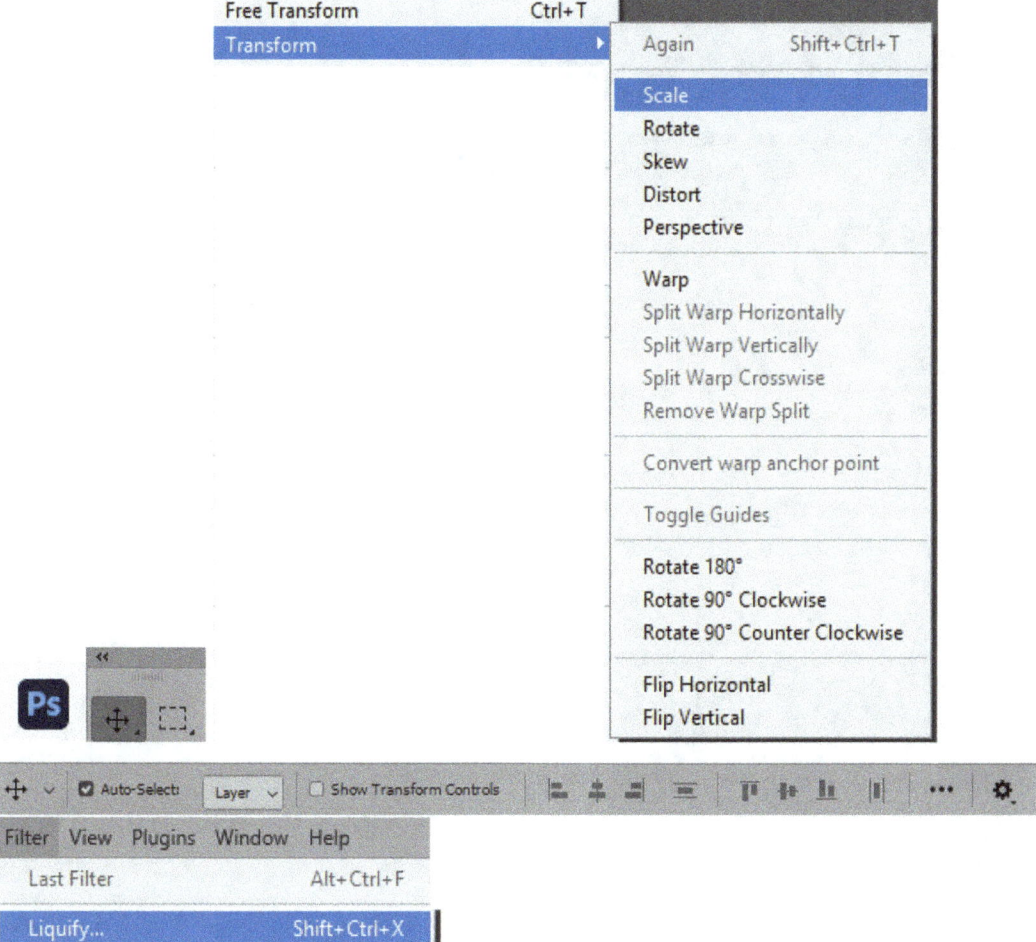

Figure 4-2. *Photoshop examples of Move and Transform tools found in its main menu and Options bar panel*

In Illustrator, there are also similar tools which perform similar tasks for movement and distortion. They can be found when using the Selection tool or in the Toolbar panel. Or you can do various warps and distortions as well as using the menu commands under Object ➤ Transform or with the Transform panel. Refer to Figure 4-3.

CHAPTER 4 EXPLORING THE WORKSPACE OF FRESCO AND ITS TOOLS: PART 2

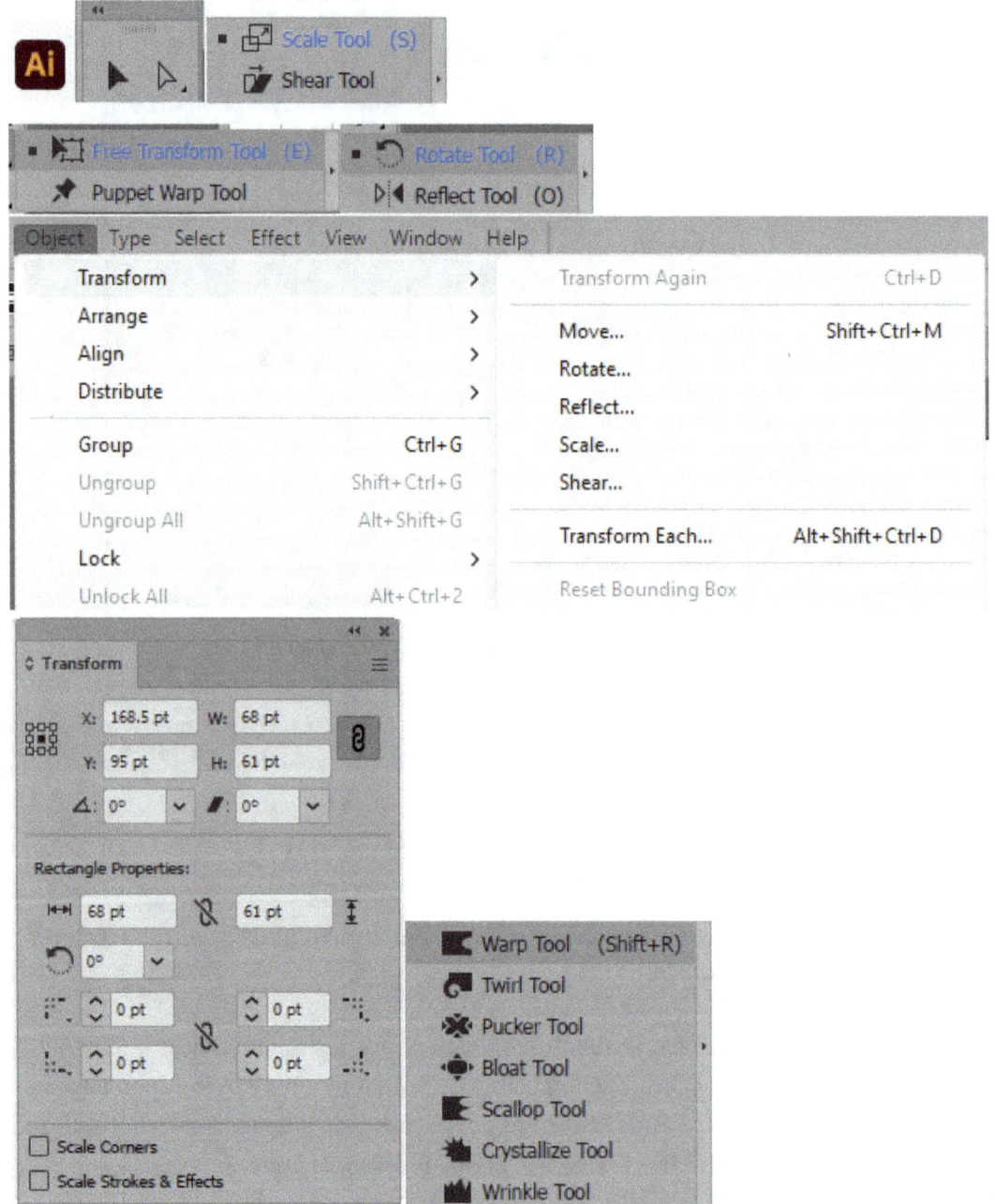

Figure 4-3. *Illustrator examples of Move and Transform tools found in its Toolbar main menu and panels*

You can learn more about transformation in Photoshop and Illustrator in the following links if you need to later compare to Fresco or review:

https://helpx.adobe.com/photoshop/using/transforming-objects.html
https://helpx.adobe.com/illustrator/using/transforming-objects.html

Transform (Ctrl+T): Scale, Rotate, and Constraint Options

In Fresco, this Move and Transform tool allows you to move, scale, and rotate your brush strokes or shapes on the canvas or layers. When you select the tool, the bounding box handles appear around the current selected set of pixel or vector strokes on a layer. In this example, I am using the file **FlowerPainting.psd** which you can find and open from the Home page ➤ Import and open in Fresco for practice, or continue on with your own painted image and select a pixel layer. Then, select the tool to enter the Transform workspace. Refer to Figure 4-4.

CHAPTER 4   EXPLORING THE WORKSPACE OF FRESCO AND ITS TOOLS: PART 2

Figure 4-4. *Import and open; then, in the Transform workspace, you can use this tool to move artwork while surrounded by the bounding box*

By holding down the mouse key, while that layer is selected in the center of the bounding box area, you can drag the artwork to a new location on the page.

If you just need to nudge the item up, down, left, or right, then use the nudge arrow keys to move in very small increments. Use the (=) lines if you need to drag and move the nudge arrows nearer to your artwork. Refer to Figure 4-5.

CHAPTER 4   EXPLORING THE WORKSPACE OF FRESCO AND ITS TOOLS: PART 2

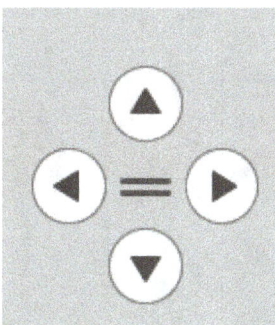

Figure 4-5. *Nudge arrow keys for moving selected items on a layer*

Use the Touch shortcut (double-click) to enable the primary circle; if you find that the nudge arrow keys have become disabled or moving in too small increments, this will increase it to larger 10 px increments of movement. Doing this will also constrain your drag movements in the X/Y vertical/horizonal positions of 90° with guides to assist for better alignment. Disable the Touch shortcut by double-clicking again to return to free-form movements. Refer to Figure 4-6.

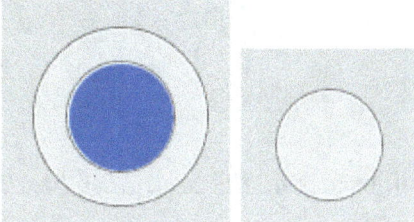

Figure 4-6. *Enabled Touch shortcut circle and the Touch shortcut disabled*

Scaling will allow you to reduce or increase the brush strokes or artwork on the layer. Use any of the eight bounding box handles to drag and scale the size by dragging inward to decrease or dragging outward to increase. Using the Touch shortcut primary circle (double-click), you can scale from the center. Refer to Figures 4-6 and 4-7.

195

Chapter 4 Exploring the Workspace of Fresco and its Tools: Part 2

Figure 4-7. *Scale your artwork using the bounding box handles*

Then, to rotate, use the upper round handle and drag left (counterclockwise) negative or right (clockwise) positive to change the angle of the strokes, and a preview of the degrees, you have turned, will appear as you work. Use the Touch shortcut primary circle (double-click), and you will be guided to rotate in 15-degree increment alerts indicated by the message of the degrees changing color. Refer to Figure 4-8.

CHAPTER 4 EXPLORING THE WORKSPACE OF FRESCO AND ITS TOOLS: PART 2

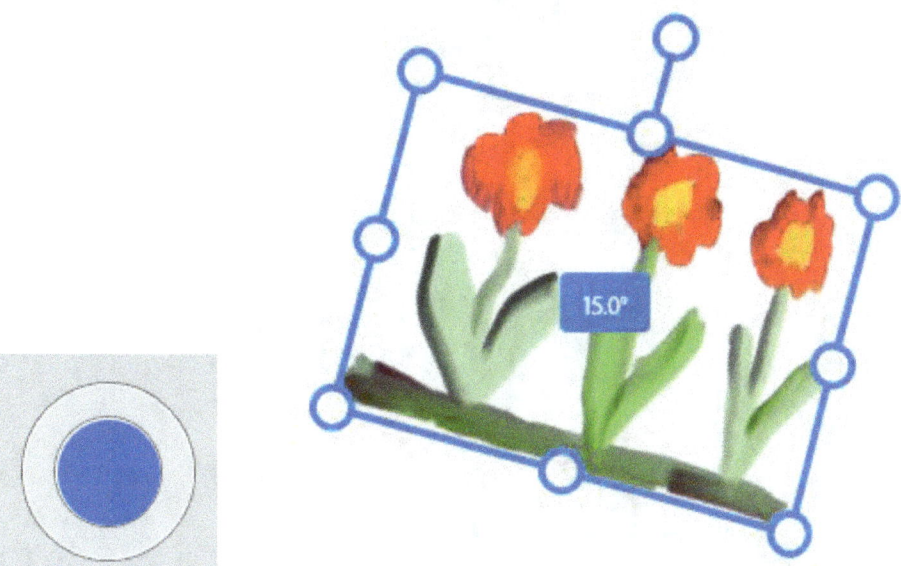

Figure 4-8. *Enabled the Touch shortcut circle when you want to rotate 15 degrees at a time*

You can review this link if you need more details on free transforming:

https://helpx.adobe.com/fresco/using/free-transform-tool.html

While in the Transform workspace, additional options for transforming can be found in the upper right menu alongside undo and redo. These are Flip vertically and Flip horizontally. You can click these to quickly change the orientation of your artwork. Refer to Figure 4-9.

197

CHAPTER 4 EXPLORING THE WORKSPACE OF FRESCO AND ITS TOOLS: PART 2

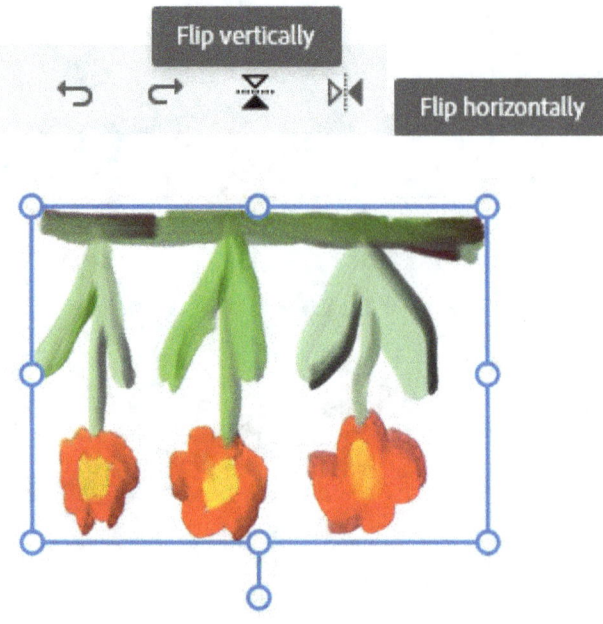

Figure 4-9. *Use the Flip vertically and Flip horizontally button icons to change the orientation of the artwork*

Likewise, also in the upper right, you can also edit a grid for better alignment. But I will discuss this more, later in this chapter and then in Chapters 5 and 6. To turn the nudge key buttons off and on, you can toggle the Nudge icon. Refer to Figure 4-10.

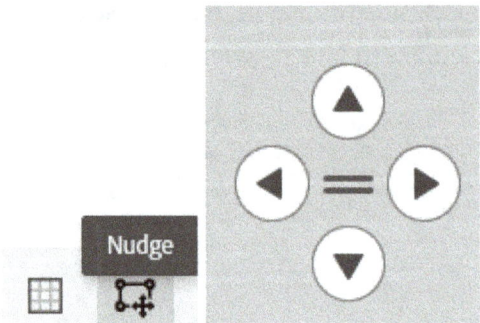

Figure 4-10. *Use the icons to edit the grid or hide/show the nudge keys*

CHAPTER 4　EXPLORING THE WORKSPACE OF FRESCO AND ITS TOOLS: PART 2

Skew

The Skew tool contains many of the same available sub-tools as Transform, in the upper right of the workspace, and still lets you move or nudge your brush strokes and artwork shapes. However, this time, when selected, you can use the bounding box handles to distort, shift, and alter the brush strokes. Refer to Figure 4-11.

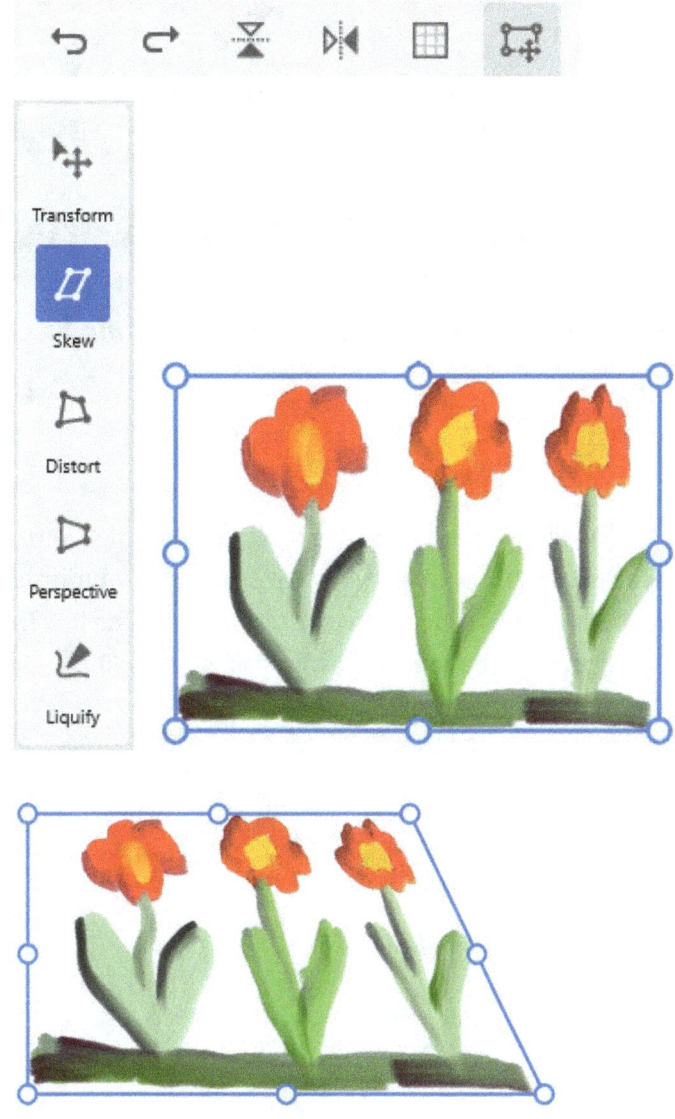

Figure 4-11. *Transform workspace with sub-tool options and artwork altered using the bounding box after Skew tool was selected*

Use the secondary source outer ring of the Touch shortcut circle to allow you to constrain opposite edges when you drag on one edge. Remember to double-click the circle first to activate and then select the ring. Refer to Figure 4-12.

Figure 4-12. *Touch shortcut enabled ring is used to constrain the Skew*

Distort

The Distort tool contains many of the same available sub-tools as Transform, in the upper right of the workspace, and still lets you move or nudge your brush strokes and shapes. Refer to Figure 4-11. This time, you can use the bounding box handles to do a free distortion, warping the brush strokes or artwork shapes. Refer to Figure 4-13.

CHAPTER 4   EXPLORING THE WORKSPACE OF FRESCO AND ITS TOOLS: PART 2

Figure 4-13. *Artwork altered using the bounding box after Distort tool was selected*

Using the Touch shortcut when double-click is enabled, the primary circle changes this tool to a Skew, and the secondary ring constrains the opposite edges. Refer to Figure 4-14.

201

CHAPTER 4 EXPLORING THE WORKSPACE OF FRESCO AND ITS TOOLS: PART 2

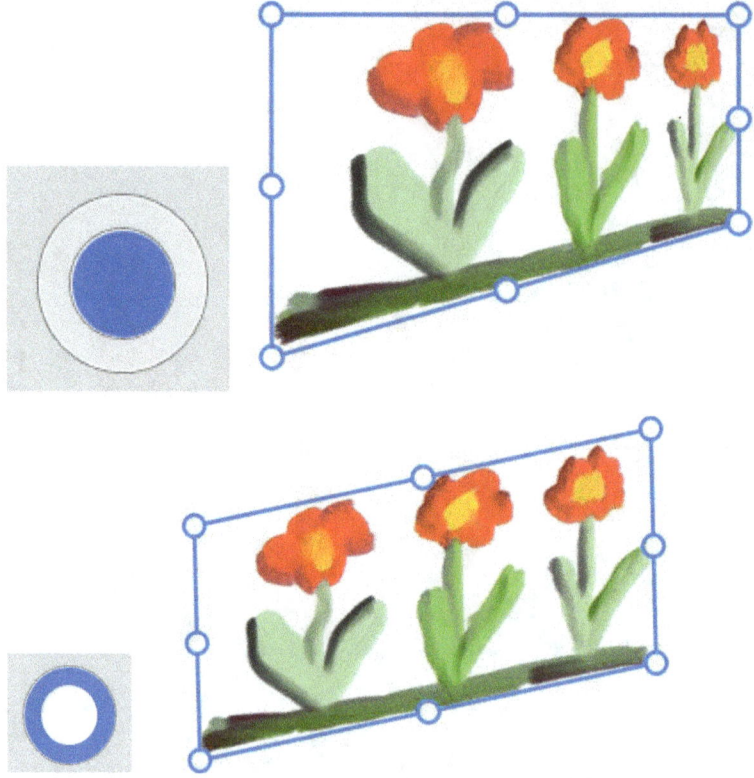

Figure 4-14. *Use the Touch shortcut primary circle or secondary ring when you want to alter the Distort and constrain the movement*

Perspective

The Perspective tool lets you create a warp that gives the appearance that the brush strokes are stretching into the distance or expanding in the foreground. You can use this tool more efficiently when working with a grid (see "Additional Grid and Future Settings" section). I will discuss grids later in more detail and again in Chapters 5 and 6. Refer to Figure 4-15.

CHAPTER 4   EXPLORING THE WORKSPACE OF FRESCO AND ITS TOOLS: PART 2

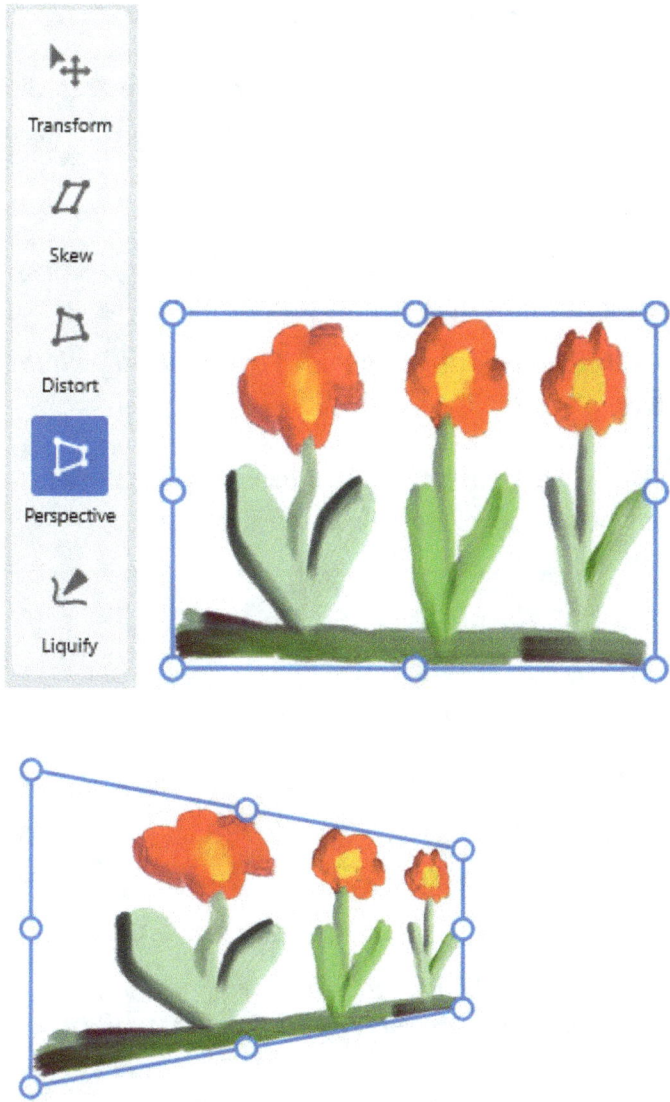

Figure 4-15. *Artwork altered using the bounding box after Perspective tool was selected*

Note   This tool does not have any additional Touch shortcut primary or secondary options for the Touch shortcut.

203

CHAPTER 4 EXPLORING THE WORKSPACE OF FRESCO AND ITS TOOLS: PART 2

Exiting and Entering the Workspace

When you are done using these tools and adjusting your art, you can click Done in the upper right of the Transform workspace to confirm the changes. Doing this will allow you to exit the workspace. Refer to Figure 4-16.

Figure 4-16. *Click the Done button to commit changes and exit the Transform workspace*

Next, click the Move and Transform tool again, and then, return to the Transform workspace to look at the next set of tools. Refer to Figure 4-17.

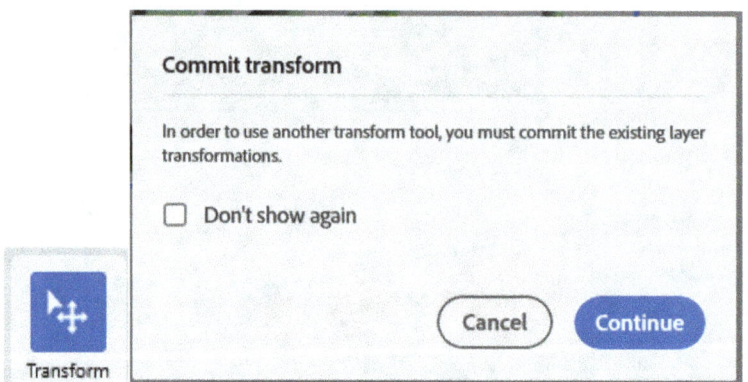

Figure 4-17. *Use the Toolbar Move and Transform tool to enter and exit the Transform workspace or follow instructions in the alert while in the workspace*

Or click Continue if you receive a warning message while remaining in the workspace. Refer to Figure 4-17.

Or click the Cancel button in the upper left to exit the workspace without committing any changes. Refer to Figure 4-18.

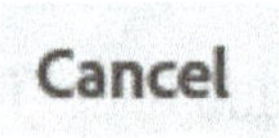

Cancel

Figure 4-18. *Transform workspace Cancel button*

204

Liquify

As mentioned earlier in this section, Liquify in Photoshop is a filter, and in Illustrator, this tool or set of tools can be used to do such things as warp, reconstruct, smooth, twirl, pucker, bloat, and push left, on all pixel layers. Refer to Figures 4-2 and 4-3 for reference.

You can refer to these links if you need to review them in those applications:

https://helpx.adobe.com/photoshop/using/liquify-filter.html
https://helpx.adobe.com/illustrator/using/scaling-shearing-distorting-objects.html#distort-using-liquify-tool

However, in Fresco, we can find these same or similar tools as well. Refer to Figure 4-19.

CHAPTER 4 EXPLORING THE WORKSPACE OF FRESCO AND ITS TOOLS: PART 2

Figure 4-19. *Fresco Transform Liquify tools and the sub-tools found in the Toolbar with their settings*

Note that currently, all Vector brush strokes are excluded from the Liquify Transform, but you can use all the other previously mentioned Transform settings. A Vector layer must be converted to pixel layer in order to use the Liquify tools.

CHAPTER 4   EXPLORING THE WORKSPACE OF FRESCO AND ITS TOOLS: PART 2

We will now look at the options for each of the options in Fresco, for warp, reconstruct, smooth, twirl, pucker, bloat, and push left. Use a pixel layer as you work with each tool, and hold down the mouse key to enable the brush. Refer to Figure 4-20.

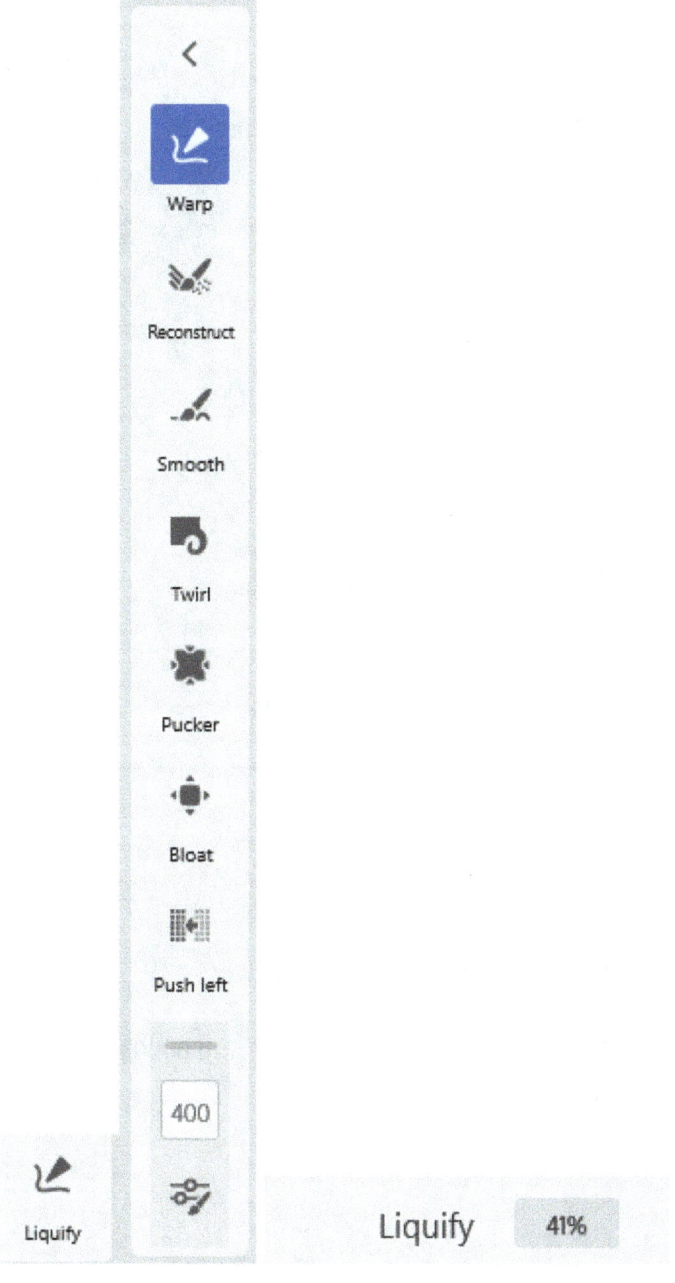

Figure 4-20. *Liquify tool active in the Transform workspace with the first sub-tool Warp selected*

207

Warp

The Warp tool uses your round brush as you drag, push your brush, and bend the brush strokes. Refer to Figure 4-21.

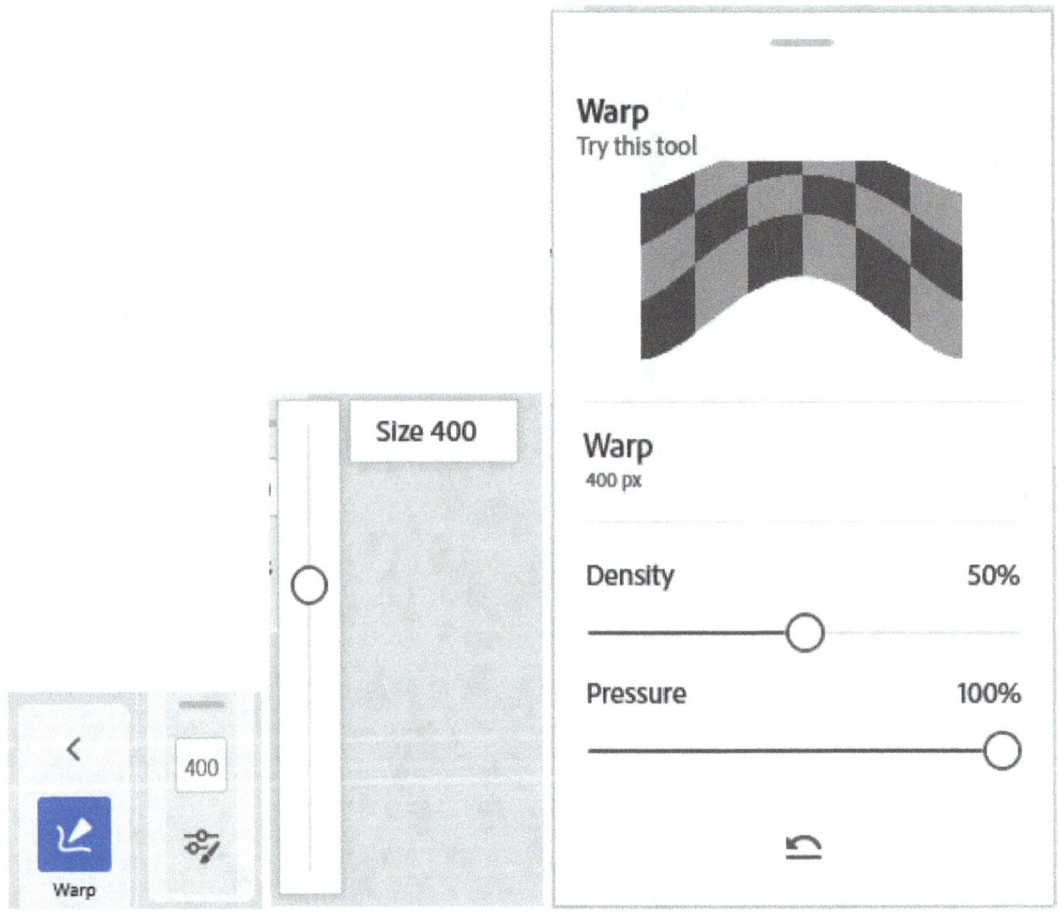

Figure 4-21. Liquify Warp tool and settings panel

The warp brush size or width can be between 1 and 8000 pixels. 400 px is default and it is always round. Refer to Figure 4-22.

CHAPTER 4 EXPLORING THE WORKSPACE OF FRESCO AND ITS TOOLS: PART 2

Figure 4-22. *Use the Warp brush to alter the artwork*

Other Warp settings that you can adjust with the sliders are

- Density (0–100%): Controls feathering at the edge of the brush

- Pressure (1–100%): Controls speed of distortion while dragging the tool and mouse key is pressed down

You can reset the settings using the left pointing arrow icon. Refer to Figure 4-21.

Additionally, while you work in the upper right, you can use the undo and redo icons as well as enable the pin edges icon to prevent distortion at the edges of the canvas. By default, the pin is disabled, and when enabled, a darker background appears around the icon. Refer to Figure 4-23.

CHAPTER 4   EXPLORING THE WORKSPACE OF FRESCO AND ITS TOOLS: PART 2

Figure 4-23.   Sub-tools used with Liquify

You can use the reset icon (left pointing arrow) to reset any changes in this workspace that you made while using any Liquify tool. Refer to Figure 4-23.

For Warp, the Touch shortcut (double-click) enables the primary circle for reconstruction. However, the secondary ring of the Touch shortcut will allow you to reconstruct as well. Alternatively, you can use the next tool instead. Refer to Figure 4-24.

Figure 4-24.   Use the Touch shortcut primary circle or secondary ring when you want to reconstruct while using the Warp tool

Reconstruct

The Reconstruct tool allows you to reconstruct areas that you may have warped by accident while using another Liquify tool. Refer to Figure 4-25.

CHAPTER 4　EXPLORING THE WORKSPACE OF FRESCO AND ITS TOOLS: PART 2

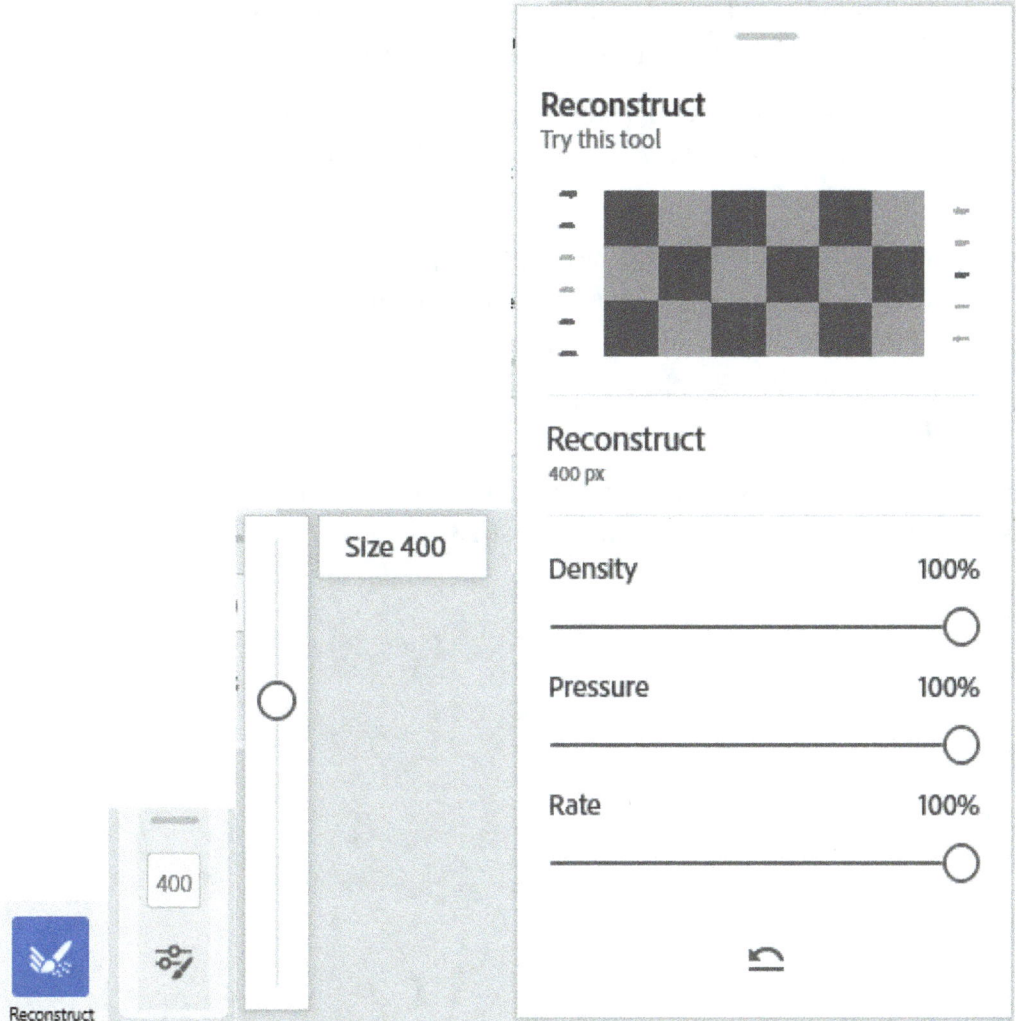

Figure 4-25. *Liquify Reconstruct tool and settings panel*

The round brush allows you to control, with the sliders, the following Reconstruct settings:

- Brush Size (1–8000) Pixels: The default is 400 px.
- Density (0–100%): Controls feathering at the edge of the brush.

CHAPTER 4　EXPLORING THE WORKSPACE OF FRESCO AND ITS TOOLS: PART 2

- Pressure (1–100%): Controls speed of distortion or repair while dragging the tool and the mouse key is pressed down.
- Rate (0–100%): Controls the speed at which the distortions are repaired while the brush is stationary and you have the mouse pressed down.

The settings can be reset using the left pointing arrow icon. Refer to Figure 4-25.

Like with the Warp tool, you have access to the mentioned sub-tools in the upper right; refer to that tool if you need more details.

Smooth

The Smooth tool allows you to blend and smooth rougher edges that you may have distorted with the Warp tool. Refer to Figure 4-26.

CHAPTER 4 EXPLORING THE WORKSPACE OF FRESCO AND ITS TOOLS: PART 2

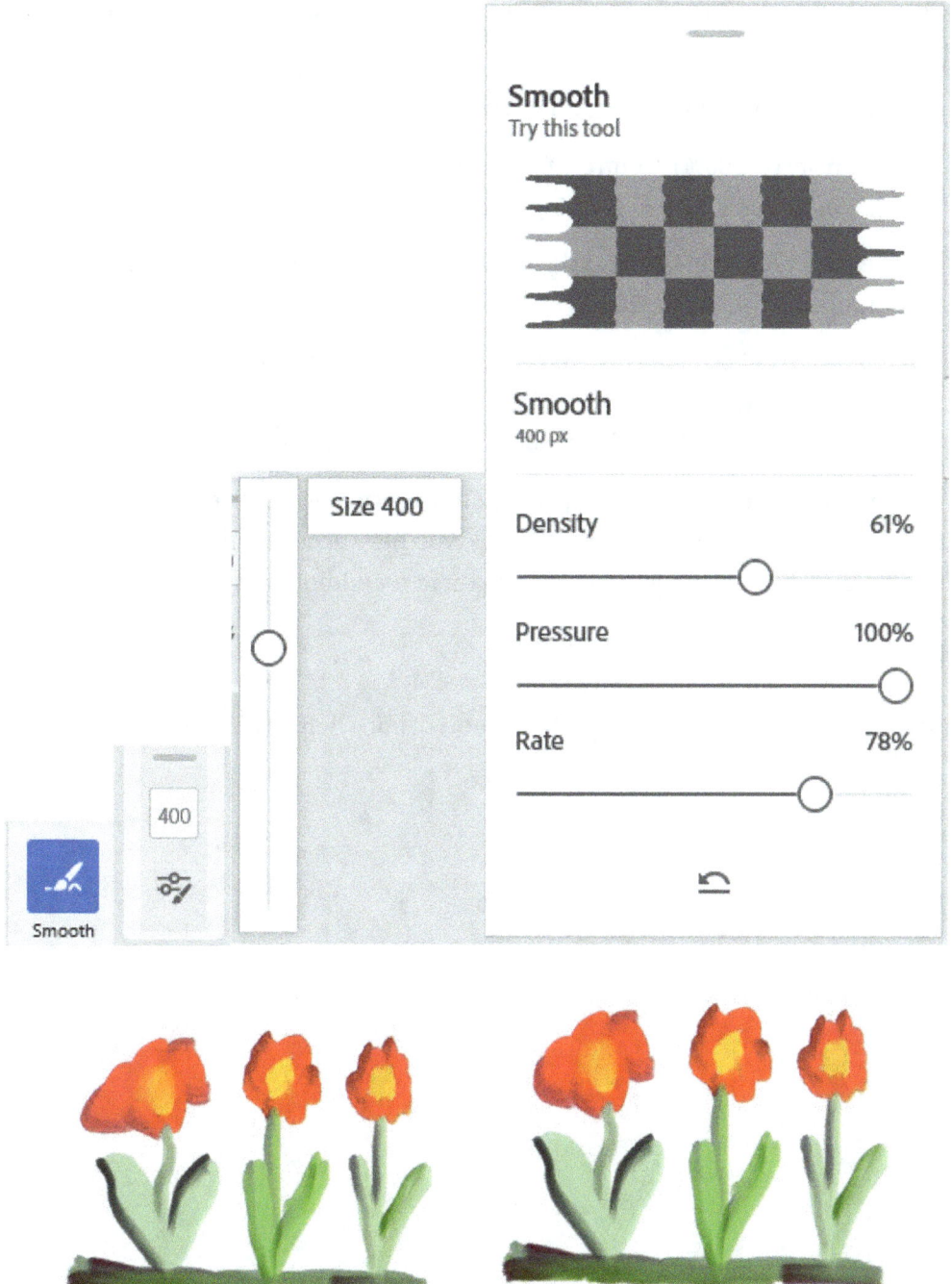

Figure 4-26. *Liquify Smooth tool and settings panel. Use the tool on jagged sharp edges to smooth out a bit more*

The round brush allows you to control, with the sliders, the following Smooth settings:

- Brush Size (1–8000) Pixels: The default is 400 px.
- Density (0–100%): Controls feathering at the edge of the brush. The default is 50%. I used a setting of 61%.
- Pressure (1–100%): Controls speed of distortion while dragging the tool and holding down the mouse key. The default is 100%.
- Rate (0–100%): Controls the speed at which the distortions are constructed while the brush is stationary and you have the mouse pressed down. The default is 80%. I used a setting of 78%.

The settings can be reset using the left pointing arrow icon. Refer to Figure 4-26.

Like with the Warp and Reconstruct tools, you have access to the mentioned sub-tools in the upper right, and you can refer to them for additional setting details.

Twirl

The Twirl tool allows you to spin and blend and distort. Refer to Figure 4-27.

CHAPTER 4   EXPLORING THE WORKSPACE OF FRESCO AND ITS TOOLS: PART 2

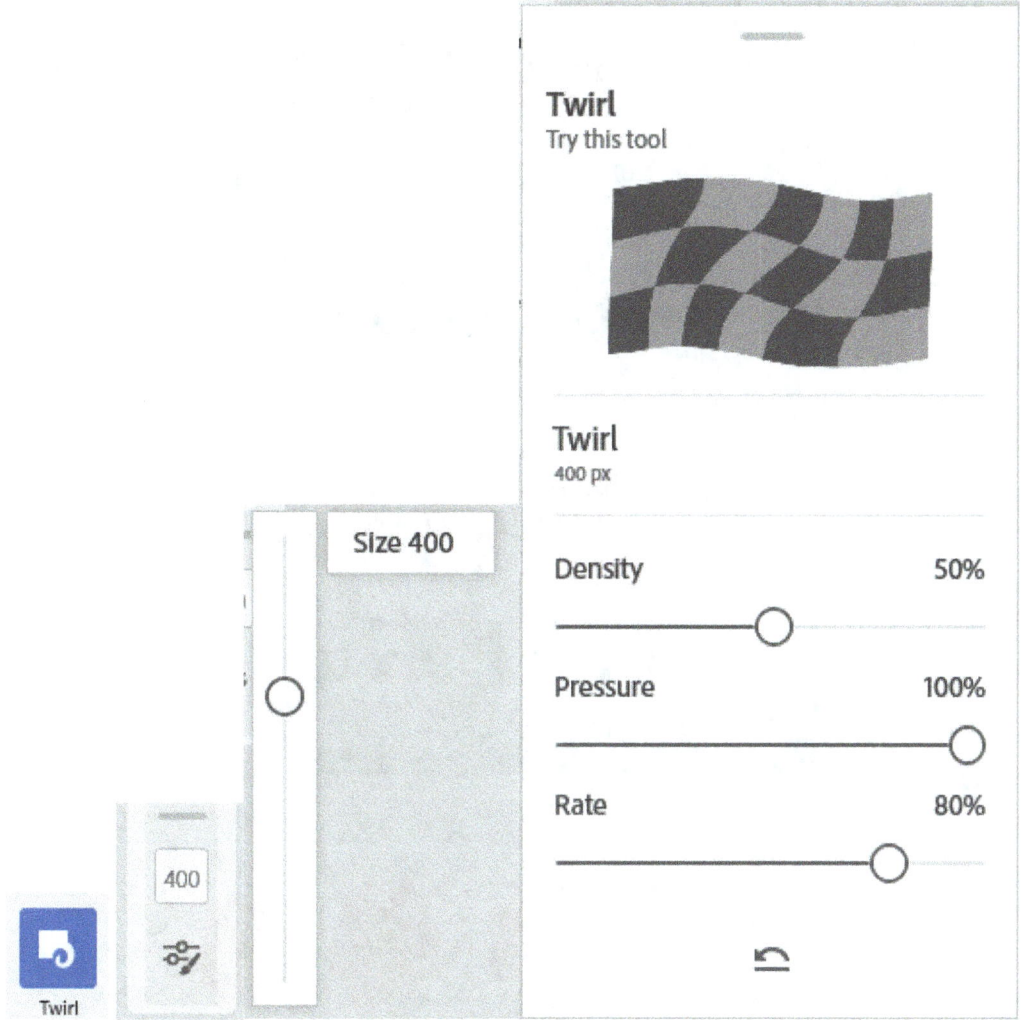

Figure 4-27. *Liquify Twirl tool and settings panel*

The default is to spin clockwise as you hold down the mouse. However, if you want to spin or twirl counterclockwise, then you need to enable (double-click) the circle of the Touch shortcut primary source so that you can hold or drag while you work. The secondary ring will allow you to reconstruct. Refer to Figure 4-28.

215

CHAPTER 4　EXPLORING THE WORKSPACE OF FRESCO AND ITS TOOLS: PART 2

Figure 4-28.　*The Twirl tool allows you to alter the distortion while the Touch shortcut is disabled and the primary circle or secondary ring is enabled*

CHAPTER 4   EXPLORING THE WORKSPACE OF FRESCO AND ITS TOOLS: PART 2

Disabling the Touch shortcut (double-click) will return the tool back to the clockwise settings. The round brush allows you to control, with the sliders, the following Twirl settings. Refer to Figure 4-27.

- Brush Size (1–8000) Pixels: The default is 400 pixels.
- Density (0–100%): Controls feathering at the edge of the brush.
- Pressure (1–100%): Controls speed of distortion while dragging the tool and holding down the mouse key.
- Rate (0–100%): Controls the speed at which the distortions are constructed while the brush is stationary and you have the mouse pressed down.

The settings can be reset using the left pointing arrow icon.

Like with the Warp and Reconstruct tools, you have access to the mentioned sub-tools in the upper right, and you can refer to them for additional setting details.

Pucker

The Pucker tool allows you to squeeze the brush stroke or artwork shape inward as you hold down the mouse. Refer to Figure 4-29.

CHAPTER 4 EXPLORING THE WORKSPACE OF FRESCO AND ITS TOOLS: PART 2

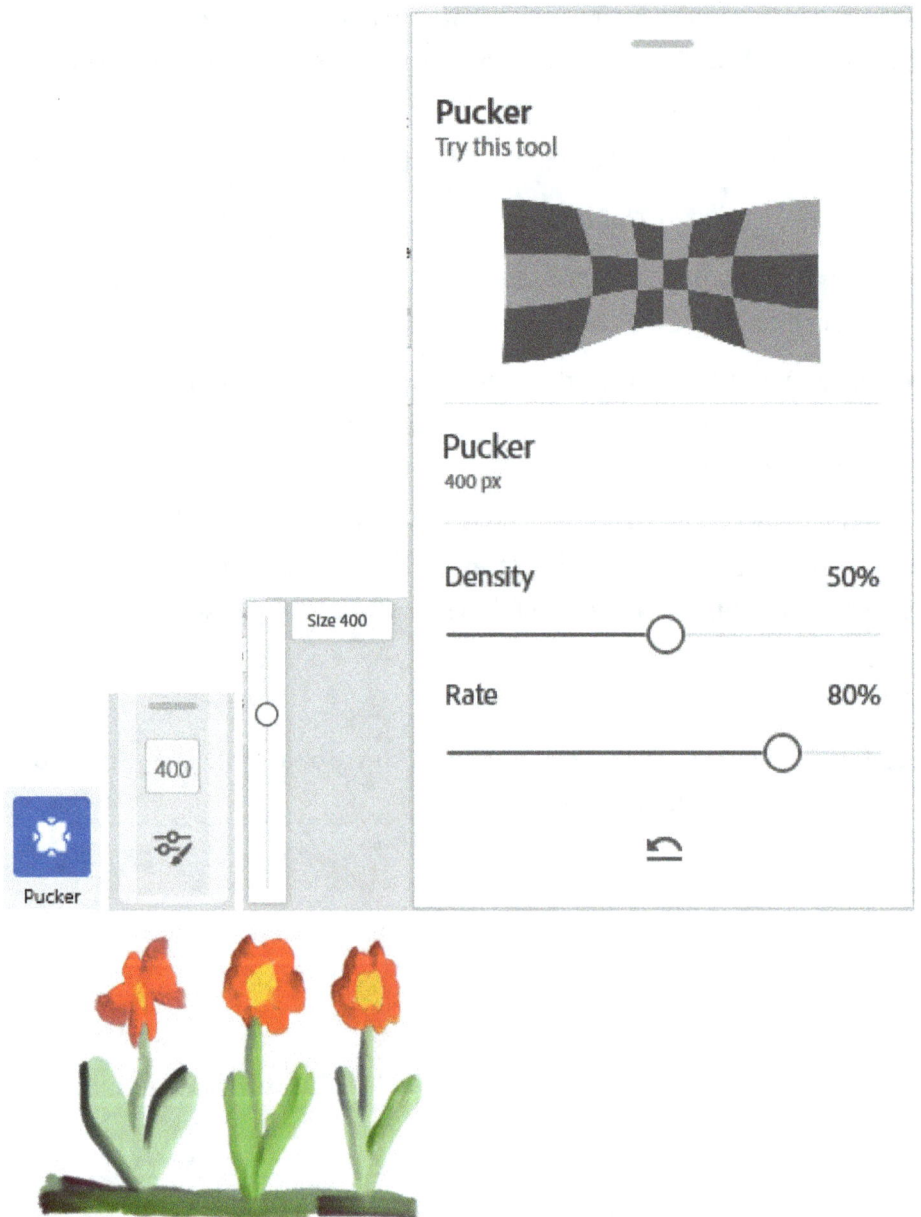

Figure 4-29. *Liquify Pucker tool and settings panel and brush settings applied to the artwork's left flower head*

To switch to bloating, you can enable (double-click) the Touch shortcut primary circle. The secondary ring will allow you to reconstruct. Refer to Figure 4-30.

CHAPTER 4   EXPLORING THE WORKSPACE OF FRESCO AND ITS TOOLS: PART 2

Figure 4-30. *The Pucker tool allows you to alter the distortion while the Touch shortcut primary circle or secondary ring is enabled*

Disabling (double-click) the Touch shortcut will return it back to the Pucker tool.

The round brush allows you to control, with the sliders, the following Pucker settings. Refer to Figure 4-29.

- Brush Size (1–8000) Pixels: The default is 400 px.

- Density (0–100%): Controls feathering at the edge of the brush.

- Rate (0–100%): Controls the speed at which the distortions are constructed while the brush is stationary and you have the mouse pressed down.

The settings can be reset using the left pointing arrow icon. Refer to Figure 4-29.

Like with the Warp and Reconstruct tools, you have access to the mentioned sub-tools in the upper right, and you can refer to them for additional setting details.

CHAPTER 4 EXPLORING THE WORKSPACE OF FRESCO AND ITS TOOLS: PART 2

Bloat

The Bloat tool allows you to expand the stroke or shape outward as you hold down the mouse. Refer to Figure 4-31.

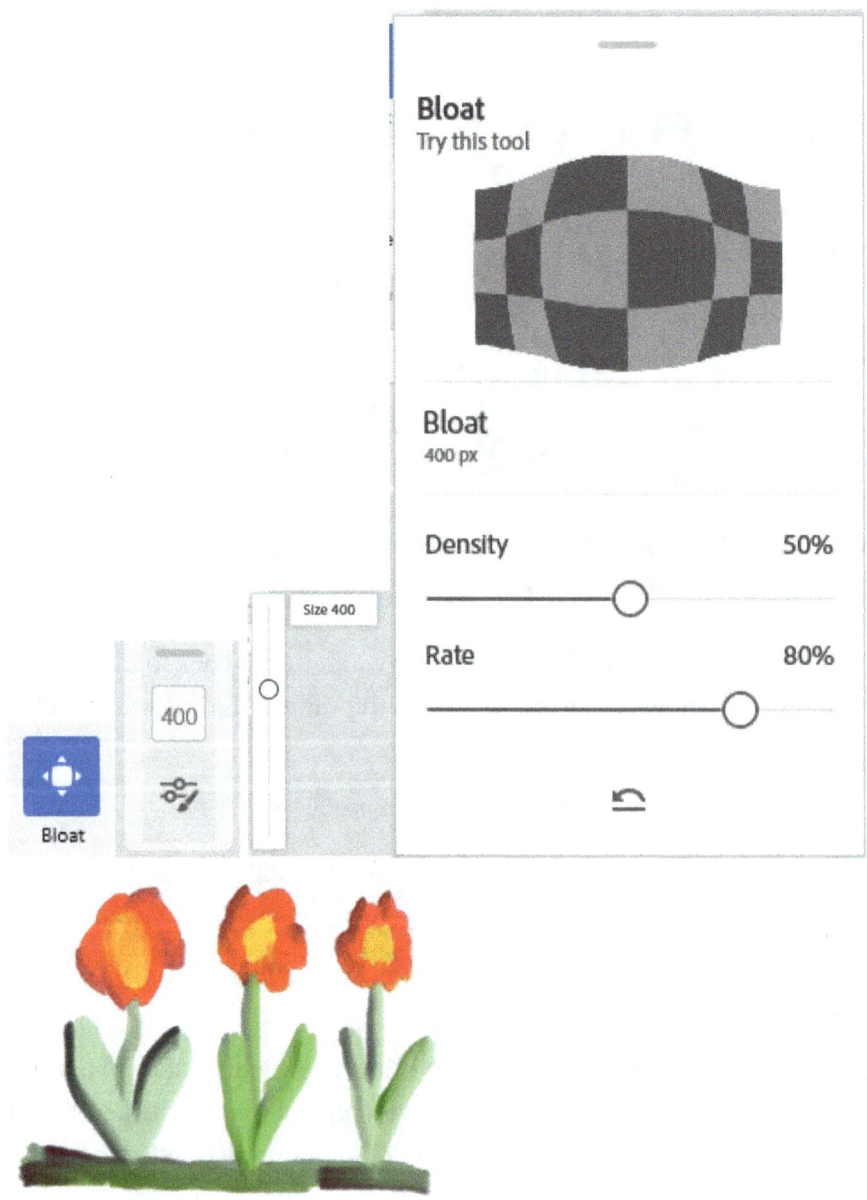

Figure 4-31. *Liquify Bloat tool and settings panel and brush settings applied to the artwork's left flower head*

CHAPTER 4   EXPLORING THE WORKSPACE OF FRESCO AND ITS TOOLS: PART 2

To switch to puckering, you can enable (double-click) the Touch shortcut primary circle. The secondary ring will allow you to reconstruct. Refer to Figure 4-32.

Figure 4-32. *The Bloat tool allows you to alter the distortion while the Touch shortcut primary circle or secondary ring is enabled*

Disabling (double-click) the Touch shortcut will return it back to the Bloat tool.

The round brush allows you to control, with the sliders, the following Bloat settings. Refer to Figure 4-31.

- Brush Size (1–8000) Pixels: The default is 400 px.
- Density (0–100%): Controls feathering at the edge of the brush.
- Rate (0–100%): Controls the speed at which the distortions are constructed while the brush is stationary and you have the mouse pressed down.

The settings can be reset. Refer to Figure 4-31.

Like with the Warp and Reconstruct tools, you have access to the mentioned sub-tools in the upper right, and you can refer to them for additional tool setting details.

CHAPTER 4   EXPLORING THE WORKSPACE OF FRESCO AND ITS TOOLS: PART 2

Push left

The Push left tool allows you to push pixels left and upward as you hold down the mouse or drag. Refer to Figure 4-33.

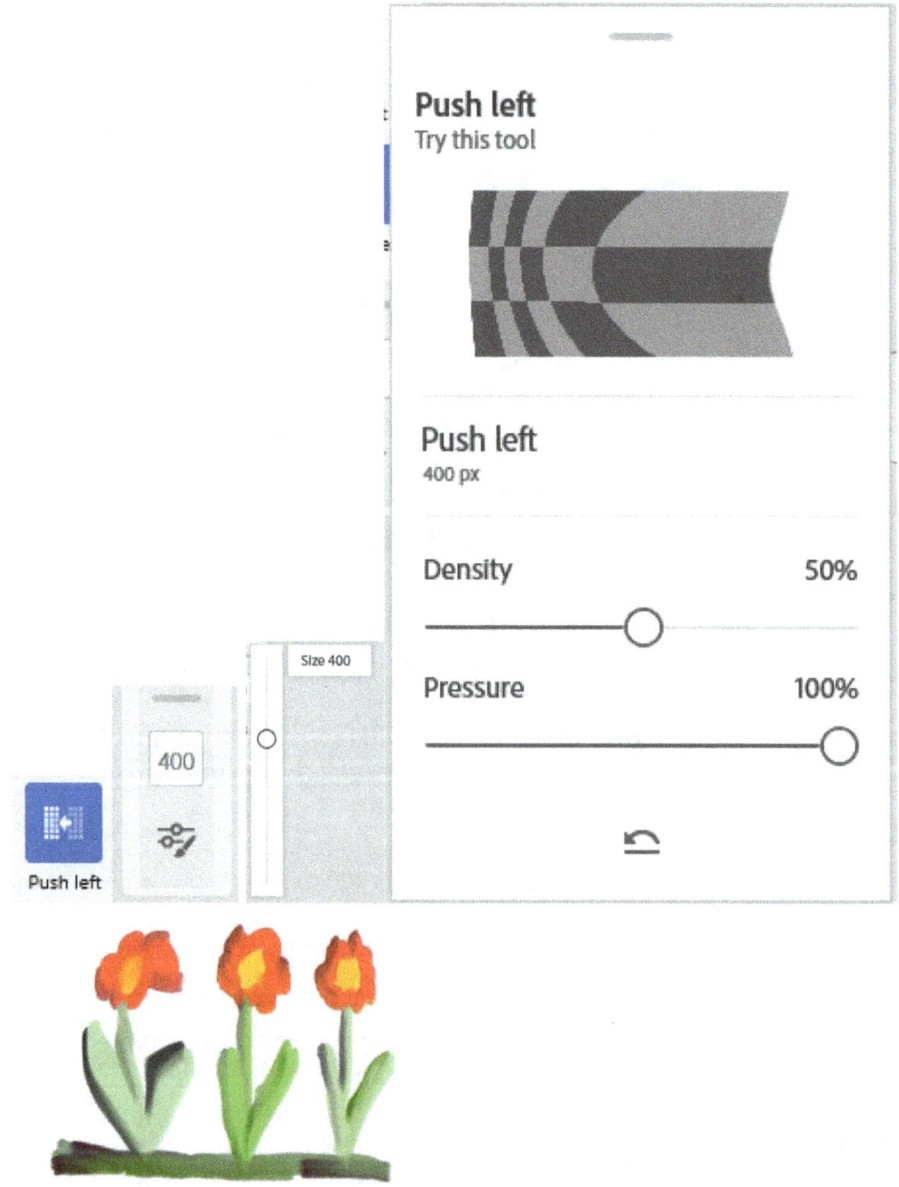

Figure 4-33. *Liquify Push left tool and settings panel and brush settings applied to the artwork's left flower head*

CHAPTER 4   EXPLORING THE WORKSPACE OF FRESCO AND ITS TOOLS: PART 2

To push right and downward, you would enable (double-click) the Touch shortcut circle for the primary source so that you can drag while you work. The secondary source ring, however, allows for reconstruction. Refer to Figure 4-34.

Figure 4-34. *The Push left tool allows you to alter the distortion while the Touch shortcut primary circle or secondary ring is enabled*

Disabling (double-click) the Touch shortcut will return the tool to the original Push left settings.

The round brush allows you to control, with the sliders, the following Push left settings. Refer to Figure 4-33.

- Brush Size (1–8000) Pixels: The default is 400 px.

- Density (0–100%): Controls feathering at the edge of the brush.

- Pressure (1–100%): Controls speed of distortion while dragging the tool.

The settings can be reset using the left pointing arrow icon.

Like with the Warp and Reconstruct tools, you have access to the mentioned sub-tools in the upper right, and you can refer to them for additional setting details.

CHAPTER 4　EXPLORING THE WORKSPACE OF FRESCO AND ITS TOOLS: PART 2

You can review more about the Liquify tool in Fresco from the following link:

https://helpx.adobe.com/fresco/using/liquify-tool.html

Click the left arrow on top of the Liquify Toolbar if you want to return to other distortion transform tools or Done to exit the workspace and confirm your changes. Click Cancel when you want to exit without saving changes. Refer to Figure 4-35.

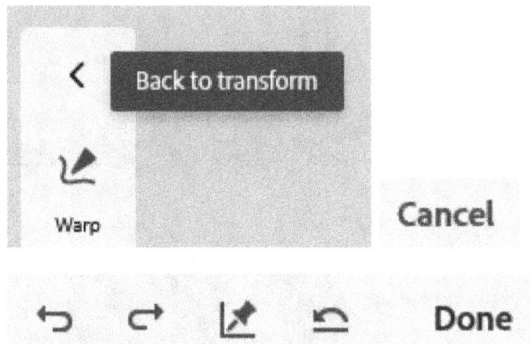

Figure 4-35. *To exit the Liquify tools, use the arrow, and then, exit the Transform workspace by clicking Cancel or Done to commit changes*

Additional Grid and Future Settings

As mentioned, when working with these Move and transform tools, there are sub-tools in the upper right corner of the menu bar for undoing and redoing steps or flipping shapes. Refer to Figure 4-36.

Figure 4-36. *Transform workspace sub-tools*

However, for better alignment, one icon to use is the Grid or Precision tool which is found outside the transformation workspace. Once you exit the tool to adjust its settings, it can be found in the right Vertical Taskbar. Refer to Figure 4-37.

CHAPTER 4   EXPLORING THE WORKSPACE OF FRESCO AND ITS TOOLS: PART 2

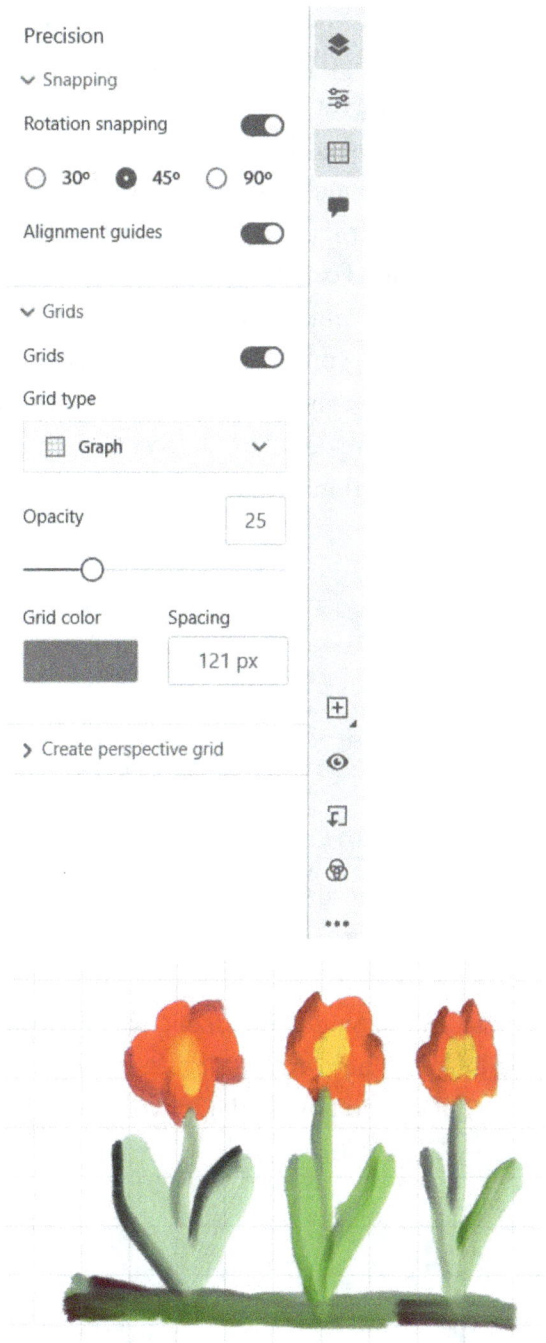

Figure 4-37. *Use the right Vertical Taskbar and Precision panel to activate a grid on the canvas*

CHAPTER 4   EXPLORING THE WORKSPACE OF FRESCO AND ITS TOOLS: PART 2

This Precision area can control your snapping as you rotate in various increments and align using the grid. In Chapters 5 and 6, as you work with multiple layers, shapes, and drawing aids, rather than just using the nudge arrows, you will need, at times, to create a grid type of graph or perspective grid.

Enable the toggle when you want to make your graph visible. For example, to alter the grid graph, you can set its opacity, grid color, and spacing. Refer to Figure 4-37.

The perspective graph as mentioned can be used with the Transform perspective tool. You can set one, two, or three vanishing points as well as edit the vanishing points.

The Grid Type of Perspective allows you to Snap to grid axis for drawing purposes. You will also be able to see the grid lines, set the density of lines, the opacity, and the grid color. We will review perspective in more detail in Chapter 6 when we work with drawing aids. Refer to Figure 4-38 for the two options in the list.

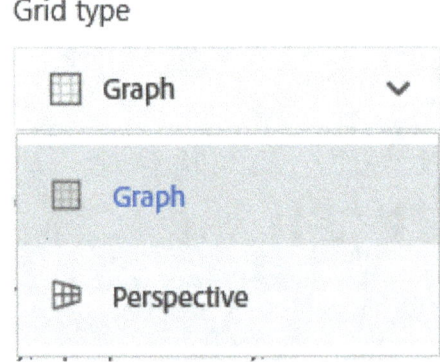

Figure 4-38. Set the grid type using the Precision tool panel

You also have the option to set or create the perspective grid from an image, layer, or document. More details can be found here and will be discussed in Chapter 6.

Toggle the grid off to hide it if you do not need it for your artwork. Refer to Figure 4-39.

Figure 4-39. Turn the grid off using the Precision Tool panel

You can review this link if you need more information on this topic:

https://helpx.adobe.com/fresco/using/grids-alignment.html

Symmetry Grid

An additional option which appears for the tablet but will eventually be available to future Fresco versions on the desktop is the Symmetry Grid and tool. You can use it to create symmetrical grids and patterns in Fresco and can learn more about it at this link:

https://helpx.adobe.com/fresco/using/symmetry.html

Tip What if you can't wait to use symmetry in Fresco? Are there any equivalents in Photoshop and Illustrator for your next art project? Indeed, there is. Photoshop allows you to use Symmetry paint, and Illustrator has Object ➤ Repeat. You can learn more about these at the following links:

https://helpx.adobe.com/photoshop/using/paint-symmetry.html

https://helpx.adobe.com/illustrator/using/repeat-patterns-desktop.html

---

Selection Creation Tools and Their Options

To create selections around an area of your drawing, you can use the following tools to add and subtract from the selection. These tools can be used on Pixel and Vector layers except for the Magic wand which can only be used on a Pixel Layer for selection creation.

They are the Lasso, Magic wand, Paint selection, Rectangle, Ellipse, and Polygon tools. Refer to Figure 4-40.

CHAPTER 4　EXPLORING THE WORKSPACE OF FRESCO AND ITS TOOLS: PART 2

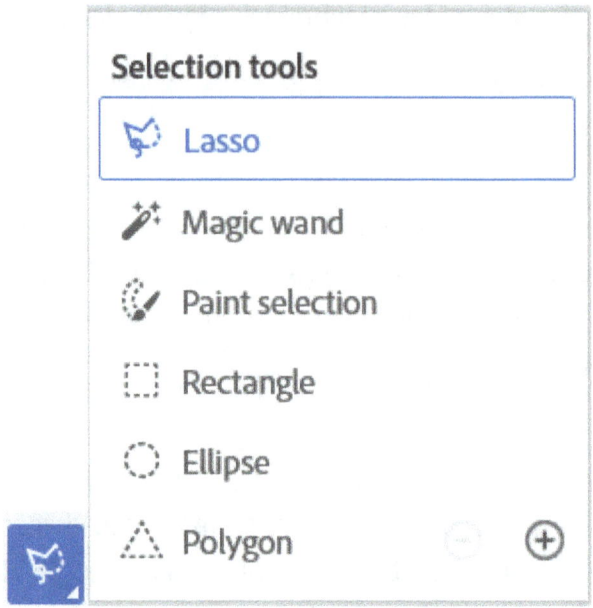

Figure 4-40. *Under the Selection tools icon, there are several to choose from*

Selections are crucial when you do not want to paint beyond a certain boundary as the paint may spread beyond, into an unwanted area of your artwork. We can think of selections much like stencils when we work with media in the real world as they block or prevent paint or the pen from going out of or into a boundary. Refer to Figure 4-41.

Figure 4-41. *In the real world, we use stencils when we want to create a selection*

CHAPTER 4　EXPLORING THE WORKSPACE OF FRESCO AND ITS TOOLS: PART 2

Let's review each of these Selection tools next.

Lasso (L)

To create a Lasso selection, select the tool, and then, click and drag out an area that you would like to paint within before you use one of your brush tools mentioned earlier in Chapter 3. Clicking out points rather than dragging creates a more angular selection. Refer to Figure 4-42.

Figure 4-42. *Lasso tool and its settings and then dragging out or clicking selections on the canvas*

CHAPTER 4 EXPLORING THE WORKSPACE OF FRESCO AND ITS TOOLS: PART 2

As you do these actions, you will find that within the Contextual taskbar, you have the options to Cancel lasso or Close lasso as you work if you do not reach the start point dot and click it. Refer to Figure 4-43.

Figure 4-43. *Use the Contextual Task bar to assist you to cancel or close a lasso selection*

Cancel will remove the lasso and you will have to redraw it. In this case, click Close lasso, and you will see a selection, much like marching ants or moving stripes, appear, and the Contextual Task bar will change. We will review that in a moment. Refer to Figure 4-44.

CHAPTER 4   EXPLORING THE WORKSPACE OF FRESCO AND ITS TOOLS: PART 2

Figure 4-44. *Once the selection is active on the artwork, the Contextual Task bar changes*

For now, look at the lower part of the Toolbar panel options. You can choose to add to the selection or subtract from the selection as you drag and draw. Currently, it is set to add to the selection. You can click the lower icon to then subtract as you drag over a current selection. Refer to Figure 4-45.

231

CHAPTER 4　EXPLORING THE WORKSPACE OF FRESCO AND ITS TOOLS: PART 2

Figure 4-45. *After adding to the selection, change the setting in the Toolbar to subtract*

Likewise, while using this Lasso tool, the Touch shortcut primary touch circle can be enabled (double-click) to toggle between subtracting with the circle or adding with the ring to a selection as you work. This order is also dependent on what was the last selection setting you used, prior to activating the Touch shortcut. Refer to Figure 4-46.

Figure 4-46. *Using the Touch shortcut circle and ring to subtract and add from a selection*

CHAPTER 4 EXPLORING THE WORKSPACE OF FRESCO AND ITS TOOLS: PART 2

Once a selection is complete, it will appear like marching ants, and you can continue to paint with a brush within the boundary of the section, and the paint will not pass outside of that selection. Refer to Figure 4-47.

Figure 4-47. *Using a Pixel brush to paint inside of a selection with a color chosen from the color chip*

Tips on Using the Contextual Task Bar While Working with a Selection and Other Tools

While working with Selection tools, you will be presented with additional options found in the lower Contextual Task bar that will appear as required. Refer to Figure 4-48.

Figure 4-48. *Selection tool Contextual Task bar options*

233

CHAPTER 4   EXPLORING THE WORKSPACE OF FRESCO AND ITS TOOLS: PART 2

These options include the following:

- Transform: This will allow you to only adjust the size of the painted area on the canvas in the Transform workspace. Refer to Transform tool selection earlier in this chapter if you need to review the types of transformations you can make and when you need to confirm the transformation. Note that Liquify will allow you to use the selection to control how far the warp will move within the boundary. This is equivalent to the Freeze and Thaw Mask in Photoshop. To exit the Transform workspace, click the Done key, and the selection will again be active outside of the Transform workspace. Refer to Figure 4-49.

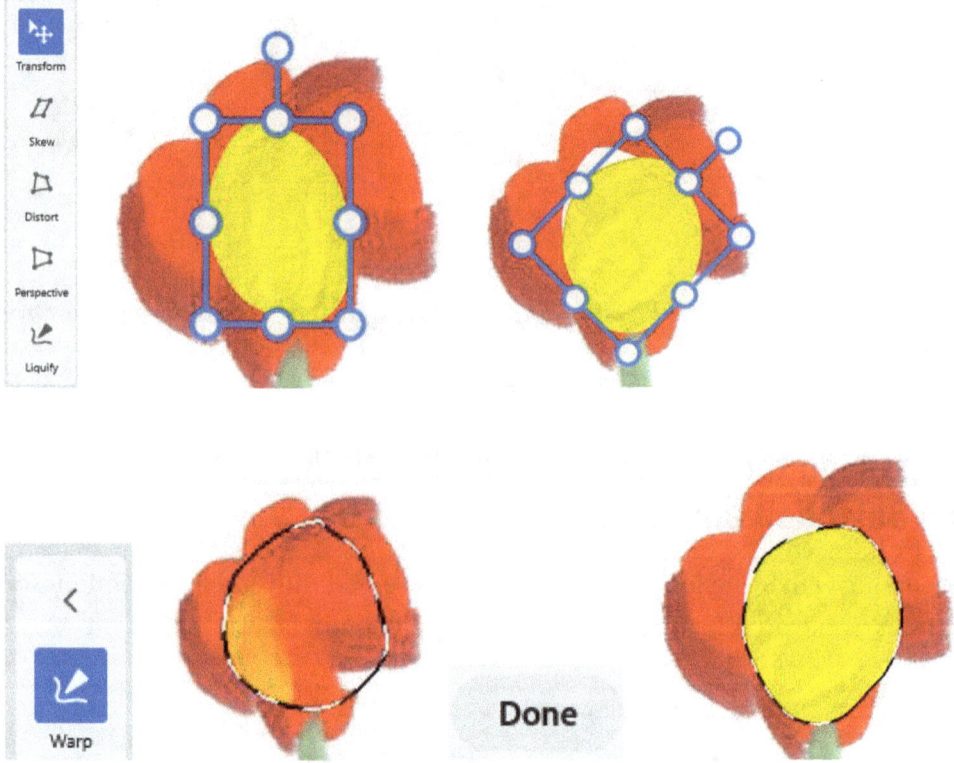

Figure 4-49. *Transform the area within the selection, or move the selected area in the Transform workspace, and click Done to exit*

You can use your undo icon or (Ctrl+Z) if you need to reset the transformation.

- Erase: This erase setting can be used to quickly subtract pixels from the selection when enabled and you are working outside of the transformation with other tools like a brush and the selection is active. Refer to Figure 4-50.

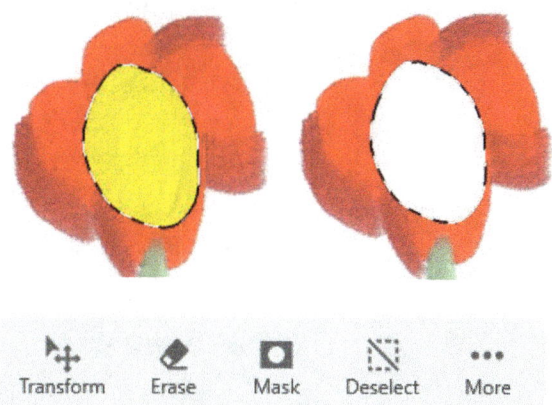

Figure 4-50. *Use the Contextual Task bar to erase while a selection is active*

- Mask: This option, which we will look at in more detail in Chapter 5, will allow you to create a masking effect on a layer to hide areas of paint or a shape entirely, and this mask can later be edited. Use your undo key if you need to remove the mask for now. Refer to Figure 4-50 and Figure 4-51.

Figure 4-51. *Use the Contextual Task bar to mask while a selection is active and then undo the mask*

- Deselect: Allows you to remove the selection and continue to paint anywhere on the canvas. Refer to Figure 4-50.

The More icon (…) when clicked reveals a few additional selection options. Refer to Figure 4-52.

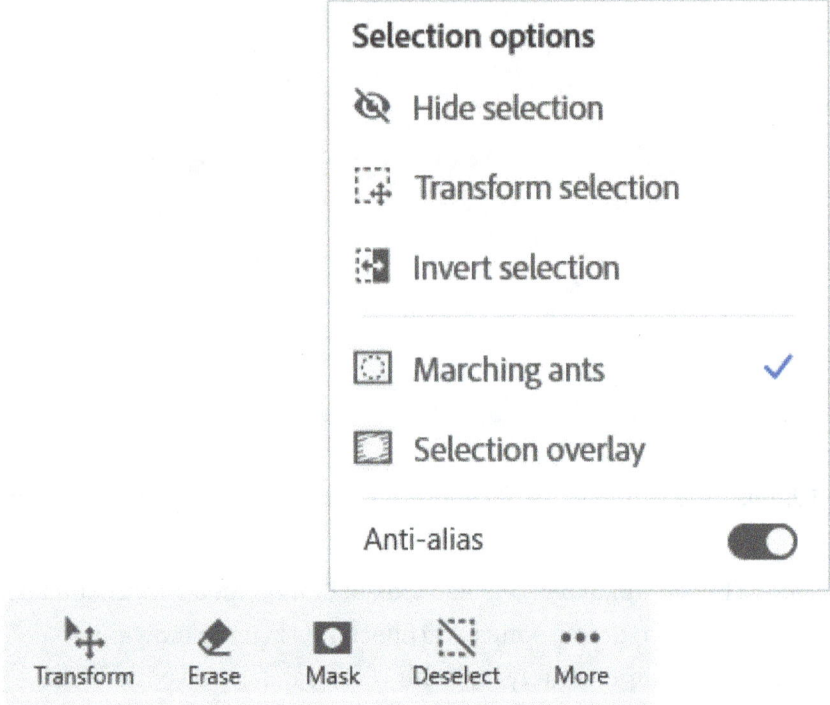

Figure 4-52. *The Contextual Task bar reveals more settings in the pop-up menu when clicked*

They include

- Hide Selection/Show Selection: This is good for when you need to view how the artwork looks currently without losing the selection. Refer to Figure 4-53.

CHAPTER 4 EXPLORING THE WORKSPACE OF FRESCO AND ITS TOOLS: PART 2

Figure 4-53. *Contextual Task bar options for hiding and showing selection*

- Transform Selection: This option affects the selection only on the artwork. You can use the options of Transform, Skew, Distort, or Perspective in the Transform workspace. You cannot Liquify. Refer to the Move and Transform tool earlier in the chapter if you need to review these options. Click Done to exit the workspace to commit your selection transformation. Refer to Figure 4-54.

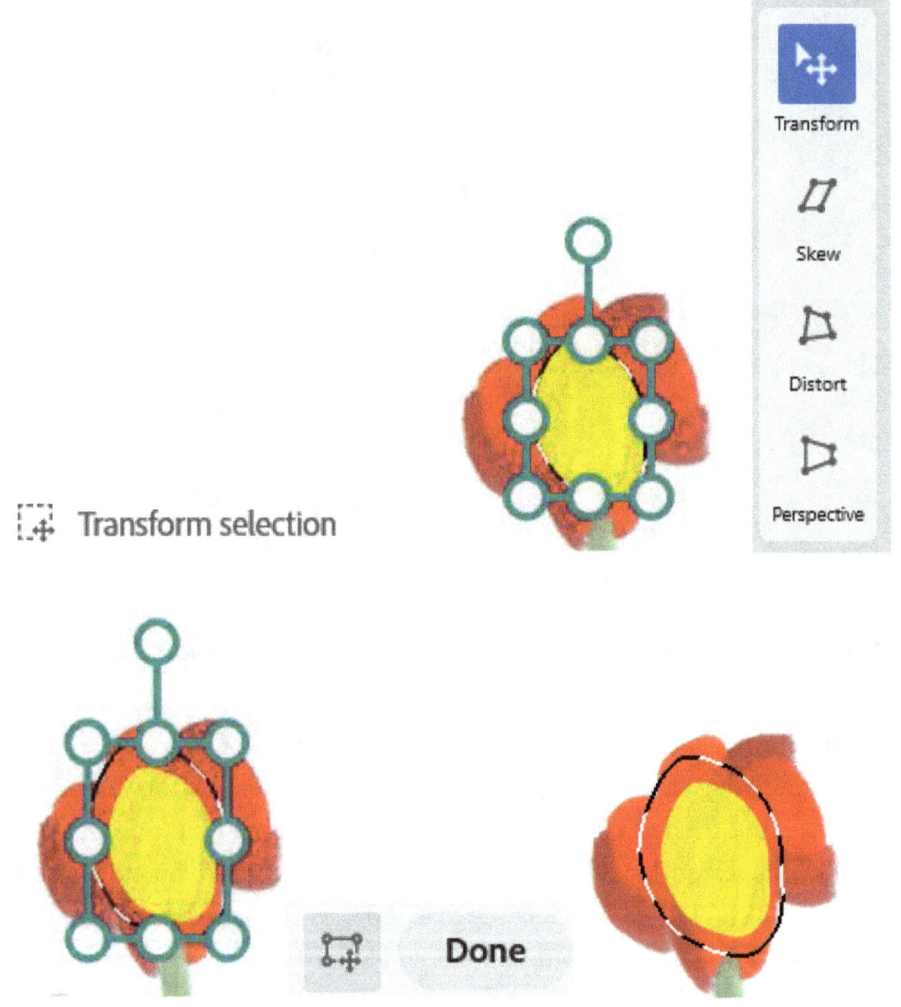

Figure 4-54. *More Contextual Task bar options for transformation of selection using the Transform workspace*

- Invert Selection: Click this option to have the opposite of the current selection you created. In this case, now you can paint outside of the boundary. Click invert again if you need to return to the previous selection. This is also useful when working in Liquify. Refer to Figure 4-55.

CHAPTER 4 EXPLORING THE WORKSPACE OF FRESCO AND ITS TOOLS: PART 2

Figure 4-55. *Before inverting the selection, you can paint inside; after clicking the option in the Contextual Task bar, you can paint outside*

- Preview either as Marching ants or Selection overlay. The Marching ants preview is easier to work with, so I leave it on this setting. Refer to Figure 4-56.

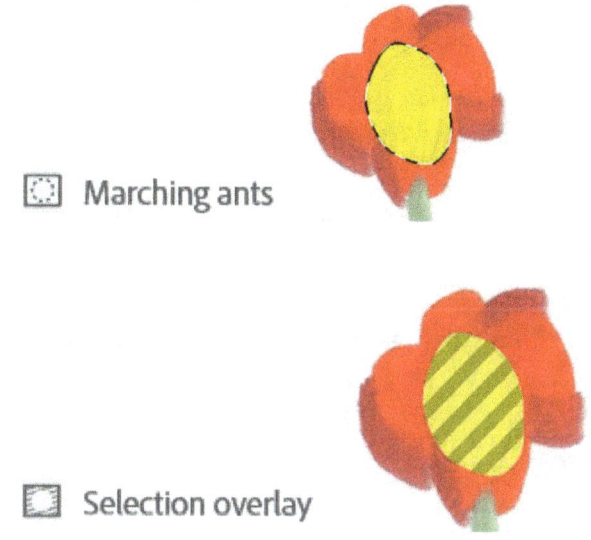

Figure 4-56. *Contextual Task bar options of Marching ants and Selection overlay as they appear on the artwork*

- Anti-alias can be either on or off, which affects how the paint overlaps at the edge boundary. By default, it is toggled on so that the transition is smooth. This can be better visualized if the selection is hidden and you zoom in close (Ctrl++) to the selection area. Refer to Figure 4-57.

Figure 4-57. Working with the Contextual Task bar Anti-alias disabled on the upper blue stroke then enabled in the lower blue stroke with a less jagged boundary

In my case, when I painted with a blue brush stroke, the blue on top near the edge is slightly jagged with the Anti-alias turned off. However, when turned on, we can see the lower brush stroke transition is smoother.

Continue to use the Contextual Task bar as you review the remaining Selection tools. Refer to Figure 4-52.

Magic Wand (W)

Magic wand is a Selection tool that will allow you to create selections based on the colors you click on and can only be used with all its settings on a Pixel layer. Refer to Figure 4-58.

CHAPTER 4   EXPLORING THE WORKSPACE OF FRESCO AND ITS TOOLS: PART 2

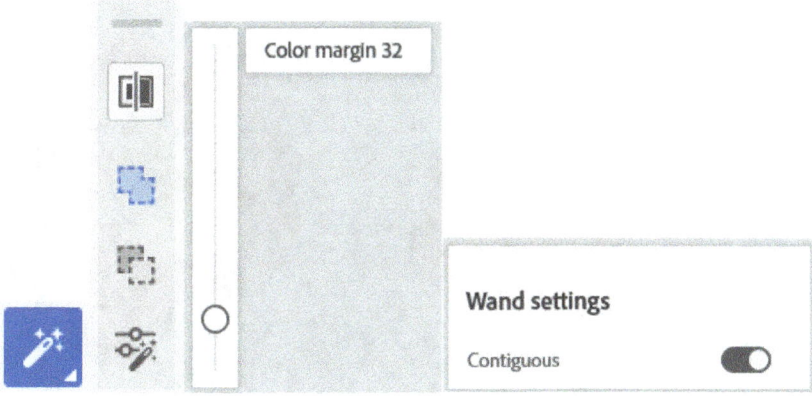

Figure 4-58. *Toolbar Magic wand Selection tool with its setting and clicking some artwork*

When the tool is selected in the Toolbar, by default, the color margin range is set to 32, but you can adjust it between 0 and 255 if you need to decrease or increase what color area is selected.

You can either, when you click, add to the selection or subtract from the selection if you choose that option. Refer to Figure 4-59.

241

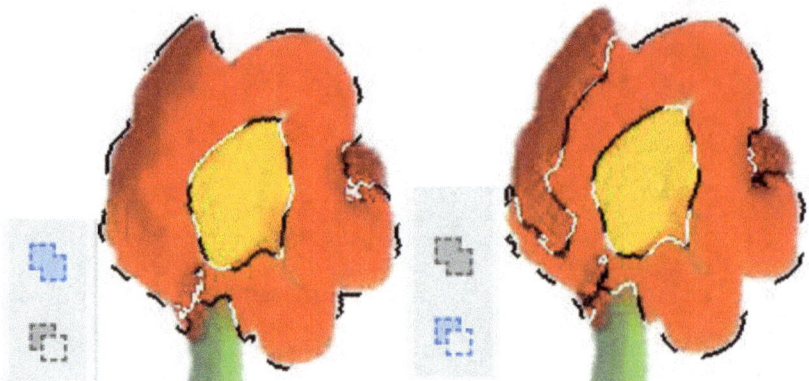

Figure 4-59. *Use the Magic wand settings to add or subtract from the selection*

Additional wand settings in the Toolbar allow for Contiguous which is on by default, and you can select the color of the disconnected area as well by toggling off the setting. Refer to Figure 4-60.

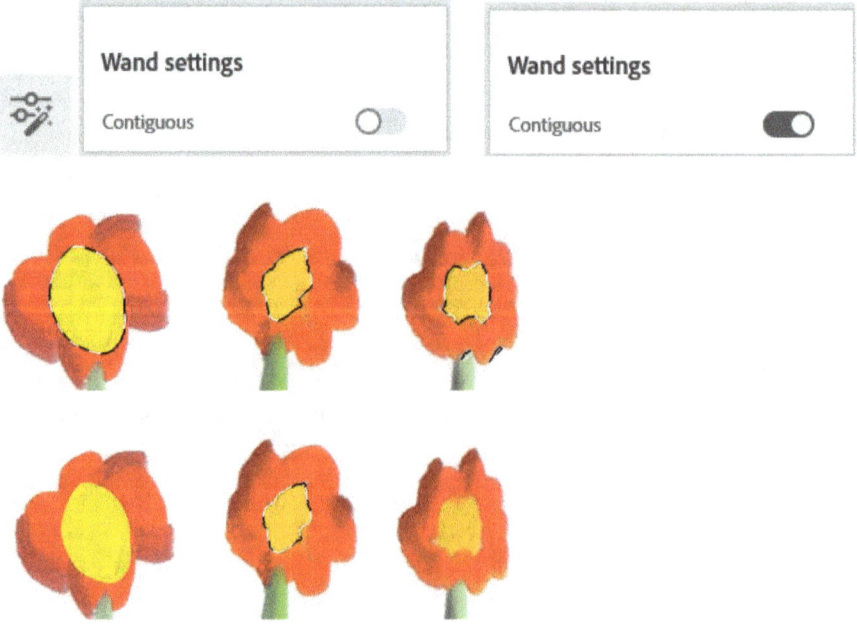

Figure 4-60. *Practice with the wand settings of Contiguous off and on to get the ideal selection*

Likewise, the Touch shortcut primary circle can be used when enabled (double-click) to toggle between subtracting or adding using the ring from a selection as you work. This order is also dependent on what was the last selection setting you used, prior to activating the Touch shortcut. Refer to Figure 4-61.

Figure 4-61. *Use the Touch shortcut when you want to subtract or add to a selection with the Magic wand*

The same options found in the Contextual Task bar for the Lasso are also available for the Magic wand.

More details on the Magic wand tool can be found here:

https://helpx.adobe.com/fresco/using/magic-wand-tool.html

Paint Selection

This tool is similar to the Lasso tool. When the tool is selected, using the settings found in the Toolbar, you can drag out and paint an area using a brush size between 1 and 300 px and then add or subtract from the selection. Refer to Figure 4-62.

CHAPTER 4   EXPLORING THE WORKSPACE OF FRESCO AND ITS TOOLS: PART 2

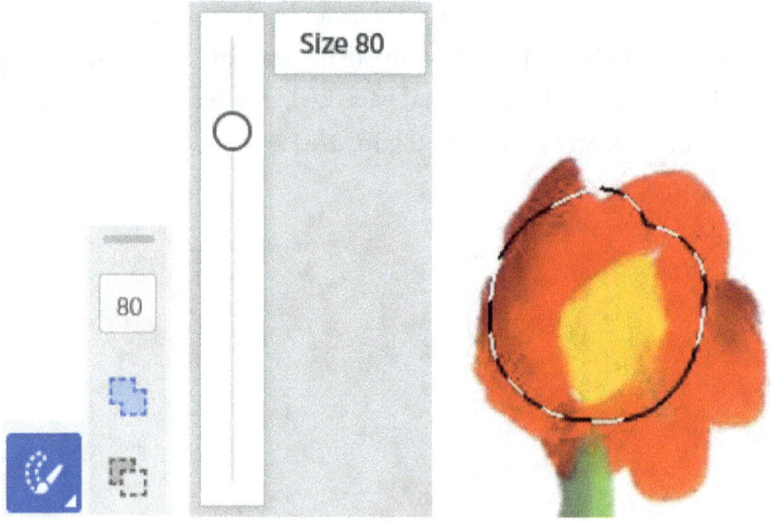

Figure 4-62. *Toolbar Paint selection tool with its setting and clicking on some artwork*

With this tool, however, you cannot use the Touch shortcut.

The same options found in the Contextual Task bar for the Lasso are also available for Paint selection.

CHAPTER 4   EXPLORING THE WORKSPACE OF FRESCO AND ITS TOOLS: PART 2

Rectangle Selection

Use this tool to create a rectangular selection. While the tool is selected, use the options in the Toolbar to add or subtract from the selection as you mouse drag over the artwork and then paint inside. Refer to Figure 4-63.

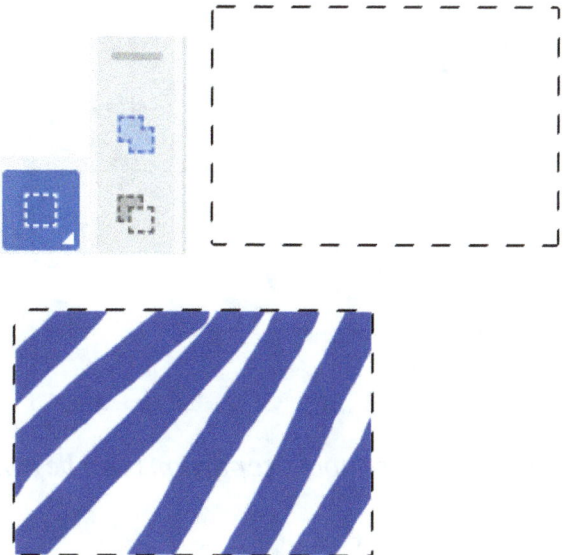

Figure 4-63. *Toolbar Rectangular selection tool with its setting and painting some artwork inside*

Likewise, the Touch shortcut primary circle can be used when enabled (double-click) to constrain the proportions to a square as you work. The secondary ring will leave the proportions unconstrained. Refer to Figure 4-64.

245

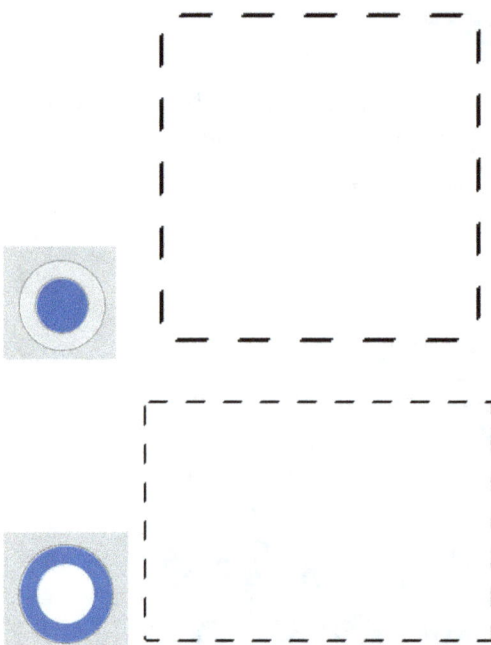

Figure 4-64. *Rectangular selection tool proportions can be constrained using the Touch shortcut*

The same options found in the Contextual Task bar for the Lasso are also available for Rectangle selection.

Ellipse Selection

Use this tool to create an elliptical selection. While this tool is selected, use the options in the Toolbar to add or subtract from the selection as you mouse drag over the artwork. Refer to Figure 4-65.

CHAPTER 4   EXPLORING THE WORKSPACE OF FRESCO AND ITS TOOLS: PART 2

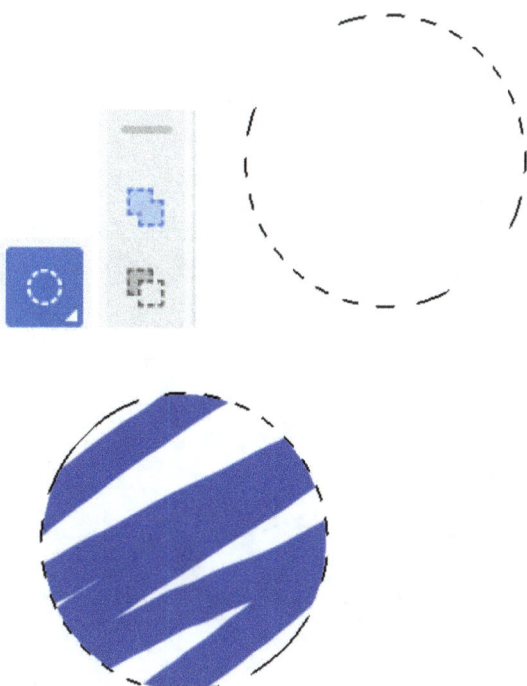

Figure 4-65. *Toolbar Ellipse selection tool with its setting and painting some artwork inside*

Likewise, the Touch shortcut primary circle can be used when enabled (double-click) to constrain the proportions to a circle as you work. The secondary ring will leave the proportions unconstrained. Refer to Figure 4-66.

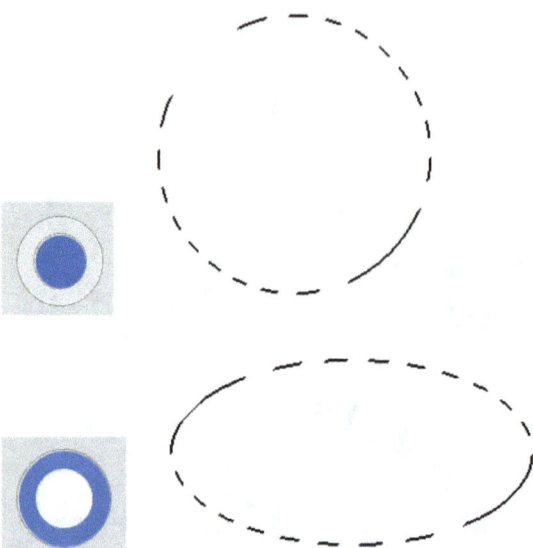

Figure 4-66. *Ellipse selection tool proportions can be constrained using the Touch shortcut*

The same options found in the Contextual Task bar for the Lasso are also available for Ellipse selection.

Polygon: Adding or Subtracting Sides from the Selection

Use this tool to create a polygonal selection. While the tool is selected, use the options in the Toolbar to add or subtract from the selection as you mouse drag over the artwork. Refer to Figure 4-67.

CHAPTER 4   EXPLORING THE WORKSPACE OF FRESCO AND ITS TOOLS: PART 2

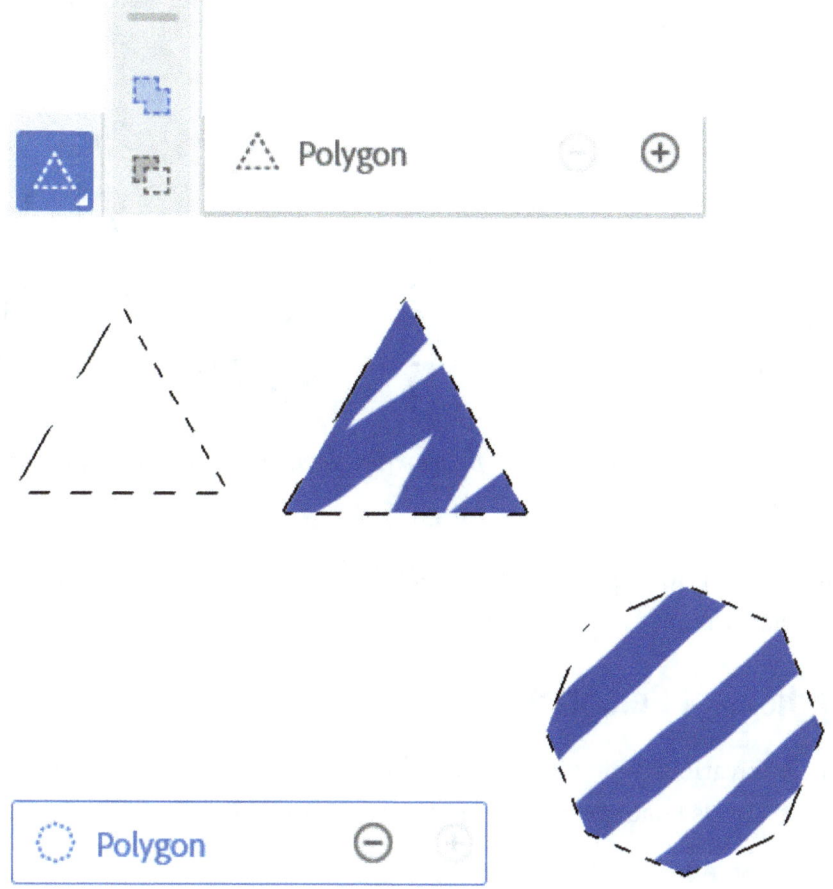

Figure 4-67. *Toolbar Polygon selection tool with its setting and painting some artwork inside*

You can remove or add more sides to the selection by clicking the minus and plus buttons before you drag out the selection. Between 3 and 8 sides are possible.

Likewise, the Touch shortcut primary circle can be used when enabled (double-click) to constrain the proportions of the selection shape as you work. The secondary ring will leave the proportions unconstrained. Refer to Figure 4-68.

CHAPTER 4 EXPLORING THE WORKSPACE OF FRESCO AND ITS TOOLS: PART 2

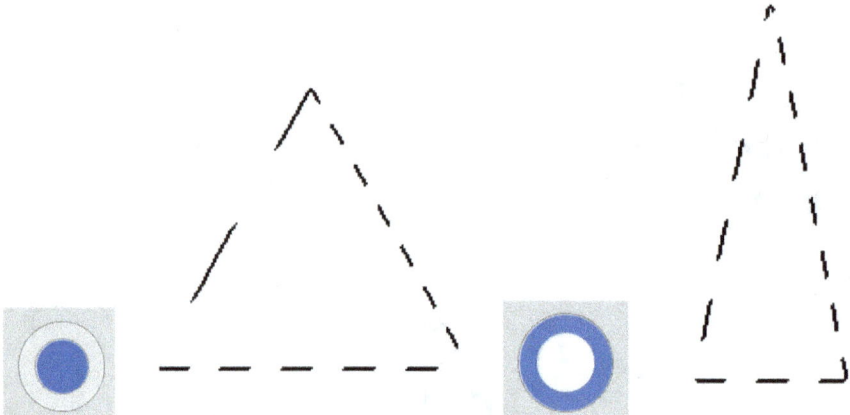

Figure 4-68. Polygon selection tool proportions can be constrained using the Touch shortcut

The same options found in the Contextual Task bar for the Lasso are also available for Polygon selection.

Loading the Last Selection

As you work with various selections, another option will appear in the Selection tools area in the list. This is Load last selection. Refer to Figure 4-69.

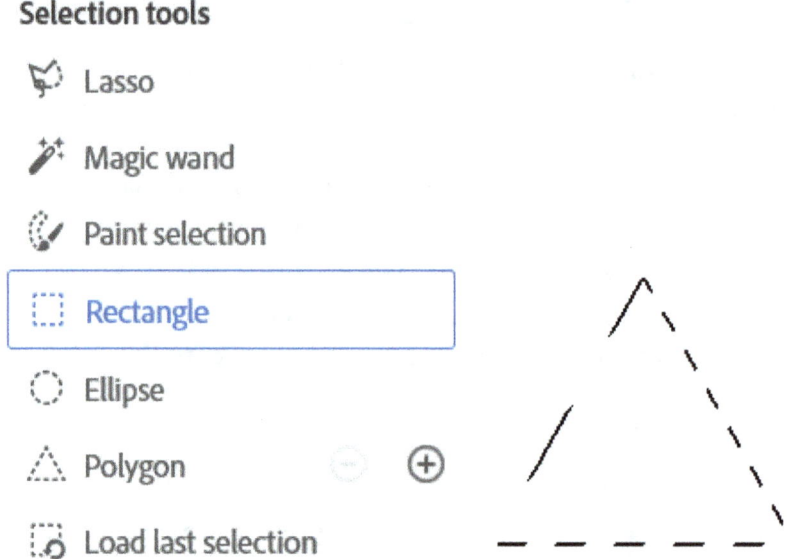

Figure 4-69. Load last selection is added to your options as you create more than one selection

This is a previous selection that you have created. Note that clicking this option may remove your last selection allowing you to redraw it again. Selections are ideal as the selection will remain active as you move to another layer. However, to prevent losing any sections if you deselect and then perform other tasks, an option is to save it on a layer as a mask which can be applied to another layer. Masks will be look at more in Chapter 5.

Key Commands Deselecting or Inverting an Active Selection

Two other helpful key commands for quickly working with selections rather than using the Contextual Task bar are

- Ctrl+D to deselect
- Ctrl+Shift+I to invert

Other keyboard shortcuts you may want to try while a selection is active are

- Ctrl+C to copy the selected area of artwork
- Ctrl+X to cut the selected area of artwork from the selection
- Ctrl+V to paste the selected area of artwork in a new location or layer

Knowing these key commands will be useful once you start working with multiple layers in Chapter 5.

Fill (G) Paint Bucket Tool

While a selection is active, you can use the Paint Bucket to fill a selection on a Vector or Pixel layer by clicking into the area and fill with color. While the tool is selected, the settings in the Toolbar for the Fill tool allow you to adjust the Color margin (0–255) as well as the toggles Preserve transparency and Contiguous, both of which are by default on. They can affect how the color fills the selection which may be more apparent in complex selections. Note that if a color area already occupies the selection, based on the setting chosen when clicked the Fill may only add to the transparent area but not the area already filled, unless you click separately on that area again Refer to Figure 4-70.

CHAPTER 4   EXPLORING THE WORKSPACE OF FRESCO AND ITS TOOLS: PART 2

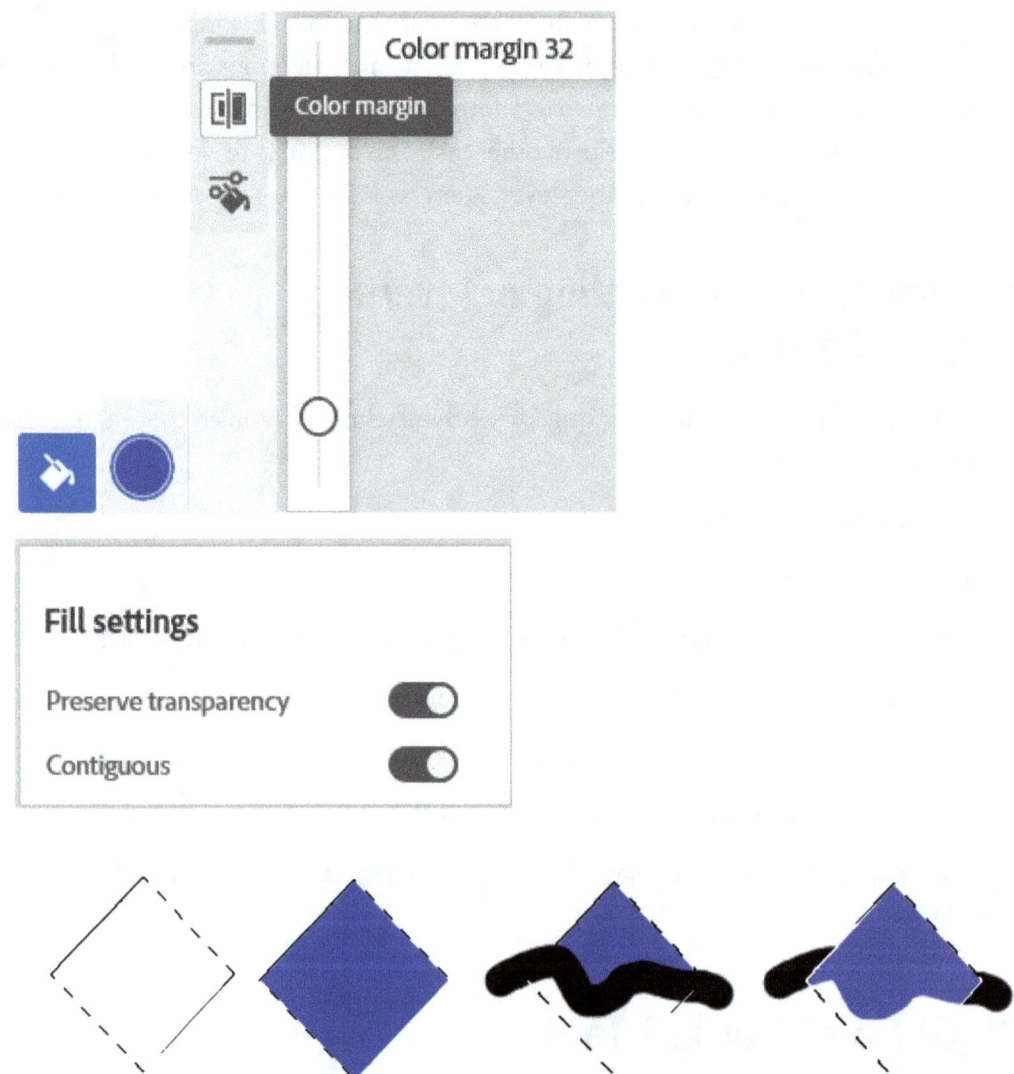

Figure 4-70. *Paint Bucket tool and its settings and painting inside an active selection*

When the Touch shortcut primary circle is enabled (double-click), the tool can also function as an eraser and remove details in the selection area. However, be aware that a thin line may remain around the border of the selection. The secondary ring will then be used to fill the selection area again with a color. Refer to Figure 4-71.

CHAPTER 4　EXPLORING THE WORKSPACE OF FRESCO AND ITS TOOLS: PART 2

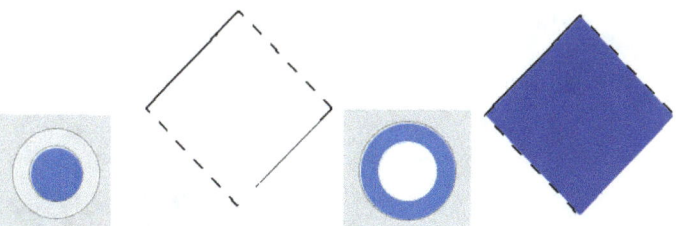

Figure 4-71. *Use the Touch shortcut to erase or fill from a selection with the Paint Bucket tool*

Remember to double-click the Touch shortcut again to deactivate and return to normal settings. You will be using the Fill tool again with layers in Chapter 5.

Shape Tools

Shape tools are more complex designs that can be used as selections or like stencils or stamps. We will discover this as we look at them next along with the Contextual Task bar. Refer to Figure 4-72.

CHAPTER 4   EXPLORING THE WORKSPACE OF FRESCO AND ITS TOOLS: PART 2

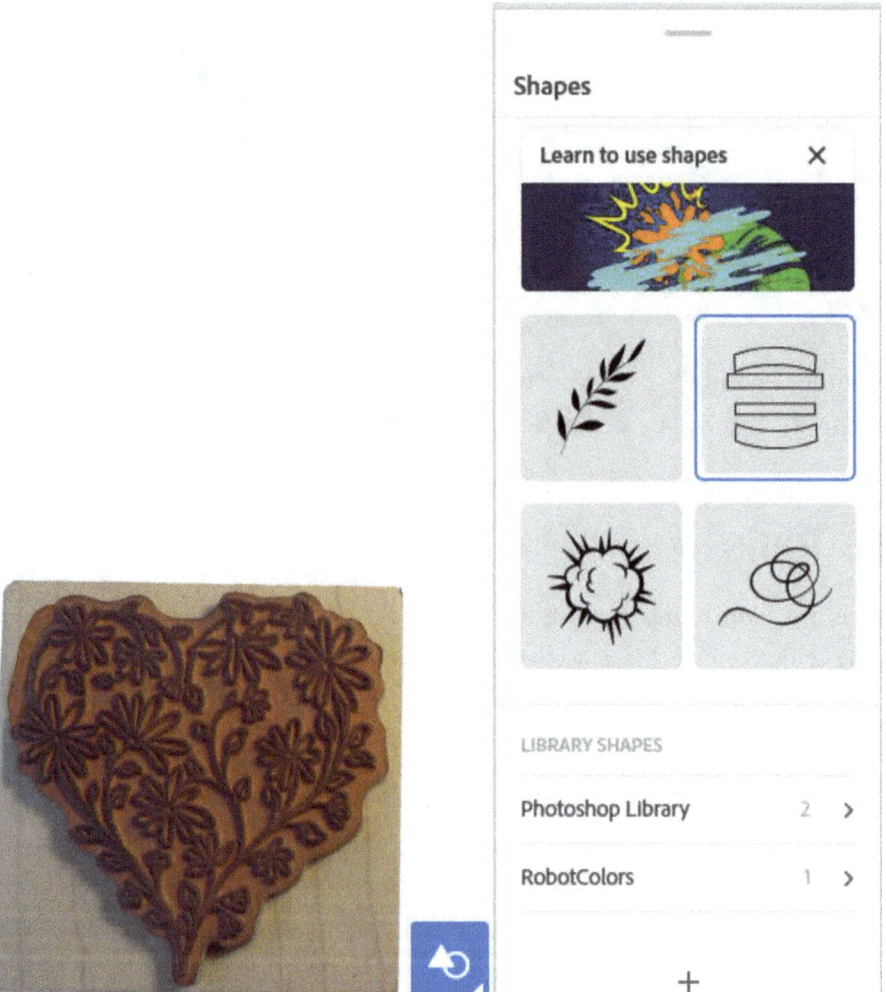

Figure 4-72.   A real stamp and Fresco's Shape tool and Shapes panel

Shapes can be created in Photoshop and stored in Photoshop but can also be accessible to Fresco via the Creative Cloud Library as I will explain later in this next section. For now, we will remain in Fresco and work with some default shapes.

Working with Default Shapes

To work with the default shapes, you need to click and hold down the Shapes tool icon in the Toolbar to display the menu or panel. You can use either a Vector or Pixel layer with the Shape tool.

CHAPTER 4   EXPLORING THE WORKSPACE OF FRESCO AND ITS TOOLS: PART 2

By default, the current shape that is selected will appear on the canvas with a bounding box surrounding it, allowing you to move, scale with the bounding box handles, and rotate it using the upper circular ring. Refer to Figure 4-73.

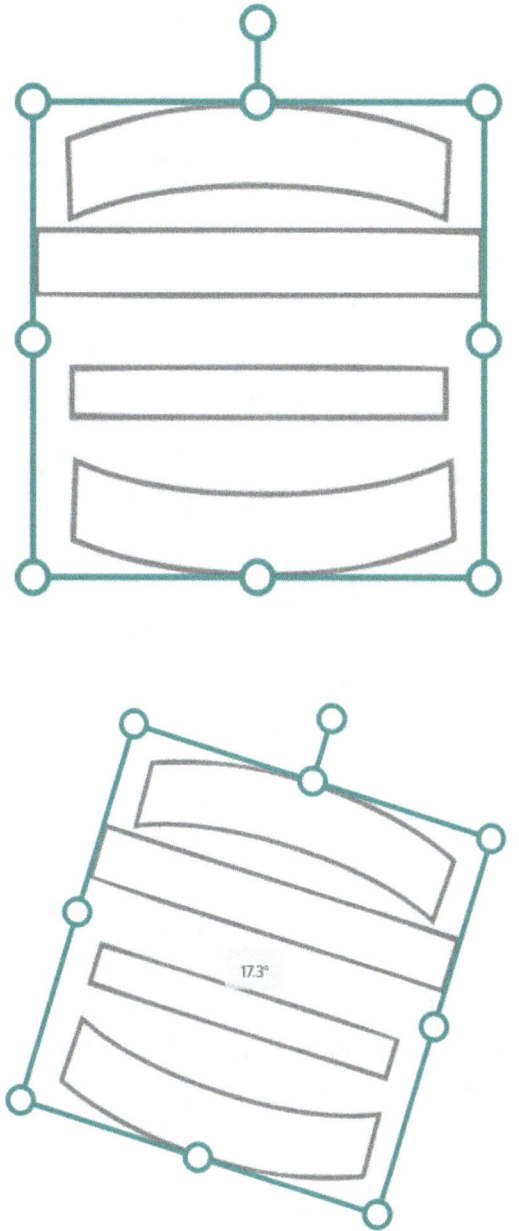

Figure 4-73. *A shape on the canvas can be easily transformed*

CHAPTER 4   EXPLORING THE WORKSPACE OF FRESCO AND ITS TOOLS: PART 2

For more details on these types of transformations, refer to the Move and Transformation tool section of this chapter.

Selecting another shape from the menu list will change the shape automatically on the canvas. Refer to Figure 4-74.

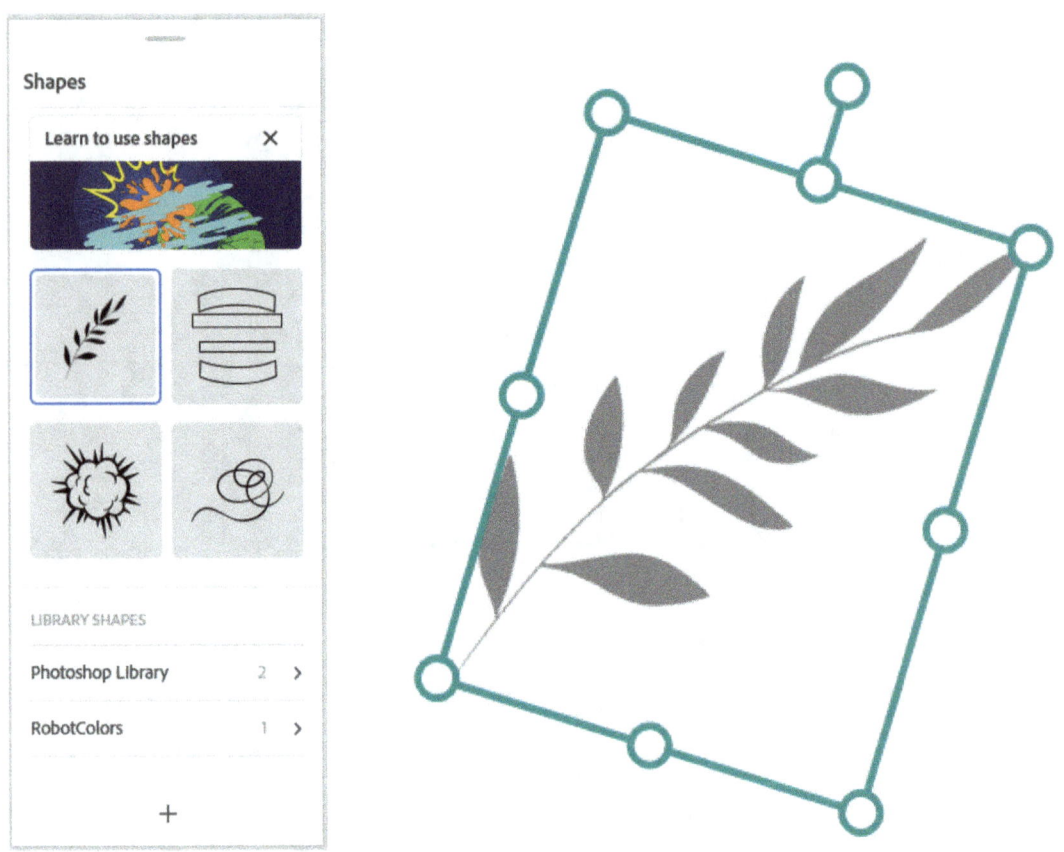

Figure 4-74. *The Shapes panel and a new shape selected on the canvas*

Then, you can also select Library shapes if you have some currently in your Libraries which we will look at in more detail shortly in the "Project: Learning to Import Shapes (SVG) from Photoshop" section. Refer to Figure 4-75.

CHAPTER 4   EXPLORING THE WORKSPACE OF FRESCO AND ITS TOOLS: PART 2

Figure 4-75. *Some custom shapes may be found in the Shapes panel and can be selected from the library*

You can also click the plus symbol at the bottom of the shape panel to Discover new shapes and Add these new shapes that were created by Adobe. Click Done if you need to exit this area. Refer to Figure 4-76.

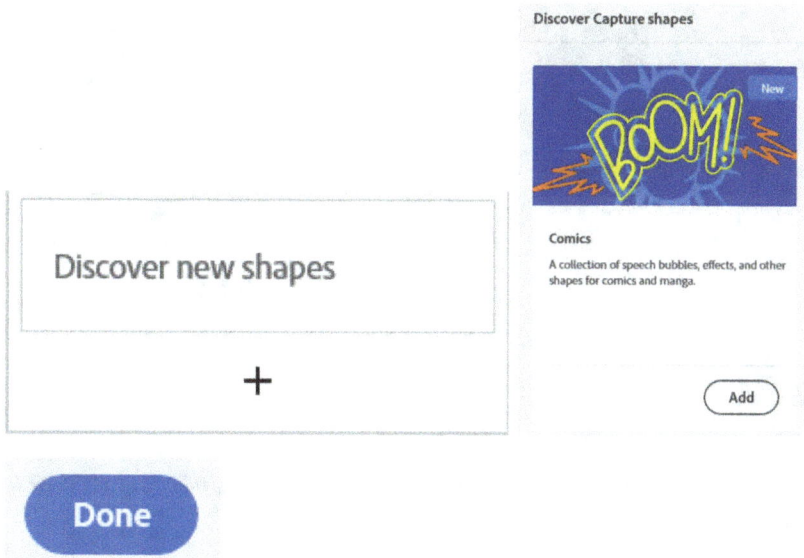

Figure 4-76. *You can acquire more shapes using the Shapes panel and Discover Capture shapes dialog box and exit with the Done button*

Tips on Using the Contextual Task Bar with Shapes

While working with the shapes, the Contextual Task bar has a few other options. Refer to Figure 4-77.

257

CHAPTER 4   EXPLORING THE WORKSPACE OF FRESCO AND ITS TOOLS: PART 2

Figure 4-77. Shapes Contextual Task bar

The options are

- Fill: Like a stamp, the Fill option allows you to fill the shape area with the color found in the color chip. I talked about color chips while working with brushes earlier in Chapter 3, but we will review this further later in the chapter as well. Refer to Figure 4-78.

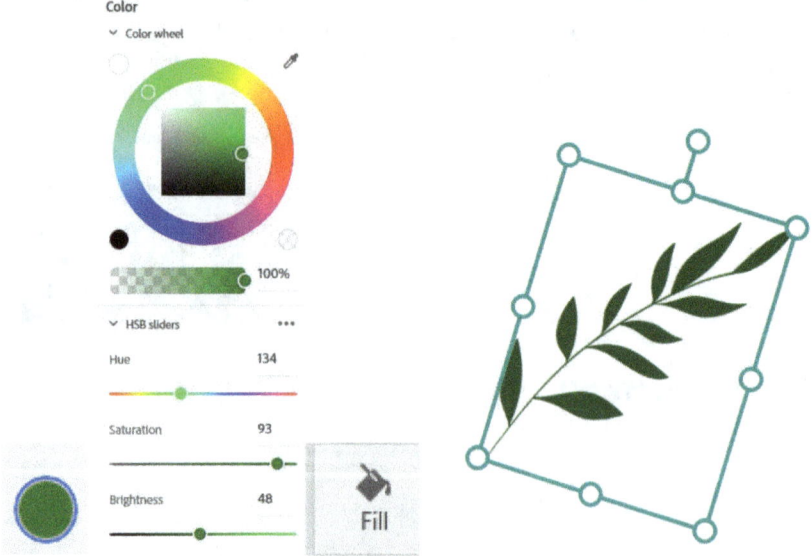

Figure 4-78. Use your color chip and shape, and then, fill the shape to add the color to the canvas

When the Touch shortcut primary circle is enabled (double-click), the tool can also fill shapes, and the secondary ring can be used to erase when you click on the shape. You can then move the shape to use it to fill a new area when you click again. Refer to Figure 4-79.

Remember to double-click again the Touch shortcut if you need to disable it.

258

Figure 4-79. *Use the Touch shortcut to fill or erase the shape when you click it*

- Erase: Allows you to use the shape area to erase areas of paint which is similar to working with selection. Refer to Figure 4-80.

Figure 4-80. *Erase part of the shape using the Contextual Task bar*

- Mask: Allows you to add a layer mask to a layer based on how the shape appears, which we will explore more in Chapter 5 while working with layers. Use your undo key (Ctrl+Z) if you need to remove the mask for now. Refer to Figure 4-81.

CHAPTER 4　EXPLORING THE WORKSPACE OF FRESCO AND ITS TOOLS: PART 2

Figure 4-81. *Turn a shape into a mask using the Contextual Task bar*

- Select: Creates a selection as you saw earlier with selections in this chapter. Shapes are a good way to store selections that you want to frequently use and are complex. A selection can then be painted within, using a brush, and you can use the selection Contextual Task bar to do further editing or to deselect the selection. Note that you cannot fill with a shape outside a selection; at least part of the shape must be inside. Refer to Figure 4-82.

Figure 4-82. *Create a selection using the Contextual Task bar and paint inside and then use the selection settings in Contextual Task bar to edit*

Note that as you use a shape, it will remain in the last used transformation state. To reset the shape, you may need to temporarily select another shape and then return to that shape. Also, you may need to rotate the shape back to the original angle.

260

CHAPTER 4   EXPLORING THE WORKSPACE OF FRESCO AND ITS TOOLS: PART 2

Project: Learning to Import Shapes (SVG) from Photoshop

As mentioned, Photoshop is a great way to create your own custom shapes that you can use in Adobe Fresco and can be imported into a Creative Cloud Library from the panel. These shapes are in the format of SVG or Scalable Vector Graphic using the Capture Features. Refer to Figure 4-83.

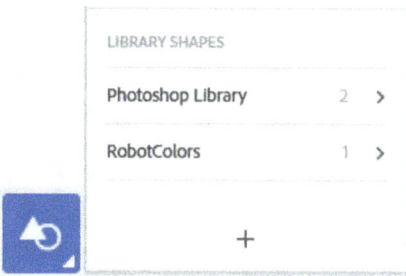

Figure 4-83. *Shapes tool and panel access to Library shapes*

Photoshop has at least two methods for creating initial shapes which I will mention here so that you can expand your custom shape collection on your own. Refer to Figure 4-84.

Figure 4-84. *Work in Photoshop to create shapes*

Note   If you are not familiar with using Photoshop to draw shapes, you can find some information at these links as well, for shape creation:

`https://helpx.adobe.com/photoshop/using/drawing-shapes.html`

`https://helpx.adobe.com/photoshop/using/drawing-pen-tools.html`

261

CHAPTER 4 EXPLORING THE WORKSPACE OF FRESCO AND ITS TOOLS: PART 2

Photoshop Shapes

In Photoshop, various basic and custom shapes are found in the Toolbar and also in the Window ➤ Shapes panel. Before dragging out a shape to the canvas, we can edit the color and edges of these shapes using the Options bar panel. Then, upon dragging out the shape, they appear on a shape layer. Refer to Figure 4-85 and Figure 4-86.

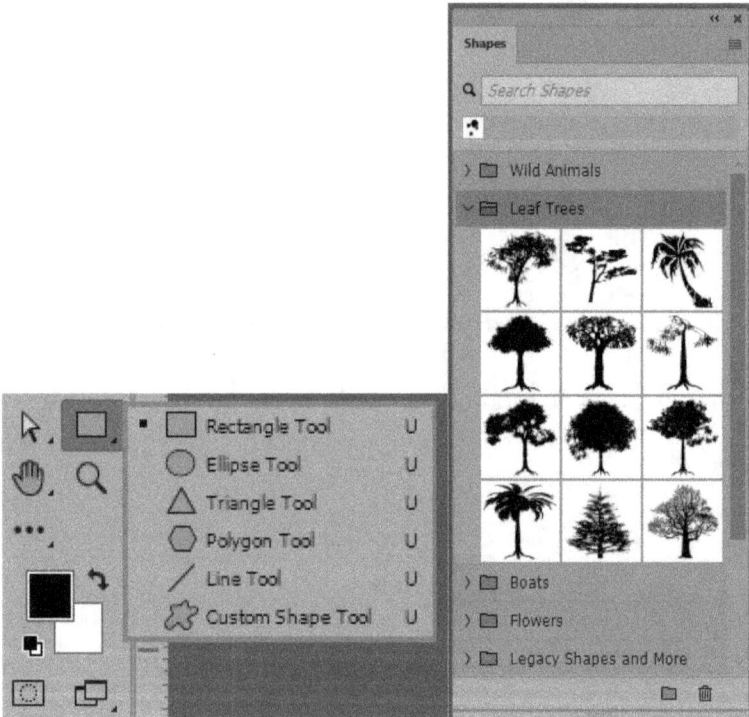

Figure 4-85. *Photoshop Shapes can be accessed via the Toolbar and the Shapes panel*

262

CHAPTER 4 EXPLORING THE WORKSPACE OF FRESCO AND ITS TOOLS: PART 2

Figure 4-86. *Edit and select shapes using the Options panel, and then, view the shapes on the layer and in the Layers panel*

In Photoshop, the first way that you can create a custom shape is by creating a new document, as you saw in Chapter 3 when we create a brush. However, this time, it is to store the shape on a layer.

For a beginner, using a custom shape with the custom shape tool is often ideal if you have never drawn a shape before, and holding down the Shift key will scale that shape proportionally. I make sure before I start to drag out the shape to set the Options bar panel with the custom shape and then set a black fill color with no stroke. Refer to Figure 4-86.

However, you can also use a Pen tool to create a solid shape on a blank layer, when set to shape in the Options bar panel with a black fill and no stroke. As mentioned, I will not be going into the operation of the Pen tool, as learning how to create curves takes practice.

263

CHAPTER 4   EXPLORING THE WORKSPACE OF FRESCO AND ITS TOOLS: PART 2

You can refer to the earlier link if you need to review how to use the Pen tool along with its sub-tools of Add Anchor Point, Delete Anchor Point, and Convert Point, as well as the Selection tools of Path Selection and Direct Selection. These are often used with Pathfinder options and Layers panel for merging complex shapes into one layer. Refer to Figure 4-87.

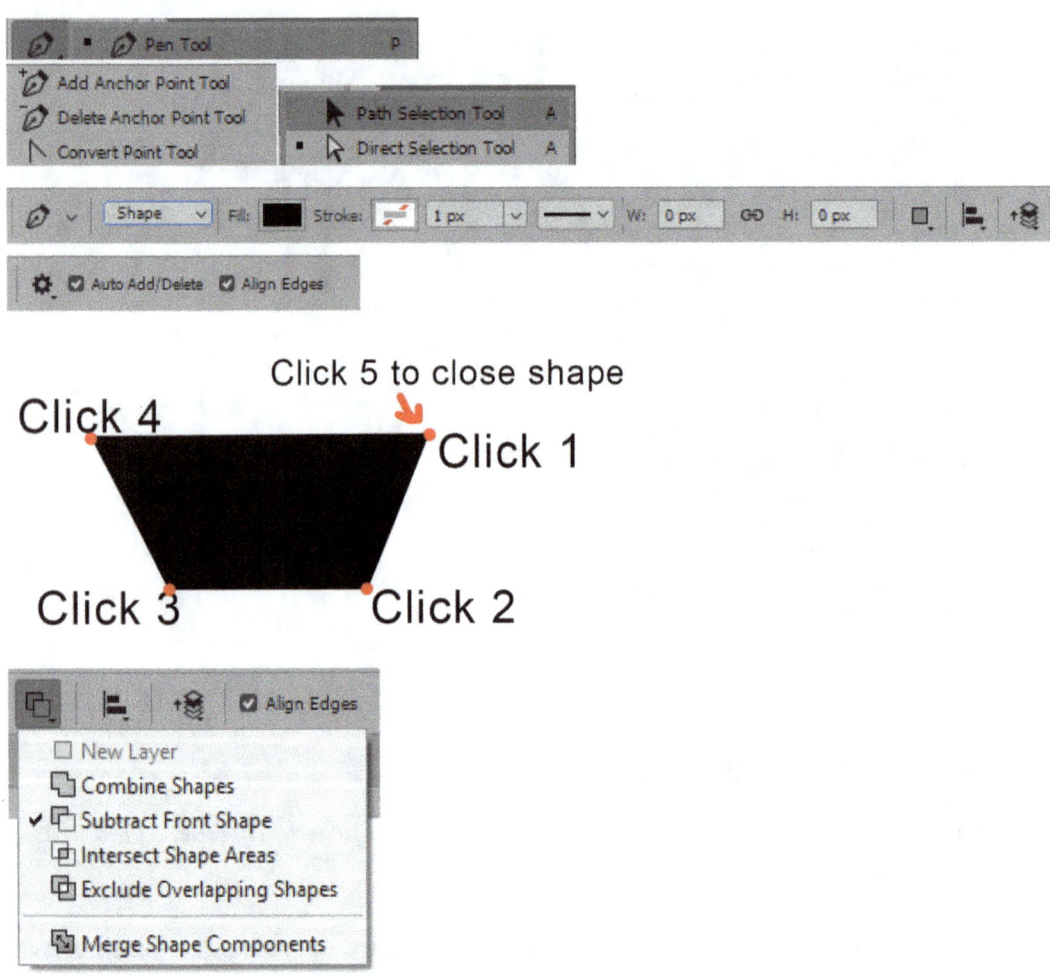

Figure 4-87. *Photoshop has various Pen and Selection tools for creating complex shapes and combining them*

Tip   For those of you who are Illustrator users and familiar with using a Pen tool or Shape tool, you can copy (Ctrl/CMD+C) a selected shape and then paste (Ctrl/CMD+V) your selected shapes into Photoshop as a Shape layer. Refer to Figure 4-88.

CHAPTER 4   EXPLORING THE WORKSPACE OF FRESCO AND ITS TOOLS: PART 2

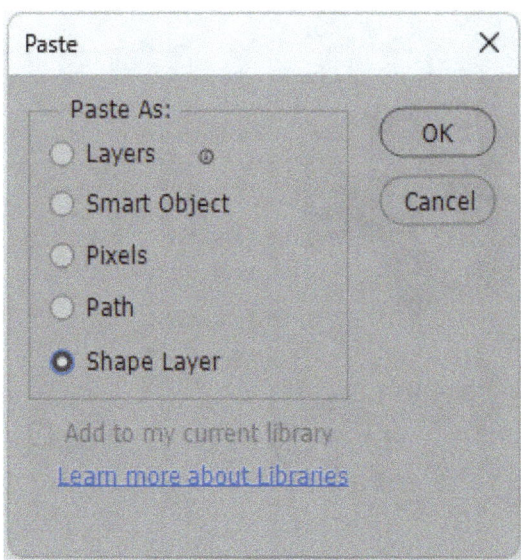

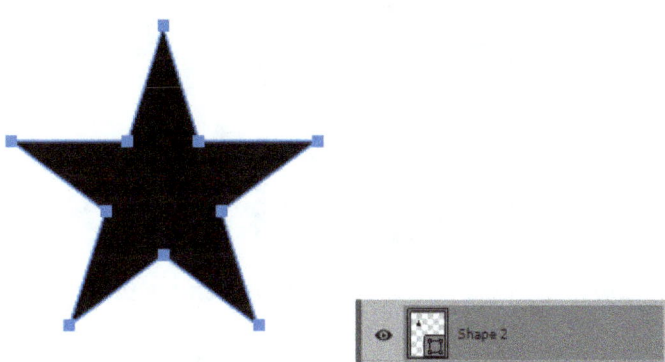

Figure 4-88. *Photoshop paste dialog box for pasting a shape and it appears as a shape layer*

We will discuss copying and pasting from Illustrator more in Chapters 7 and 9.

The focus of this chapter is the quick creation of a custom shape in Photoshop for Fresco. So, feel free to drag out one of the custom shapes from the Shapes panel using the Options bar panel, or you can in this case use the custom shapes I have created or add to various layers in the file **CustomShapes.psd** to follow along. Refer to Figure 4-89.

CHAPTER 4   EXPLORING THE WORKSPACE OF FRESCO AND ITS TOOLS: PART 2

Figure 4-89. *Custom shapes and the Photoshop Layers panel*

Either way, you need to make the shape artwork in black fill with a stroke of none for areas to stamp or optionally, with white, for areas that will not stamp. This is how it must be done for the shape to be saved correctly. In your own designs, as I have done, you may want to save certain shapes as separate components or layers so that you can reuse them elsewhere in your projects. In my case, using the Layers panel menu, I merged certain shapes together and then altered them using the Options bar panel and arrow Selection tools.

Once you have created the custom shape, you can then select that shape layer and choose the option from the Photoshop menu. Edit ➤ Define Custom Shape. Give the shape a custom name and click OK. Refer to Figure 4-90.

CHAPTER 4   EXPLORING THE WORKSPACE OF FRESCO AND ITS TOOLS: PART 2

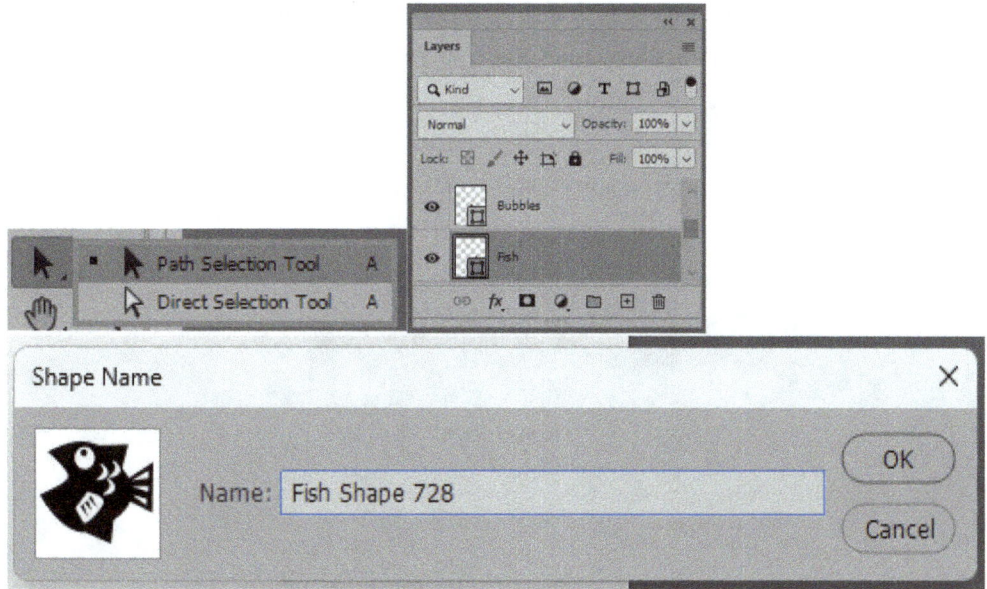

Figure 4-90. *Path Selection tool active and Photoshop Layers panel with a layer selected and the Shape Name dialog box*

It will automatically be added to your Shapes panel. Repeat those steps for any additional shapes you want to add. Refer to Figure 4-91.

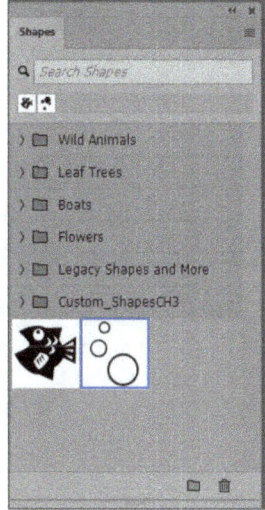

Figure 4-91. *Adding custom shapes to the Photoshop Shapes panel*

267

CHAPTER 4　EXPLORING THE WORKSPACE OF FRESCO AND ITS TOOLS: PART 2

You can then store those shapes in a Group Folder by selecting the button in the Shapes panel. Name it and click OK, and you can drag them into the folder. They will be available when you select your custom shape tool. If you need to see the original shapes I created, you can also import the shape file **Custom Shapes.csh** using the Shapes panel menu. Refer to Figure 4-91 and Figure 4-92.

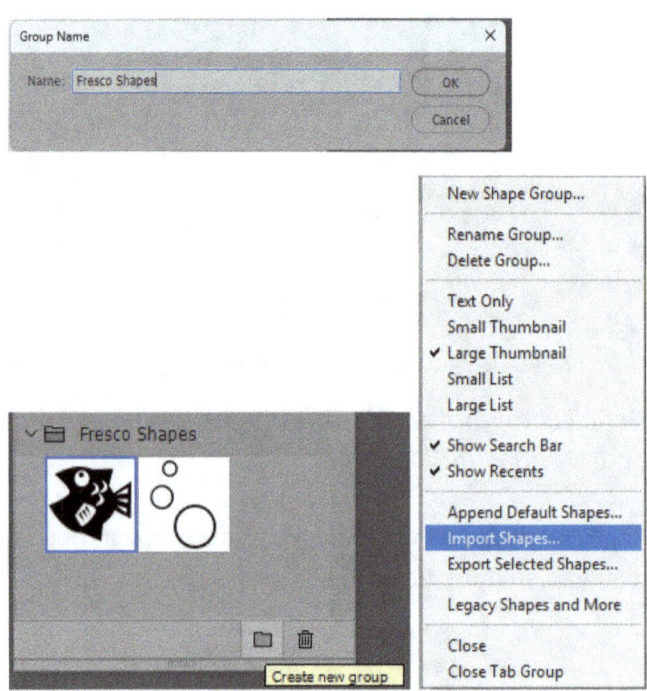

Figure 4-92. *Create a group name folder, add your shapes, or import more shapes using the Shapes panel menu*

When you select a shape, however, you will discover that you cannot add the shape directly to the Libraries panel and the only option that may first seem correct under the plus (+) icon is to add as a Graphic, but this is not a shape. It is only selecting the current layer, which is not helpful in Fresco, in this instance. Refer to Figure 4-93.

CHAPTER 4　EXPLORING THE WORKSPACE OF FRESCO AND ITS TOOLS: PART 2

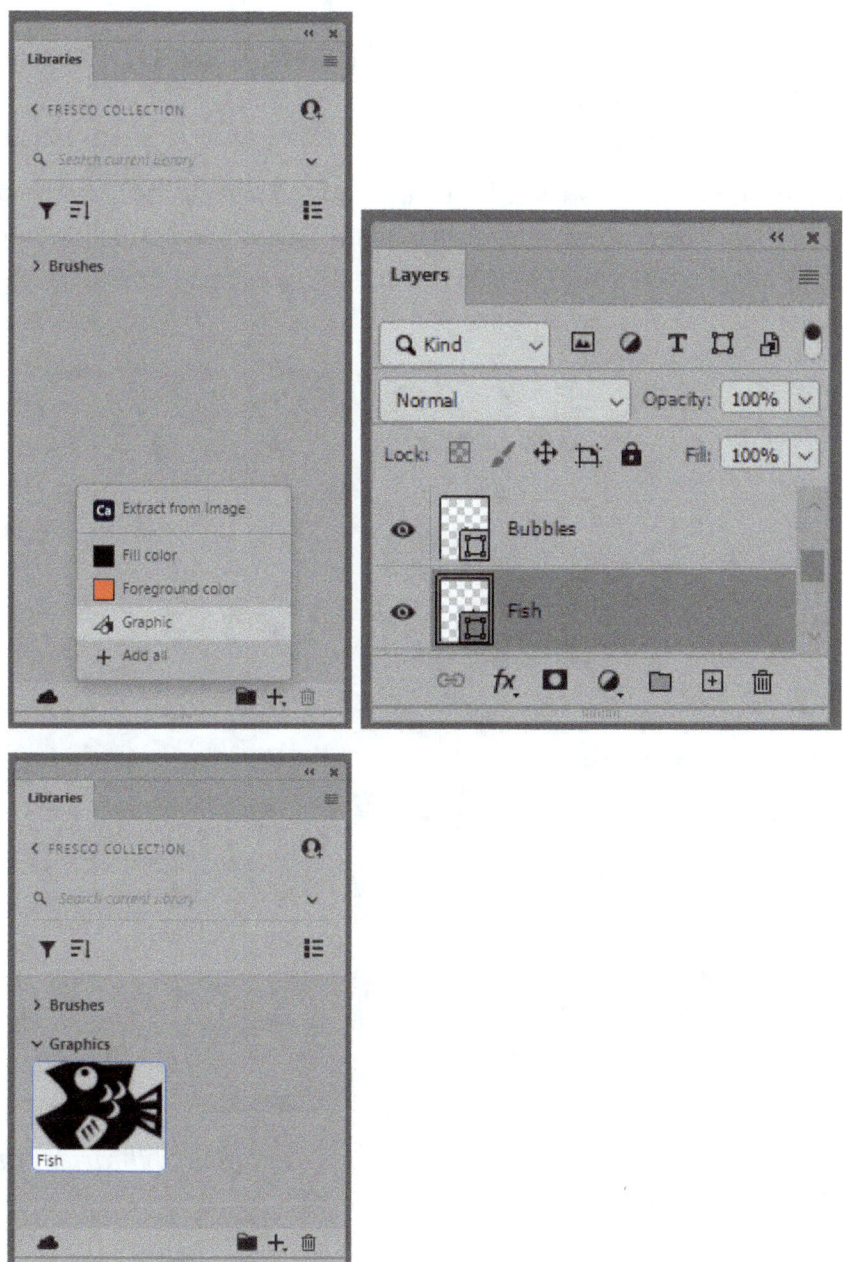

Figure 4-93. *Photoshop Libraries Layers panel and a Graphic added to the Libraries panel*

CHAPTER 4   EXPLORING THE WORKSPACE OF FRESCO AND ITS TOOLS: PART 2

Tip For details on how to create a library in Photoshop, refer to my section on library creation for brushes in Chapter 3.

In this case, to get a shape, we need to do a second step using the Libraries panel. Make sure the shape layer you want is selected in the Layers panel, and this time, select from the add elements plus (+) icon menu options Extract from Image. Refer to Figure 4-94.

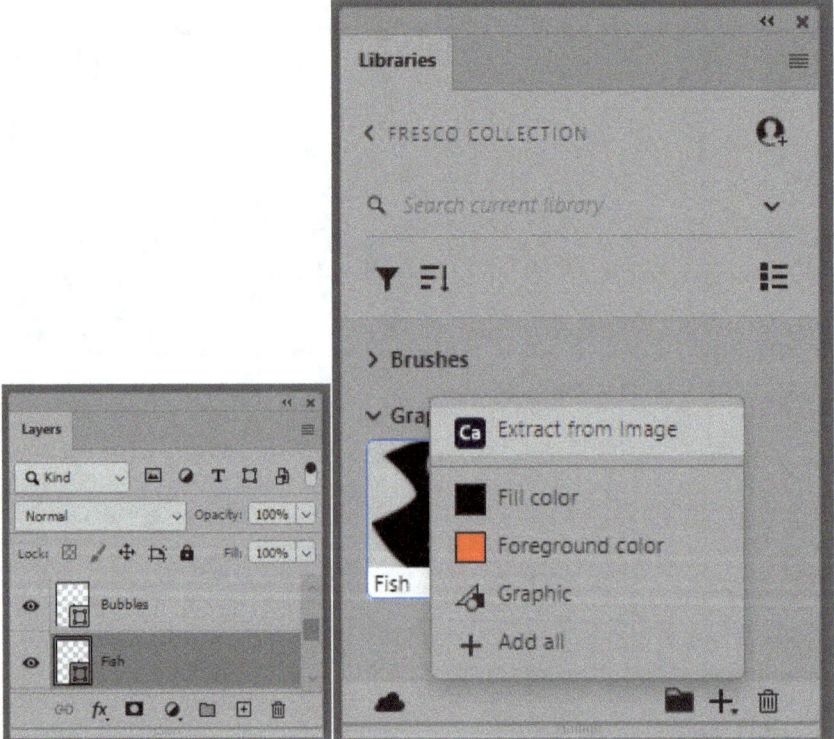

Figure 4-94.* Select your layer in the Layers panel, and in the Libraries panel, choose Extract from Image*

This opens the Adobe Capture app which is accessed through Photoshop via the Libraries panel. Refer to Figure 4-95.

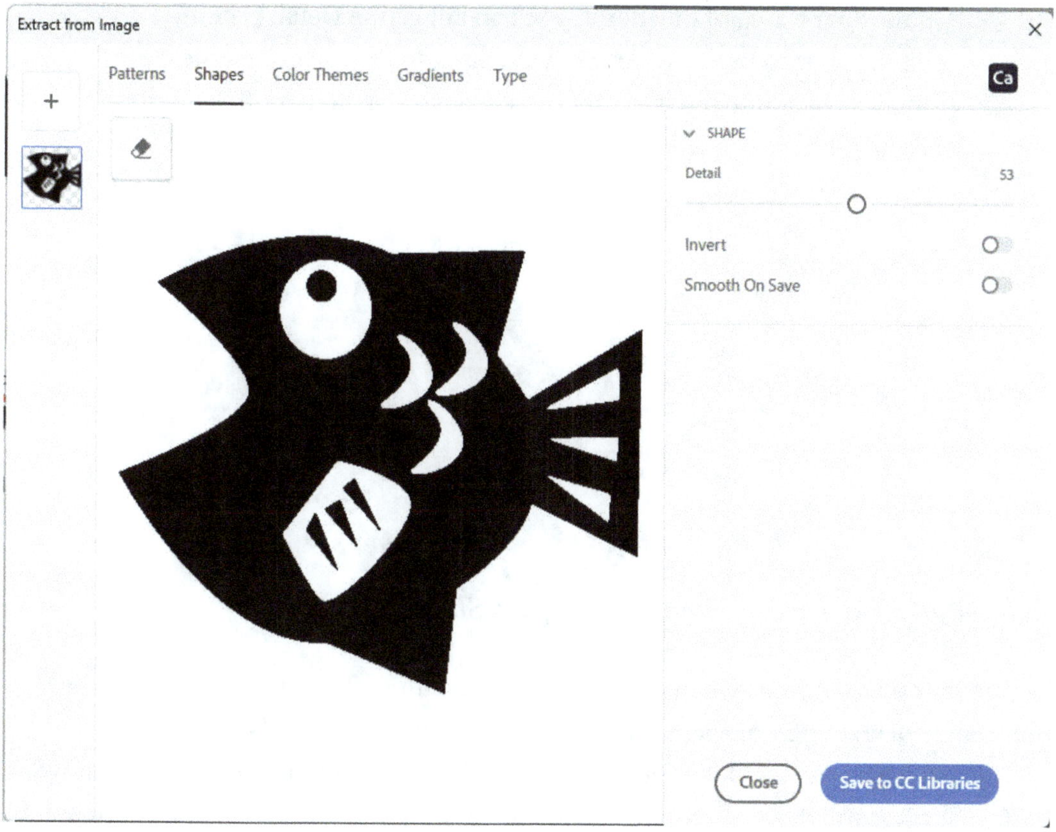

CHAPTER 4 EXPLORING THE WORKSPACE OF FRESCO AND ITS TOOLS: PART 2

Figure 4-95. Extract from Image dialog box Shapes tab

You are now in Capture workspace, "Extract from Image."

This workspace allows you to capture assets for your library such as Patterns, Shapes, Color Themes, Gradients, and Type. In this case, our focus is just on capturing a shape. Go to the Shapes tab.

The Shapes tab allows you to do such things as

- Add (+) an image that you would like to turn into a shape. In this case, we have already done that.

- Erase unwanted details that you do not want to include in the shape. Move the slider to adjust the size of the eraser. Refer to Figure 4-96.

Figure 4-96. Extract from Image dialog box erase tool

271

- In the Shape area of the menu, you can adjust the Detail (1–100) slider, toggle to Invert, or Smooth On Save. In this case, I left the Detail at 58 and Invert and Smooth On Save disabled or off. Refer to Figure 4-97.

Figure 4-97. *Extract from Image dialog box Shape settings*

For your own projects, you may have different settings, but you can see here the importance of creating a black and white copy for maximum details in your shape.

Once you have adjusted the settings to your liking, you can then click the button Save to CC Libraries, and the shape is now added to your library. Then, click the Close button to exit the Capture app. Refer to Figure 4-98.

Figure 4-98. *Extract from Image dialog box Close and Save to CC Libraries buttons*

You can return to this app any time if you have more shapes on other selected layers to add.

Now, in the Libraries panel, you can see that the graphic is now stored as a Capture Shape. Refer to Figure 4-99.

CHAPTER 4   EXPLORING THE WORKSPACE OF FRESCO AND ITS TOOLS: PART 2

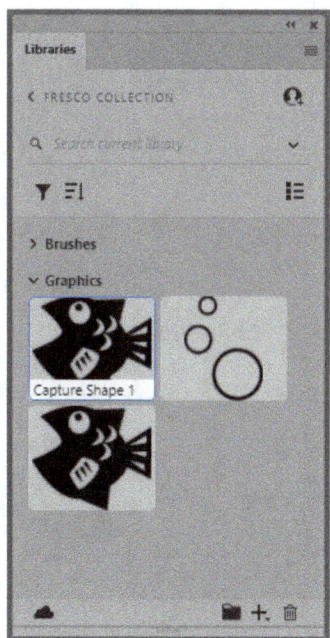

Figure 4-99. *Photoshop Libraries panel with Capture Shapes added*

You can then return to Fresco to locate the shape from that library in the Shapes tool and use it as you would the default shapes with the Contextual Task bar to paint, create masks, or selections. Refer to Figure 4-100.

CHAPTER 4 EXPLORING THE WORKSPACE OF FRESCO AND ITS TOOLS: PART 2

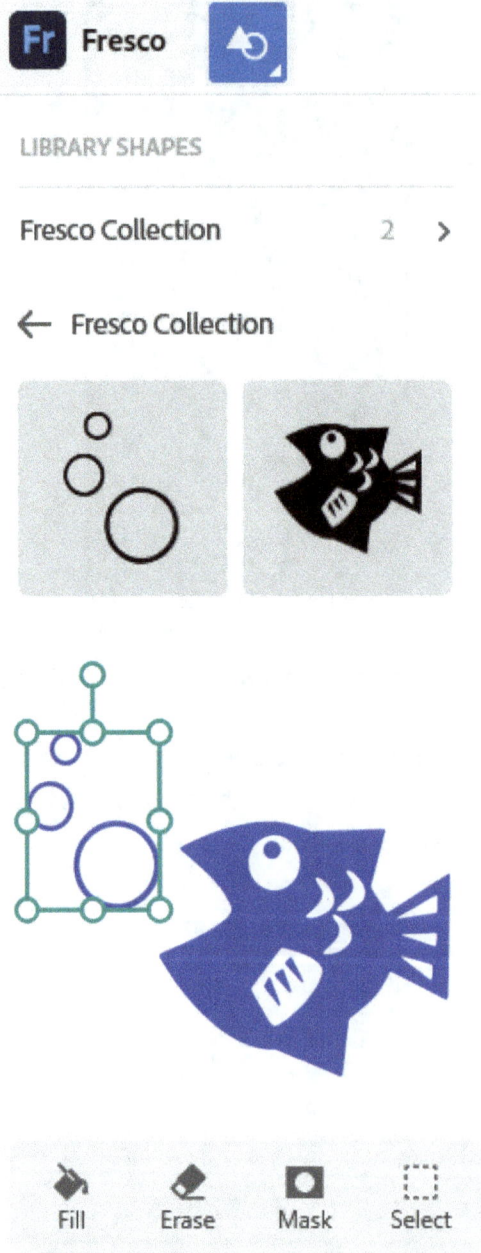

Figure 4-100. *Fresco shape added to the Shapes panel and then stamped on the canvas; the Contextual Task bar can also assist*

CHAPTER 4   EXPLORING THE WORKSPACE OF FRESCO AND ITS TOOLS: PART 2

Tip   While not required for this book for designers who are also familiar with InDesign, the CC Libraries panel also offers the Adobe Capture option of Extract from Image under the plus (+) icon allowing you to add shapes when you select the Shapes tab. All Photoshop options for shapes are here as well, and you can follow those same steps in the Extract from Image dialog box to create a Capture Shape. Refer to Figure 4-101.

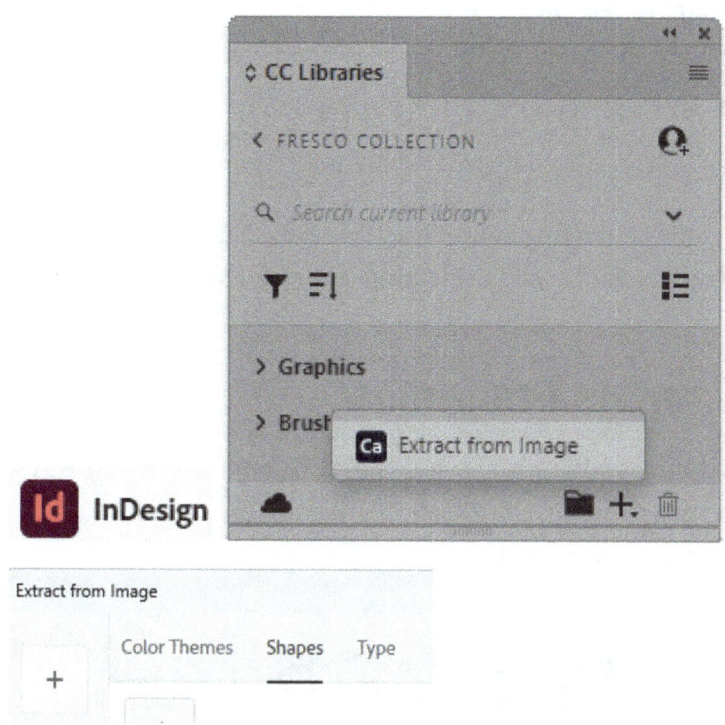

Figure 4-101. *InDesign CC Libraries panel and Extract from Image dialog box Shapes tab*

Note for Illustrator users: While it is true that Capture Shapes can be dragged into Illustrator from its Libraries panel, as mentioned earlier, a shape cannot be just a graphic created in Illustrator and added to the CC Library, as the Illustrator Libraries panel does not have an Extract from Image Capture option.

To add shapes from Illustrator, they will need to be converted to a Shape or Pixel layer in Photoshop first before any shape extraction can take place using Capture. Details on how to copy an Illustrator shape or Image to Photoshop for use in Fresco will be explained in Chapter 7.

More details on Fresco shapes can be found here:

https://helpx.adobe.com/fresco/using/shapes.html

We will also look at drawing aids as they relate to shapes in Chapter 6. For reference, you can see my library file **Fresco Collection_shapes_colors.cclibs**.

Text Tool and Its Properties

The Text tool is used for adding text somewhere on your canvas. The text will remain as an editable layer as long as it is a Text layer. We will explore text layers along with the different kinds of layers in more detail in Chapter 5. Refer to Figure 4-102.

Figure 4-102. *Text tool, Color chip, and Text layer*

To add some text to a Text layer, you can click on the canvas, and some placeholder text will automatically be added. The text at this stage can be moved, transformed, and scaled proportionally using the bounding box handles. Use the upper handle to rotate. Refer to Figure 4-103.

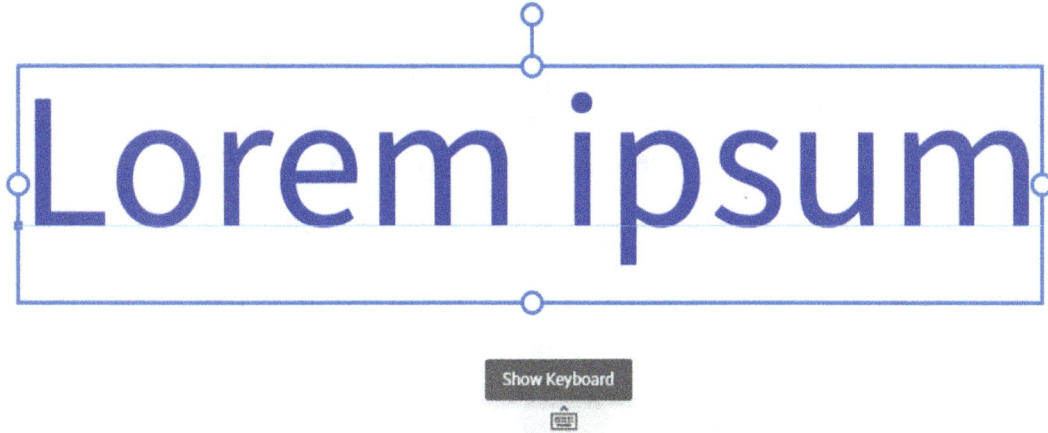

Figure 4-103. *Text from the Text layer on the canvas*

However, if you want to edit the text, click the Show Keyboard icon below the text. Refer to Figure 4-103.

The text and the text color can be changed while the text is highlighted, and you can use the color chip to alter the color as you would for brushes in Chapter 3. Refer to Figure 4-104.

CHAPTER 4　EXPLORING THE WORKSPACE OF FRESCO AND ITS TOOLS: PART 2

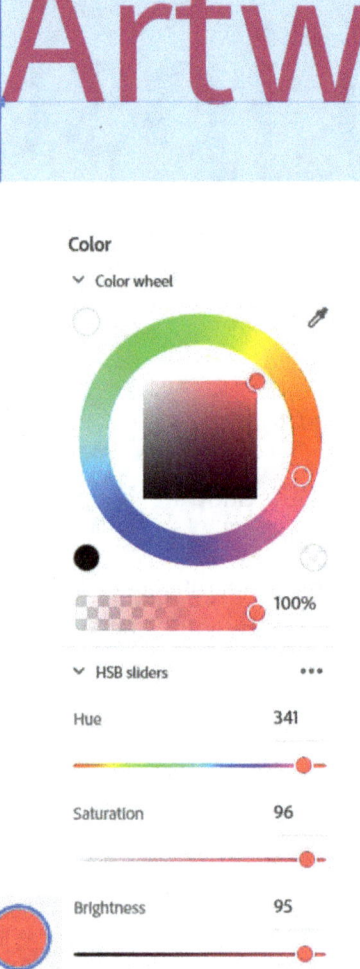

Figure 4-104. *Alter the text color using the color chip color wheel while the text is highlighted*

Other settings you can use while in this mode are the icons of cut, copy, and paste as well as options to undo and redo. Or for more properties, click Style text to access the Layer properties for that Text layer. Refer to Figure 4-105.

Figure 4-105. *Additional text editing options while text is highlighted: cut, copy, paste inactive, undo, redo, paste active, and Style text button*

CHAPTER 4 EXPLORING THE WORKSPACE OF FRESCO AND ITS TOOLS: PART 2

To return the text to transformation mode, click the Hide Keyboard icon, or click again to show keyboard. Showing allows you to retype highlighted text. Refer to Figure 4-106.

Figure 4-106. *Hide and Show Keyboard options for Text tool*

To change the other properties of the text, you need to access the Layer properties panel on the right-hand side using the Vertical Taskbar, which we will explore more in Chapter 5. Refer to Figure 4-107.

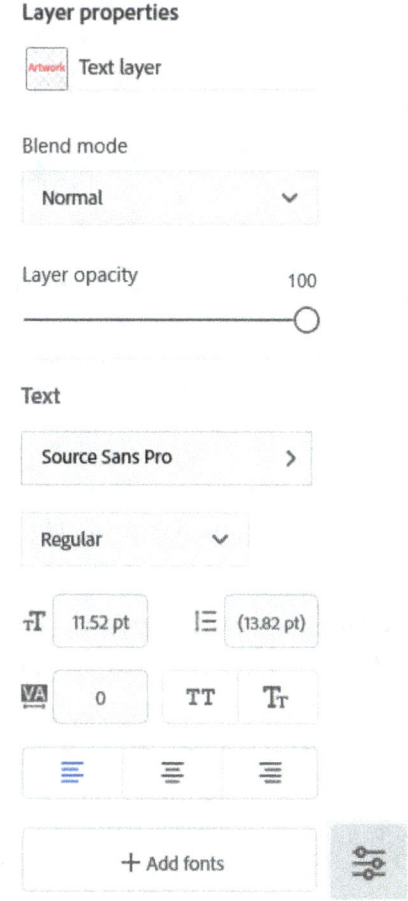

Figure 4-107. *Layer properties for Text tool*

However, for fonts, the main areas in the properties panel that you can review are

- Layer Name: In this case, it is called a Text layer, but you can rename it by typing a new name in that area if required.

- Blend Mode: Like the brushes, these are the color options that will alter the colors as the text layer is overlayed above other pixels of color on an underlying layer. Colors can appear differently or disappear altogether. The options include Normal (default), Darken, Multiply, Color burn, Linear burn, Darker color, Lighten, Screen, Color dodge, Linear dodge Lighter color, Overlay, Soft light, Hard light, Vivid light, Linear light, Pin light, Hard mix, Difference, Exclusion, Subtract, Divide, Hue, Saturation, Color, and Luminosity. We will look at this more closely in Chapter 5. Refer to Figure 4-108.

Figure 4-108. Adding a layer Blend mode to the overlaying text

- Layer Opacity: The opacity or transparency of the layer (0–100%). By default, it is set to 100% but can be lowered when more pixels behind need to show through or you want a lighter color, such as if you are creating a watermark. Refer to Figure 4-109.

CHAPTER 4   EXPLORING THE WORKSPACE OF FRESCO AND ITS TOOLS: PART 2

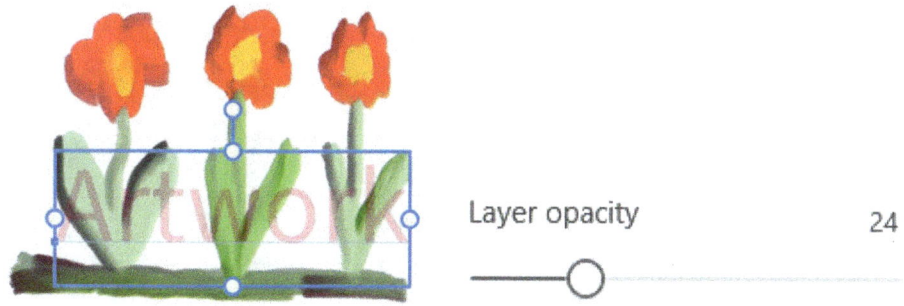

Figure 4-109. Altering the Layer opacity of the Text layer

- Text Properties: These include the following:

    - Fonts: Your fonts on your computer or More fonts from Adobe. Refer to Figure 4-110.

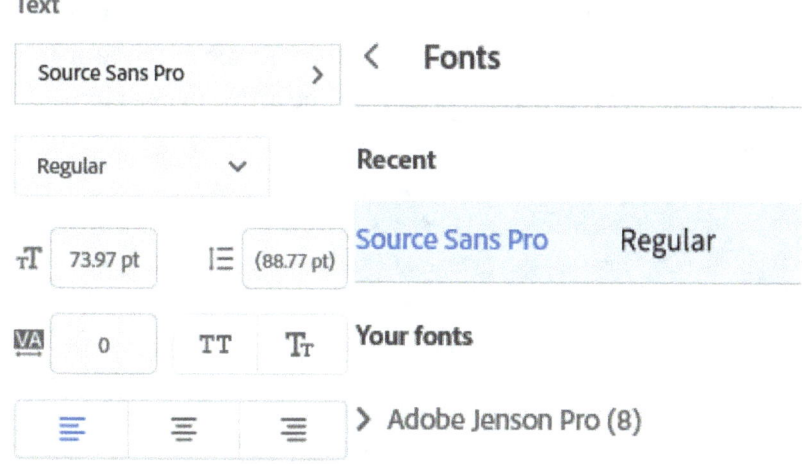

Figure 4-110. Text properties in the Layers panel

    - Style: For example, Regular, Bold, Italic, or whatever custom style your font comes with. Refer to Figure 4-110.

    - Font Size: You can enter the size using your plus (+)/minus (−) scale or numeric keyboard. Refer to Figure 4-111.

281

CHAPTER 4　EXPLORING THE WORKSPACE OF FRESCO AND ITS TOOLS: PART 2

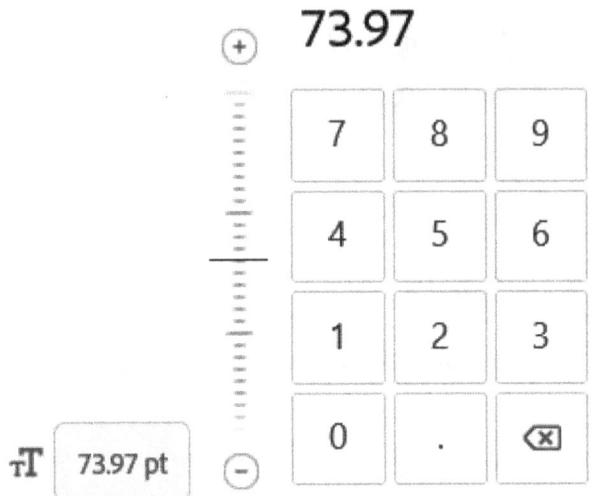

Figure 4-111. *Text size settings*

- Line Spacing Between Two Lines on the Text: You can enter the spacing using your plus (+)/minus (−) scale or numeric keyboard. You can use the back pointing arrow to reset line spacing to default. Refer to Figure 4-112.

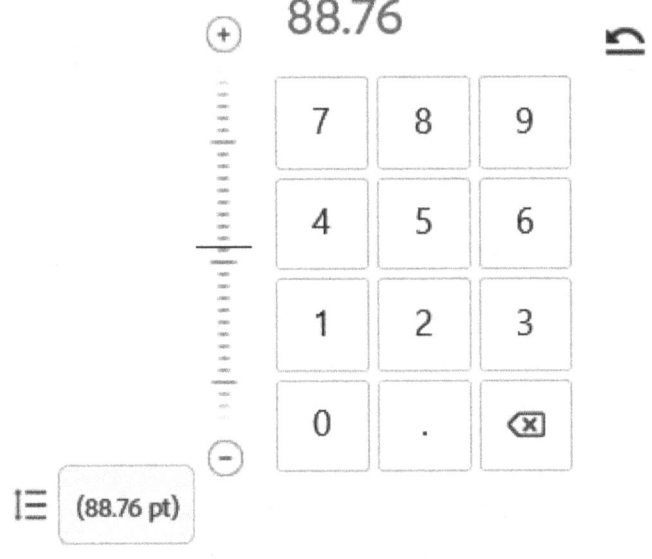

Figure 4-112. *Text line spacing settings*

- Letter Spacing Between Letters: You can enter the spacing using your plus (+)/minus (−) scale or numeric keyboard. Use the +/− icon to toggle between positive and negative numbers. You can use the back pointing arrow to reset line spacing to default. Refer to Figure 4-113.

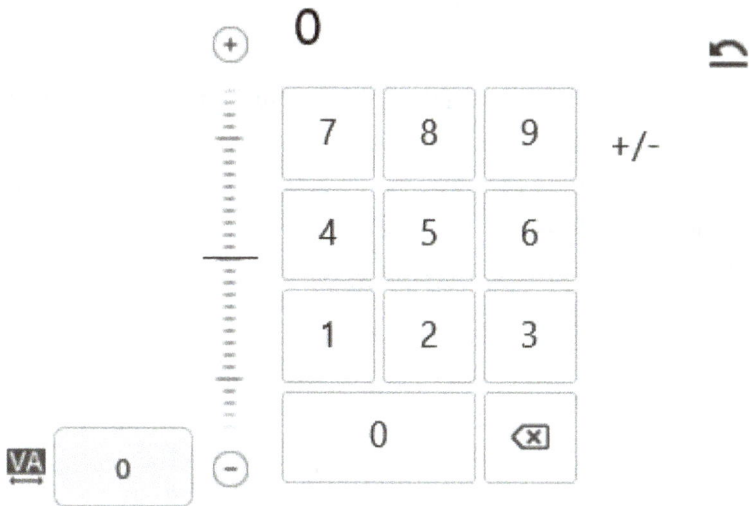

Figure 4-113. *Text letter spacing settings*

- Toggle on and off between all caps, small caps, and back to default. Refer to Figure 4-114.

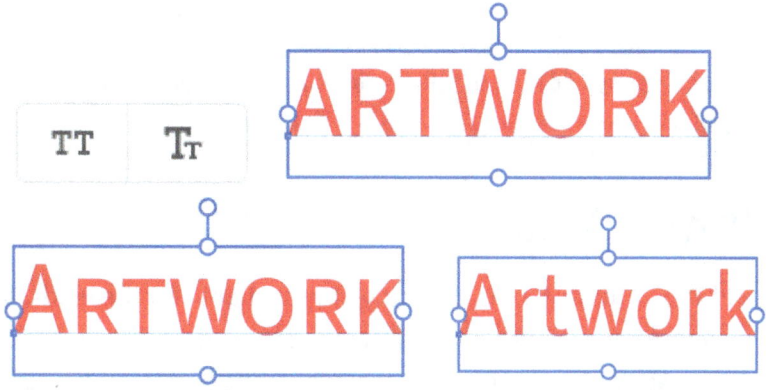

Figure 4-114. *Text caps settings buttons for all, small, and default*

CHAPTER 4 EXPLORING THE WORKSPACE OF FRESCO AND ITS TOOLS: PART 2

- Align: Left align, Center align, and Right align. Refer to Figure 4-115.

Figure 4-115. *Text alignment settings buttons*

- Add Fonts: you can find more fonts either in the Font drop-down menu, under More fonts, or click the Add fonts button to access more fonts online through your Creative Cloud account with Adobe fonts. Refer to Figure 4-116.

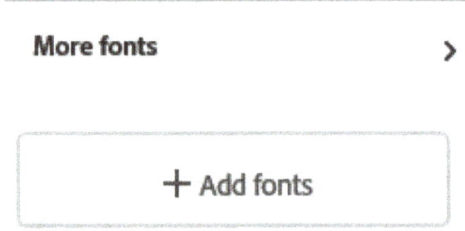

Figure 4-116. *Text option buttons for accessing additional fonts*

More information on fonts and working with them can be found at the following links, including how to work with East Asian type, add fonts, or update the fonts in your list:

```
https://helpx.adobe.com/fresco/using/create-text-font.html
https://helpx.adobe.com/fresco/using/add-your-own-font.html
https://fonts.adobe.com/
```

Creating Vertical Type

To create Vertical Type, this option is currently only available for the iPad. However, as a workaround, you can kind of recreate this effect for a word or two using the cursor and press your Enter key after every letter, and then, adjust the line spacing property and alignment as required. Refer to Figure 4-117.

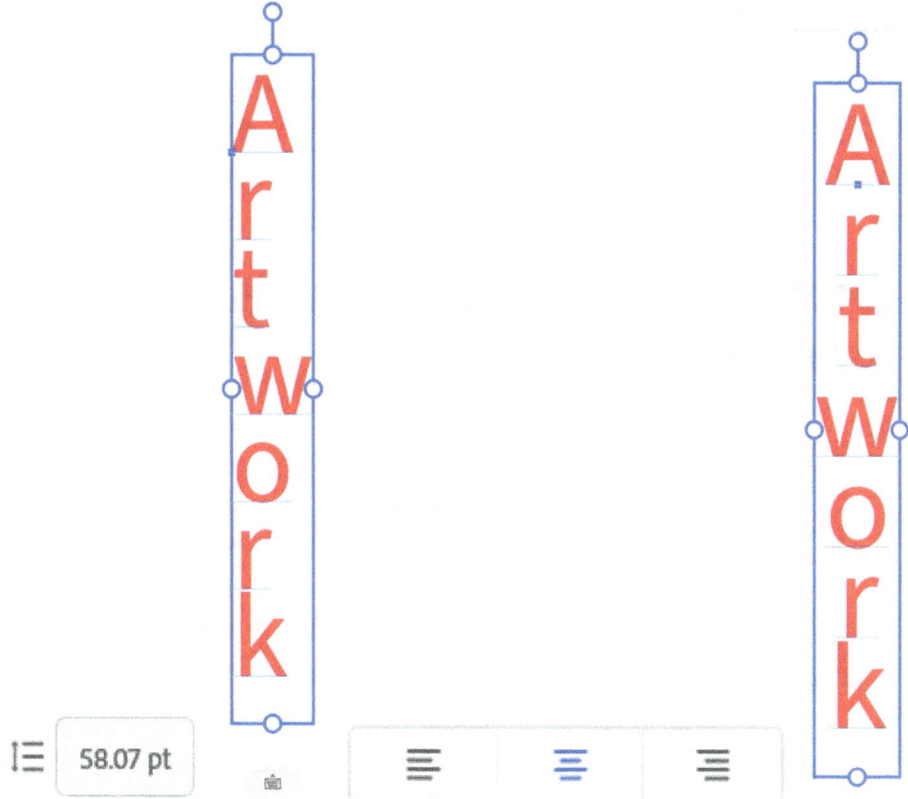

Figure 4-117. *Create some vertical text with the Text tool layer properties*

If you have more complex font designs, I recommend doing the layout in Photoshop or, later, in a layout application like Illustrator or InDesign once you have exported your files. Exporting a Fresco file will be reviewed in Chapter 9.

Tip Font layers in Fresco can be edited with the Move and Transform tools; however, they will need to be converted to a Pixel or Vector layer first. I will discuss this conversion more in Chapter 5.

CHAPTER 4 EXPLORING THE WORKSPACE OF FRESCO AND ITS TOOLS: PART 2

Note on Troubleshooting Missing Fonts

If a font is not available in Fresco document, it may substitute the font with the closest matching font until you have altered or updated it in your file. This is done using Adobe Fonts and the Creative Cloud Desktop app as described in the earlier link.

Eyedropper Tool (I): Single and Multiple Color Eyedropper

The Eyedropper tool is good for acquiring single or multiple colors at once. For the single color Eyedropper, make sure that setting is selected in the Toolbar when you click on colors on a specific layer. The area is magnified and the color will be added to the color chip. Refer to Figure 4-118.

Figure 4-118. *Use the Toolbar Eyedropper tool to add a single color to the color chip*

Fresco will then jump back to the last previously used tool like a selection, shape, or pixel brush, and you can begin to fill or paint in that color now that it is in the color chip, which I will talk about again shortly. Refer to Figure 4-119.

CHAPTER 4   EXPLORING THE WORKSPACE OF FRESCO AND ITS TOOLS: PART 2

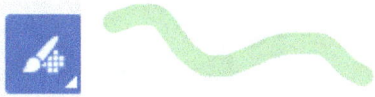

Figure 4-119. *Continue to paint with your brush with the new color*

For multicolor options, click on the setting for the multicolor Eyedropper in the Toolbar. This adds a multicolor chip, you can again click on your artwork, and you can begin to paint in several colors with your brush. Refer to Figure 4-120.

Figure 4-120. *Create a multicolor chip for painting with your desired brush using the Eyedropper tool*

Tip Use the Touch shortcut primary circle when enabled (double-click) which can be used with the solid or multicolor Eyedropper as well. Refer to Figure 4-121.

Figure 4-121. *The Eyedropper tool with the Touch shortcut enabled*

Altering the Color Chip (RGB, HSB) Solid and Multicolor Swatches

In Chapter 3, as you worked with brushes, you looked at the color chip as well as the color wheel to be used when you need to alter the color or opacity as you paint. You can either work with the HSB slider or RGB slider as you work with the single solid color before painting with your brush or filling a selection as you did in this chapter. Refer to Figure 4-122.

CHAPTER 4   EXPLORING THE WORKSPACE OF FRESCO AND ITS TOOLS: PART 2

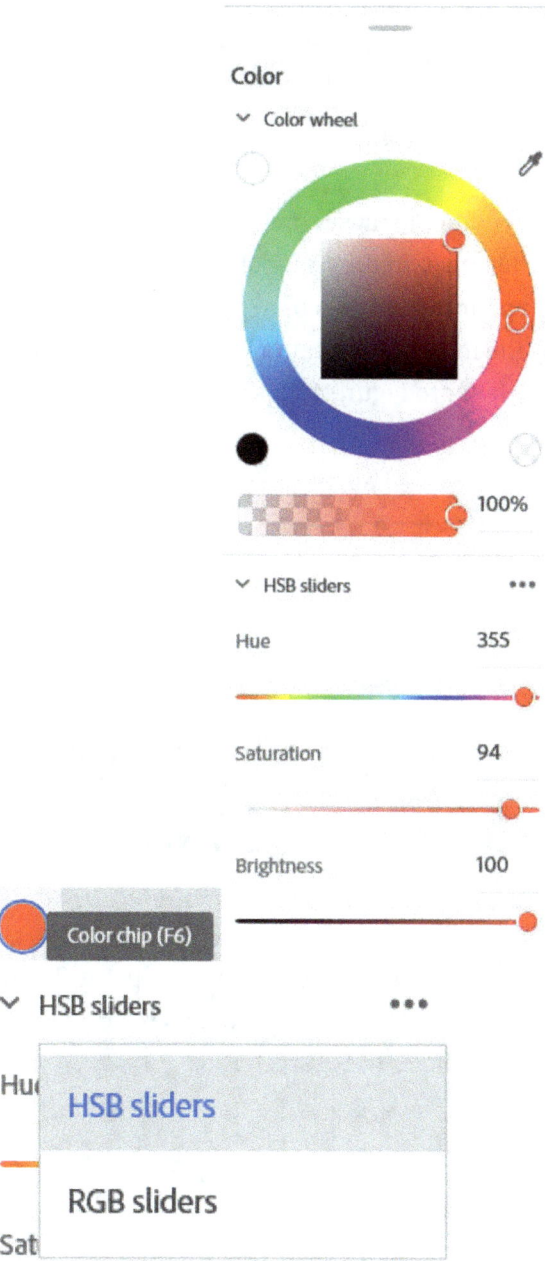

Figure 4-122. *Solid color chip and the color wheel with slider options*

However, as mentioned in this chapter, you have to use the Eyedropper tool to capture a multicolored swatch. But you will not see that color initially in the panel area but only as a chip preview. Refer to Figure 4-123.

CHAPTER 4   EXPLORING THE WORKSPACE OF FRESCO AND ITS TOOLS: PART 2

Figure 4-123. *Multicolor color chip*

To access that recent multicolor swatch, if you need to use it again while working in the file, you will need to locate it. In the Color chip panel, go to the All tab and then click the Recents color tab. Remember the All colors will list all colors in the libraries, but the Recents tab will display the multicolor swatch if it was recently created and used as a chip that you can access. Refer to Figure 4-124.

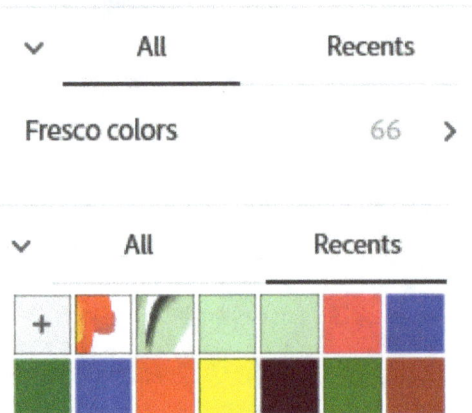

Figure 4-124. *Access the Recents tab for multicolor chips*

You can then select that chip again and continue to paint. Then, you can also use your HSB sliders and alter the multicolor chip's colors to add more interest to your design and continue to paint. Refer to Figure 4-125.

Chapter 4   Exploring the Workspace of Fresco and its Tools: Part 2

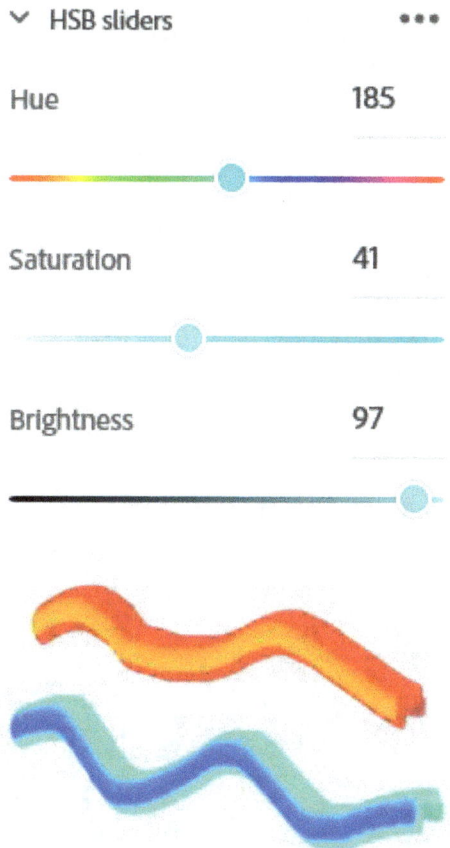

Figure 4-125. *Use the Color panel to access the HSB sliders to alter the color and begin to paint*

However, note that for the Pixel brushes settings, Color dynamics may be disabled when working with a multicolor swatch. Review this setting in Chapter 3.

More information about color in Fresco can be found at the following link:

https://helpx.adobe.com/fresco/using/colors.html

Note that all Live and most Pixel brushes support multicolor painting except for Marker, and Vector brushes.

CHAPTER 4 EXPLORING THE WORKSPACE OF FRESCO AND ITS TOOLS: PART 2

Project: Add Some Colors from the Creative Cloud Library Using Photoshop or Illustrator

Photoshop and Illustrator can be used to add individual color swatches or themes (five colors maximum) to your library if you need them for another Fresco project. In Photoshop, you can drag swatches from your Swatches panel into the Libraries panel, and they will be added as colors that can be accessed in Fresco. Refer to Figure 4-126.

Figure 4-126. *Photoshop Swatches and Libraries panels*

With Illustrator, however, you can select the Swatch or Swatch Group (color theme) with a maximum of five colors, and from the Swatches panel, click "Add selected Swatches and Swatch Groups to my current Library," and they will be added as well. Refer to Figure 4-127.

CHAPTER 4   EXPLORING THE WORKSPACE OF FRESCO AND ITS TOOLS: PART 2

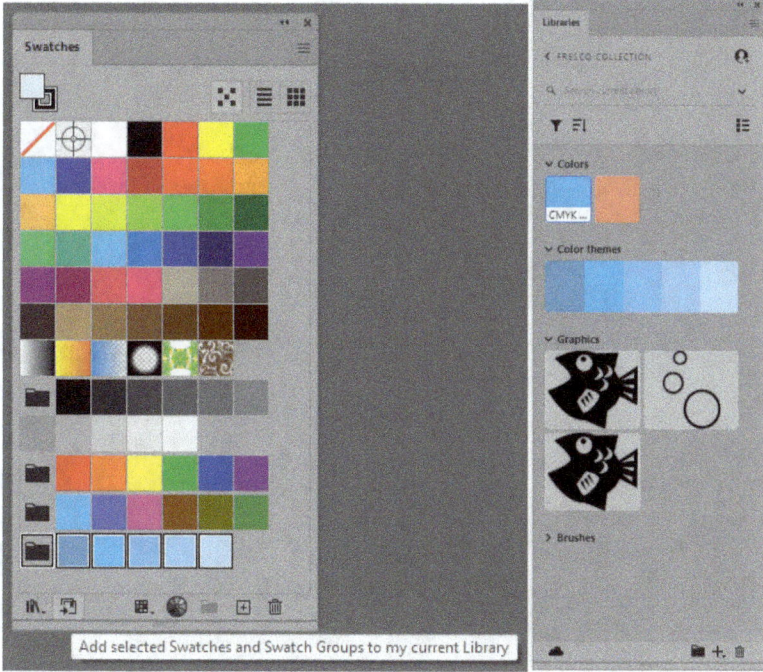

Figure 4-127. *Illustrator Swatches and Libraries panels*

Refer to the earlier section in Chapter 3 if you need to review Creative Cloud Library creation.

In Photoshop, another way to capture your colors from a selected layer via the library is using the Library "Extract from Image" Capture app under the menu plus (+) icon to add elements. To follow along, use the File ➤ Open and locate **Extract_ColorsThemes.psd.** Refer to Figure 4-128.

CHAPTER 4   EXPLORING THE WORKSPACE OF FRESCO AND ITS TOOLS: PART 2

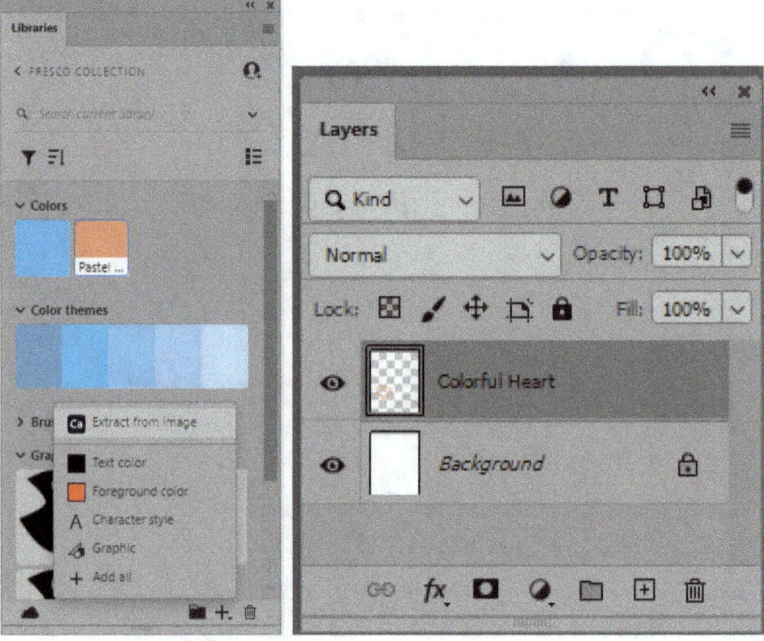

Figure 4-128. *Photoshop Libraries panel Extract from Image option*

This time, choose the Color Themes tab. The theme is created from colors on a previous selected layer, and you can choose to alter them using the plus circles on the left, choose a Color Mood from the list, and current swatch colors labels are listed on the right. Refer to Figure 4-129.

CHAPTER 4   EXPLORING THE WORKSPACE OF FRESCO AND ITS TOOLS: PART 2

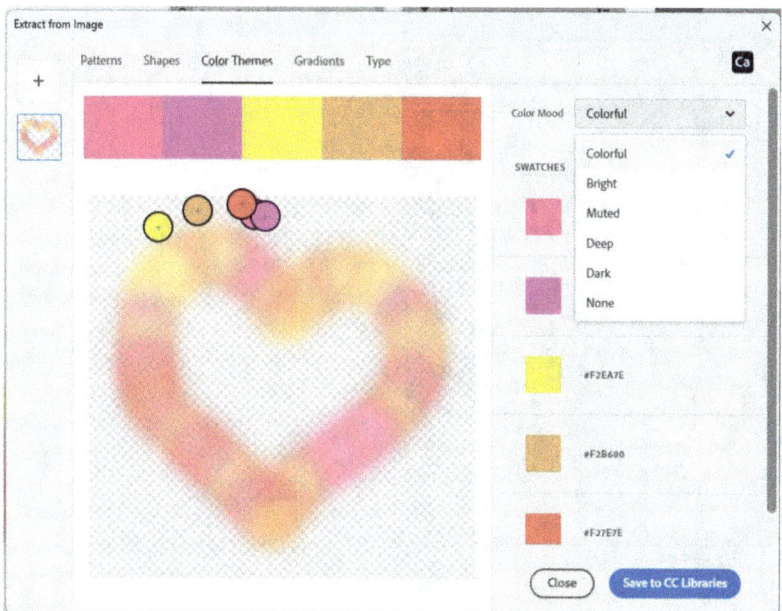

Figure 4-129. *Extract from Image dialog box*

Click the Save to CC Libraries button if you want to add these colors as a theme to your library. Click the Close button to exit when you are done with the Extract from Image dialog box. The color theme can now be viewed in the Libraries panel, and then, you can return to Fresco, and these colors swatches are now available in the color chip panel under the All tab when that library is selected. Refer to Figure 4-130.

295

CHAPTER 4 EXPLORING THE WORKSPACE OF FRESCO AND ITS TOOLS: PART 2

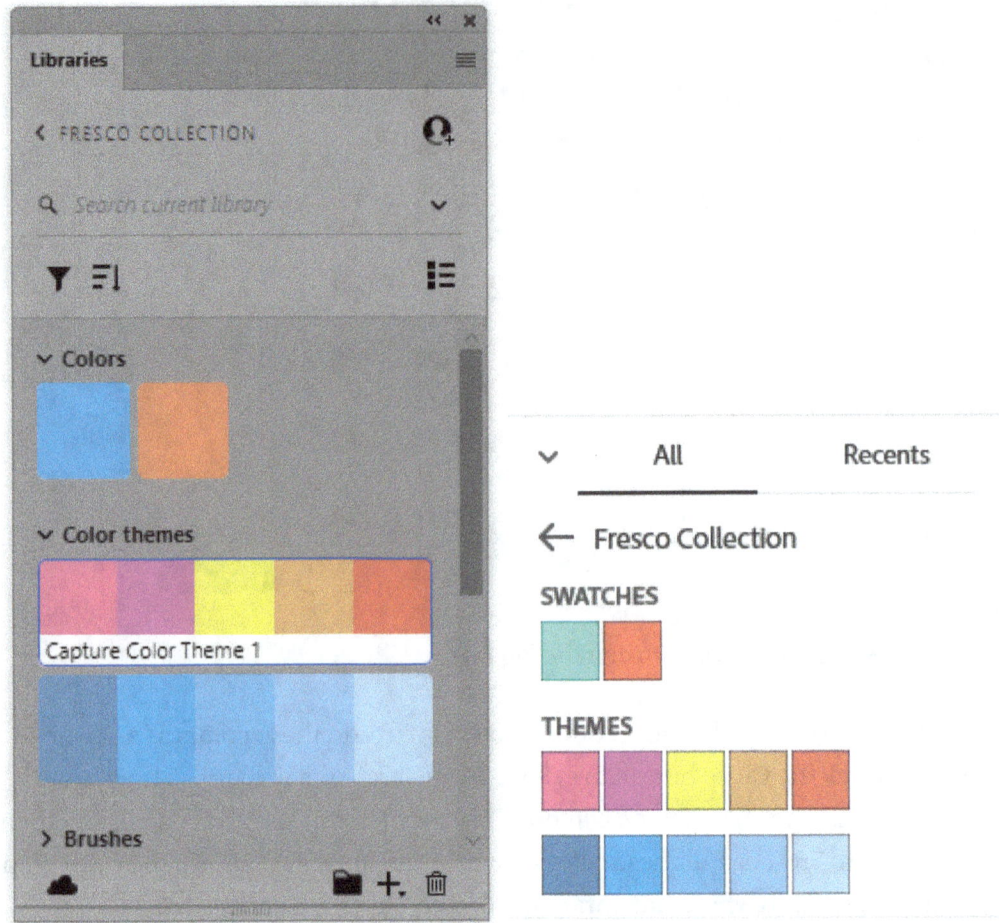

Figure 4-130. *Themes are added to the Photoshop Libraries panel and then available as colors in Fresco*

Remember for InDesign users, you can also use the CC Libraries Panel (+) Extract from Image Capture app to acquire Color Themes as well. Refer to Figure 4-131.

CHAPTER 4 EXPLORING THE WORKSPACE OF FRESCO AND ITS TOOLS: PART 2

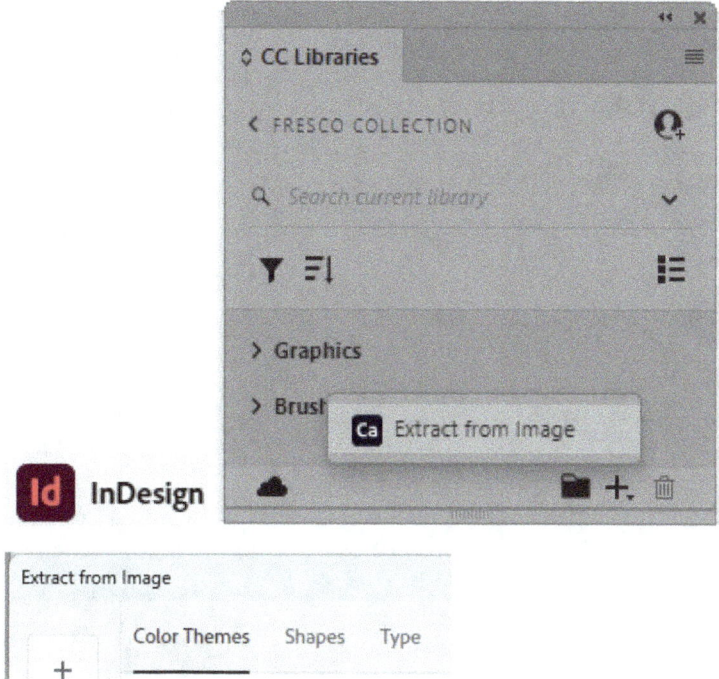

Figure 4-131. *InDesign CC Libraries panel and Extract from Image dialog box for Color Themes*

If you want the exact library file for the shapes and colors that I used, you can import **Fresco Collection_shapes_colors.cclibs**.

Note Currently, Fresco does not allow you to import Gradient Swatches via the Libraries, and for now, you must work with your multicolor color chips.

Overview of Place Tool for Graphics

The Place tool is the last main tool in the Toolbar panel. Its purpose is to place a graphic from either a camera, file, or one of your Creative Cloud Libraries Graphic Assets (not Capture Shapes). In this chapter, we will not go into any detail on this topic but will discuss this Place tool in more detail in Chapter 7. Refer to Figure 4-132.

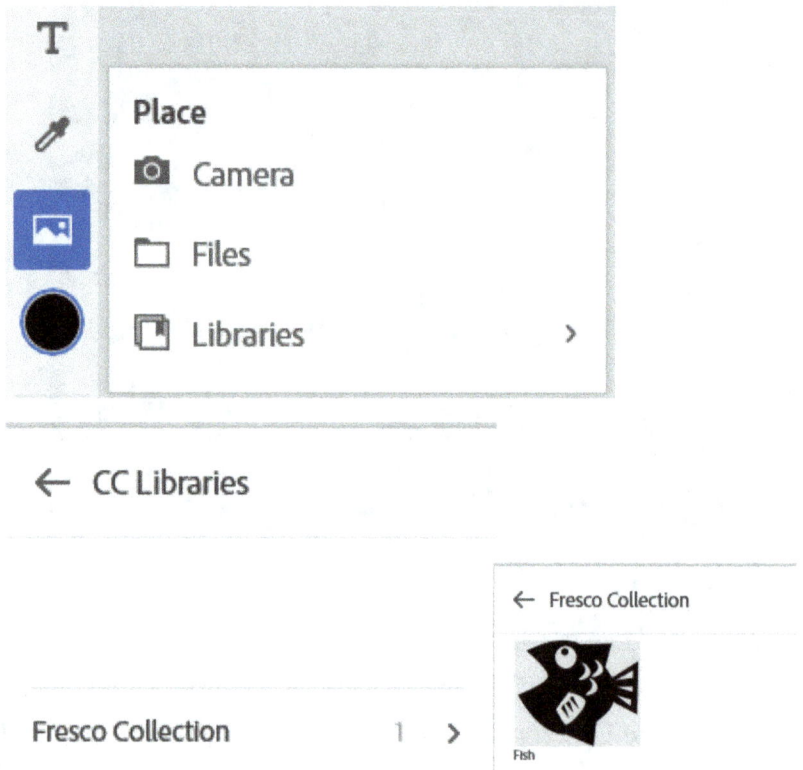

Figure 4-132. *Toolbar Place tool options and CC Libraries*

File ➤ Save any Photoshop files that you may have open at this point.

Project: Practicing with Your Brushes and Selections on a Single Layer

In this project, you will continue to work with the brushes and other tools that you have used to paint with, to create different brush effects. Use the skills you have gained in the previous Chapter 3 and now in this chapter.

Either use the Creative Cloud Desktop Files ➤ Files area or from Fresco Home page ➤ Import and Open to open and work with the file **SeascapeBackgroundStart.psd.** As mentioned in Chapter 2, upon upload into Your files or Recent area, it will become a (.psdc). Refer to Figure 4-133.

CHAPTER 4 EXPLORING THE WORKSPACE OF FRESCO AND ITS TOOLS: PART 2

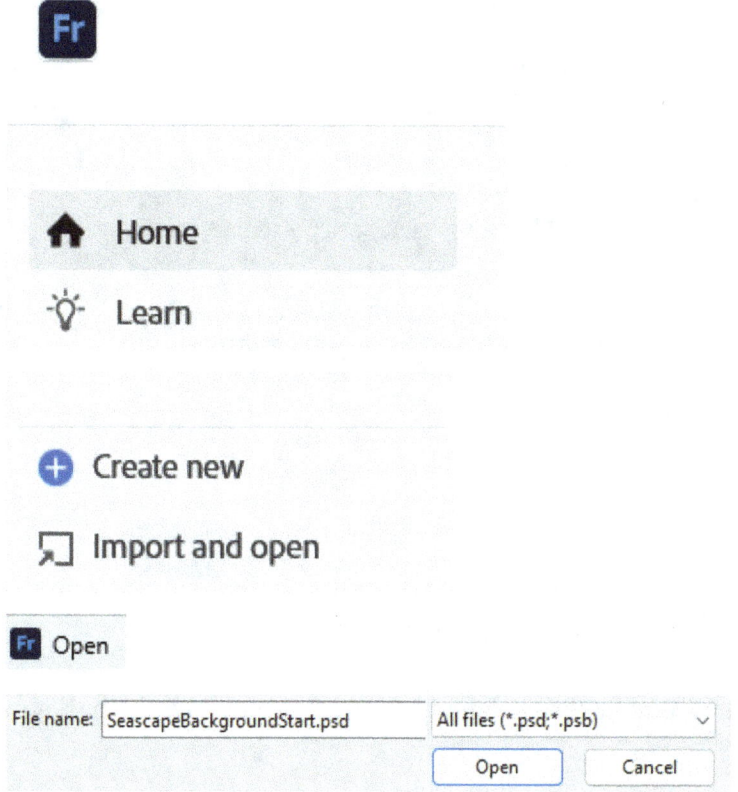

Figure 4-133. *Open a project file in Fresco*

Locate your file, select it, and click Open. Refer to Figure 4-133.

If you get a warning message that says your Photoshop layers are preserved, click OK as the background was edited in Photoshop. Refer to Figure 4-134.

CHAPTER 4　EXPLORING THE WORKSPACE OF FRESCO AND ITS TOOLS: PART 2

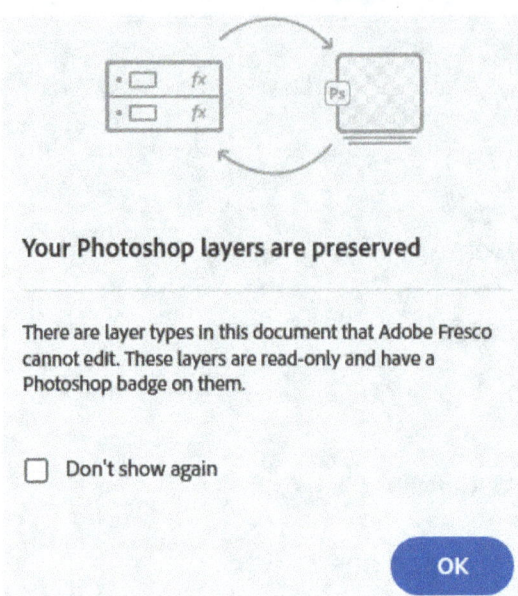

Figure 4-134. *Fresco layer warning message*

The file is now open with a default blank Pixel layer above the background. Refer to Figure 4-135.

CHAPTER 4   EXPLORING THE WORKSPACE OF FRESCO AND ITS TOOLS: PART 2

Artwork by Jennifer Harder

Figure 4-135. *Artwork opened in Fresco with two layers, with the blank pixel layer selected*

In this case, we are working with a background layer of a sketch that I scanned and edited for the purpose of adding painterly effects over using the Fresco paint brushes. For now, try using your various brushes to paint over the image on the blank Pixel layer. On the Pixel layer, use the following brush types such as Pixel, Live, Eraser, and Smudge. Refer to Figure 4-136.

301

CHAPTER 4   EXPLORING THE WORKSPACE OF FRESCO AND ITS TOOLS: PART 2

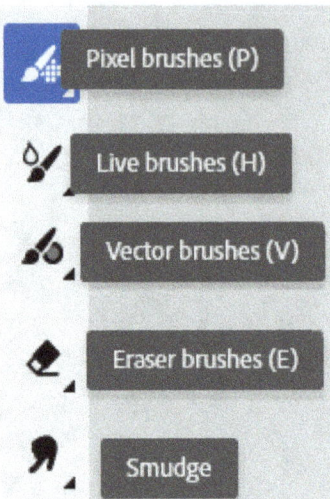

Figure 4-136. Fresco Toolbar brush options

If you do decide to use Vector brushes that will create a new additional vector layer, make sure you select the appropriate layer when you work with a specific brush. If you get stuck, we will review layers in Chapter 5 in more detail. Refer to Figure 4-137.

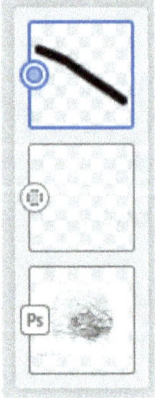

Figure 4-137. Various layers are added based on brushes used

For this project, in this case, I used pixel Mixer brushes, then experimented with some brushes such as Blocky mixer and Brushy mixer, and varied the size of the brush as I worked over the sketch. Refer to Figures 4-138 and 4-139.

CHAPTER 4   EXPLORING THE WORKSPACE OF FRESCO AND ITS TOOLS: PART 2

Figure 4-138. *Painting on the blank layer with brushes*

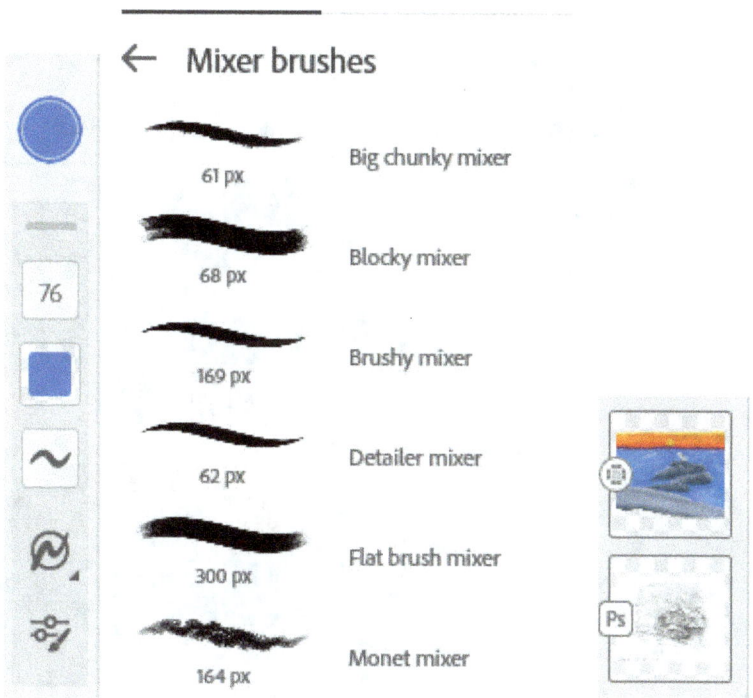

Figure 4-139. *Pixel mixer brushes used to create the artwork*

When I made a mistake, I used my undo icon right away, but I also used my Eraser tool to remove some brush strokes as required. I sure wish that painting in reality had an undo button! Refer to Figure 4-140.

303

CHAPTER 4   EXPLORING THE WORKSPACE OF FRESCO AND ITS TOOLS: PART 2

Figure 4-140. *Use a combination of the undo key and your Eraser brushes if you make a mistake*

As I paint, I can continue to change my colors by accessing the Color wheel panel via the color chip. As you build up more colors, they appear in the Recents area as you work. Refer to Figure 4-141.

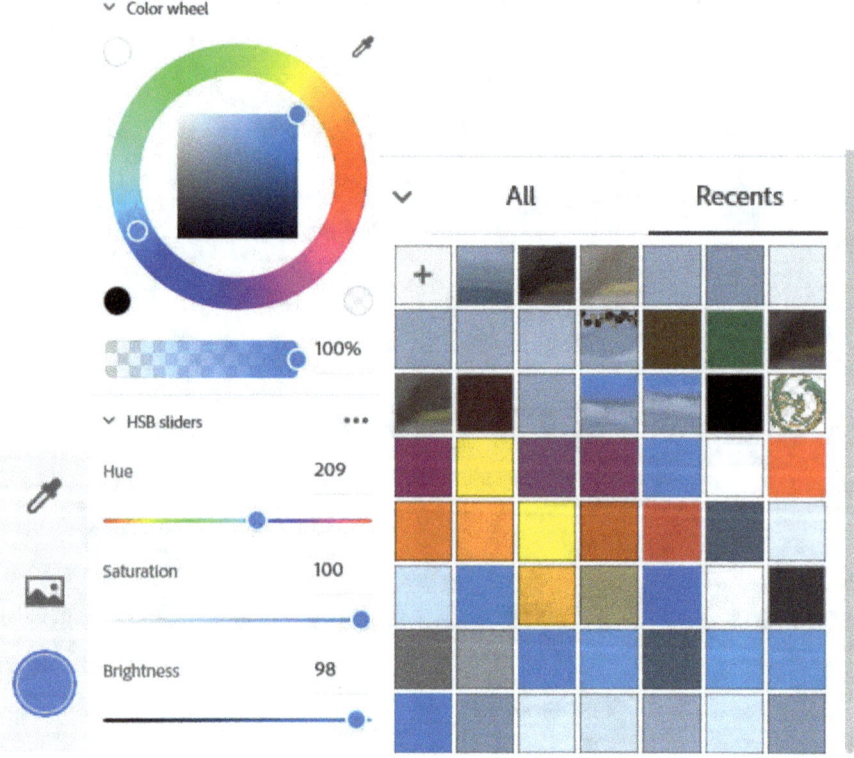

Figure 4-141. *Color chip with a current color and colors that I recently used while painting*

As well, you can use this in conjunction with your Eyedropper tool so that you can return to your current brush quickly. Refer to Figure 4-141.

CHAPTER 4   EXPLORING THE WORKSPACE OF FRESCO AND ITS TOOLS: PART 2

The colors I focused on near the water and rocks were blues, grays, and purples. The seagull had some gray and white but also had some yellow in his beak and legs. Looking at images online of the seaside may help you get the colors you want, as you are in this case dealing with a black and white sketch and not original photos as we will look at in Chapter 7. The water moves around the rocks in various ways causing variations in color, which is ideal for a Mixer brush to create highlights and shadows. Refer to Figure 4-138.

To blur areas, I can use a combination of my Smudge brushes tool but also the Transform Liquify tools as well. However, in this case, I want to keep my brush strokes as authentic as possible, so I did not use those tools for this project.

Remember, if you need to prevent paint from going beyond a boundary, then use one of the Selection tools such the Paint selection when you needed to create a tight area around the seagull, as well as by Contextual Task bar to select, invert, or deselect. Using smaller brush sizes or reducing the flow of the brush can help as well. Refer to Figure 4-142.

Figure 4-142. *Use a Paint selection tool and your Contextual Task bar to create the ideal selection before you paint again*

Other kinds of selection such as Rectangular may be used to differentiate between the horizon of water and sky. Refer to Figure 4-143.

CHAPTER 4 EXPLORING THE WORKSPACE OF FRESCO AND ITS TOOLS: PART 2

Figure 4-143. *Use the Rectangular selection to create a sky area*

In the sky, I then added colors of whites, yellows, oranges, reds, and purples for mountains and then inverted the selection to add some shadow in the water of those mountains. Refer to Figure 4-144.

CHAPTER 4 EXPLORING THE WORKSPACE OF FRESCO AND ITS TOOLS: PART 2

Figure 4-144. Invert a selection when you want to paint in the outside of the previous location

You could also continue and add an Ellipse selection to create a sun, painting yellow within, and then back to some purple to cover it partly by the mountains. Refer to Figure 4-145.

CHAPTER 4   EXPLORING THE WORKSPACE OF FRESCO AND ITS TOOLS: PART 2

Figure 4-145. *Using an elliptical selection to paint the sun and then adding color over to blend with the mountains*

You can then Deselect the selection using the Contextual Task bar. Refer to Figure 4-145.

CHAPTER 4   EXPLORING THE WORKSPACE OF FRESCO AND ITS TOOLS: PART 2

To avoid altering the brush strokes too much, at this point with other brushes, in my case, I created a new layer to add a brush stroke of stones along the beach. The brush I used was Comics ➤ Krackle. Then, I created a multicolor swatch with my Eyedropper tool and adjusted the HSB sliders as required, varying the browns and grays and adjusting brush properties, such as size and scatter to get the type of shapes I wanted. Refer to Figure 4-146 and Figure 4-147.

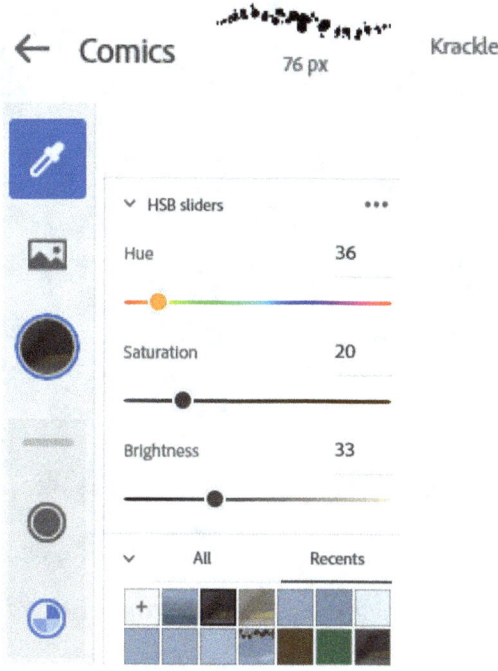

Figure 4-146. *Choosing a brush and then creating a multicolor swatch with the Eyedropper and color chip HSB sliders*

CHAPTER 4   EXPLORING THE WORKSPACE OF FRESCO AND ITS TOOLS: PART 2

Figure 4-147. *Artwork with the layer of beach stones added*

In other instances, you may want to use Shape tools and libraries that you created to add additional designs across the beach, but in that case, you would want to have more layers to control your work so that brush strokes would not blend together. We will look at that and how to add layers with the Vertical Taskbar in Chapter 5 using the plus [+] icon and other actions.

In this case, I did add one more layer to create moss/algae on the rocks and some grasses; I used the Mixer brushes ➤ Monet mixer. I varied the size of the brush stroke as I worked. Refer to Figure 4-148 and Figure 4-149.

CHAPTER 4　EXPLORING THE WORKSPACE OF FRESCO AND ITS TOOLS: PART 2

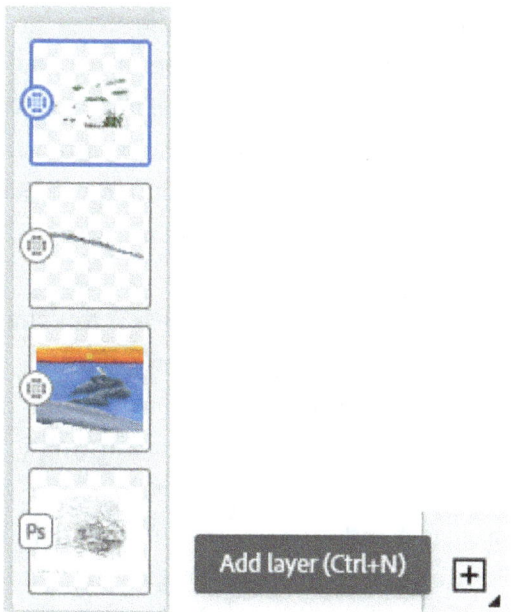

Figure 4-148. *Artwork with multiple pixel layers*

CHAPTER 4 EXPLORING THE WORKSPACE OF FRESCO AND ITS TOOLS: PART 2

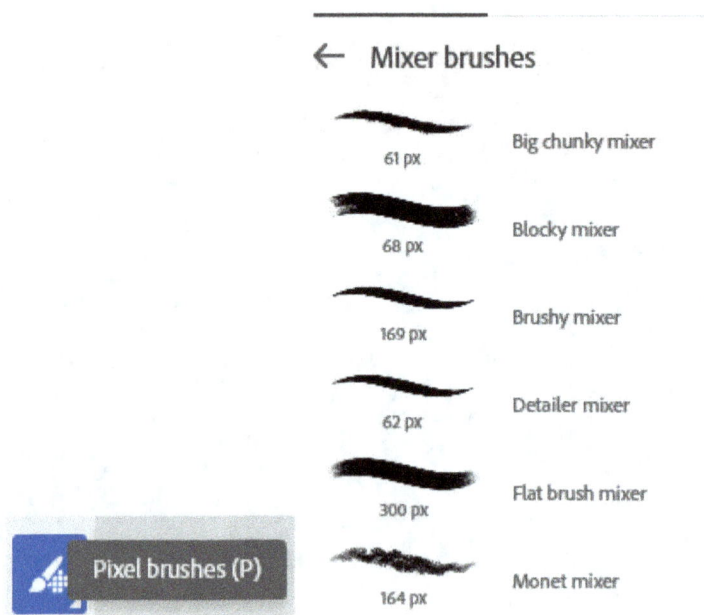

Figure 4-149. *Mixer brush added*

Colors that I focused on were greens and browns and then returned to my Comics ➤ Krackle brush to add a few more stones in the foreground on the new layer.

Take your time to work on the piece as it is said, "Art should not be rushed," and so, just like painting on the canvas in reality, you may want to take several hours or days to work on your artwork. The great thing about Fresco is that the paint dries instantly and you can add as little or as much as you want without worrying that your art will become a muddy mess, and you can always remove a layer or some paint and try again with a different color or brush.

Later, as you progress through the chapters, you may want to return to this chapter with your own images that you upload and review these steps or create variations of the same image with different brush strokes or more layers. For now, just work with one to three layers, and we will look at how multiple layers can enhance your work in the next chapter.

Once this project is complete, you can close it and then upload, open, and review the following file **SeascapeBackgroundFinal.psd** if you need to compare my work to yours as everybody's work will be different. Your paint strokes and color choices will be different than mine. For your work, you can now close and exit the file as well as Fresco and any other Adobe applications like Photoshop or Illustrator you may have open, using File ➤ Exit.

Summary

In this chapter we explored working with color, transformations, liquify options, selections, shapes, and text. We also used the Libraries panel to acquire custom assets from other applications such as Photoshop and Illustrator.

Then, we reviewed what we had learned from previous chapters with a project and created our first landscape painting.

In the next chapter, we will look at, in more detail, multiple layers and their properties that can be found in the right Vertical Taskbar, as well as other panels found there as well.

CHAPTER 5

Working with Layers in Fresco and the Vertical Taskbar

In this chapter, we will continue to work with the previous panels and tools but now will further explore working with the Layer panel to add and alter layers in Fresco. Layers, as you will discover, are not just for keeping your artwork organized but can add additional enhancements to the artwork such as opacity and basic color adjustments. Layers can also be used to create different kinds of masks to block part of the artwork as well. You will also look at other tools that work with layers. In a project, we will then continue to work with the artwork from the previous chapter. Refer to Figure 5-1.

Figure 5-1. Fresco Vertical Taskbar has the following tools and panels available with layers at the top

© Jennifer Harder 2025
J. Harder, *Beginner's Guide to Adobe Fresco*, https://doi.org/10.1007/979-8-8688-1557-7_5

Note The project files for this chapter can be found in the Chapter 5 folder. Refer to the link in the introduction.

Remember, as you work with layers, to zoom in (Ctrl++), zoom out (Ctrl+-), and hold down the spacebar key on your keyboard which becomes the hand tool when you want to move about the canvas without moving the artwork by mistake.

In Fresco, you can continue to work with one of your files you created, or Import and Open my file **Cat_Fish_ReviewLayers_project.psd** to follow along for the topic of layers in this chapter. Use the various layers if you need to try various actions and experiment.

Layer Panel

If you have worked in applications like Photoshop and Illustrator, then you will be familiar with working with layers. Refer to Figure 5-2.

CHAPTER 5   WORKING WITH LAYERS IN FRESCO AND THE VERTICAL TASKBAR

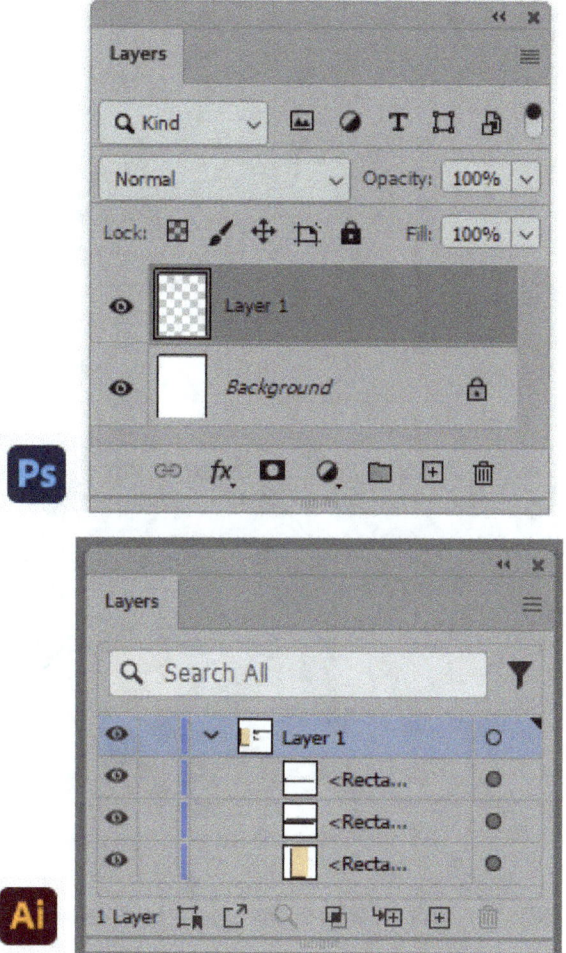

Figure 5-2. *Photoshop Layers panel and Illustrator Layers panel*

Just like in those applications, in Fresco, Layers are essential to keeping parts of your project organized in groups or above each other. Layers that are above each other block areas or pixels below other layers. Layers can be moved and dragged up and down in the Layer panel. Fresco has different kinds of layers as we will look at in this chapter and the remainder of this book. Refer to Figure 5-3.

CHAPTER 5   WORKING WITH LAYERS IN FRESCO AND THE VERTICAL TASKBAR

Figure 5-3. *Fresco Layer panel with images of fish and cat behind a fish bowl*

Some kinds of single layers which will appear with badges that you will look at in this chapter are presented next:

- Background: Often a white blank layer that is the canvas or starting canvas for a Fresco document. A background may have been created in Photoshop. Refer to Figure 5-4.

Figure 5-4. *Example of a background layer*

- Blank Layer: A clear transparent layer which can become either a Pixel or Vector layer depending upon which brushes or shapes you use, as seen in Chapter 3. At some point, you may get a message asking you how you would like to fill this layer before you begin to add a shape as seen in Chapter 4. Refer to Figure 5-5.

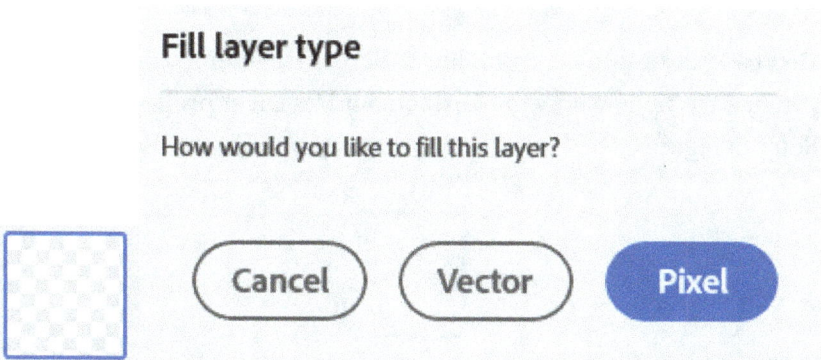

Figure 5-5. *Example of a blank layer with no badge and alert message asking how to fill a shape or selection to create a Vector or Pixel layer*

- Pixel Layer: Similar to a Photoshop layer which you paint on with a Pixel brush or shape, while items on the layer can be scaled or transformed, they can lose quality if downsized and then upsized again. Refer to Figure 5-6.

Figure 5-6. *Example of a Pixel layer*

- Vector Layer: Similar to working with an Illustrator layer, which in this case you paint on with a Vector brush or shape. The Vector brush strokes can be scaled or transformed up and down in size without losing quality. Refer to Figure 5-7.

Figure 5-7. *Example of Vector layer with shape*

- Text Layer: Contains text and letter elements. Refer to Chapter 4 if you need to review how the Text tool and its Layer properties work. Refer to Figure 5-8.

Figure 5-8. *Example of a Text layer*

- Image Layer: Can display imported and placed images. Similar to a Pixel or background layer, we will look at these more in Chapter 7. Refer to Figure 5-9.

Figure 5-9. *Example of an Image layer*

- Motion Layer (Animation): While a badge does not show up directly in the Layer panel on the left as the layer can also be a Pixel layer, you will know that this is an animation layer due to the Contextual Task bar and the icon in the lower right of the layer which we will look at later in Chapter 8. Refer to Figure 5-10.

CHAPTER 5　WORKING WITH LAYERS IN FRESCO AND THE VERTICAL TASKBAR

Figure 5-10. *Example of a Motion layer*

- Ps or Photoshop Layers: These are often merged layers that have been worked on in Photoshop before the file is imported to Fresco, or part of an animation, and you can identify them by the warning that appears when the document is open and the Ps badge. These layers are locked and can only be edited if changed into a flattened Pixel layer or you return to Photoshop. If you left the background layer blank white in Photoshop, it will remain as a separate layer when imported into Fresco. Refer to Figure 5-11.

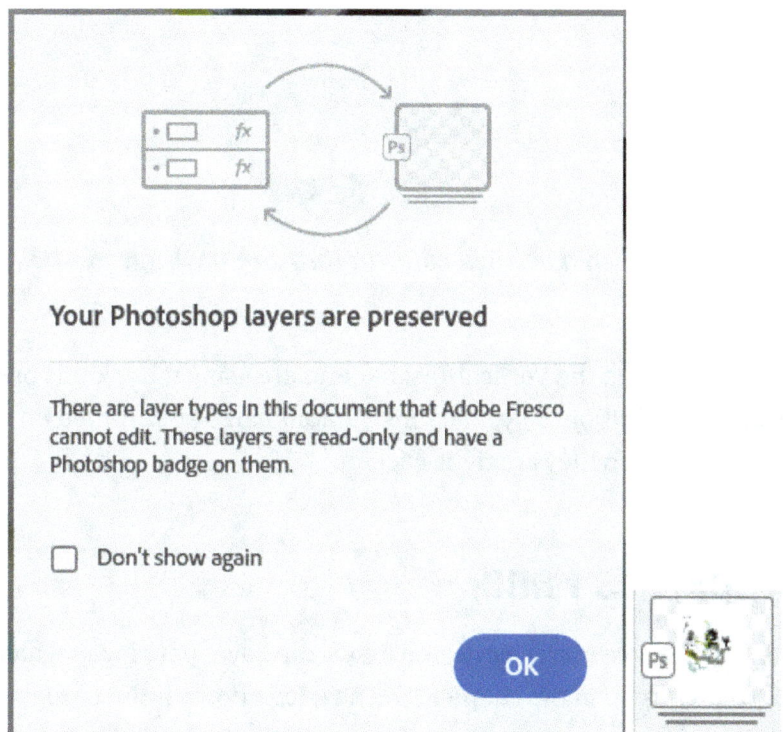

Figure 5-11. *Example of a Photoshop layer and message that appears when Fresco is opened*

321

To display your Layer panel, click that icon in the Vertical Taskbar on the right. Refer to Figure 5-12.

Figure 5-12. *Layer panel icon*

Layers can be dragged up and down with your mouse in the panel so that they can overlap one another in a specific order with the top layer being the most visible and all other layers below with parts hidden. For example, the fish hides part of the cat's face. Refer to Figure 5-13.

Figure 5-13. *Layers are in a vertical column that can be dragged up and down to alter the order*

As we progress through the Vertical Taskbar and are using these kinds of layers, we will also look at some additional layer actions. Actions can be performed on each Layer or with several layers when they are right-clicked.

Layer Properties Panel

In the Vertical Taskbar are several icons; the first is the Layer panel icon which we just looked at and will return to in the chapter. The next icon down is the Layer properties panel; when a layer is selected, this reveals the properties of that layer that you can edit. Refer to Figure 5-14.

CHAPTER 5 WORKING WITH LAYERS IN FRESCO AND THE VERTICAL TASKBAR

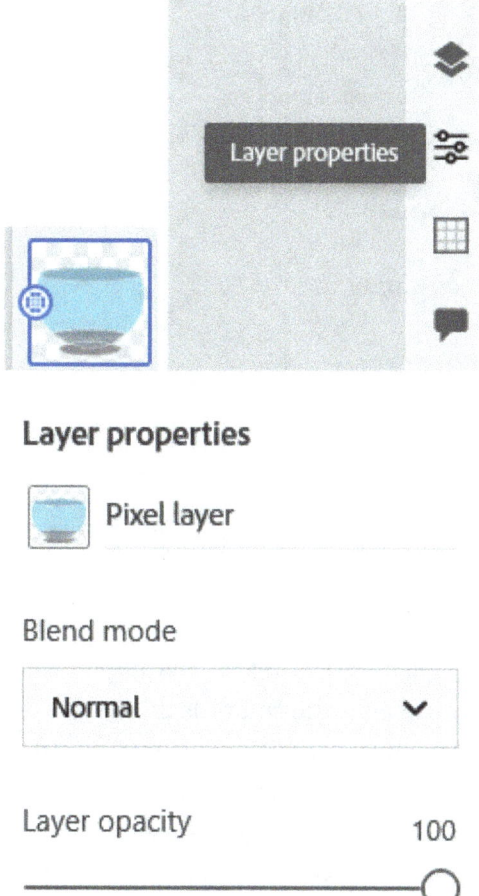

Figure 5-14. Vertical Taskbar accessing the Layer properties panel

Layer Blending Modes and Layer Opacity

For example, if you select a Blank, Pixel, Text layer, or Vector layer, you can in the Layer properties panel change the name of that layer by editing the text next to the image thumbnail. Then, click outside the area to confirm the text. Refer to Figure 5-15.

CHAPTER 5 WORKING WITH LAYERS IN FRESCO AND THE VERTICAL TASKBAR

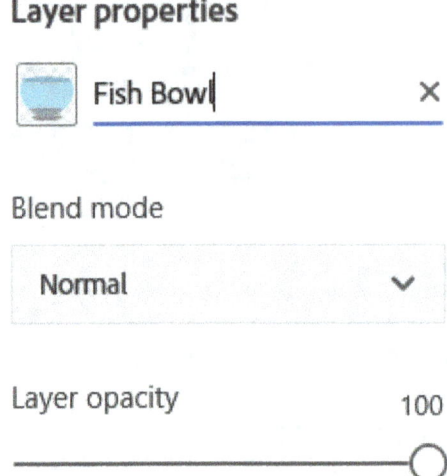

Figure 5-15. Layer properties panel adding a new name to the selected layer

You can also set the following options such as

- Blend Mode: Like the brushes, as seen in Chapter 3, these are the color options that will alter the colors as the layer is overlayed above other pixels of color on an underlying layer. The options include Normal (default), Darken, Multiply, Color burn, Linear burn, Darker color, Lighten, Screen, Color dodge, Linear dodge, Lighter color, Overlay, Soft light, Hard light, Vivid light, Linear light, Pin light, Hard mix, Difference, Exclusion, Subtract, Divide, Hue, Saturation, Color, and Luminosity. Refer to Figure 5-16 and Figure 5-17.

CHAPTER 5 WORKING WITH LAYERS IN FRESCO AND THE VERTICAL TASKBAR

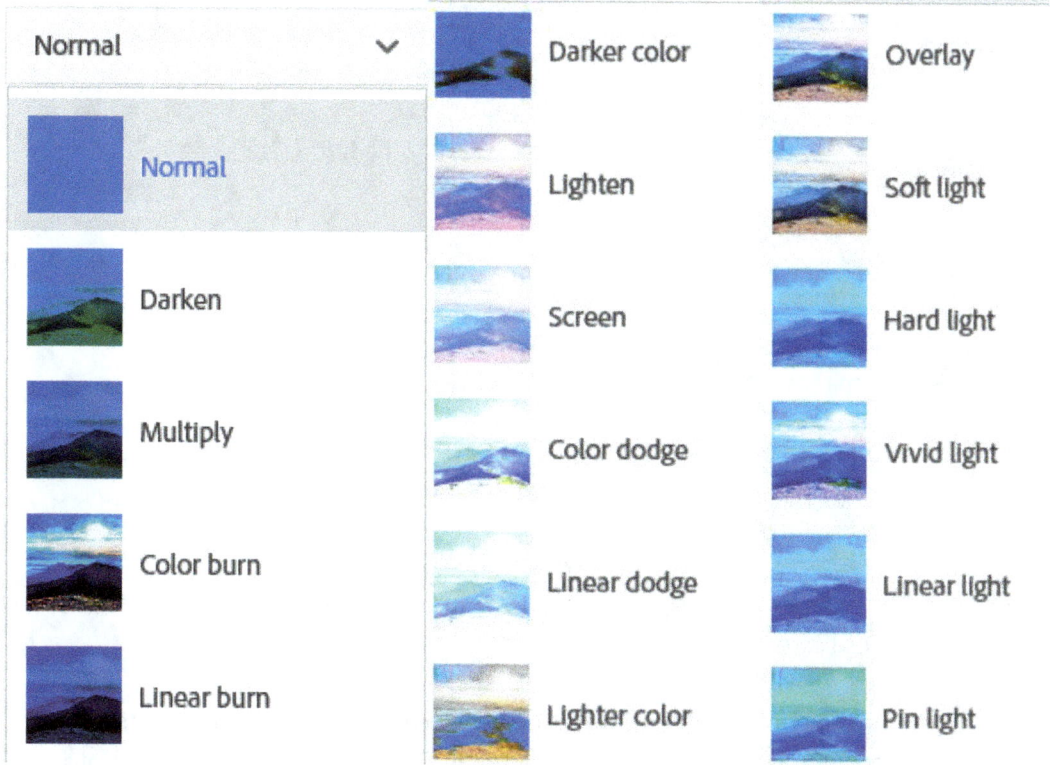

Figure 5-16. *Layer properties; many blend modes can be found in the list*

CHAPTER 5   WORKING WITH LAYERS IN FRESCO AND THE VERTICAL TASKBAR

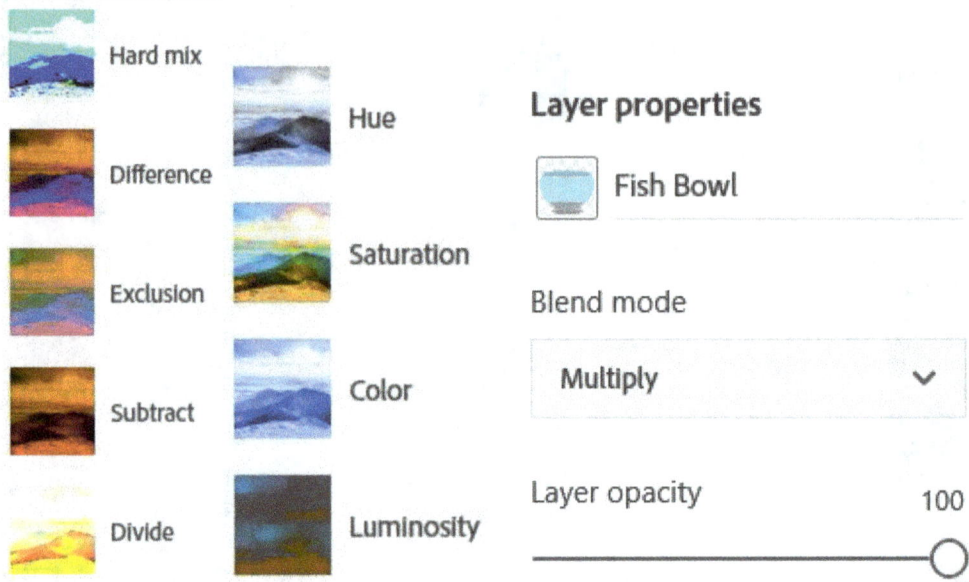

Figure 5-17. *Layer properties; many blend modes can be found in the list and then set in the Layer properties panel*

Next, you can see how the blending of the layers interacts here with the Fish Bowl layer, and in the following link is an example that is similar to what is seen in Photoshop and gives more detail on how each blend works:

https://helpx.adobe.com/photoshop/using/blending-modes.html

Colors from the above layer blend and change as they pass over the lower layers, and this can vary, depending on which blend mode is chosen from the list. Refer to Figures 5-17 and 5-18.

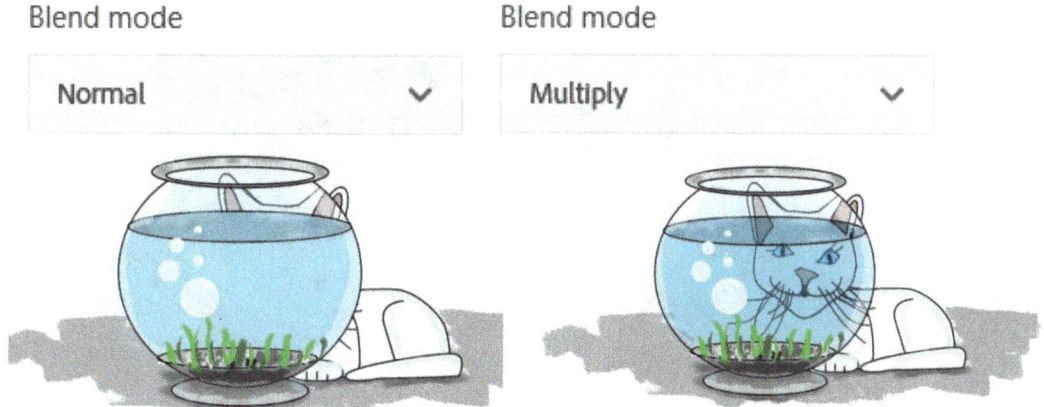

Figure 5-18. *A blend mode of Normal and of Multiply applied to the water in the fish bowl*

Caution In Photoshop, there is one additional layer blend mode called Dissolve. In Fresco, this blend mode is only available for painting with brushes. If you apply this blend mode to a layer prior to importing and opening in Fresco, it will cause the layer to turn into a Photoshop layer, and it will not be editable.

- Layer Opacity: Controls the opacity/transparency of the layer. By default, it is set to 100%, but the range is 0–100%. You can change it as you move the slider. In a way, we can think of opacity in art much like a sponge soaking up some of the color, based on what setting you choose, but in Fresco's case, you can instantly add it back by moving the slider. Refer to Figure 5-19 and Figure 5-20.

CHAPTER 5 WORKING WITH LAYERS IN FRESCO AND THE VERTICAL TASKBAR

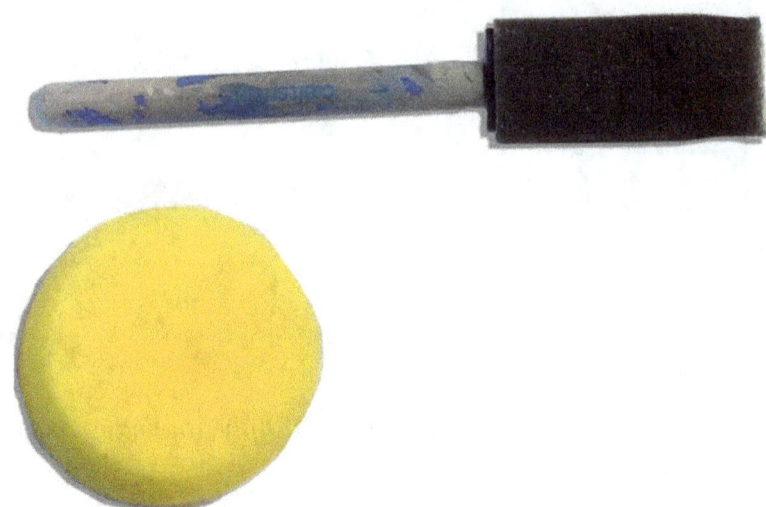

Figure 5-19. *Sponges are often used in Painting to draw up extra moisture and lighten an image*

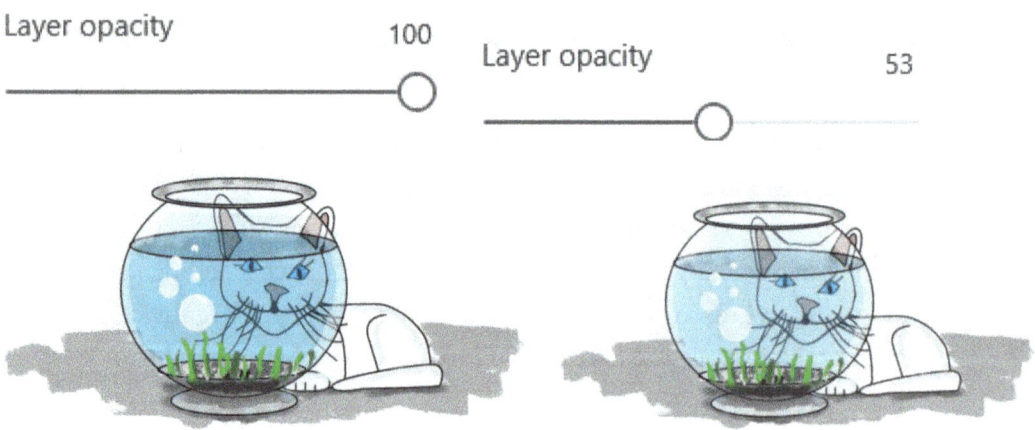

Figure 5-20. *Fresco used the Layer opacity slider to lighten or make more transparent a layer by lowering the opacity*

Opacity only alters the transparency on that layer, and so items behind the affected layer will show through. However, in combination with a blend mode, this can also alter the transparency effect as well. Different layers can have different levels of transparency as they overlap. Refer to Figure 5-21.

CHAPTER 5 WORKING WITH LAYERS IN FRESCO AND THE VERTICAL TASKBAR

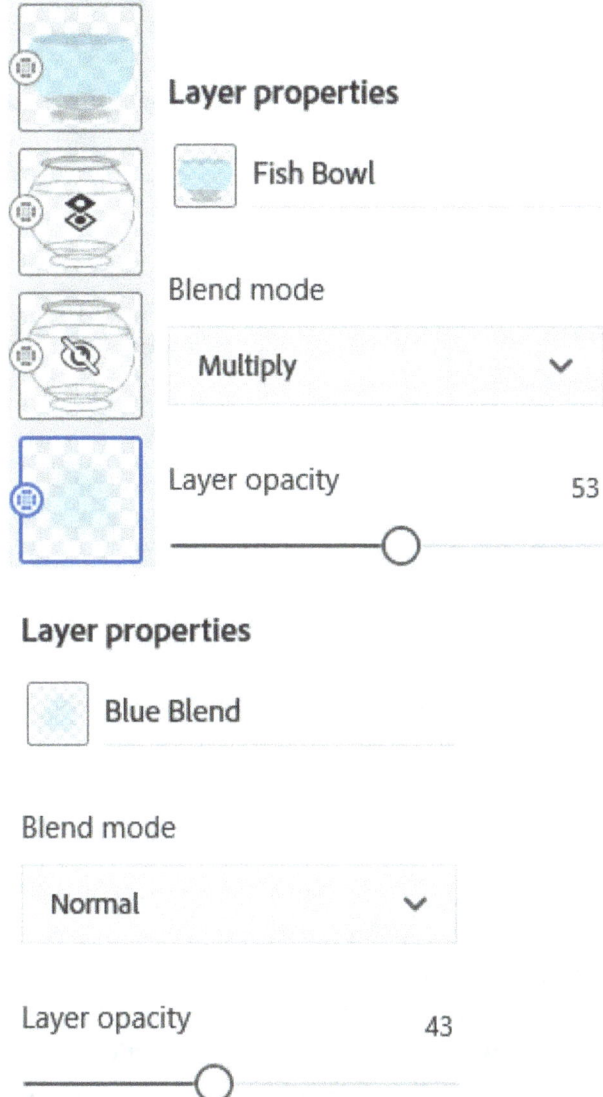

Figure 5-21. *Layer properties for various layers with different blend modes and opacities*

However, as with the text layer mentioned in Chapter 4, you can also set other text-related properties such as font kind, font style, font size, line spacing, letter spacing, all caps, small caps, and alignment (left, center, right). Refer back to that chapter if you need to review those properties again. Refer to Figure 5-22.

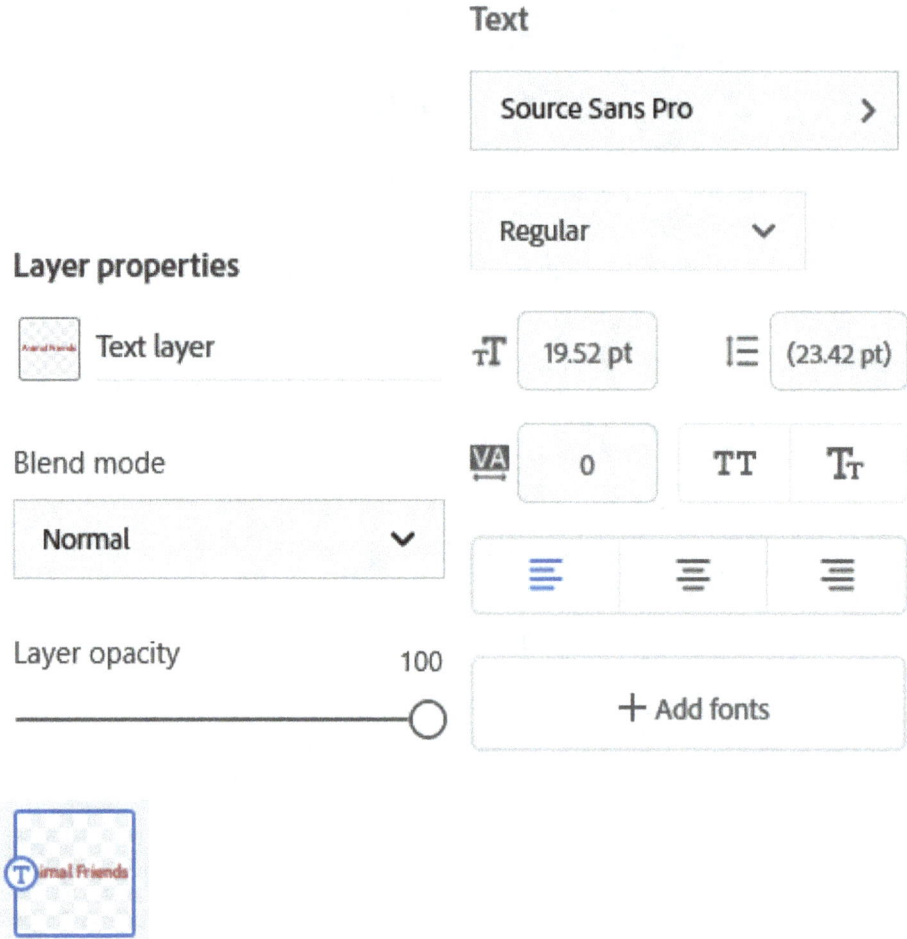

Figure 5-22. *Layer properties for text*

Later, in this chapter, we will look at some more properties for Appearance layers and look at how they interact with layers below them. In Chapter 8, we will look at Animation properties.

Precision Tool

The next icon in the Vertical Taskbar is the Precision tool which is ideal for when you need to work with a grid, as we'll see in more detail in Chapter 6.

Grids are good for alignment of shapes, as we saw earlier in Chapter 3, as well as creating perspective grids for your artwork projects. Refer to Figure 5-23.

CHAPTER 5 WORKING WITH LAYERS IN FRESCO AND THE VERTICAL TASKBAR

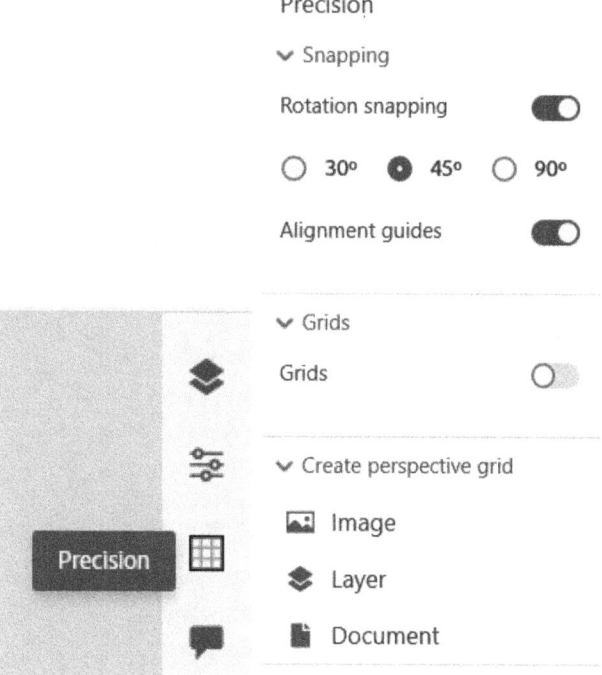

Figure 5-23. Precision tool and its panel

Comments Tool

The Comments tool allows you to add comments to your document which is ideal if you are working in a group setting where sharing and collaboration are important. In this book, you are working alone so you will not be using this tool in the book. Refer to Figure 5-24.

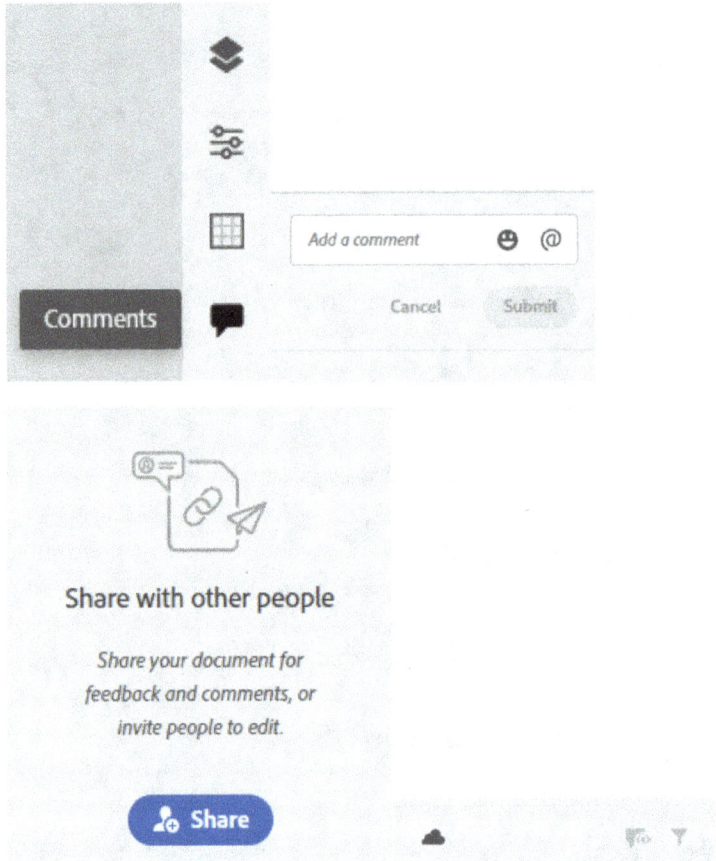

Figure 5-24. *Comments tool and its panel*

Adding and Editing Pixel and Vector Layers with Layer Actions and Icons

Returning to the Layer panel, your Fresco document will have various layers for your brush's strokes, images, and text. As you work with the layers and their properties, you will then encounter different possible actions that you will use to alter or move the layer. Here are some easy to find additional actions that you can use from the Vertical Taskbar and when you click the Layer tool and reveal the panel.

CHAPTER 5 WORKING WITH LAYERS IN FRESCO AND THE VERTICAL TASKBAR

- Add Layer (Ctrl+N) (Vector or Pixel): This plus icon adds a blank layer that you can then paint on with either a Vector or Pixel brush. However, optionally, you can hold down the mouse key on the icon and then select from the list, Pixel layer or Vector layer, so that you have the chosen layer kind right away. This then adds the badge to that layer. Refer to Figure 5-25.

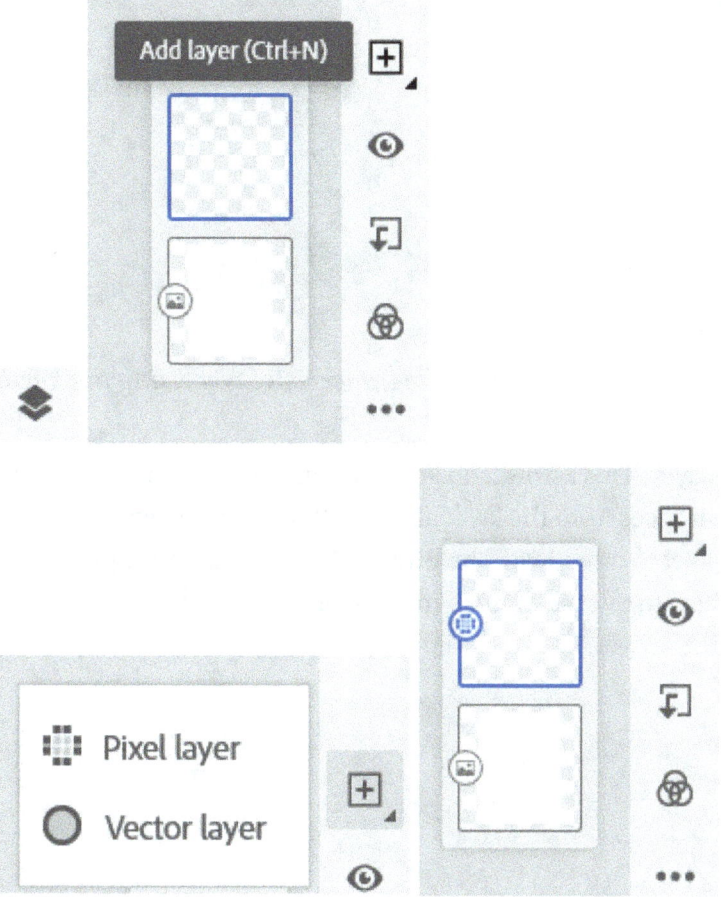

Figure 5-25. *Layers panel adding a new layer of either Pixel or Vector using the Vertical Taskbar. In this case, pixel was chosen*

- Layer Visible (Ctrl+,): This action eye toggles the layer's visibility on or off. When a layer is off, you cannot edit it, and it is hidden on the canvas. Refer to Figure 5-26.

333

CHAPTER 5 WORKING WITH LAYERS IN FRESCO AND THE VERTICAL TASKBAR

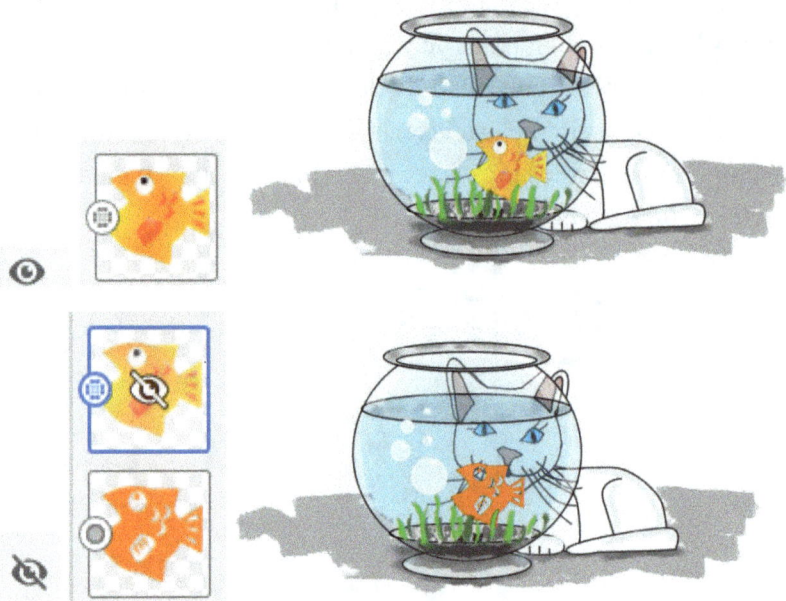

Figure 5-26. *Showing and hiding the upper fish layer using the Vertical Taskbar*

- Clip Layer: This arrow icon applies some text, brush designs, or appearances from the layer above to that layer below; it will not apply the effect to other layers below that. We will explore clipping masks and how to release them in more detail later in the chapter. Refer to Figure 5-27.

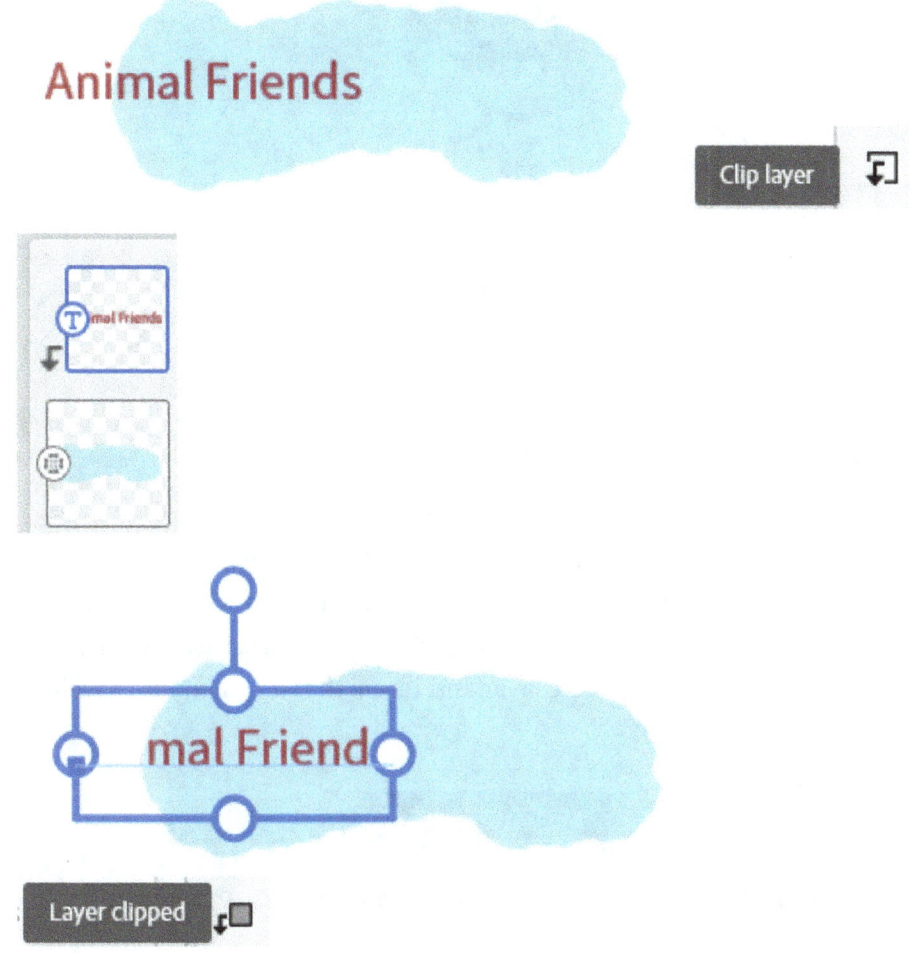

Figure 5-27. *Text on a layer being clipped to an image using the Vertical Taskbar*

- Appearances: This allows you to access special kinds of color adjustment layers that we will look at later in this chapter in more detail. Refer to Figure 5-28.

CHAPTER 5   WORKING WITH LAYERS IN FRESCO AND THE VERTICAL TASKBAR

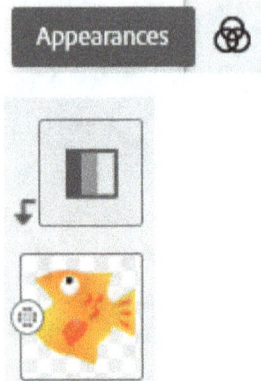

Figure 5-28. *Adding Appearances or Adjustment layers to the Layer panel as well as clipping actions*

- More Layer Options or Actions Ellipsis (…): This provides a pop-up menu, based on the kind of layer on which you are working. These various added additional actions, likewise, can be accessed when you right-click on a specific layer and reveal the same actions as well. Refer to Figure 5-29.

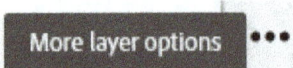

Figure 5-29. *Using the Vertical Taskbar to access More layer actions*

Let's look at that area next.

More Layer Options and Actions

Select a Pixel layer for example. Then, in the Vertical Taskbar, click now the ellipsis (…) or right-click the layer to reveal the pop-up menu and review the Layer actions selected. Refer to Figure 5-30.

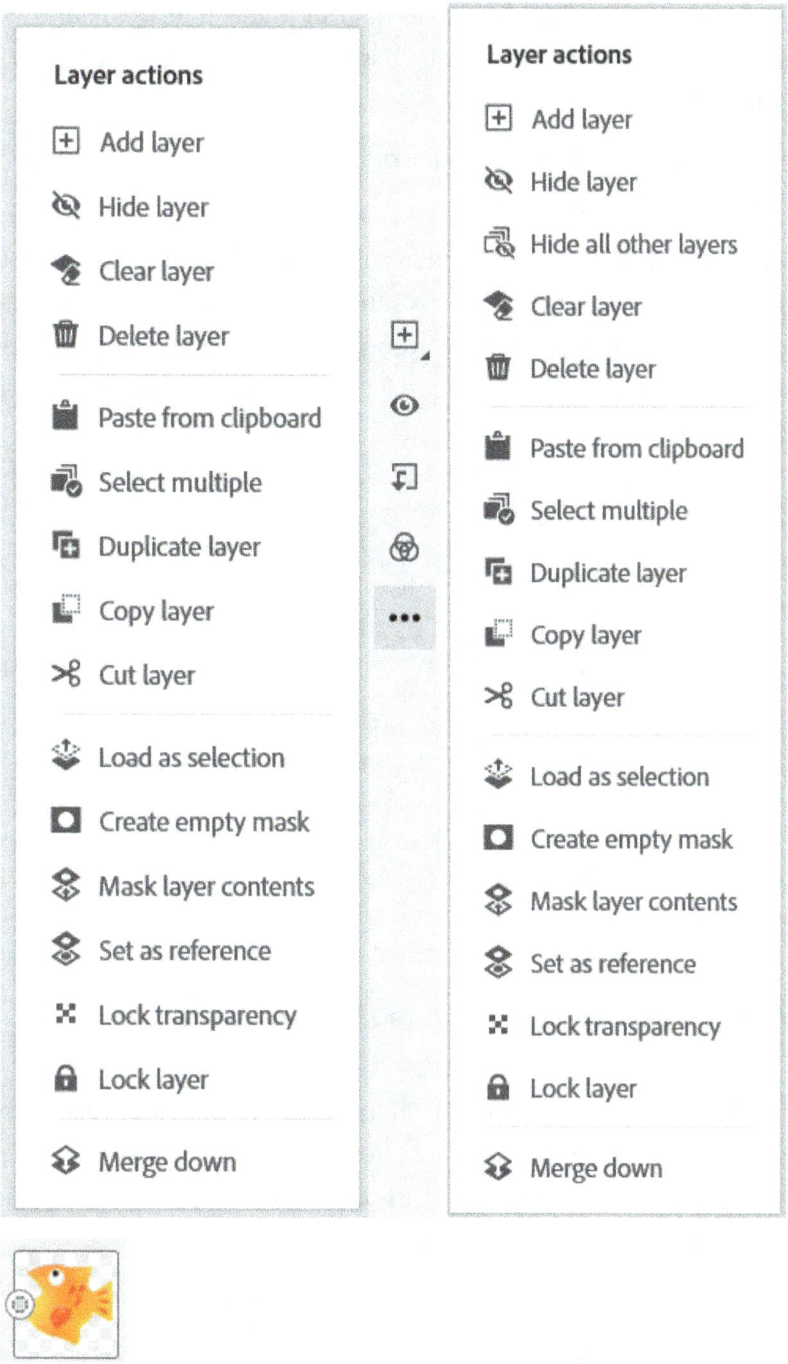

CHAPTER 5 WORKING WITH LAYERS IN FRESCO AND THE VERTICAL TASKBAR

Figure 5-30. Layer actions vary slightly depending on whether accessed from the Vertical Taskbar (left) or you right-click on a layer (right)

CHAPTER 5   WORKING WITH LAYERS IN FRESCO AND THE VERTICAL TASKBAR

- Add Layer: Adds a blank transparent layer that will be blank until painted on, which will determine if it is Pixel or Vector. Refer to Figure 5-30.

- Hide/Show Layer: Toggles the current selected layer on (Show) or off (Hide). Refer to Figure 5-30.

- Hide/Show All Other Layers: Hides or shows the surrounding layers but does not affect the one that is selected. Refer to Figure 5-31. Note that the background layer may in some instances remain visible and may need to be separately hidden if it continues to display.

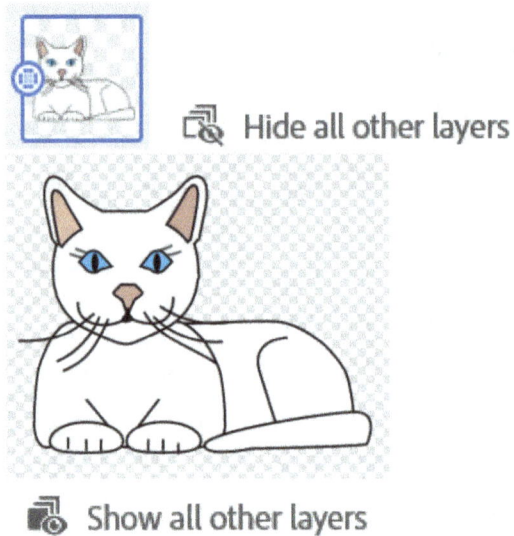

Figure 5-31. *Layer actions let you hide or show all other layers*

- Clear Layer: Removes content from the current layer such as Vector or Pixel layer returning it to blank, but the layer itself is not deleted. If the layer is locked or hidden, this option is not available. Refer to Figure 5-32.

Figure 5-32. *Layer actions Clear layer removes all the artwork on the layer*

- Delete Layer: Removes the entire layer from the Layer panel. Use your Undo key now if you realize you made a mistake and removed a layer. Refer to Figure 5-33.

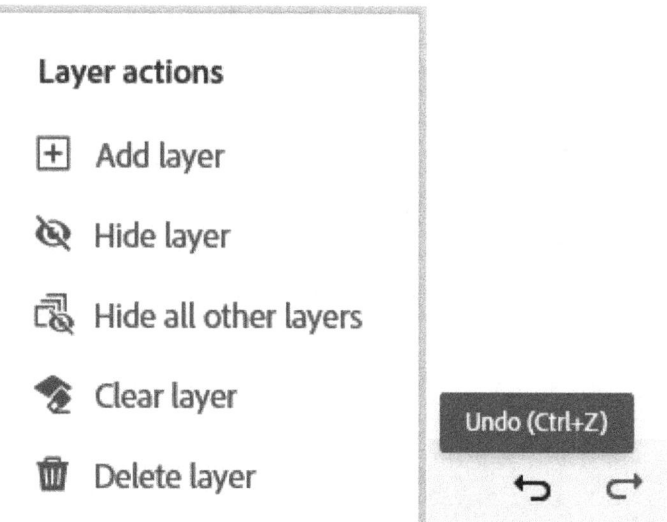

Figure 5-33. *Layer action Delete layer removes the selected layer. Undo key is used to return the layer*

- Paste from Clipboard: Paste any image item that has been copied to the computer clipboard. Refer to Figure 5-34.

Figure 5-34. *Layer action Paste from clipboard*

- Select Multiple: When more than one layer is selected, you can then move, copy, merge, transform, or delete the layers as one unit or group. These layers can have different blend modes and opacities. A group selection is good when you need to move and transform multiple layers at the same time when using the move and transform tool in the Transform workspace.

  Clicking the X in the blue box above the layers allows you to cancel the multiselect. Refer to Figure 5-35 and Figure 5-36.

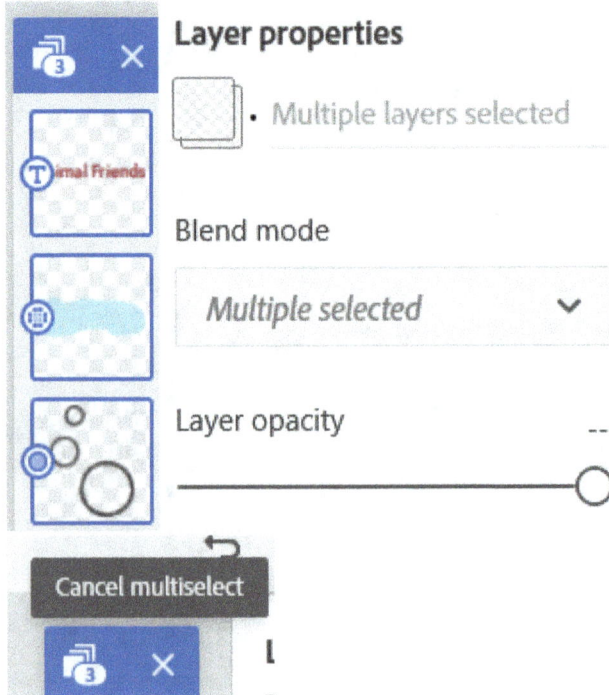

Figure 5-35. *Layer action Select multiple with several layers selected and then canceling the multiselect*

CHAPTER 5 WORKING WITH LAYERS IN FRESCO AND THE VERTICAL TASKBAR

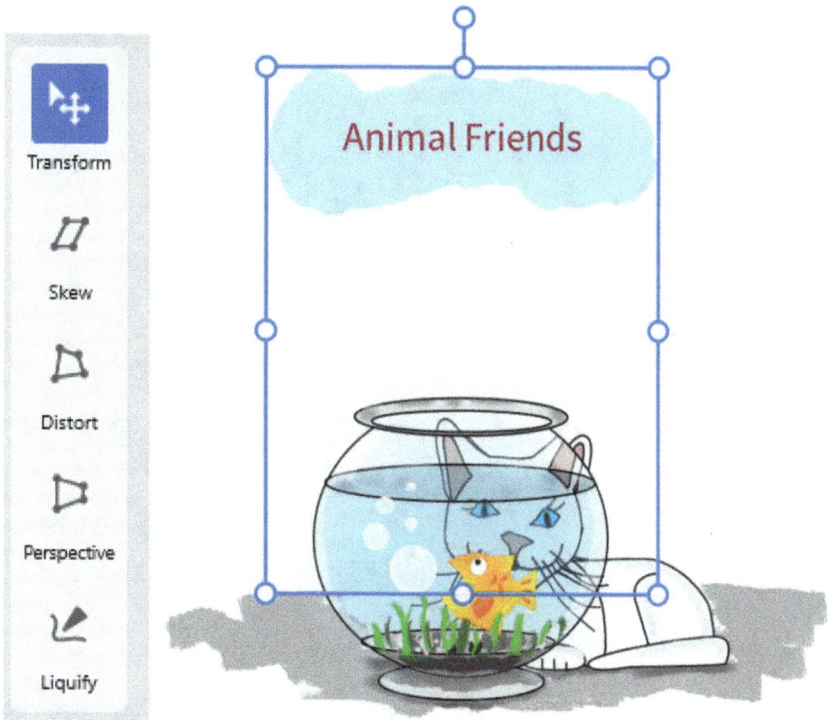

Figure 5-36. *When multiple layers are selected, they can be moved and transformed at the same time within the Transform workspace*

Note The Touch shortcut (double-click) primary circle can also be used to assist you in selecting multiple layers. Refer to Figure 5-37.

CHAPTER 5 WORKING WITH LAYERS IN FRESCO AND THE VERTICAL TASKBAR

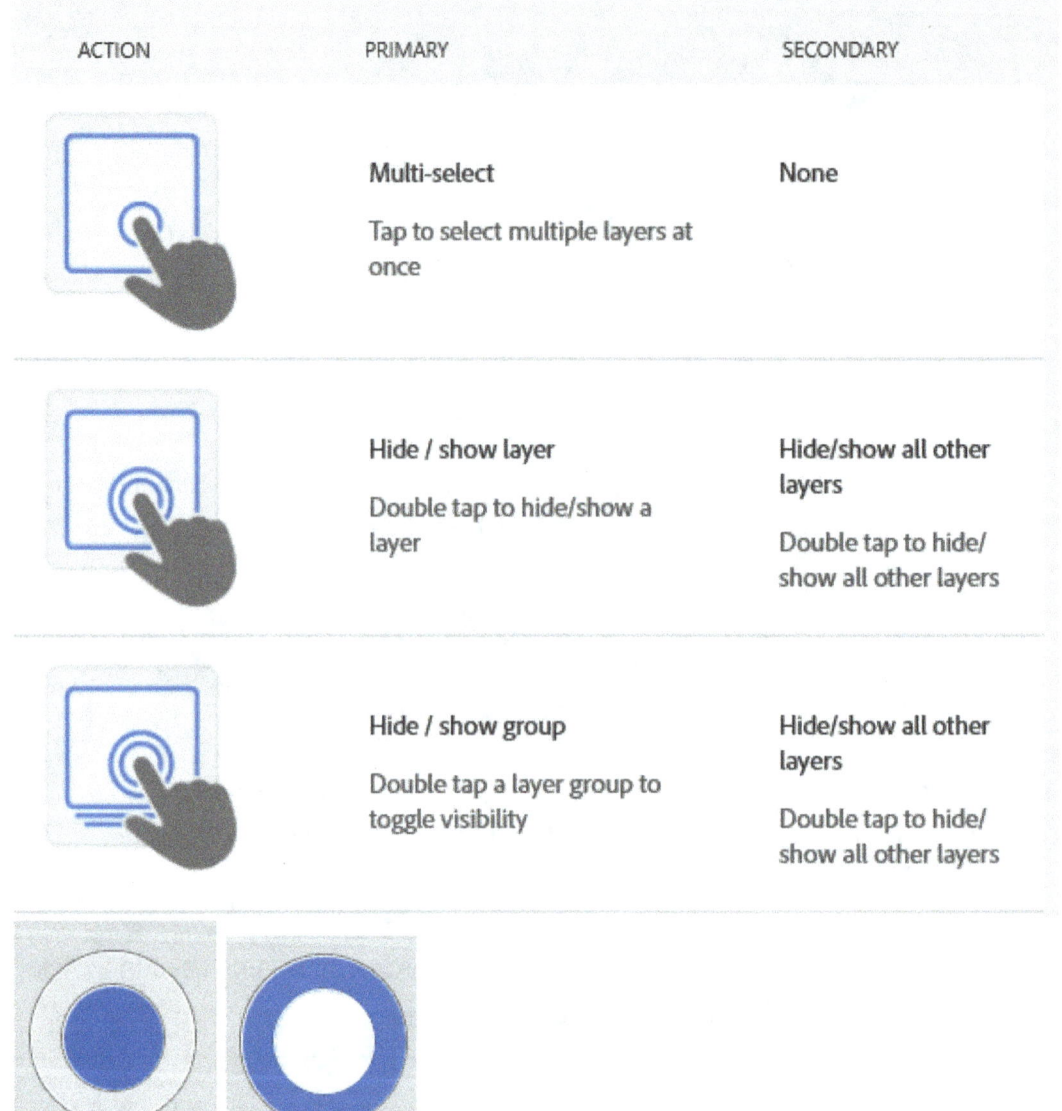

Figure 5-37. Touch shortcut can be used to assist in selecting multiple layers

CHAPTER 5   WORKING WITH LAYERS IN FRESCO AND THE VERTICAL TASKBAR

- Duplicate Layer: Creates a layer exactly the same as the one that is selected. Refer to Figure 5-38.

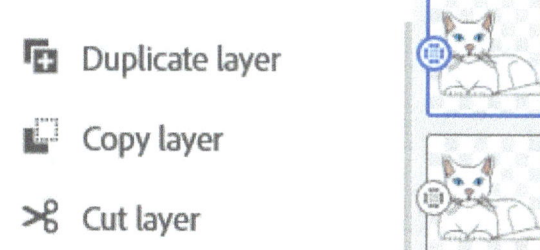

Figure 5-38. *Layer actions of Duplicate layer, Copy layer, and Cut layer when a single layer is selected*

- Copy Layer: Same as using the key command Ctrl+C and allows you to copy brush strokes from one layer and then layer paste onto another layer.

- Cut Layer: Same as using the key command Ctrl+X and allows you to cut brush strokes from one layer and then optionally layer paste onto another layer.

- Paste Layer: Same as using the key command Ctrl+V and allows you to paste brush strokes from one layer onto another new layer from a previous cut or copy action. The strokes can then be transformed, and you can click Done when complete. Refer to Figure 5-39.

CHAPTER 5   WORKING WITH LAYERS IN FRESCO AND THE VERTICAL TASKBAR

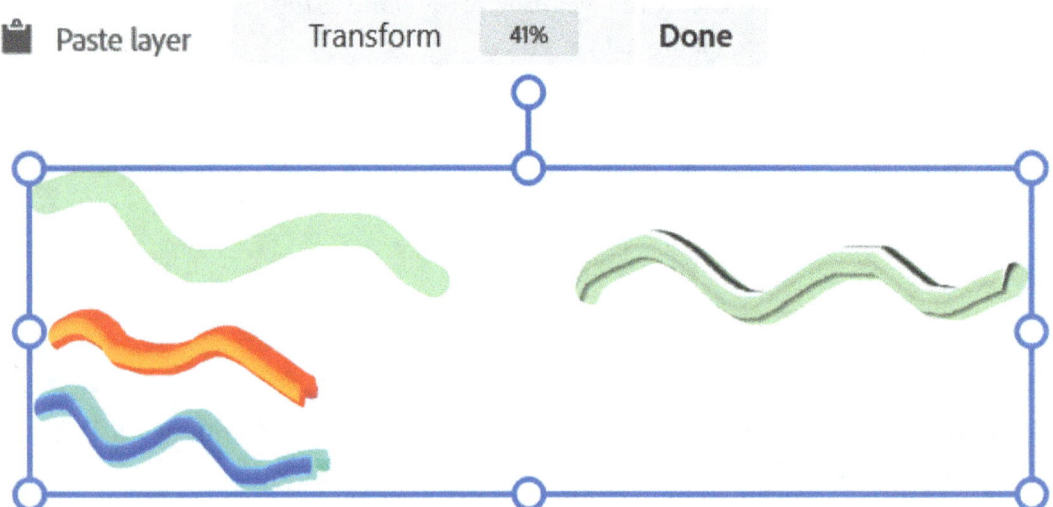

Figure 5-39. *Layer action of Paste layer can be used to transform a selection in the Transform workspace*

- Load As Selection: Loads that Pixel layer as a selection that can then be used to confine where painting will occur, as seen in Chapter 4 regarding selections. This option is not available for Vector layers. Refer to Figure 5-40.

CHAPTER 5   WORKING WITH LAYERS IN FRESCO AND THE VERTICAL TASKBAR

Figure 5-40. Layer action Load as selection can be used to select an area on a layer

- Create an Empty Mask: Allows you to create a mask to block content. We will look at masks in the next section shortly. Refer to Figure 5-41.

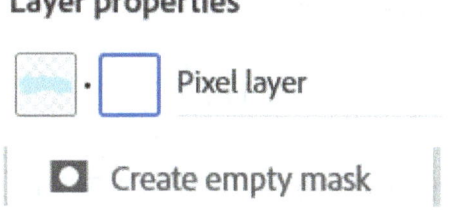

Figure 5-41. Layer action Create empty mask creates a blank mask on a Pixel layer

345

- Mask Layer Contents: Allows you to cover or surround the current content of the layer with a layer mask which you can later edit. Refer to mask section for more details. Refer to Figure 5-42.

Layer properties

Figure 5-42. *Layer action Mask layer contents creates a mask selection on a Pixel layer that can later be edited*

- Set As Reference: Used as a primary reference when you plan to create either a Pixel or Vector layer design above to fill in line art. See the section on reference layers for more details. Refer to Figure 5-43.

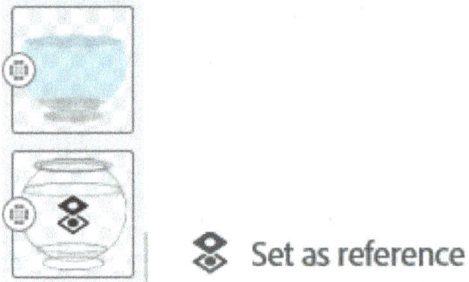

Figure 5-43. *Layer action Set as reference sets the layer to a layer for reference for other layers above that require coloring*

- Lock Transparency: Locks only the transparent areas of the layer so extra brush strokes cannot be added to those areas of the layer. You can only add color to areas that already have pixels. You can then, from the Actions list, Unlock transparency. This option is not available for Vector layers. Refer to Figure 5-44.

CHAPTER 5 WORKING WITH LAYERS IN FRESCO AND THE VERTICAL TASKBAR

Figure 5-44. *Layer action Lock transparency can either lock or unlock transparent areas on a layer*

- Lock Layer: Makes a layer non-editable so it can't move or transform. You can then, from the Actions list, Unlock layer. Refer to Figure 5-45.

Figure 5-45. *Layer action Lock layer can either lock or unlock the selected layer*

- Merge Down: Flattens two or more layers down into one Pixel layer. These layers can no longer be split. Use the Undo icon right away if you realize you made a mistake. Refer to Figure 5-46.

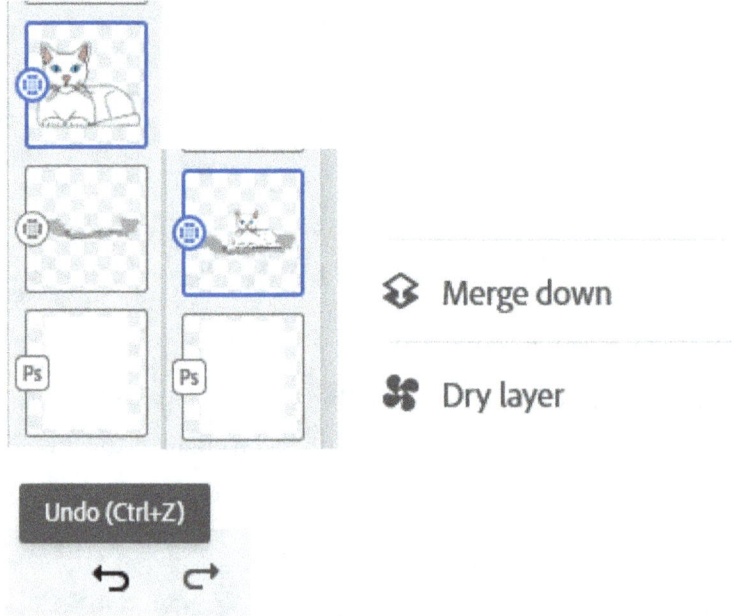

Figure 5-46. *Layer action Merge down can merge one layer into the next lower layer*

- Convert to Pixel Layer: Converts certain layers, such as a blank, Vector layer, or Photoshop layer, to a Pixel layer. There is currently no option to convert a Pixel layer to Vector layer. You will only get that option if working with text. Refer to Figure 5-47 and Figure 5-48.

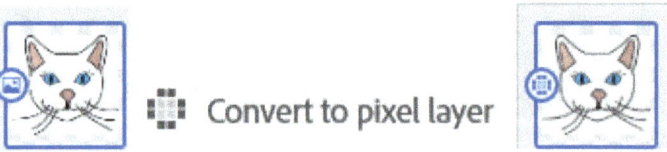

Figure 5-47. *Layer action Convert to pixel layer can change an image layer into a Pixel layer for editing*

Note One other layer action that that you may encounter is Dry layer. This action only appears with layers that contain Watercolor strokes using Live brushes. Applying this action will turn the Live paint into pixel paint and may affect how it blends layer on. Once applied, the action is removed. However, you can undo this step if you need to keep Live paint editable on the Pixel layer. Refer to Figure 5-46 for the icon.

Text Layer Warnings

In the case of Text layers, if you plan to edit with the Move and Transform tools, you will get a warning message that to use some Transform tools such as Skew, Distort, and Perspective, you will need to convert the layer first to a Vector layer before you can proceed. To use the Liquify tool, you will need to convert to a Pixel layer. The text will at this stage no longer be editable as it was before. If you made a mistake and converted the layer, you can use the Undo key right away and create a duplicate of the layer for transforming, so that you have a backup of the text layer which you can hide. Optionally, use layer actions to convert the layer to Pixel or Vector. Refer to Figure 5-48.

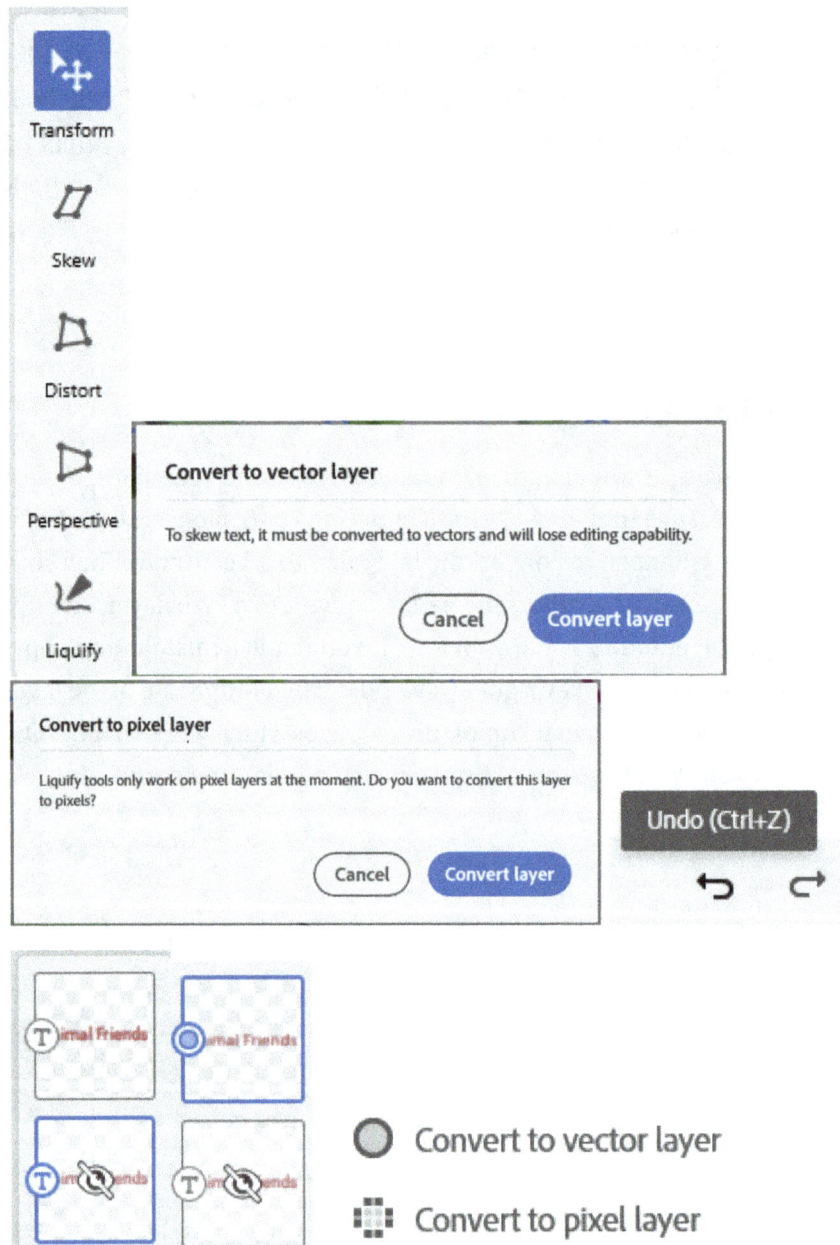

Figure 5-48. *Text layers if edited with the Move and Transform tools may create an alert asking if you want to convert the layer to a Vector or Pixel layer before transformation can progress*

CHAPTER 5   WORKING WITH LAYERS IN FRESCO AND THE VERTICAL TASKBAR

Multiple Layer Actions

When multiple layers are selected, use the ellipses (…) in the Vertical Taskbar. You will find they can have Multiple layer actions which include the following:

- Delete layers, Paste layer, Duplicate layers, Copy layers, Merge selected which allows you to merge multiple selected layers, and Lock layers which allows you to lock or unlock several layers at once. Refer to Figure 5-49.

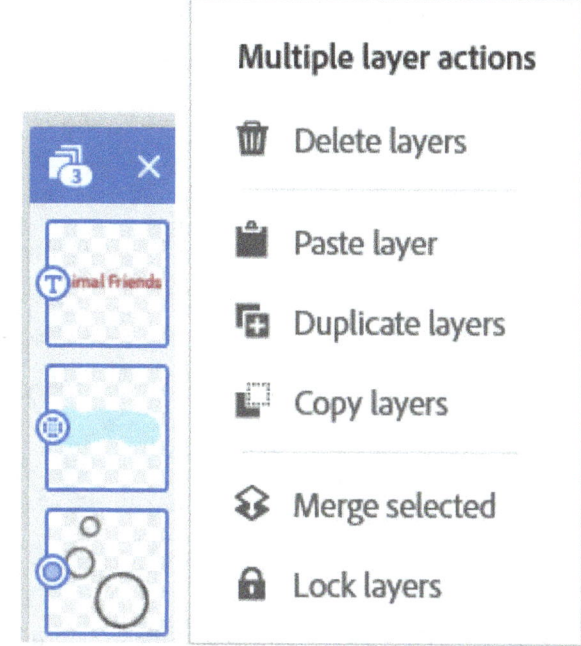

Figure 5-49. *When multiple layers are selected, they can have their own set of actions*

CHAPTER 5 WORKING WITH LAYERS IN FRESCO AND THE VERTICAL TASKBAR

Grouping Layers

To create grouped layers, they need to be dragged one upon another to be a group.

They have their own set of similar actions to single layers, and they can be ungrouped by choosing that option in the menu of Ungroup layers. A group is a better option to choose than Merge down if you are still editing your artwork. Groups of layers are good when you want to keep the Layer panel organized and uncluttered. For properties, they can have blend modes, but it is by default set to Pass through so that the layers within the group are affected, and, like single layers, you can adjust the opacity of the group. Optionally, grouped layers can later be merged into a flatten layer. Refer to Figure 5-50 and Figure 5-51.

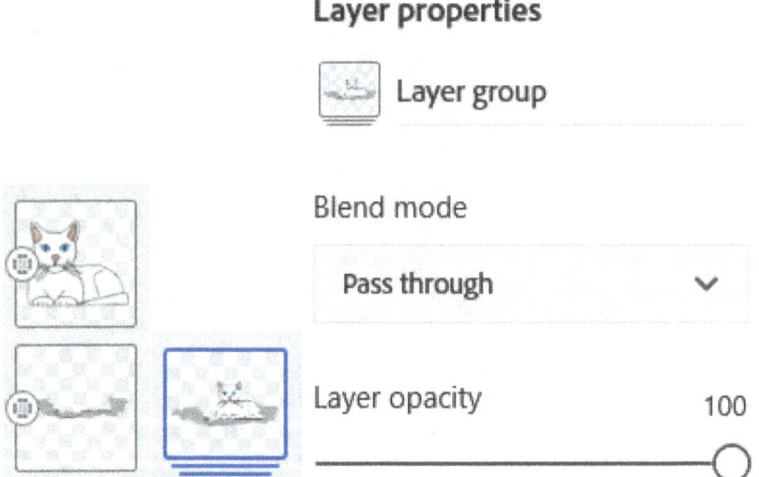

Figure 5-50. *Layers are grouped, and then the Layer properties of the group can be reviewed in the panel*

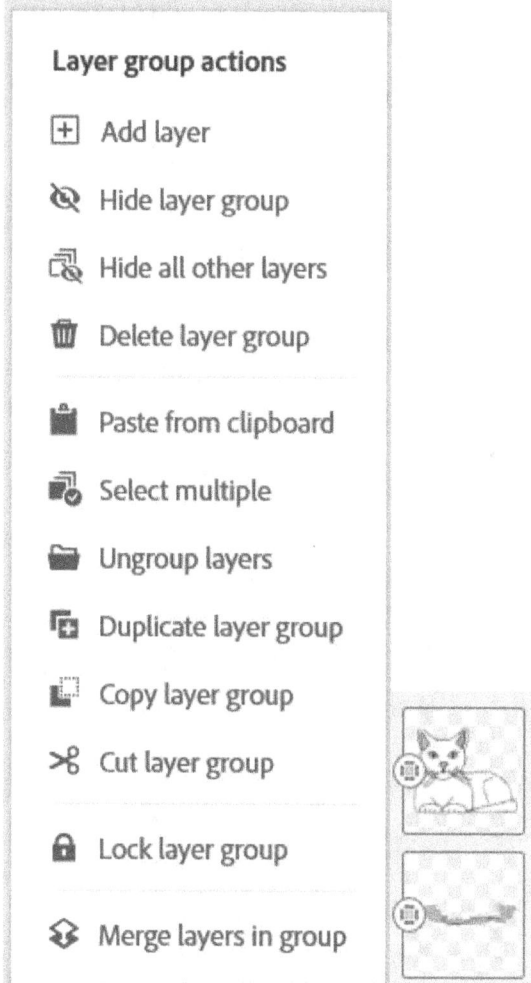

Figure 5-51. *Layer group actions have an additional action allowing you to Ungroup layers to return them to the original single layers*

Reference Layer (Line Art, Selections, and Shapes)

A reference layer, as mentioned, can be used as a primary source for your artwork to assist in adding color to a layer. You can create several blank layers (either vector or pixel) and then use a reference layer to set your boundaries of where the paint goes.

This is great since you can keep your line art and your fill area separate without using selections to control where the paint appears. You can have one reference layer in the document.

Your line art in this case may be a drawing that you created in Illustrator with shapes and copied into Photoshop and then turned into a Raster or Pixel layer before importing and opening in Fresco. Refer to Figure 5-52.

Figure 5-52. *Illustration of a fish bowl in Photoshop and the layer has been rasterized in the Layers panel*

We will look at that process more in Chapter 7 and 9.

Regardless of how you created your line art, whether externally or within Fresco with the paint brush or as a shape, it will now have sections that you want to color. You can then turn that Pixel layer drawing or even Vector layer shape into a reference layer to color; choose the Layer action Set as reference. Refer to Figure 5-53.

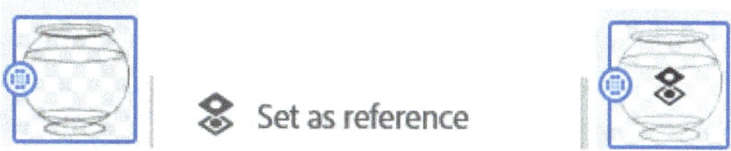

Figure 5-53. *Layer action Set as reference and with the reference badge*

Then, create a new blank Pixel or Vector layer (click the Add layer button), and select the new layer. Refer to Figure 5-54 and Figure 5-55.

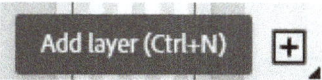

Figure 5-54. *Add a new layer using the Vertical Taskbar*

You can use the Fill (Paint Bucket) to fill in the areas of spaces with color. Refer to Figure 5-55.

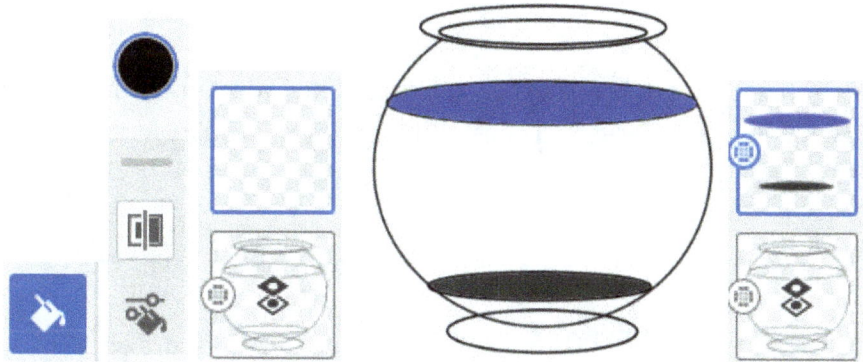

Figure 5-55. *Fill tool and settings and a painting on a new layer using the reference layer*

Refer to Chapter 4 if you need to review how to use the Fill tool and adjust settings.

> Note that a Vector layer will appear with a more solid fill than a Pixel layer whether it is a reference or regular layer. However, if your file is at 300 ppi, the resolution should be high, and you will not notice a loss in quality.

Also, make sure the blank layer is selected and not the reference layer as you fill the section, as you can still edit the reference layer. Use the Undo button if you made that mistake. Locking the reference layer may be good to do as well. Alternatively, to avoid accidental editing, I recommend keeping a duplicate of a reference layer hidden in case you make this mistake and then need to replicate the layer again. Refer to Figure 5-56.

Figure 5-56. *Reference layer painted on by mistake; use the Undo icon to undo the step; use the Layer action to lock the layer or create a duplicate layer to hide for use later*

If you no longer want the layer to be a reference layer, you can choose from the pop-up menu action Release reference. Then, unlock the layer if you need to edit it. Refer to Figure 5-57.

Figure 5-57. *Layer action Release reference layer and then Unlock layer so it can be edited*

When you need to set a new reference layer, the reference icon will switch to that layer and remove itself from the previous layer.

For more information on reference layers, you can refer to this link:

https://helpx.adobe.com/fresco/using/layers.html

Masking Different Kinds of Layers and Their Content Setting

Masking can be used to cover parts of a shape or brush strokes as well as control transparency of an area. In this section, we will look at some of the actions used for layer masking, and later, in the Appearance section, we will look more at the clipping mask.

To create a mask, you can start with either an empty layer mask or mask the current layer contents. Refer to Figure 5-58.

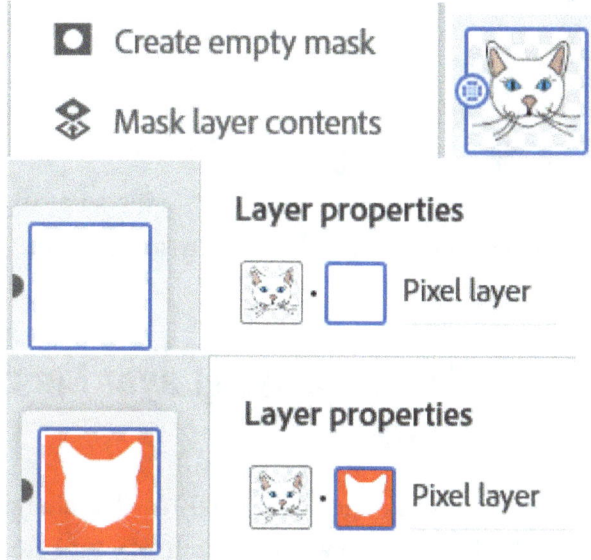

Figure 5-58. *Layer actions for creating a mask and their layer properties displayed*

You can also start with creating a selection using a Selection tool, as seen in Chapter 4, and create a mask using the Contextual Task bar. Refer to Figure 5-59.

357

CHAPTER 5   WORKING WITH LAYERS IN FRESCO AND THE VERTICAL TASKBAR

Figure 5-59. Create a selection and use the Contextual Task bar to create a mask

Editing the Mask and Reveal/Hide Layer Masking in the Contextual Task Bar

Once you have created the layer mask, the Contextual Task bar changes and allows you to reveal the layer or hide the layer as you work with one of your Pixel brushes. Refer to Figure 5-60.

CHAPTER 5   WORKING WITH LAYERS IN FRESCO AND THE VERTICAL TASKBAR

Figure 5-60. *Paint with a Pixel brush on the mask to reveal and hide parts of the image on the layer*

On the mask, you can paint with any Pixel brush that you like while Reveal layer is clicked. This will show areas of the original art, but if Hide layer is clicked, then red will cover and mask parts of the art. They are not erased permanently, and you can use the mask to reveal the art on the layer at any time. Refer to Figure 5-61.

CHAPTER 5   WORKING WITH LAYERS IN FRESCO AND THE VERTICAL TASKBAR

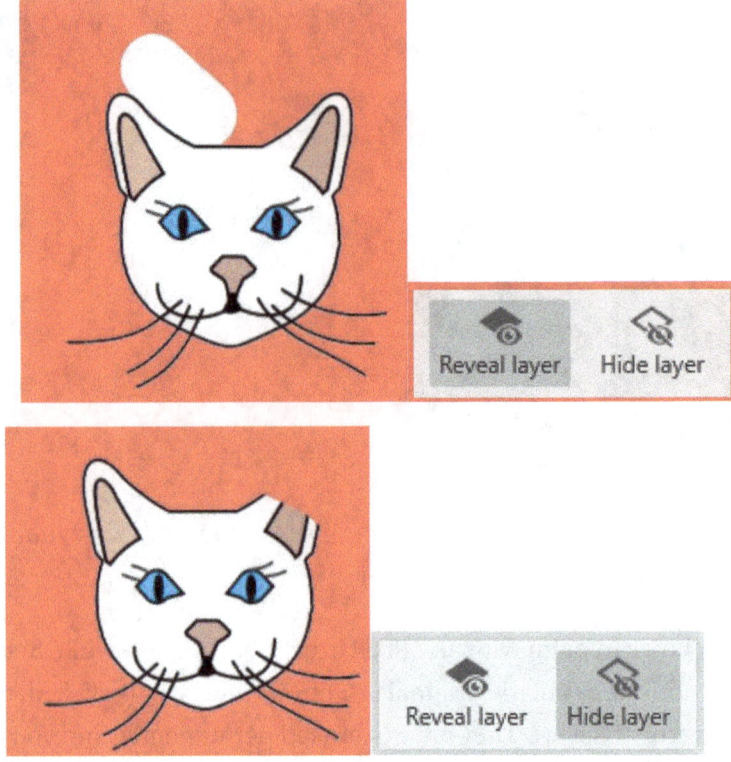

Figure 5-61. *Paint with a Pixel brush on the mask to reveal and hide parts of the image on the layer, and switch settings using the Contextual Task bar*

You can further refine the areas you want to mask by using various Selection, Fill, and Shape tools along with your Touch shortcut tool that you saw in Chapter 4. Refer to Figure 5-62.

CHAPTER 5　WORKING WITH LAYERS IN FRESCO AND THE VERTICAL TASKBAR

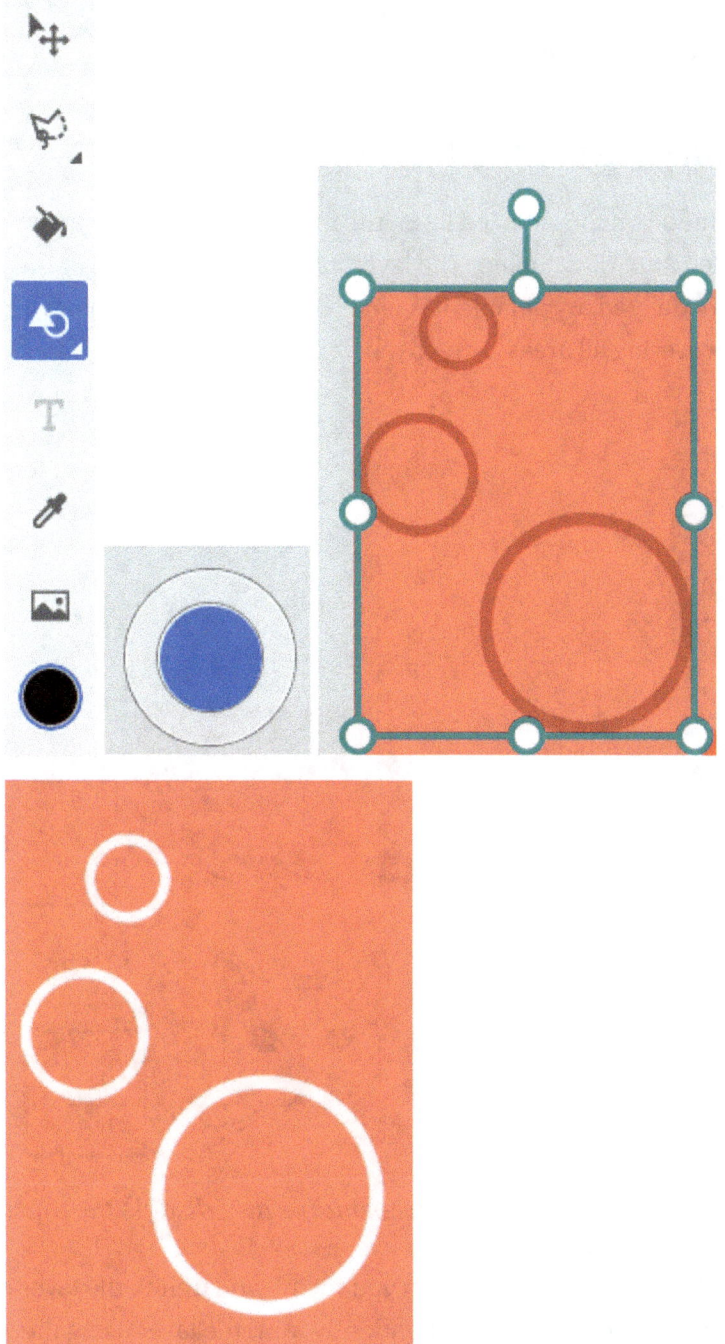

Figure 5-62. *Use shapes and the Touch shortcut to stamp on the mask*

CHAPTER 5   WORKING WITH LAYERS IN FRESCO AND THE VERTICAL TASKBAR

Note, however, right now if the Move and Transform tools are used to transform the layer, it will also transform the mask because both are linked.

Mask Enabled and Mask Linked

While in mask mode on the selected layer, the following two icons can be toggled on and off, Mask enabled and Mask linked. The layer mask can be enabled or disabled while you work but it is not deleted. By default, it is enabled. This is useful when you need to check if your mask is covering all areas correctly. Refer to Figure 5-63.

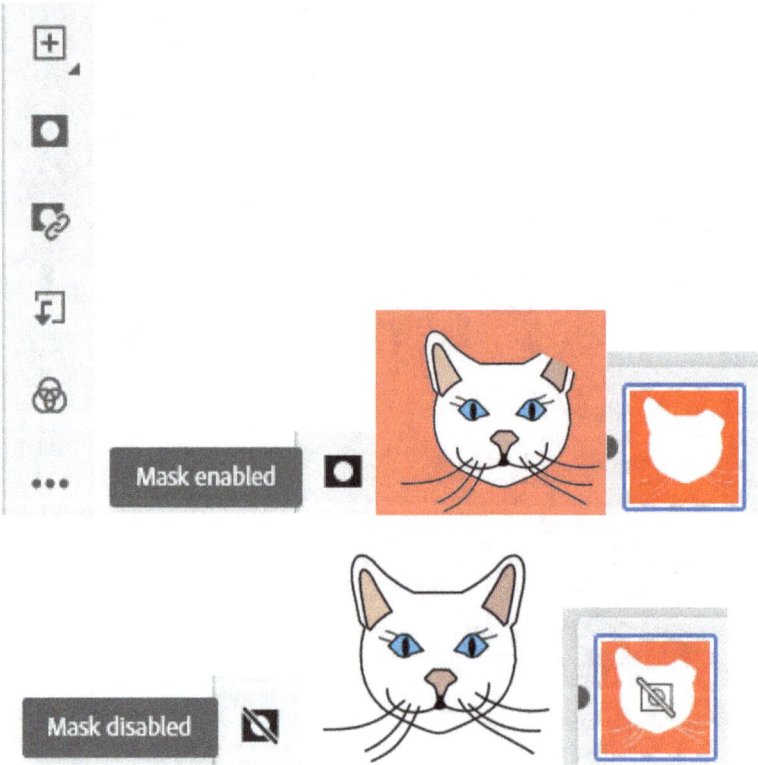

Figure 5-63. *Use the Vertical Taskbar to enable and disable the mask*

The second icon, Mask linked, allows you to link and unlink the layer mask from the layer so that it can move independently from the layer using the Move and Transform tools. By default, the mask is linked so the layer and mask move together. While unlinked, you can also move and transform the layer mask separately. Refer to Figure 5-64.

CHAPTER 5   WORKING WITH LAYERS IN FRESCO AND THE VERTICAL TASKBAR

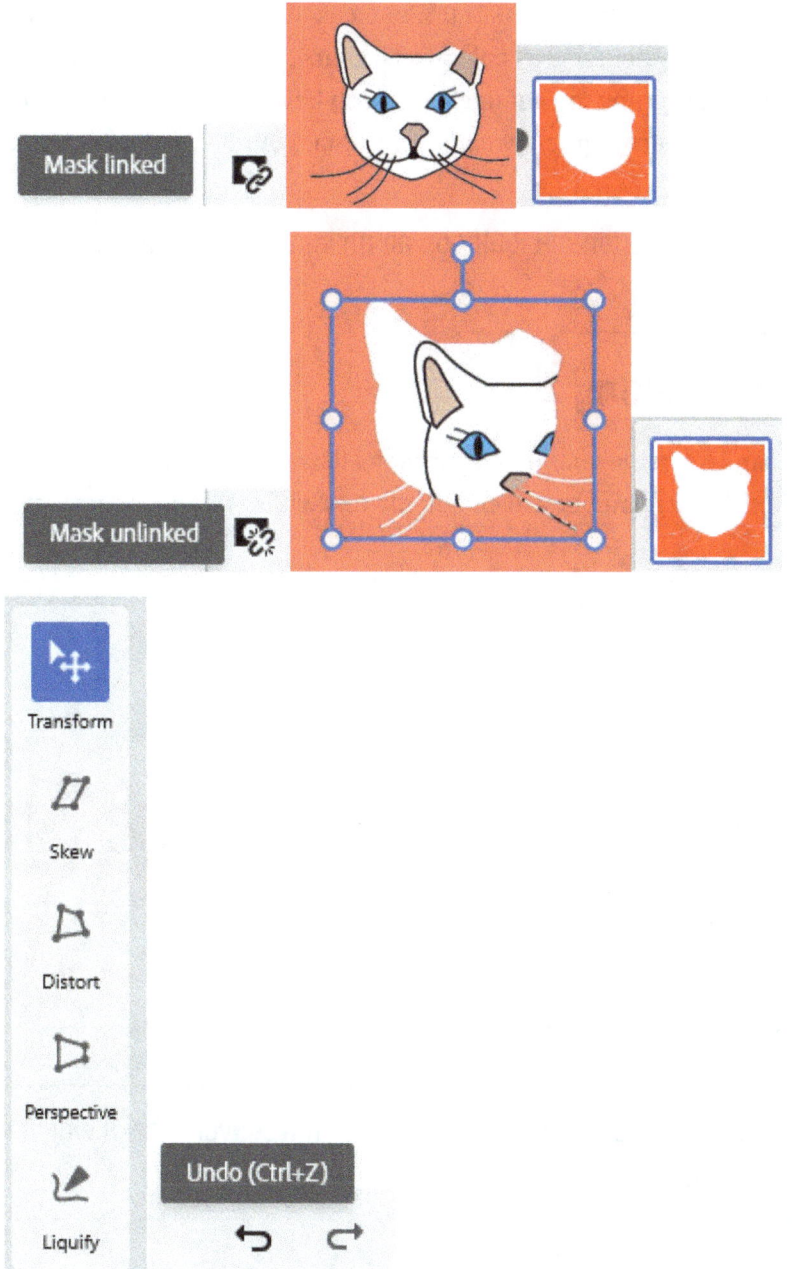

Figure 5-64. *Use the Vertical Taskbar to link and unlink the mask, transform the mask, and use the Undo key to undo any transformation*

You will also know that the mask is unlinked as the gray dot between the mask and image will be a slightly lighter gray color. Click cancel if you need to exit the Transform workspace without keeping the changes. Or if you have clicked Done to exit, use the Undo button if you need to quickly realign your mask, and then, lock it again.

> **Note** The transformation of Liquify on an unlinked mask will only work for Pixel layers.

Text Layer Masking

Besides Pixel and Vector layers, Text layers can all have a layer mask applied to them, and it can be edited. You cannot, however, edit the text while you are in Mask mode. Refer to Figure 5-65.

Figure 5-65. *Masks can be applied to Text layers*

> **Note** Appearance adjustment layers can also have layer masks which we will look at later in this chapter.

Mask Properties: Mask Density

Like other layers, masks can have their own properties. While the layer and mask are selected, in this case, Mask density can be set to a range of 0–100% to hide or reveal more of the artwork by reducing the density. Refer to Figure 5-66.

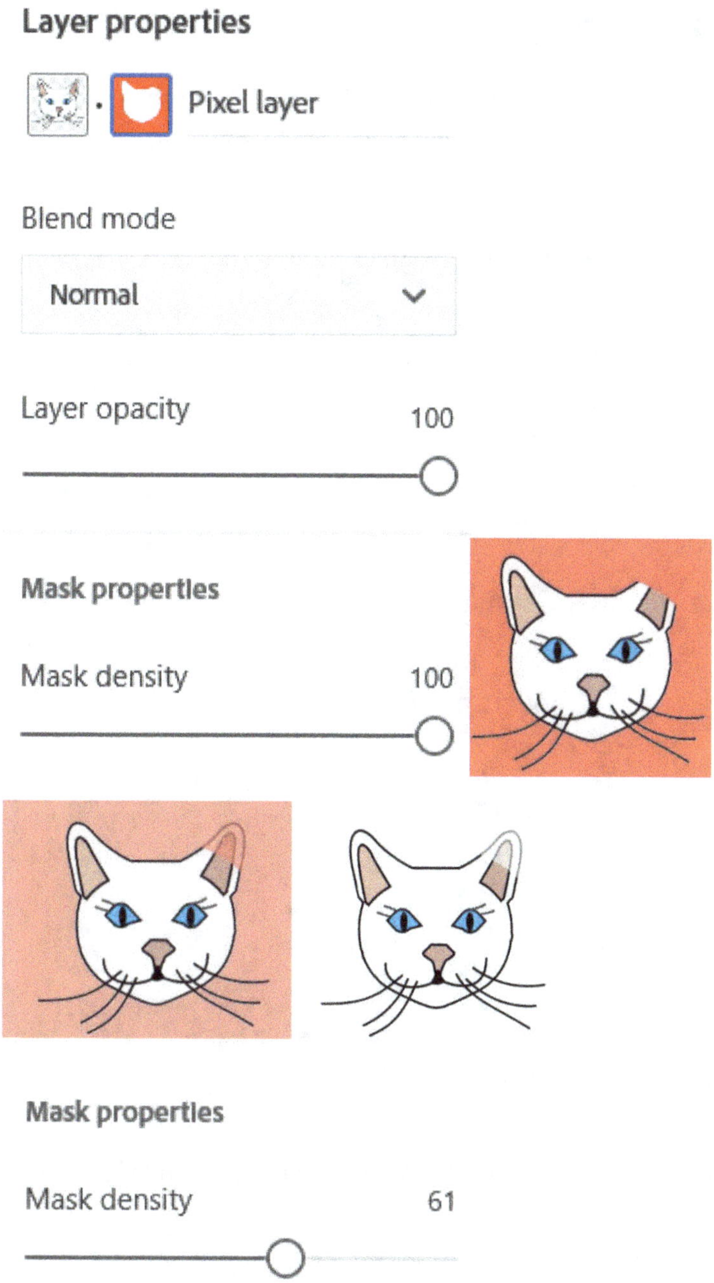

CHAPTER 5　WORKING WITH LAYERS IN FRESCO AND THE VERTICAL TASKBAR

Layer properties

Pixel layer

Blend mode

Normal

Layer opacity　　　100

Mask properties

Mask density　　　100

Mask properties

Mask density　　　61

Figure 5-66. *Once a mask is applied, use the Layer properties panel to adjust the density of the mask*

Layer Mask Actions

Masks also have their own set of actions which appear from the pop-up menu while in Mask mode, and you click a selected mask. Refer to Figure 5-67.

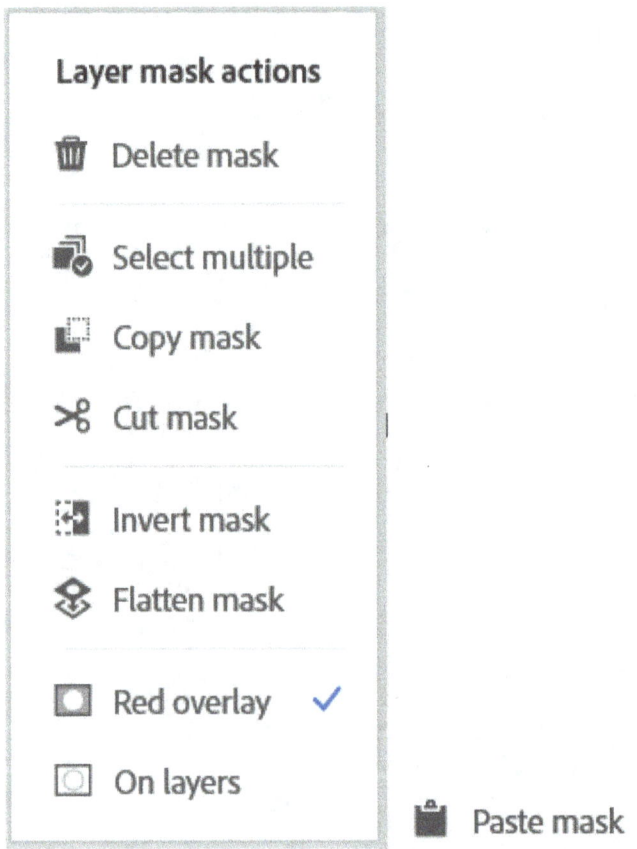

Figure 5-67. *Layer mask actions*

Delete Mask: Remove the mask from the layer. Refer to Figure 5-68.

Figure 5-68. *Removal of the layer mask with a Layer mask action*

CHAPTER 5   WORKING WITH LAYERS IN FRESCO AND THE VERTICAL TASKBAR

- Select Multiple: This action is not for selecting masks but for selecting multiple layers while the mask is active. Refer to Figure 5-69.

Figure 5-69. *Selection of multiple layers including those that have masks*

- Copy Mask: Copy or duplicate the layer mask so that it can be applied to another layer with a mask when you use the action Paste mask. Refer to Figure 5-70.

- Cut Mask: Remove the layer mask from one layer to paste it on another layer when you use the action Paste mask. Refer to Figure 5-70.

- Paste Mask: Paste the mask on another layer after it has been cut or copied from a previously selected layer. The mask can then be transformed, and click the Done button when complete. Refer to Figure 5-70.

CHAPTER 5   WORKING WITH LAYERS IN FRESCO AND THE VERTICAL TASKBAR

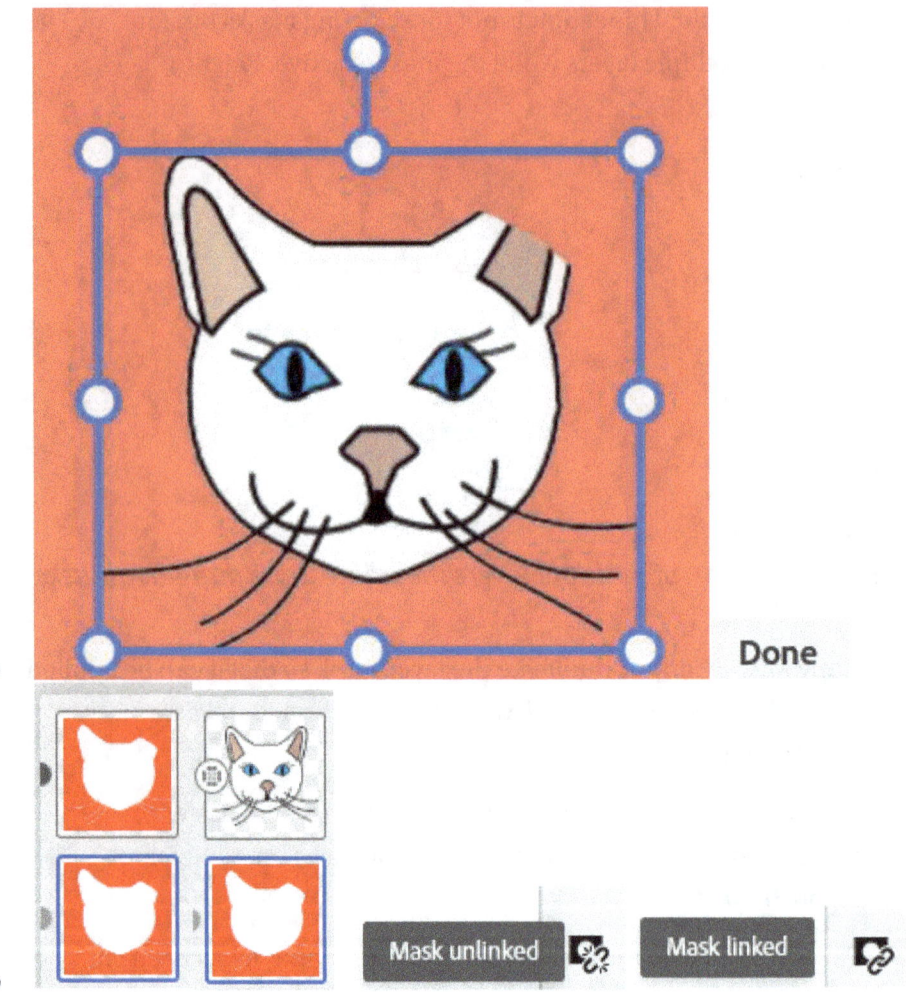

Figure 5-70. *Copying or cutting and then pasting a mask onto a new layer and relinking the mask*

Note that after a mask is pasted, it may need to be relinked.

- Invert Mask: Creates the opposite of the original mask; what was hidden is now revealed and vice versa. Click the Invert mask action again if you need to return to the original mask state. Refer to Figure 5-71.

CHAPTER 5   WORKING WITH LAYERS IN FRESCO AND THE VERTICAL TASKBAR

Figure 5-71. *Layer mask action of inverting the layer mask*

- Flatten Mask: Flattens or applies the mask so it is now part of the image. Use your Undo key right away if you realize you made a mistake to return the mask. Refer to Figure 5-72.

Figure 5-72. *Layer mask action of flattening the mask*

- Red Overlay: Work with a traditional quick mask Red overlay or toggle to the traditional black grayscale layer mask of On layers. Red conceals and white areas reveal. Refer to Figure 5-73.

369

CHAPTER 5 WORKING WITH LAYERS IN FRESCO AND THE VERTICAL TASKBAR

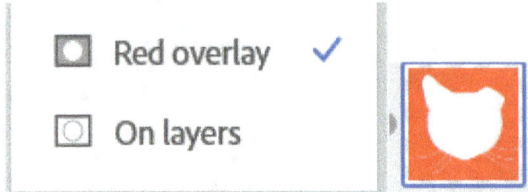

Figure 5-73. *Layer mask action set to Red overlay*

- On Layers: A layer mask color of black may be easier to work with on some projects where red might be distracting. White areas are revealed and Black areas are concealed. Note, however, the mask itself will appear transparent in Mask mode and not in red. Refer to Figure 5-74.

Figure 5-74. *Layer mask action set to On layers*

When you no longer want to work on the red mask, slide it horizontally right back into the Layer panel so that the red color is hidden, and you can see the masked areas more clearly. This will allow you to select your layer area for further editing separately from the mask. Refer to Figure 5-75.

Figure 5-75. *Slide the mask over so you can see the image thumbnail on the layer*

Slide the image left if you need to return to Mask mode.

For more information on layers, you can refer to this link:

https://helpx.adobe.com/fresco/using/layer-masks.html

CHAPTER 5   WORKING WITH LAYERS IN FRESCO AND THE VERTICAL TASKBAR

Appearances

As in Photoshop, you can add Adjustment layers to your project. The following are Brightness/Contrast, Hue/Saturation, and Color balance. Color adjustments affect the color and tonal range of pixels. However, these adjustments are done over the top of the layer on their own dedicated layer and are therefore editable and nondestructive to the layers below and can be deleted, hidden, and shown at any time. Refer to Figure 5-76.

Figure 5-76. *Adding an Appearance or Adjustment layer above a Pixel layer*

On the Vertical Taskbar, these Adjustment layers can be accessed from the pop-up menu as well as be set to the Clip state. Let's look at the Layer properties options for each one. Refer to Figure 5-77.

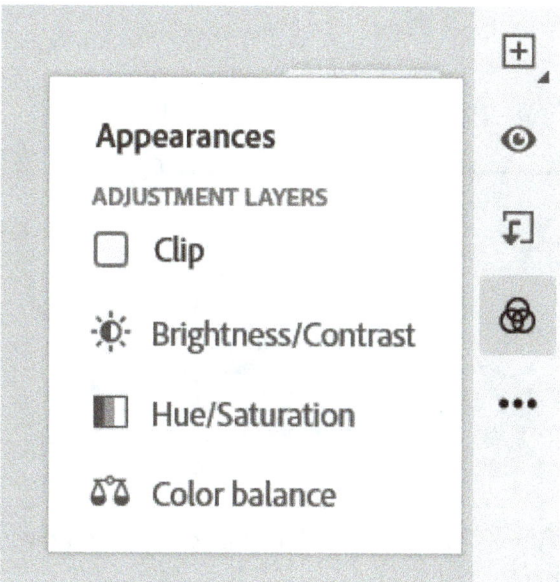

Figure 5-77. *Appearance Adjustment layers found via the Vertical Taskbar*

371

Brightness/Contrast

This Adjustment layer can be used to affect Brightness and the Contrast of the artwork below. Click and hold to reveal this appearance in the pop-out menu, and select Brightness/Contrast from the menu to add to your Layer panel. You can then work with the following sliders and drop-down menu for additional color blending options which will affect those layers below. Refer to Figure 5-78.

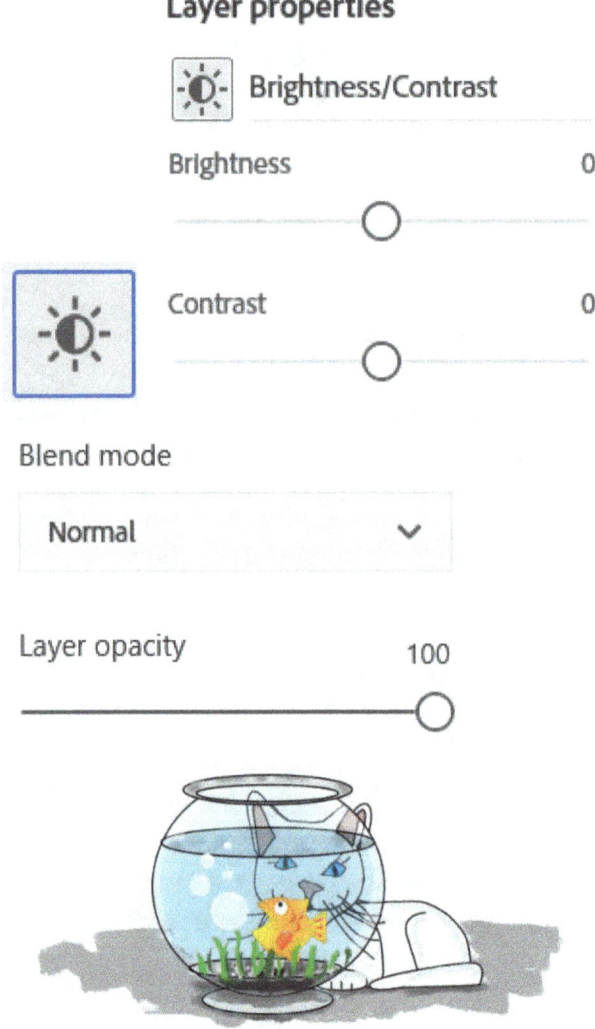

Figure 5-78. *Brightness/Contrast Adjustment layer applied to an image using the Layer properties panel*

- Brightness (−150, 0, 150): Decrease or increase brightness.

- Contrast (−50, 0, 100): Decrease or increase contrast.

- Blend Mode: By default, it is set to Normal. Refer to the "Layer Blending Modes and Layer Opacity" section in this chapter if you need more details.

- Layer Opacity (0–100%): Alters the intensity of how the adjustment affects the underlying colors. By default, it is set to 100%.

Here, we can see how the overall image is affected if I change the Brightness/Contrast. Refer to Figure 5-79.

CHAPTER 5　WORKING WITH LAYERS IN FRESCO AND THE VERTICAL TASKBAR

Figure 5-79. *Brightness/Contrast Adjustment layer applied to an image using the Layer properties panel while moving the sliders*

Likewise, altering the Blend mode and Layer opacity would cause other color alterations as well. Refer to Figure 5-80.

CHAPTER 5   WORKING WITH LAYERS IN FRESCO AND THE VERTICAL TASKBAR

Figure 5-80. *Brightness/Contrast Adjustment layer applied to an image using the Layer properties panel while moving the sliders and adjusting Blend mode and Layer opacity*

Hue/Saturation

This Adjustment layer, also known as HSL, can be used to affect all the colors in the artwork below. Click and hold to reveal this appearance in the pop-out menu, and select Hue/Saturation from the menu to add as a layer to your Layer panel. You can then work with the following sliders and drop-down menu for additional color blending options which will affect those layers below. Refer to Figure 5-81.

CHAPTER 5   WORKING WITH LAYERS IN FRESCO AND THE VERTICAL TASKBAR

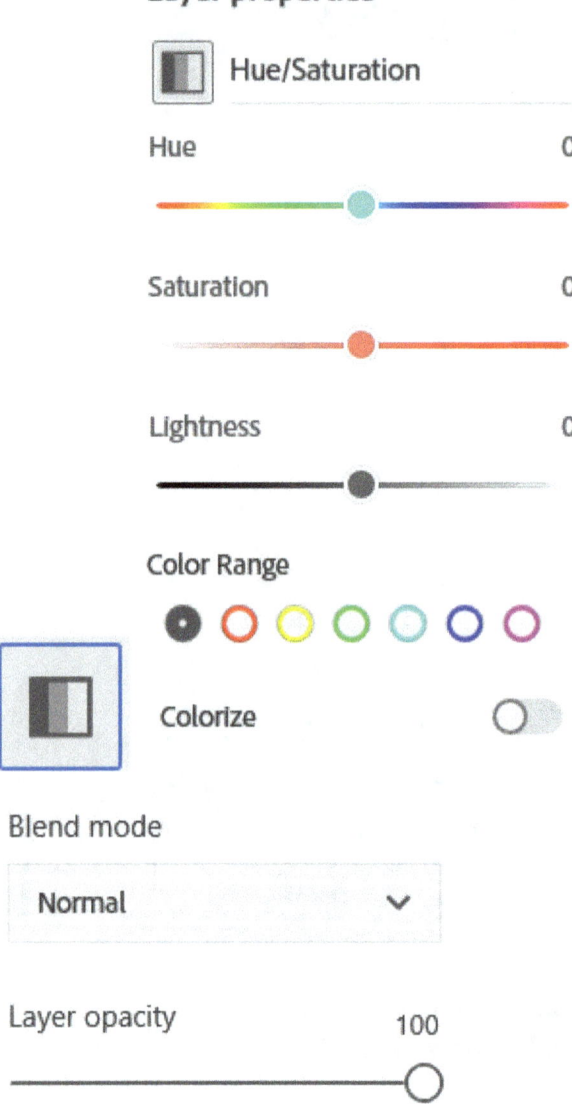

Figure 5-81. *Hue/Saturation Adjustment Layer properties*

The options are

- Hue (−180, 0, 180): Like a color wheel, you can alter the overall hue of colors by moving the sliders. Refer to Figure 5-82.

CHAPTER 5 WORKING WITH LAYERS IN FRESCO AND THE VERTICAL TASKBAR

Figure 5-82. *Hue/Saturation Adjustment layer applied to an image using the Layer properties panel Hue slider*

- Saturation (−100, 0, 100): Decrease or increase the level of saturation. Refer to Figure 5-83.

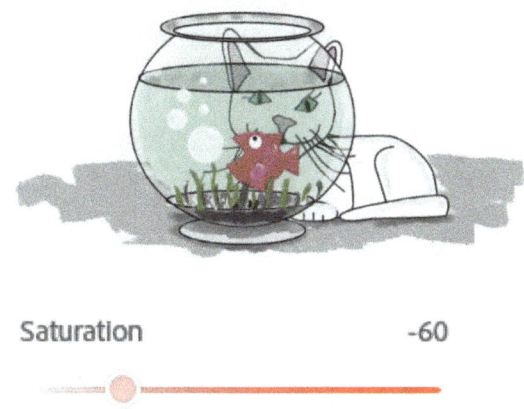

Figure 5-83. *Hue/Saturation Adjustment layer applied to an image using the Layer properties panel Saturation slider*

- Lightness (−100, 0, 100): Decrease or increase the level of lightness. Refer to Figure 5-84.

377

CHAPTER 5   WORKING WITH LAYERS IN FRESCO AND THE VERTICAL TASKBAR

Figure 5-84. *Hue/Saturation Adjustment layer applied to an image using the Layer properties panel Lightness slider*

- Color Range: Click one of the color dots to adjust for various color ranges (Master/All Colors, Reds, Yellows, Greens, Cyans, Blues, Magentas). By default, it is set to All. But if set to Red, then you can target the reds in that image. Refer to Figure 5-85.

CHAPTER 5   WORKING WITH LAYERS IN FRESCO AND THE VERTICAL TASKBAR

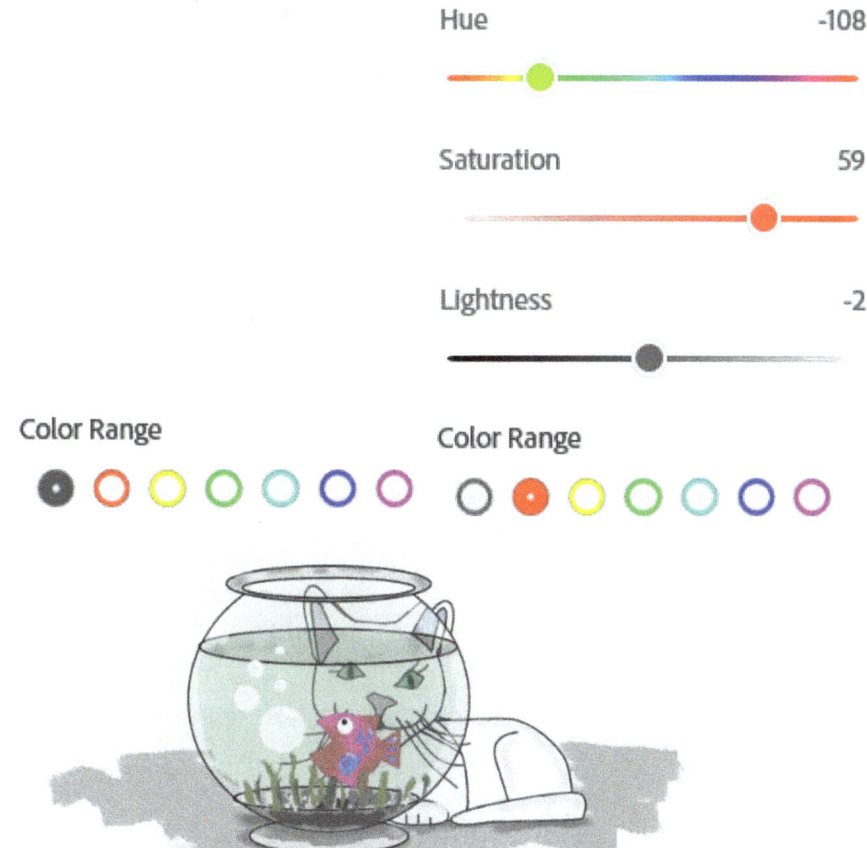

Figure 5-85. *Hue/Saturation Adjustment layer applied to an image using the Layer properties panel Color Range and HSL sliders and altering the red color range*

- Colorize Toggle: Creates a monochromatic sepia tone that can be controlled with the HSL sliders when the toggle is enabled. Note that the Color Range option becomes disabled. Refer to Figure 5-86.

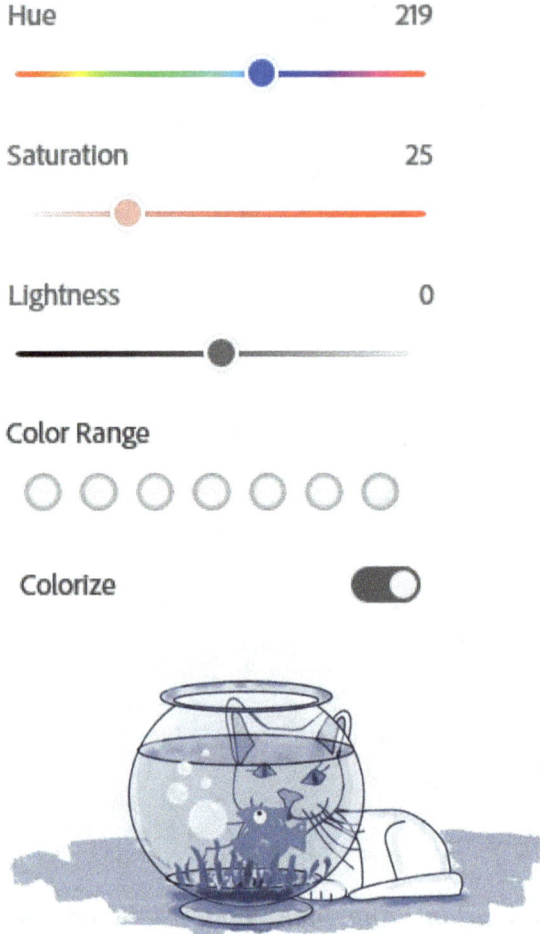

Figure 5-86. *Hue/Saturation Adjustment layer applied to an image using the Layer properties panel Colorize toggle*

- Blend Mode: By default, it is set to Normal. Refer to the "Layer Blending Modes and Layer Opacity" section in this chapter if you need more details.

- Layer Opacity (0–100%): Alters the intensity of how the adjustment affects the underlying colors. By default, it is set to 100%.

When you alter the Blend mode or Layer opacity, you can affect the underlying colors. Refer to Figure 5-87.

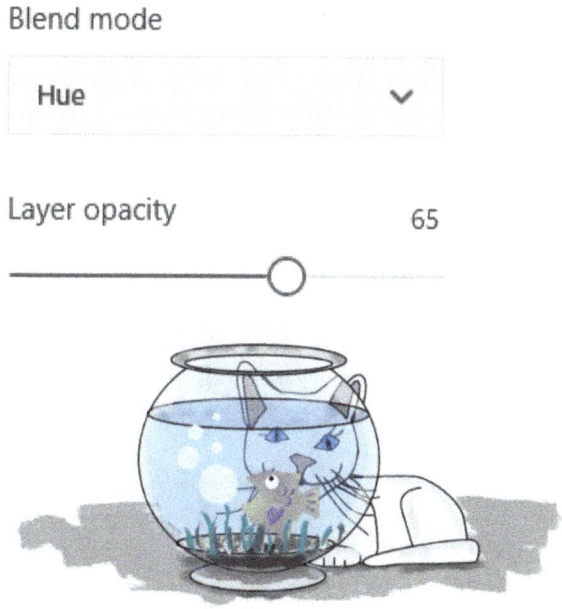

Figure 5-87. *Hue/Saturation Adjustment layer applied to an image using the Layer properties panel, Blend mode, and Layer opacity*

Color Balance

This Adjustment layer can be used to affect the color intensity on the artwork below. Some colors may become more vibrant, and shadows become isolated. Click and hold to reveal this appearance in the pop-out menu, and select the Color Balance menu to add as a layer to your Layer panel. You can then work with the following sliders, drop-down menus, and toggle for additional color blending options which will affect those layers below. Refer to Figure 5-88.

CHAPTER 5 WORKING WITH LAYERS IN FRESCO AND THE VERTICAL TASKBAR

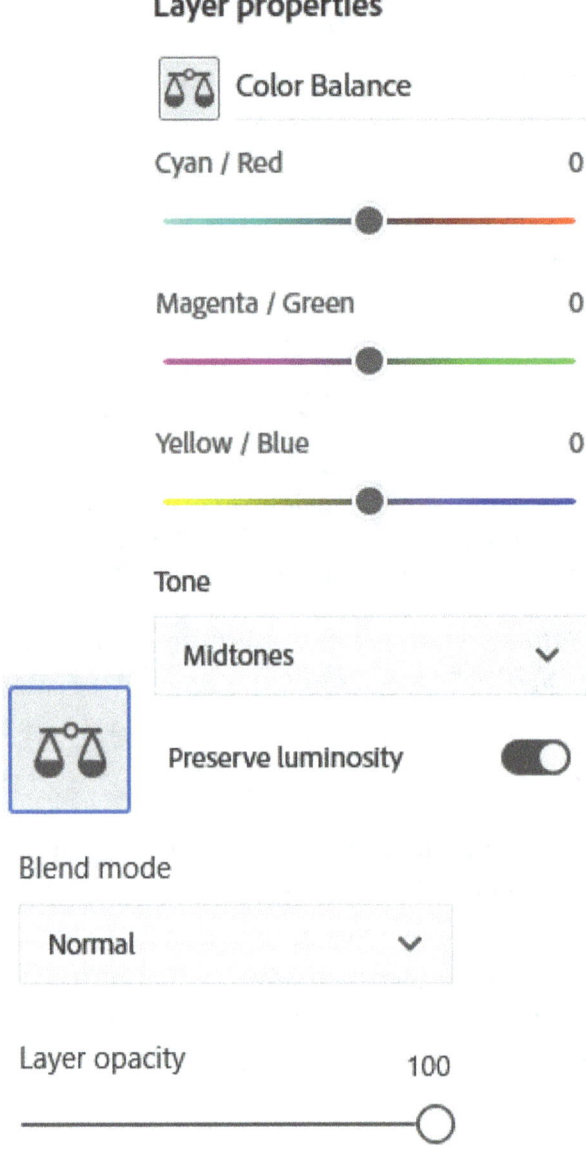

Figure 5-88. Color Balance Adjustment Layer properties

- Cyan/Red (−100, 0, 100): Decrease or increase the balance of cyan to red.

- Magenta/Green (−100, 0, 100): Decrease or increase the balance of magenta to green.

- Yellow/Blue (−100, 0, 100): Decrease or increase the balance of yellow to blue.

- Tone: From the list, you can choose to affect the tone of the Shadows, Midtones, or Highlights. Then, you can adjust the previously mentioned slider differently for each tone.

- Preserve Luminosity Toggle: This can be turned off or on. By default, it is on and controls how the color luminosity appears.

- Blend Mode: By default, it is set to Normal. Refer to the "Layer Blending Modes and Layer Opacity" section in this chapter if you need more details.

- Layer Opacity (0–100%): Alters the intensity of how the adjustment affects the underlying colors. By default, it is set to 100%.

In this example, we can see how altering the properties affected the Color Balance of the image in the midtones. Refer to Figure 5-89.

CHAPTER 5　WORKING WITH LAYERS IN FRESCO AND THE VERTICAL TASKBAR

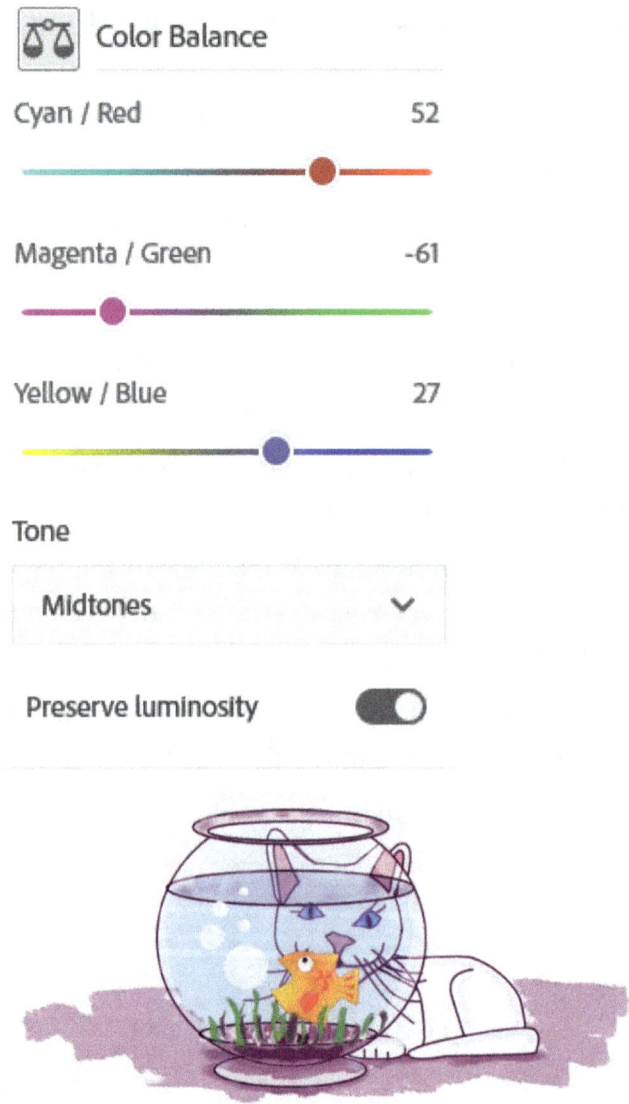

Figure 5-89. *Color Balance Adjustment layer applied to an image using the Layer properties panel sliders, Tone list, and Preserve luminosity toggle*

You could then further edit by adjusting Blend mode and Opacity. Refer to Figure 5-90.

CHAPTER 5   WORKING WITH LAYERS IN FRESCO AND THE VERTICAL TASKBAR

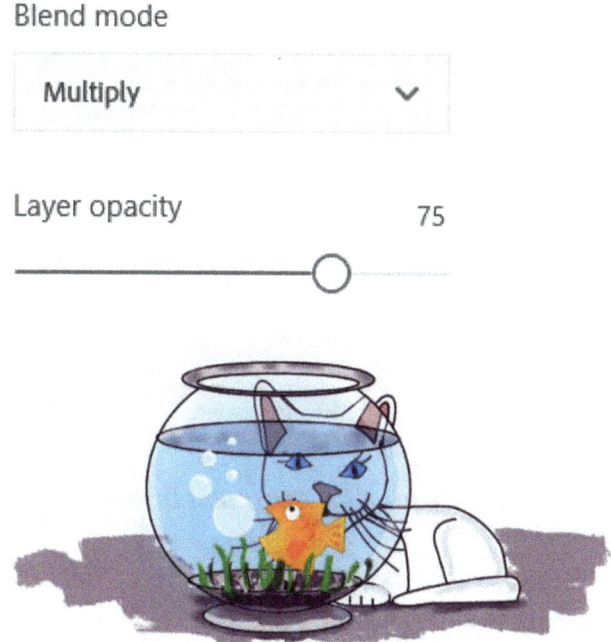

Figure 5-90. *Color Balance Adjustment layer applied to an image using the Layer properties Blend mode and Layer opacity*

Here are some important tips to remember.

When you want to affect multiple areas or add intensity, you can use the same Adjustment layer multiple times by duplicating the layers. Refer to Figure 5-91.

Figure 5-91. *Duplication of an Adjustment layer*

Adjustment layers can also be grouped like other layers. They can be dragged one on top of another, and you can ungroup them as well. Refer to Figure 5-92.

Figure 5-92. *Grouped and ungrouped Adjustment layers*

While working with Adjustment layers to find the correct settings, you can turn the visibility on and off. Refer to Figure 5-92.

Clipping Masks

Clipping masks are used for creating a mask by clipping one or more layers to another layer or a layer group below. These clipped layers can be Pixel or Vector layers. However, Adjustment layers can also be used to apply or clip an adjustment of color to a specific layer. Refer to Figure 5-93.

CHAPTER 5   WORKING WITH LAYERS IN FRESCO AND THE VERTICAL TASKBAR

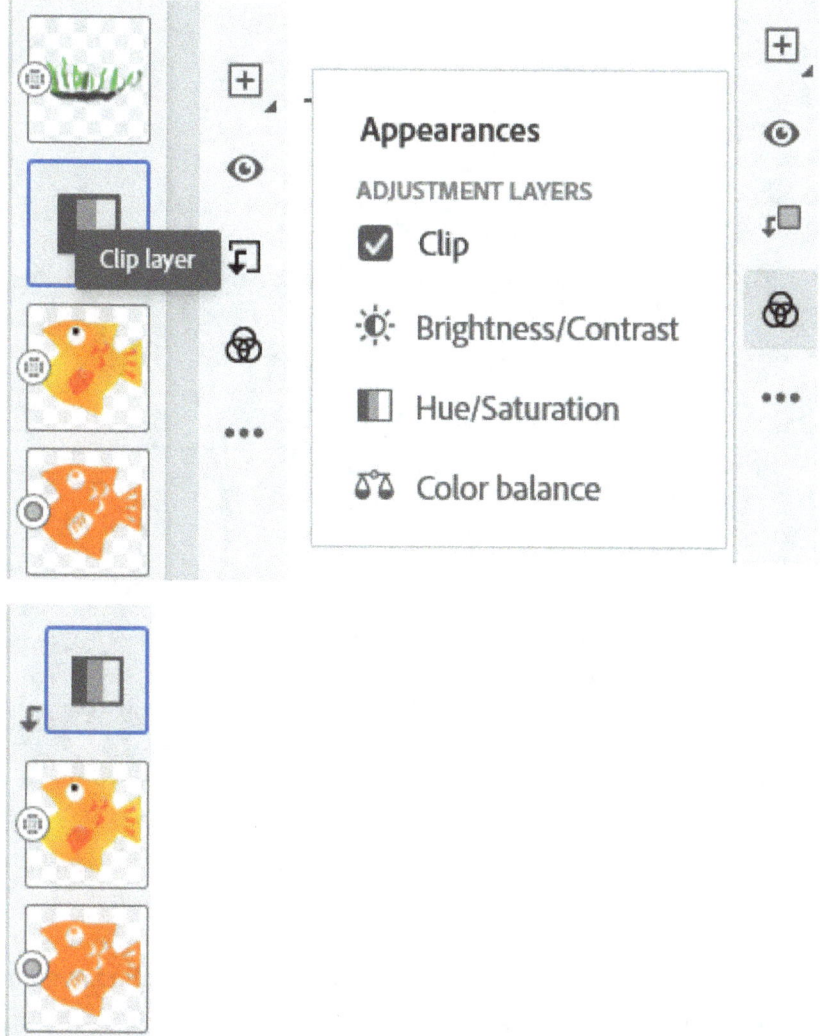

Figure 5-93. *Applying an Adjustment layer clipping mask via the Vertical Taskbar*

When we want to apply an Adjustment layer, we can automatically apply a clipping mask state by enabling the Clip check box in the pop-up menu before selecting the Adjustment layer.

However, if you decide to apply the clipping mask later manually, you can still do this by clicking the icon Clip layer in the Vertical Taskbar while the Adjustment layer is selected. Refer to Figure 5-93.

This means that the Adjustment layer will then only affect that Adjustment layer or layer group but not the rest below it. Refer to Figure 5-94.

387

CHAPTER 5   WORKING WITH LAYERS IN FRESCO AND THE VERTICAL TASKBAR

Figure 5-94. *Clipping mask applied to the image overall (above) and only applied to the fish layer (below). Note slight color change in shadow areas*

In this case, the Adjustment layer of Hue/Saturation, when applied overall, lightened all areas which I did not want to do. But when applied only to the upper fish as in Figure 5-93 and Figure 5-94, the colors surrounding or below returned to a more darkened state, such as some of shadows. Subtle changes like this can be important. Refer to Figure 5-95.

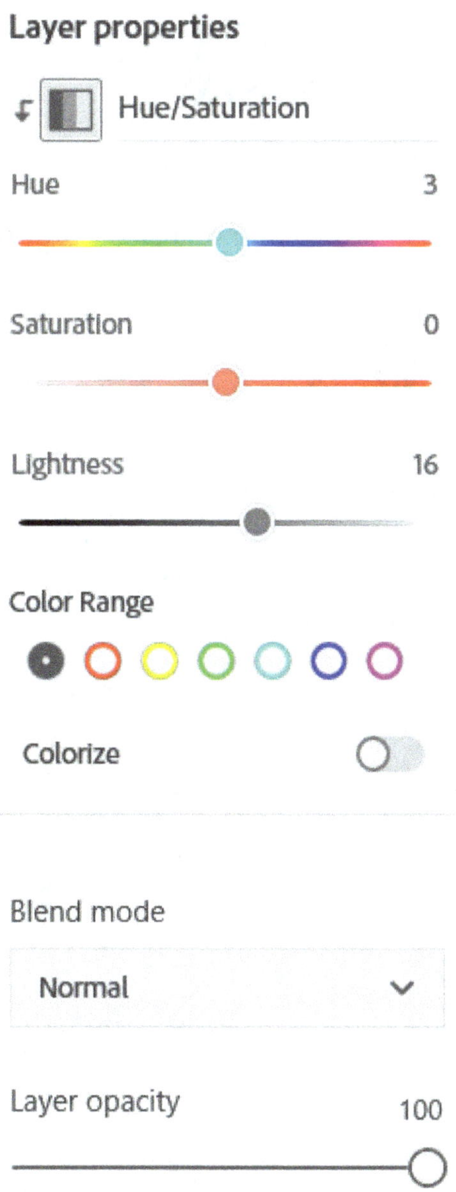

CHAPTER 5   WORKING WITH LAYERS IN FRESCO AND THE VERTICAL TASKBAR

Layer properties

Hue/Saturation

Hue   3

Saturation   0

Lightness   16

Color Range

Colorize

Blend mode

Normal

Layer opacity   100

Figure 5-95. *Clipping mask applied to the Adjustment layer displayed in the Layer properties*

As mentioned, if you want the effect for all layers and below, then remove the clipping mask from the selected Clip layer any time by choosing that action from the Vertical Taskbar again. Refer to Figure 5-96.

CHAPTER 5   WORKING WITH LAYERS IN FRESCO AND THE VERTICAL TASKBAR

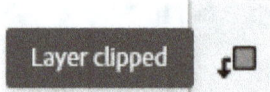

Figure 5-96. *Use the Vertical Taskbar icon to remove the clipping of a layer*

A clipping mask could also be used with animation, as we will look at in more detail in Chapter 8.

Adjustment Layer Masks

Another way to alter the area your Adjustment layer affects is to create a layer mask. When you create a layer mask for these layers, you can then make selective color adjustments. This is possible when you use the Layer actions of Load as selection from a selected layer then return to the Adjustment layer before applying the mask using the Contextual Task bar. Refer to Figures 5-97, 5-98, and 5-99.

Figure 5-97. *Load a selection of a select layer*

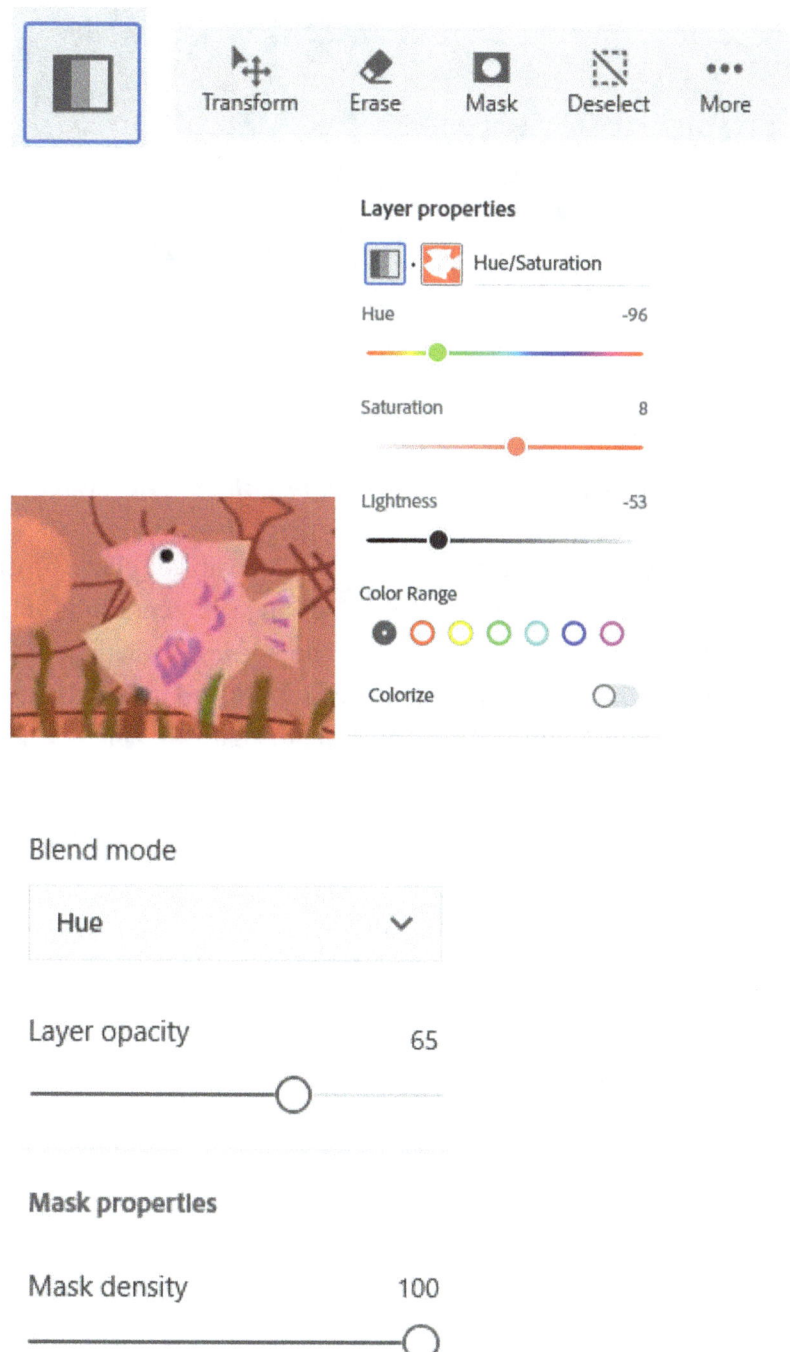

Figure 5-98. *Use the Adjustment layer and Contextual Task bar to create a mask, and then use the Layer properties to change the color of the masked area*

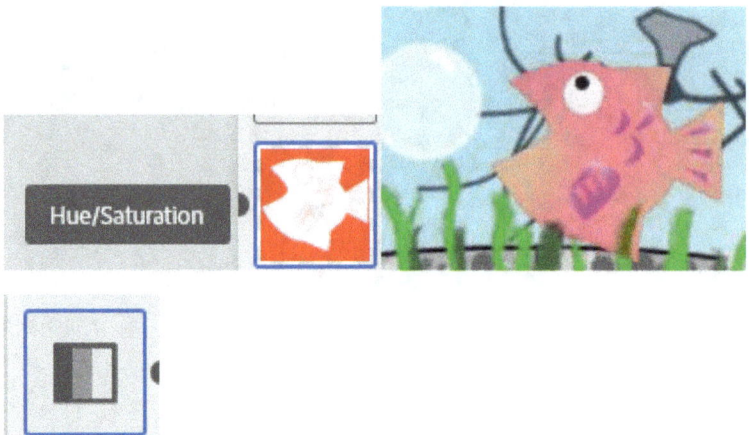

Figure 5-99. *A mask applied to a Hue/Saturation Adjustment layer*

Just like the other layer masks, you can edit and paint with your Pixel brush on them to adjust your areas of color. Review the section "Masking Different Kinds of Layers and Their Content Setting," as discussed earlier in this chapter, if you need more details.

Note that the three mentioned Adjustment layers discussed in this chapter are compatible with Photoshop Adjustment layers. Refer to Figure 5-100.

CHAPTER 5   WORKING WITH LAYERS IN FRESCO AND THE VERTICAL TASKBAR

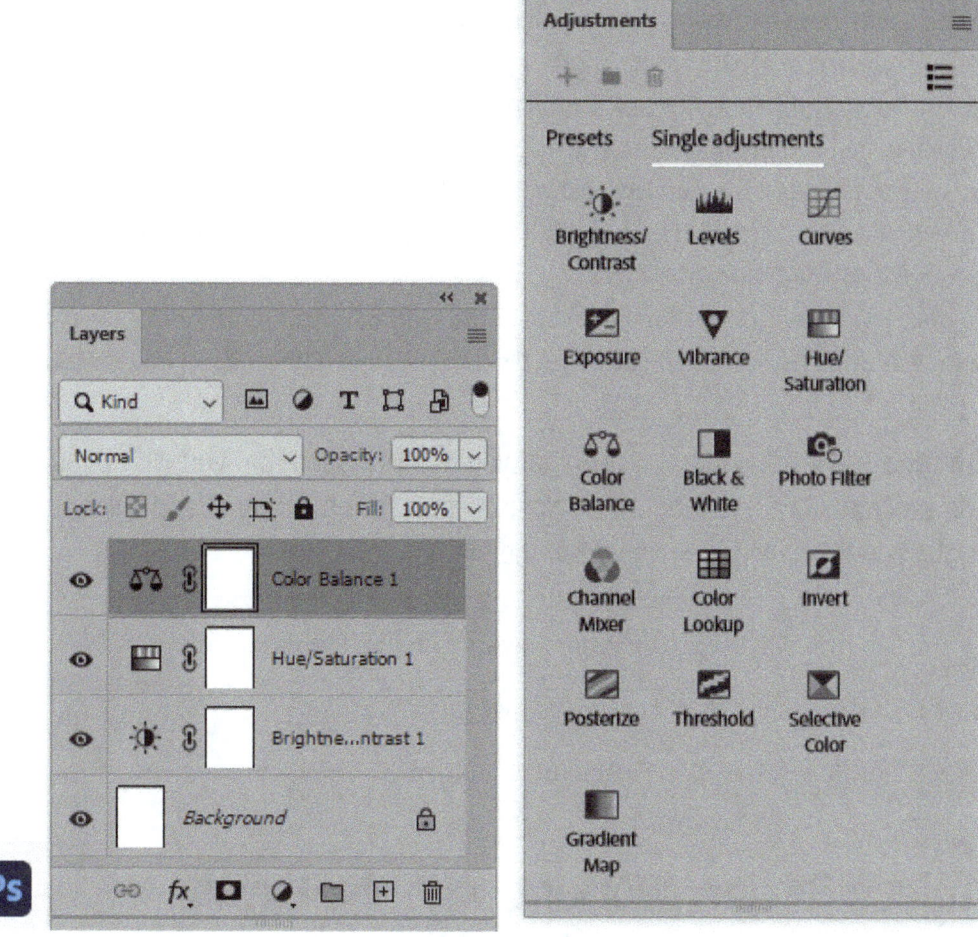

Figure 5-100. *Adjustment layers found in Photoshop in the Layers panel and Adjustments panel under the Single adjustments tab*

Because these three are also available in Fresco, I recommend putting a blank or Pixel layer between each before importing the file into Fresco. While they can be added using Photoshop, it's important to be aware that on occasion they can in Fresco, if placed on top of all the layers, cause the file to revert to one grouped Photoshop layer which is impossible to edit in Fresco as separate layers. Be aware of this with Hue/Saturation, as the Photoshop Adjustment layer has a few new custom features (Prominent colors) which have been added beyond the color range settings in Fresco. If you run into an issue of combined Adjustment layers, I recommend downloading the file, opening it in Photoshop and then in a duplicate of the file, deleting/removing any Adjustment layer you may have added before importing and opening in Fresco. Then import the file into Fresco again. Alternatively, you can just continue to work on the file in Photoshop, which I will discuss in Chapter 9.

However, Photoshop has additional Adjustment layers such as Levels and Curves, which can be used prior to working in Fresco, but these will not be accessible in Fresco and may appear as a merged Photoshop layer. This is important to note because if, for example, Levels was placed on top of all other Adjustment layers that would cause them to merge into one Photoshop layer.

Also, as mentioned earlier, be aware of the kind of layer blend modes that you apply as, for example, Dissolve will cause the layer to become a Photoshop layer upon import.

Caution Any Adjustment layers that you add in Fresco that you did not alter with the sliders will be removed, upon closing, from the Layer panel and will not appear in the panel the next time you open the file.

You can review Fresco Adjustment layers from the following link:

https://helpx.adobe.com/fresco/using/layers.html

You can close the earlier opened file and then look at the project.

Project: Review Working with the Layers in a Fresco Document

Continuing on with the previous project in Chapter 4, we will now look at the current layers that are in the document and then additional layers that I added to the artwork.

Refer to the file **SeascapeLayersStart_Part2.psd** and open it if you want to from the Home page ➤ Import and open into Fresco. Refer to Figures 5-101 and 5-102.

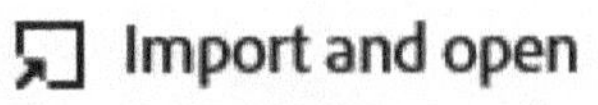

                     🗂 Import and open

Figure 5-101. *Import and open a file in Fresco*

CHAPTER 5　WORKING WITH LAYERS IN FRESCO AND THE VERTICAL TASKBAR

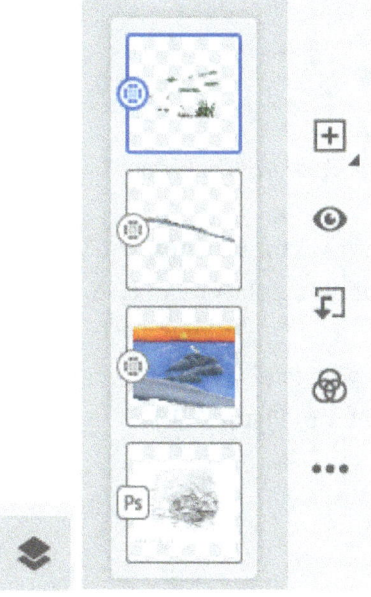

Figure 5-102. *Reviewing the current layers found in the project and the artwork on the canvas*

CHAPTER 5   WORKING WITH LAYERS IN FRESCO AND THE VERTICAL TASKBAR

You can also, at the end of the chapter, look at the file **SeascapeLayersFinal2.psd** if you later need to compare the work done in this chapter.

Review of Previous Layers

In Chapter 4, as the project was completed, there were a few layers present and then added to the document. In my example, there were, if we look from bottom to top in the Layer panel, four:

- A Photoshop Background Layer (Ps): This was the sketch that I had earlier scanned and then cleaned up in Photoshop.

- Pixel Layer: In Photoshop, I had also created a blank new layer or Pixel layer, and then, I proceeded to paint on that layer with my Pixel Mixer brushes to create most of the scene.

- I then proceeded to paint on two other Pixel layers with Pixel brushes. To create those layers, I clicked the Add layer button each time and then began to paint such things as rocks, grasses, and algae. Refer to Figure 5-103.

Figure 5-103. *Adding layers to a project with the Vertical Taskbar*

Optionally, in your project, if you had worked with Vector brushes, you would have clicked the same button and then proceeded to paint on that layer, but it would have been a transformed Vector layer.

Another step that I did as I painted was to turn layer visibility off and on so that I could compare my work to the underlying sketch. Refer to Figure 5-104.

CHAPTER 5　WORKING WITH LAYERS IN FRESCO AND THE VERTICAL TASKBAR

Figure 5-104. *Hiding layers to see other layers using the Vertical Taskbar*

Alternatively, I could also use the Layer properties panel to temporarily reduce the Layer opacity so that I could still see some of the painted color as I worked and then return the Layer opacity back to 100%. Refer to Figure 5-105.

CHAPTER 5   WORKING WITH LAYERS IN FRESCO AND THE VERTICAL TASKBAR

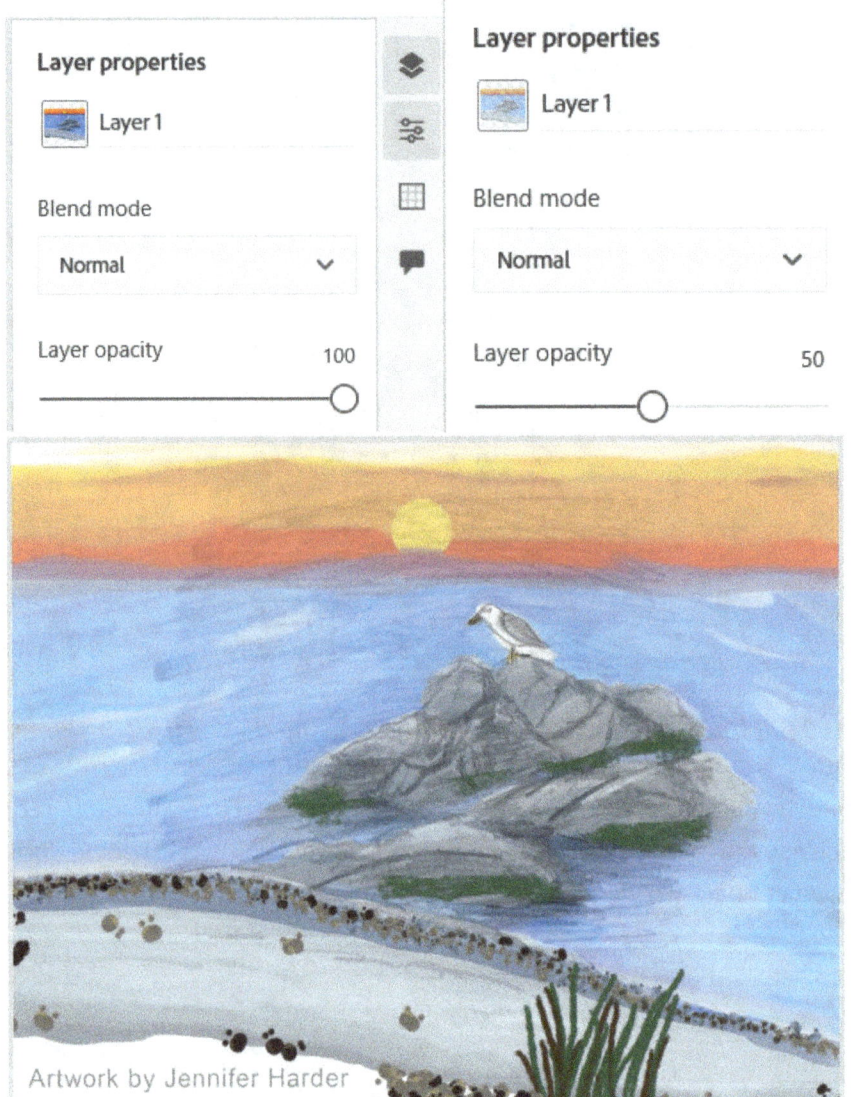

Figure 5-105. *Changing the opacity of a selected layer in the Layer properties*

These are considered basic repetitive steps that you would do as you work with Pixel and Vector layers in your artwork.

You would also use the key command of zoom in (Ctrl++) and out (Ctrl+-) and use and hold down the spacebar key (hand tool) when you do not want to move objects on the layer by mistake.

CHAPTER 5 WORKING WITH LAYERS IN FRESCO AND THE VERTICAL TASKBAR

Adding Additional Layers

As you discovered in this chapter, it is important, when adding additional Pixel or Vector layers to your project, to keep them organized so that you can visualize your artwork correctly. However, the other benefit of layers is to prevent certain brush strokes or shapes from mixing with others, especially when adding fine details or new shapes that you may want to move, transform, and repaint.

For example, in my final file on separate Vector layers, I added the shapes of a starfish and two shells that may be found on the beach. Refer to Figure 5-106.

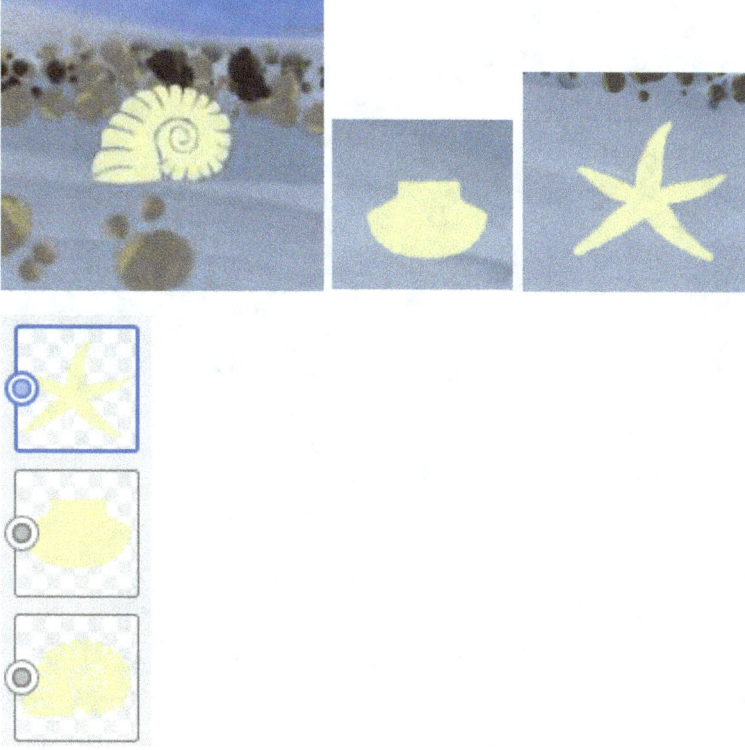

Figure 5-106. Adding stamped shapes to Vector layers

To review, in Chapter 4, we looked at how to create custom shapes, either our own using Shapes tools and pen or from the Shapes panel. You also learned how to add them into a Creative Cloud Library via the Photoshop Libraries panel and the Capture app. Refer to Figure 5-107.

CHAPTER 5   WORKING WITH LAYERS IN FRESCO AND THE VERTICAL TASKBAR

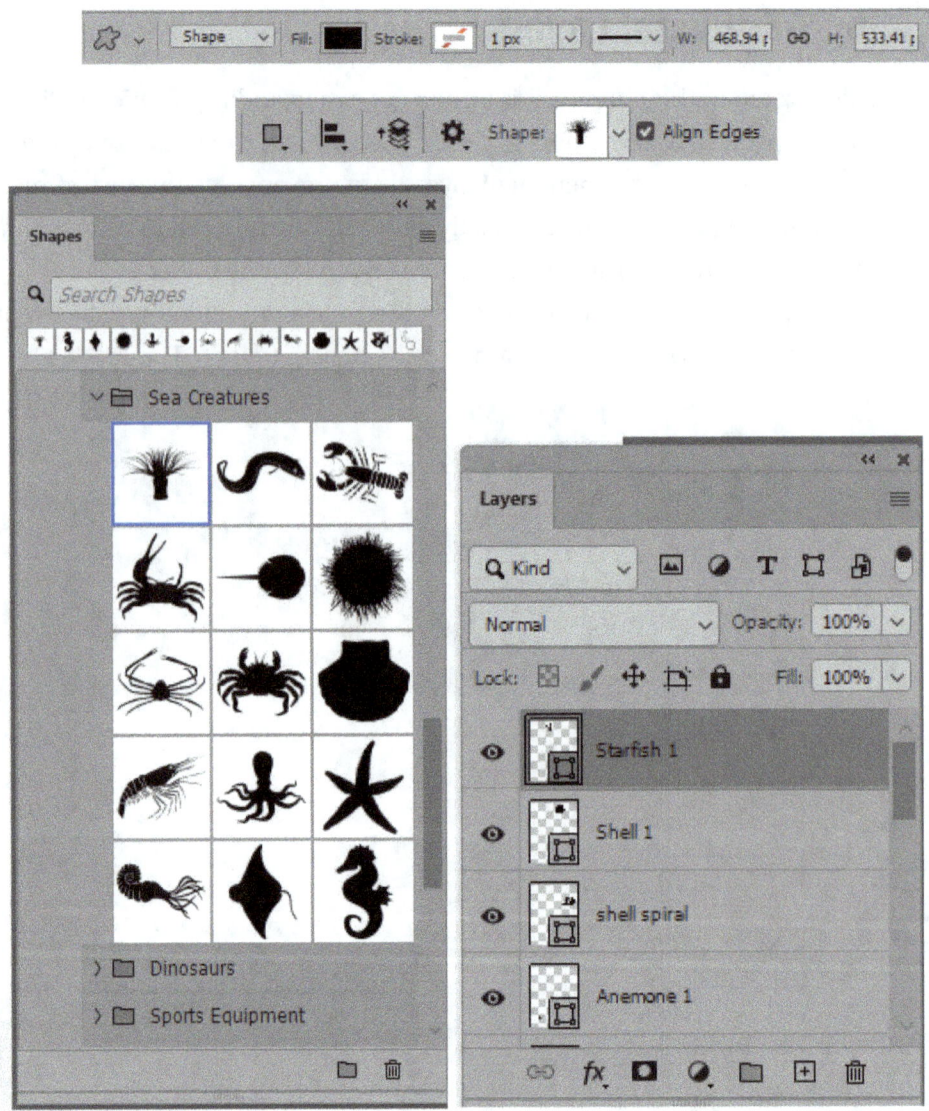

Figure 5-107. *Review where shapes are accessed in Photoshop's Options bar, Shapes panel, and Layers panel*

The shapes that I used in this chapter came from the Photoshop Shapes panel Legacy Shapes and More ➤ 2019 Shapes ➤ Sea Creatures folder.

After dragging them onto a layer in Photoshop, I adapted a copy of one of the creatures using Pen and Selection tools to be more shell-like. To do that, I removed anchor points and then added back some anchor points on the shape. In addition, I used the Transform main menu option as Edit ➤ Transform ➤ Rotate to adjust the alignment of the shape. Refer to my file **shape_sealife.psd**. Refer to Figure 5-108.

CHAPTER 5   WORKING WITH LAYERS IN FRESCO AND THE VERTICAL TASKBAR

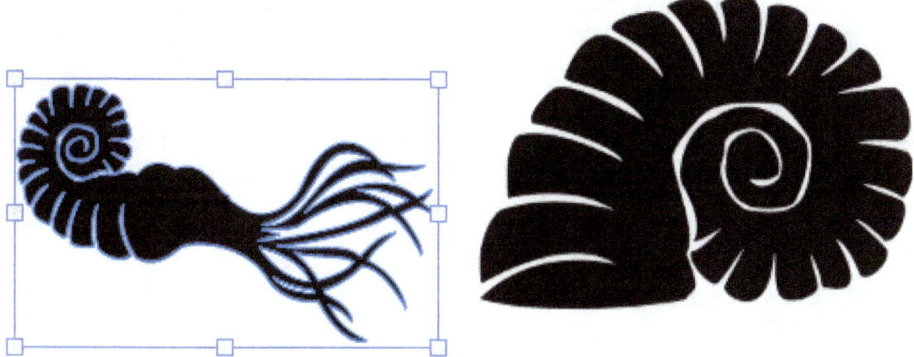

Figure 5-108. *Shapes can be modified in Photoshop*

In my case, I created a new library in the Libraries panel called **SeaCreaturesFresco.cclibs**. You can use the panel's menu if you want to import my Library file. Refer to Chapter 3 if you need to review how to do that. Refer to Figure 5-109.

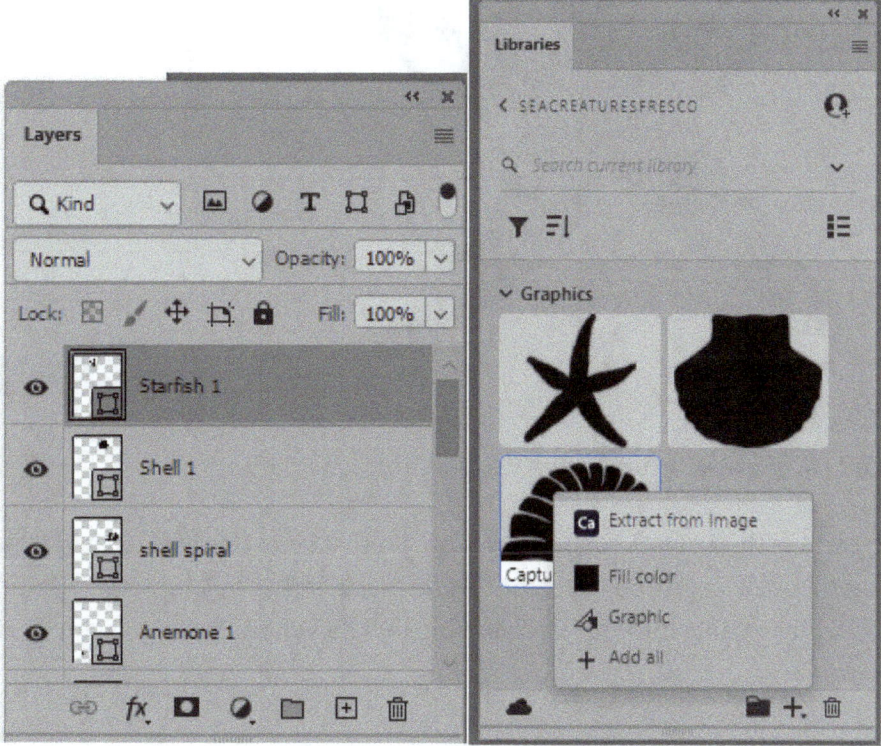

Figure 5-109. *Adding a Shape layer from the Layers panel to the Libraries panel via the Extract from Image Capture app*

CHAPTER 5   WORKING WITH LAYERS IN FRESCO AND THE VERTICAL TASKBAR

Once I created the library, I added some shapes by selecting each layer in the Layers panel one at a time. While the layers were selected, in the Photoshop Libraries panel, I used the plus (+) icon and clicked the Extract from Image option. In the Capture dialog box, I turned the layers, one at a time, into Capture Shapes and Saved to the CC Libraries. Review Chapter 4 if you need more details on this topic. Refer to Figure 5-110.

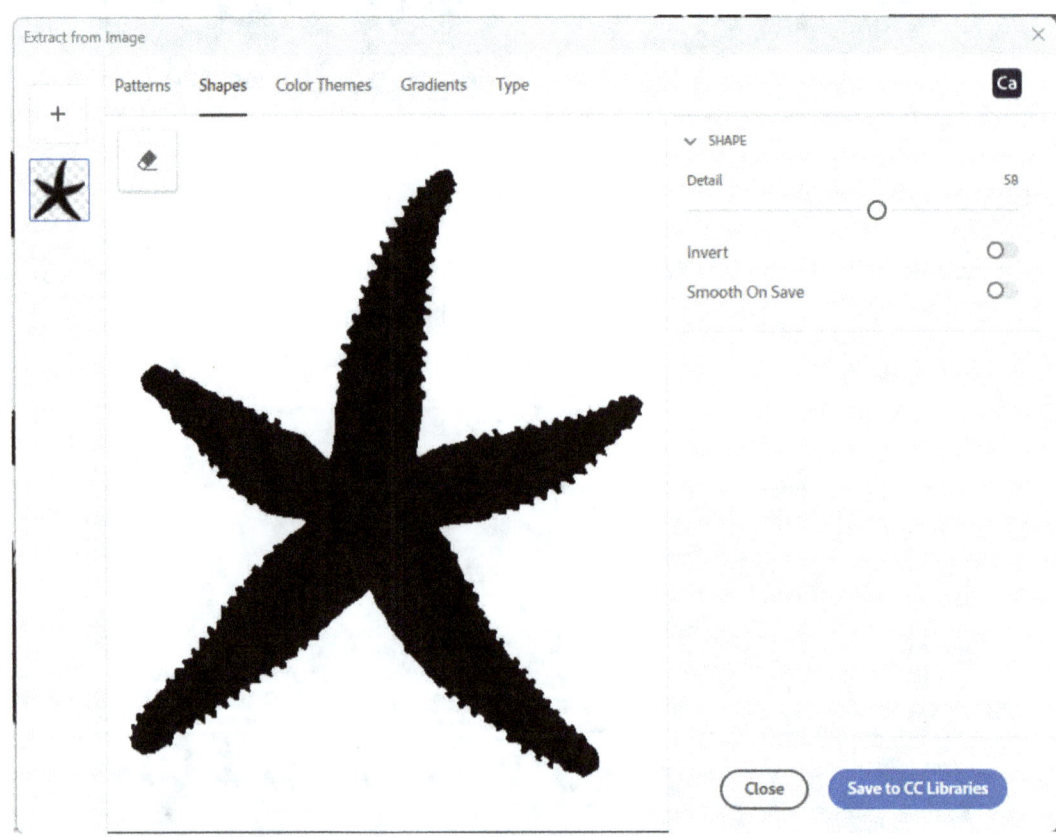

Figure 5-110. *Extract from Image Capture app dialog box*

After I added these to my shape collection, I returned to Fresco, I located the shape in the Shapes tool library, and using the Contextual Task bar Fill, I stamped the shape on a new Vector layer using the current color chip of light yellow. Refer to Figure 5-111.

CHAPTER 5   WORKING WITH LAYERS IN FRESCO AND THE VERTICAL TASKBAR

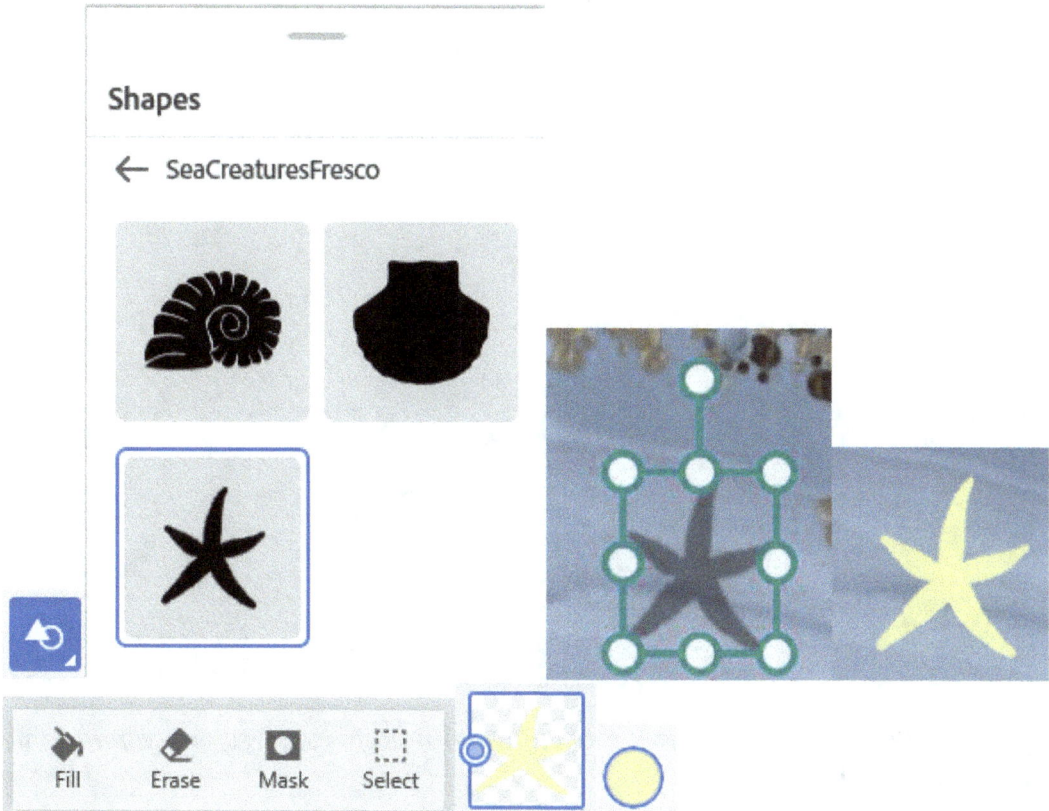

Figure 5-111. *Fresco Shapes tool panel adding a shape to a Vector layer using the fill on the Contextual Task bar with a color chip selected*

Now, you may wonder why did I choose to stamp each of my shapes on a separate Vector layer rather than on Pixel layers? There are several reasons.

If the shape is not in correct perspective, I may want to move and transform it. I want to keep the shape in high-resolution quality if I need to transform it several times. Keeping shapes on separate layers means I can move them independently without destroying another shape. Refer to Figure 5-112.

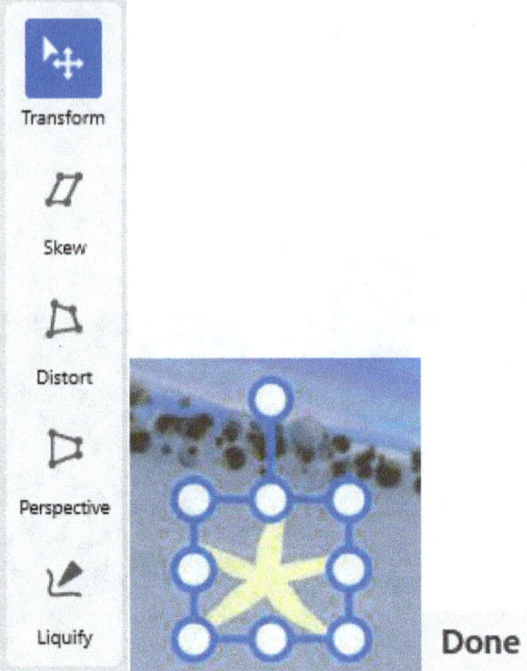

Figure 5-112. *Use the Transform tool to further modify your Vector layer and then exit by clicking Done*

Once I have transformed the shapes on the Vector layers to the size I want, I click Done to exit the Transform workspace.

I then may want to decorate them with less solid colors using Pixel brushes. Rather than transform these Vector layers into Pixel layers, right-click on the layer using the Layer actions. I will create a duplicate layer and then, on the top copy, convert it to a Pixel layer. Refer to Figure 5-113.

CHAPTER 5   WORKING WITH LAYERS IN FRESCO AND THE VERTICAL TASKBAR

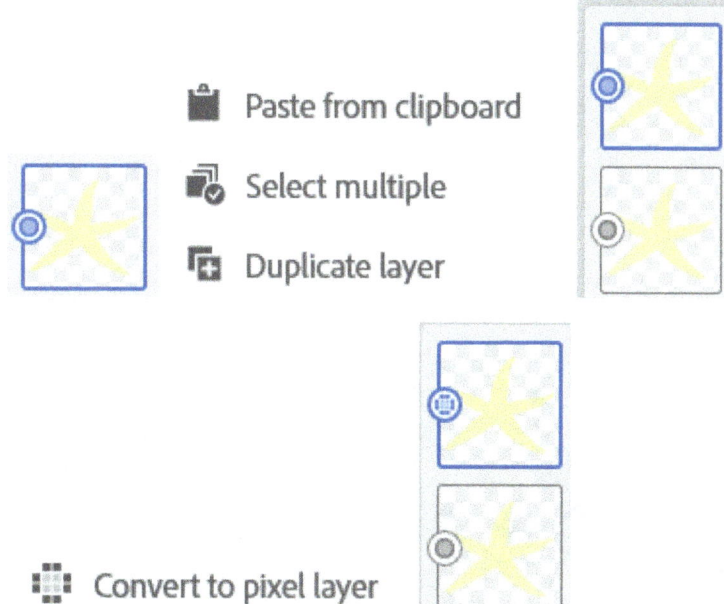

Figure 5-113. *Duplicate a Vector layer and then convert a copy to a Pixel layer*

With the Pixel copy layer selected, I can then right-click on the layer and, from the Layer actions, choose Load as selection. Refer to Figure 5-114.

Figure 5-114. *Load the selected layer as a selection*

Then, with a Pixel brush and a new color chip color, paint within the selection to add texture and design to a shell or starfish. In this case, I used the Pixel brush Mixer brushes ➤ Monet mixer. Refer to Figure 5-115.

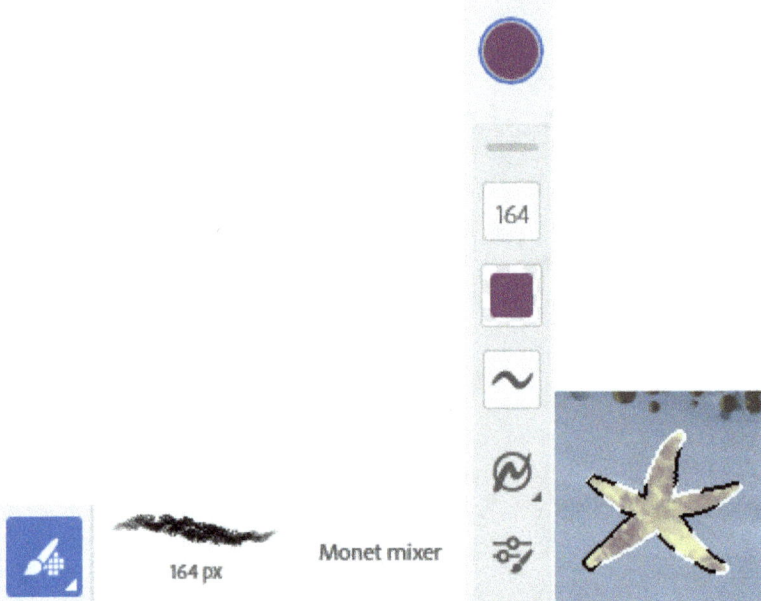

Figure 5-115. *Use a Pixel brush to paint with in the selection with a color chip*

Then, using the Contextual Task bar, deselect the selection. Refer to Figure 5-116.

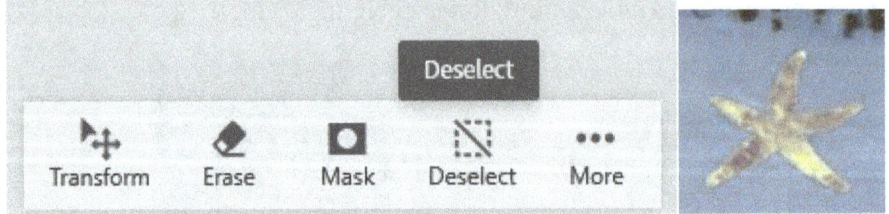

Figure 5-116. *Use the Contextual Task bar to deselect the selection to see the result*

I then repeated these steps again for the other Vector layers by turning the duplicate copies into Pixel layers, loading each duplicate Pixel layer as a selection, and then painting on the selected copy with a Pixel brush. I used different colors and varied the brush sizes. Sometimes you will have to load the layer as selection several times and then deselect for smaller items as you paint them. Refer to Figure 5-117.

CHAPTER 5   WORKING WITH LAYERS IN FRESCO AND THE VERTICAL TASKBAR

Figure 5-117. *Duplicate other layers, convert to Pixel layers, and paint those layers when selected*

Remember, if you need to move two layers at once, such as a Vector and Pixel layer, use the Layer action of Select multiple to select both, before using the Move and Transform tools. Click Done to commit any movements. Refer to Figure 5-118.

CHAPTER 5　WORKING WITH LAYERS IN FRESCO AND THE VERTICAL TASKBAR

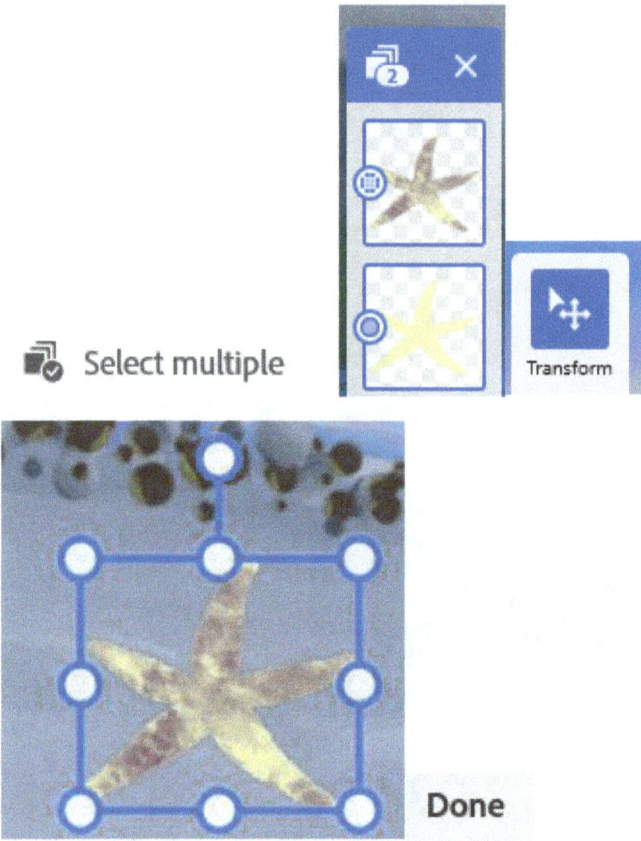

Figure 5-118. *Select multiple Layer action when you want to move or transform more than one, and click Done to exit that workspace*

Then, cancel any multiselect and select a single layer again. Refer to Figure 5-119.

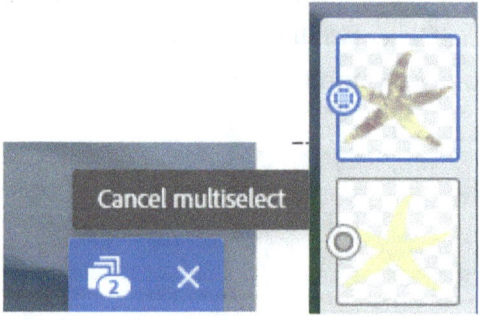

Figure 5-119. *Cancel your multiselect when you want to go back to a single layer*

CHAPTER 5 WORKING WITH LAYERS IN FRESCO AND THE VERTICAL TASKBAR

Going beyond Vector and Pixel layers and painting on them, I will then add an Appearance/Adjustment layer of Hue/Saturation above all the layers. Refer to Figure 5-120.

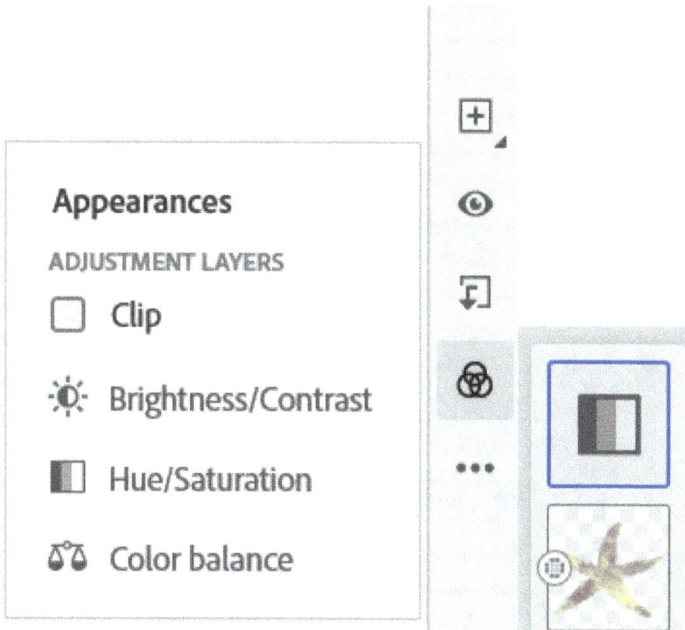

Figure 5-120. *Apply an Adjustment layer above all or some layers using the Vertical Taskbar Appearances*

The reason that I am doing this is because, instead painting on a Pixel layer, I want to alter the colors in select areas to add some color changes to the water. Because it is a sunset picture, I do not want to destroy my original brush strokes.

In the Layer properties panel, I begin by figuring out what colors make the sunset. This will alter the overall color for the moment, but that is OK as I will adjust for this afterward. For the moment, I will move my Hue over to -180 and set my Blend mode to Linear light. Refer to Figures 5-121 and 5-122.

CHAPTER 5 WORKING WITH LAYERS IN FRESCO AND THE VERTICAL TASKBAR

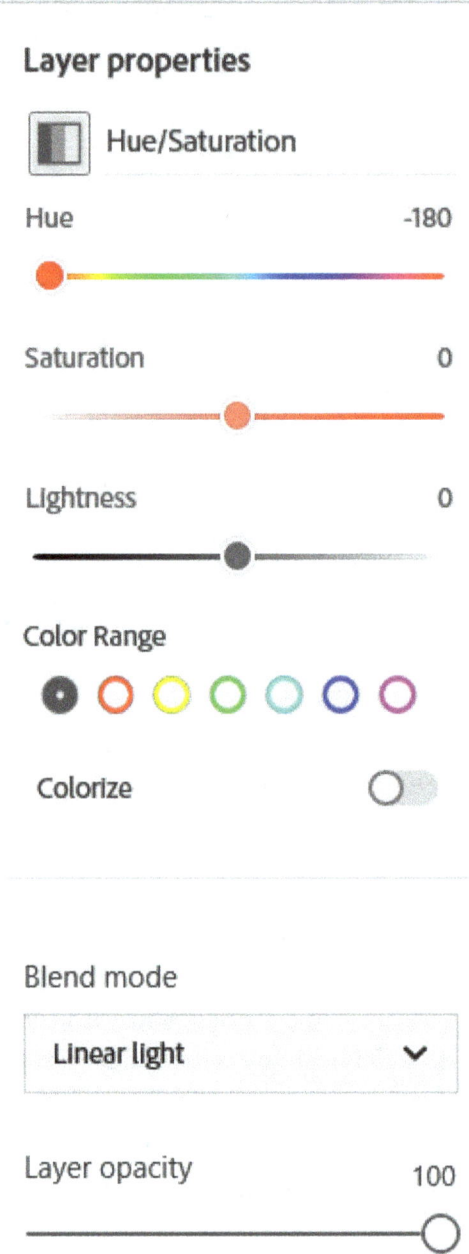

Figure 5-121. *Layers properties settings for Hue/Saturation Adjustment layer*

CHAPTER 5　WORKING WITH LAYERS IN FRESCO AND THE VERTICAL TASKBAR

Figure 5-122. *Result of adding an Adjustment layer overall*

Next, I will create a mask and hide and reveal areas of color. While on the Adjustment layer, I will use the Rectangle selection tool to drag around the water and sand areas below the sky horizon. Refer to Figure 5-123.

CHAPTER 5   WORKING WITH LAYERS IN FRESCO AND THE VERTICAL TASKBAR

Figure 5-123. *Using the Rectangle selection tool on an Adjustment layer*

Then, from the Contextual Task bar, choose Mask. Refer to Figure 5-124 and Figure 5-125.

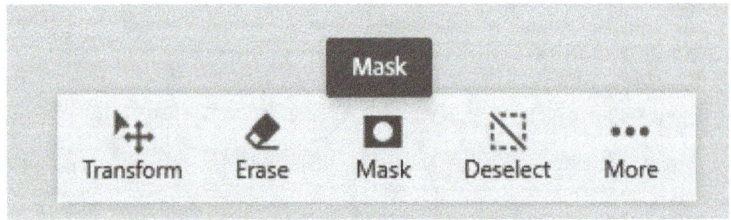

Figure 5-124. *Masking that areas of the selection with the Contextual Task bar*

412

CHAPTER 5   WORKING WITH LAYERS IN FRESCO AND THE VERTICAL TASKBAR

Figure 5-125. *Viewing the masked area of the artwork with the mask on the Hue/Saturation layer*

This then creates a mask on that layer which you can slide right to see what areas of color are now affected by the Adjustment layer. The sky is not part of the color adjustment, and so, that part is hidden. Refer to Figure 5-126.

Figure 5-126. *Sliding the mask over on the Adjustment layer to see the artwork as it is*

This is getting better, but we really do not want all the water, rocks, and sand to be orange so you will need to edit the water and sand area further.

Back in Mask mode, use one of your Pixel brushes while you hide and reveal areas of the mask. Working with the setting On layers may help you to visualize this better, as you would in Photoshop with a layer mask. Refer to Figures 5-127 and 5-128.

CHAPTER 5　WORKING WITH LAYERS IN FRESCO AND THE VERTICAL TASKBAR

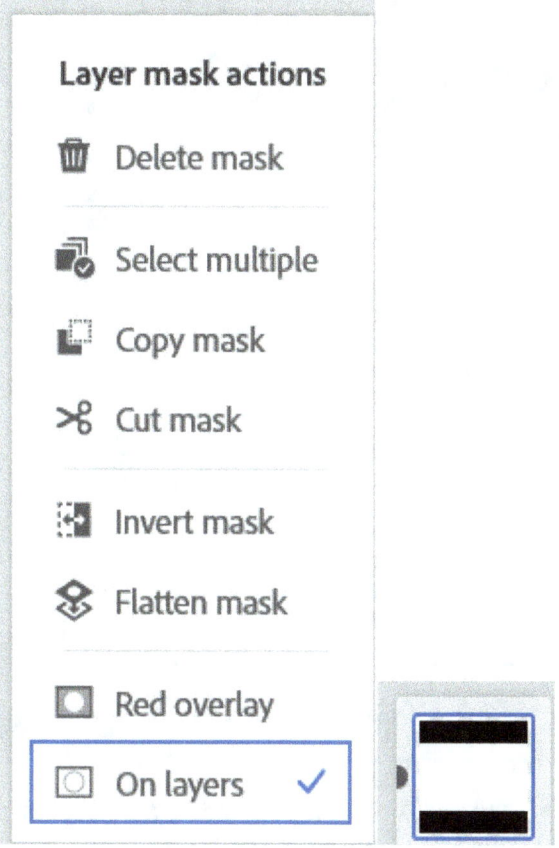

Figure 5-127. *Using Layer mask action to change the layer mask settings from Red overlay to On layers*

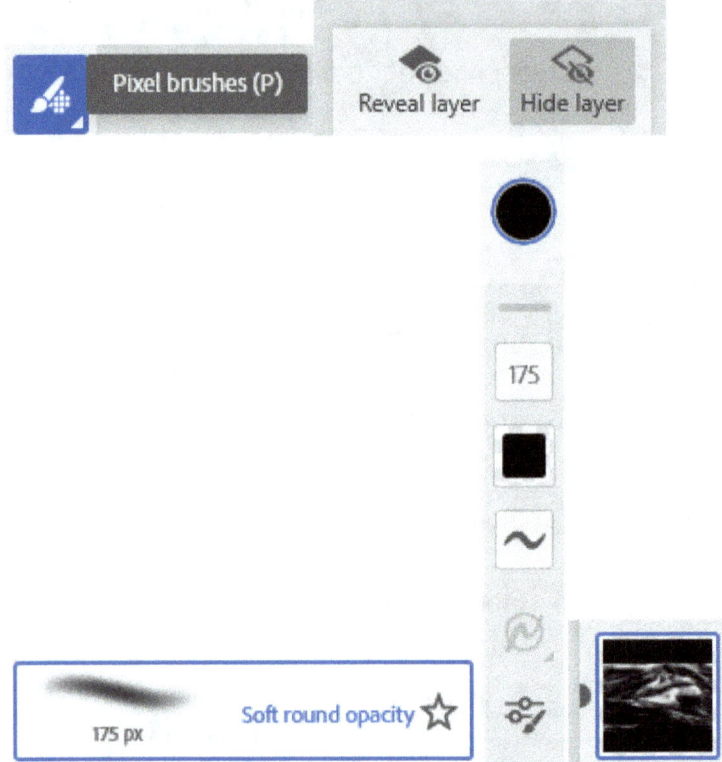

Figure 5-128. *Paint on the masks with your Pixel brush, and use the Contextual Task bar and other brush settings to alter the mask*

Try, maybe, a Basic brush of Soft round opacity and brush with black as required, to leave some orange glow in certain areas moving between hiding and revealing areas. Refer to Figure 5-128.

As I worked on the Adjustment layer, I then reduced the Saturation a bit to (−16) to make it less intense. Refer to Figure 5-129.

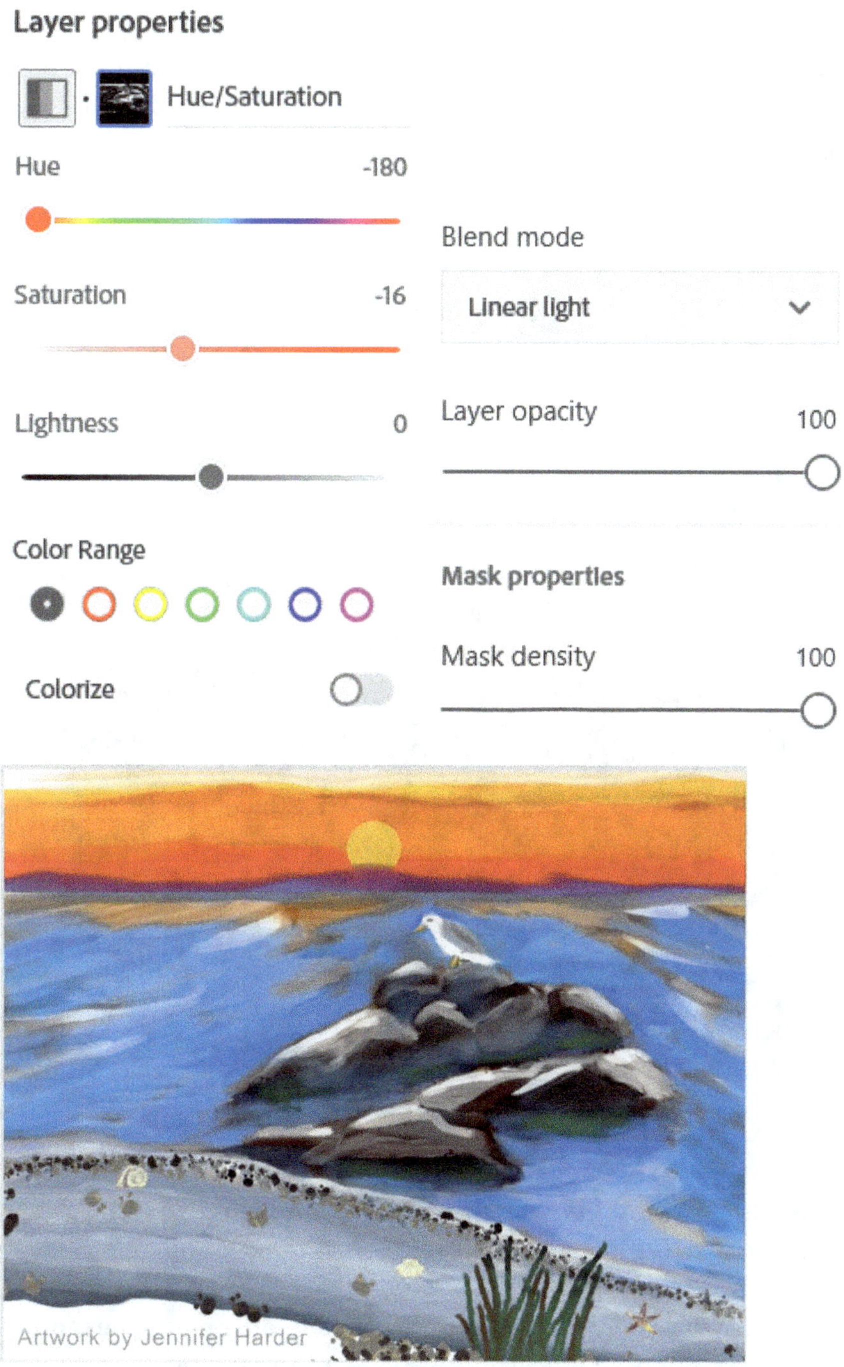

Layer properties

Hue/Saturation

Hue   -180

Saturation   -16

Lightness   0

Color Range

Colorize

Blend mode

Linear light

Layer opacity   100

Mask properties

Mask density   100

Artwork by Jennifer Harder

Figure 5-129. *Make color adjustments to the final layer mask using the Layer properties Hue/Saturation*

CHAPTER 5   WORKING WITH LAYERS IN FRESCO AND THE VERTICAL TASKBAR

This is a clever way to adjust the color of the water and rocks for the sunset rather than altering the brush strokes on another layer. To other layers above and below, you can continue to add more Adjustment layers, such as Brightness/Contrast, to create more shadow in certain areas around the rocks. I set the Brightness to -42 and Contrast to 100. Refer to Figure 5-130.

Figure 5-130. Make color adjustments to another layer mask using the Layer properties Brightness/Contrast

Adding another Hue/Saturation layer for where the water meets the mountains and then altering the mask with a few brush strokes can be an additional step. I set the Hue to 85, left Saturation at 0, and set the Lightness to -13. Refer to Figure 5-131.

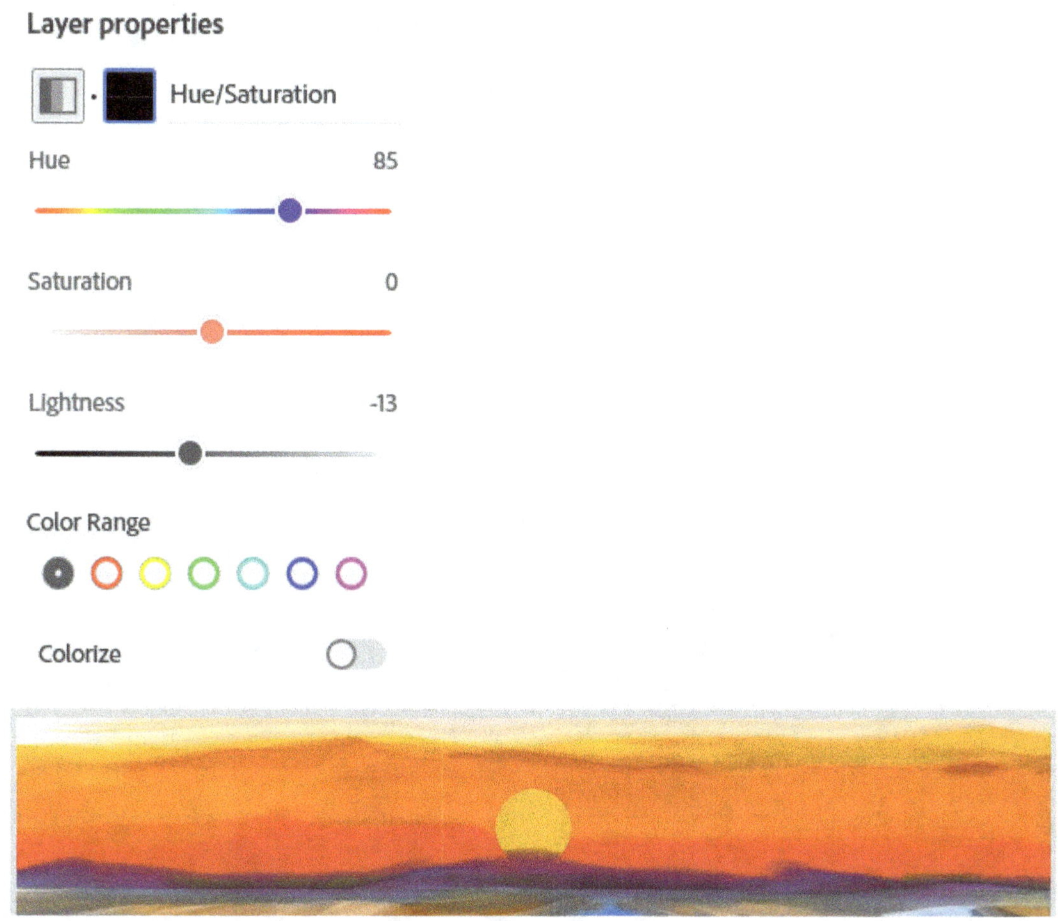

CHAPTER 5   WORKING WITH LAYERS IN FRESCO AND THE VERTICAL TASKBAR

Layer properties

Hue/Saturation

Hue   85

Saturation   0

Lightness   -13

Color Range

Colorize

Figure 5-131. *Make color adjustments to another layer mask in the mountain area using the Layer properties Hue/Saturation*

Alternatively, in your own project, you may want to add an Adjustment layer with a clipping mask which I could do to alter the color of the starfish separately. I set the Hue: −25, Saturation: 45, and Lightness: 4 with a Blend mode of Multiply and Layer opacity 100%. Refer to Figure 5-132.

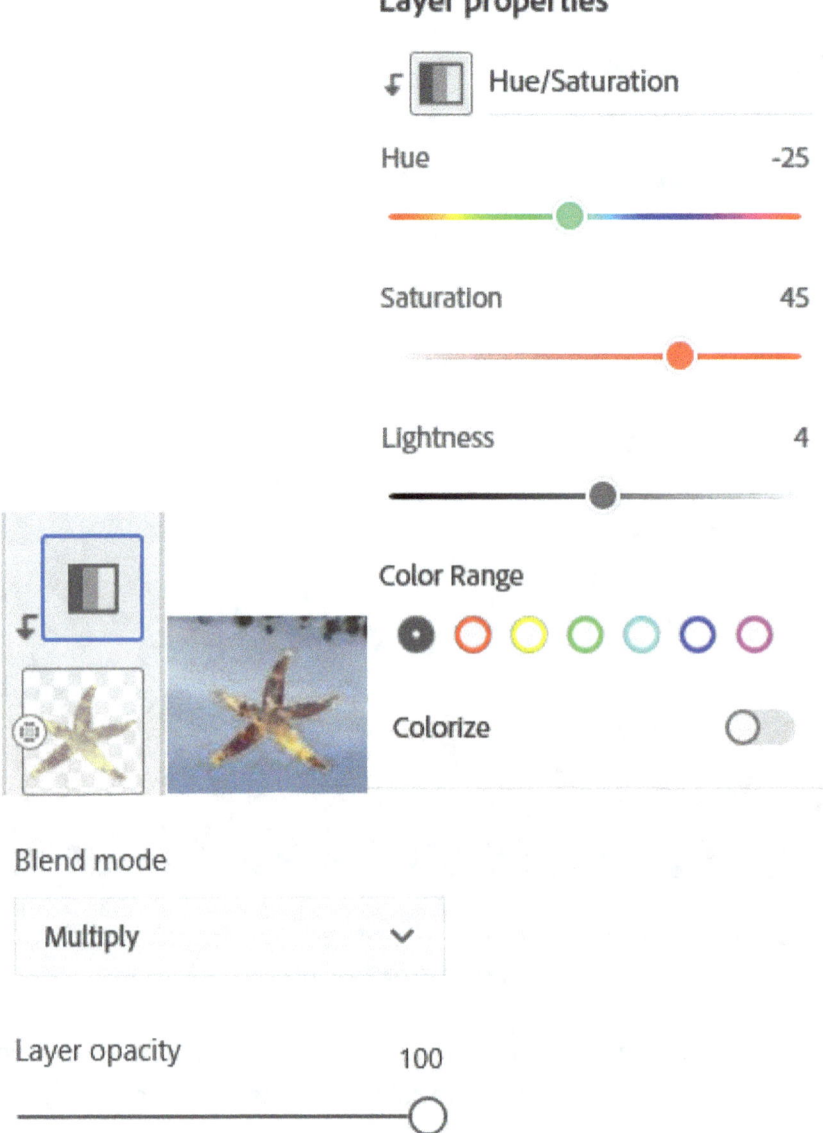

Figure 5-132. Make color adjustments to another layer mask that is clipped using the Layer properties Hue/Saturation and adjusting the Blend mode

You may, at this point, continue to add shadows or other brush strokes to your image. I added additional layers for shadow under the shells and starfish on the beach as well as added a few pink layer masked starfish near the rocks in the shadows. I used the masks to hide some of their limbs in the water and, on the image area, altered the color while in selection mode, as you saw earlier with a Pixel brush. Refer to Figure 5-133.

CHAPTER 5　WORKING WITH LAYERS IN FRESCO AND THE VERTICAL TASKBAR

Figure 5-133. *The completed artwork on the canvas*

Once you have completed your project, you can save a copy of it and review my file **SeascapeLayersFinal2.psd**.

You can see many more layers were added to the original. Refer to Figure 5-134.

CHAPTER 5   WORKING WITH LAYERS IN FRESCO AND THE VERTICAL TASKBAR

Figure 5-134. *Many more layers have been added to the Layers panel as you work on the project*

Remember to use either your Creative Cloud Desktop Files area or from the Fresco Home page if you need to download a copy later. Review Chapters 7 and 9 later if you need to know how to do that.

You have completed the project. You can close your project in Fresco to auto save your file.

Summary

In this chapter, we reviewed layers, layer properties, clipping masks, layer masks, and Adjustment layers that are available via the Vertical Taskbar. You also completed a painting project using the skills you learned in this chapter and the previous chapters.

In the next chapter, we will look at drawing aids for working on the canvas.

CHAPTER 6

Working with Drawing Aids on the Canvas

In Chapter 4, you saw how you can create your own free shapes for designs. Now, you will discover you can use drawing aid tools to enhance your artwork further. We will also look at how the drawing aids can be used with the perspective grid. Then, this chapter will also conclude with three project ideas that you may want to try.

Note The project files for this chapter can be found in the Chapter 6 folder. Refer to the link to files in the introduction.

Open the Adobe Fresco application.

In this chapter, you may want to create a blank Fresco Letter document, as described in Chapter 2, if you want to follow along, and you can create several layers to practice on. Refer to Figure 6-1.

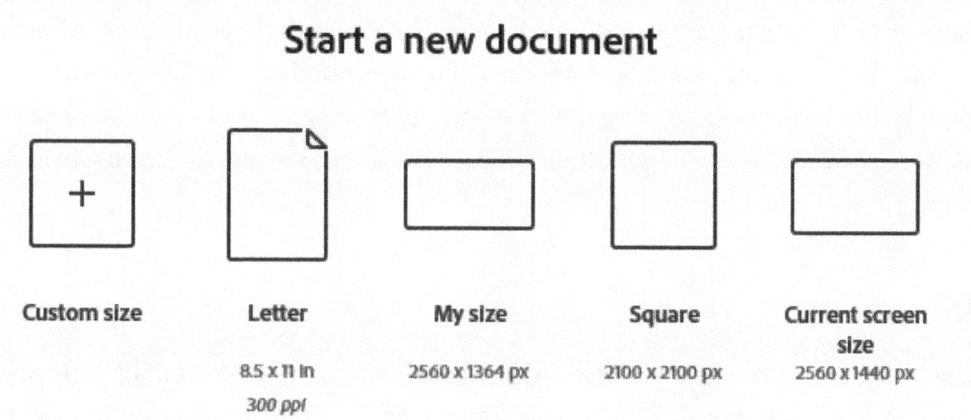

Figure 6-1. Fresco Home page Start a new document preset area

© Jennifer Harder 2025
J. Harder, *Beginner's Guide to Adobe Fresco*, https://doi.org/10.1007/979-8-8688-1557-7_6

CHAPTER 6 WORKING WITH DRAWING AIDS ON THE CANVAS

Working with the Drawing Aids

Drawing aids, as you will discover, are similar to shapes and can be used with the various brushes for painting, as you saw in Chapter 3. Refer to Figure 6-2.

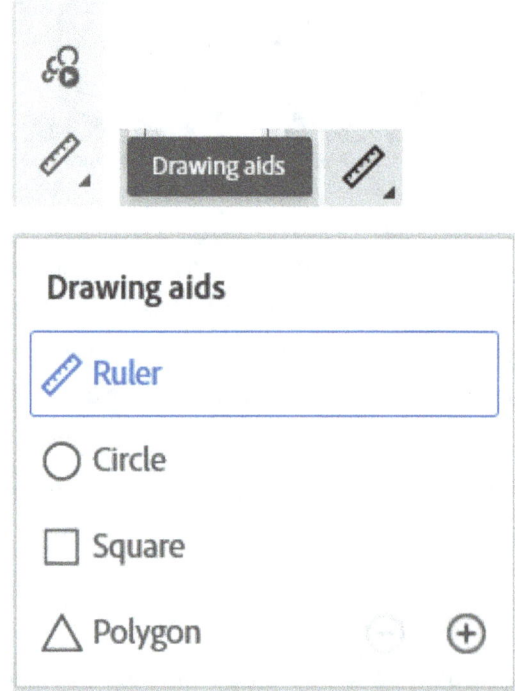

Figure 6-2. *Vertical Taskbar selection of the drawing aids and the menu of options*

They can even be used on layer masks which were discussed in Chapter 5.

The icon and panel for these tools can be found in the lower right area of the Vertical Taskbar below the animation tab. Animation will be discussed later in Chapter 8.

For now, click the lower drawing aid icon and hold down the mouse to reveal what options are available. They are the Ruler, Circle, Square, and Polygon and you will look at each next.

Ruler

The ruler is similar to a ruler in the real world. It can be used to draw straight vertical, horizonal, or diagonal lines with your brush on a layer. It is great for creating primitive shapes. Refer to Figure 6-3.

CHAPTER 6 WORKING WITH DRAWING AIDS ON THE CANVAS

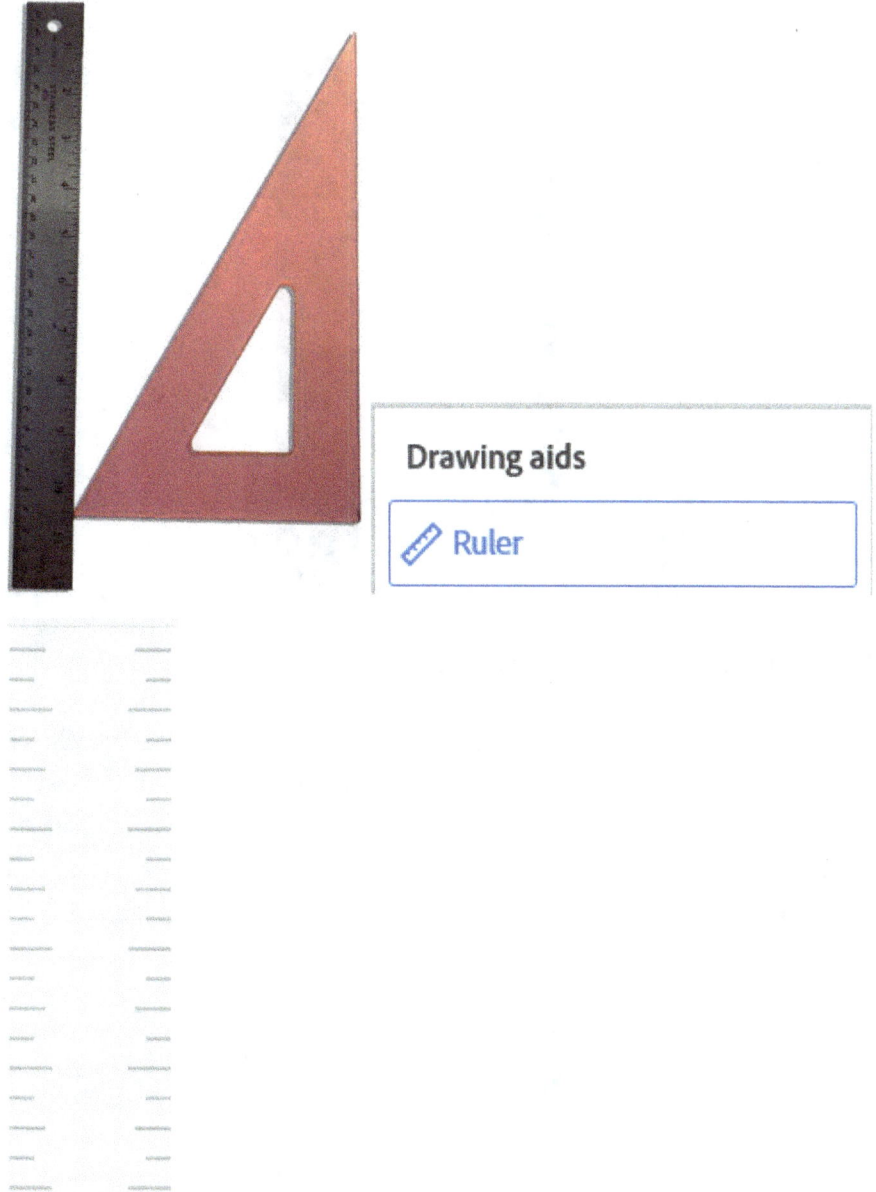

Figure 6-3. *Example of real-world drawing aids, a ruler and triangle, and Fresco's ruler*

You can drag your ruler anywhere on the canvas, and it will not move as you draw even if you zoom in (Ctrl++) and out (Ctrl+-). Refer to Figure 6-4.

CHAPTER 6   WORKING WITH DRAWING AIDS ON THE CANVAS

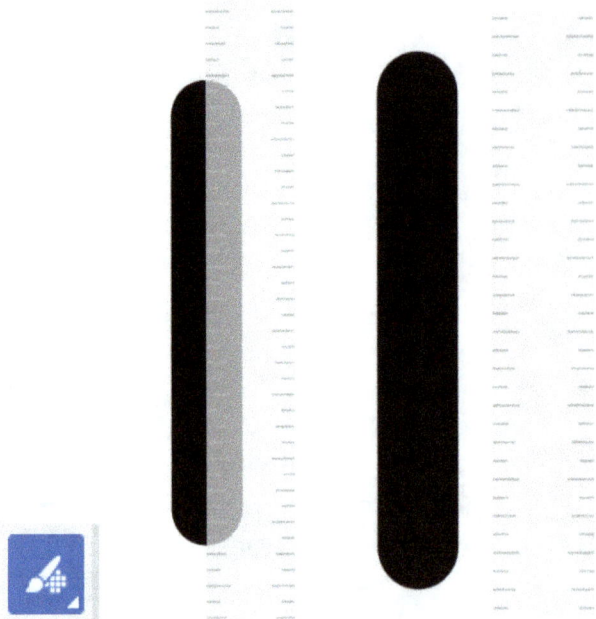

Figure 6-4. *Using a Pixel brush to draw with a ruler*

With your Touch shortcut enabled (double-click), use your primary circle when you want to constrain the movement of the ruler to vertical and horizonal or the secondary ring when you want to move the ruler free-form. However, remember to disable the Touch shortcut again by double-clicking, such as when you want to select a Pixel brush. If you do not, you may be using the brush instead to erase. Refer to Figure 6-5.

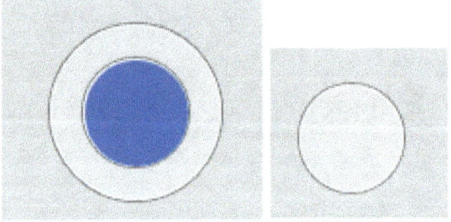

Figure 6-5. *Enabling Touch primary shortcut circle and the Touch shortcut disabled afterward*

When you want to rotate the ruler, hold down the R key on your keyboard. Note that the R key can also be used to rotate the canvas so make sure you press the R key and are holding down the ruler and do not touch the canvas as you rotate the ruler. Refer to Figure 6-6.

428

Figure 6-6. *Use the R key when you want to rotate the ruler before you draw*

Once rotated, then you can paint again with one of your brushes on a layer. With the Touch shortcut primary circle enabled for all drawing aids, you can confine the rotation to snap to 15° while rotating.

CHAPTER 6   WORKING WITH DRAWING AIDS ON THE CANVAS

Tip   The Precision grid tool can also help you with snapping and rotation snapping. We will look at this in more detail after we have reviewed the remaining drawing aid tools. Refer to Figure 6-7.

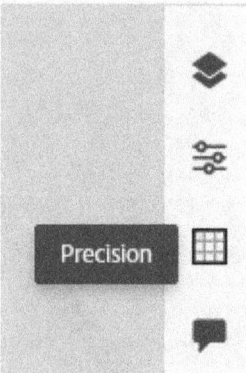

Figure 6-7. *Vertical Taskbar where Precision tools can be accessed*

As you draw, you will also see a display of how many pixels your brush has covered. When you release the mouse or stylus, the message will disappear.

Circle

When the drawing aid called Circle is selected, use your brush on a layer to trace around the circle. This is very much like using a stencil. You can draw around part of the aid or the whole circle. Refer to Figure 6-8.

CHAPTER 6   WORKING WITH DRAWING AIDS ON THE CANVAS

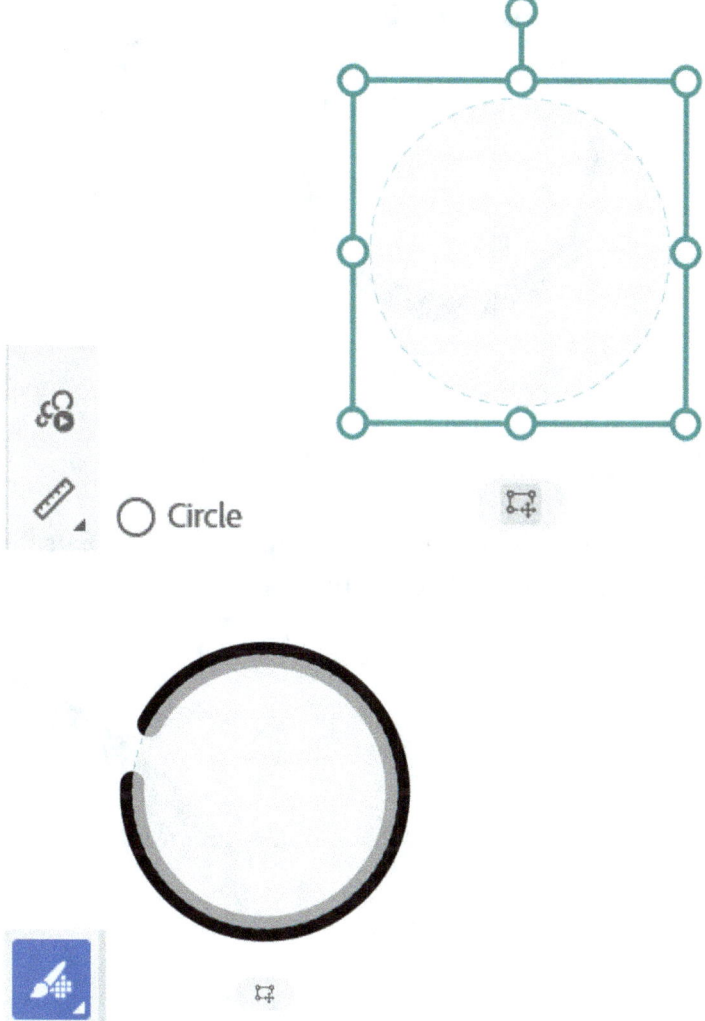

Figure 6-8. *Accessing the Circle drawing aid from the Vertical taskbar in edit mode and the painting*

When first selected, you can use the bounding box handles to scale the circle so that it is more of an oval ellipse. Refer to Figure 6-8. Holding down the Shift key can also help constrain proportions as you drag on one of the handles. Optionally, you can use the Touch shortcut primary circle if you need to scale from the center of the aid. Refer to Figure 6-9 to see an example of drawing around an ellipse.

CHAPTER 6   WORKING WITH DRAWING AIDS ON THE CANVAS

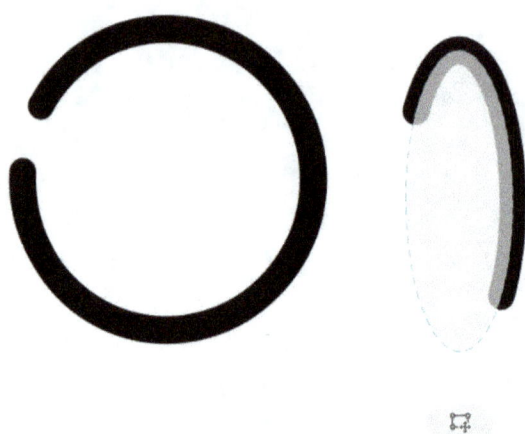

Figure 6-9. *The circle drawing aid is for perfect circles or ellipses*

Move the aid to a new location by dragging from the center. Rotate the circle using the upper rotation handle. Refer to Figure 6-10.

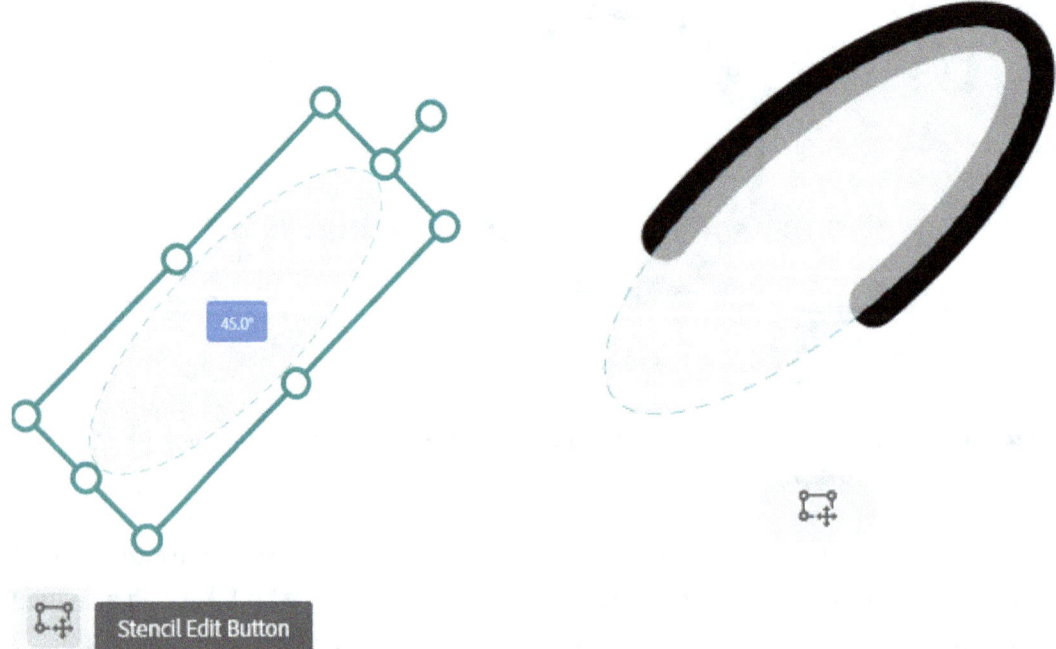

Figure 6-10. *Rotation of the circle drawing aid while edited with the Stencil Edit Button and then the brush used to create a stroke*

Use the Stencil Edit Button below the aid when you need to toggle between adjusting the stencil and painting with it on the canvas. A darker gray box appears around it when in edit mode. Refer to Figure 6-10. When not in edit mode, you will still be able to move the aid even if the bounding box handles are not visible but not edit it unless you click that icon button.

The drawing aid is reset when the application is closed and you open a new document. Or while working with the aid in your current document, you can continue to scale the shape using the handles.

Square

Use your brush on a layer to trace around the square stencil-like drawing aid. You can use the bounding box handles to scale the square so that it is more rectangular. Holding down the Shift key can also help constrain proportions as you drag on one of the handles. Refer to Figure 6-11. Optionally, like the Circle drawing aid, you can also use the Touch shortcut primary circle if you need to scale from the center of the aid.

CHAPTER 6 WORKING WITH DRAWING AIDS ON THE CANVAS

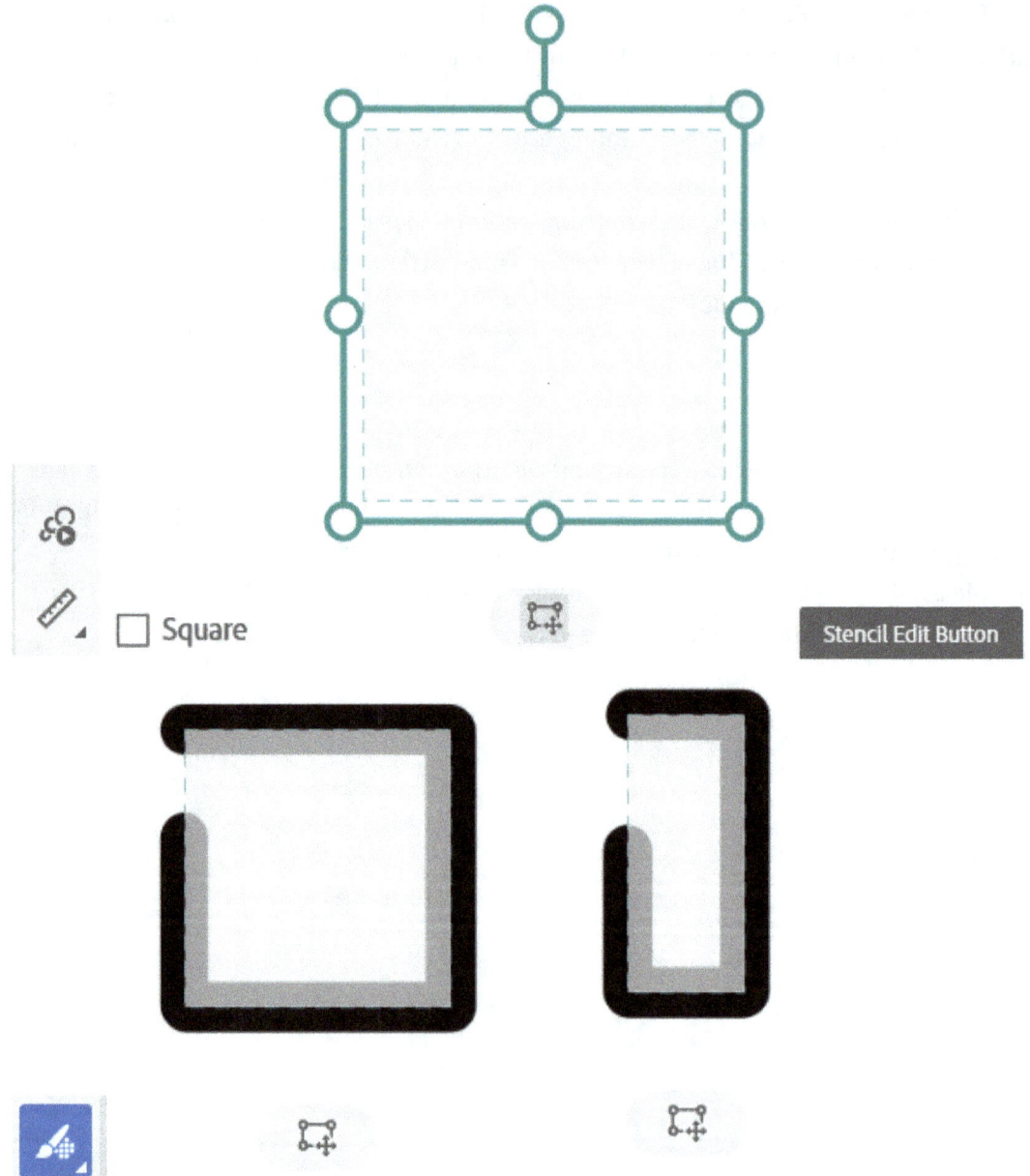

Figure 6-11. Vertical Taskbar Square drawing aid selected and edited, and then draw around to create a square or rectangle with a Pixel brush

Move the aid to a new location by dragging from the center. Rotate the square using the upper rotation handle. Refer to Figure 6-12.

CHAPTER 6   WORKING WITH DRAWING AIDS ON THE CANVAS

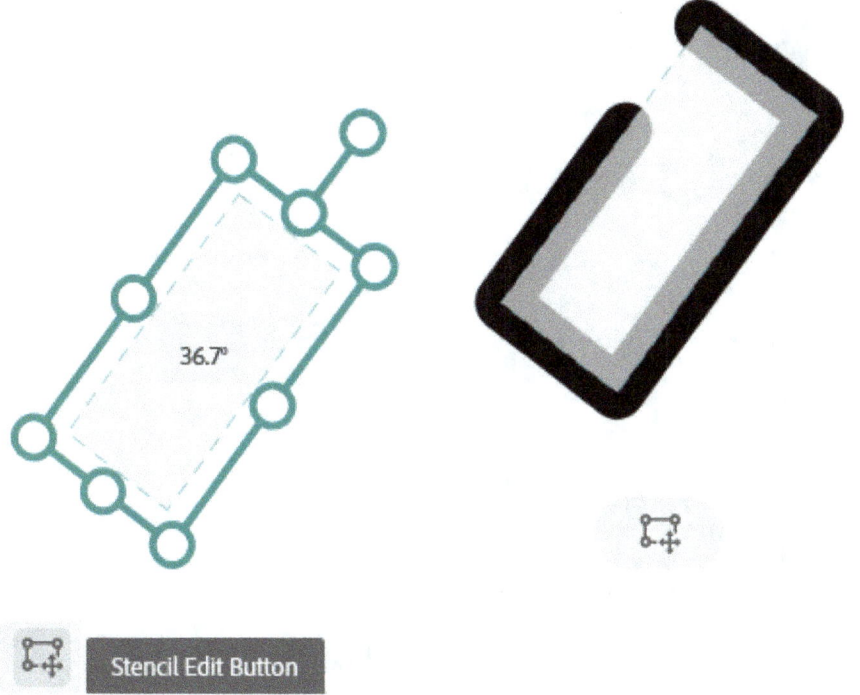

Figure 6-12. *Drawing aid is rotated while in Stencil Edit mode and then disabled to draw around aid*

Use the Stencil Edit Button when you need to toggle between adjusting the stencil and painting with it on the canvas. When not editing the stencil, you will still be able to move the aid even if the bounding box handles are not visible but not edit it unless you click that icon button.

The drawing aid is reset when the application is closed and you open a new document. Or, while working in the current document with the aid, you can continue to scale the shape using the handles.

Polygon

Click the drawing aid icon to reveal the Polygon option. You can create a polygon drawing aid stencil that is between three and eight sides using the minus (–) and plus (+) icons. It will change while on the canvas as you press the button icons from the list. Refer to Figure 6-13.

CHAPTER 6 WORKING WITH DRAWING AIDS ON THE CANVAS

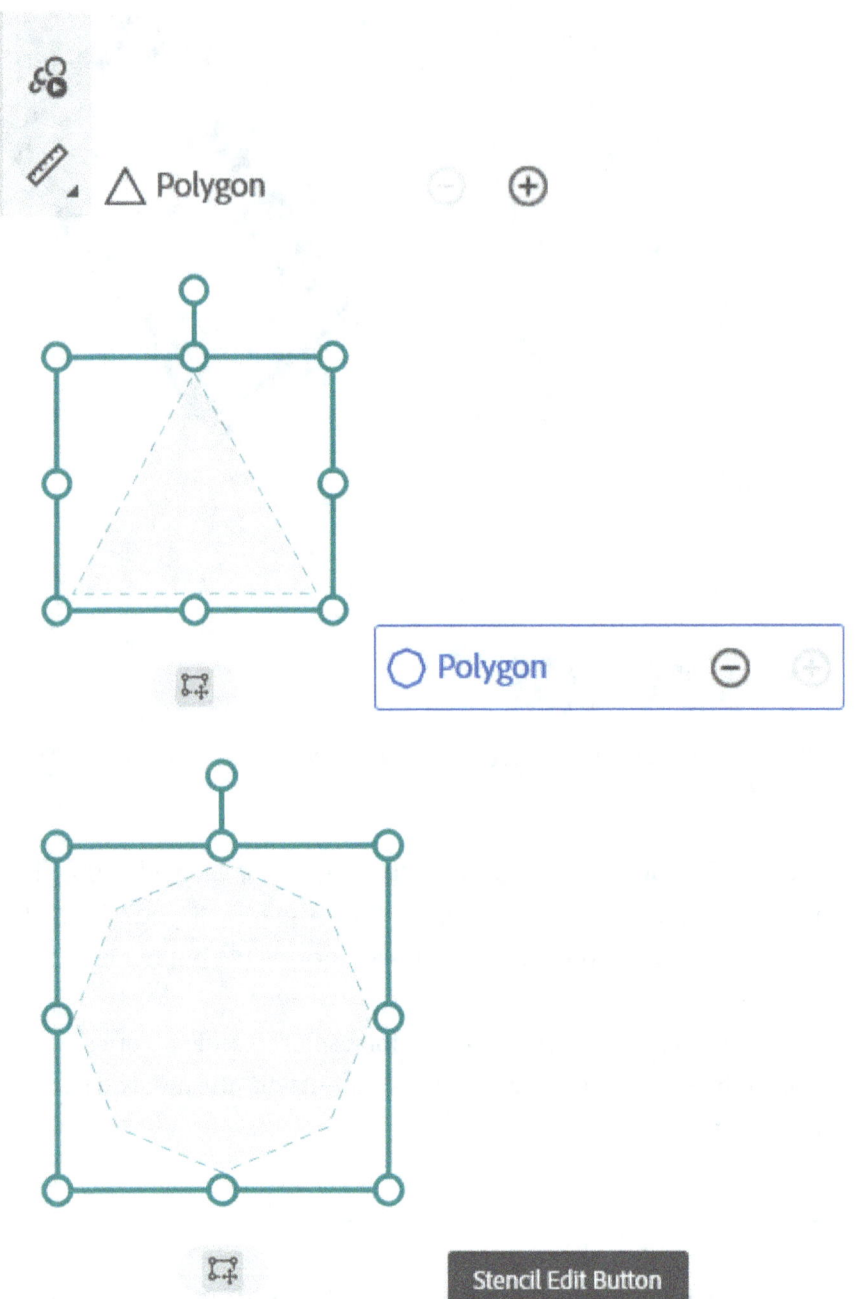

Figure 6-13. *Vertical Taskbar starts with an aid that is a triangle, and click the plus icon until the Polygon drawing aid is an octagon*

CHAPTER 6   WORKING WITH DRAWING AIDS ON THE CANVAS

Once you have chosen your number of sides, click the Stencil Edit Button, then click that button again, and then use your brush on a layer to trace around the polygon stencil. Refer to Figure 6-14.

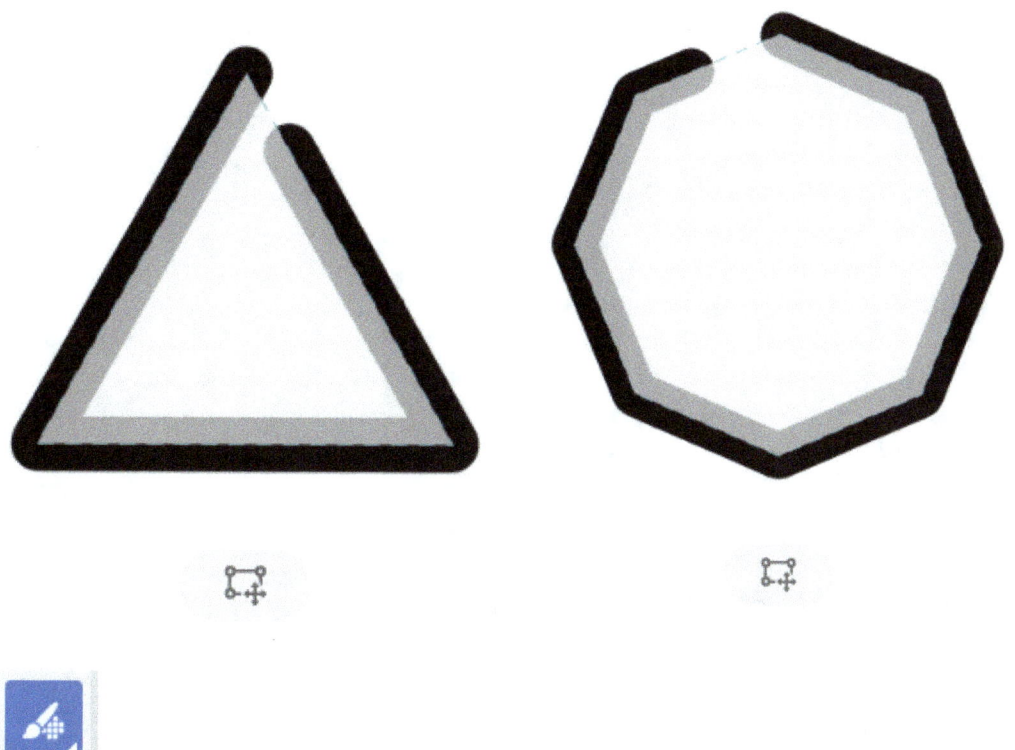

Figure 6-14. *Drawing with your brush around two kinds of Polygon drawing aids after editing*

Use the Stencil Edit Button when you need to toggle between adjusting the stencil and painting with it on the canvas. You will still be able to move the aid even if the bounding box handles are not visible but not edit it unless you click that icon button again.

You can use the bounding box handles to scale the polygon so that it is more proportionate. Holding down the Shift key can also help constrain proportions as you drag on one of the handles. Refer to Figure 6-15. Optionally, you can also use the Touch shortcut primary circle if you need to scale from the center of the aid, and then, disable the Touch shortcut (double-click).

437

CHAPTER 6   WORKING WITH DRAWING AIDS ON THE CANVAS

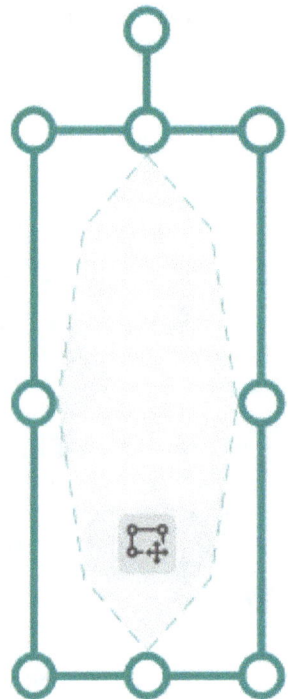

Figure 6-15. *Scaling the Polygon drawing aid*

Move the aid to a new location by dragging from the center. Rotate the polygon using the upper rotation handle. Refer to Figure 6-16.

CHAPTER 6 WORKING WITH DRAWING AIDS ON THE CANVAS

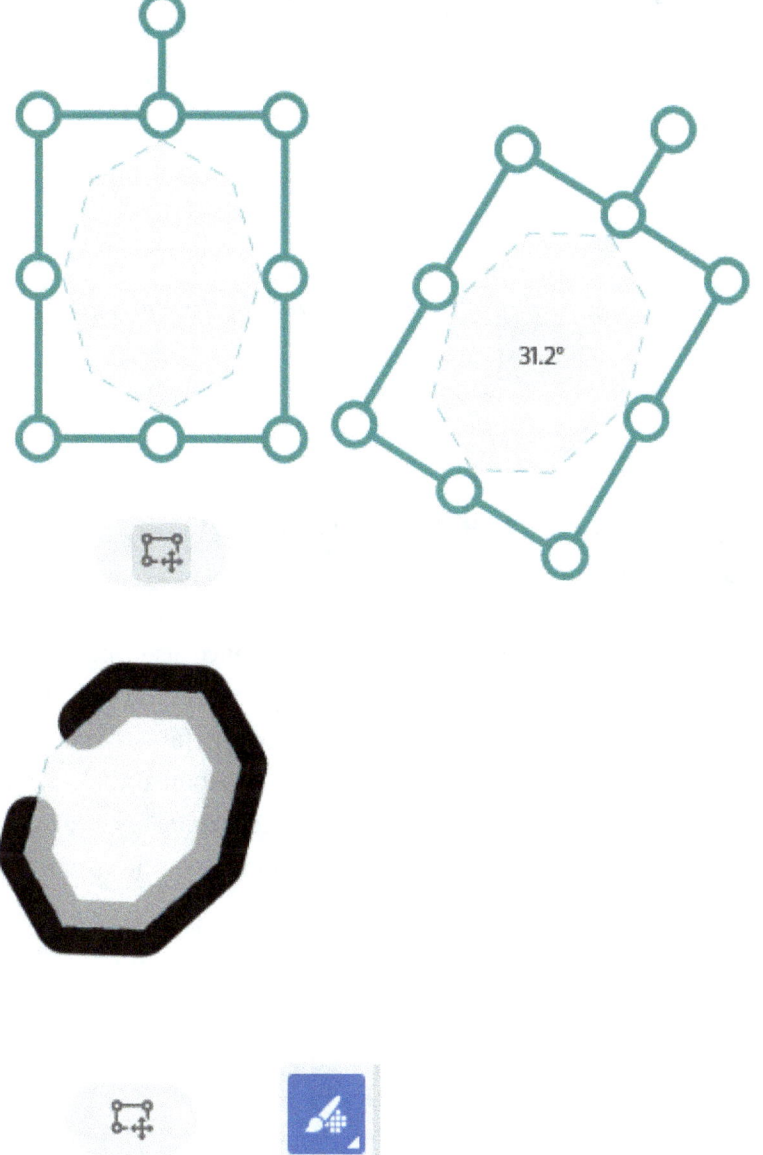

Figure 6-16. *Rotating the upper rotation handle of the Polygon drawing aid and then painting around the aid*

The drawing aid is reset when the application is closed. Or, while working with the aid, you can continue to scale the shape using the handles.

Adjusting Settings, Hiding, and Showing

When you no longer want to use the rulers or aids, you can click the icon to remove them from view and continue to use your brushes free-form. Refer to Figure 6-17.

Figure 6-17. *Turning on and off the drawing aids in the Vertical Taskbar*

For now, keep your drawing aid visible as you will want to use it with the Precision options.

Working with the Grid and Perspective in Precision Options

The ruler and the drawing aid stencils mentioned also have a setting called Change Perspective Plane. You will not see this setting if the grid lines have not been enabled and set to Perspective, which we will look at in a moment. By default, when you want to see your grid lines, click the precision icon in the Vertical Taskbar, and check your settings if they are toggled on. We will now review this area in more detail as it relates to drawing aids and later with other tools. In this case, try practicing with the square or ruler aids. Refer to Figure 6-18.

CHAPTER 6　WORKING WITH DRAWING AIDS ON THE CANVAS

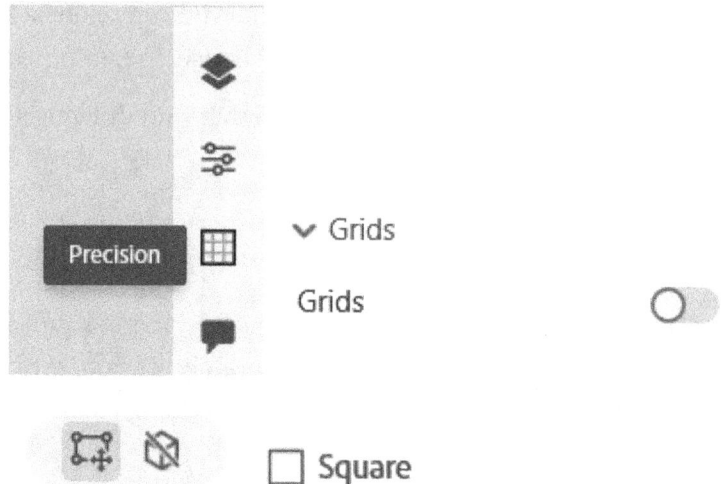

Figure 6-18. Use the Vertical Taskbar to access the Precision grids and access additional settings for the drawing aids such as the Square

While working with the stencil and rulers, working with your grid and perspective lines can enhance your drawing accuracy.

Snapping

While working with drawing aids, Precision ➤ Snapping has two settings you can use. Refer to Figure 6-19.

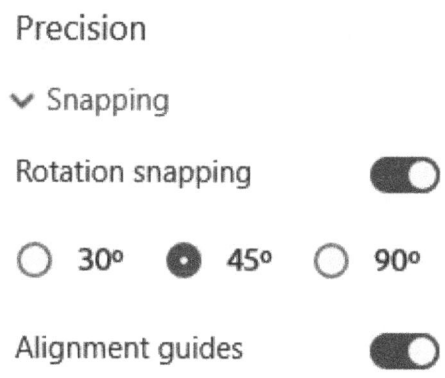

Figure 6-19. Precision panel options for Snapping

441

CHAPTER 6   WORKING WITH DRAWING AIDS ON THE CANVAS

- Rotation Snapping: Enable this setting so that you can rotate at 30°, 45°, or 90°, depending on what setting you choose. I set mine to 45°.

- Alignment Guides: Toggle this setting on so that your drawing aids can snap to guides as well as grids.

Displaying Grids

Now, you want to toggle on the grids so that they are visible. In most projects, when you are done, you will toggle them off so that you can accurately see your artwork, but turn them on for now so you can work with the next settings. Refer to Figure 6-20.

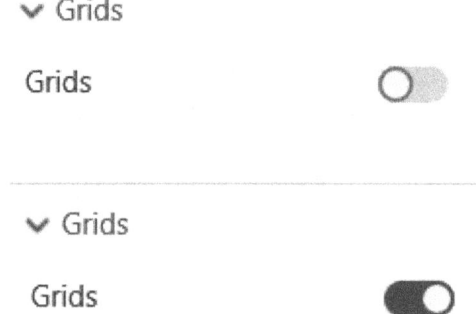

Figure 6-20. *Precision panel option for disabling and enabling the grids*

You will have two kinds of grid types that you can choose from the drop-down menu:

- Graph: This type is ideal for 2D drawing as well as for creating patterns. Graph allows you to change the opacity of the graph lines (1–100%); by default, it is set to 25. The grid color is gray, but you can set a custom color using the color wheel and sliders when you click that color chip. Here, you can also adjust the spacing of the lines; by default, they are set to 121 pixels. Refer to Figure 6-21.

CHAPTER 6 WORKING WITH DRAWING AIDS ON THE CANVAS

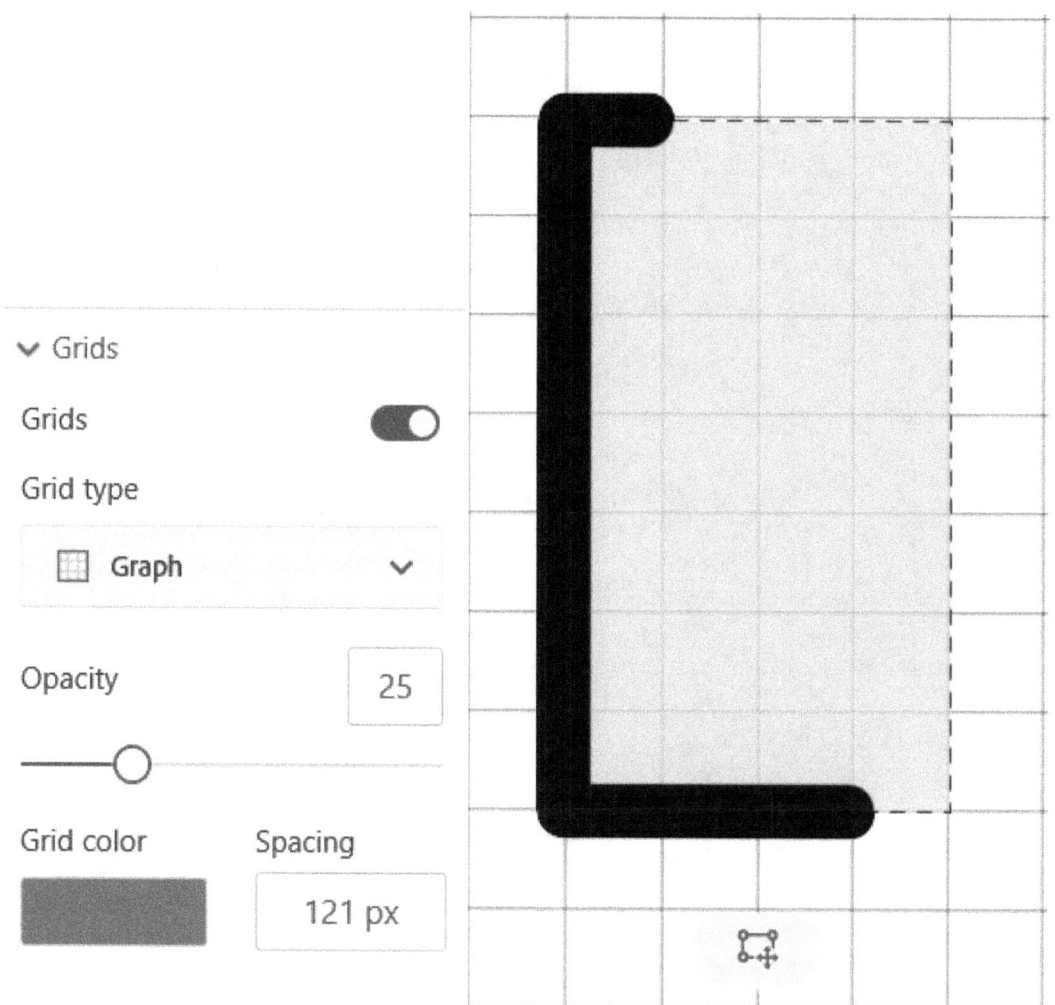

Figure 6-21. *Precision panel options to enable grid type of Graph and how it displays on the canvas with a drawing aid that has had an outline started*

- Perspective: This grid type is for 3D-like drawings where you want to create some sense of realism or distance. Perspective is the art of drawing solid objects on lines on a two-dimensional surface such as on your canvas so as to give the right impression of their height, width, depth, and position in relation to each other when viewed from a particular point or altitude. You will be trying to give the illusion of a three-dimensional space. Refer to Figure 6-22.

CHAPTER 6   WORKING WITH DRAWING AIDS ON THE CANVAS

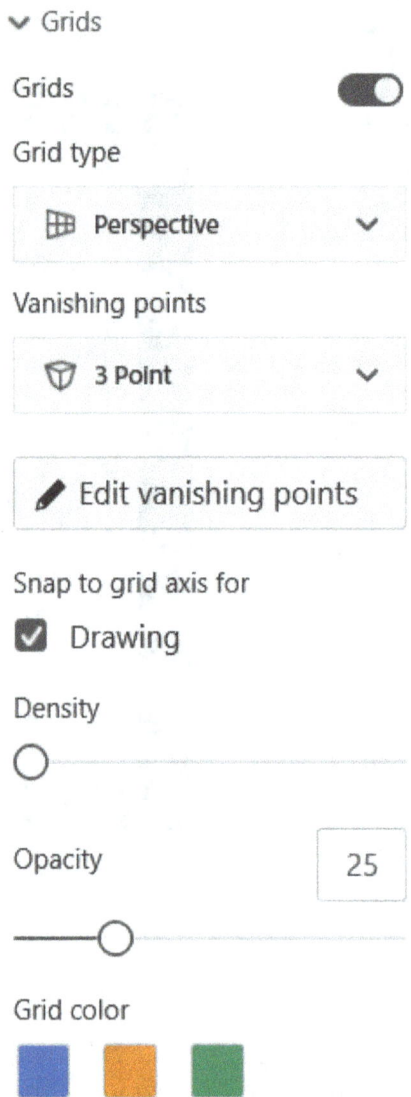

Figure 6-22. Precision panel options to enable grid type of Perspective Vanishing points: 3 Point

- Fresco creates various perspective lines or guides to assist us with our drawing or painting. They can be accessed by the drawing aid when we enable the Change Perspective Plane button by clicking multiple times the icon, None, Left, Right, and Top/Bottom (Horizontal). This can be done while the Stencil Edit Button is enabled or disabled. Refer to Figure 6-23.

CHAPTER 6　WORKING WITH DRAWING AIDS ON THE CANVAS

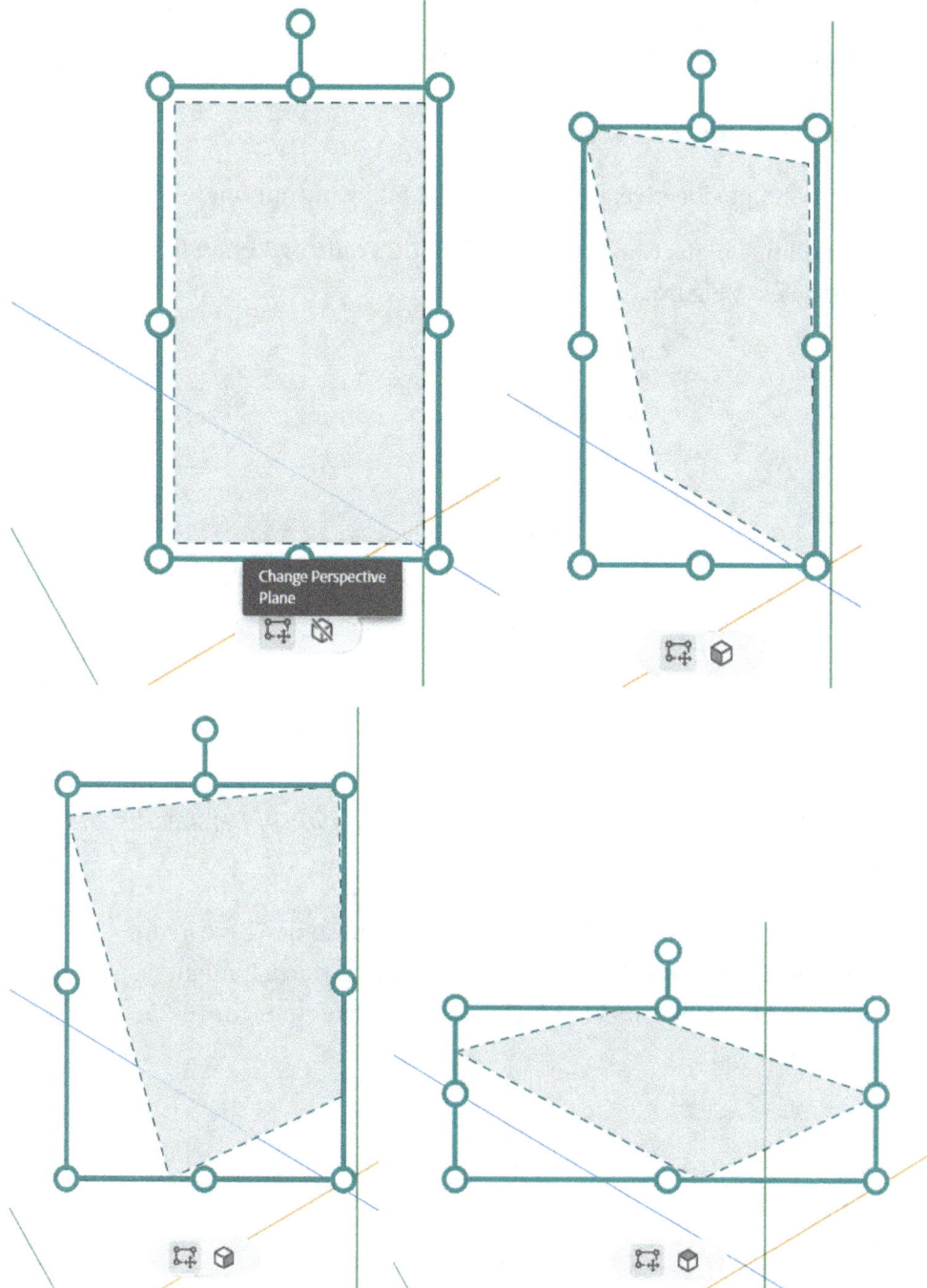

Figure 6-23. *Stencil Edit Button is enabled for the Square drawing aid while the Change Perspective Plane is clicked for the following options None, Left, Right, and Top/Bottom (Horizontal) based on 3 Point perspective*

The drawing aid will change in perspective as well, based on where it is moved or placed on the grid and how many vanishing points are set.

Additional Perspective Settings

While working with perspective, you can alter the following options:

- Vanishing Points: Choose either 1 Point, 2 Point, or 3 Point from the list. Refer to Figure 6-24.

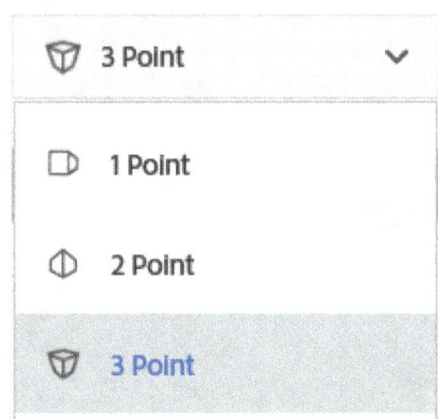

Figure 6-24. *Precision panel options to enable grid type of Perspective Vanishing points list with a current setting of 3 Point*

1 Point: Gives the look of traveling to a central point somewhere in the distance, much like if we were drawing the rails of a train track. It might be a track heading toward a possible tunnel or maybe a sunset. Refer to Figure 6-25.

CHAPTER 6   WORKING WITH DRAWING AIDS ON THE CANVAS

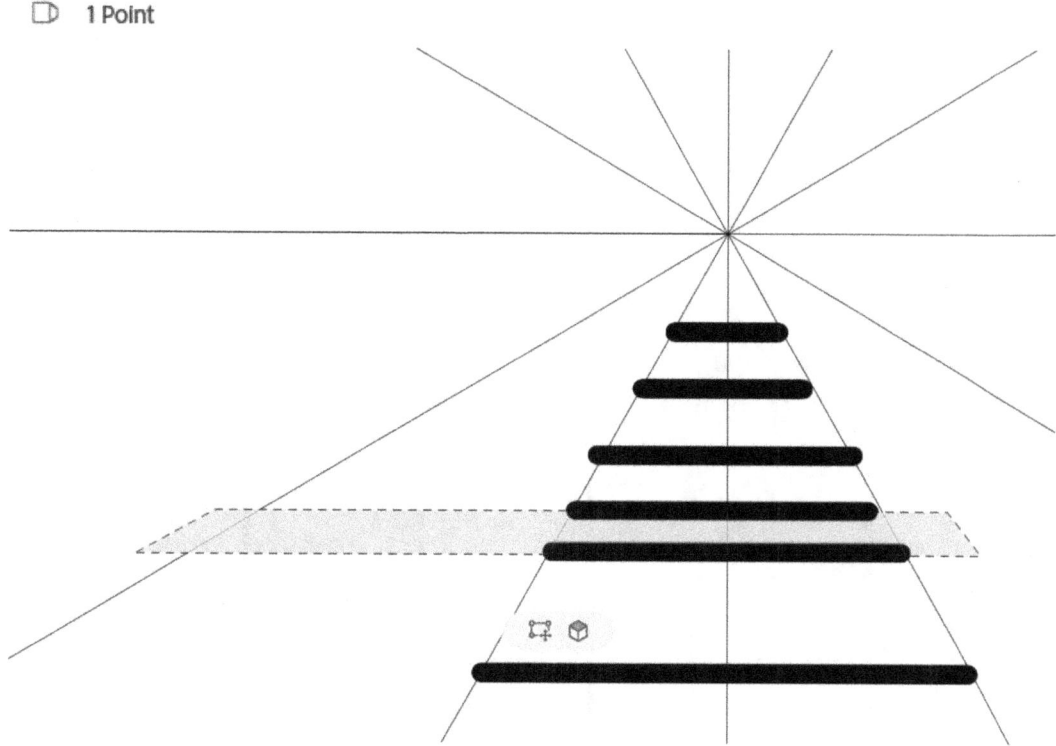

Figure 6-25. *Grid type of Perspective Vanishing points list with a current setting of 1 Point on the canvas while creating artwork*

While this figure is just an example of adding lines to the 1 Point perspective in your own art, as the lines go further into the distance, you may want to place them closer together or make the brush strokes that are farther away progressively thinner, reducing their size.

2 Point: Is like looking at the corner of a building or where two blocks meet. Using this perspective, you may want to create a cityscape of many buildings. We will look at that later in the project. Refer to Figure 6-26.

447

CHAPTER 6   WORKING WITH DRAWING AIDS ON THE CANVAS

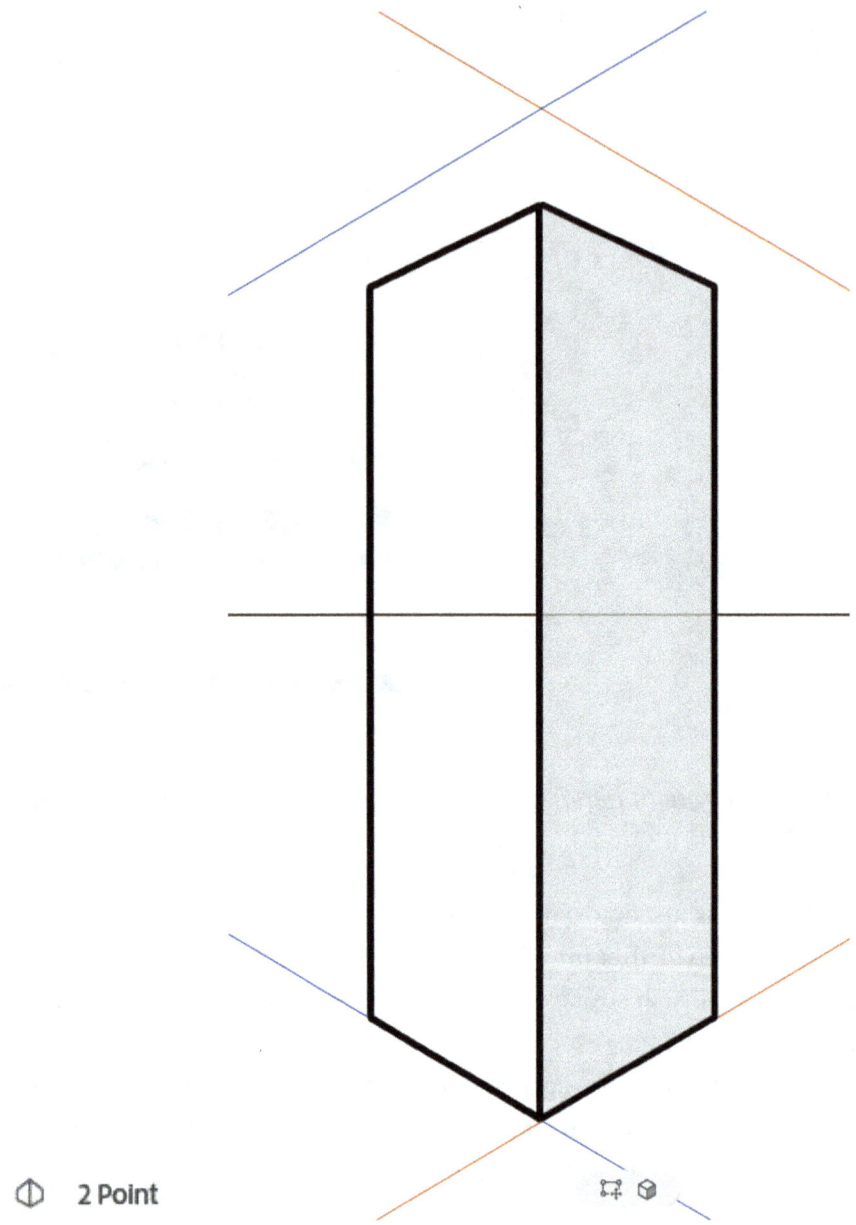

Figure 6-26. *Grid type of Perspective Vanishing points list with a current setting of 2 Point on the canvas while creating artwork*

3 Point: Is like looking down at that street corner while in the sky. It is how you would see a scene if you were traveling by plane or even looking down at the top of a table. Refer to Figure 6-27.

CHAPTER 6   WORKING WITH DRAWING AIDS ON THE CANVAS

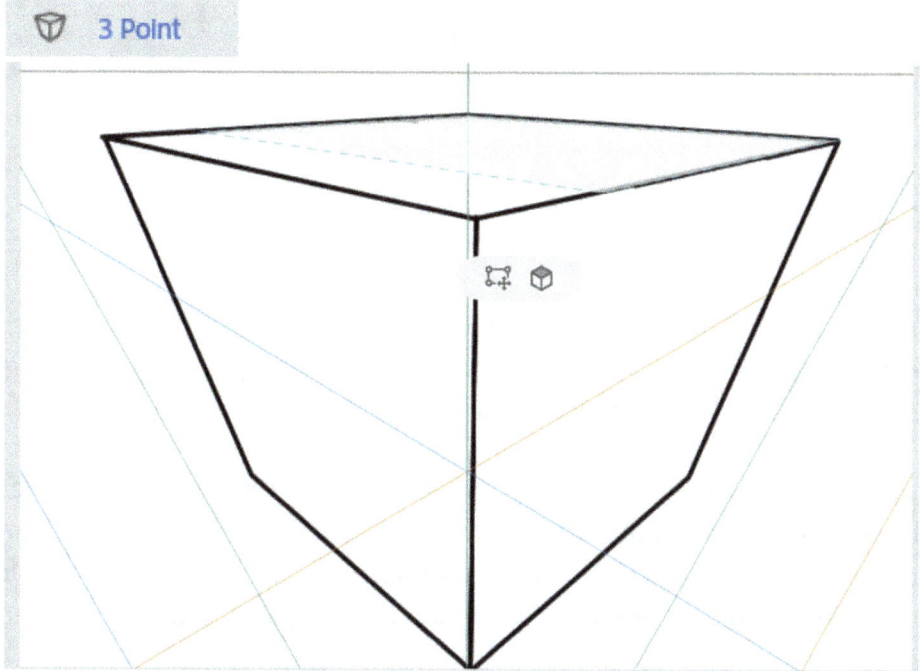

Figure 6-27. *Grid type of Perspective Vanishing points list with a current setting of 3 Point on the canvas while creating artwork and moving the aid*

Drawing in 3 Point perspective is often the most challenging of the three as you need to make frequent changes to the perspective plane as well as move the drawing aid around or transform it to match your grid lines.

Note that as you work, if you find your Change Perspective Plane icon has removed itself from the options, choose another perspective from the Vanishing points list, and then return to the previous Vanishing point in the list you were using.

- Edit Vanishing Points Button: For each vanishing point setting, you can adjust the placement of the converging lines or planes while in this workspace.

This is good to do when you need to adjust the horizon or, after working, reset one or more vanishing points. Refer to Figure 6-28.

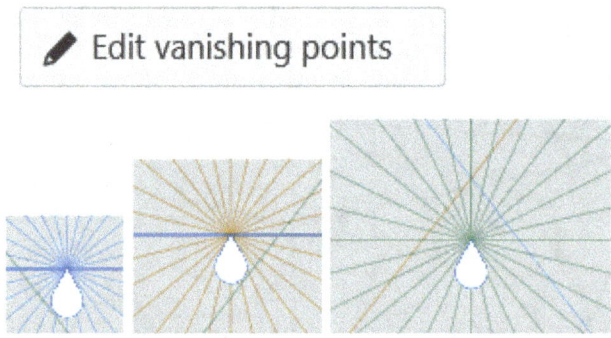

Figure 6-28. *Precision panel options to enable grid type of Perspective and the Edit vanishing points button while in the Edit perspective grid workspace*

To exit this workspace, you can click Cancel without making changes. Or remain and edit all three Vanishing point kinds from the list, zoom in or out, and use the undo and redo icons while you work. If you have made changes that you want to commit, click Done to exit, and then, continue to review the rest of the grid settings. Refer to Figure 6-29.

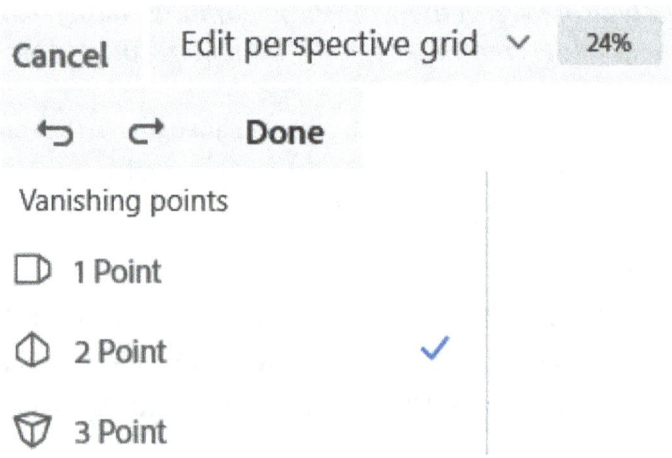

Figure 6-29. *Inside the Edit perspective grid workspace*

Often, when working on a project, it is best to edit the Vanishing points when you start rather than later as your perspective is now altered.

- Snap to Grid Axis for Drawing: You can then use this setting for each drawing aid when you enable the Change Perspective Plane (cube) on the aid. Refer to Figure 6-30.

CHAPTER 6 WORKING WITH DRAWING AIDS ON THE CANVAS

Figure 6-30. *Precision panel options to enable grid type of Perspective and the options for Snap to grid axis for Drawing and it works with the Change Perspective Plane button*

Remember, depending on how many planes there are, you can click the icon while using the aid until you return to the default or ideal setting.

Note that for the ruler, you would still need to rotate it before drawing as you work. However, in perspective, the ruler changes shape so that you can draw the sides of the plane more accurately. Refer to Figure 6-31.

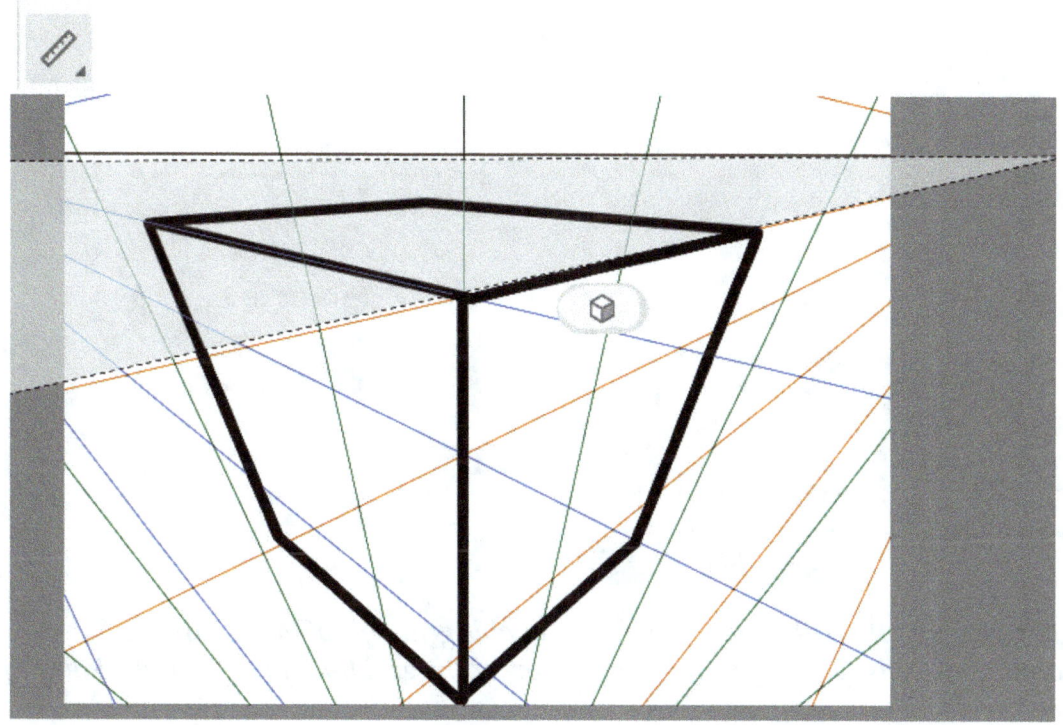

Figure 6-31. *Drawing with the Ruler drawing aid on the canvas and Change Perspective Plane enabled on the left*

451

CHAPTER 6   WORKING WITH DRAWING AIDS ON THE CANVAS

Other settings that you can adjust for Perspective in the Precision area are

- Density: This is for the grid line and how many lines you want visible. I keep the slider relatively in the center as too many lines many make the artwork difficult to visualize.

- Opacity of the lines (1–100%) by default is set to 25. However, you can set higher to 44 if you find it easier to see the lines on the screen.

- Grid Color: Depending on how many planes there are, each will have a different grid color. For example, in 3 Point, the lines can be blue, orange, and green, while 2 Point will have blue and orange and 1 Point gray. An additional gray line will also appear on the canvas in which would be the horizon line based on how the other grid lines are placed. Refer to Figures 6-31 and 6-32.

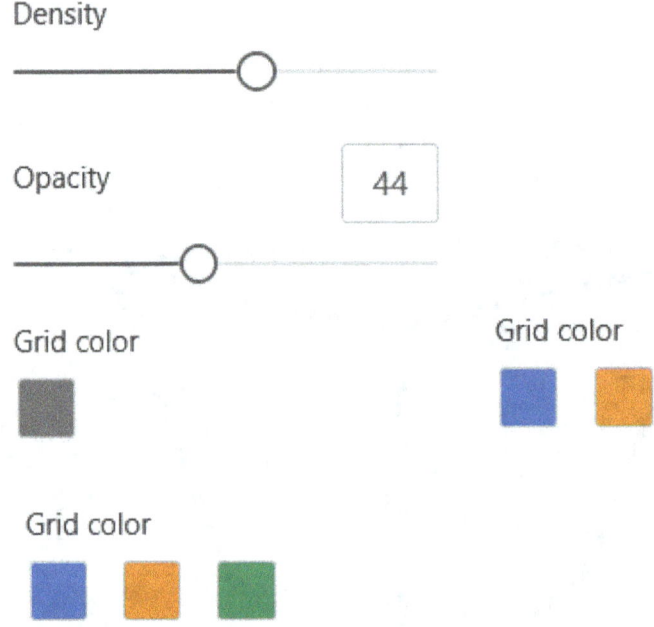

Figure 6-32. *Precision panel options to enable grid type of Perspective and the options of Density, Opacity, and Grid color for the grid lines for 1, 2, and 3 Point perspective*

CHAPTER 6   WORKING WITH DRAWING AIDS ON THE CANVAS

However, when you click that square chip, you can set a custom color for each with the Grid color wheel panel and sliders. Refer to Figure 6-33.

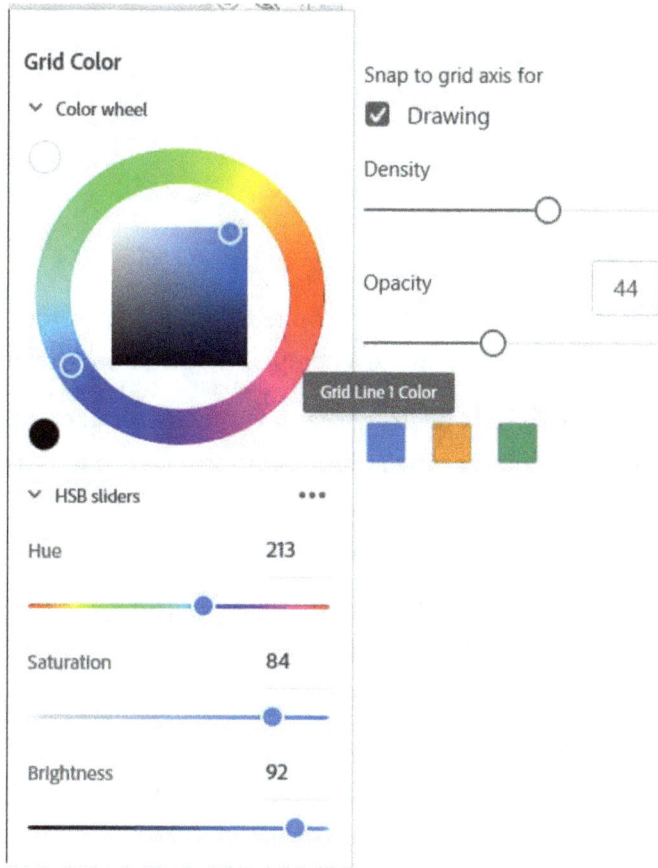

Figure 6-33. *Setting the grid line color using the Grid color panel for each color chip in the Precision panel*

Note   While working in perspective, as you scale the drawing aid, you may get a warning if you scale too large. This will cause the drawing aid to appear with a red outline and prevent you from scaling any higher. In this case, you must reduce the size of the drawing aid to change the perspective plane. Refer to Figure 6-34.

453

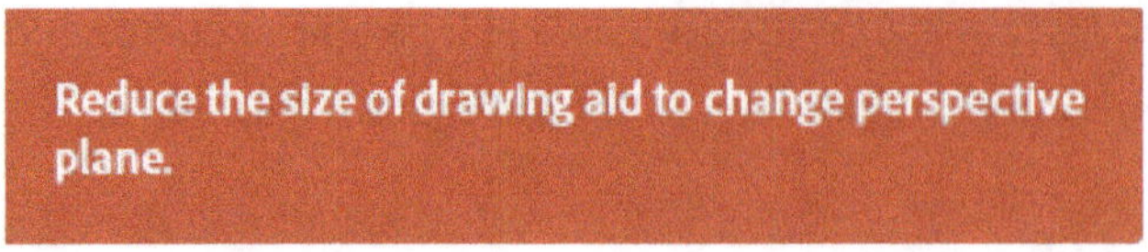

Figure 6-34. Warning that may appear when you try to scale a drawing aid too much while in a certain perspective

Create a Perspective Grid

While working with your documents, there is one final area in the Precision tool for perspective grids that allows you to create a perspective grid from the following choices:

- Image: The image could be from a camera, files on your computer, or graphics from your Creative Cloud Libraries. I will get into more detail about adding images in Chapter 7 when we look at how to import or place an image in Fresco.

- Layer: Work with the current layer and edit the grid. Click Cancel or Done to exit this area. Be aware that the grid may become misaligned based on what is on the current layer.

- Document: Work with the current document and edit the grid. Click Cancel or Done to exit this area. However, based on some image shapes in the document Fresco may not be able to adjust the perspective in all cases using this option. As noted earlier, you can manually reset the grid by entering the editing area again via the Edit vanishing points button. Refer to Figure 6-35.

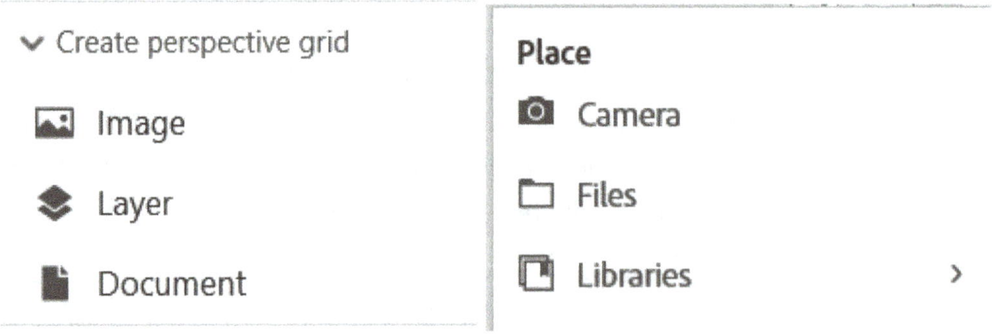

Figure 6-35. Precision panel options for Create perspective grid

CHAPTER 6　WORKING WITH DRAWING AIDS ON THE CANVAS

Using Other Tools with the Perspective Grid

For more complex drawing aids, I recommend using the Shapes tools mentioned in Chapter 4. They too can be used on a perspective grid. However, in order to change the perspective plane, you need to first select a drawing aid. Then, set the perspective plane, and then, choose your shape and move into place. And fill the shape as required on your layer using the Contextual Task bar. Refer to Figure 6-36.

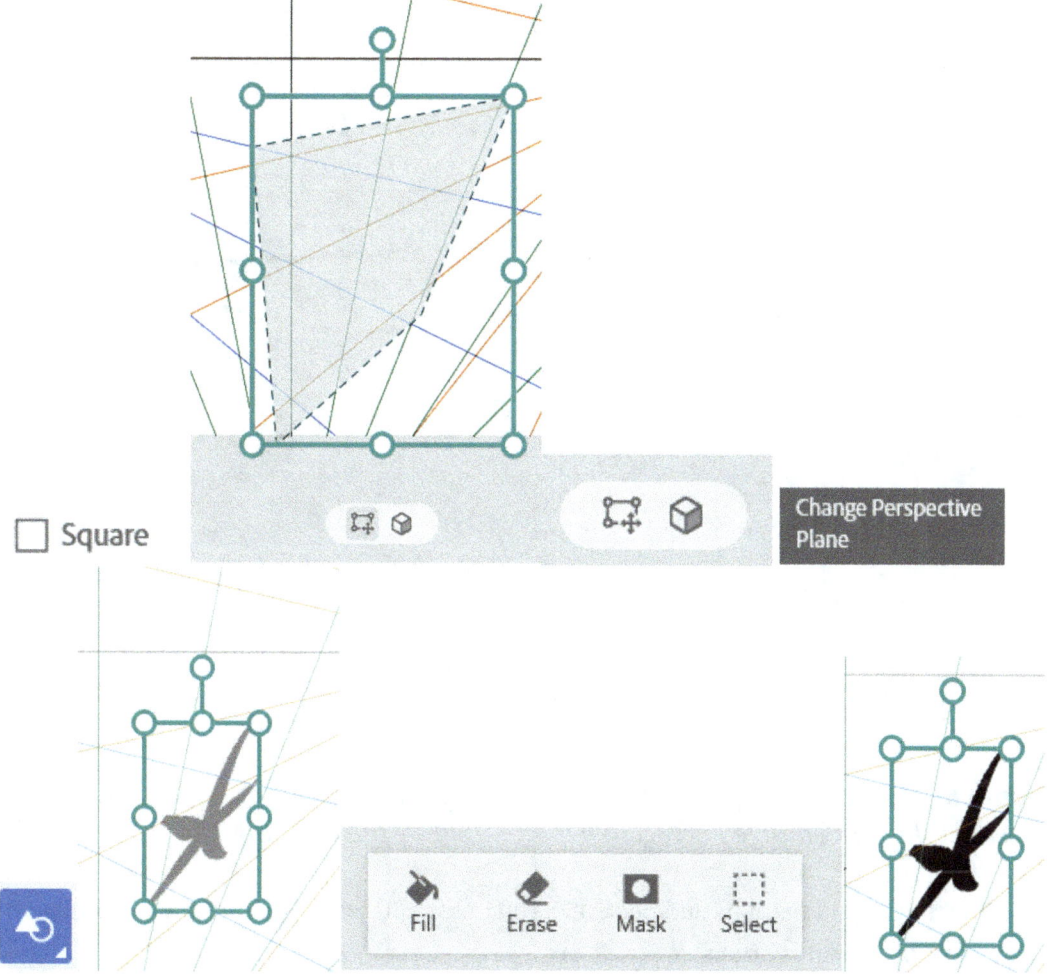

Figure 6-36. *While using a drawing aid on your perspective grid, switch to a shape from the Toolbar instead and fill, erase, mask, or create a selection in Perspective based on the last Change Perspective Plane used by the drawing aid and shape filled using the Contextual Task bar*

Likewise, as long as your perspective grid is on and you have set a perspective plane, you can use your brushes and erasers from Chapter 3 to paint in perspective while the drawing aids are not visible or off. This is especially useful when you need to fill your outline or paint over your reference layer afterward with a solid fill on a separate layer. Refer to Figure 6-37.

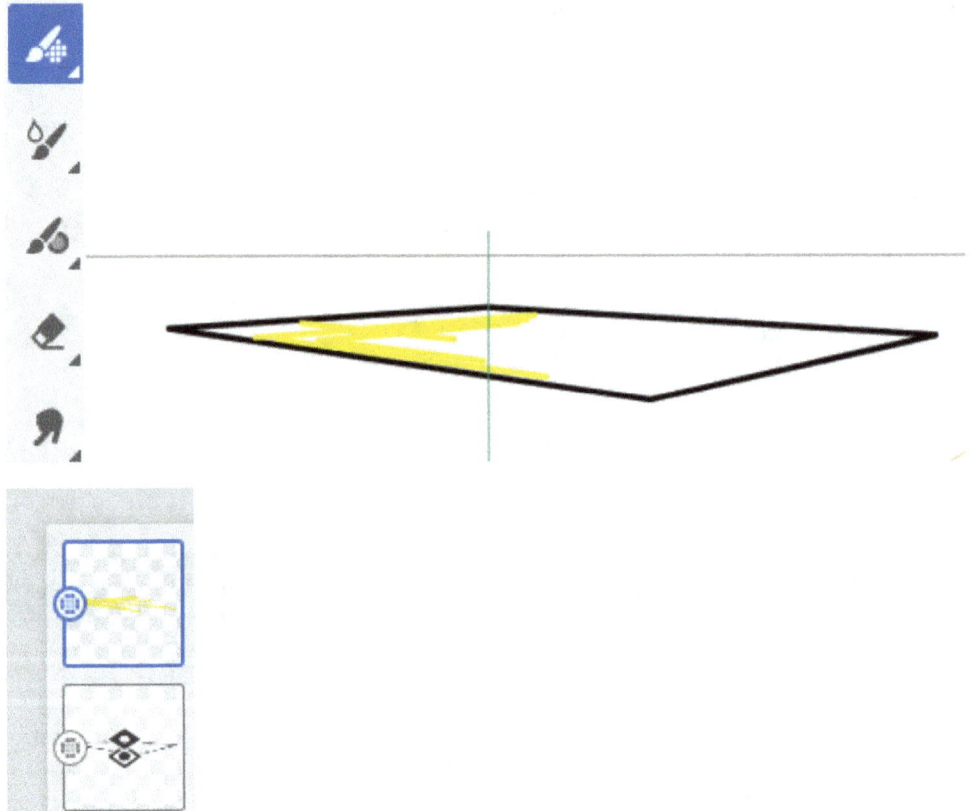

Figure 6-37. Use your brushes to paint on a layer while you are in perspective based on the last Change Perspective Plane used by the drawing aid

Note that as you paint in perspective, a red cross hair will appear that will control the movement of the paint brush.

Tip Selections of brush strokes can also be scaled in perspective while in the Transform workspace. See Project 3 in this chapter for more information on how to do this.

Remember, to change the plane, you must turn your drawing aid icon back on, use Change Perspective Plane icon, and then, turn off the drawing aid again before continuing to paint with your chosen brush.

For more details on drawing aids, you can refer to these links:

```
https://helpx.adobe.com/fresco/using/ruler.html
https://helpx.adobe.com/fresco/using/shapes.html
```

Also, refer to your Learn tutorials within Fresco if you need to additionally review and practice how to work with drawing aids and shapes. Refer to Figure 6-38.

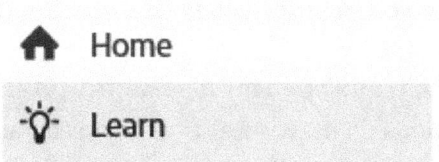

Figure 6-38. *Use the Learn page tab when you need to review tools in Fresco*

Remember, if you need to turn off the grid, use the Grids toggle, and return to free-form painting. Refer to Figure 6-39.

Figure 6-39. *Precision panel; disable the Grids when you do not need them to paint*

Project 1: Creating a Geometric Tile Pattern and Using Drawing Aids

For this project, you can work on a new Letter document. Refer to Figure 6-40.

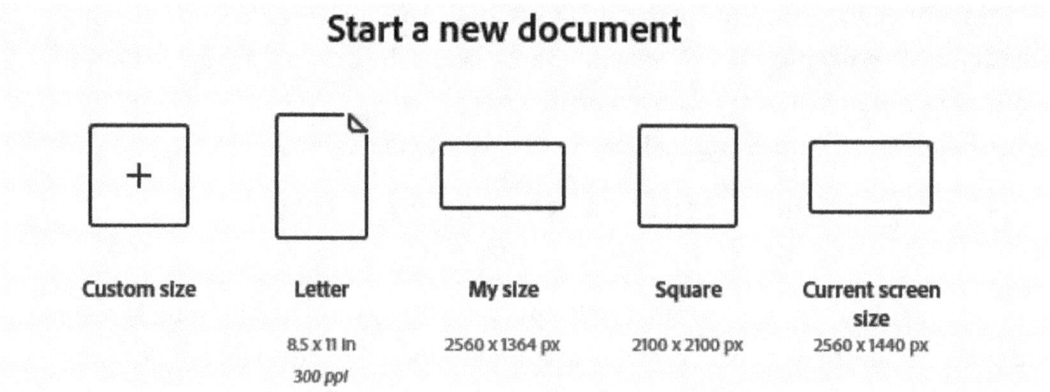

CHAPTER 6   WORKING WITH DRAWING AIDS ON THE CANVAS

Start a new document

Custom size	Letter	My size	Square	Current screen size
	8.5 x 11 in 300 ppi	2560 x 1364 px	2100 x 2100 px	2560 x 1440 px

Figure 6-40. *Fresco Home page Start a new document with the preset of Letter*

Afterward, you can import and open my file **Drawing_Aids_Final.psd** for reference.

Our focus in this chapter is on drawing aids, but you can add more layers if you want to for your project. Review Chapter 5 on layers if required.

Using different brushes from past chapters, you can create a geometric tile background. Shapes that are good for creating interlocking tile patterns are triangles, squares, hexagons, and octagons, but be as creative as you want. In my example, on a new Pixel layer, I used a Pixel brush of Hard round to first draw the outlines of my shapes at 28 px. Move the drawing aid, in this example, a polygon with three sides, over each time and scale or edit the size of the drawing aid as required. Refer to Figure 6-41 and Figure 6-42.

CHAPTER 6   WORKING WITH DRAWING AIDS ON THE CANVAS

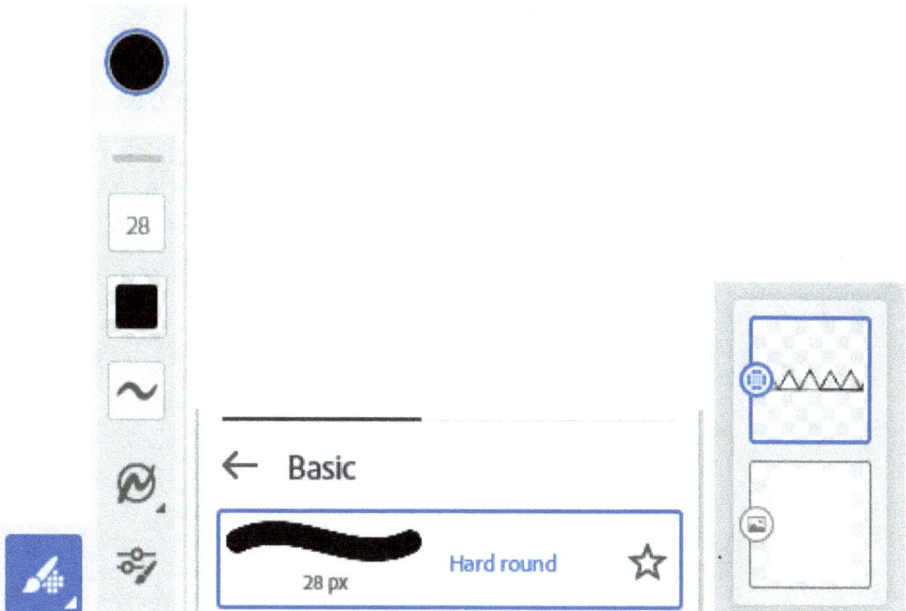

Figure 6-41. *Choose a Pixel brush of Basic ➤ Hard round and paint on a Pixel layer with a brush size of 28 px*

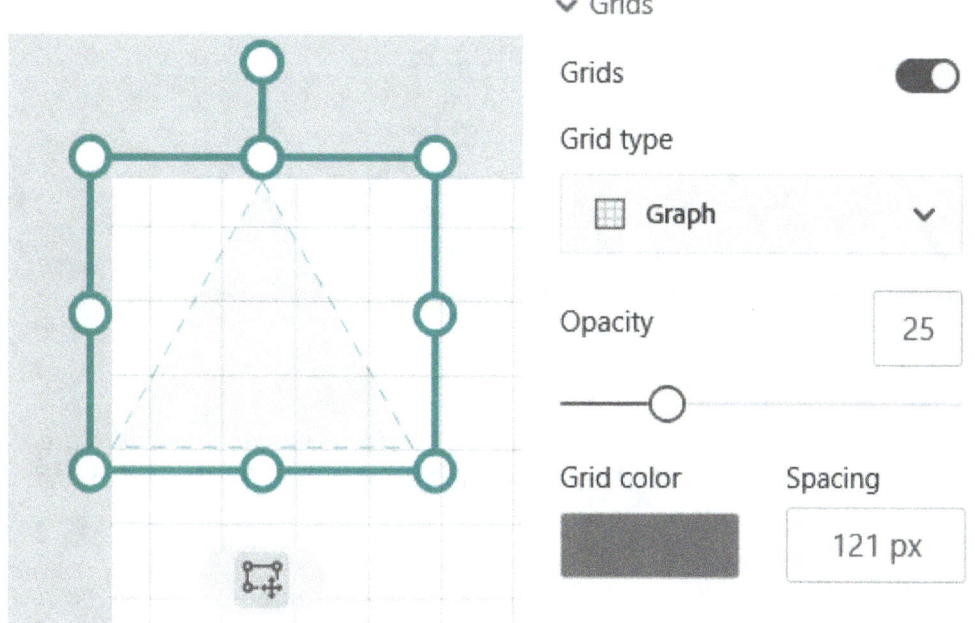

Figure 6-42. *Use one of your drawing aids like a polygon triangle, and in the Precision panel, enable a Grid type of Graph*

459

CHAPTER 6   WORKING WITH DRAWING AIDS ON THE CANVAS

In this case, I also double-clicked the Touch shortcut primary circle, then moved the aid so that the movement was level, but double-clicked again to disable for painting with the Pixel brush to prevent erasing by mistake. Also, using a graph grid is also a good idea, as well, to keep the movement of aids even. Refer to Figure 6-42 and Figure 6-43.

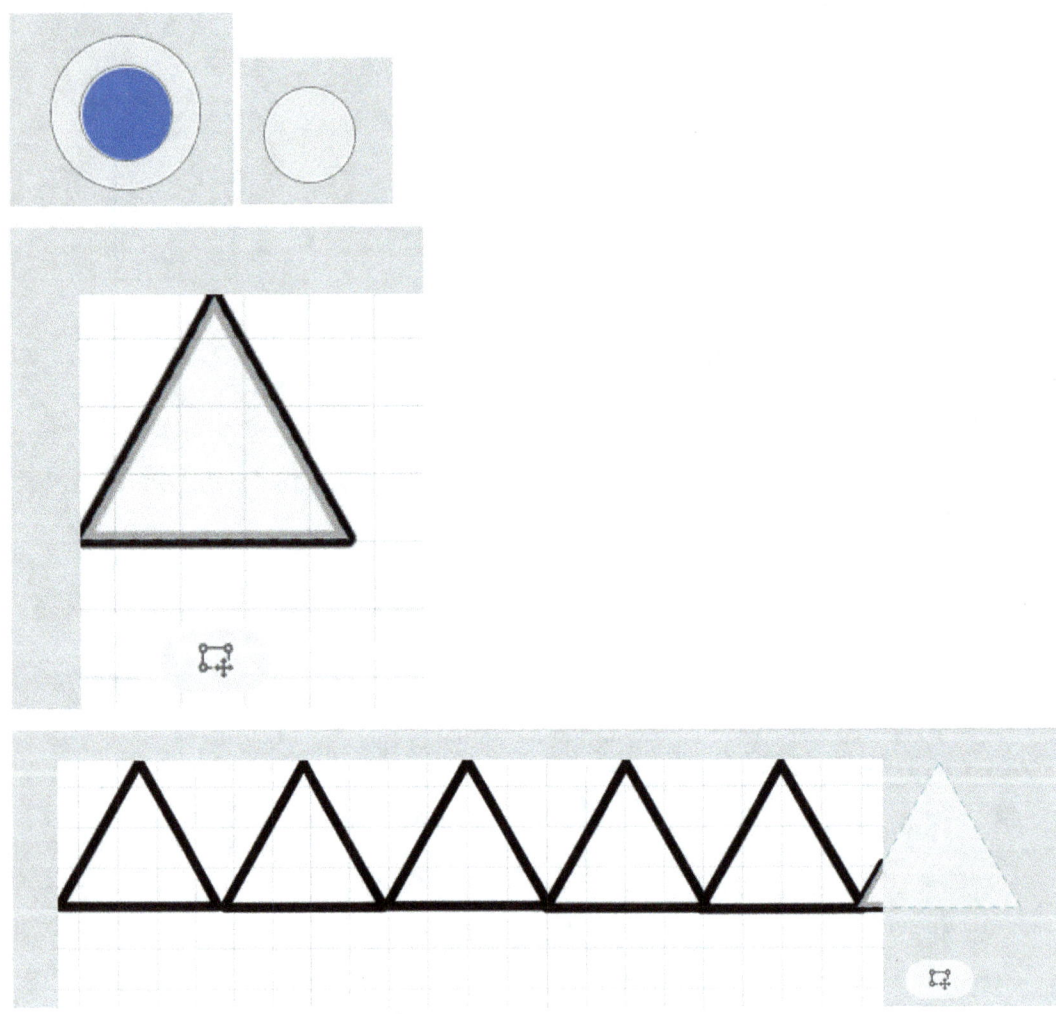

Figure 6-43. *Use the Pixel brush, then move the drawing aid either with the Touch shortcut enabled or disabled to paint your pattern with the Pixel brush on the canvas*

CHAPTER 6 WORKING WITH DRAWING AIDS ON THE CANVAS

Continue on drawing a pattern, this time maybe rotating the shape or changing the color using the color chip with the color wheel. Refer to Figure 6-44 and Figure 6-45.

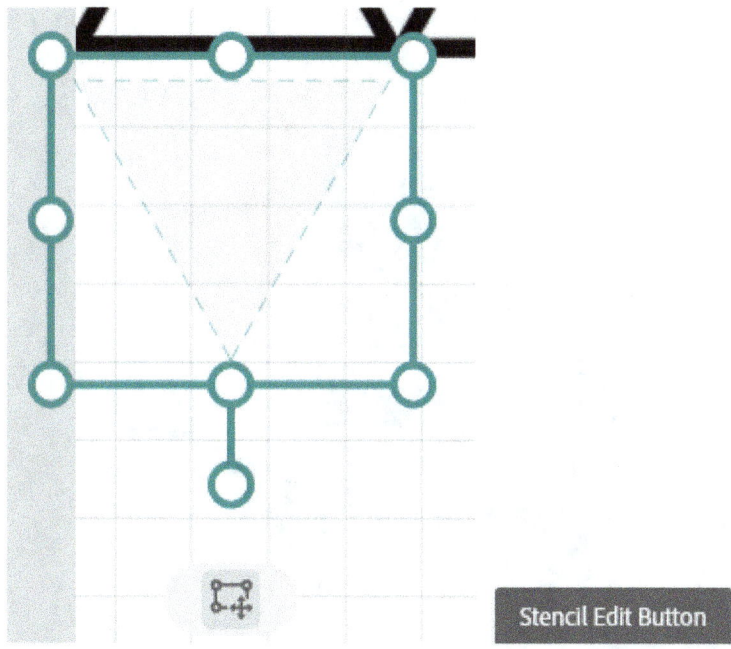

Figure 6-44. *Rotate the drawing aid on the canvas and align with the grid*

CHAPTER 6   WORKING WITH DRAWING AIDS ON THE CANVAS

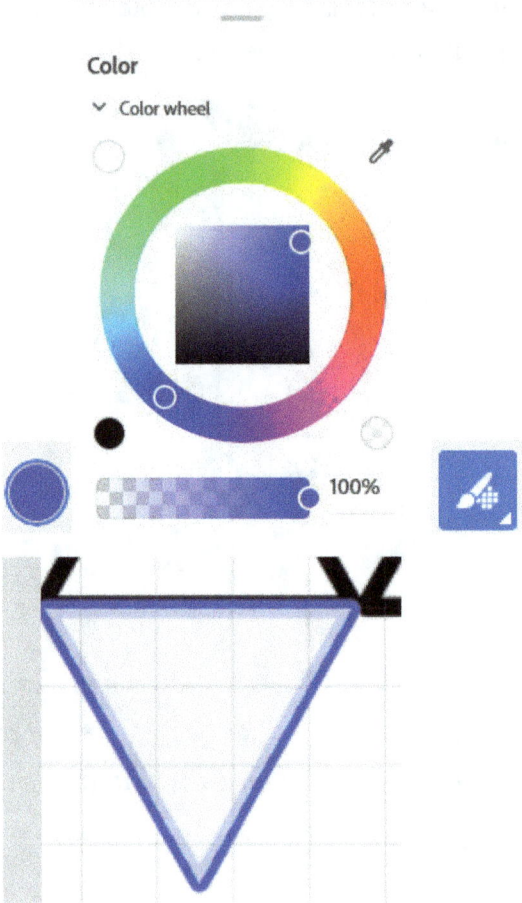

Figure 6-45. *Choose another color from the color chip and Color panel, and paint again with the drawing aid*

Continue across and down the page with other drawing aid shapes until you have a unique pattern. Try using a square, then a Polygon hexagon with six sides, and last an octagon with eight sides. Remember to edit and move them, by enabling then disabling the Stencil Edit Button again to continue painting. Refer to Figure 6-46.

CHAPTER 6   WORKING WITH DRAWING AIDS ON THE CANVAS

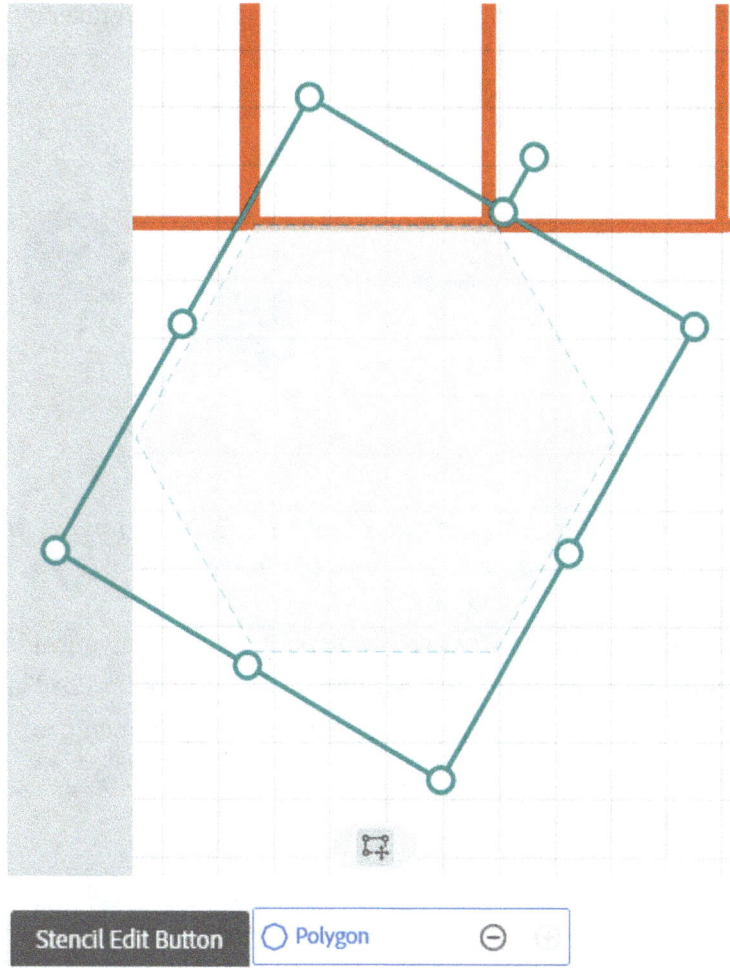

Figure 6-46. *Use the Stencil Edit Button or choose a new drawing aid setting to create a pattern*

Remember to zoom in (Ctrl++) or use your spacebar key so that you can move about the canvas without moving the drawing aids.

Use the undo (Ctrl+Z) and redo (Ctrl+Shift+Z) keys if you make a mistake or need to go forward a step. Refer to Figure 6-47.

Figure 6-47. *Use the undo and redo keys in the Title bar as you work*

Likewise, use your Ruler drawing aid to add lines, or even an eraser by selecting that tool, or using your Touch shortcut key (double-click) while you have the current brush selected if you need to remove some lines. Refer to Figure 6-48.

Figure 6-48. *Use the Ruler drawing aid, enable the Touch shortcut primary circle with your brush, or use an eraser brush tool to remove lines*

After you have created the outlines you want with various drawing aids, then set that layer as a reference layer using the Layer action and create another Pixel layer above. Use the Fill tool to fill in those shapes with other colors from the color chip and Color wheel. Refer to Figures 6-49, 6-50, and 6-51.

CHAPTER 6　WORKING WITH DRAWING AIDS ON THE CANVAS

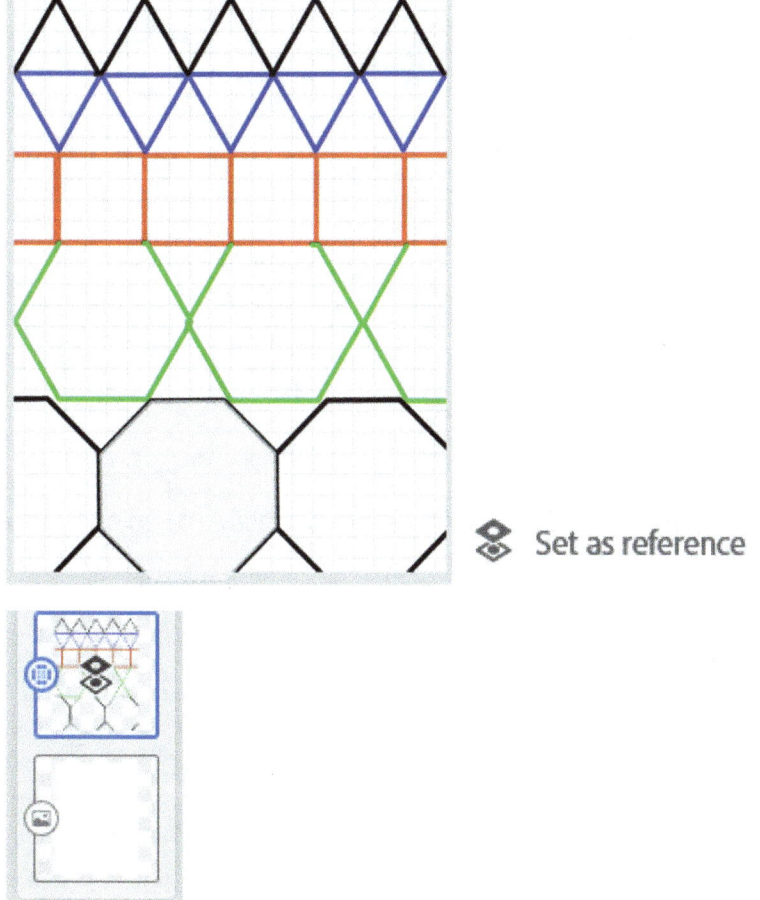

Figure 6-49. *Finished artwork on the Pixel layer which is then set to a Layer action of Set as reference in the Layer panel*

CHAPTER 6 WORKING WITH DRAWING AIDS ON THE CANVAS

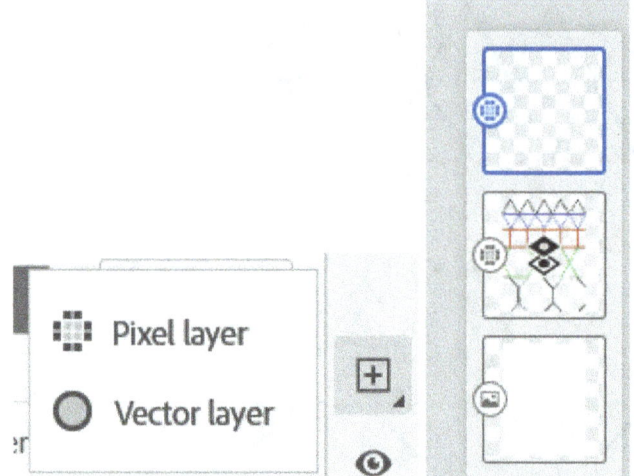

Figure 6-50. *Create a new Pixel layer above the reference layer*

CHAPTER 6 WORKING WITH DRAWING AIDS ON THE CANVAS

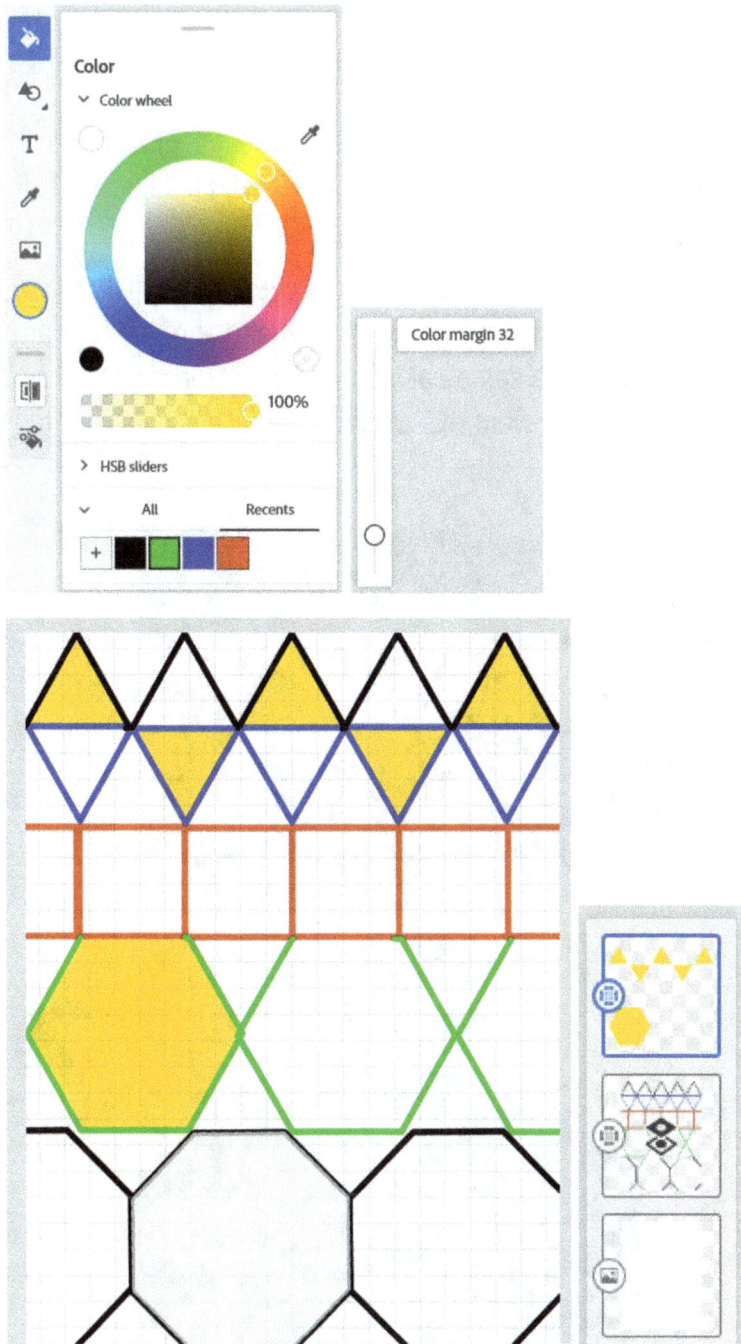

Figure 6-51. *Use the Fill tool on the new layer with a set color margin to fill in the transparent areas of the shapes with new colors from the color chip and Color panel*

CHAPTER 6   WORKING WITH DRAWING AIDS ON THE CANVAS

Continue to fill with colors using the Eyedropper to change to various colors of your choice, and remember to use the Recents tab in the Color chip panel when you want to add a past color.

I left the Color margin at 32, but you may want to set it higher to 253 if you do not want a slight white gap to appear between the outline and fill. Refer to Figure 6-51.

Note that if there is a gap between shapes and lines, it will fill in that region as well. This may or may not be what you want so make sure to close any gaps on your reference layer with the same color you used for the outline to prevent any kind of spread, if you do not want this as part of your design. Refer to Figure 6-52.

Figure 6-52. *Colors filled in on the blank area of the new Pixel layer with some spread due to gaps between shapes as seen with the space of triangles between the hexagon and octagons*

468

CHAPTER 6 WORKING WITH DRAWING AIDS ON THE CANVAS

You can toggle the grid off in the Precision panel at this point if you no longer need it.

Or leave the grid on and continue to add more shapes with the drawing aids, on another Pixel layer to create more stroke outlines this time in white. Then, set this new layer as reference layer and create a final new layer above and use different brush strokes or fills to add more colors. Refer to Figure 6-53.

Figure 6-53. *A new layer of shapes created which is then set to a reference layer and a new layer with additional filled shapes added with Grids turned off*

This is a great starting point for creating a unique background that could have other drawing elements over the top. Later, you could combine or group some layers or reduce their opacity using the Layer properties as mentioned in Chapter 5. You can review my file **Drawing_Aids_Final.psd** for reference.

CHAPTER 6   WORKING WITH DRAWING AIDS ON THE CANVAS

Project 2: Drawing Creatures with the Drawing Aids

Another way you can be creative with drawing aids is to create a unique illustration like this spider or a beetle. From the Home page, import and open the file **Spider_web_start. psd**. In this project, I will demonstrate the spider. Refer to Figure 6-54.

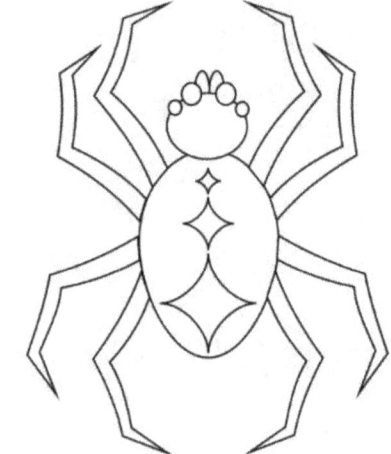

Figure 6-54. *Import and open a file that contains illustrations or sketches that you can trace over with drawing aids like a spider and beetle*

In this project, I have created some starter drawing lines in Illustrator and Photoshop ahead of time that you can practice with your ruler or another drawing aid, such as the Circle, to create various drawing lines and curves. In your own projects, these may be sketches that you have scanned and add onto a layer earlier in Photoshop. Work on a new Pixel layer above the other layers. Refer to Figure 6-55.

CHAPTER 6 WORKING WITH DRAWING AIDS ON THE CANVAS

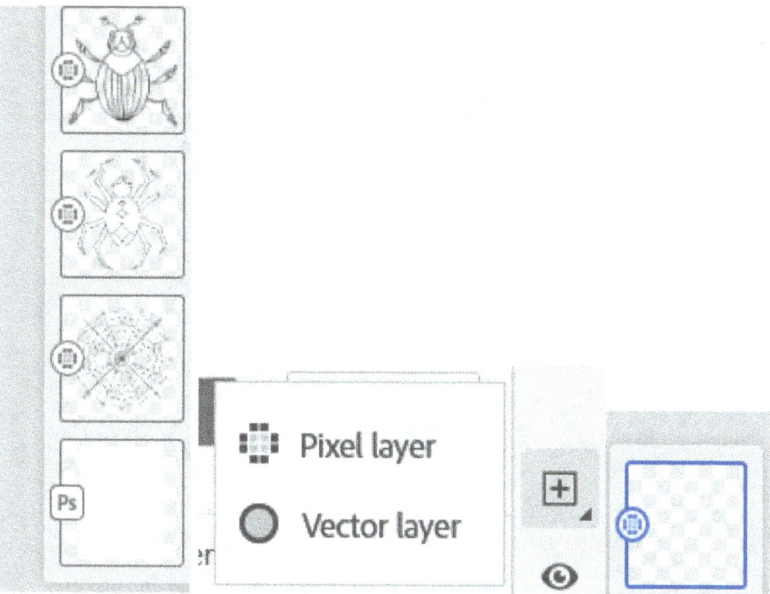

Figure 6-55. *Pixel layers in the Layers panel that contain various illustrations; then create a new layer to work on above all the other layers*

When working with the Circle drawing aid to trace complex curves, you may have to scale the aid several times, for example, with the spider's body abdomen, which is not a perfect ellipse. In this example, I am drawing with a blue outline, with the Pixel brush Basic Hard round, but use any color you want from the color chip. The size of the brush is 12 px. Refer to Figure 6-56 and Figure 6-57.

CHAPTER 6   WORKING WITH DRAWING AIDS ON THE CANVAS

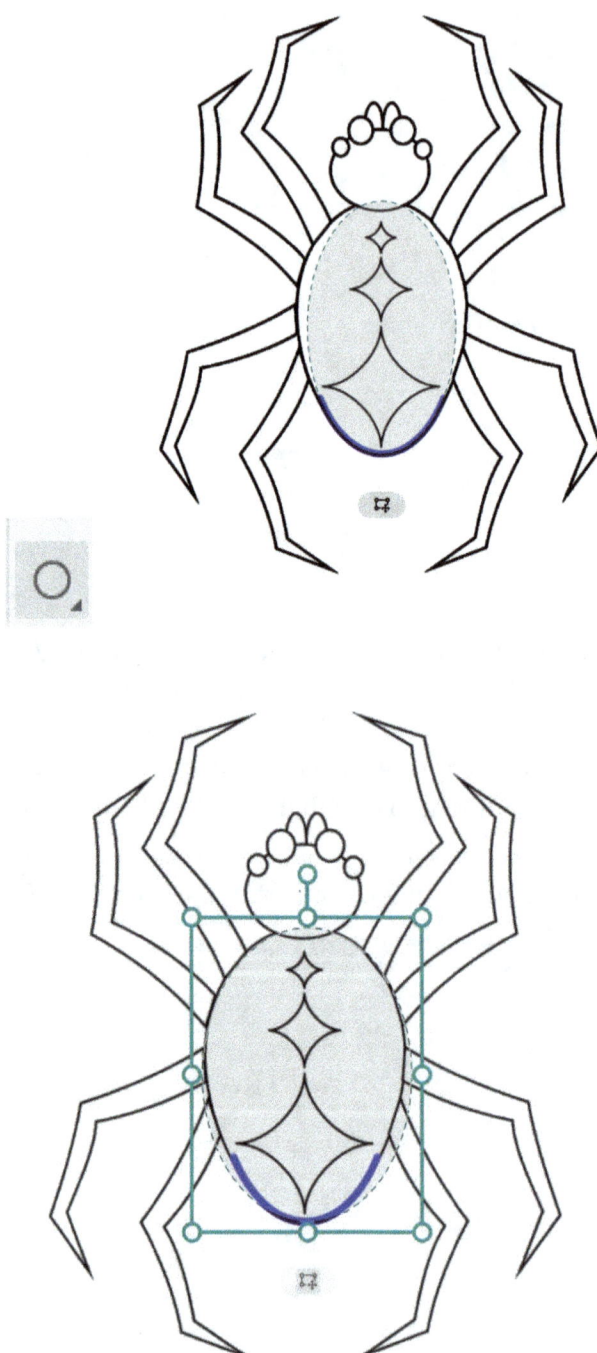

Figure 6-56. *Circle drawing aid must be scaled and moved many times so that you can then start to draw the outline of the body of the spider with the brush*

CHAPTER 6   WORKING WITH DRAWING AIDS ON THE CANVAS

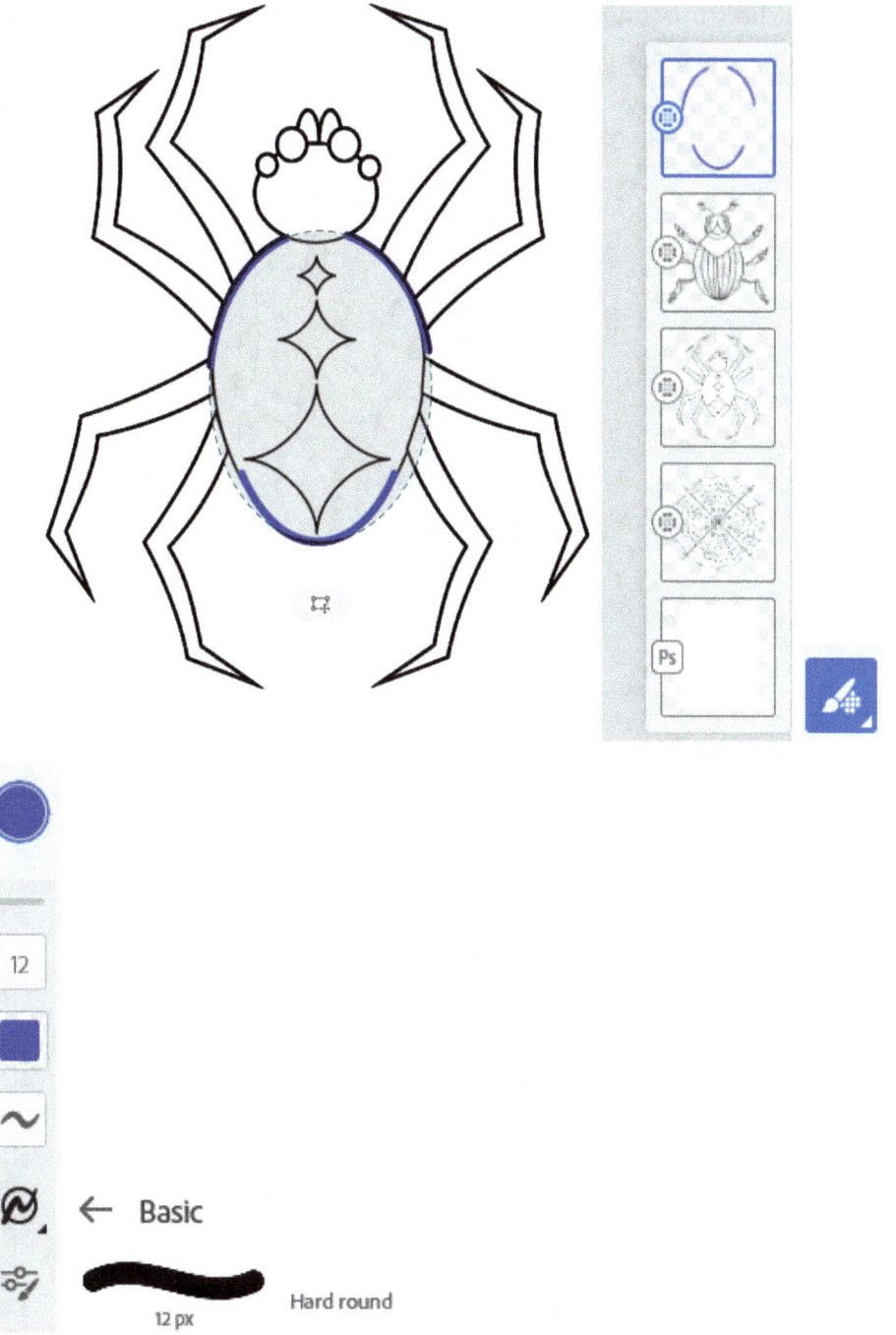

Figure 6-57. *The body of the spider is not a perfect ellipse so continue to make adjustments to paint the abdomen and observe how the paint appears on the new Pixel layer with a Pixel brush of 12 px set in the Toolbar*

CHAPTER 6   WORKING WITH DRAWING AIDS ON THE CANVAS

You can see here how much of the spider's body outline can be colored by carefully rotating or scaling the Circle drawing aid, clicking the Stencil Edit Button for enabling, then disabling, and moving the aid into place, and then using the brush to paint that part of the curve. Refer to Figure 6-58 and Figure 6-59.

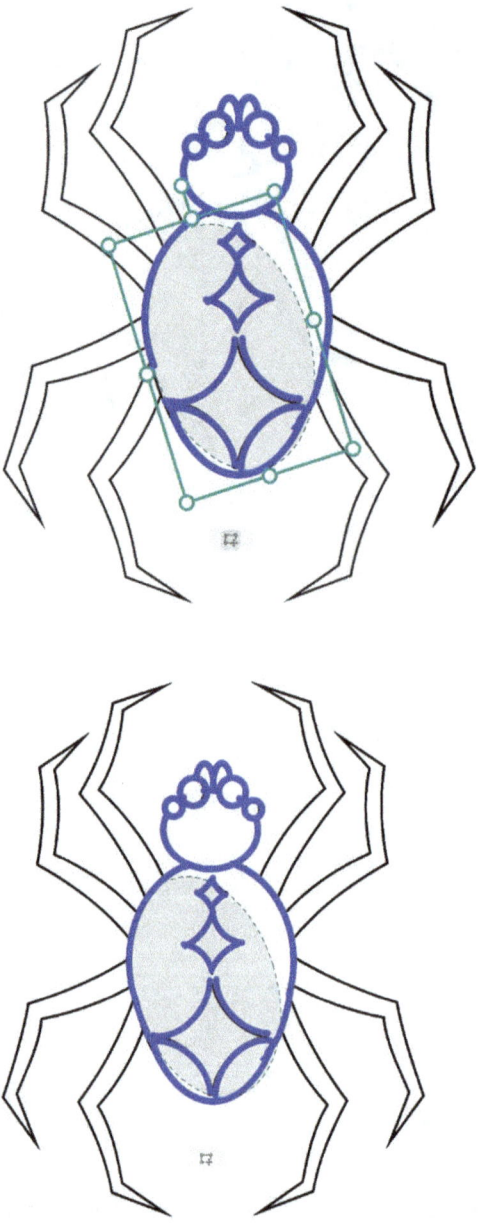

Figure 6-58. *The Circle drawing aid may need to be rotated or moved to a new location before painting with it again*

CHAPTER 6 WORKING WITH DRAWING AIDS ON THE CANVAS

The eyes are more perfect circles, and so they can be easily outlined, while for the rounded diamonds on the abdomen, an ellipse or circle can be used for the edges, but the aid may need to be scaled. Refer to Figure 6-59.

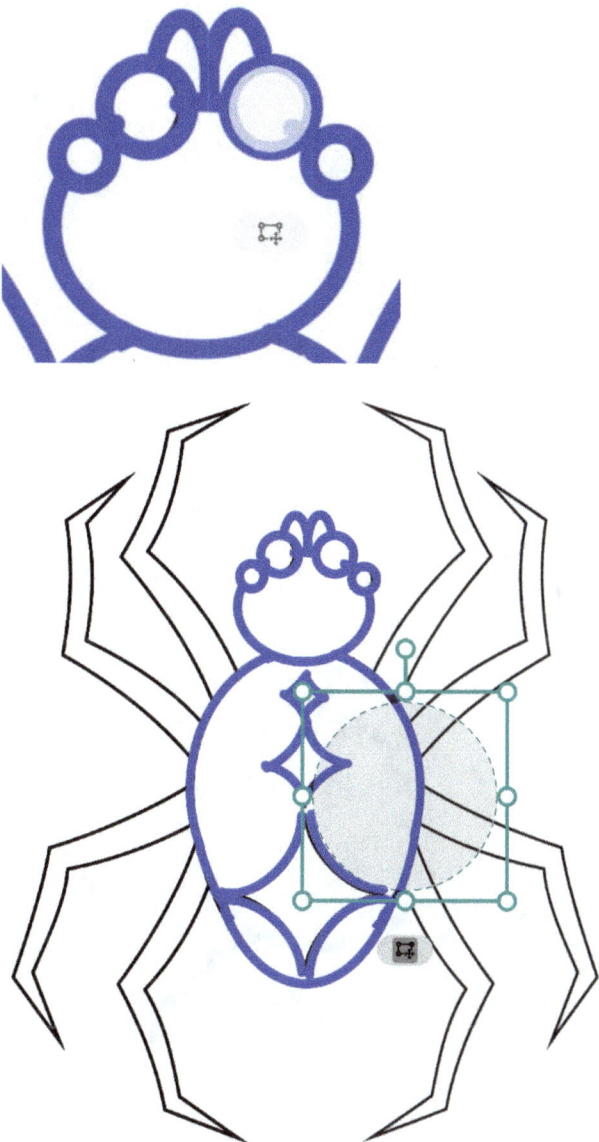

Figure 6-59. *In some cases, the eyes of the spider or part of a rounded diamond can be easily painted with the Circle drawing aid once it is scaled and moved into place*

475

CHAPTER 6　WORKING WITH DRAWING AIDS ON THE CANVAS

Note that in the case of the legs, however, you could use the Ruler drawing aid as well for the tips of the legs. Remember to use the R key when you want to rotate the ruler. Refer to Figure 6-60.

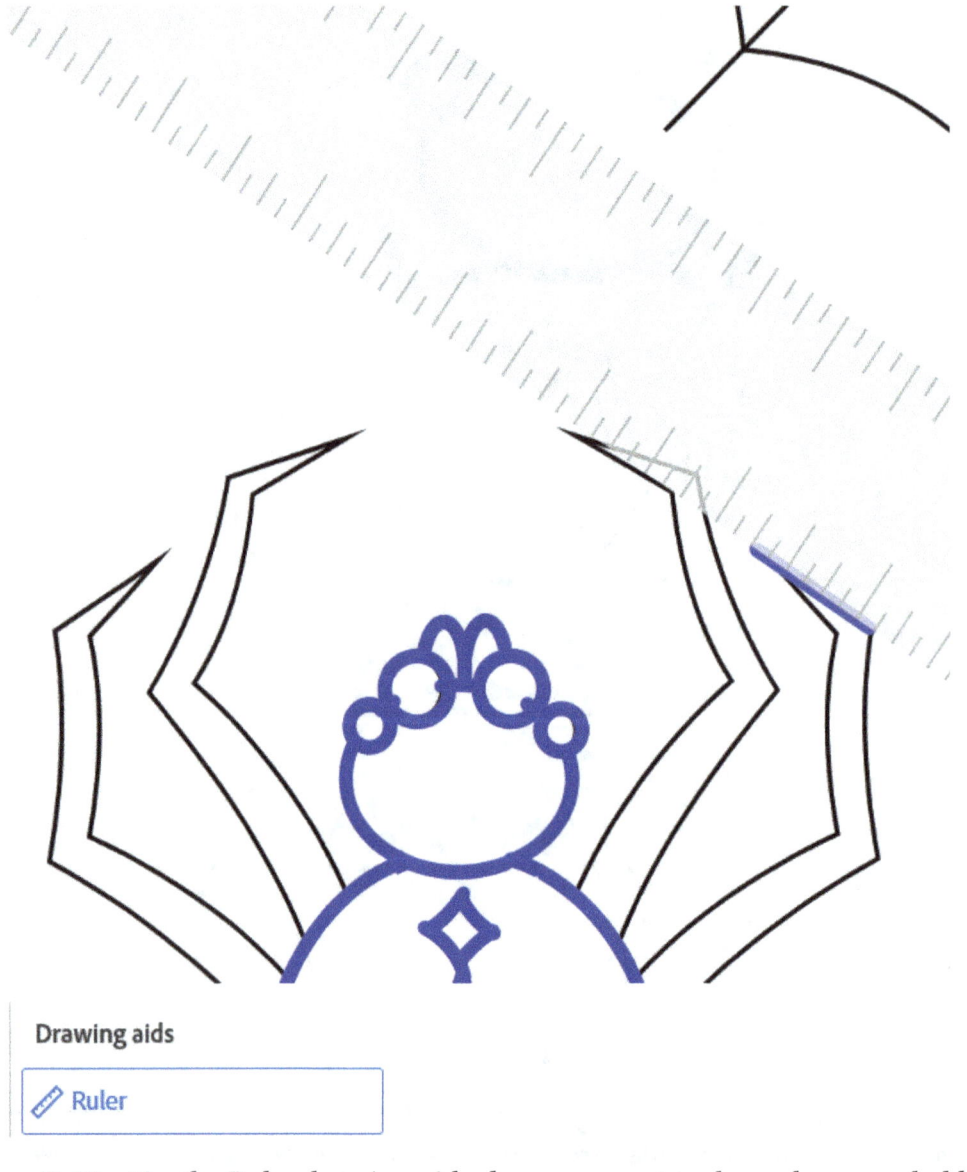

Figure 6-60. *Use the Ruler drawing aid when you want to draw sharp angled lines like the tips of the spider's legs*

However, because other areas of the legs are curved, you could use the Circle drawing aid again, but it may have to be quite large to get an accurate arch. Refer to Figure 6-61.

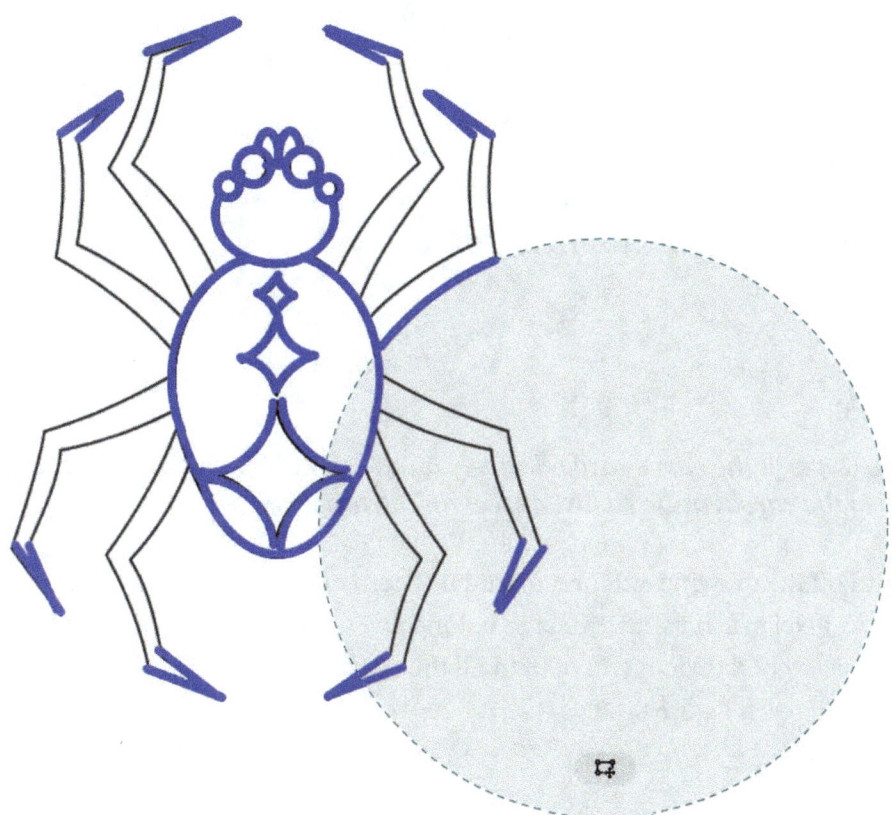

Figure 6-61. *Return to the Circle drawing aid when you want to paint large arches and curves on the spider's legs*

You may notice how, by moving the same Circle drawing aid around, you can accomplish drawing all the leg curves with minimal scaling. Refer to Figure 6-62.

Figure 6-62. *If the curves are relatively all the same, then you may be able to draw many of the curves quite easily, as seen in the top layer*

Turn off the drawing aid for a moment. Then, make sure you close any minor gaps with your Pixel brush using the same color, in this case blue and same brush size of 12 px. This is good to do if you plan to fill the spider with color just like the shapes in Project 1. Refer to Figure 6-63.

Figure 6-63. *Disable the drawing aid and make sure to fill in any small gaps so that you can later fill on the layer above the spider*

CHAPTER 6   WORKING WITH DRAWING AIDS ON THE CANVAS

Afterward, you can color your spider using a separate new Pixel layer and turn the outline you just created into a reference layer. Making the spider appear more solid, use the Fill tool, and set a higher color margin of about 253 to avoid white gaps. Refer to Figure 6-64.

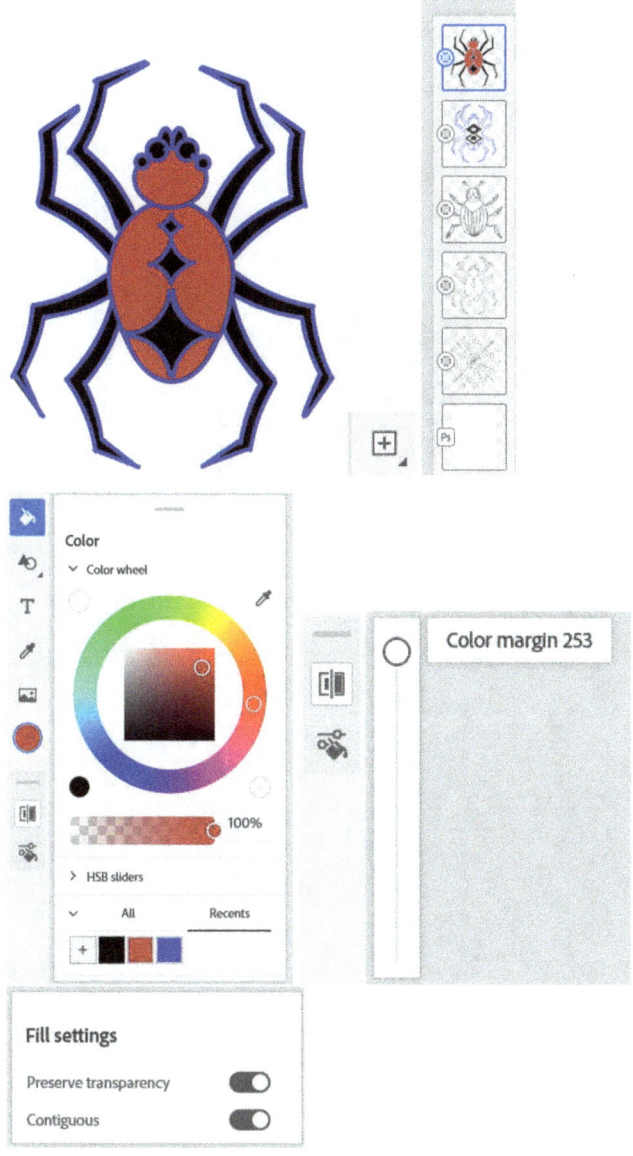

Figure 6-64. *On a new layer above the reference layer, you can fill the transparent areas above the spider with color using the Fill tool, color chip, and Color panel, and adjust the Color margin or Fill settings*

479

CHAPTER 6 WORKING WITH DRAWING AIDS ON THE CANVAS

Refer to file **Spider_web_Final.psd** if you would like to review the layers and see the colored beetle as well. In your file, again practice with your Circle drawing aid and Ruler on a new layer above the beetle sketch as seen in red outline, and then, make that layer into a reference layer and then fill the new Pixel layer above with colors as was done with the spider. These final drawings could be later used with the web in a final art piece. Refer to Figure 6-65.

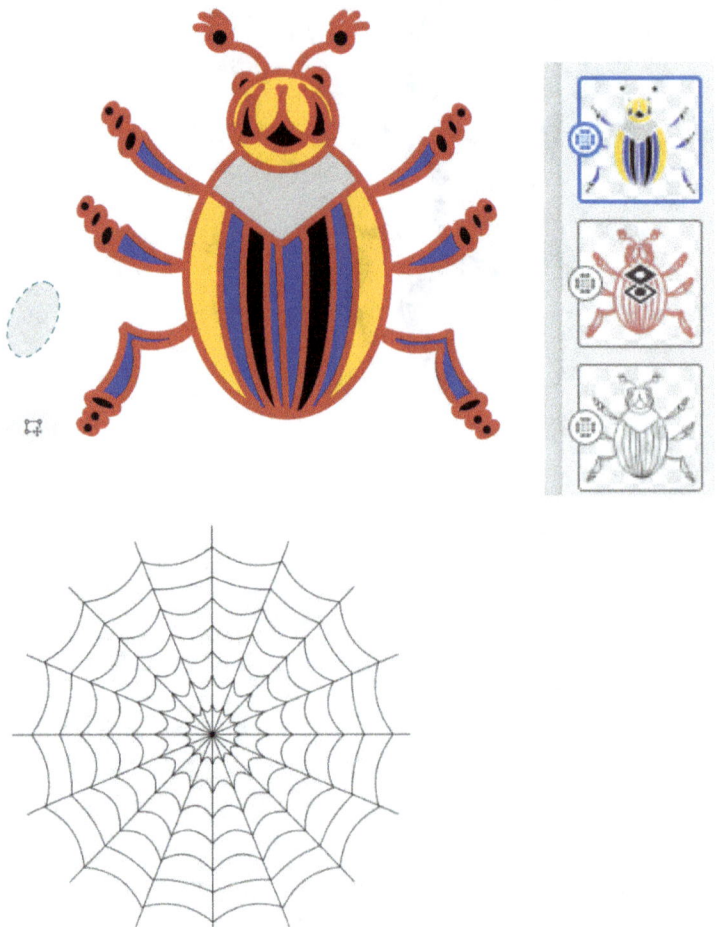

Figure 6-65. *Try drawing the beetle with the drawing aids on a new layer, and turn into a reference layer, and fill another new layer with color, and add it to the web illustration*

Optionally, if you are working over your own sketches, you could then hide or delete those layers that contain the sketches, if you no longer need them to be visible.

CHAPTER 6　WORKING WITH DRAWING AIDS ON THE CANVAS

Project 3: Drawing a Cityscape

For a third idea, you may want to practice your perspective. Use the perspective grid and try creating a cityscape drawing on multiple layers. Make sure, as you did in Project 1, to start with a new Letter document.

Using the Square drawing aid, scale the sides of it using your bounding box handles for your building wall as required, to start creating the urban landscape. Refer to Figure 6-66.

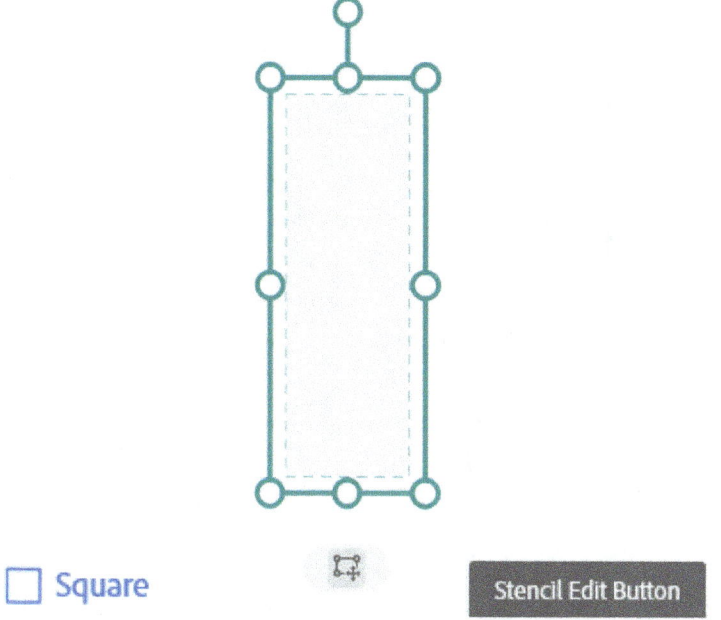

Figure 6-66. *Square drawing aid in Stencil Edit Button mode*

Then, using the Vertical Taskbar Precision panel, enable the grid and set the Grid type to Perspective.

In my example, I am using a Vanishing points 2 Point perspective. Refer to Figure 6-67.

CHAPTER 6 WORKING WITH DRAWING AIDS ON THE CANVAS

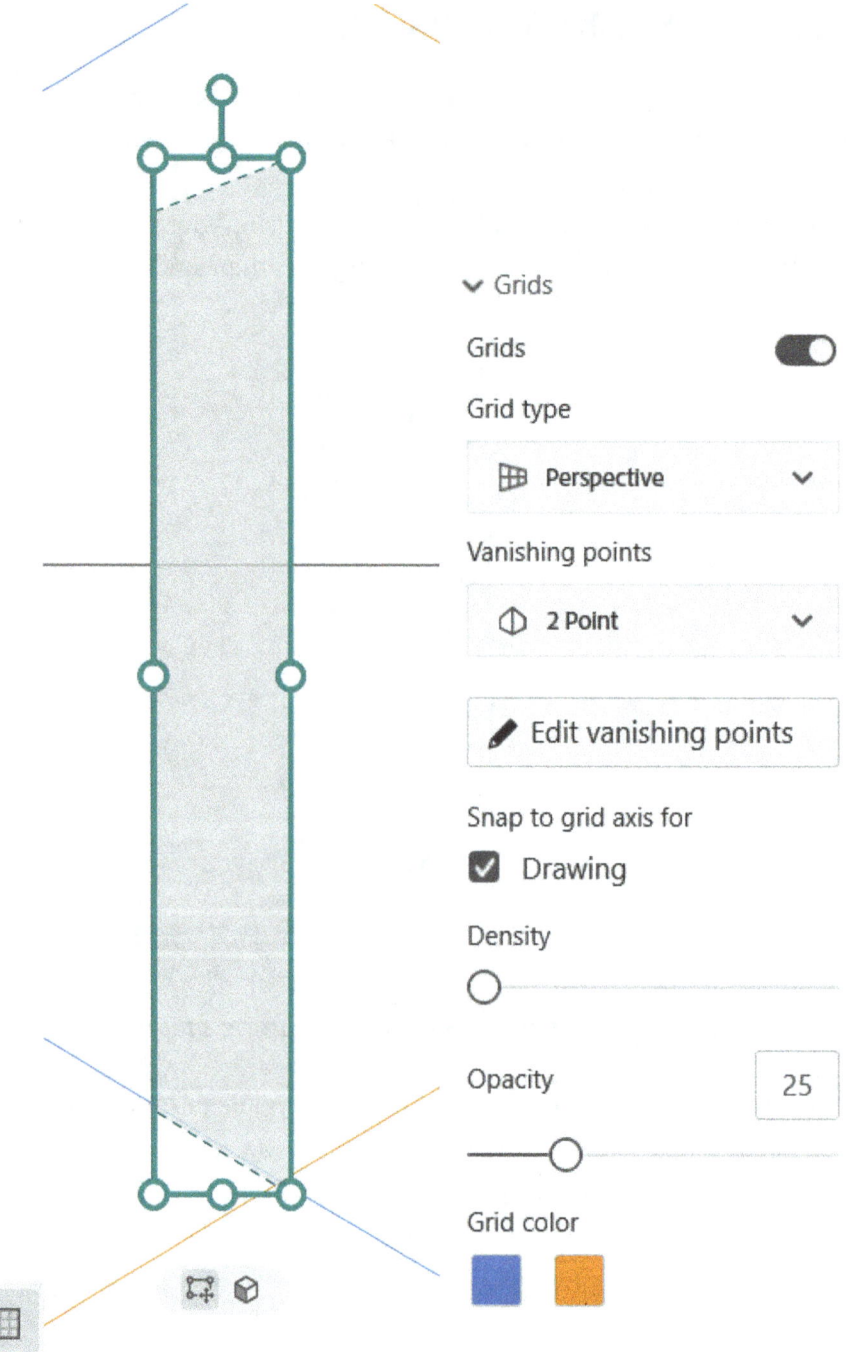

Figure 6-67. *Setting the Precision grid settings for perspective for the drawing aid at 2 Point*

CHAPTER 6　WORKING WITH DRAWING AIDS ON THE CANVAS

I drew my outlines again on a Pixel layer with my Pixel brush Basic ➤ Hard round in black and about 12 points.

Change your perspective grid planes as you work. Starting your drawing from the center of the document, first draw your left perspective and then switch your grid plane to the right. In this case, there is no need to scale; just move the Square drawing aid as soon as you have changed to the new grid perspective plane and start drawing. Refer to Figure 6-68.

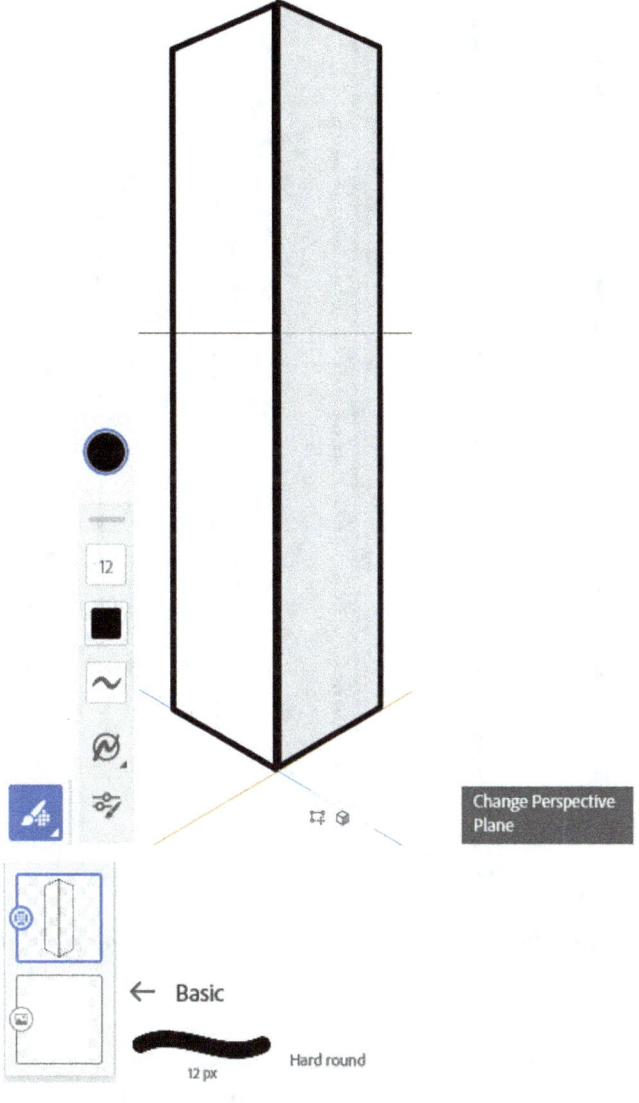

Figure 6-68. *Painting on a new Pixel layer with the drawing aid in Perspective and changing perspective plane*

CHAPTER 6   WORKING WITH DRAWING AIDS ON THE CANVAS

You may prefer, as you work, to move down one side of the page to focus on one grid plane at a time. Remember to vary the buildings' heights as not all buildings are the same. You can, at this point, use the Stencil Edit Button to scale your drawing aid, then disable the Stencil Edit, and then move it to a new location before continuing to draw. Refer to Figure 6-69.

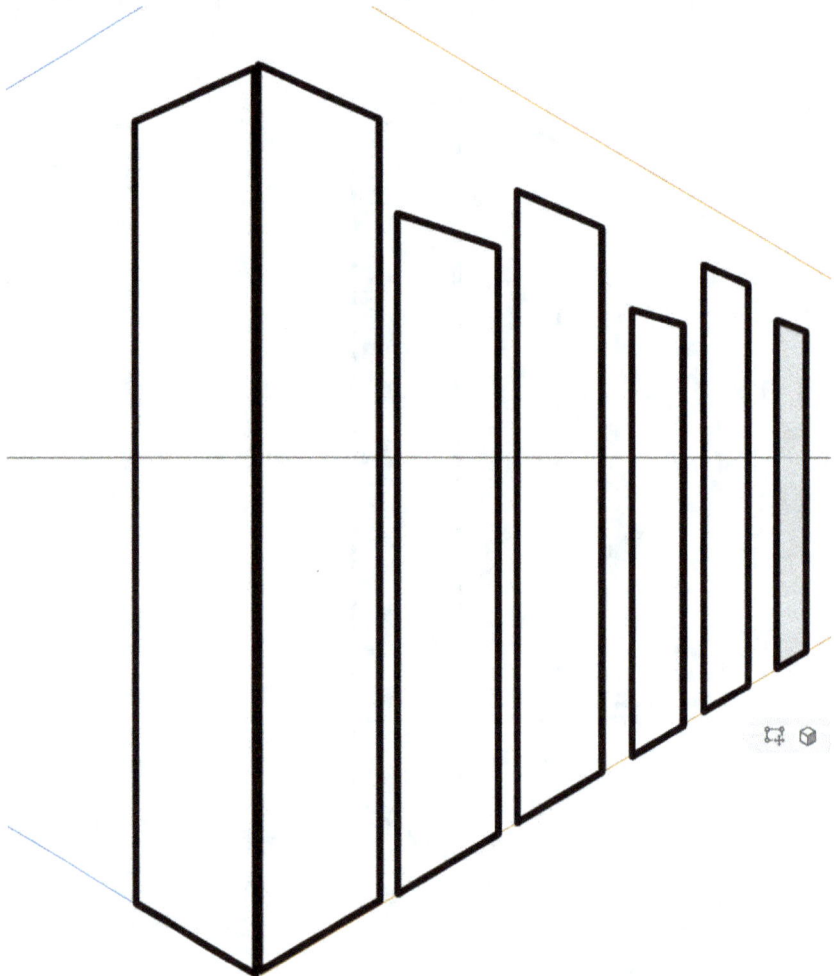

Figure 6-69. *Moving, scaling, and painting the grid on the right with the right plane*

Then, on that same grid line row, you may want to change the perspective plane and draw the left sides of those same buildings in the same row. This is what gives you the 3D effect. Again, you may need to scale your drawing aid so that it lines up with the opposite building walls for the height. Refer to Figure 6-70.

CHAPTER 6   WORKING WITH DRAWING AIDS ON THE CANVAS

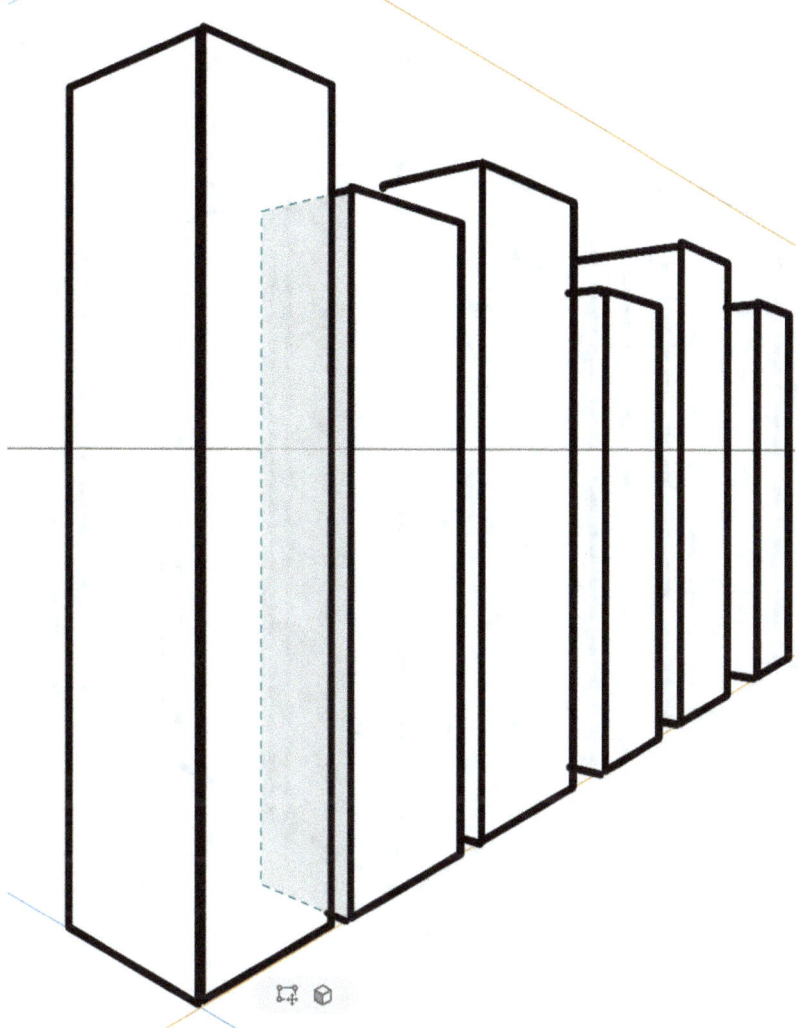

Figure 6-70. *Moving, scaling, and painting the grid on the right with the left plane to make the buildings appear more 3D-like*

Then, continue the process on the left side of the city block or row, changing from left to right grid perspective to create the 3D-like look of each building. Be aware that, as you create the visible parts of the walls, you only need to use your drawing aid to outline to a certain point just so you hit the next black line to close the gap. Refer to Figure 6-70 and Figure 6-71.

CHAPTER 6   WORKING WITH DRAWING AIDS ON THE CANVAS

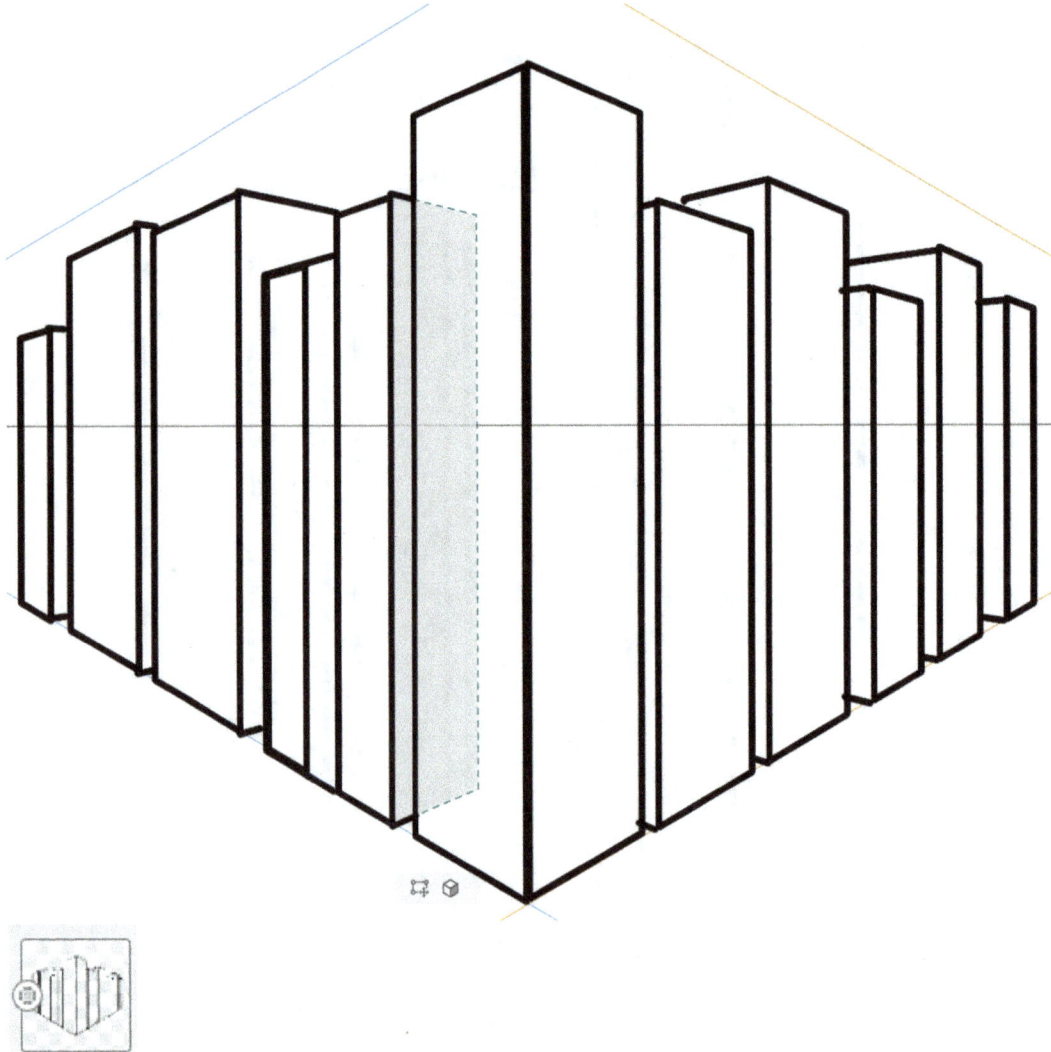

Figure 6-71. *Moving, scaling, and painting the grid on the left. Change switching from left to right plane to make the buildings appear more 3D-like*

Remember, if you make a mistake, you can always use the undo key or use your eraser tool later with the same brush by using your Touch shortcut primary circle as seen in the previous projects.

Once you have created enough buildings, then use your Ruler drawing aid in a new Pixel layer. Continue to change the perspective left or right, rotating it as it attaches to the horizon. Use your brush to create a road where the street meets at the end of the block, using your brush to create parts of the sidewalk. Refer to Figure 6-72.

486

CHAPTER 6   WORKING WITH DRAWING AIDS ON THE CANVAS

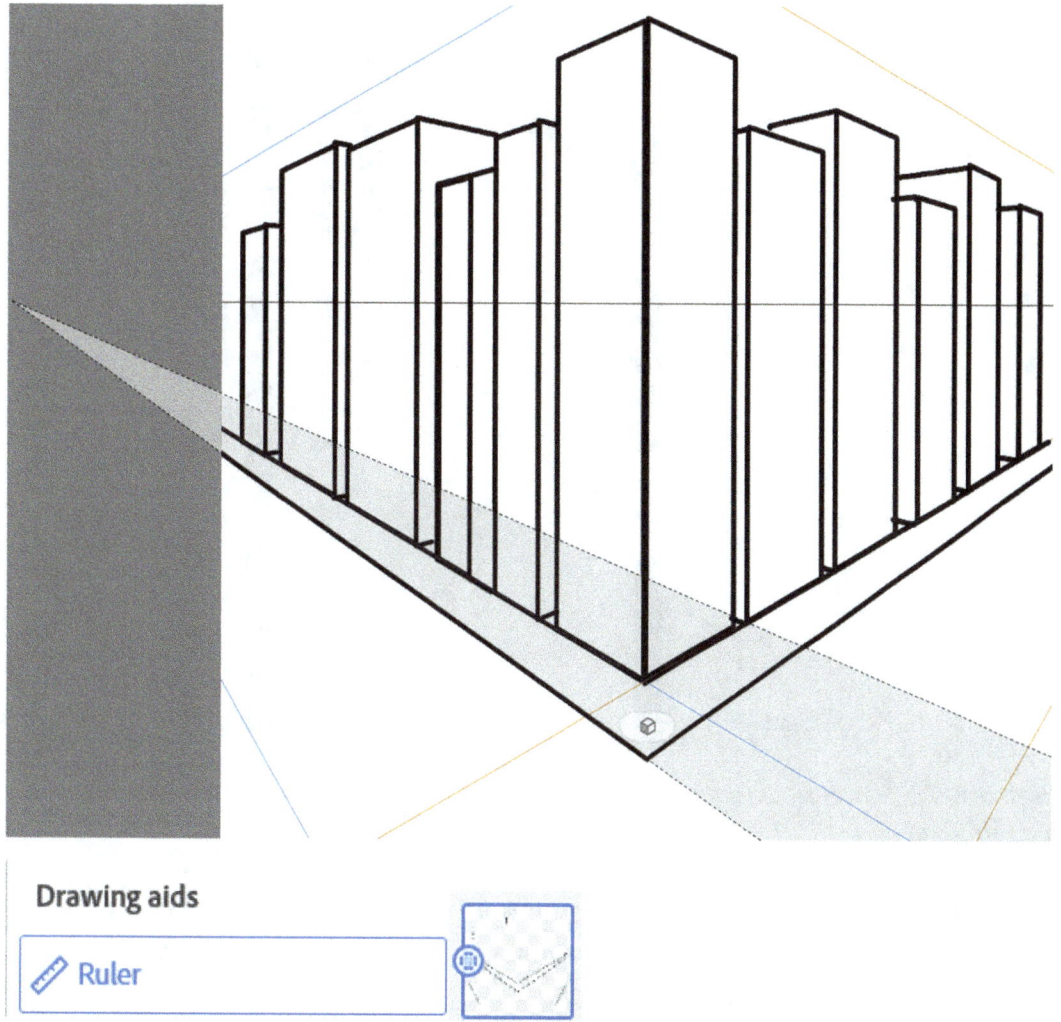

Figure 6-72. *Using the Ruler drawing aid to create a road and sidewalk in perspective on the left and right plane sides*

To make sure structures appear more building-like in your art, on another blank Pixel layer, you can return to the Square drawing aid. Then, scale the drawing aid and create small rectangles or lines for your windows on the building, always switching from left to right perspective. Then, paint the windows on the building walls. Refer to Figure 6-73.

487

CHAPTER 6   WORKING WITH DRAWING AIDS ON THE CANVAS

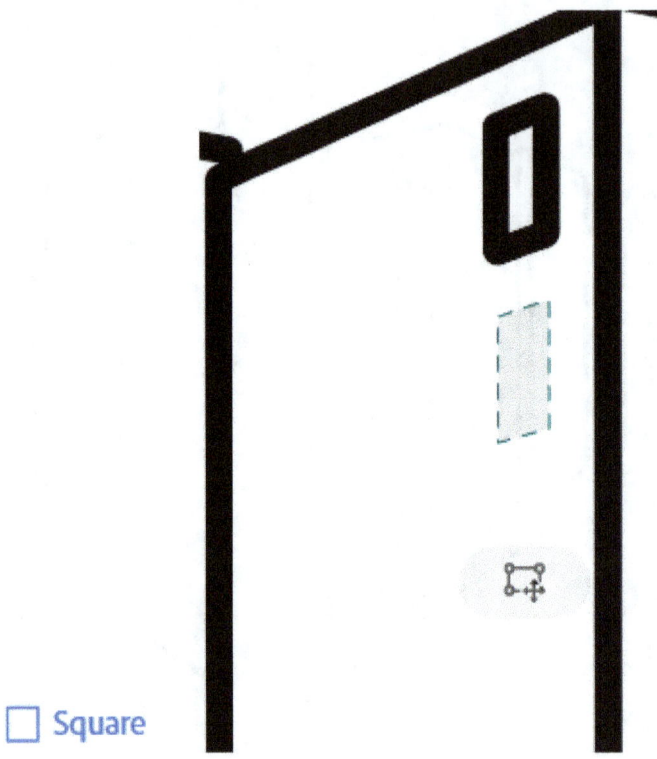

Figure 6-73. *On a new layer, create windows for each building using the Square drawing aid*

Create as many or a few windows as you like, though more may add interest later when you decide to color. Some windows you may only want as partial lines rather than drawing around the entire aid.

Tip   After creating an outline using the drawing aid, you may discover, after you have turned it off, that the stroke is not quite where you wanted it placed. In that case, you can use your Magic wand Selection tool that you saw in Chapter 4 to select the color stroke. Then, use the Transform tool and nudge or scale that painted area into place using your arrow nudge keys and bounding box handles. Click Done to exit the workspace, and then, Deselect the selection around the stroke using the Contextual Task bar. Refer to Figures 6-74, 6-75, and 6-76.

CHAPTER 6   WORKING WITH DRAWING AIDS ON THE CANVAS

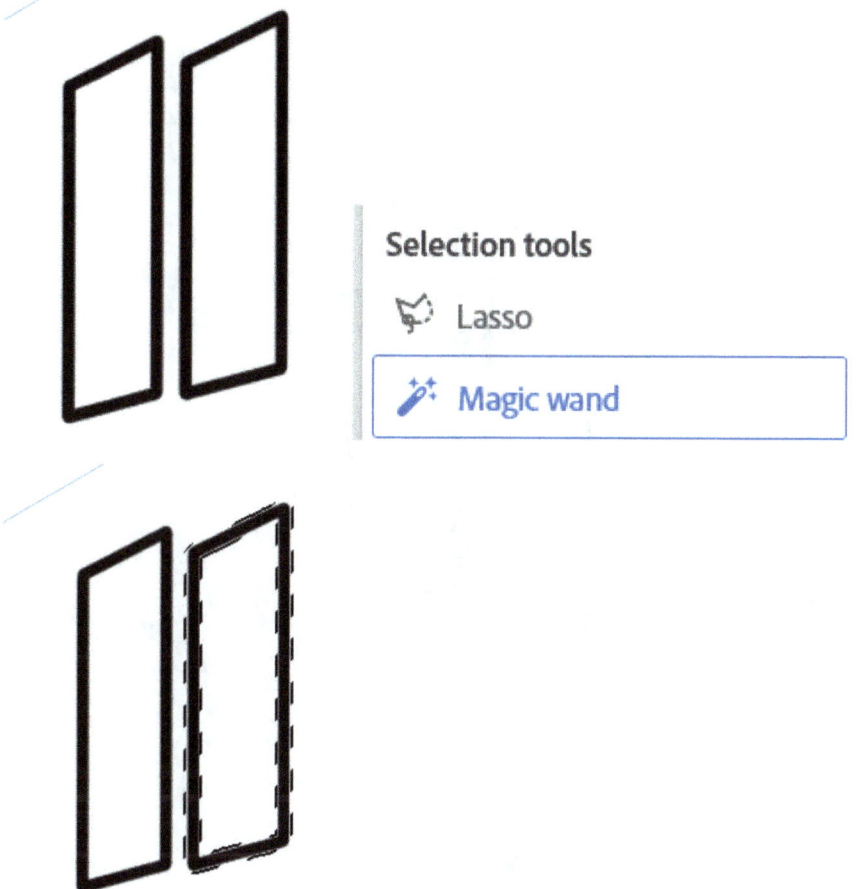

Figure 6-74. *Use the Magic wand Selection tool when you need to select some brush strokes that you want to move and transform on the layer*

CHAPTER 6 WORKING WITH DRAWING AIDS ON THE CANVAS

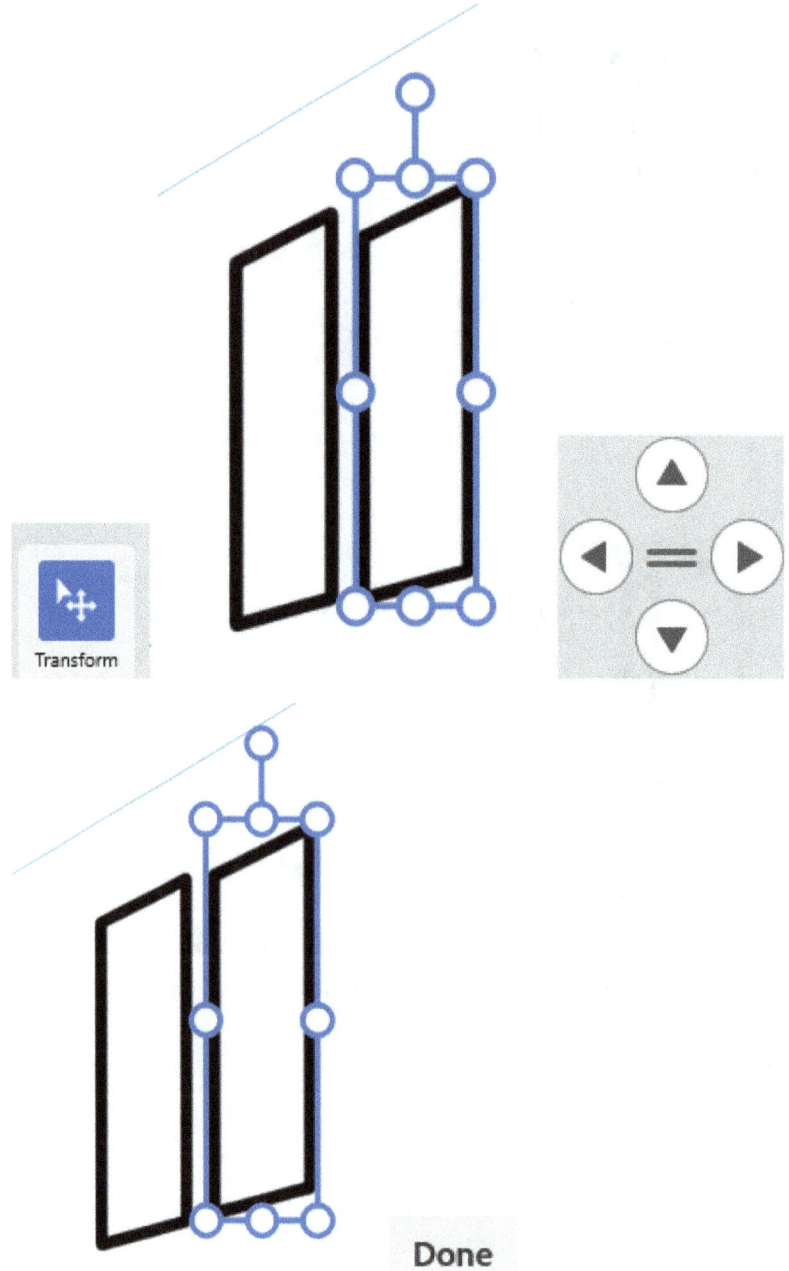

Figure 6-75. *Enter the Transform workspace and then use the nudge arrows, or drag and scale in perspective the brush strokes and click Done to exit the workspace*

CHAPTER 6   WORKING WITH DRAWING AIDS ON THE CANVAS

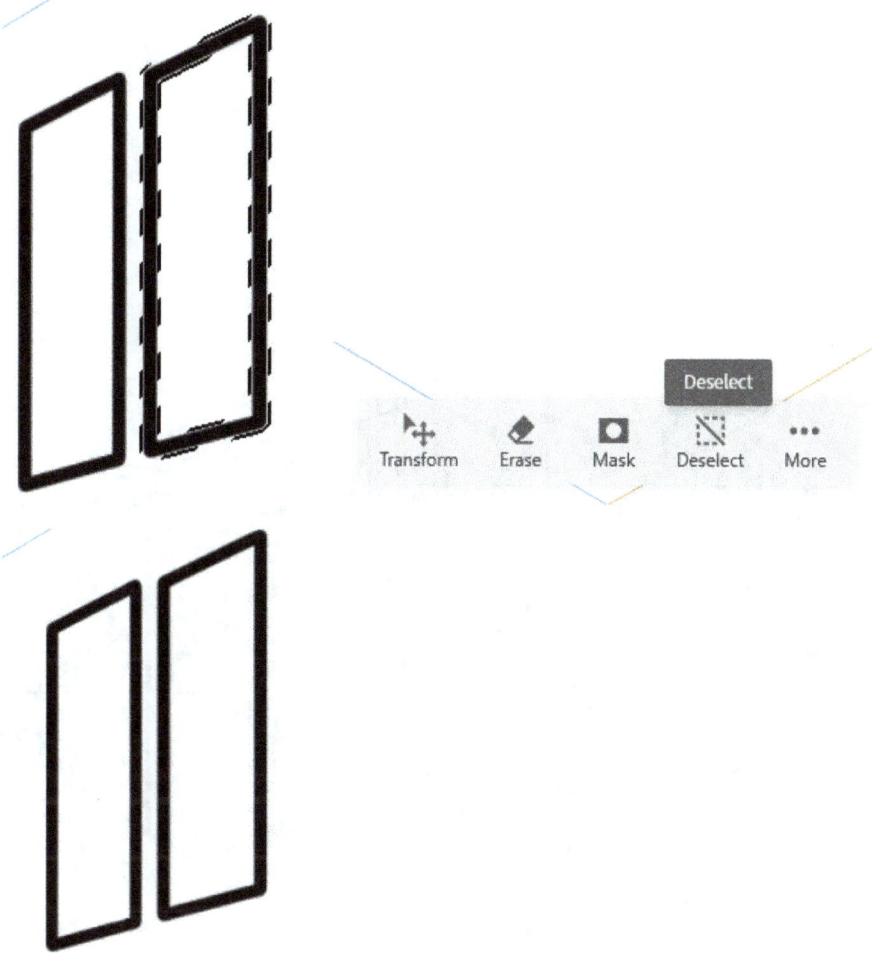

Figure 6-76. *While the selection is still active, click the Deselect button on the Contextual Task bar to remove the selection*

You can also just use the Square drawing aid to add lines or lower doors. Or another suggestion is to use the Square to create an awning above the door or window when you are using the Change Perspective Plane (cube) top/bottom setting.

You can then continue to use the Ruler to add another side to the road where there could be other sidewalks. Refer to Figure 6-77 and 6-78 for how this might look.

491

CHAPTER 6   WORKING WITH DRAWING AIDS ON THE CANVAS

Figure 6-77. *The current city scene in outline with the layer containing the windows selected*

CHAPTER 6 WORKING WITH DRAWING AIDS ON THE CANVAS

Once you have city outlines the way you want, use these outlines as a reference layer, and use other Pixel layers to spend time coloring the areas of your city using the Fill bucket tool, as you did in Projects 1 and 2. You can do such things as add yellow lights for windows and various grays for the buildings and streets to create shadows. Remember to adjust your Fill color margin to a higher setting if you are concerned with gaps.

Or use a brush to paint areas on the street in perspective without the drawing aids. Refer to Figures 6-78 and 6-79.

CHAPTER 6   WORKING WITH DRAWING AIDS ON THE CANVAS

Figure 6-78. *The full city scene with multiple layers added with some background colors*

CHAPTER 6   WORKING WITH DRAWING AIDS ON THE CANVAS

Figure 6-79. *Many layers found in the Layer panel that are used to create the city*

Later, you can turn off the grid. Then, you can add a background solid color on another layer with the Fill paint bucket for the night sky. Also, with Grids turned off for your drawing aid, add a pale yellow moon outline using the Circle drawing aid and fill with white.

Or above the night sky on a new layer, add some clouds with the large Basic soft round opacity brush with a size 272 px in a very light gray but dark enough to cover the white of the moon. You may want to alternate grays and then remove some with the same brush but as an eraser with the Touch shortcut primary circle enabled. Refer to Figure 6-80.

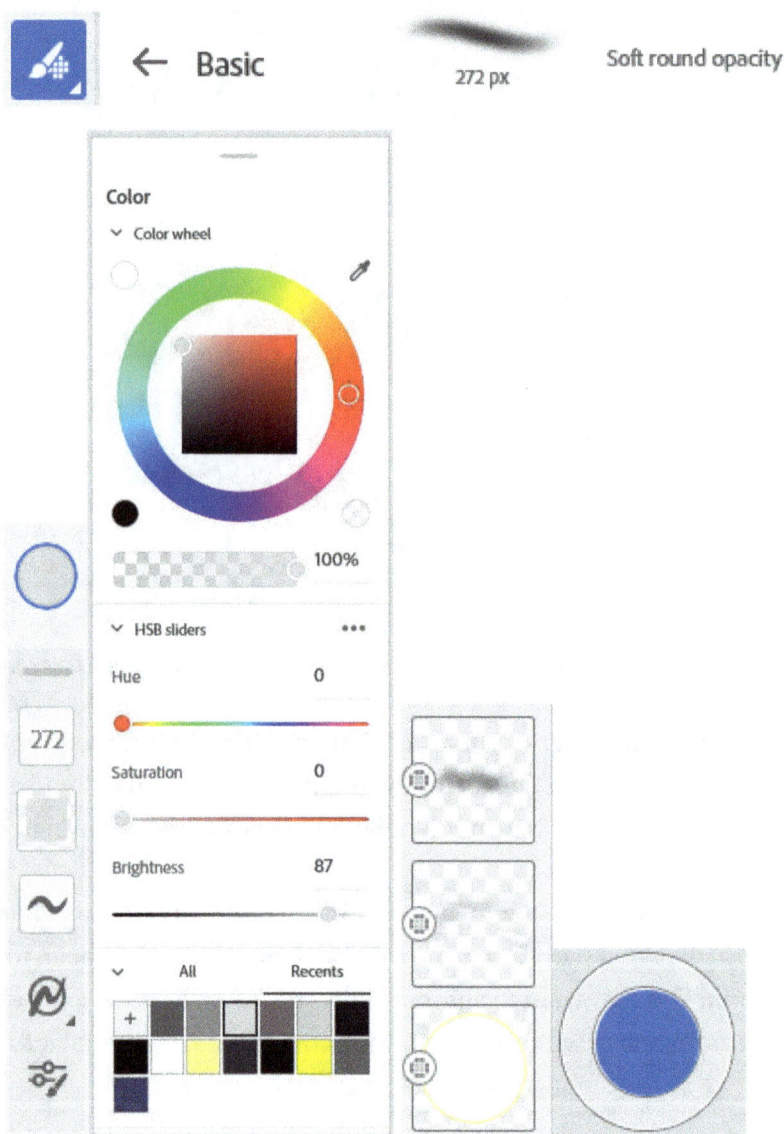

Figure 6-80. *For cloud wisps in the sky and over the moon, try the Basic Soft round opacity brush with a light gray using the color chip and Color panel. Erase with the Touch shortcut circle enabled*

Be as creative as you want on new layers in front and behind. Adding details with a Pixel brush Dry media Soft chalk in dark gray size 149 px can also, on additional layers, add grit and texture to buildings in front or behind and on the street. Refer to Figures 6-78, 6-79, and 6-81.

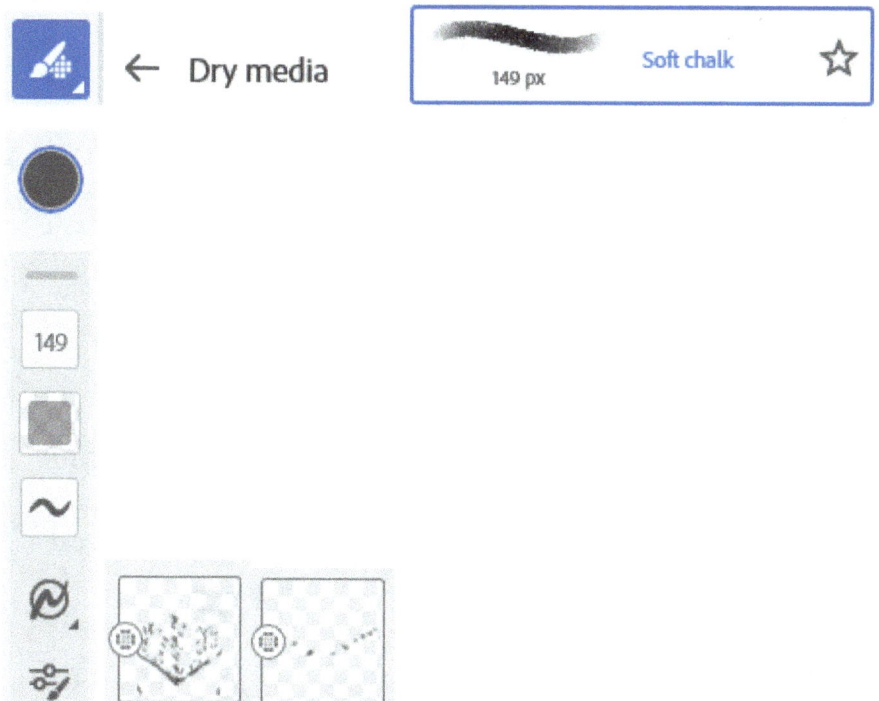

Figure 6-81. *For grit and dirt on the buildings, try a Dry media Soft chalk in darker to medium gray while painting on a new Pixel layer or layers if you need to, in front or behind other layers*

You can view my file **Cityscape_Perspective_Final.psd**. Make sure to save any documents before closing Fresco.

Summary

In this chapter, we reviewed drawing aids as well as the grid graph and perspective with their options. We also looked at how perspective can be used with tools from previous chapters. Then, you worked on a new project and looked at a few additional project ideas that can be accomplished using the skills learned in this chapter.

In the next chapter, you will return to the Toolbar and will look at importing or placement of images and editing.

CHAPTER 7

Importing Images and Editing

Many projects in the previous chapters were created in a freehand style, using your imagination, in a new document on a blank canvas. Then, in other projects, you imported and opened files that contain images, and this was a better solution when you needed to accurately trace or paint over a sketch or enhance your artwork. However, in your own project, you may have started to work on the canvas and realized that now you want to include an image for the purpose of tracing or transforming as part of the current artwork.

In this chapter, I will show you how to place and add images to the document already in progress so that you can edit and paint over, using your new layers. Refer to Chapter 5, if you need to review layers. Later, we will work on a few projects which involve formatting graphics correctly to import into Fresco. Finally, we'll review saving a copy of the file from Fresco and learn how to remove a Fresco file from the Creative Cloud Desktop and from the Fresco Home page.

Note The project files for this chapter can be found in the Chapter 7 folder. Refer to the link in the introduction.

You can, in this case, start with a blank document from the Home page or import and open a file you created if you want to follow along. Refer to Figure 7-1.

CHAPTER 7　IMPORTING IMAGES AND EDITING

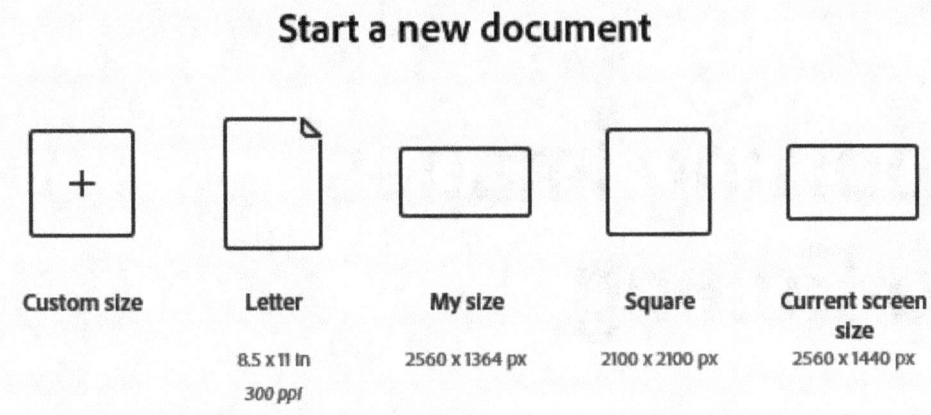

Figure 7-1. *Fresco Home page create a new document for practice*

Later, refer to Chapters 8 and 9 if you need to save your files in other formats not discussed in this chapter.

Placing and Importing Options

As noted in Chapter 4 for tools, and in Chapter 6 when working with the Precision perspective grid, images can be added to Fresco in several ways to the current document. Let's refer to the Toolbar panel as seen in Chapter 4 for these examples. Click the Place image icon, and you will see three placement options. Refer to Figure 7-2.

CHAPTER 7   IMPORTING IMAGES AND EDITING

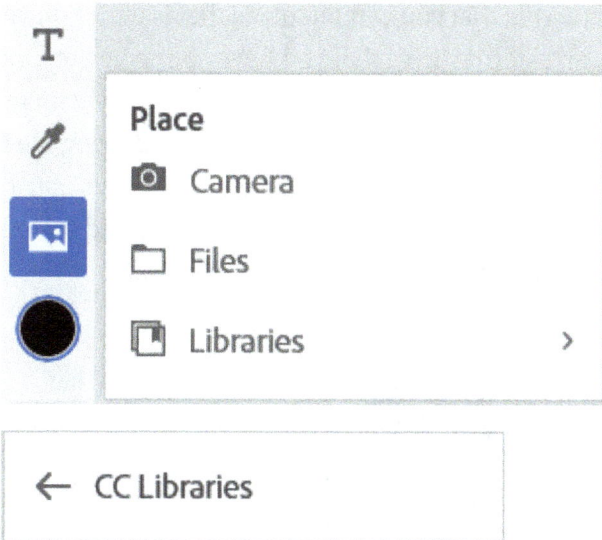

Figure 7-2. *Fresco Toolbar Place tool options for images*

Let's look at each option:

- Camera: In this case, if you have your camera directly connected to your computer via a USB, Fresco should be able to detect it if the drivers are up to date. However, if it cannot detect the camera, you can get more information from the alert with some links. The Learn more and Get help buttons may be able to assist you if you get an error code. However, if you do not want to use the images on your camera, then I would recommend using one of the two next options. Click the X if you need to exit this dialog box. Refer to Figure 7-3.

Figure 7-3. *A warning message that appears if your camera is not connected when trying to place images from a camera*

CHAPTER 7   IMPORTING IMAGES AND EDITING

- Files: Locate a file that you want to place that is either on your computer, an external drive that you have connected to, or USB flash drive stick. In a project in this chapter, we'll work over an imported image and edit and enhance it. However, the following file formats are ideal for placing in Fresco (.jpg, .jpeg, .png, .bmp, .gif, .tif) as an Image layer. For now, select this option to locate and try to Place the file called **flower_image.jpg**. Refer to Figure 7-4.

Figure 7-4. *Use the Open dialog to locate and open an image in a chosen format*

Select and click the buttons Open or Cancel and do not apply the image.

When you click the Open button, it will be placed on an Image layer so you can continue to transform the image. Transform options would include Movement, Scaling, Rotation, Skew, Distort, and Perspective. Refer to Chapter 4 if you need to review the Transform workspace. Refer to Figure 7-5.

CHAPTER 7　IMPORTING IMAGES AND EDITING

Figure 7-5. *In the Transform workspace, you can alter your placed image on a layer using the tool's sub-tools and nudge arrows*

CHAPTER 7   IMPORTING IMAGES AND EDITING

To complete the transformation and embedded placement of the image, you need to click Done to exit the Transform workspace. Refer to Figure 7-5.

Note that because the Image layer is currently not a Pixel layer in the Transform workspace, you did not have access to Liquify tools. To set an Image layer to Pixel layer, use the Layer action when you right-click on the selected layer and choose Convert to pixel layer. Then, when you want to distort the image further, now the Liquify options will be available in the Transform workspace. Refer to Figure 7-6.

Figure 7-6. *Image layer is converted to a Pixel layer to gain access to the Transform Liquify tools*

However, use the Undo key (Ctrl+Z) right away if you want to keep the layer as an Image layer to prevent further distortion. Refer to Figure 7-7.

Figure 7-7. *Use the Undo icon button when you need to undo a step and the alteration a layer kind*

- Libraries: As with other assets reviewed in previous chapters such as colors, brushes, and shapes, you can also add graphics that have been stored in your Creative Cloud Library that you created in Photoshop. To locate a Library, look in the pop-out list, select a library to view the graphic, and then double-click the image icon to add to the canvas as a layer. As with the image you acquired from the Files option, you can then edit it in the Transform workspace and click Done to exit. Refer to Figure 7-8.

CHAPTER 7 IMPORTING IMAGES AND EDITING

***Figure 7-8.** Images can be added to Fresco from a Creative Cloud Library and transformed in Fresco*

Next, I will give a brief demo on how to add a graphic to a Photoshop library, but for now, you can use the **Fresco Collection.cclibs** library you created in Chapter 4, if you need to practice as you would have already imported this library from Photoshop earlier. Again, library images can appear as Image layers in the Layer panel of Fresco. However, regarding graphics from an Illustrator library, because they are Vector graphics, that option or library will not be available. Note that for iPad and iPhone users only, you may encounter a new forth way to place images known Elements or free stock assets. This is not available for the Desktop, but if you need information on this topic refer to the following link. https://helpx.adobe.com/fresco/using/elements.html.

Color Profile and Color Mode Conversion Tips for Photoshop Users

The images that I have used in this application have been created with a color profile sRGB, in the color mode of RGB and a resolution of 300 ppi (pixels/inch). Many digital cameras will have a color profile of sRGB. However, other files you use may have a different color profile like RGB (1998). The type of color profile is also dependent on which color mode you are working in RGB or CMYK. Keep this in mind if you run into any errors while importing a file as you may need to adjust the color profile in Photoshop. Refer to Figure 7-9.

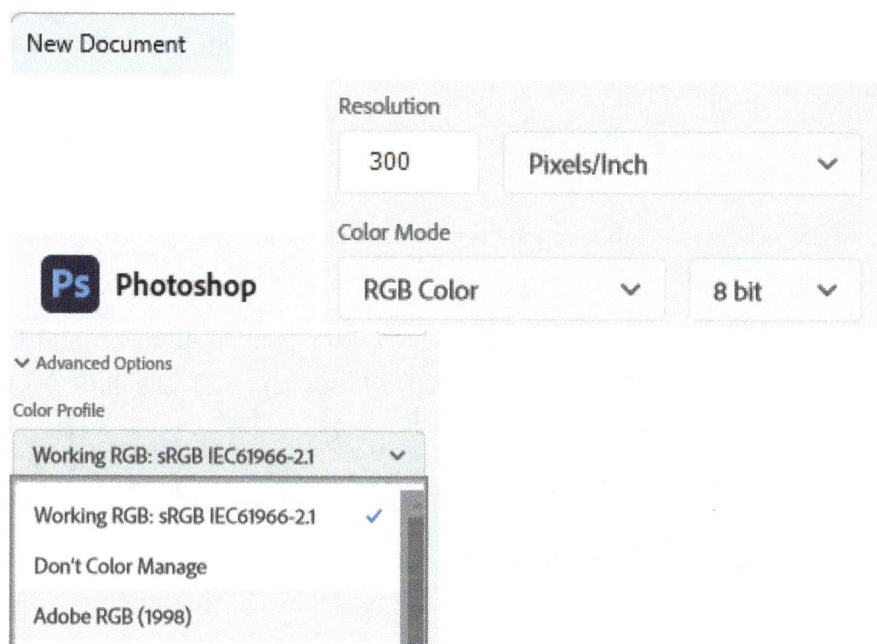

Figure 7-9. *When a new document is created in Photoshop, you can easily set the resolution, color mode, and color profile before creating the document*

In Photoshop, color profiles can be quickly adjusted under Edit ➤ Assign Profile dialog box. In this case, no adjustment was required to the image **flower_image.jpg** because it was already in sRGB, and you can click Cancel to edit the dialog box. Refer to Figure 7-10.

Figure 7-10. *Settings in the Assign Profile dialog box for a specific image*

Another advanced Photoshop option is Edit ➤ Convert to Profile which will do a similar but more drastic color conversion task.

More details for Photoshop color conversion and information on color profiles can be found at this link:

`https://helpx.adobe.com/photoshop/using/working-with-color-profiles.html`

Note If your Photoshop document is in CMYK mode, use Image ➤ Mode ➤ RGB color to adjust, and make sure to save a copy of the file. Refer to Figure 7-11.

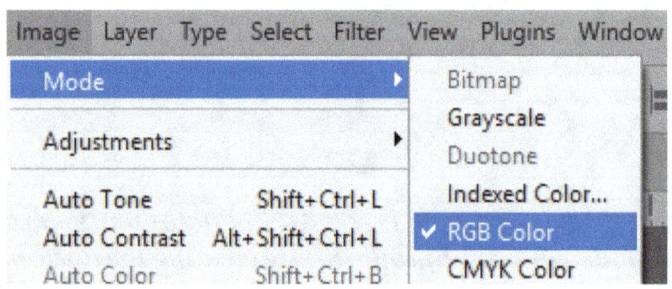

Figure 7-11. *Photoshop image Color Mode menu*

CHAPTER 7 IMPORTING IMAGES AND EDITING

Tip If you are in Photoshop and need to adjust your resolution or dimensions prior to placing your file in Fresco, make sure to use your Image ➤ Image Size dialog box. Refer to the following link for more details on how to do that:

`https://helpx.adobe.com/photoshop/using/image-size-resolution.html`

Otherwise, you can scale in your Fresco document image while in the Transform workspace. Refer to Figure 7-5.

Project: Steps to Adding Graphics to a Creative Cloud Library Using Photoshop

To work on this project with the Creative Cloud Library, open the Photoshop application, and you can then File ➤ Open the following **graphics_start.psd** to begin the process of adding a graphic to a Photoshop library via the Libraries panel. Refer to Figure 7-12.

Figure 7-12. *A Photoshop document can have several flower graphic images displayed*

CHAPTER 7 IMPORTING IMAGES AND EDITING

This file contains two layers, one that is a photo, and the other is a shape layer of a flower that I dragged into the Layers panel earlier from the Photoshop's Shapes panel that we reviewed in previous chapters such as Chapters 4 and 5. Refer to Figure 7-13.

Figure 7-13. Photoshop Layers panel with a layer selected

In Chapter 3, you looked at the steps to create a library. You can return to the chapter if you need to review those steps. I named my library **Fresco Flower Graphics** in this case; I have selected my shape layer Flower first and am starting my new library. Refer to Figures 7-13 and 7-14.

CHAPTER 7　IMPORTING IMAGES AND EDITING

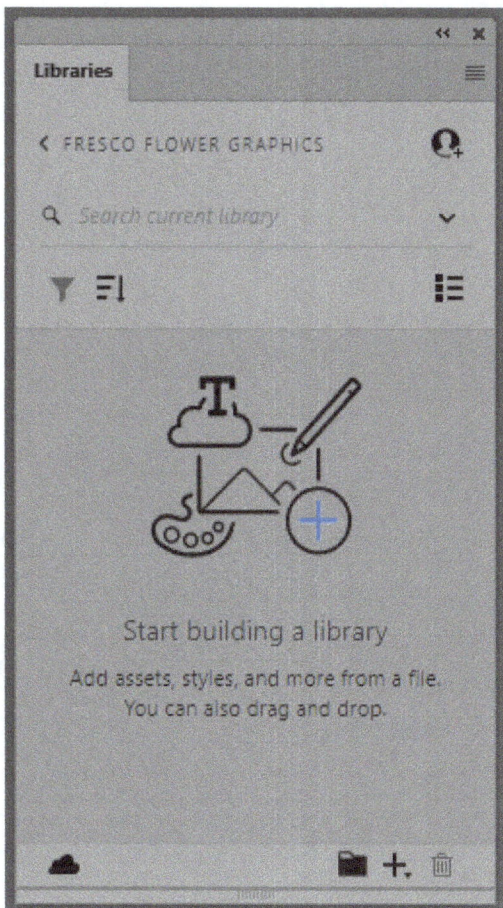

Figure 7-14. *Photoshop Libraries panel with a new library started*

In Chapter 4, you looked at how you could select a layer and turn it into a Capture Shape using the Capture app. This was done when you selected the plus icon (add elements) from the Libraries panel and then that option "Extract from Image" from the list. However, in this case you just want to import it as a graphic, so select that option from the list. Refer to Figure 7-15.

CHAPTER 7　IMPORTING IMAGES AND EDITING

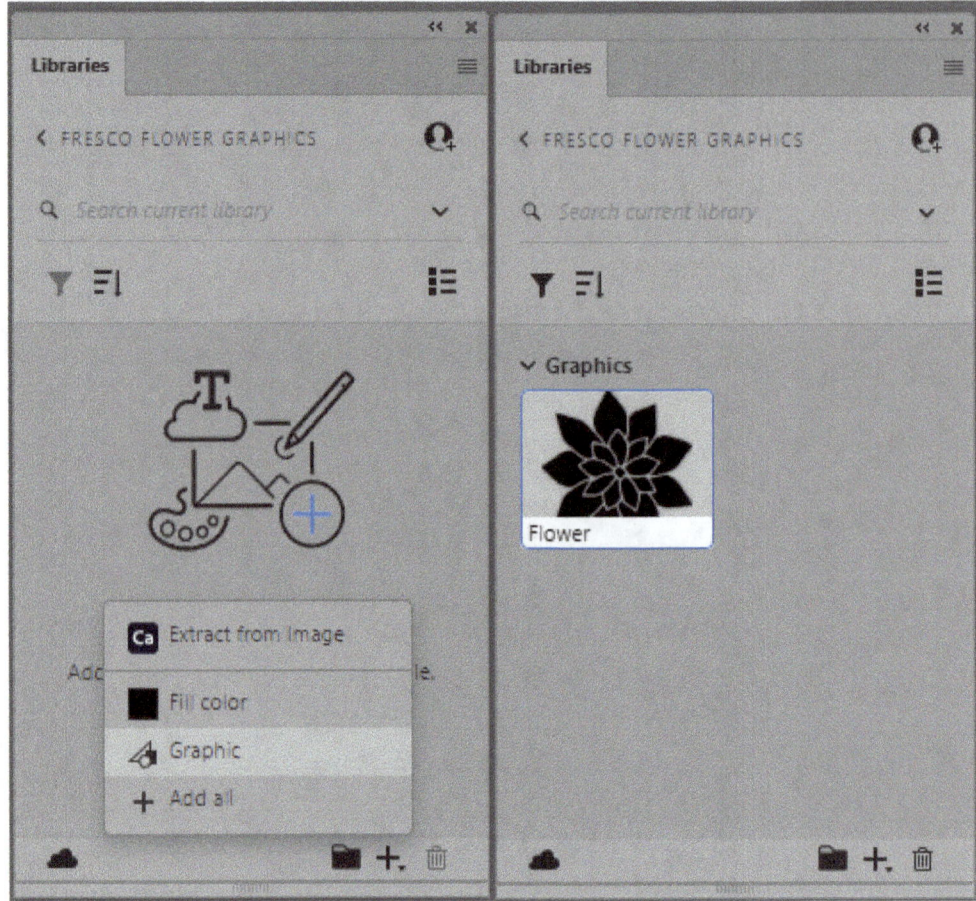

Figure 7-15. *Use the Libraries panel to add a graphic to a library*

The graphic is now added to the Libraries panel. You can then return to Fresco, and you will find that graphic in the Place image ➤ Libraries list, in this case added to the Libraries as Fresco Flower Graphics, and the graphic has the same layer name it was exported with. Refer to Figure 7-16.

CHAPTER 7   IMPORTING IMAGES AND EDITING

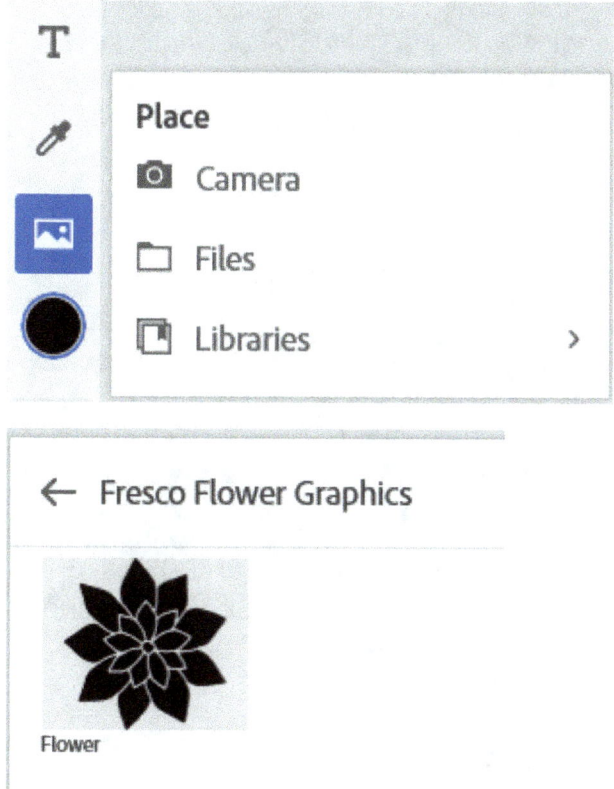

Figure 7-16. *Fresco Toolbar with Place tool Libraries selected and the graphic is displayed*

You can then double-click it if you want to add it to your Fresco document as an Image layer. Click Done, as mentioned earlier, if you want to exit the Transform workspace. Refer to Figure 7-17.

Figure 7-17. *Once the graphic is an Image layer, you can click the Done button to commit the layer*

Graphic assets can be illustrations that you want to trace over, but they can also be photographic images. Again, if you return to Photoshop, if you have a small photographic image or element on a layer that you want to add to the library, then just repeat the same process and add it to your Libraries panel. Refer to Figure 7-18.

513

CHAPTER 7 IMPORTING IMAGES AND EDITING

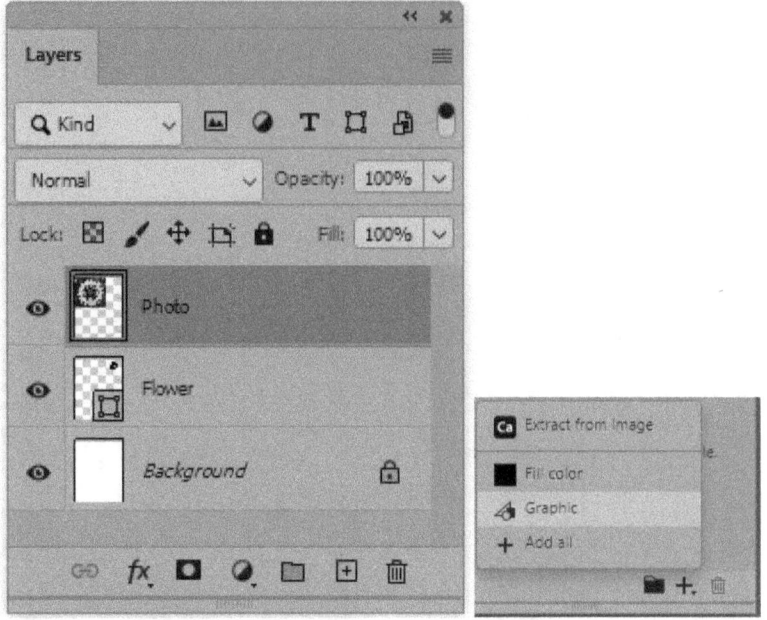

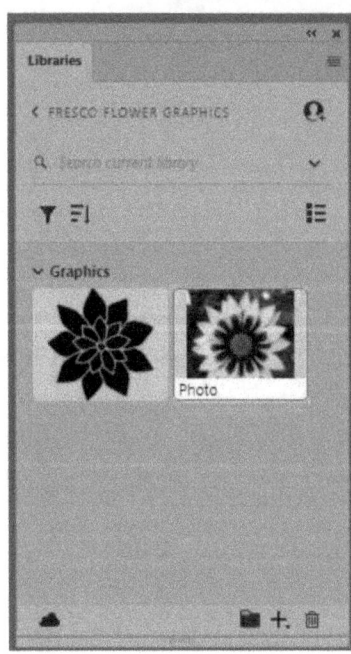

Figure 7-18. *Photoshop Layers panel with the layer selected and Graphic options chosen in the Libraries panel and the layer added as a graphic asset to the Libraries panel*

CHAPTER 7   IMPORTING IMAGES AND EDITING

You can refer to Chapter 3 if you need instructions on how to import my **Fresco Flower Graphics.cclibs** file into Photoshop to view in Fresco.

Either way, in Fresco, graphics are applied to an Image layer which you can edit and transform using the tools in Fresco. Refer to Figure 7-19.

Figure 7-19. *Fresco Library open with images placed on layers*

Afterward, on the Image layer, you can use the Layer action to lock the layer and then paint over the layer on a new layer with, for example, a Live brush like Watercolor wash soft. Now, use the Eyedropper tool and color chip panel to locate colors found within the image to paint with. See file **Image_placement.psd** for reference. Refer to Figures 7-20 and 7-21.

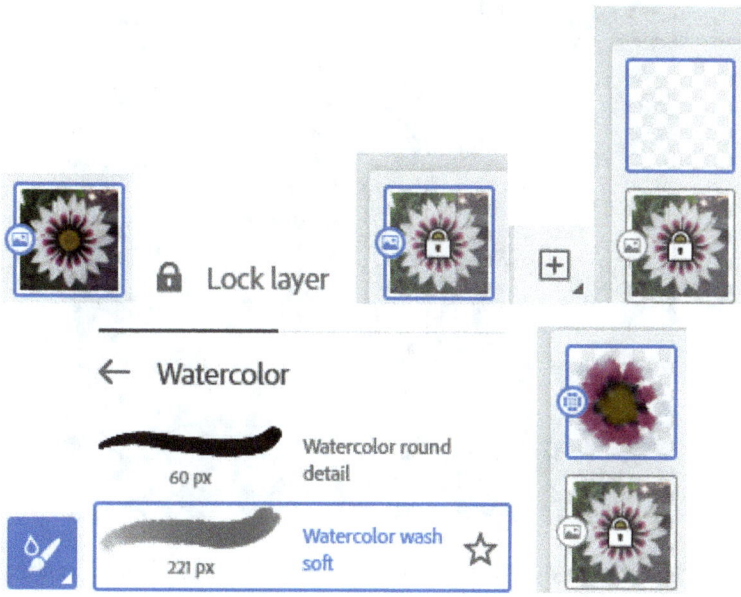

Figure 7-20. *Add a new layer above your locked Image layer to paint over with a brush*

515

CHAPTER 7 IMPORTING IMAGES AND EDITING

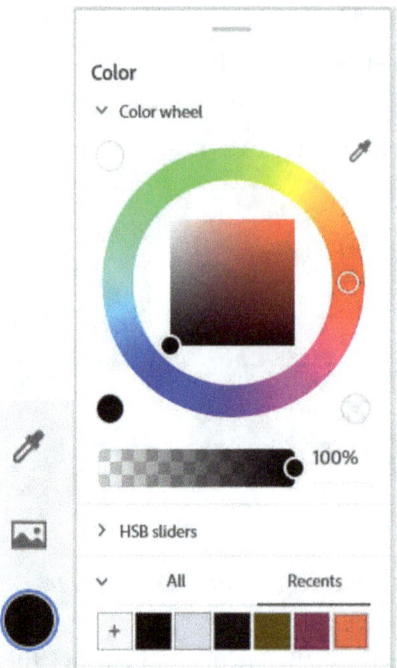

Figure 7-21. *Choose colors from your image with the Toolbar Eyedropper and color chip and color panel, and then, continue to paint on a Pixel layer over the image*

CHAPTER 7　IMPORTING IMAGES AND EDITING

Other Importing Options

It should be noted that there are additional workarounds when you want to add images from other Adobe applications, like Illustrator, directly to your file. Here, I will show you some quick steps you can use. However, be aware that the image will now either be a Pixel layer or Image layer and no longer Vector.

Steps to Copying and Pasting an Image from Photoshop or Illustrator Directly into Fresco

Using Photoshop, you can select a layer, then Select ➤ All (Ctrl+A) and Edit ➤ Copy (Ctrl+C), and then in Fresco, using the Layer action from the ellipsis on a blank layer, Paste from clipboard or Ctrl+V. This will paste the image onto the Image layer. Refer to Figure 7-22.

Figure 7-22. *Use Photoshop to directly copy an image on a layer and then paste it into a layer in Fresco*

Remember to click Done to exit the Transform workspace.

Likewise, in Illustrator, with the Open file **graphics_movements.ai**, you can use your Selection tool to marquee around or click to select a graphic and choose Edit ➤ Copy (Ctrl+C), and then, in Fresco, on a blank layer, paste (Ctrl+V). However, the graphic may have a white background on the Image layer. Refer to Figure 7-23.

CHAPTER 7   IMPORTING IMAGES AND EDITING

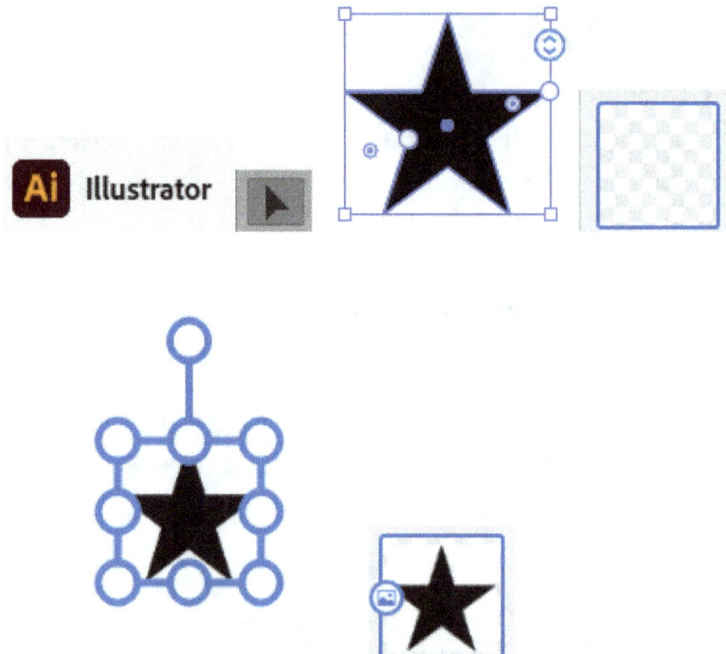

Figure 7-23. *Graphics can be copied from Illustrator and then pasted directly into Fresco but only as an Image layer, not a Vector layer*

A better solution when you need a transparent layer for simple shaped graphics is to Edit ➤ Copy (Ctrl+C) that graphic first into Photoshop and Edit ➤ Paste (Ctrl+V) as a Shape layer. Click OK. And later, adjust the color of the shape to black if required. Refer to Figure 7-24.

CHAPTER 7   IMPORTING IMAGES AND EDITING

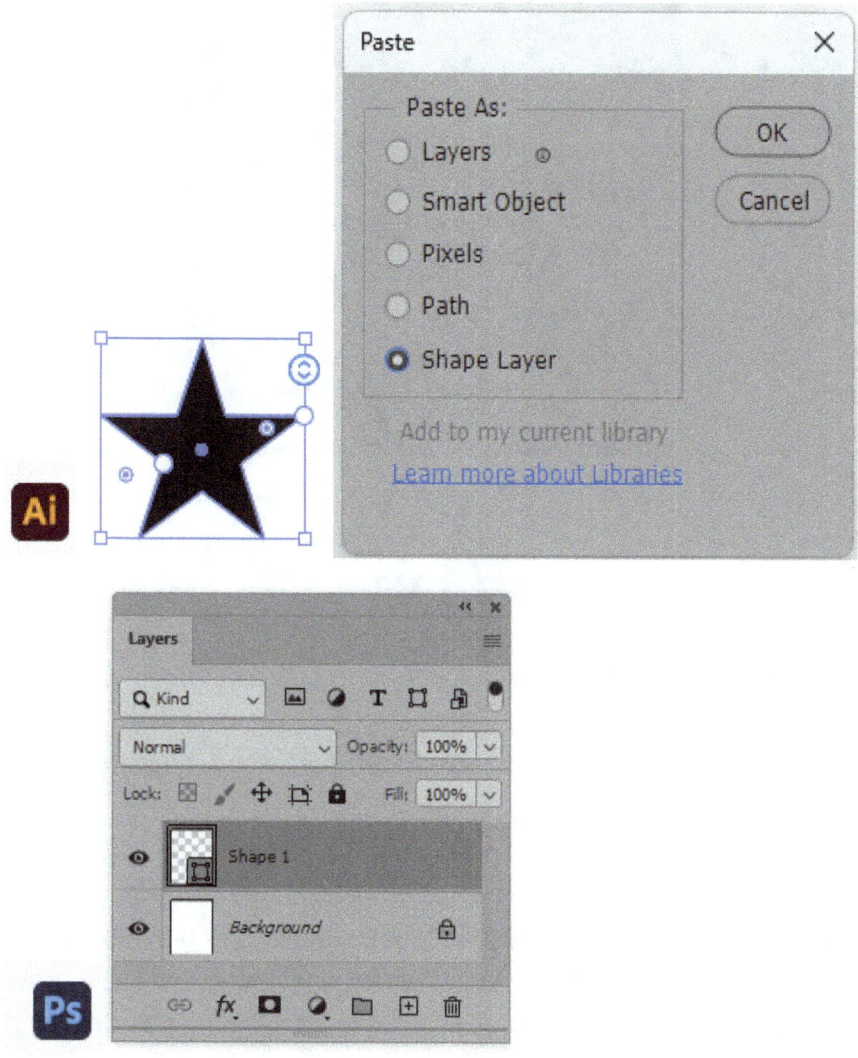

Figure 7-24. *Adding an Illustrator graphic to Photoshop using the Paste dialog box and added to the Layers panel*

Note that if the Illustrator graphic is CMYK, when it enters the RGB Photoshop document as it converts to RGB, a slight color adjustment may occur.

Then, use your Libraries panel to create a Capture Shape using the steps as seen in Chapter 4. Refer to Figure 7-25.

519

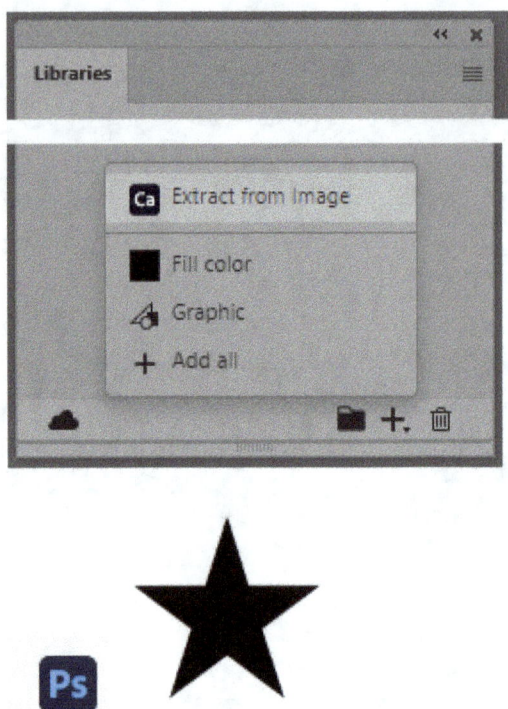

Figure 7-25. *Add your graphic as a Capture Shape (Extract from Image) to the Photoshop Libraries panel*

Advanced Tip For those who like to create animations, Adobe Animate, which has some similarities to Illustrator, is another application that will also allow selecting of an object or simple graphic from a layer using Edit ➤ Copy and using the Fresco action of Paste from clipboard or (Ctrl+V), but again, you will get a white background surrounding the image. Nevertheless, this is a good tip to remember if you are planning to use an element from an animation created in Animate for animation later in Fresco. Animation will be discussed in Chapter 8, and a link to information on Animate is included in Chapter 9. Refer to Figure 7-26.

Figure 7-26. *Adobe Animate app icon*

CHAPTER 7 IMPORTING IMAGES AND EDITING

However, you cannot copy/paste images directly from Adobe InDesign, and in that case, images should be imported as a Capture Shape via the CC Libraries panel, as was briefly mentioned in Chapter 4. Refer to Figure 7-27. Or if a graphic, open the original image in Photoshop first, and then, drag or add that graphic layer into the library as described earlier in the chapter.

Figure 7-27. *Adobe InDesign icon and CC Libraries panel*

Steps to Rasterizing an Illustrator File in Photoshop So That It Can Be Imported As an Image Layer with Transparency

When you want to add a more complex colorful illustration that you created in Illustrator, I recommend you do the following steps to keep the surrounding transparent areas. Refer to Figure 7-28.

CHAPTER 7   IMPORTING IMAGES AND EDITING

Figure 7-28. *A drawing of some colorful flowers created in Adobe Illustrator and selected with the Selection tool*

Use your Selection tool to marquee select the entire graphic. Refer to Figure 7-28. Edit ➤ Copy and then in Photoshop Edit ➤ Paste, but this time choose, from the dialog box, Paste as a Smart Object directly into Photoshop. Click OK, and then, click the check in the Options bar panel or Done in the Contextual Task bar to commit the paste. Refer to Figure 7-29.

CHAPTER 7   IMPORTING IMAGES AND EDITING

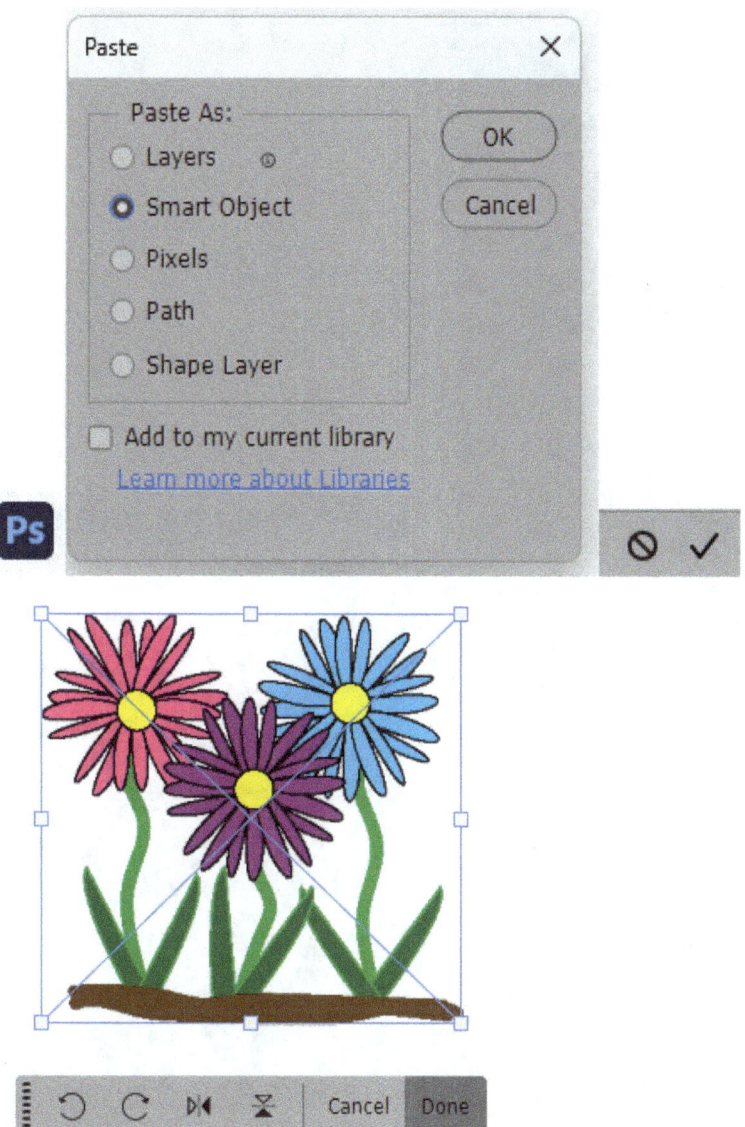

Figure 7-29. *Paste an Illustrator graphic directly into Photoshop as a smart layer object, and confirm using the Options panel or Contextual Task bar*

You can then use the Layers panel menu to rasterize that layer but still keep the transparency as one separate Pixel layer. Refer to Figure 7-30.

CHAPTER 7 IMPORTING IMAGES AND EDITING

Figure 7-30. *Photoshop Layers panel with a Smart Object Vector file that can be rasterized using the Layers panel menu and turning into a Pixel layer and saved on your computer*

In Photoshop you would then File ➤ Save as a .psd file on your computer, and then open and import the file into Fresco.

Regardless, the rasterized layer will be a Pixel layer in Fresco. Refer to Figure 7-31.

CHAPTER 7   IMPORTING IMAGES AND EDITING

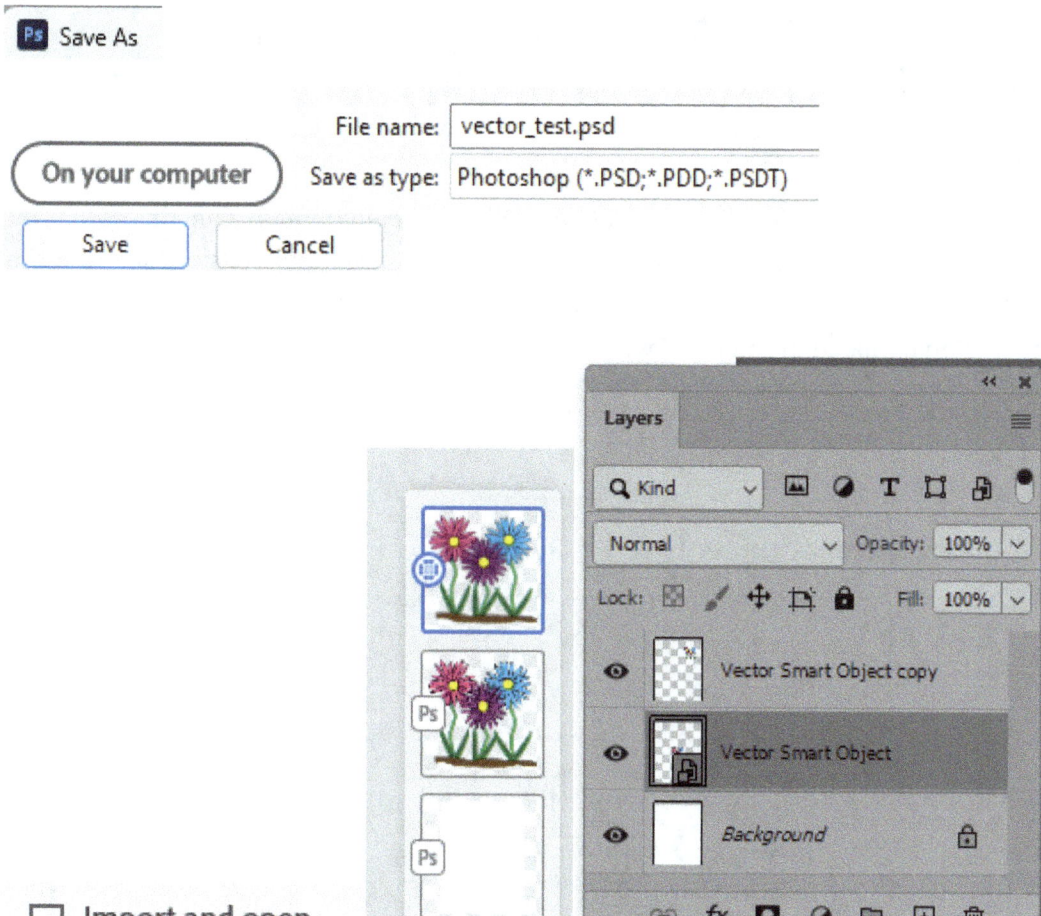

Figure 7-31. After saving your file, you can then Import and open the file in Fresco and observe how Fresco displays the Photoshop layers (Ps) from the Layer panel, and choose the action of Convert to pixel layer in Fresco

However, if you leave the layer as a Smart Object Layer, it will appear as a Photoshop layer in Fresco. Refer to Figure 7-31. You can see this in the example file **vector_test.psd** where I created a copy of the layers to compare. Both layers have transparent areas. Like an Image layer, you must convert a Photoshop layer using your Layer action Convert to pixcl layer before you transform it.

525

CHAPTER 7 IMPORTING IMAGES AND EDITING

Project: Painting over an Image Layer and Overlaying a Pixel Layer to Edit with Brushes and Layer Properties

For this project, you can start with either a blank document or open a file that you have been working on in Fresco. In this case, the image I am using was a custom size of width of 14 inches by height of 9 inches. I made sure that my document was in landscape orientation to match the picture I will be placing. Refer to Figure 7-32.

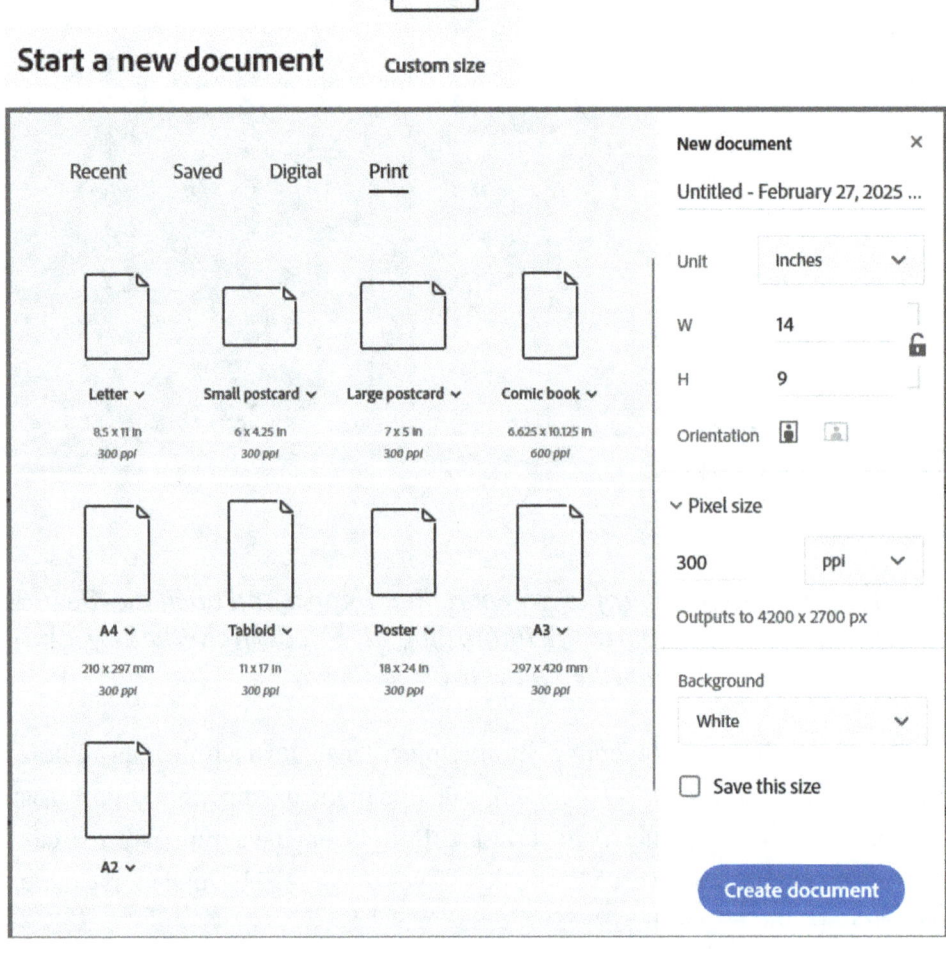

Figure 7-32. Fresco Custom size document setting for a New document

CHAPTER 7   IMPORTING IMAGES AND EDITING

I then clicked the Create document button to create my new canvas.

Now, using the Place tool from the Toolbar, from the chapter's project folder, locate the file **farm_barn_start.jpg** to place the file. Select it and click Open. Refer to Figure 7-33.

Figure 7-33. *Use your Place tool to locate and open the file you want to place into a new Fresco document*

While in the Transform workspace, you can click Done to exit and confirm the placement. However, in your own projects, you may want to do some moving, scaling, or rotating in this workspace before you exit. Refer to Chapter 4 if you need to review working in the Transform workspace. Refer to Figure 7-34.

Figure 7-34. *The image is placed into the Transform workspace with the various tool options*

In my case, using Photoshop, this was a drawing that I created using a photograph, color corrected, adjusted the sky, and later added the filter from the Filter Gallery of Sketch ➤ Stamp to create the sketch-like background for my painting. Refer to Figure 7-35.

CHAPTER 7   IMPORTING IMAGES AND EDITING

Figure 7-35. *Use Photoshop to apply Stamp filters to an image that can edit the image before it is added to Fresco*

Since this is an advanced Photoshop topic, I will not be going into any detail on the creation of its layers. But I will note that to create an accurate image with this Stamp filter, you need to apply the filter to multiple copies or layers of the same image, of at least seven, with the same smoothness settings of 1 but with different Light/Dark balances to achieve the ideal look overall. Settings I used for Light/Dark Balance were 1, 5, 8, 14, 25, 34, and 48. Refer to Figure 7-35.

Black and white were also the foreground and background colors used prior to entering the filter as seen in the Toolbar.

Then, afterward, extensive layer masking on each layer was required. Every project is different, but this kind of technical preparation is sometimes necessary before starting a project in Fresco. Color correction and filters are definitely Photoshop's strengths.

Here is how the Layers panel in Photoshop appeared prior to me flattening a copy of the file using the panel's menu and saving as a (.jpeg) for Fresco. Refer to Figure 7-36.

529

CHAPTER 7   IMPORTING IMAGES AND EDITING

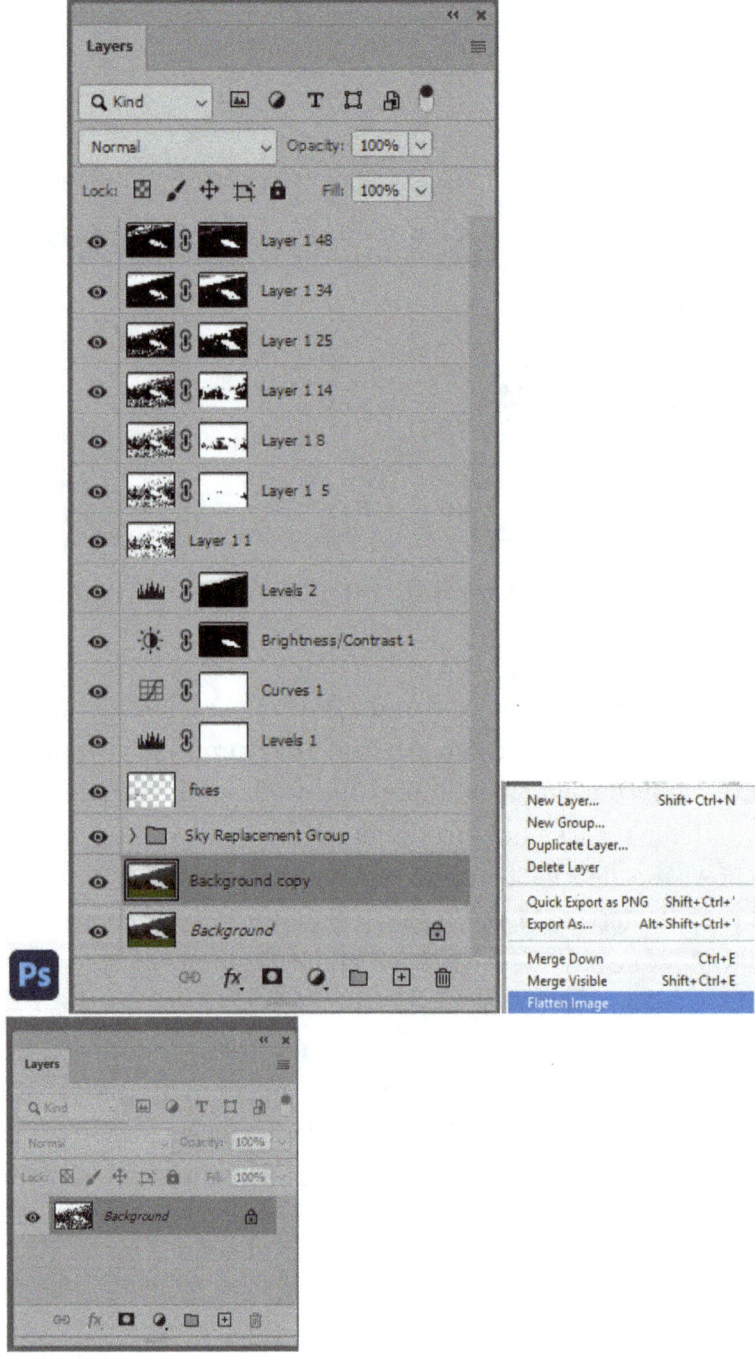

Figure 7-36. *Photoshop requires many layers to be created to generate a sketch-like image and then flattened with the panel's menu prior to import so that the file is not too large*

CHAPTER 7 IMPORTING IMAGES AND EDITING

However, if you do not have such an image for your own work, you can use your own digitized sketch or a favorite photo that you may have earlier color adjusted in Photoshop.

To avoid distortion or error, I made sure in this case that the image was 300 ppi and in RGB color mode so that it would match the presets in Fresco. Refer to Figure 7-37.

Figure 7-37. *The completed sketch with the correct color and resolution settings applied*

The size in this case was custom, which was OK, but as you saw earlier, when I created my Fresco file, I made sure to match to the orientation of landscape and made the dimensions of width and height just a bit larger than the image. In your case, you may have to scale your image if you already started a project or go to the Settings gear icon, as you saw in Chapter 2, to change the document size. Refer to Figure 7-38.

CHAPTER 7   IMPORTING IMAGES AND EDITING

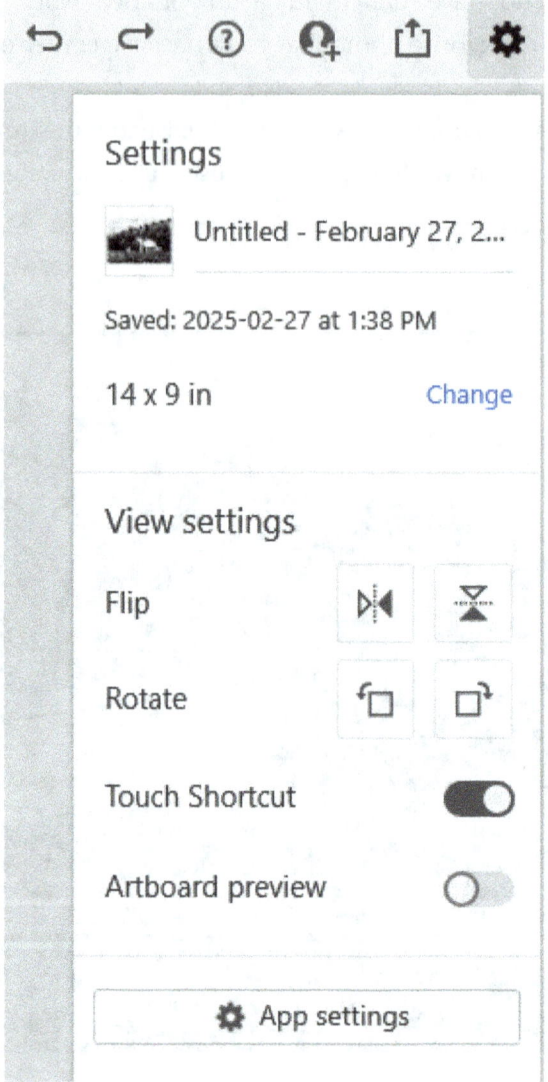

Figure 7-38. *Fresco Settings panel menu area*

Now that the image is on an Image layer, you can decide to keep it as is or, using the Layer actions, convert it to a Pixel layer if I want to transform it further or use it as a reference layer as you saw in Chapter 6. Refer to Figure 7-39.

CHAPTER 7   IMPORTING IMAGES AND EDITING

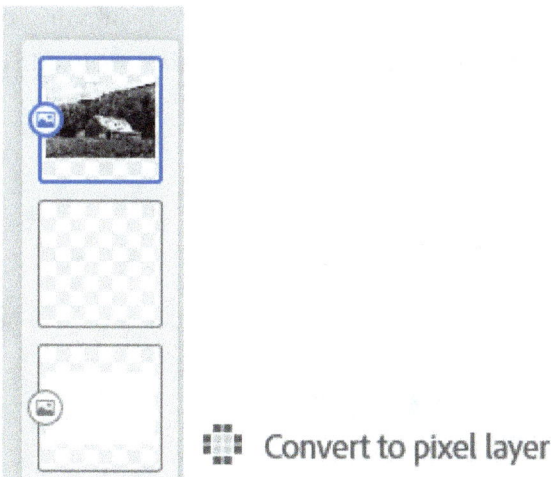

Figure 7-39. *The placed Image layer, on the top of the Layers in Fresco, can remain as is or converted to a Pixel layer*

In this case, I will keep it as an Image layer and am going to lock the layer and then drag the blank layer above it so that I can paint on that layer over top. If you do not have a blank new layer, then add one now. Refer to Figure 7-40.

Figure 7-40. *Layer panel image is locked, and a new blank layer is added above for painting*

533

CHAPTER 7   IMPORTING IMAGES AND EDITING

Then, on the blank layer, I am going to paint with an Oilpaint round brush from Live brushes and paint over the top, varying the brush sizes to add details. Refer to Figure 7-41.

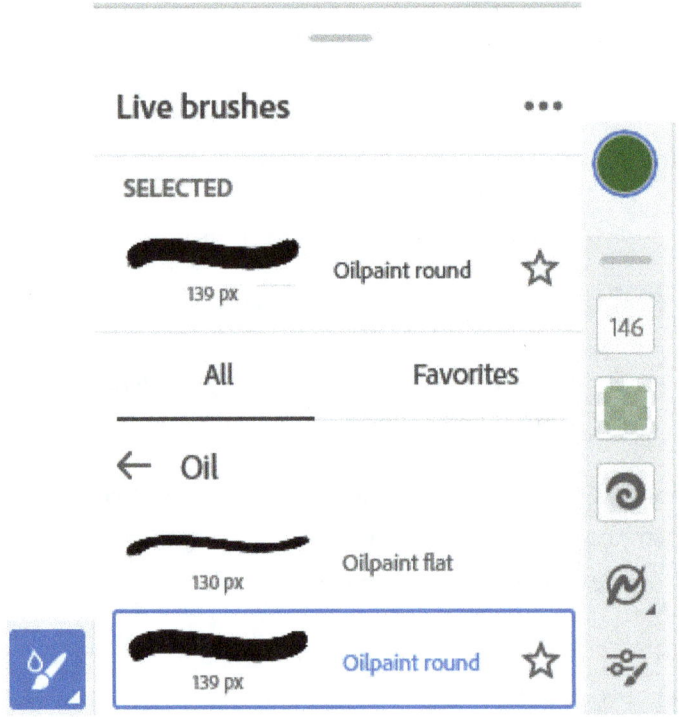

Figure 7-41. *Use a Live brush to paint with on your painting and adjust the settings as required*

The nice thing about digital oil painting is that you can erase your brush's oily strokes if you make a mistake which is hard to do with real oil paints. In this case, use your Eraser tool Pixel eraser like Hard round opacity, or with a Pixel brush and your Touch shortcut primary circle (double-click), do the erase. You should not use the Live brushes to erase as they may smear or blend like a dry brush rather than erase your artwork. In their case, as mentioned in Chapter 3, when the primary Touch shortcut is used, they only paint with clear or smear color so the result is different than erasing. For Watercolor brushes with the primary Touch shortcut, the result is "Pure water" or another kind of smearing. Refer to Figure 7-42.

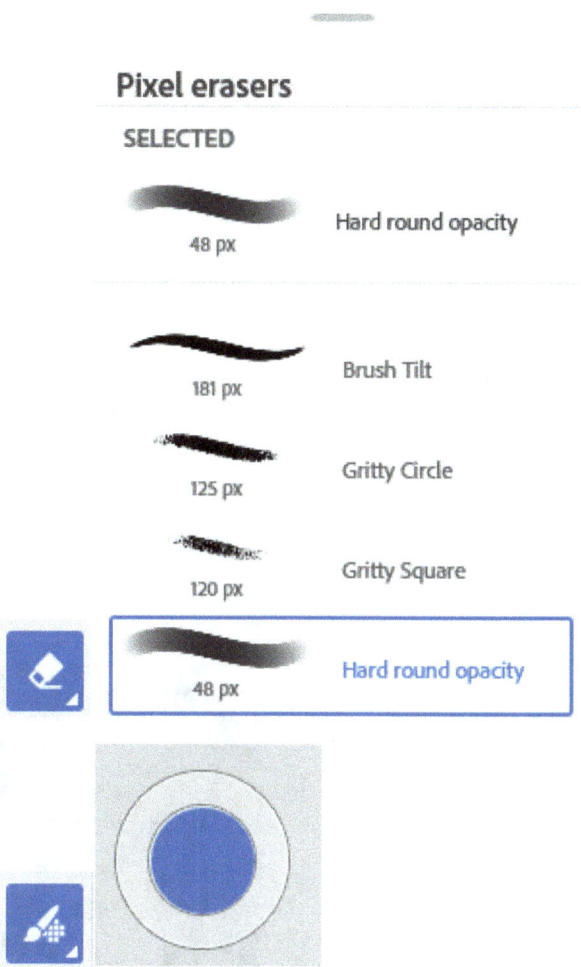

Figure 7-42. *Use the Eraser or a Pixel brush of your choice with the Touch shortcut enabled*

Then, return to your Live brushes after disabling the Touch shortcut.

Before or while you paint on various layers, set Layer properties in some cases from the Default or Normal to Multiply or other blending modes. For example, you can use Pin light, Color, Soft light, Divide, Color dodge, Lighter color, Linear light, or Multiply. They are all good for painting over black areas and allow some color to show.

Then, vary the Layer opacity between 35% and 100% depending on the blend mode and colors you use. Everyone's artwork will be different. This is a great way to color and paint, so you can see your artwork and at the same time adjust your colors or paint over other colors to create better blends. Refer to Figures 7-43 and 7-44.

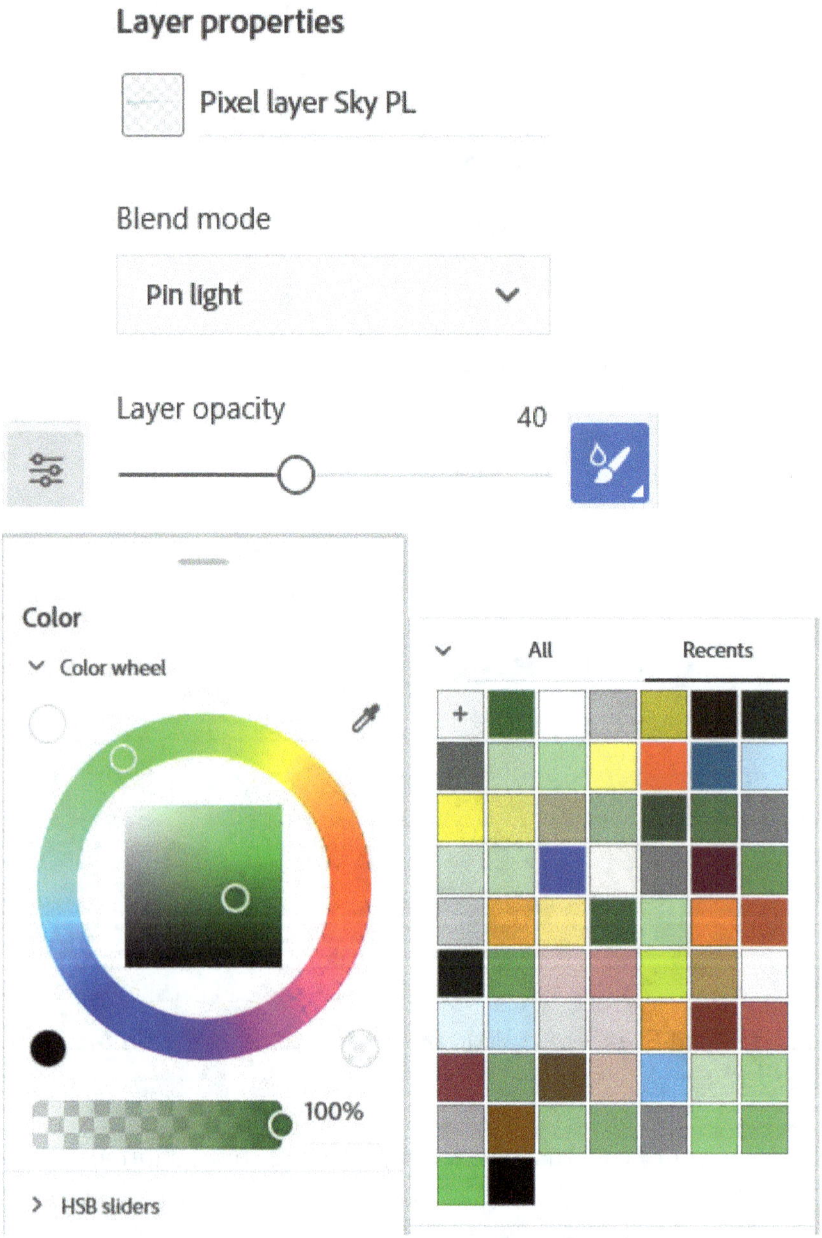

CHAPTER 7　IMPORTING IMAGES AND EDITING

Figure 7-43. *Adjust your Vertical Taskbar Layer properties for selected layers, and then, continue to paint with your Live brush altering colors in the Color panel and returning to recently used colors*

You can refer to my file **farm_barn_final.psd** if you need to review the image and the layer settings used. Refer to Figure 7-44.

CHAPTER 7   IMPORTING IMAGES AND EDITING

Figure 7-44. *Final painting in Fresco with all the layers found in the Layers panel*

I added my signature on the top layer in white with a Pixel Sketching ➤ Pencil brush.

On your own, now practice one of the other image placing options and consider which method of importing you prefer for your projects.

File ➤ Save or close any Photoshop documents you may have open, and then, close your own Fresco files as well to return to the Home page.

CHAPTER 7   IMPORTING IMAGES AND EDITING

Saving Your Files Review

As noted in each of the chapters, as you work on a project in Fresco, it will auto save when it closes as you exit and return to the Home page. However, be aware that if you open the project in Photoshop and alter something and then import back into Fresco, sometimes layers may combine and become Photoshop layers or read-only the next time that you open the file in Fresco. Refer to Chapter 5 to review how this can happen with blend modes or Adjustment layers that are not the same as the ones found in Fresco.

This is why it is important to keep backups of your files off the cloud as well, which we'll look at next and later in Chapter 9.

How to Remove or Download Files from the Creative Cloud Desktop or Fresco Home Page

Files that you do not intend to keep can be removed from the Creative Cloud Desktop. This is good as there may be situations where you, by accident, created a blank document or a test document that you no longer need in your Creative Cloud. Refer to Figure 7-45.

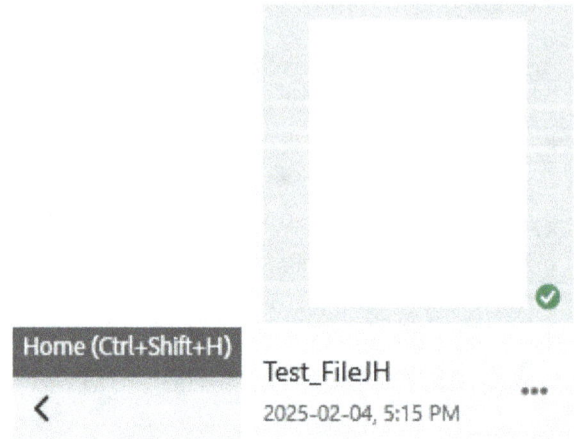

Figure 7-45. *Files auto save when you return to the Home page, and there you can see any unwanted files*

CHAPTER 7   IMPORTING IMAGES AND EDITING

To remove a file, you can either go from your Fresco application Home page ➤ Recent, or Your files areas, or from your Creative Cloud Desktop console, to go to Files ➤ Files. This area will display all the files that you have created in Fresco. Refer to Figure 7-46.

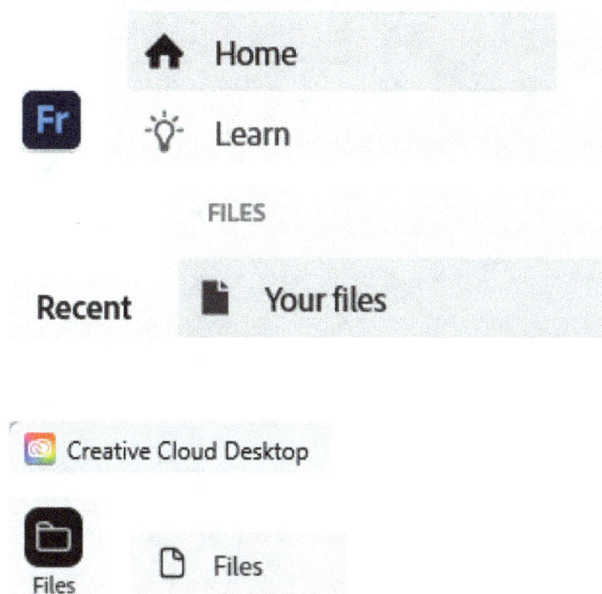

Figure 7-46. *You can search in either Fresco or the Creative Cloud Desktop for your files*

If you want to delete a file in the Creative Cloud Desktop, click the ellipsis on the image and choose Delete from the menu. This will send it to the Delete folder, and after 30 days, that file will be removed from the Creative Cloud, but you can enter that folder, click the ellipsis, and restore it before that happens. Refer to Figure 7-47.

CHAPTER 7   IMPORTING IMAGES AND EDITING

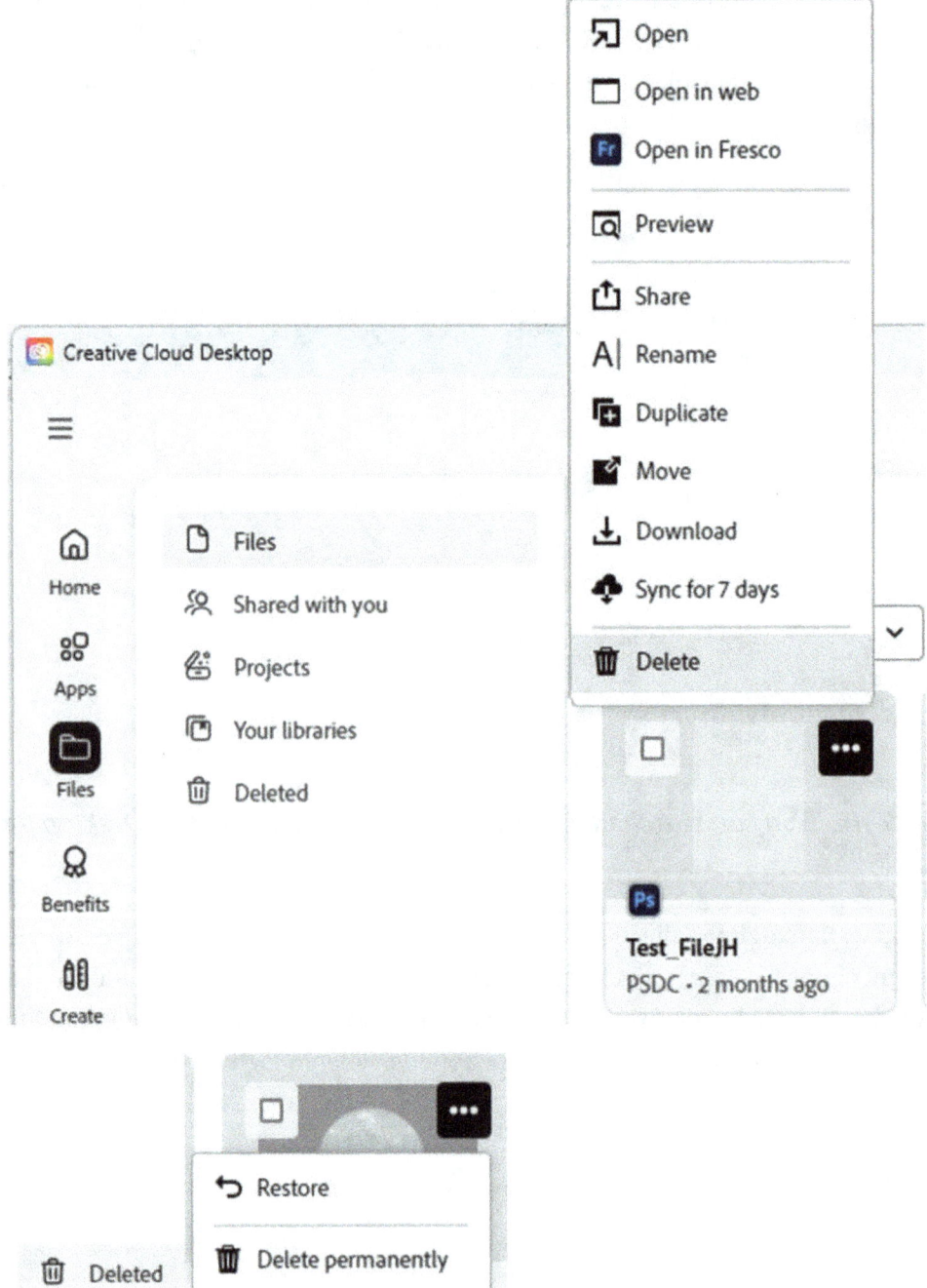

Figure 7-47. *From the Creative Cloud Desktop, you can delete any files you do not want to keep or restore them when found in the Deleted folder*

CHAPTER 7 IMPORTING IMAGES AND EDITING

On the Fresco Home page, you can access a similar menu using the ellipsis (...) More actions at the bottom of each thumbnail image and choose Delete and then check in your Deleted folder if you made a mistake. From this menu, you can always choose to restore or permanently delete the file. Refer to Figure 7-48.

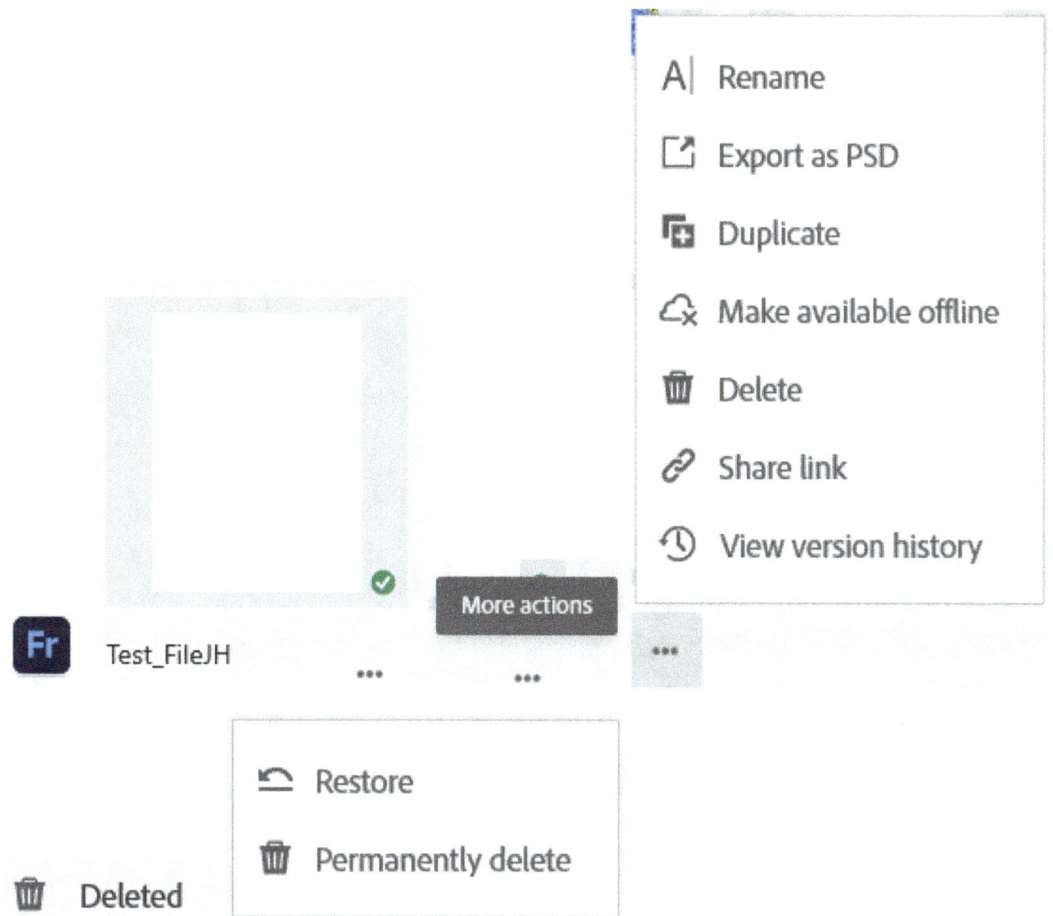

Figure 7-48. *Use Fresco Home page to delete or restore files from the Deleted folder*

This actions menu also allows for other tasks such as renaming and duplication if you need to make a copy of the file you are working on. Refer to Figure 7-48.

However, if you still want to keep the file on your computer's desktop but also on Creative Cloud Desktop, then right-click the thumbnail's ellipsis and choose Download from the menu. Refer to Figure 7-47. The equivalent to that on the Fresco Home page menu is to Export as PSD. Refer to Figure 7-48.

CHAPTER 7 IMPORTING IMAGES AND EDITING

Once you choose this option, then for Creative Cloud Desktop, use the Select Folder dialog box to navigate to a folder that you want to download to and then click the Select Folder button. Refer to Figure 7-49.

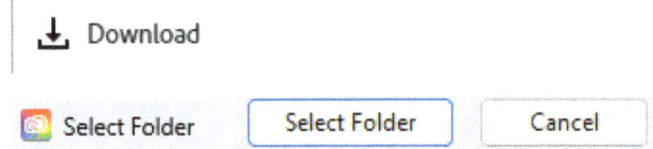

Figure 7-49. *Download a file from the Creative Cloud Desktop*

Or from the Fresco Home page, when you choose Export as PSD, then use the Save As dialog box to navigate to a folder and click the Save button. Refer to Figure 7-50.

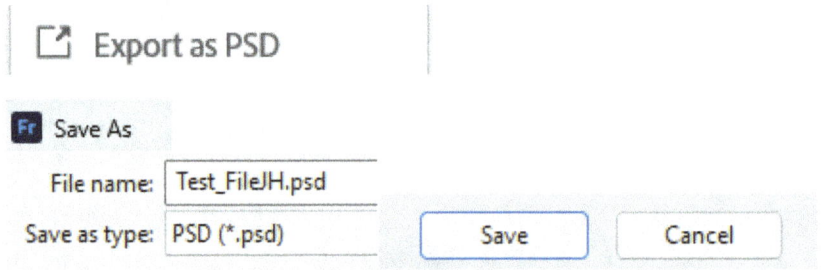

Figure 7-50. *Export as PSD from Fresco with the Save as dialog box*

Either way, you have a backup copy (.psd) on your desktop computer that you can keep in a folder and use in Photoshop at any time off the cloud. We will look at that in more detail in Chapter 9.

Optionally, you could then delete the same file from the Creative Cloud if space is an issue or you are done with a project.

Remember, if you need to upload the file at any time, follow the instructions found in Chapter 2 on importing and opening files for Fresco.

Summary

In this chapter, we looked at how to import image files directly into a Fresco file which could be images from a camera, your own files on your computer, or graphics from one of your Creative Cloud Libraries folders. Then, we worked on a project to create a paint effect and reviewed how to save, download, and then remove unwanted files from the Creative Cloud.

In the next chapter, we will look at how to create a basic animation as well as additional saving and exporting options.

CHAPTER 8

Basic Animation in Fresco

In the application Photoshop, you can create a GIF or an MP4 file for animation, using the Timeline panel. This is a benefit when you want to create a basic animation with some illustrations or photos. Refer to Figure 8-1.

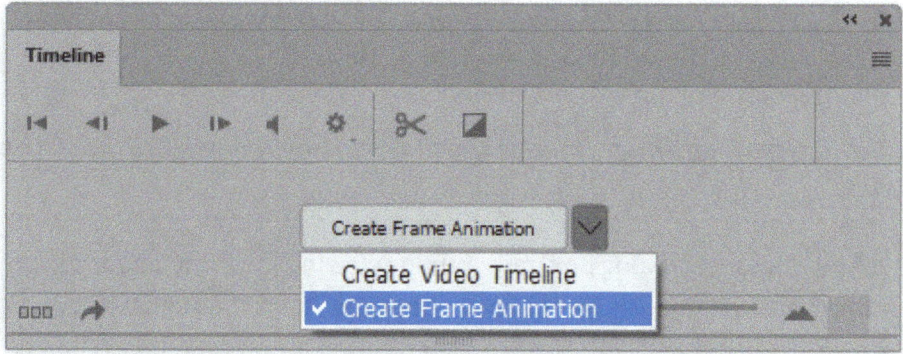

Figure 8-1. Photoshop icon and the application's Timeline panel

However, did you know that you can also create similar animations in Fresco as well? In this chapter, we will explore how to create an animation in Fresco and then look at how to export the file in similar formats, including the option of PNG files for an image sequence. The chapter will also discuss possible new features that may be added to Fresco for animation creation in future versions, and then we will complete the chapter by reviewing an additional project.

Note The project files for this chapter can be found in the Chapter 8 folder. Refer to the link in the introduction.

CHAPTER 8 BASIC ANIMATION IN FRESCO

Creating a New Document for Animation

In this example, if you are creating your own animation, you may want to work with a page size specifically for animation. From the Home page, click the Custom size button icon. Refer to Figure 8-2.

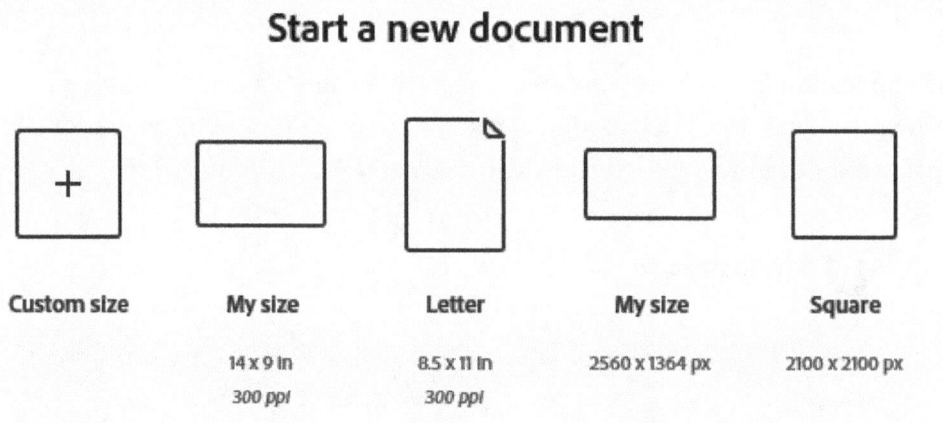

Figure 8-2. Fresco Home page presets used for starting a new document from Custom size

In the New document dialog box, rather than selecting the Print tab for the preset documents as you have done in past chapters, this time, click the Digital tab, or create a custom size at 72 ppi rather than 300 ppi which we used for print. Refer to Chapter 2 if you need to review this information and refer to Figure 8-3. In this case, I am also using the unit of pixels rather than inches as this is appropriate for the Web and video. I will also be working in a landscape orientation as this is appropriate for most animations.

You can choose one of the presets or type in your own custom settings for width (W) and height (H). Refer to Figure 8-3.

A good custom practice size for a GIF animation that I recommend is W:720 by H:480 pixels for display on a web page. However, if you are thinking of creating an MP4 video, then I recommend the size of the preset Full HD: 1920 × 1080px. However, this entirely depends on where the animation will be used so you may need to consult with your other coworkers first if this is a team project. Once confirmed, then click the Create document button. Refer to Figure 8-3.

CHAPTER 8 BASIC ANIMATION IN FRESCO

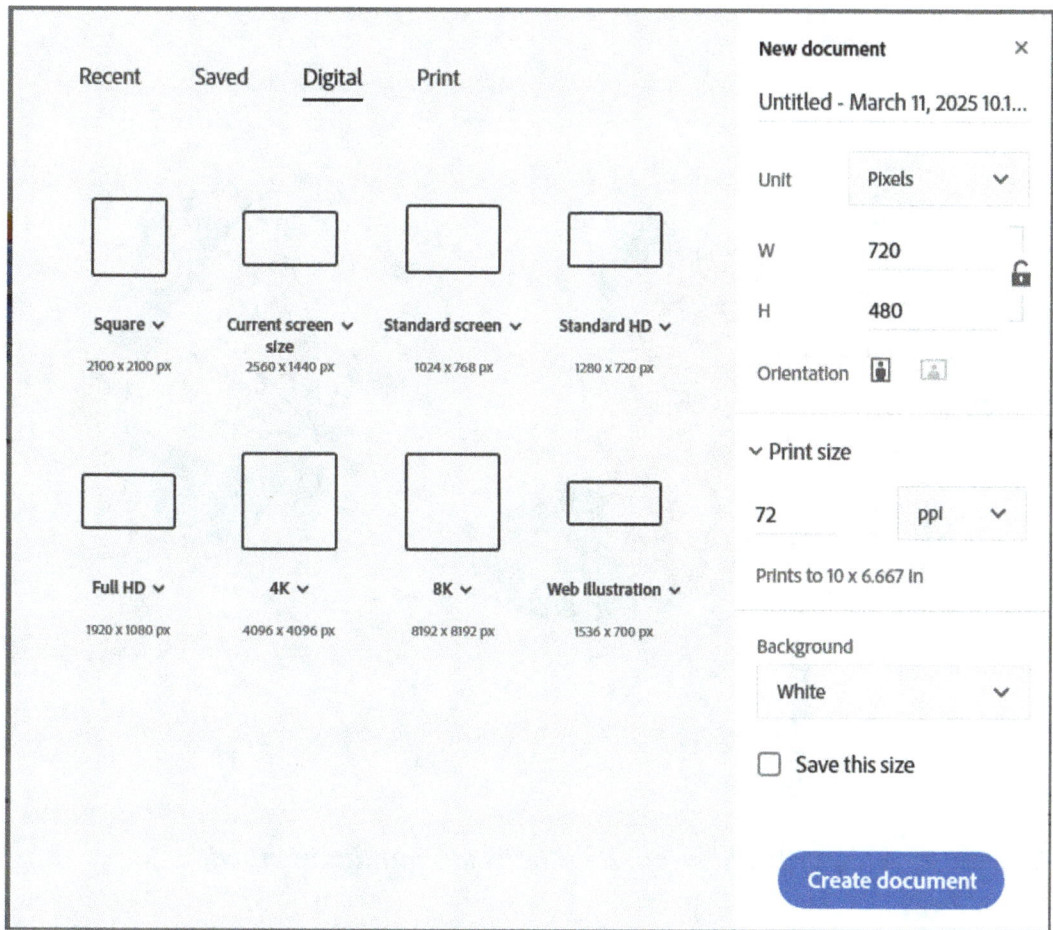

Figure 8-3. *Fresco New document dialog box with a Digital custom size created for the Web*

At this point, you would start creating layers and painting a scene for your animation which would eventually have stationary layers (Pixel and Vector) and Motion layers which we will explore shortly.

However, if you want to follow along with my example, then import and open the file **butterfly_frame_by_frame_start.psd** for practice. Refer to Figure 8-4.

CHAPTER 8   BASIC ANIMATION IN FRESCO

⤴ Import and open

Figure 8-4. *A file with a flower and butterfly for animation practice*

As you can see in the settings, the file's width and height are 720 × 480 px, and if you click the word Change, its resolution (print size) is 72 ppi. Refer to Figure 8-5.

CHAPTER 8 BASIC ANIMATION IN FRESCO

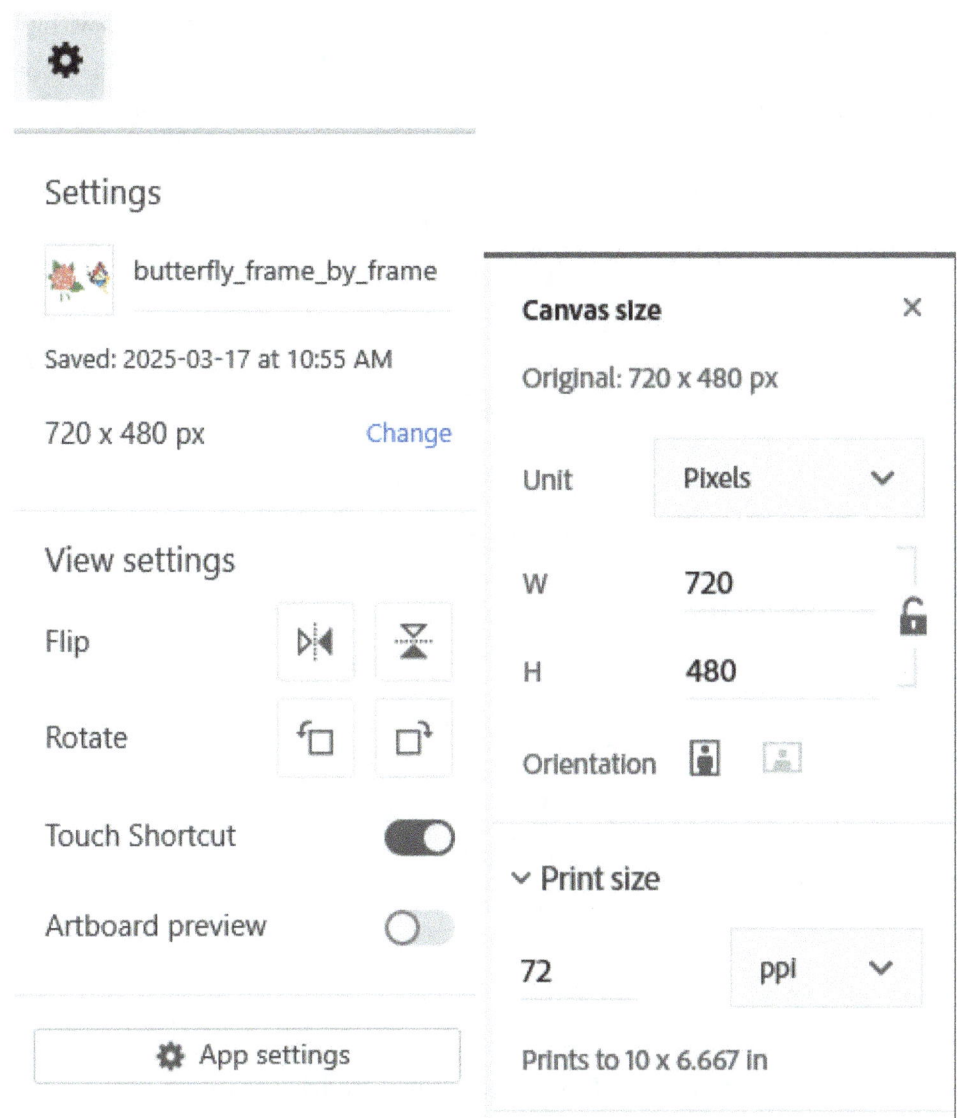

Figure 8-5. Settings drop-down panel and Canvas size dialog box settings

Click the X to exit so that you do not alter the canvas size. Refer to Figure 8-5. Later in the chapter, we'll look at a larger project for additional practice.

Many of the components for the animation were sketched out or designed in Illustrator and then added to separated rasterized (pixel) layers in Photoshop. At this point, some additional layers were added for brush embellishments using Fresco. I used the Magic wand tool to select areas of flower's petals and leaves and then painted on

CHAPTER 8 BASIC ANIMATION IN FRESCO

some new layers using the Pixel painting brush of Cezanne 2 in various sizes with pinks for the rose and greens for the leaves. This is a good workflow when you need to blend the more precise art with your artistic designs. Refer to Figure 8-6 and Figure 8-7.

Figure 8-6. *Layers found in the Layer panel for the current document*

CHAPTER 8 BASIC ANIMATION IN FRESCO

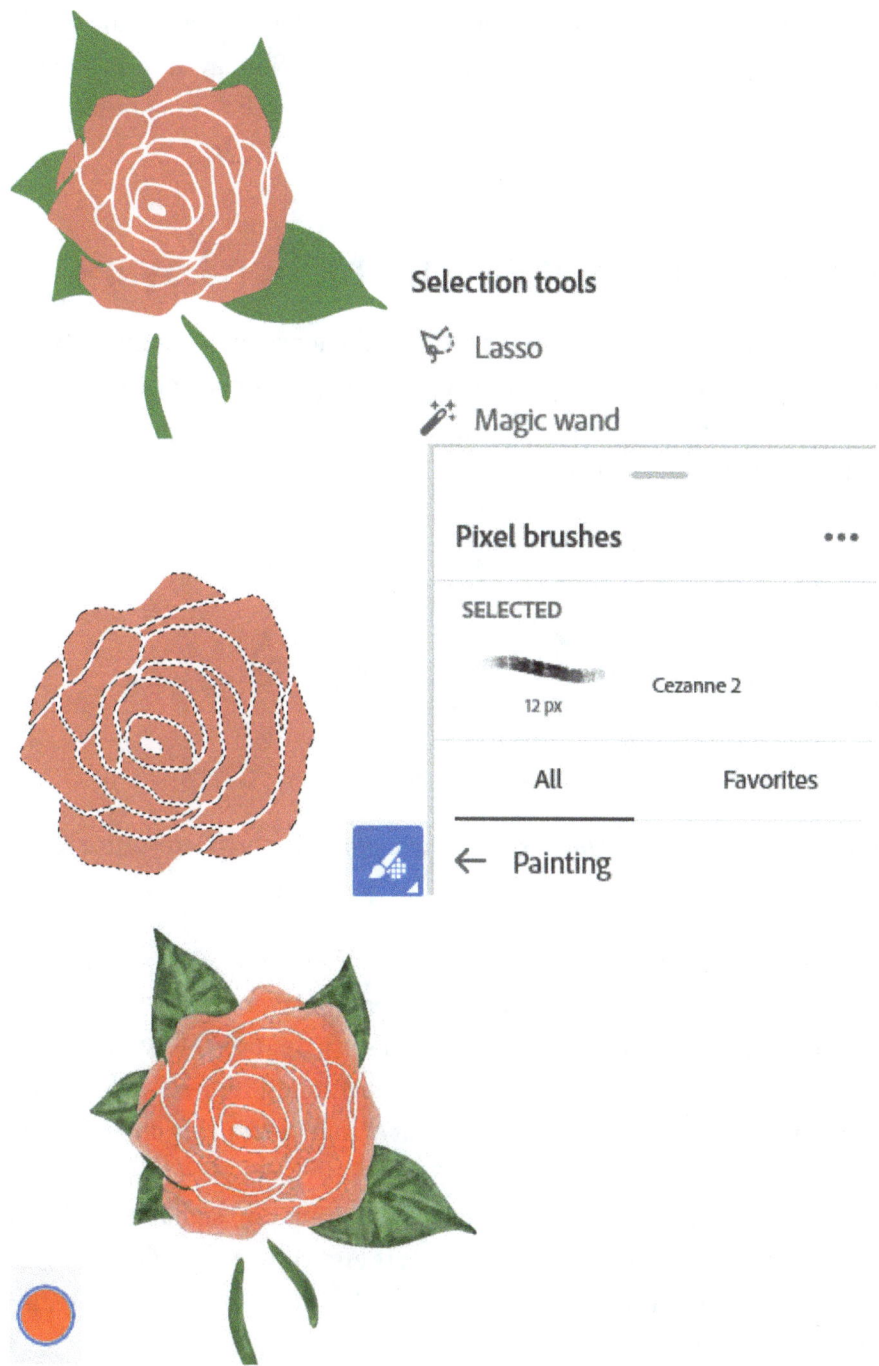

Figure 8-7. *Painting effects added Pixel layers with the Magic wand selection tool, a Pixel brush (Cezanne 2), and color chip to add embellishments to the animation*

You will notice that I initially hid some of the layers that are part of the butterfly as these will be used to create the frame by frame for the Motion layer. Refer to Figure 8-6.

Now, we will take some time to focus on the creation of the animation with Motion layers.

Creating GIF Animations with Motion Layers

When you want to create or review an animation, that icon can be found in the lower area of the Vertical Taskbar above the drawing aids which were discussed in Chapter 6. It is also used in conjunction with the Layers and Layer properties panels which were discussed in Chapter 5. Refer to Figure 8-8.

Figure 8-8. *Vertical Taskbar layers, Layer properties, and Animation panel icons selected*

For any animation, working on separate layers is best practice, if you think that your animation might have a few moving components. More layers ensure you will have greater control over your artwork. Also, when you start creating the actual Motion layer, it may be best to keep some of these layers as a backup and hidden so that you always have access to the originals if you make a mistake that cannot be quickly corrected using undo (Ctrl+Z).

When you start creating, don't expect to get the animation sequence right the first time as this chapter is for more intermediate users and you will need to take some time to prepare what you intend your animation to do. The purpose of this chapter is to practice and help you figure that out.

For your own project to begin, I would suggest starting with a few sketches or illustrations that you have digitized and place them on layers. This could be hand drawings or ones that you created in Illustrator or Photoshop. Then write down a few notes about what you would like your animation to do in regard to movement,

CHAPTER 8   BASIC ANIMATION IN FRESCO

scaling, and opacity changes. As you work though this chapter, you will gain a greater understanding of what Fresco can or cannot animate or workarounds you may have to implement for greater control.

Most animations you will want to keep short; a duration of under 30 seconds is best to keep the file size small. In Chapter 9, for larger more complex animations, I will mention another Adobe application which I think is more suitable for your lengthy, more precise projects.

In Fresco, make sure that your Layer panel is always visible. As you will discover, some of your layers will have no movement (stationary), and others will have the Motion layer badge applied to them. Refer to Figure 8-9.

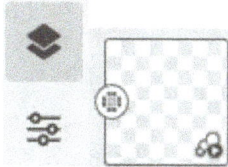

Figure 8-9. *Layer panel icon with a Motion layer displayed*

Both Pixel and Vector layers can be used to create an animation, though I find it easier to work with the Pixel layers as there are more Transformation options.

To create the animation, you first need to select your starting layer and then click the Animation icon to see all the options in the Contextual Task bar and layer timeline. In this case, it is the Layer B Frame 1. Refer to Figure 8-10.

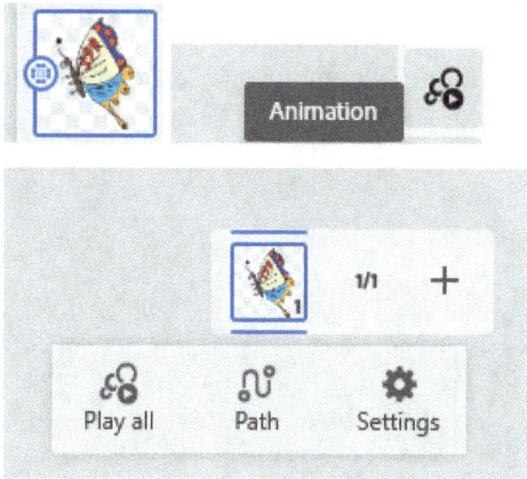

Figure 8-10. *Pixel layer selected with Animation icon, Timeline, and Contextual Task bar displayed*

553

CHAPTER 8　BASIC ANIMATION IN FRESCO

The Timeline, as you edit it, will include all frames in the selected layer and displays the total number of frames created, as well as the current frame on which you're working on and have selected.

In this example, we read on the right 1/1. This indicates that you're working on the first frame of 1, but shortly, we will add more frames as the animation is built. However, some layers which are stationary, like the flower and its leaves, will always have one frame even when the total number of frames are listed for the entire animation. Refer to Figure 8-11.

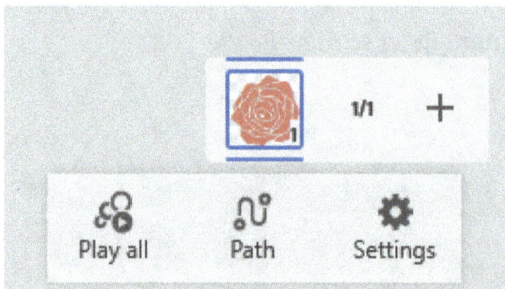

Figure 8-11. *A Pixel layer displayed in the Timeline panel with the Contextual Task bar below*

Let's review in more detail how these frames are added and what each frame actions mean.

Adding a Frame-by-Frame Layer Motion and Its Actions

To add other frames to the Layer B Frame 1, you need to make sure that layer is now selected. Refer to Figure 8-12.

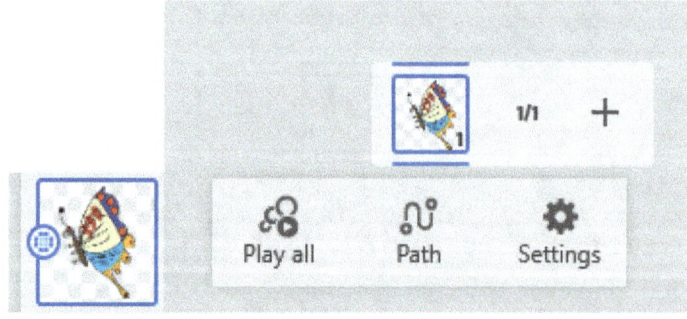

Figure 8-12. *A chosen layer selected to become a Motion layer and it is displayed in the Timeline panel with the Contextual Task bar below*

CHAPTER 8 BASIC ANIMATION IN FRESCO

The following frame actions will be available even if you have not set the animation to a path when you click on a frame. We will look at how to create a path later in this chapter. Refer to Figure 8-13.

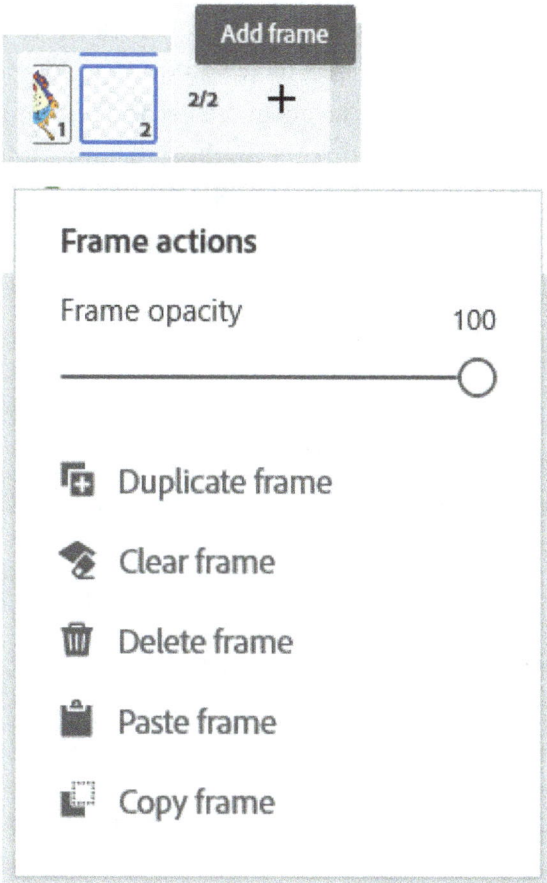

Figure 8-13. Timeline panel with a new frame added and the panel displaying the frame actions

Each frame in the animation needs to appear different, or is like a separate drawing, as the frames play, turning on and off. This gives the appearance of change or the impression of movement. Each frame will appear off to the side or horizontal when that layer is selected. However, the Timeline panel also moves upward or downward to a parallel layer or layer's frame when another layer is selected in the Layer panel.

555

You can then do the following Frame actions. Refer to Figure 8-13.

- Adding Frames: Click the plus icon (+) to add a new blank frame.

- Drag frames manually on the timeline to a new location to alter their order. However, when you just want to select a frame, click directly on it, and do not drag. For example, later, you will see situations where there are multiple frames or layers in the list and only half a layer or frame is showing. In that case, click on the half frame or layer rather than drag to avoid altering the order. This is a better way to move to more frames that are hidden from view. Refer to Figure 8-14 and Figure 8-15 to see an example.

- Right-click on the frame to select the other Frame actions from the list.

- Frame Opacity (0–100%): 100% is the default which is fully visible.

- Duplicate Frame: Create an exact copy of the currently selected frame.

- Clear Frame: Clears the frame of its contents but does not remove it.

- Copy Frame: Copies the contents of the frame.

- Paste Frame: After copying a frame's contents, paste into a new frame in a different location.

- Delete Frame: Remove the frame entirely from the group. Refer to Figure 8-13.

Adding the Content to the Frames from Other Layers

Now, as mentioned, to begin by adding a new frame, the added frame is currently blank. It is frame 2 of 2. Refer to Figure 8-14.

Figure 8-14. *Timeline panel showing a blank frame added*

CHAPTER 8 BASIC ANIMATION IN FRESCO

Now, in the layer panel, select the hidden layer B Frame 2 and make it visible. Refer to Figure 8-15.

Figure 8-15. *Selecting and making a layer visible in the next panel to be used as the next frame in the animation*

Use the Layer actions by right-clicking on the layer and choose Copy layer. Refer to Figure 8-16.

Figure 8-16. *Accessing the Layer action of Copy layer*

557

CHAPTER 8   BASIC ANIMATION IN FRESCO

Now, return to the blank frame 2 in the layer B Frame 1, and choose the Frame action of Paste frame. Refer to Figure 8-17.

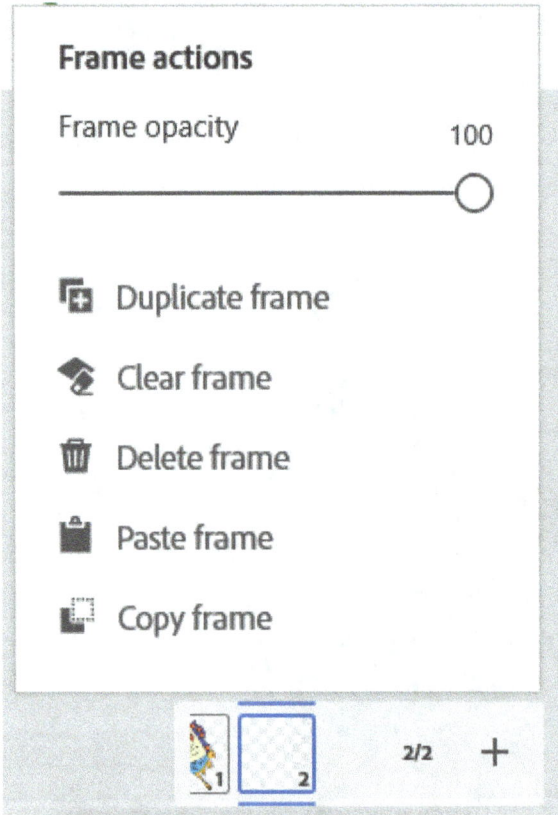

Figure 8-17. *Using the Frame action of Paste frame to add the layer image to the Timeline panel*

You will temporarily be in the Transform workspace and then click the Done button to exit. We'll discuss that area more in a moment. Refer to Figure 8-18.

Figure 8-18. *Transform workspace and the Done button to exit*

CHAPTER 8 BASIC ANIMATION IN FRESCO

But you should now have a copy of the previous layer image added to a frame, in this case to frame 3. Refer to Figure 8-19.

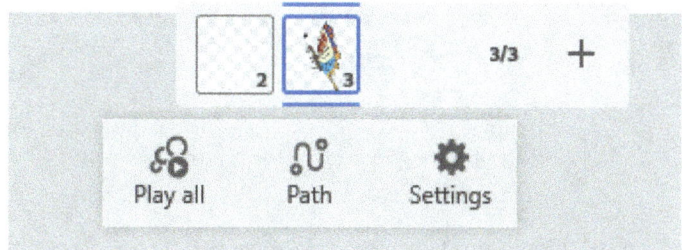

Figure 8-19. *Image 2 was added to frame 3 of the Timeline panel*

In this case, because the image was not directly pasted onto frame 2, we can now select that frame and use the action of Delete frame so that we are back to two frames. You can then hide Layer B Frame 2. Refer to Figure 8-15 and then refer to Figure 8-20.

559

CHAPTER 8   BASIC ANIMATION IN FRESCO

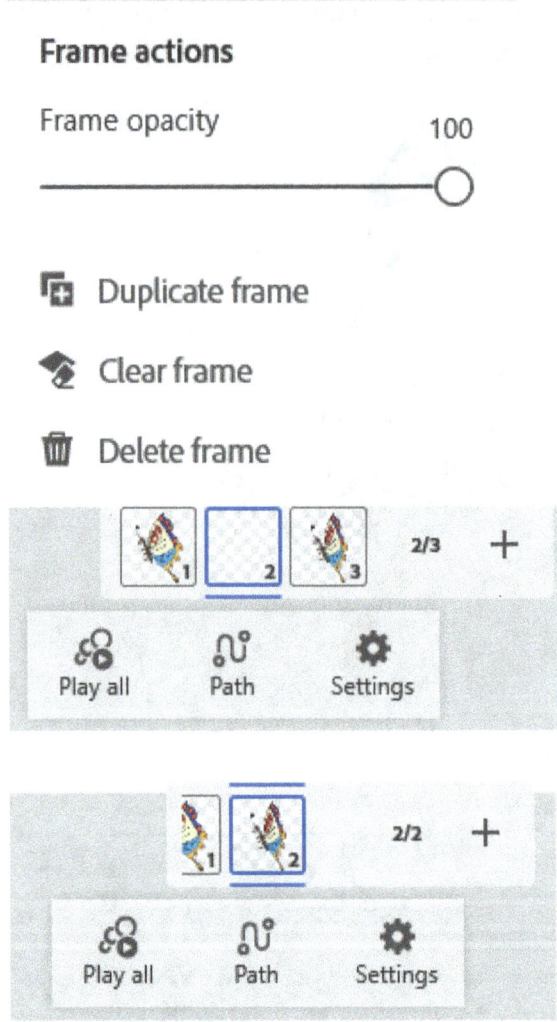

Figure 8-20. *Using the Frame actions to delete frame 2 to return the Timeline panel to two frames*

Now, repeat this process of selecting the next layer (B Frame 3) making it visible; then while selected, choose the Layer action of Copy layer. Then return to Layer B Frame 1 which is now a Motion layer and use the Frame action of Paste frame. You can then hide Layer B Frame 3. Continue to do these steps until you have six frames. You may need to show and hide the various layers as you work.

Remember each time when in the Transform workspace, click the Done button to exit for now.

Use the Layers B Frame 3, B Frame 4, B Frame 5, and B Frame 6 always adding them as frames to B Frame 1 which is now the Motion layer. Refer to Figure 8-21.

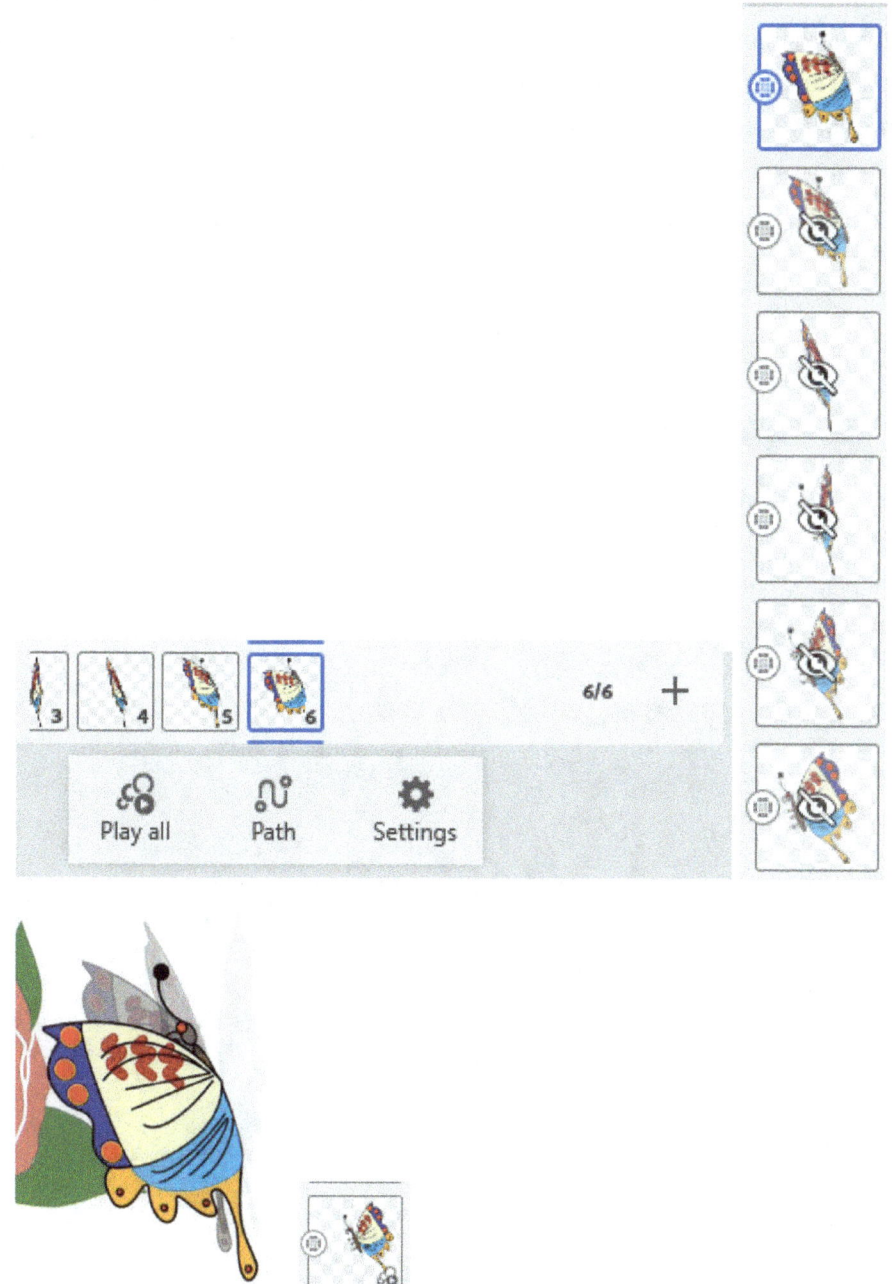

Figure 8-21. *Adding the remaining layers as frames to the Timeline panel to make the butterfly appear to flap its wings forward*

CHAPTER 8   BASIC ANIMATION IN FRESCO

As you work, check your order as mentioned earlier; you can drag the frames back and forth if you make a mistake with the frame order.

To complete the cycle of frame animation, as currently the butterfly's wings are only moving forward in one direction, you would now want to reverse that movement to get back to a starting point. You would then use the Frame action of Duplicate frame, in this case frames 5, 4, 3, and 2. Then drag them manually and move them so that they were ordered in the reverse order. Refer to Figure 8-22.

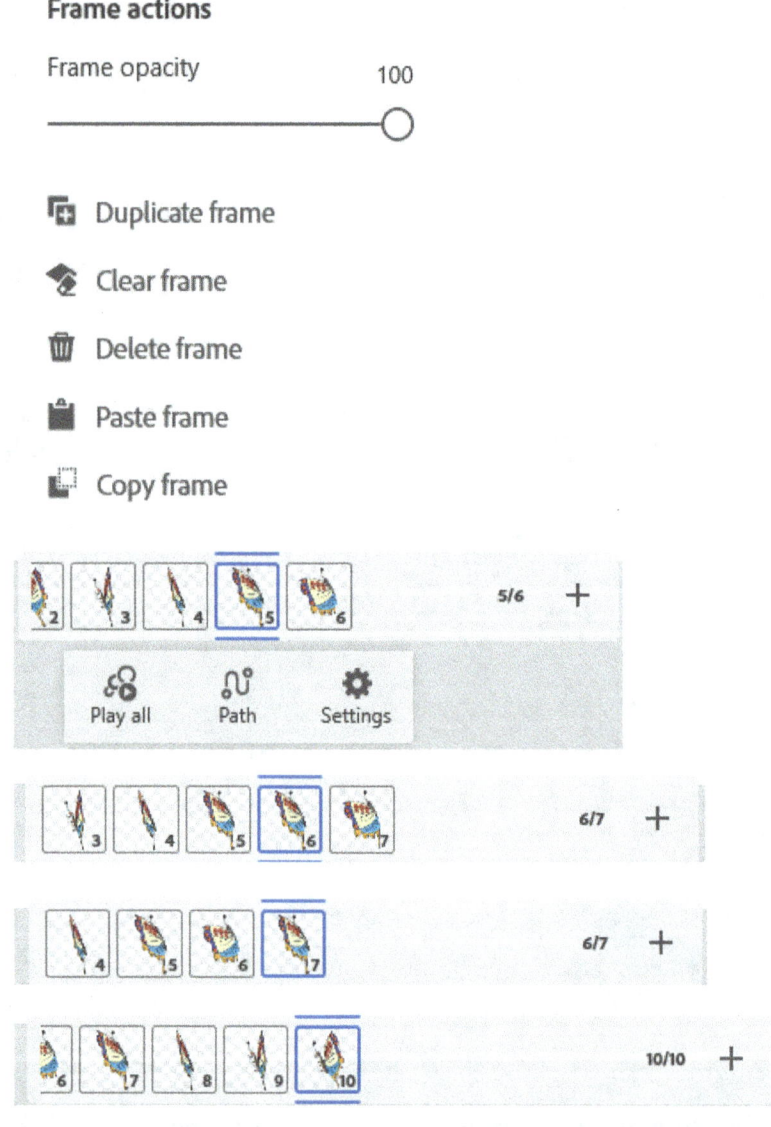

Figure 8-22. *Duplicating frames using the Frame action in the Timeline panel and then rearranging the frames to give the appearance of full flight*

You should then have a total of ten or 10/10 frames. Later, in the chapter, I will demonstrate why adding a few more frames to this Motion layer may be useful for more accurate motion in certain situations, but for now, ten frames is OK for practice. Refer to Figure 8-22.

Editing the Frames

As you create various frames, here are some additional things you can do.

You can select each frame as you would layers and paint on them as well as use drawing aids. In this example, I could use a Pixel brush like Basic ➤ Hard round in black along with the Ellipse Selection tool to touch up the edge of the antenna so that it was more rounded if I noticed a side appeared flat. This was more apparent on frames 2 and 10. Refer to Figure 8-23 and Figure 8-24.

CHAPTER 8 BASIC ANIMATION IN FRESCO

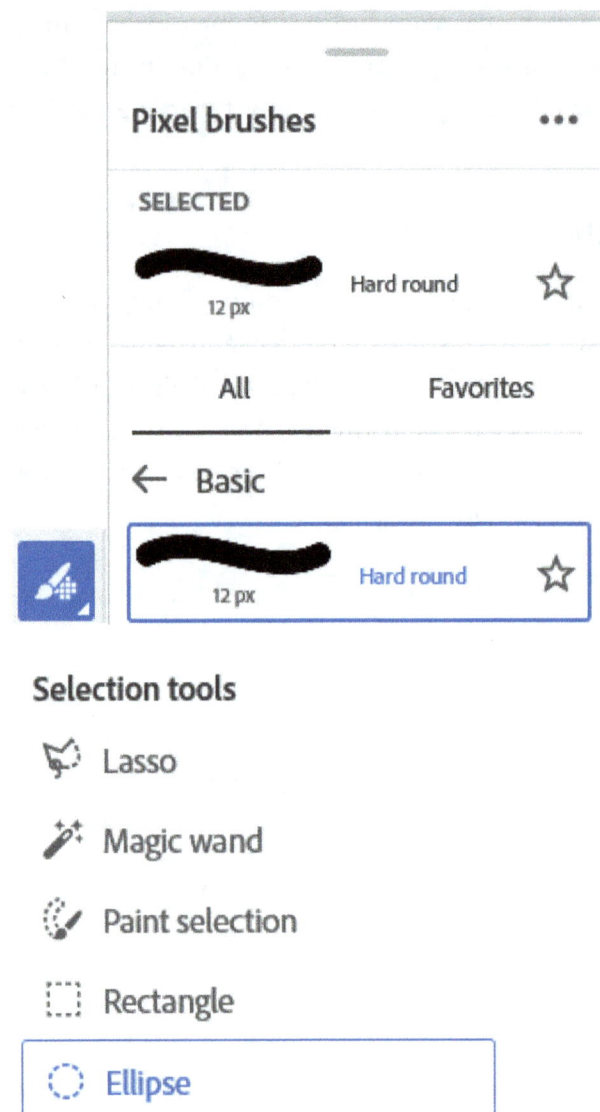

Figure 8-23. *Using the Pixel brush and the Selection tool Ellipse to touch areas on a frame*

CHAPTER 8 BASIC ANIMATION IN FRESCO

Figure 8-24. *Once the selection is complete, you can use the black color chip to paint within the selection*

Then the selection was deselected using the Selection tool's Contextual Task bar which you can review in Chapter 4. Also, using the Selection tool's Load last selection option is very helpful when the painting area you need to fill is similar on several frames. Refer to Figure 8-25.

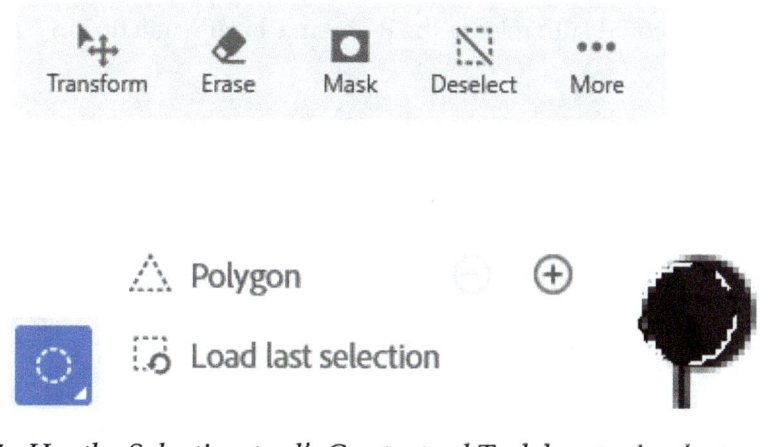

Figure 8-25. *Use the Selection tool's Contextual Task bar to deselect a selection and then load the last selection when you move to another frame*

565

In other situations, to avoid painting on a layer for more complex work, it may be better to create a separate layer with the same number of frames. We will look at an example of that when more Motion layers are added to better match the sequence in the project at the end of this chapter. Refer to Figure 8-26.

Figure 8-26. *Additional artwork can be added above a frame-by-frame animation on a parallel frame for additional embellishments*

A painting tip that Adobe recommends is to select your preferred layer or Motion layer that is below the selected Motion layer, then the more options (…) icon, and choose the Layer action Set as reference, and you apply Fill to individual frames of the targeted fill layer. This can speed up the coloring of your animation. We looked at this with single still layers in Chapters 5 and 6, but the same principles can apply here with Motion layers and frames, and you could later release the Reference layer when no longer needed. Refer to Figure 8-27.

CHAPTER 8   BASIC ANIMATION IN FRESCO

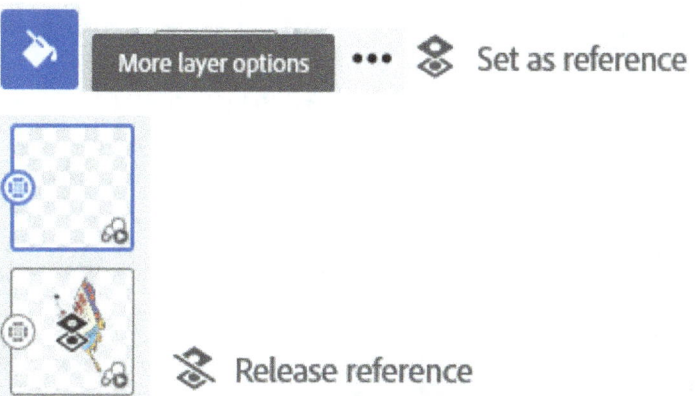

Figure 8-27. *Use the More layer options ➤ Layer actions ➤ Set as reference when you need to recolor certain frames above on another Motion layer and release reference when no longer required*

You can also set each frame to different opacities, using your Frame actions, which may be helpful when you want something to fade or appear. We will look at an example of that shortly. In this case, for the butterfly, we want the frames to remain at 100%. Refer to Figure 8-28.

CHAPTER 8　BASIC ANIMATION IN FRESCO

Figure 8-28. *Frame actions and adjusting the Frame opacity*

You can also add separate layer masks for each frame. However, layer masks are added to the Layer panel, not the Timeline itself. Refer to Figure 8-29.

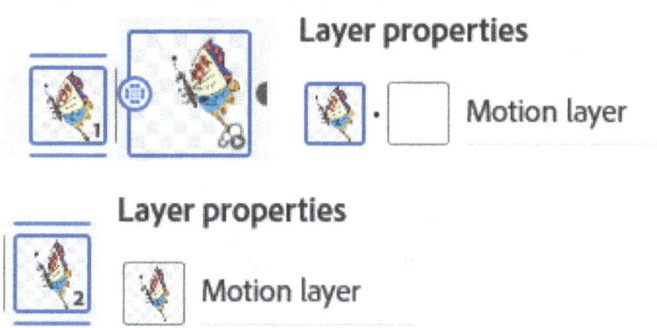

Figure 8-29. *Layer properties for a Motion layer with a layer mask applied to a specific frame and then the next frame has no layer mask*

A clipping mask can optionally be added, along with a layer mask to the Layer panel, and can be added at any point during the animation creation. However, unlike the layer mask, it will remain visible for every frame and cannot be applied to separate frames. Refer to Figure 8-30.

Figure 8-30. *A Motion layer applied as a clipping mask above a Pixel layer in the Layer panel*

We will discuss adding a clipping mask and layer masks again later in the chapter. See section "Adding Clipping Masks or Layer Masks to an Animation."

CHAPTER 8 BASIC ANIMATION IN FRESCO

Transforming Frames

Sometimes, you will notice that some frames, after you have added them, may not be exactly lined up as you hoped after you have pressed the Play all button in the Timeline Contextual Task bar to preview how the animation is progressing. Press Pause if you have done this. Refer to Figure 8-31.

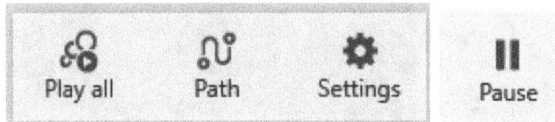

Figure 8-31. *Timeline panel's Contextual Task bar icons Play all and then click Pause*

Unlike layers, you cannot multiselect specific groups of frames at the same time. Multiselecting layers was described in Chapter 5. You can however, while on Motion layer, select a frame and then choose the Move & transform tool in the Toolbar. Refer to Figure 8-32.

CHAPTER 8   BASIC ANIMATION IN FRESCO

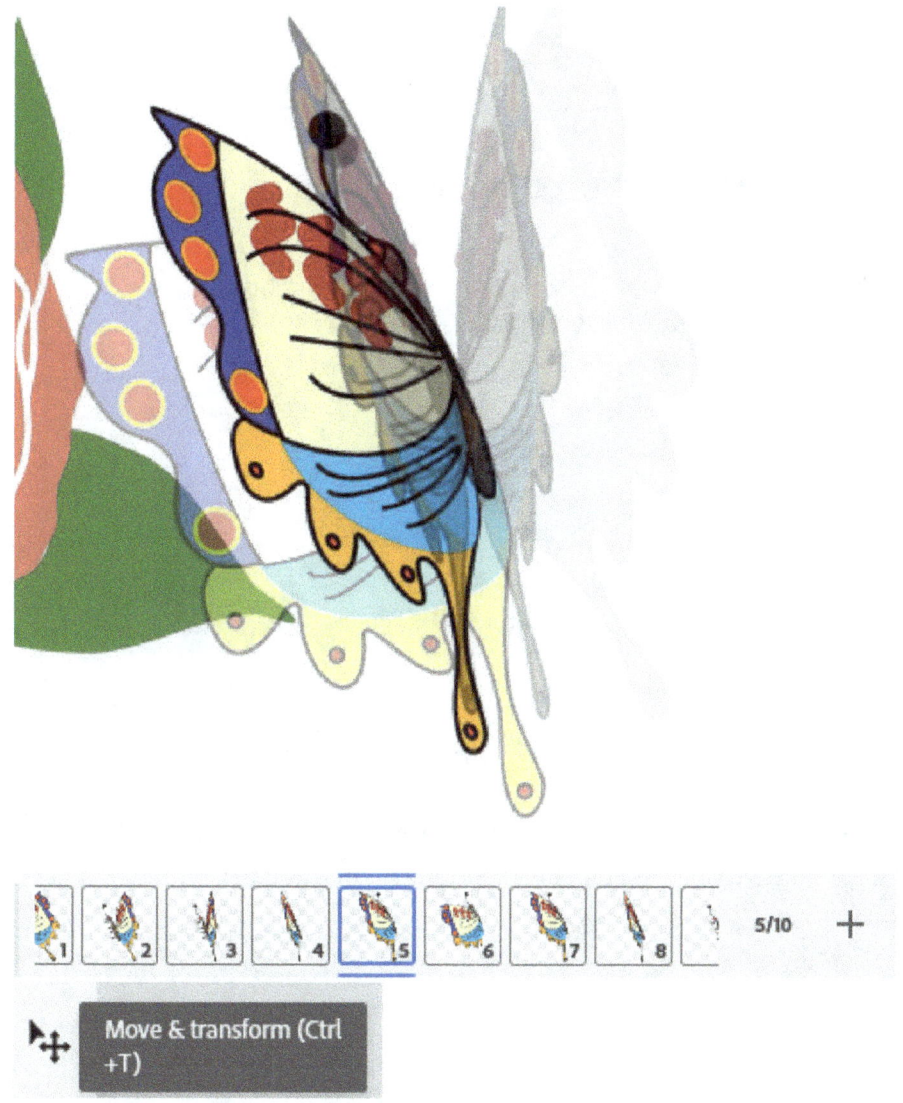

Figure 8-32. *Select a frame on a Motion layer and then select the Move & transform tool*

A dialog box will appear with two options to transform the layer or frame; you can transform the current frame or all frames. In this case, I may choose just the current frame and click the Transform button to enter the Transform workspace. Refer to Figure 8-33.

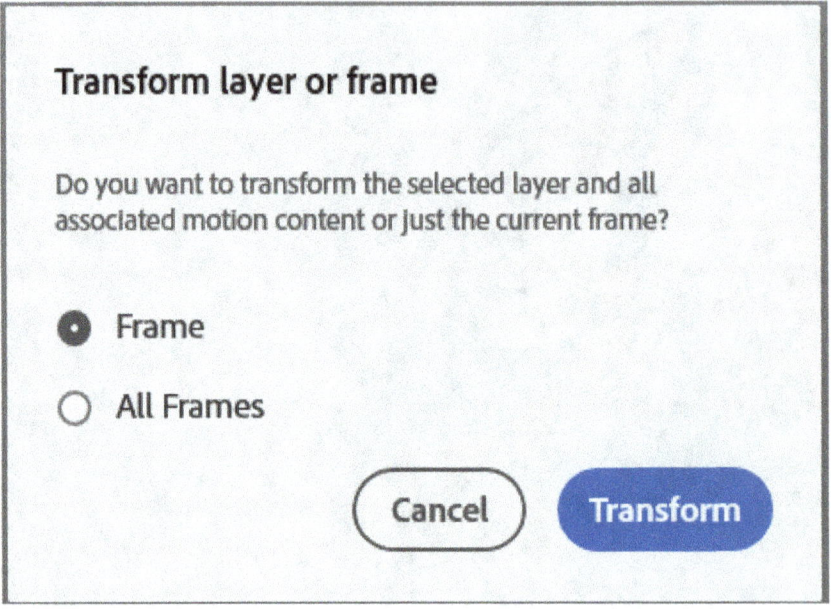

Figure 8-33. *Move & transform tool with the Transform layer or frame dialog box*

In the Transform workspace, because you are working with a Pixel Motion layer, you will have access to all the Transform options mentioned in Chapter 4. Refer to Figure 8-34.

CHAPTER 8 BASIC ANIMATION IN FRESCO

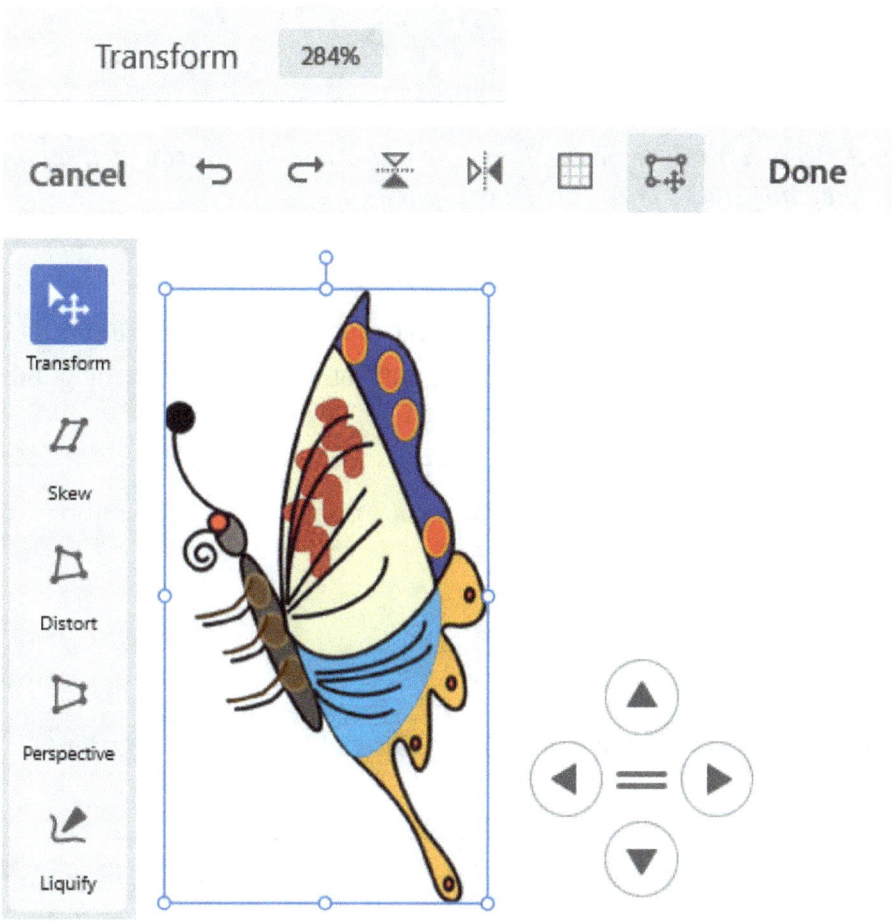

Figure 8-34. *A single frame can be selected and then transformed with the tools and sub-tool of the Transform workspace*

Often, just moving the frame using the nudge arrows is enough to align, but in other situations, you may need to work with the other transform options such as Transform to Rotate or Scale, Skew, Distort, Perspective, or Liquify, as well as any of the other sub-tools in the Title bar for flipping. Refer to Figure 8-34.

In my case, I worked on frames 4, 5, 6, and 7 that needed a nudge down and right to align in the frames better. You can work with all motion frames within a layer without exiting the Transform workspace; just select the next frame in the Timeline. Refer to Figure 8-35.

CHAPTER 8   BASIC ANIMATION IN FRESCO

Figure 8-35. *Each frame from the Timeline panel can be transformed separately and selected while in the Transform workspace*

Note that if the All Frames option had been clicked prior to entering the workspace, all the frames would be highlighted in blue, and you would be performing the transform on all at once. Refer to Figure 8-33.

I then clicked Done afterward to exit the Transform workspace and return to the other layers. Refer to Figure 8-36.

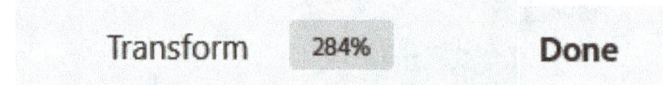

Figure 8-36. *Exit the Transform workspace by clicking the Done button*

Tip   To improve your alignment when selecting single frames, before entering the Transform workspace under the Timeline's Contextual Task bar for Settings in the Motion settings panel, you can enable the Onion skin toggle, using the default settings of previewing with Frames (3) and Opacity (40%) so that you can better align each frame on the layer as you transform it. Refer to Figure 8-37.

CHAPTER 8 BASIC ANIMATION IN FRESCO

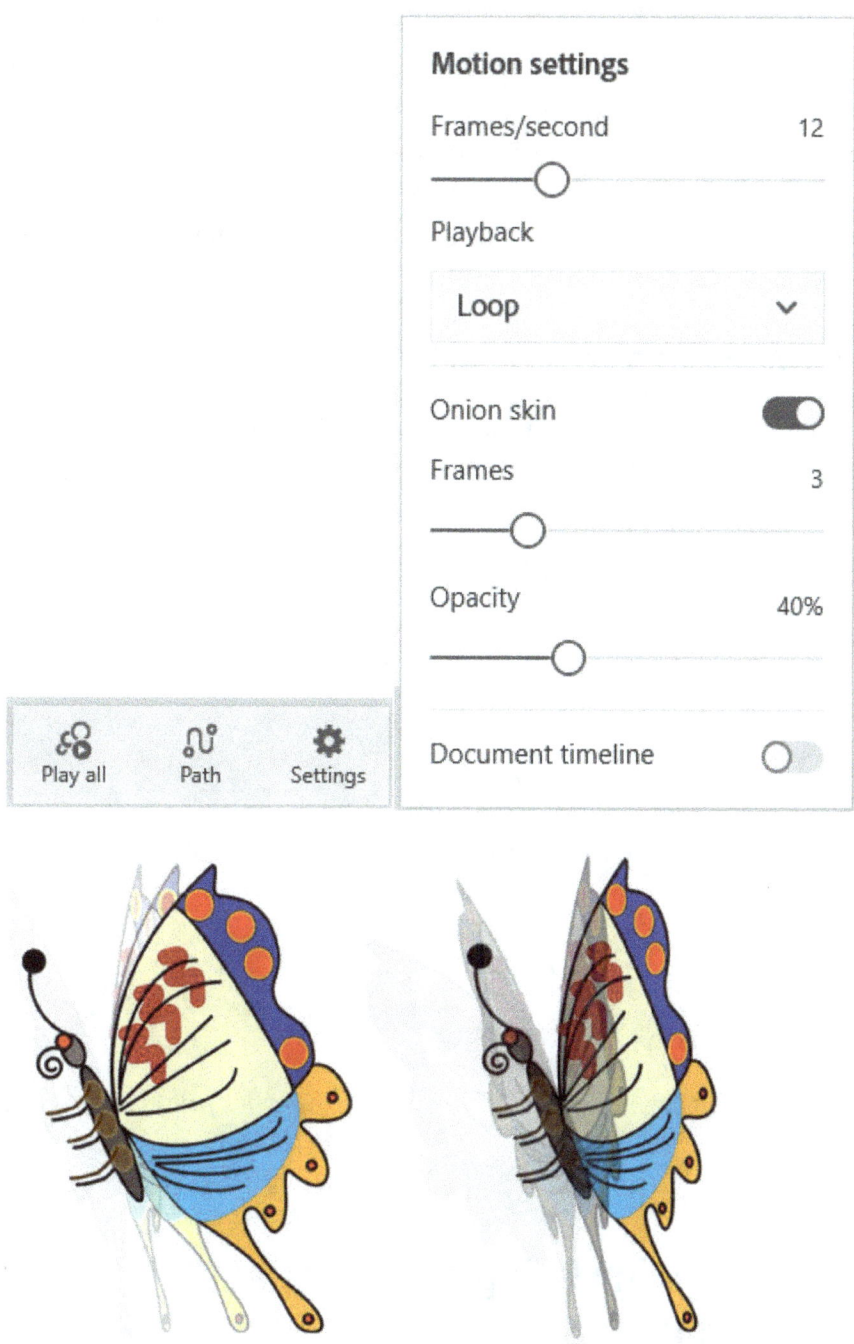

Figure 8-37. *Use the Timeline's Contextual Task bar to adjust the Motion settings for Onion skin*

575

Now, we have seen the process to add a frame-by-frame motion using the timeline. Each frame is slightly different, so it makes wings appear, in this case to move in a different direction as you change to a new frame. In your case, you may also have a fade opacity option added as well, as you will soon see.

Later, we'll look at the Motion settings panel in more depth so that you can further configure your frame setting. Refer to that area for speed (Frames/Seconds) and Playback options.

Motion Layer Properties (Frame by Frame)

The current Motion layer, which only has frames, will have the same Layer properties as the Pixel layer of Blend mode and Layer opacity which were reviewed in Chapter 5. Refer to Figure 8-38.

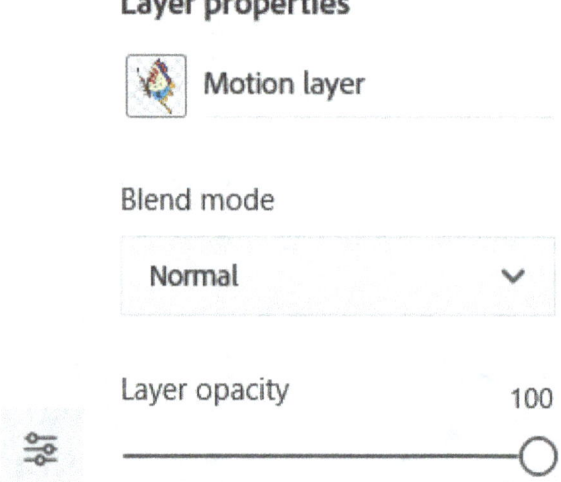

Figure 8-38. *Motion Layer setting in the Layer properties panel when only frames are present*

Define an Animation Using a Motion Path and Path Actions

Paths can be used with a frame animation to make it appear like the object is floating or moving across an area in a repetitive way. Animations that are defined by a path need to have a Vector path as a guide to control the motion.

You can continue to work with the file **butterfly_frame_by_frame_start.psd** or review the file **butterfly_frame_by_frame_Final_10.psd**. Later at the end of this section, I will also be showing examples from the file **car_outdoor_motions.psd** to illustrate some additional ideas.

In the car example, one note of caution if you are building some components of the animation on Photoshop layers is to ensure that you have, until you start the animation, all potential moving layers near but not beyond the canvas borders as this can cause parts of the drawing, upon import, to be cropped off. For layers, once you start the path animation, it's OK to allow items on layers to go beyond the borders. Refer to Figure 8-39.

Figure 8-39. *Moving car animation with a colorful scenery*

Creating the Path Layer

To continue with the butterfly animation, first, while on the Motion layer first frame, click the path icon in the Contextual Task bar to begin. Refer to Figure 8-40.

CHAPTER 8 BASIC ANIMATION IN FRESCO

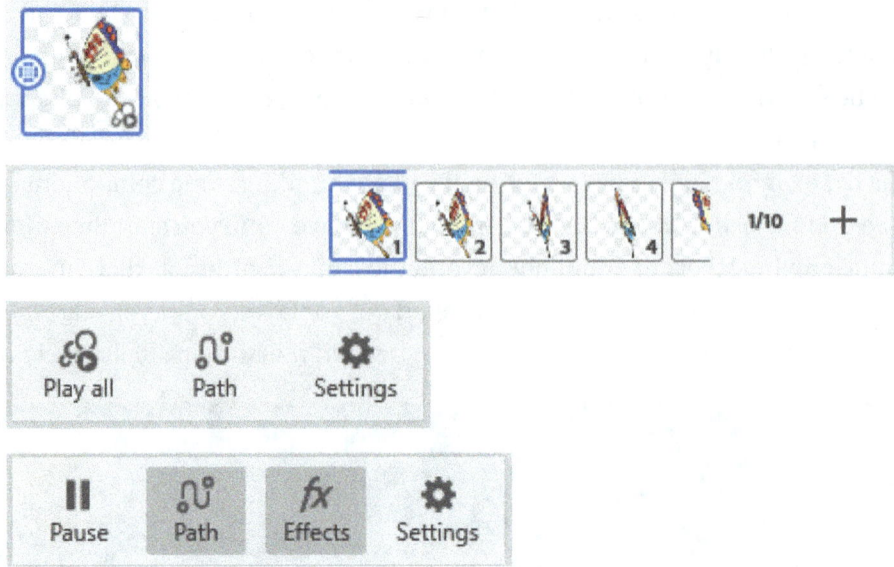

Figure 8-40. *Selecting the Motion layer and using the Timeline and Contextual Task bar to add a motion path and effects*

For your own projects, you will be using a vector brush also known as a Motion brush when you want to create a path. I suggest using a ruler or drawing aid to draw a straight or curved line. Refer to Figure 8-41.

CHAPTER 8 BASIC ANIMATION IN FRESCO

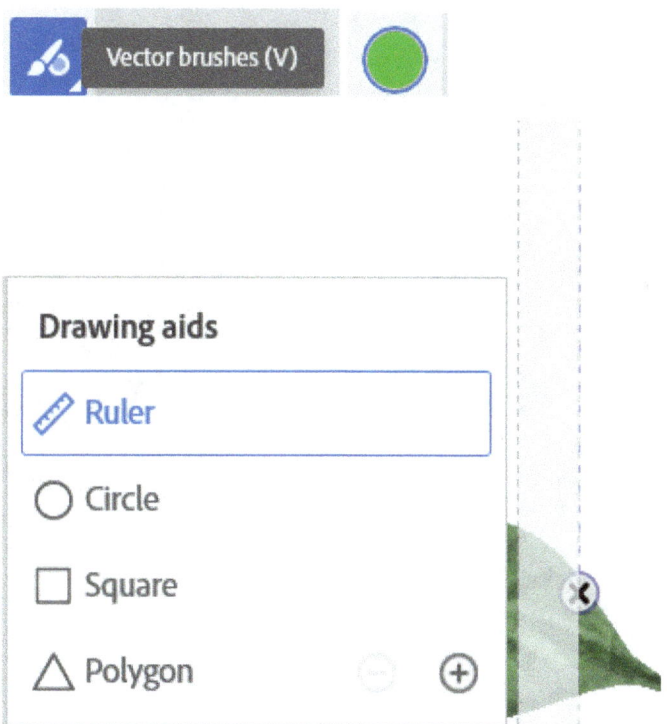

Figure 8-41. *In path mode, use the Vector brushes to draw a path along with using a drawing aid, but the color chip is not required*

Or if you prefer a freestyle path, then just use your Vector/Motion brush on the same layer while in path mode for the object to follow. The path is invisible even though a color chip option will appear on the Toolbar. The path can be open or closed if you draw back toward the (X). Refer to Figure 8-42.

579

CHAPTER 8   BASIC ANIMATION IN FRESCO

Figure 8-42. *Example of drawing a freehand path without the drawing aid that is open and closed*

In this case, I drew the path toward the flower because that is where I want the butterfly to go. The starting point is the (X). Refer to Figure 8-42.

Additionally, you can draw multiple paths with the Vector/Motion brush on the Motion layer. Drawing multiple paths will also automatically duplicate the object and the object motion on the same layer. This is helpful so you don't have to create multiple Motion layers unless you want to apply different motions to every object. Then you should add the path to a duplicate or different Motion layer. Refer to Figure 8-43.

580

CHAPTER 8   BASIC ANIMATION IN FRESCO

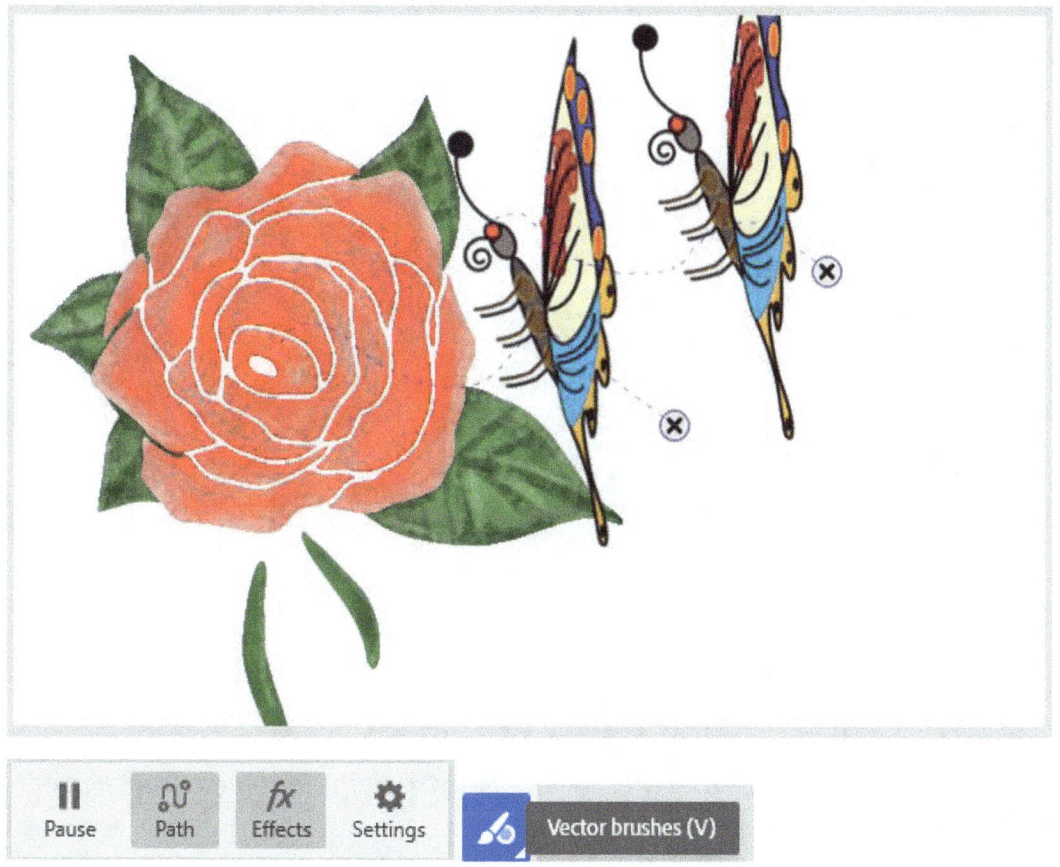

Figure 8-43. *Draw more than one path with the Vector/Motion brush when you want copies of the same item to move on different paths within the same layer*

While in path mode, a path can be deleted by clicking on the circle with the (X) and then the path redrawn if no paths are present. In this case, we only need one path or butterfly right now. Refer to Figure 8-44.

CHAPTER 8 BASIC ANIMATION IN FRESCO

Figure 8-44. *Click the (X) on paths to remove extra paths and then draw a new path for the butterfly to travel on*

Edit and Transform the Path

When you need to edit the path or frames, you can select the Move & transform tool from the Toolbar as seen earlier in the chapter and choose the following options from the dialog box. Refer to Figure 8-45.

CHAPTER 8 BASIC ANIMATION IN FRESCO

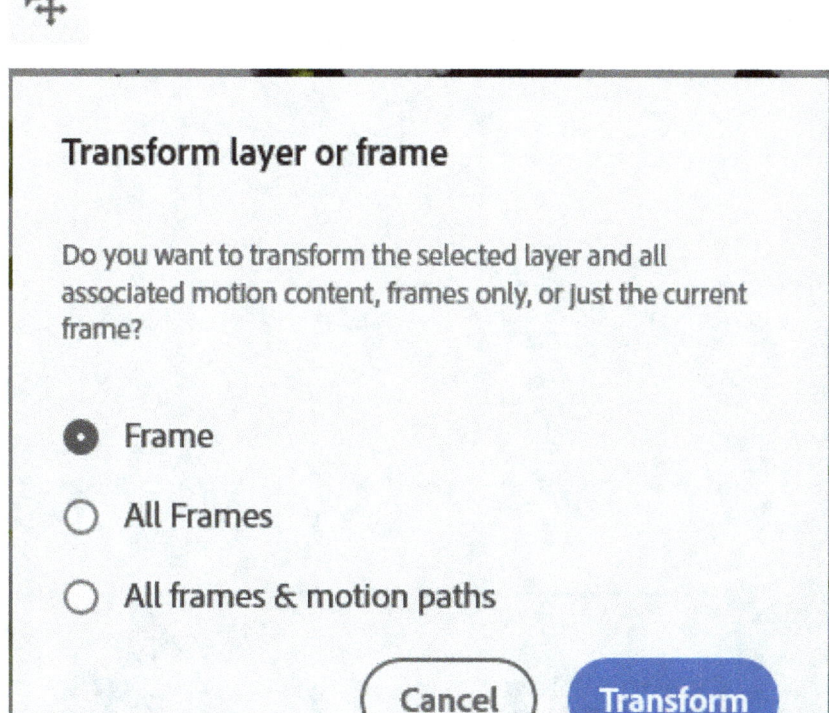

Figure 8-45. *Move & transform tool with the Transform layer or frame dialog box and a frame and motion path option added*

The options for Transform layer or frame are Frame, All Frames, or All frames & motion paths. For All frames & motion paths, after you click Transform, in the Transform workspace, you will have access to the Transform, the sub-tools, and Liquify tool only. This is good when you need to scale or rotate the path along with other frame elements. Refer to Figure 8-46.

583

CHAPTER 8　BASIC ANIMATION IN FRESCO

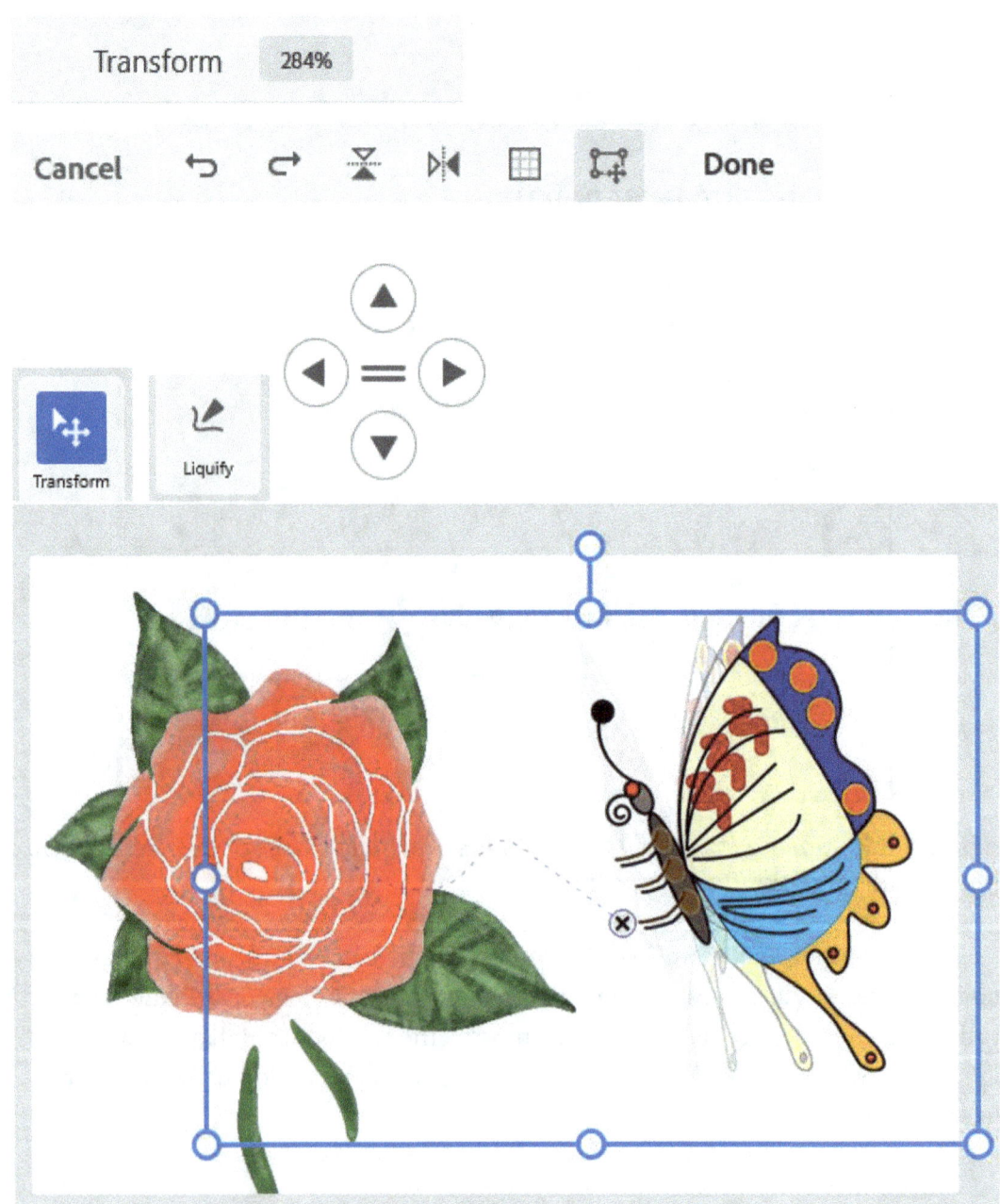

Figure 8-46. *Transform workspace with the All frames & motion paths option selected which restricts the use of certain tools*

Note However, for your own projects, if the layer has no additional frames and only motion paths, you may see a slightly different dialog box message. In this case, you would have the options to edit the Layer content or Layer content & motion paths. Refer to Figure 8-47.

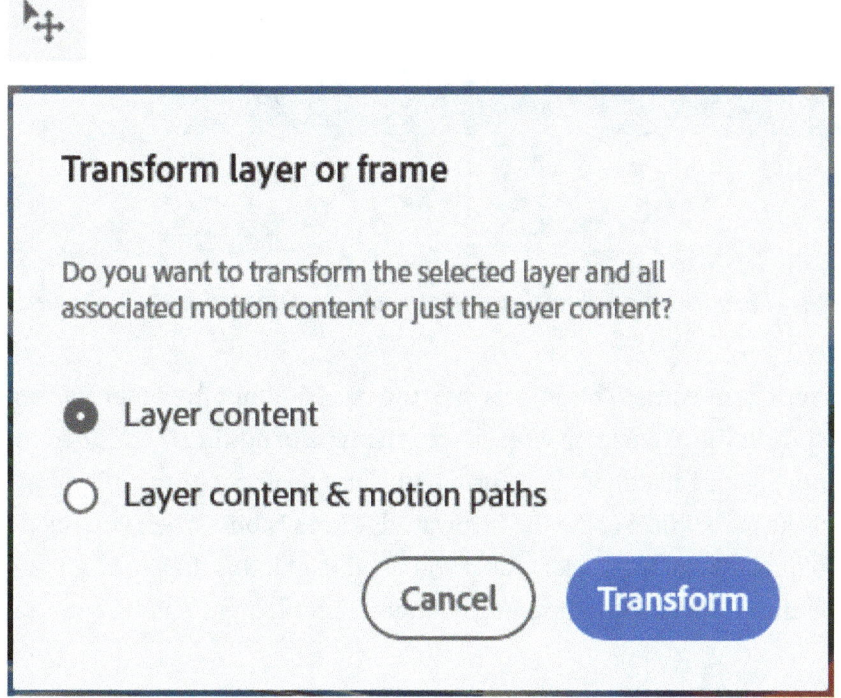

Figure 8-47. Move & transform tool with the Transform layer or frame dialog box when Motion layers only have one frame and a path

Click the Cancel or Done button to exit the Transform workspace. Refer to Figure 8-46.

Outside the Transform workspace, while working on the path animation, the following path actions are available when you click the word PATH and its bar in the Timeline panel. Refer to Figure 8-48.

CHAPTER 8 BASIC ANIMATION IN FRESCO

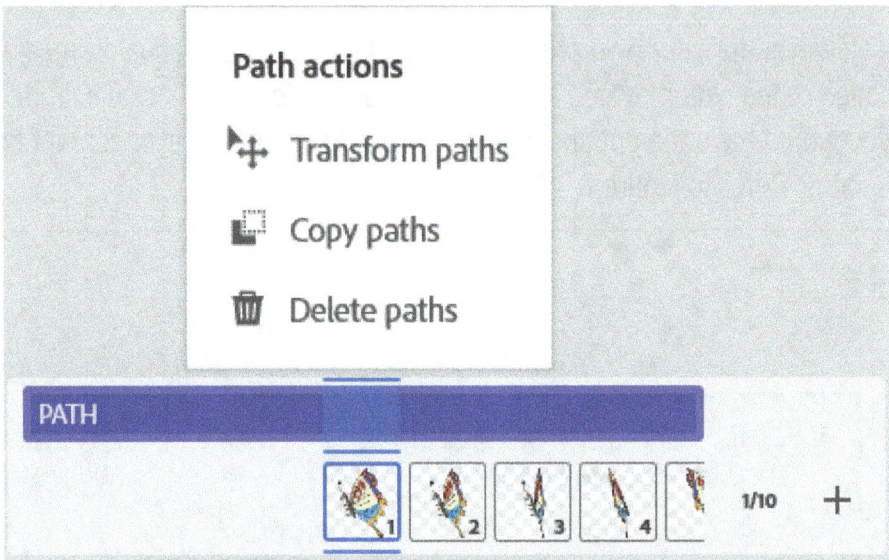

Figure 8-48. *Timeline panel with the Path action selected above a frame*

- Transform Paths: This affects only the path and not the other frames while in the Transform workspace. The type of editing is confined to moving and scaling of free-form paths and basic rotation or flipping of the path. I find using the arrow nudge keys is best when you need to move the path. Click Done if you need to exit this area to confirm or click Cancel without saving changes. Refer to Figure 8-49.

CHAPTER 8 BASIC ANIMATION IN FRESCO

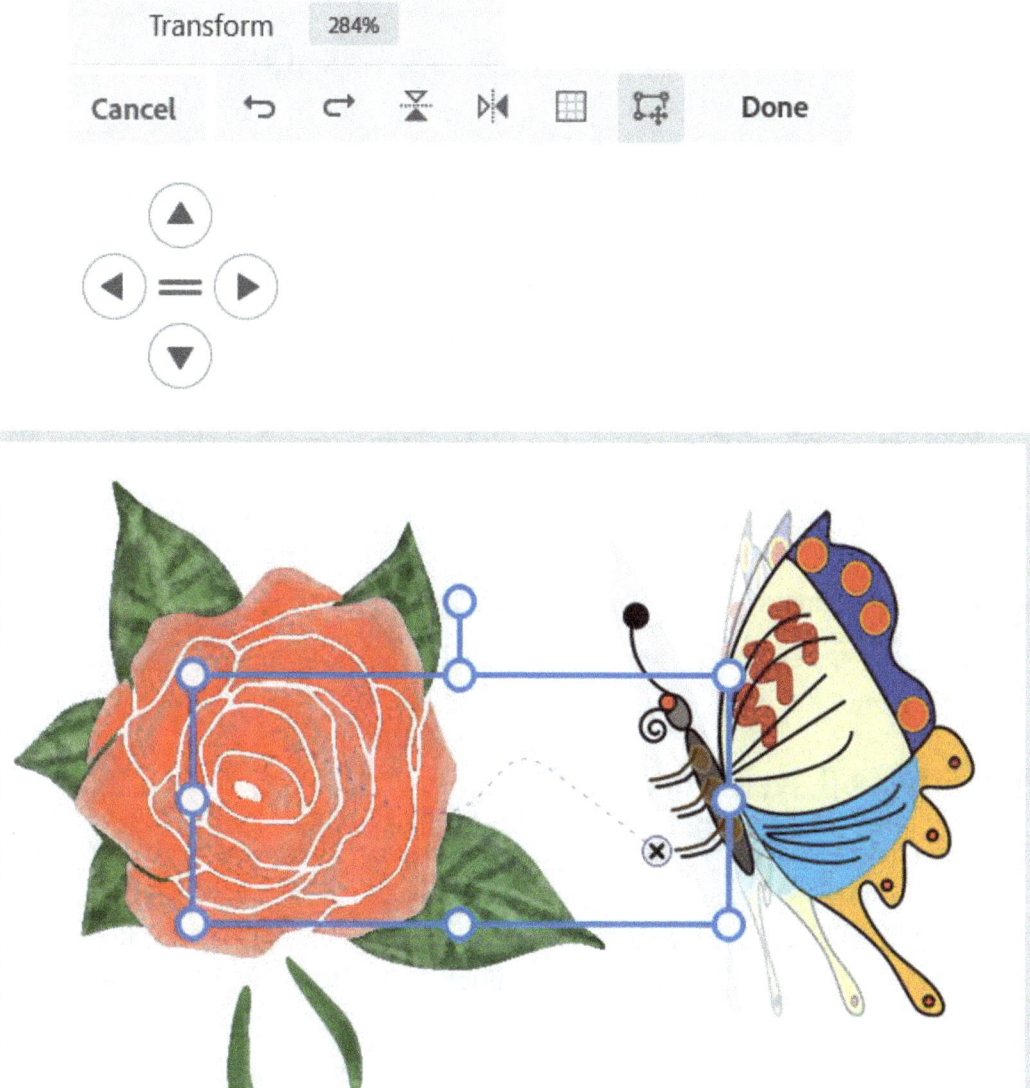

Figure 8-49. *Transform workspace has limited options for editing a motion path when selected*

The other Path actions are

- Copy Paths: Copy the selected motion path. Refer to Figure 8-48.

- Paste Motion Paths: After a path is copied, this action is available under the Layer actions either when you right-click on a layer or use the More actions in the Vertical Taskbar or under the Frame actions while the layer is selected, and choose this option to paste into the new motion path layer. Refer to Figure 8-50.

Figure 8-50. Layer and Frame actions for Paste motion panel

This option is unavailable for a regular Pixel layer with no additional frames.

- Delete Paths: Deletes any motion paths on that layer. Refer to Figure 8-48

Path Effects (Layer Properties)

The Motion layer can have various effects added when a path is present. To do that, you need to click the path icon in the Timeline's Contextual Task bar.

While the path is selected, go to the Layer properties panel or click the Effects (*fx*) button, and review and adjust based on the options provided. Refer to Figure 8-51.

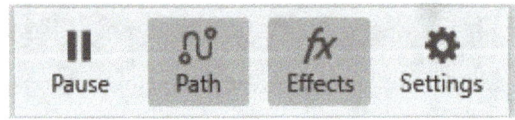

Figure 8-51. Timeline Contextual Task bar; once a path is selected, you can access the Effects (fx)

The following default path effects found in the Layer properties panel are Blend mode and Layer opacity (0–100%) which you can review in Chapter 5 and were mentioned again when we worked with frames in this chapter. However, below them in the panel are now additional Path effects that can be applied as well. Refer to Figure 8-52.

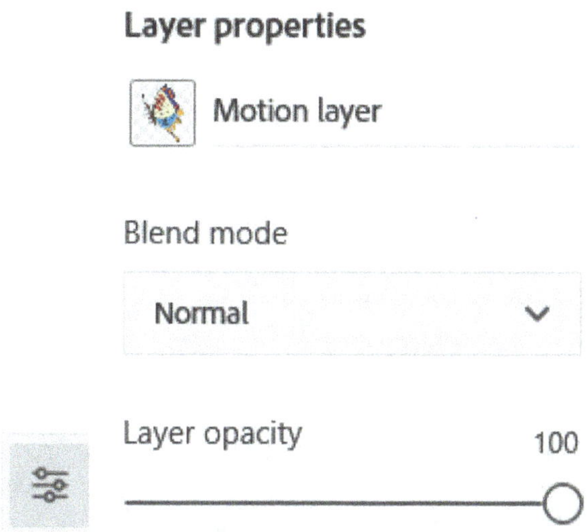

CHAPTER 8 BASIC ANIMATION IN FRESCO

Layer properties

Motion layer

Blend mode

Normal

Layer opacity   100

Figure 8-52. *Layer properties default options for the Motion layer*

Below the word Path effects, you will find the first setting.

- Add Multiples (1–20): Add multiple objects to the same path, and then preview in real time when you click Play all. Refer to Figure 8-53.

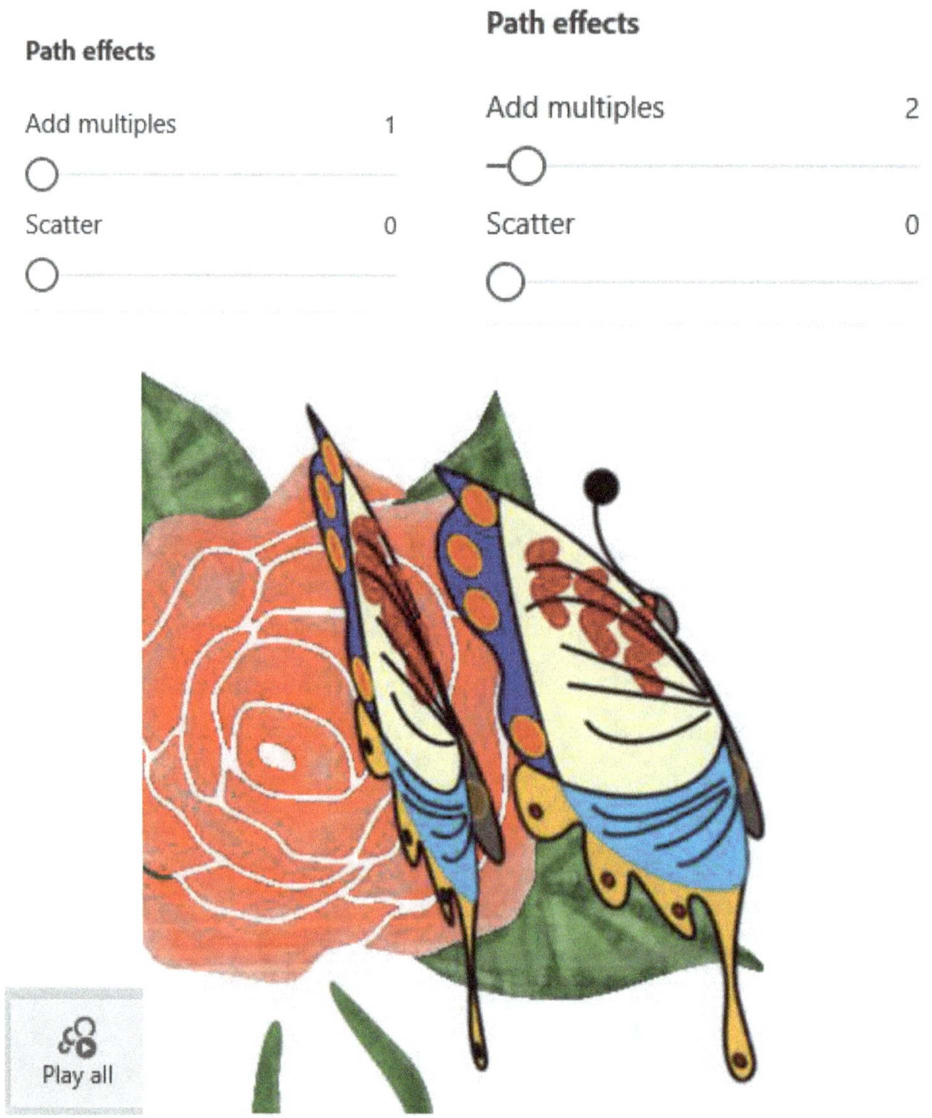

CHAPTER 8   BASIC ANIMATION IN FRESCO

Figure 8-53. *Play all when you want to review various Layer properties Path effects on the canvas, such as Add multiples and Scatter*

- Scatter (0–100): Applies the effects to corresponding objects once added; then click Play all. This can cause, in this case, the two butterfly movements on the path to be less in sync, and the movements are shifted over more to the left as I increase the setting to a higher number like 74. Refer to Figure 8-54.

CHAPTER 8   BASIC ANIMATION IN FRESCO

Figure 8-54. Layer properties Path effects are altered for Add multiples and Scatter using the sliders

Move the sliders of Add multiples back to 1 and Scatter back to 0 as you look at the next settings.

- Grow/Shrink: Allows you to decrease or increase the object's size. When enabled, you can access Percentage (−100%, 0%, 200%) and Number of times (1–20). Click Play all when you want to preview. Refer to Figure 8-55.

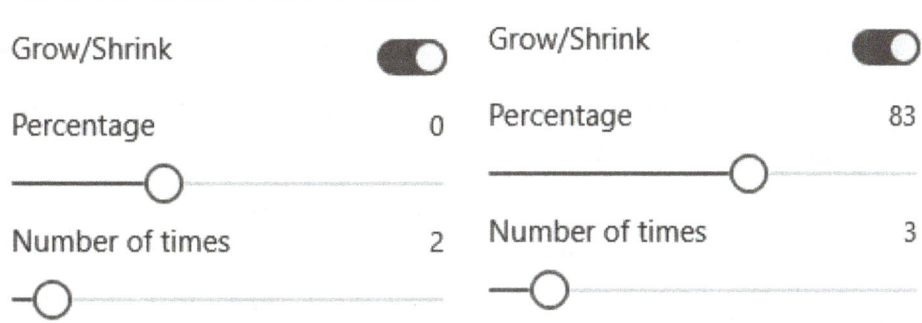

Figure 8-55. Layer properties Path effects are altered for Grow/Shrink, Percentage, and Number of times

CHAPTER 8 BASIC ANIMATION IN FRESCO

This alternation from 0 to 83 percentage will cause the butterfly to grow size and then shrink a certain number of times such as three as it moves in the air. Refer to Figure 8-56.

Figure 8-56. *The butterfly grows and shrinks as it flies along the motion path*

Disable the Grow/Shrink for now to see the next set of options.

- Rotate: When enabled, Rotate options are Sway and Spin. Click Play all when you want to preview.
  - Sway: This will alter the motion control as well as the option for Angle (−90°, 0°, 90°) and Number of times (1–20).

Currently, I had my settings on the Sway, Angle of 0, and Number of times 1. However, if I set to Angle 45 and Number of times 4, then as the butterfly files, it moves in a more erratic way swerving and rocking. Refer to Figure 8-57.

CHAPTER 8　BASIC ANIMATION IN FRESCO

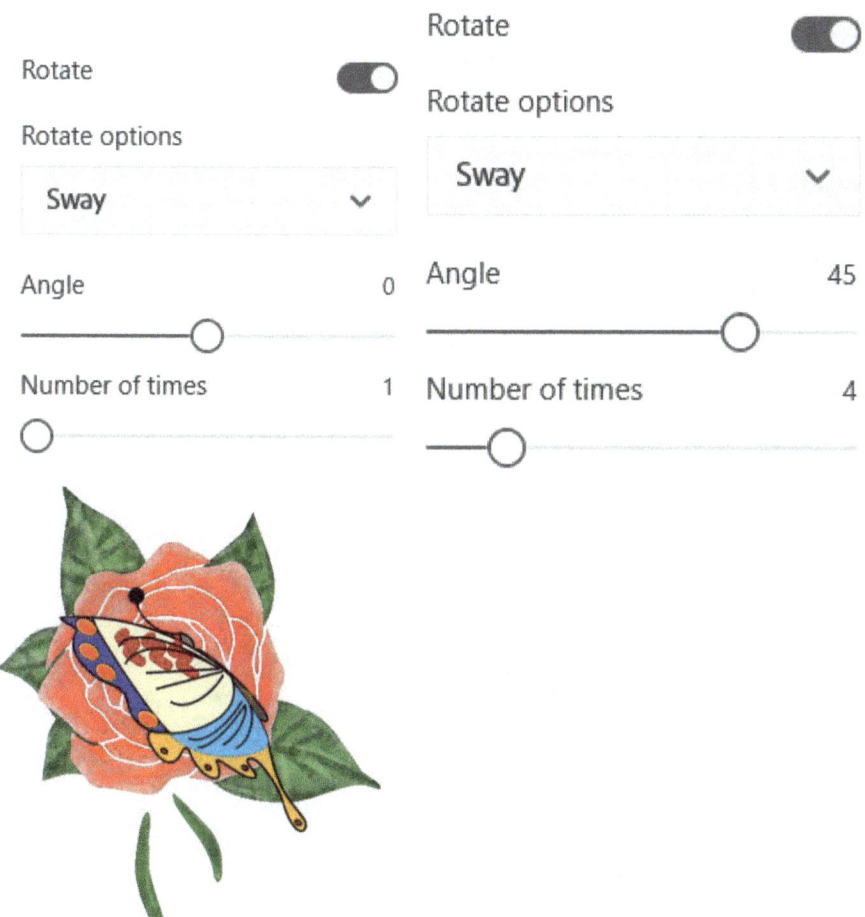

Figure 8-57. *Layer properties Path effects are altered for Rotate Sway as the butterfly moves on the path*

- Spin: Toggles off clockwise and on counterclockwise. Then set the Number of times (1–20) for the motion. By default, the number of times is set to 1. But when increased to 4, the butterfly will do a lot of loops in the air as it moves toward the flower. Refer to Figure 8-58.

593

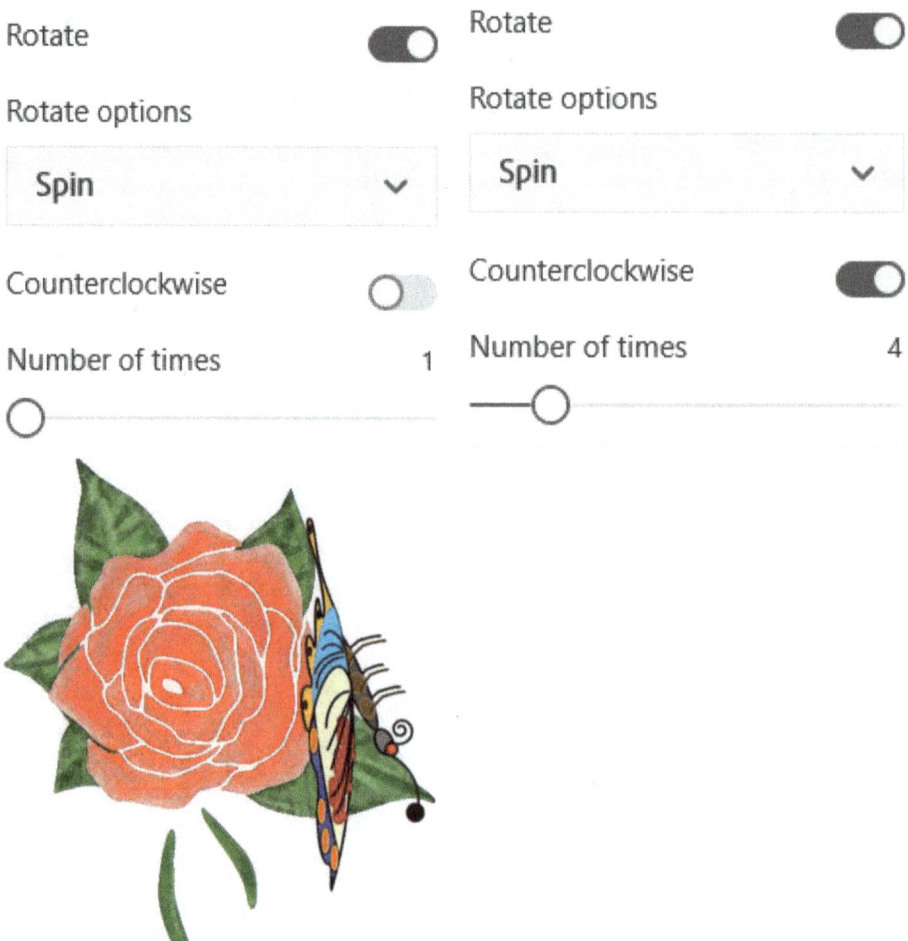

Figure 8-58. *Layer properties Path effects are altered for Rotate Spin as the butterfly moves on the path*

You can set back to the default of Rotate options Sway, Angle 0, and Number of times 1 and then toggle off the Rotate setting for now. Refer to Figure 8-59.

Figure 8-59. *Layer properties Path effects are disabled for Rotate*

CHAPTER 8   BASIC ANIMATION IN FRESCO

- Fade In/Out: You can alter an object's opacity to create smooth transitions at the beginning or end of its motion path. If you do not see this option in the current desktop version, you can alternatively alter each frame's opacity instead. For example, if you want ten frames to fade down to about 10%, start with frame 1 at 100%, and then reduce each frame opacity by 10%, like 90%, then the next 80%, and so on to whatever transition you think blends best. See Frame actions earlier in the chapter. Refer to Figure 8-60.

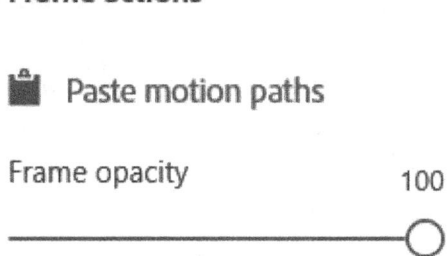

Figure 8-60. *Using the Frame actions to adjust Frame opacity for each frame*

- Align to Path: Aligns objects to the specific path or paths when enabled. By default, it is disabled, and the butterfly stays in a stable vertical position as it moves on the path, but when enabled, it follows the exact path moving more horizontally. Refer to Figure 8-61.

CHAPTER 8   BASIC ANIMATION IN FRESCO

Figure 8-61. *Layer properties Path effects are altered for Align to path when enabled and the result in the animation*

For now, disable the setting of Align to path.

- Speed Options: You can choose two options from the list, Uniform speed or Original speed. This will adjust the playing speed of the motion track. Refer to Figure 8-62.

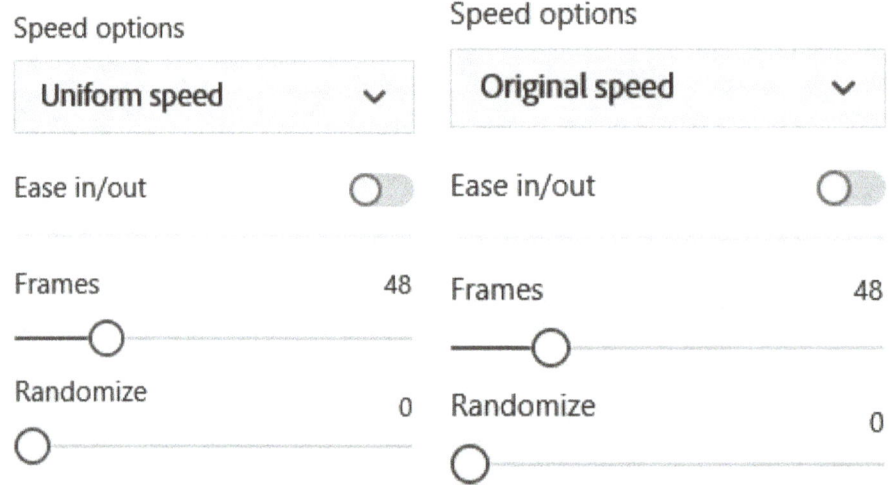

Figure 8-62. *Layer properties Path effects are altered for Speed options*

Uniform speed is currently the default setting I am using, and if you do not alter any of the next settings, it will appear very similar to Original speed.

- Ease In/Out: Enable this effect to make the object, in this case the butterfly, move slowly at first, hover, and then speed up in the animation. In this case, Uniform speed is best, but Original speed seems to break up the frames in the animation. Refer to Figure 8-63.

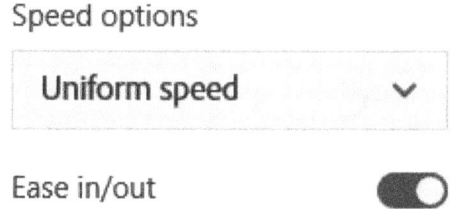

Figure 8-63. *Layer properties Path effects are altered for Speed options of Ease in/out*

- Then set the number of Frames (10–200); by default, it is set to 48, but a higher number will cause a longer pause in the hover and as it moves slowly toward the flower. This is great for insects. Refer to Figure 8-64.

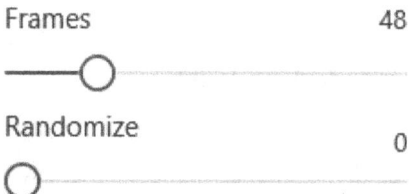

Figure 8-64. *Layer properties Path effects are altered for Speed options of Frames and Randomize*

- Altering the Randomize (0–100) slider from the default of 0 to 75 in conjunction with frames and Ease in and out can also affect the speed at which the butterfly approaches the flower. I encourage you to experiment in this area if you need to adjust the speed of any moving object. Refer to Figure 8-65.

CHAPTER 8 BASIC ANIMATION IN FRESCO

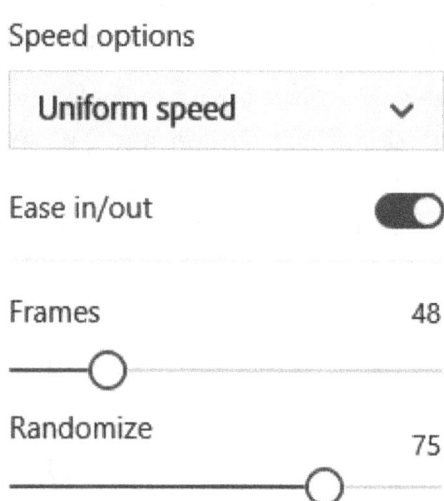

Figure 8-65. *Layer properties Path effects are altered for Speed options when you enable the toggle and move the slider in various combinations*

Note that the desktop version of the application does not have access to the following icons for prebuilt Motion preset: None, Bob, Breathe, Sparkle, Bounce, Spin, Sway, Flicker, Jitter, and Custom. If you have an iPad, you can, however, review these options at the link mentioned at the end of this chapter, and they may be added to a future Windows desktop build.

Later, we will review the additional Motion settings. However, for the moment, you can continue to use the Play all button to preview the motion path options and adjust your settings when you press Pause. Refer to Figure 8-66.

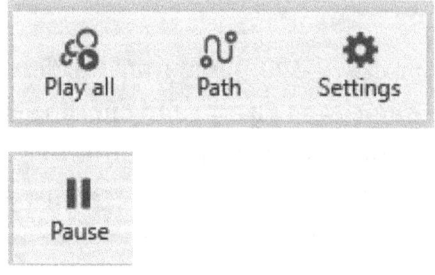

Figure 8-66. *Timeline's Contextual Task bar with Play all/Pause, Path, and Settings icons*

Once you are finished working on **butterfly_frame_by_frame_start.psd** and reviewed the file **butterfly_frame_by_frame_Final_10.psd**, you can close them for now and import and open **car_outdoor_motions.psd**.

Example of a Fresco Document with Multiple Motion Layers

The **car_outdoor_motions.psd** is an example of how complex a Fresco animation could become. In this example, I create a scene of stationary artwork using Illustrator and Photoshop that I thought might be interesting to try animating in Fresco, with two cars moving through a scene somewhere near the mountains and forest. Upon opening this file, you will notice that it has many layers in the scene that remain stationary, such as the mountains, the trees, and road. Refer to Figure 8-67.

CHAPTER 8　BASIC ANIMATION IN FRESCO

Figure 8-67. *Layers that are present in the car animation*

However, many other layers needed to be Motion layers. Those, as mentioned earlier, I made sure to move within in the scene before I imported to Fresco, because unlike Photoshop, Fresco does not understand that artwork from another application exists beyond the boundaries of the canvas. This can be concerning if you are planning to do a repeating movement with Pixel layers that will be turned into Motion layers.

Examples of Motion layers and movements that I used were as follows:

- The forward motion of the body of two cars that are blue and red. In that case, I used a drawing aid of a ruler to draw a straight path while in the timeline and also selected the Path icon in the Contextual Task bar. Refer to Figure 8-68.

Figure 8-68. *Use the Ruler drawing aid when you want to create a horizontal motion path for the car's body layers to move on*

Each layer will need its own path, and so you would need to move the ruler up or down as you work on each layer.

- The same process is true of the shadows beneath the cars. They are on their own layers. Refer to Figure 8-69.

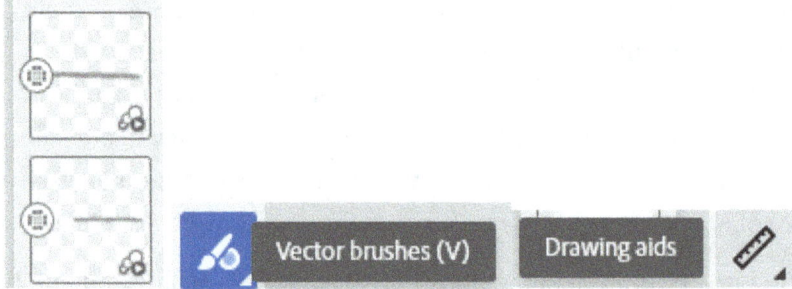

Figure 8-69. *The car's shadow layer can also use a Ruler drawing aid*

- The last component of the cars are the separate wheels, and a Ruler drawing aid is required to make sure the wheels run under the car in the same direction. Refer to Figure 8-70.

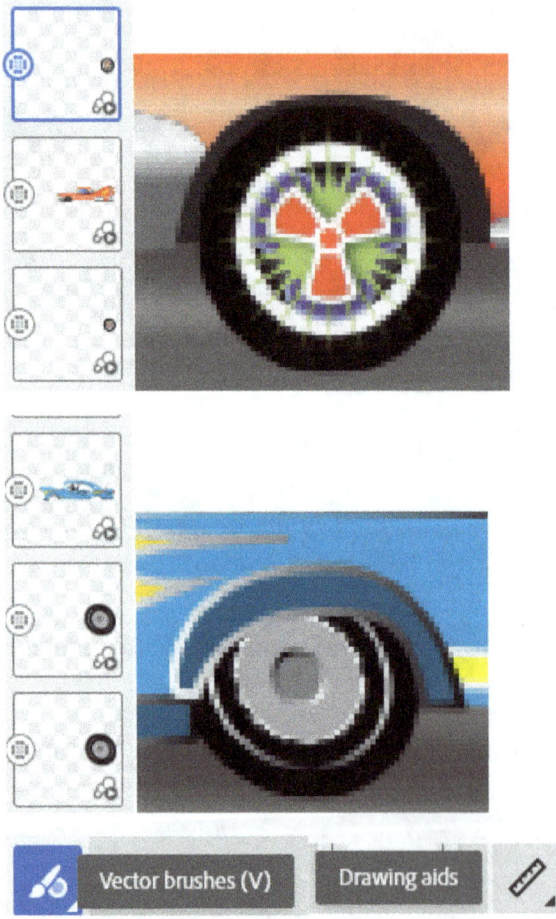

Figure 8-70. *Each car's tire layer can also use a Ruler drawing aid*

CHAPTER 8 BASIC ANIMATION IN FRESCO

If, as you draw the paths, you find that they are not level with the car, you can always use the Path action of Transform paths and then the nudge arrows in the Transform Workspace to move the path for wheels, shadow, or body of the car up or down to align. Refer to Figure 8-71.

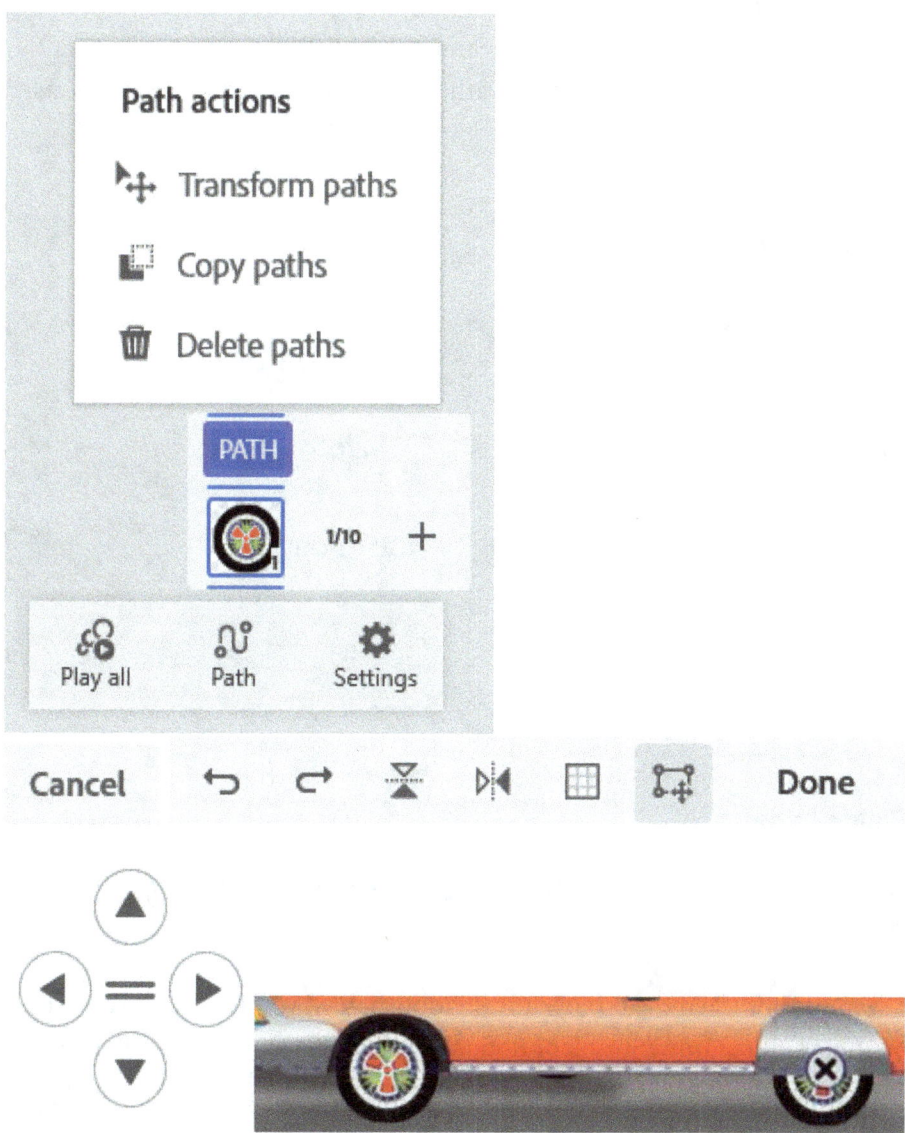

Figure 8-71. *Use the Path actions in the Timeline panel when you need to Transform or nudge a path in the Transform workspace*

603

CHAPTER 8 BASIC ANIMATION IN FRESCO

Note that straight paths unlike free-form paths cannot be scaled only moved or flipped.

Then click Done to exit the Transform workspace and click Play all to test.

Drawing motion movements like this can be a challenge, and you may want to review these Layer properties as well for Path effects, as they vary from car to car. Refer to Figure 8-72.

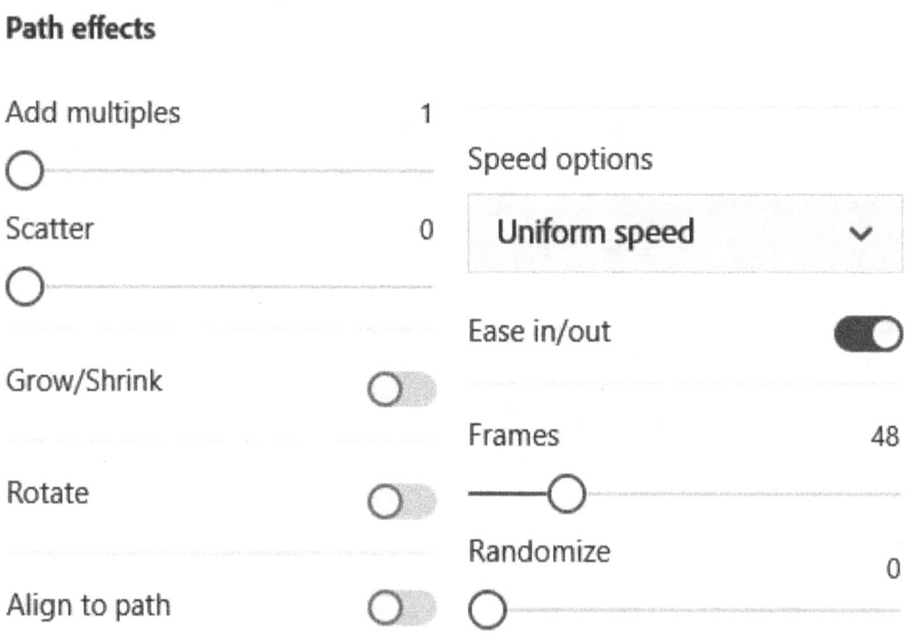

Path effects

Add multiples	1
Scatter	0
Grow/Shrink	
Rotate	
Align to path	

Speed options: **Uniform speed**

Ease in/out (on)

Frames: 48

Randomize: 0

Figure 8-72. *Making adjustments to the Layer properties Path effects for the red car body*

For example, for the red car body and shadow below, you will notice that the motion path does not require Grow/Shrink or Rotate. I do not use align to path because I want the car to remain horizontal with the road and not tip over. I keep the Speed options at Uniform speed, but I then enabled the option of Ease in/out to give the red car a bit of a forward lurch so that it would go faster than the blue car which did not have that option enabled, as it is a slower car. For the car body and shadow, I set the Frames to 48 and kept the Randomize at 0 so that they stayed in sync with the wheels. Refer to Figure 8-72.

CHAPTER 8 BASIC ANIMATION IN FRESCO

The wheels of the red car have a very similar settings to the car's body and shadow. However, they have a Rotate option of Spin, Counterclockwise, Number of times 1, and Align to path. Refer to Figure 8-73.

Figure 8-73. Making adjustments to the Layer properties Path effects for the red car's wheels

605

CHAPTER 8   BASIC ANIMATION IN FRESCO

The wheels in this case needed to be on separate layers so that the spin could be adjusted, but note that while the body of the car moves horizontally, the wheels must also move horizontally on the spin at the same time. This can be a challenge for Fresco to calculate when there are multiple spinning items. Keep this in mind as you in your own projects work on multiple paths and add more Motion layers.

Sometimes, a path may need to be redrawn to adjust the movement, or you may have to start with a frame-by-frame option in which the wheels are combined with the car and rotated for each frame prior to entering Fresco.

The Sun is another example of a Motion layer which has only a dot as path to remain in place. This is good for some spinning objects that you just want to rotate in one spot and not rotate on a path. Refer to Figure 8-74.

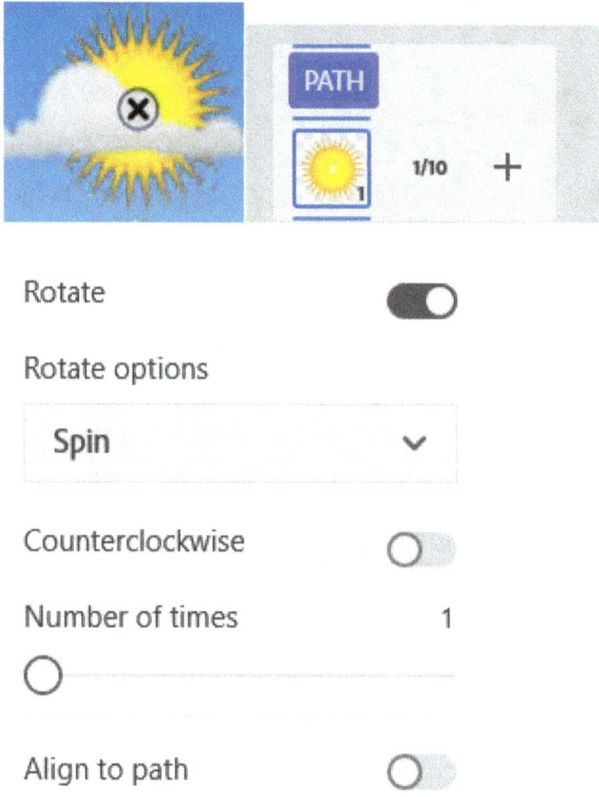

Figure 8-74. *Making adjustments to the Layer properties Path effects for the Sun which only spins and how it appears in the Timeline panel*

CHAPTER 8 BASIC ANIMATION IN FRESCO

As you explore the layers, Layer properties, and Timeline of the file, you will discover that this kind of animation mostly does not need to rely on frames. This is because only the movement is changing, but not the structure. The structure of the car is not as fluid or dynamic as the body of a butterfly which requires frames to appear alive.

Other movements in the animation include clouds. Some cloud layers had just the motion path. The path I drew was either freehand or with a drawing aid Ruler. Refer to Figure 8-75.

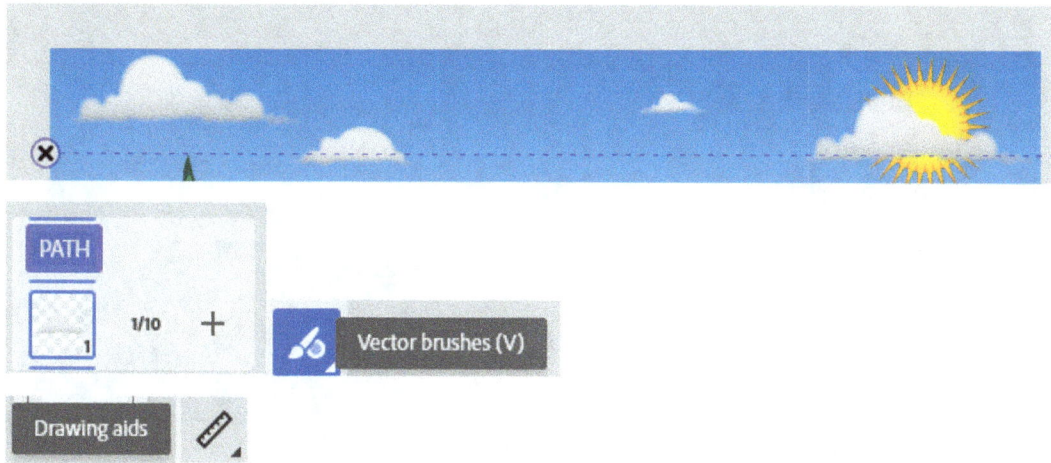

Figure 8-75. *Making adjustments to the path using drawing aids of a cloud and how it appears in the Timeline panel*

However, in one case with the upper left cloud to express how, in weather, clouds may move, appear, and then fade, I added to the motion path with a combination of ten frames so that the frame opacity could be altered to make the cloud appear like it was moving and fading away at the same time in the wind in a random kind of way. Refer to Figure 8-76.

607

CHAPTER 8 BASIC ANIMATION IN FRESCO

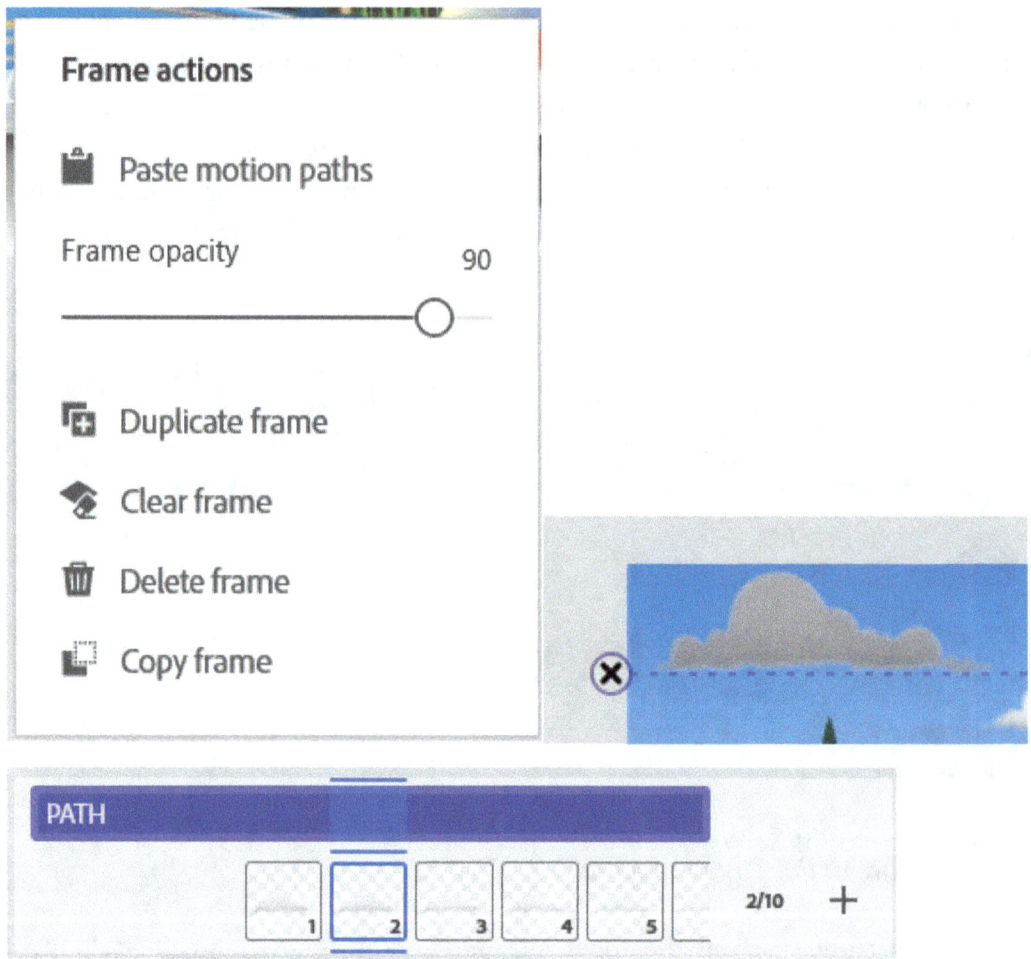

Figure 8-76. *Adjusting the Frame actions Frame opacity for select frames in one of the cloud layers by using multiple copies of the same cloud as it moves along a path*

This is why, as you select each layer, you see the number 10, as not all layers have multiple frames, only this layer, as the Timeline is showing you as a whole how many frames it has for every layer.

Then, in the Layer properties of this clouds path effect, I adjusted the Add multiples to 5 to add more clouds that would fade and in the Speed options changed the speed to Ease in/out and adjusted the Frames (21) and Randomize (57) settings. Refer to Figure 8-77.

608

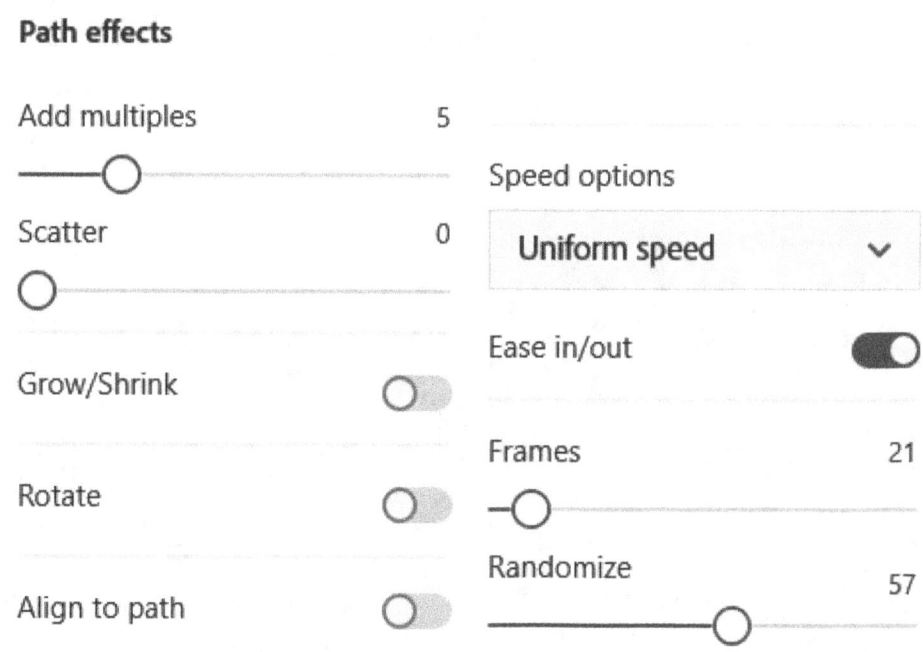

Figure 8-77. *Making adjustments to the Layer properties Path effects for the clouds adjusting Add multiples and changing the Speed options using the sliders*

Other cloud layers, while they did not have frames, also had their speed options altered, and you can click those Motion layers to compare.

As we can see, such animations can become complex. Practice and preparation are key, and such an animation takes many hours to perfect. More motion beyond this would be pushing the limits of the Fresco animation, but we can certainly see that it is capable of creating multiple motions all at once.

You can close the file and look at the next example **car_outdoor_masks_final.psd**.

Adding Clipping Masks or Layer Masks to an Animation

Clipping masks or even layer masks in general can be very useful when you need to hide and show parts of the image or display altered colors while the animation is playing. Refer to Figure 8-78.

CHAPTER 8　BASIC ANIMATION IN FRESCO

Figure 8-78. *A car animation with frames containing different masks*

In this example, one layer has a Motion layer with a layer mask applied. And you can review this in the Timeline and Layer properties panel as well. Refer to Figure 8-79.

CHAPTER 8 BASIC ANIMATION IN FRESCO

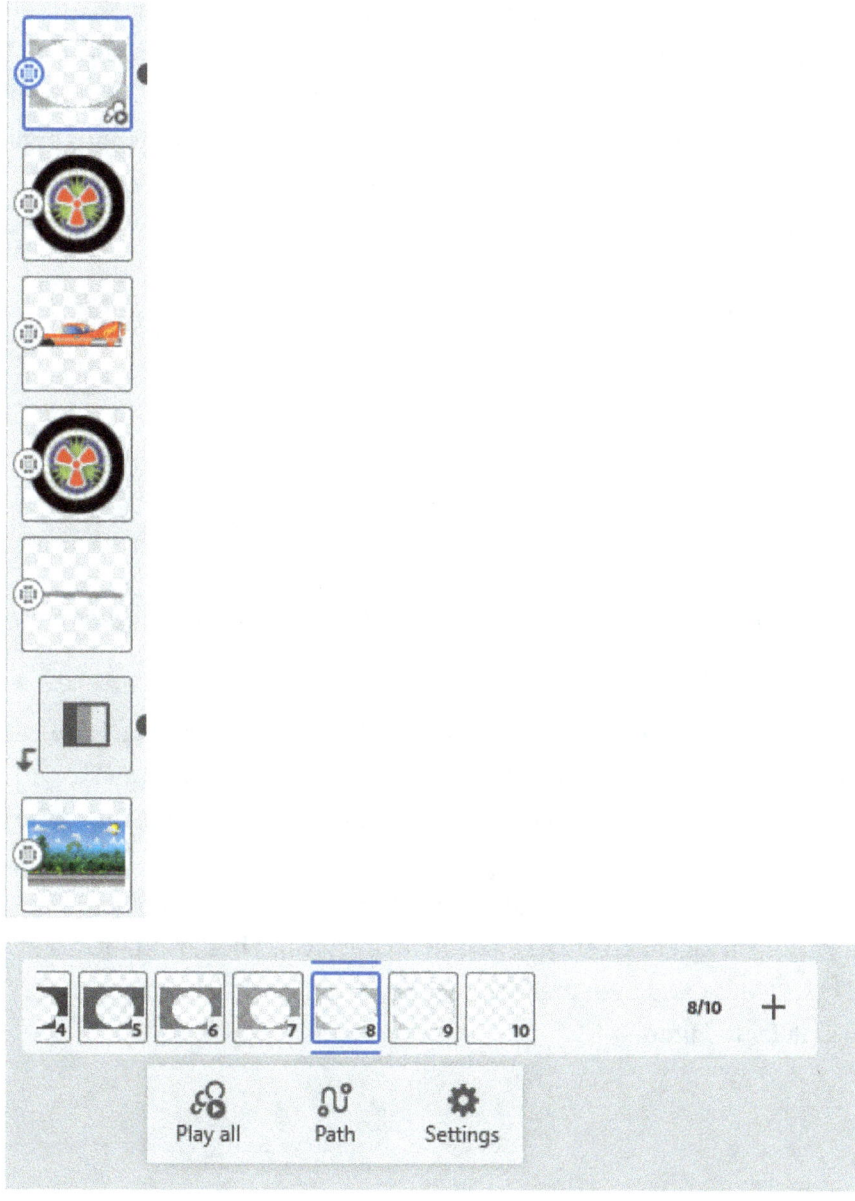

Figure 8-79. *An altered layer mask can be added to each frame to make it change and how it appears in the Layer panel and viewed in the Layer properties*

611

To add a clipping mask to a Motion layer, you need to use the Layer panel and the Vertical Taskbar to add the mask, as we reviewed in Chapter 5. However, you will notice that in the Layer panel, if the clipping mask is also an Adjustment layer, then in the Timeline panel, no additional frames can be added or Frame actions applied. Adjustment layers must remain as stationary items unless first converted to Pixel layers and then created as a Motion layer. Refer to Figure 8-80.

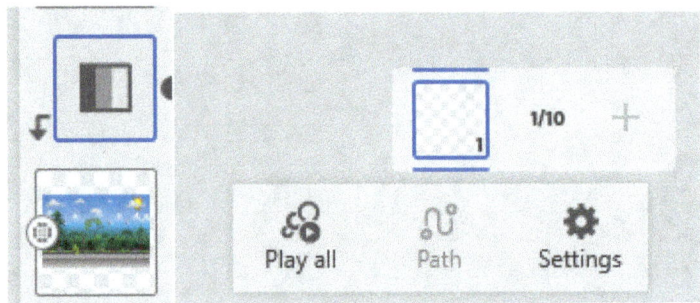

Figure 8-80. *Layer panel with a clipping mask that is also an Adjustment layer to give a unique color effect*

However, for Pixel layers that are clipping masks or Pixel layers that have been turned into Motion layers, to them, you can always add a transitioning layer mask.

To begin adding a layer mask, select the first frame that you want to add the layer mask to.

In this case, with my Fill tool, I had filled a Pixel layer with solid black. Then, I used my Selection Ellipse tool to create a selection on the layer. Then, with the Contextual Task bar, I chose Mask and then the Mask action, when I right-clicked on the layer of Invert mask. Refer to Figure 8-81.

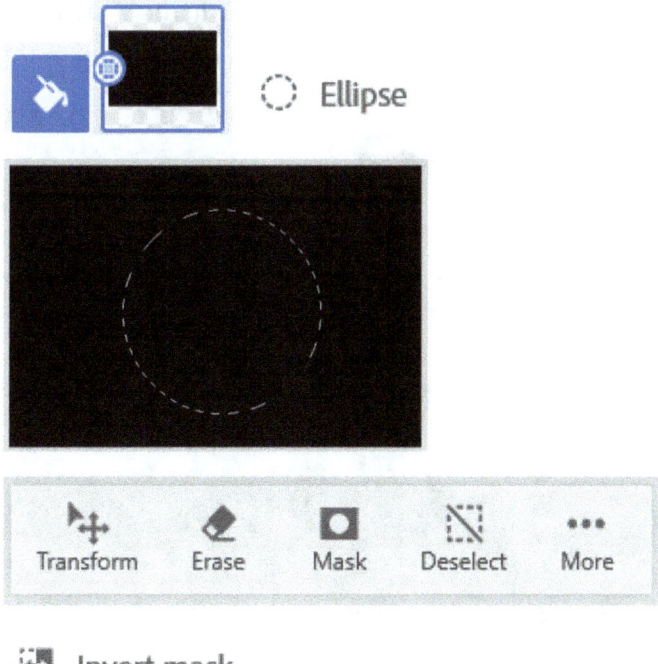

Figure 8-81. *A black layer can be filled and then a selection tool can be used to draw an ellipse with the Contextual Task bar to add the mask and then the Mask action of Invert mask afterward*

Not choosing to Invert mask would have left a black circle in the middle of the image so that step was important. This created a type of port hole to see the image behind the layer. Refer to Figure 8-82.

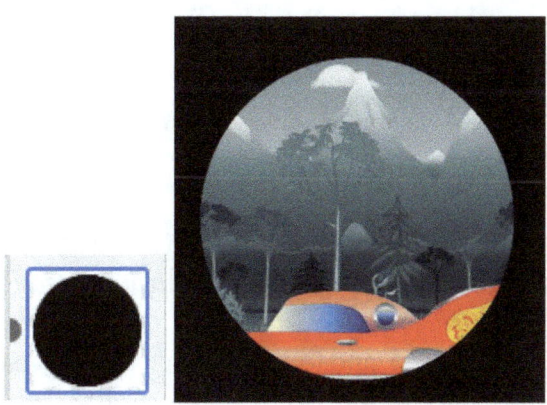

Figure 8-82. *When the circle layer mask is inverted, it can appear like a window to the background scene*

However, this only affects one frame as we can see in the Timeline. Refer to Figure 8-83.

Figure 8-83. *A layer mask is only ever applied to one frame at a time*

The layer masks, to animate, need multiple frames to appear or disappear, depending on what frame is selected. Refer to Figure 8-84.

Figure 8-84. *A layer mask needs to be transformed frame by frame if you want to see movement*

To do that, you need to duplicate your frame using the frame action several times, which I did again so I had at least nine or ten frames. Refer to Figure 8-85.

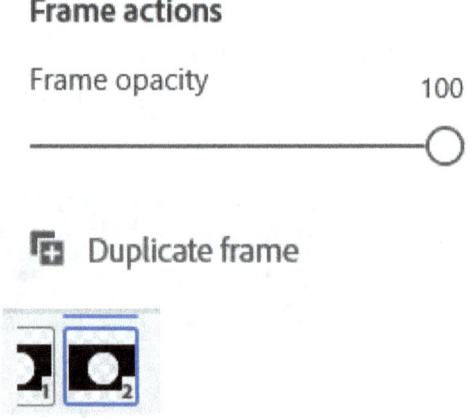

Figure 8-85. *The Frame action of Duplicate frame was used for a layer mask*

Afterward, while the layer mask and frame is selected, you can do such things as alter Frame opacity or use your Transform tool, in this case to expand and scale both the black content and the mask at the same time. Refer to Figure 8-86.

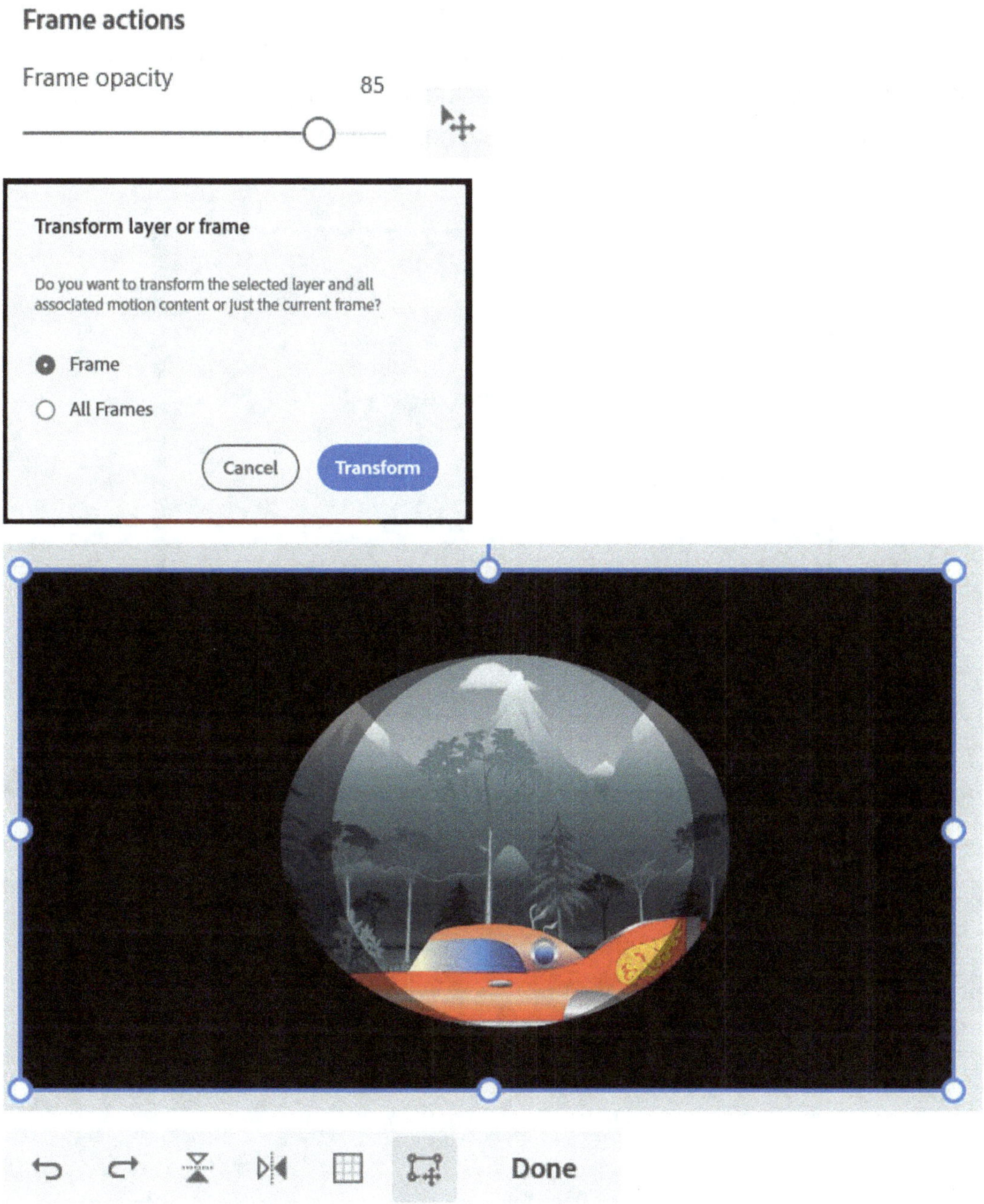

CHAPTER 8   BASIC ANIMATION IN FRESCO

Figure 8-86. *Multiple frames that contain the layer mask can each have different frame opacities, or enter the Transform workspace to change the size of the frame*

CHAPTER 8   BASIC ANIMATION IN FRESCO

Note that if you scale off the canvas and click the Done button, you may get a warning that some areas of the layer or mask may be cropped. In this case, you can click Continue or Cancel the transformation. Refer to Figure 8-87.

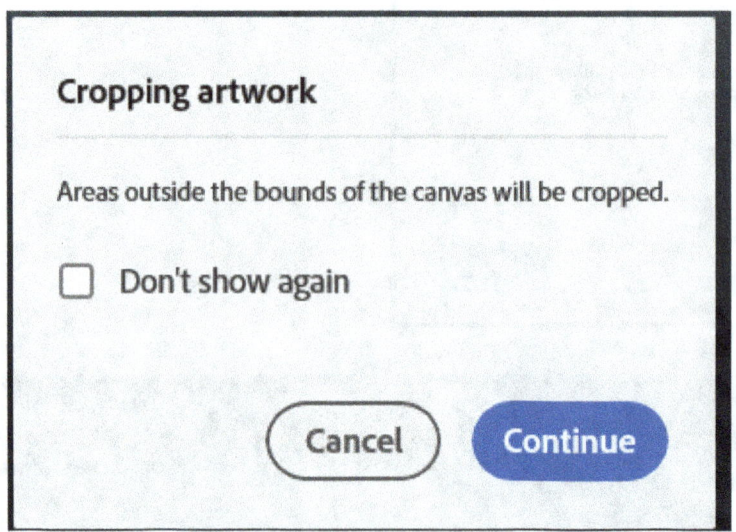

Figure 8-87. *The dialog box Cropping artwork that may appear when you scale the frame beyond it default boundaries as you try to exit the Transform workspace*

Once you click the Done button to confirm, you can exit the Transform workspace. Refer to Figure 8-87.

Also, as the final frame 10, optionally you can add a blank frame. Notice when you do this that this frame contains no layer mask, which you can review in your Layer properties as you select each frame and compare. Refer to Figure 8-88.

CHAPTER 8 BASIC ANIMATION IN FRESCO

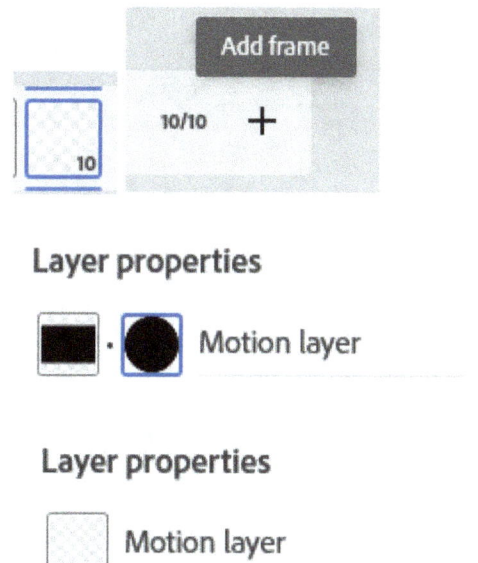

Figure 8-88. *Add a blank frame to the end of the Motion layer if you want no layer mask to appear on that frame*

Note For Text layers, they too must be converted to Pixel layers before you can convert and edit it as a Motion layer.

You can close this file and return to the file **butterfly_frame_by_frame_Final_10.psd** to review the Timeline's Contextual task bars Motion settings to complete the next set of steps.

Configuring Motion Settings

In the Timeline's Contextual Task bar, while working on the animation, you will click the Settings icon to get additional Motion settings. Refer to Figure 8-89.

CHAPTER 8 BASIC ANIMATION IN FRESCO

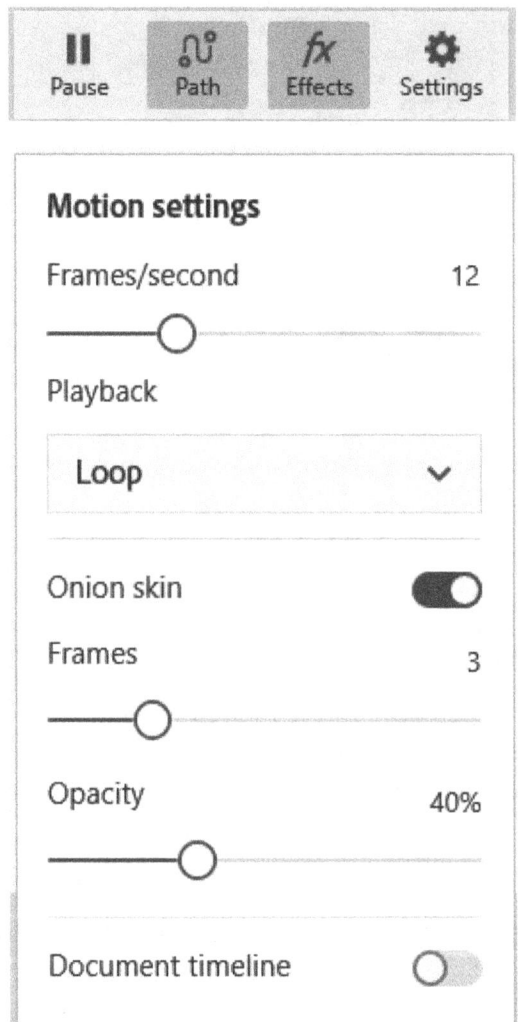

Figure 8-89. *Timeline Contextual Task bar and the Settings button Motion settings panel*

- Frames/Second (1–40): Sets the speed of the animation in frames per second (FPS). Increasing or decreasing FPS correspondingly increases or decreases the speed. GIF animations for the Web might be acceptable at a lower FPS like 5–12, but for use in another application, like for a video, the FPS would need to be increased to 24–30 for better quality, but this does increase the file size as well. More frames can make the animation less choppy, but with a frame

CHAPTER 8   BASIC ANIMATION IN FRESCO

by frame, you may also need to create enough transitional images to balance the speed of the movement if it appears to be moving too fast. In my case, I left it at the default of 12. Refer to Figure 8-89.

- Playback: Set for preview and final playback settings; the options are Loop, Boomerang, and Play once. For videos or animations that are not cyclical, Play once is a good option, but for a GIF animation, a Loop or Boomerang might be required when the animation is cyclical. I will put this butterfly animation on Play once, but for the **car_outdoor_motions.psd** animation, Loop would be a better choice. See Publish and export settings for additional final loop settings for MP4 files to publish and export or share workspace in various motion formats, later in this chapter. Refer to Figure 8-90.

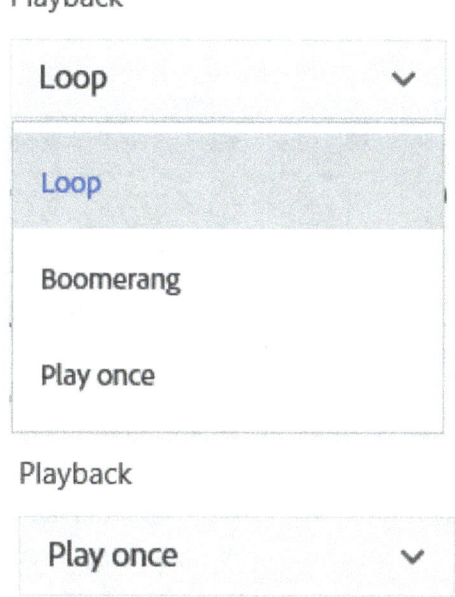

Figure 8-90. *Motion settings adjust the Playback options in the drop-down list when you want to Play all an animation*

- Onion Skin: When enabled, lets you set the number of frames (1–10) that you want to see before and after the selected frame visibly. Opacity (10–100%) adjusts the transparency of each onion skin frame to help see the frames better. This displays as a reference to the

619

contents of the previous and the following frames. As you preview the drawing, on the frame, this can help you trace or make minor Transformation changes more precisely. Refer to Figure 8-91.

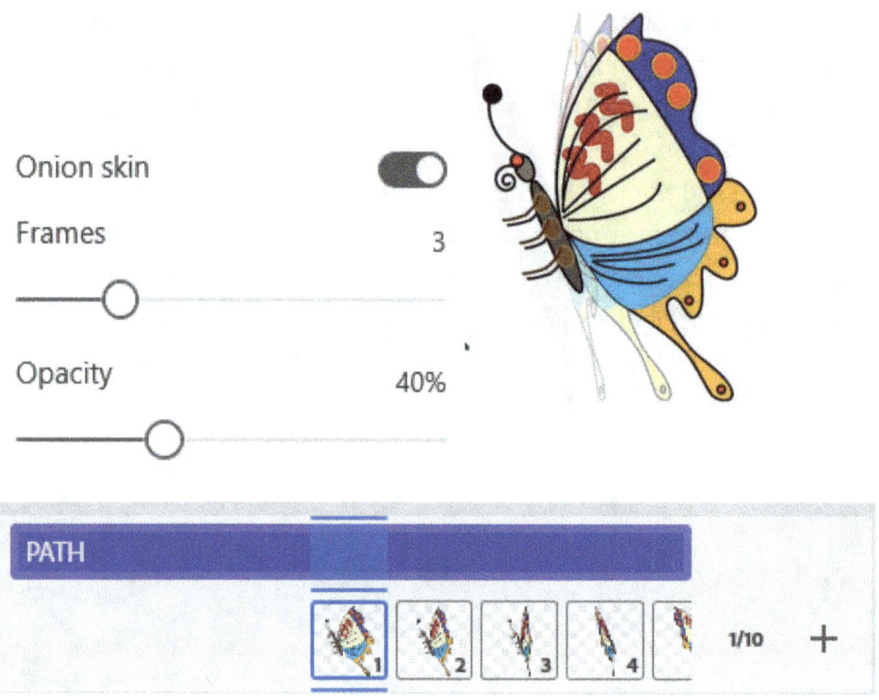

Figure 8-91. Adjust the Motion settings Onion skin when you need to preview the frames in the Timeline

Using these kinds of guides could also assist you for adjusting the opacity for each frame or, overall, using the Layers properties for Layer opacity. Note that as you work with the timeline, the frame under the play-head appears in full color. You can disable the settings at any time, and it does not affect the final export of the animation. Refer to Figure 8-91.

- Document Timeline: When enabled lets you access the toggle Show paths as frames, which is by default disabled. Refer to Figure 8-92.

CHAPTER 8   BASIC ANIMATION IN FRESCO

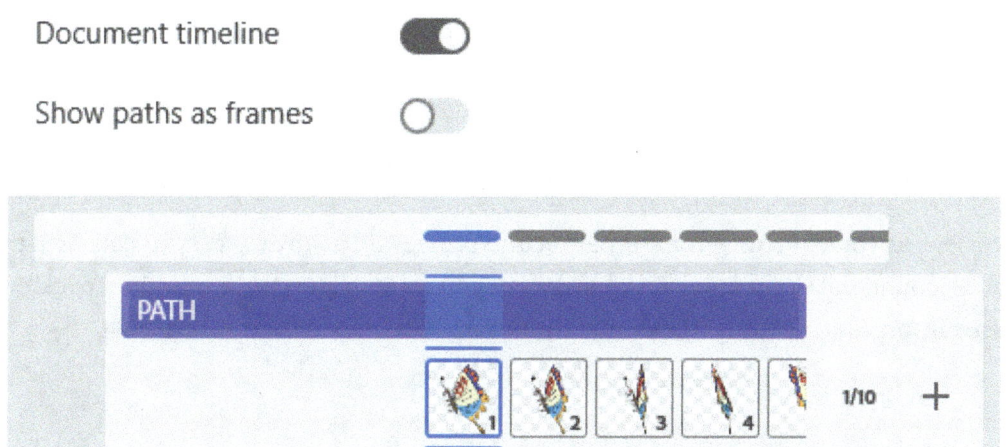

Figure 8-92. Enable the Motion settings Document timeline and review the Timeline panel

You can display all the paths as frames when you enable the Show paths as frames in timeline for better navigation, and the number in this case increases to 48. Refer to Figure 8-93.

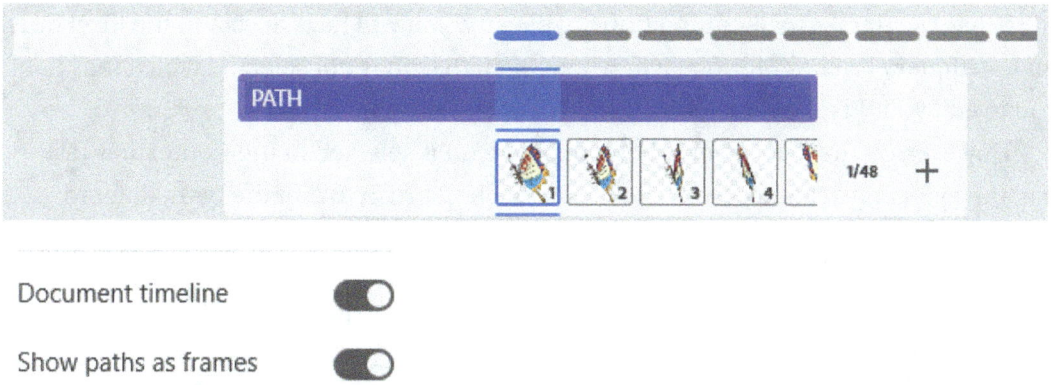

Figure 8-93. Enable the Motion settings Show paths as frames and review the Timeline panel

This setting is very useful when you click the line above the frame as it can show you exactly which area of the path and frame you are on at the same time. This is helpful when you want to paint on a new layer above the current frame set and need to match the positioning of the new frame below the lower frames. We will see an example of this in the final project.

CHAPTER 8   BASIC ANIMATION IN FRESCO

Disable these options in the panel when you don't want them visible or do not want to show the paths as frames. Refer to Figure 8-89.

Play All and Pause Animation to Adjust the Frames

To review, as you work on your animation and preview it, at any times, you can click the Play all icon in the Contextual Task bar. When you want to stop the animation, click the Pause button which causes the animation to stop moving. Refer to Figure 8-94.

Figure 8-94. *Timeline Contextual Task bar Play all options*

While the frames in the animation are playing, you will have access to the Pixel brush on a stationary layer or Motion layer when the path icon is not selected which may help you to edit your Pixel layer.

However, on the Pixel layer, when the path icon is selected in the Contextual Task bar, then you only have access to the Vector/Motion brush to edit the path. Refer to Figure 8-95.

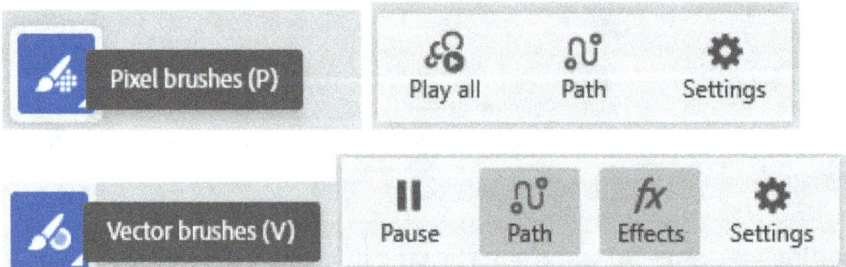

Figure 8-95. *Use a Pixel brush tool for editing frames when path in Timeline's Contextual Task bar is not selected, and use a Vector/Motion brush tool for editing paths when path in Timeline's Contextual Task bar is selected*

CHAPTER 8 BASIC ANIMATION IN FRESCO

If at any point you do not need to view the Animation Timeline and its Contextual Task bar, click the Animation icon to close it. However, the icon badge will remain on any Motion layers in the Layer panel. Refer to Figure 8-96.

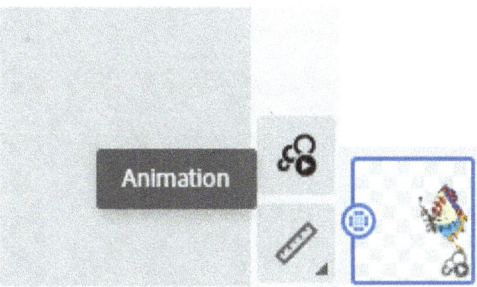

Figure 8-96. *Turn off and on the Animation settings, but the Motion Layer badge on the layer in the Layer panel remains*

Tip If you do need to remove a Motion badge from a Motion layer with many frames, currently doing so directly is not possible using the Layer action of Convert to pixel layer. It is best to copy the content of the selected frame that you want to keep in the Timeline, and then in the Layers action panel, choose the option Paste onto a new pixel layer. Refer to Figure 8-97.

CHAPTER 8   BASIC ANIMATION IN FRESCO

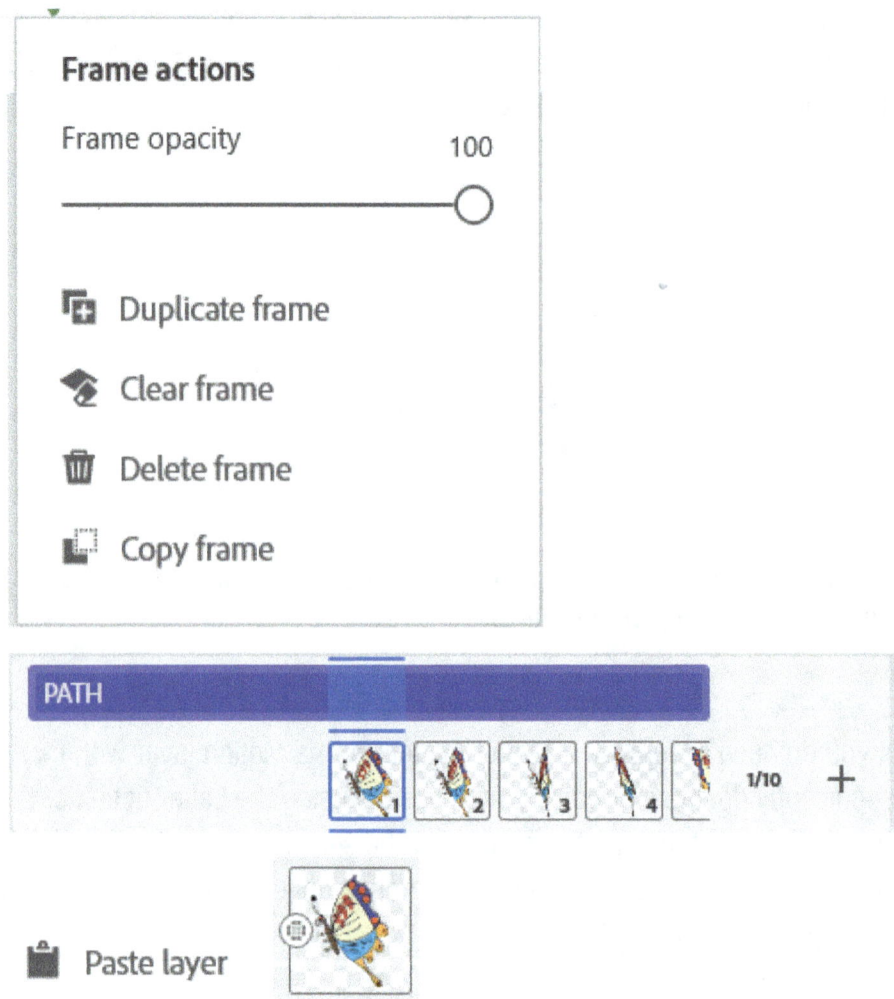

Figure 8-97. *You can select a frame in the Timeline panel and use the Frame action of Copy frame and the Layer action of Paste frame to move to a new layer*

Then, afterward, delete or hide the Motion layer.

Continue to review the file **butterfly_frame_by_frame_Final_10.psd** at this point. Notice that in this file I kept the motion layer visible and original butterfly layers hidden.

Publish and Export in Various Motion Formats

While working on the animation, at some point, once it is completed, you will want to export the animation. Based on your project, Fresco offers at least three options:

624

- MP4: A video file format. Later, in another application such as Photoshop or Premiere Pro, you can add audio or combine with other video files known as tracks. See Chapter 9 on more details regarding the application Premiere Pro.

- GIF: A motion graphic format that is often used on the Internet. This format has no sound but is ideal for small repetitive animations for your website or social media page.

- PNG Sequence: A format for animation or sequence of separate image files based on the motions in the file and frames. This file format allows for images that can contain transparent areas. You can export the PNG file for further editing in Adobe After Effects. See Chapter 9 for a link to information on this application.

To access these options, you need to use the Share icon found in the upper right of the Title bar in the menu and go to the Publish & export (Social media, other formats) arrow. Refer to Figure 8-98.

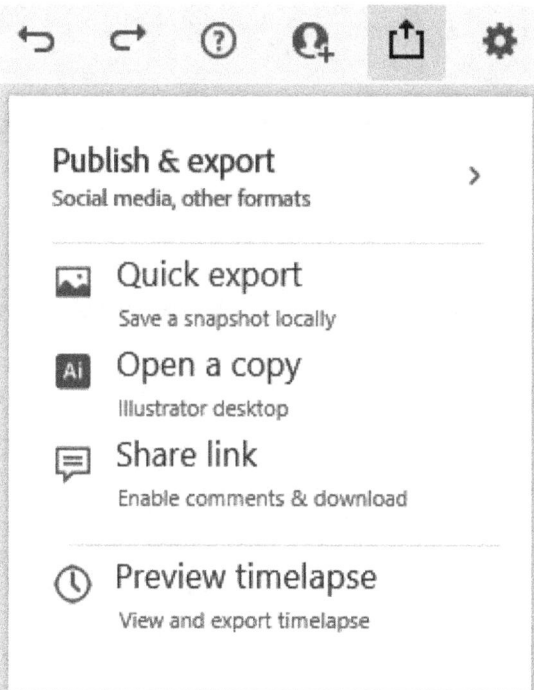

Figure 8-98. Share icon for the options of Publish & export

CHAPTER 8   BASIC ANIMATION IN FRESCO

This will take you to the Share workspace where you will see, on the left, several export tabs. They are Quick export, Export as, Timelapse export, and Motion. We will look at Quick export and Export as found in the Share workspace later in Chapter 9. Timelapse export can create a type of preview of the animation. However, for now, we will focus on the Motion tab; click the arrow to reveal the other options in the list. Refer to Figure 8-99.

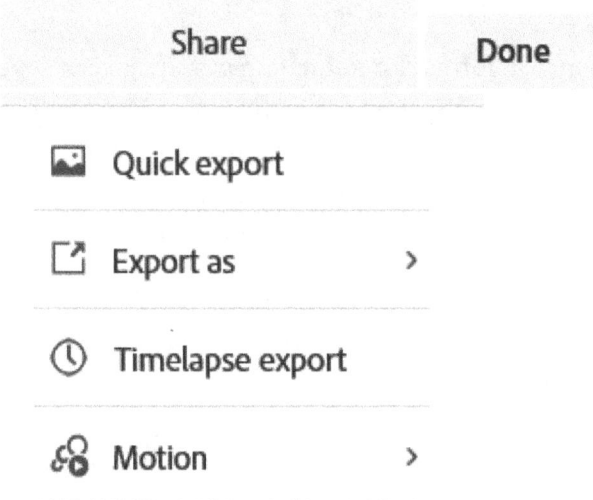

Figure 8-99. *Share workspace options when Motion layers are present in a file*

Note that if your file has no Motion layers, this option Motion, will not appear in this list. However, Timelapse Export may still appear in the list.

Motion Settings

The Motion tab lets you set the following settings:

- File Name: This can be a new name different from your Fresco file that you want to choose to export your animation as. Refer to Figure 8-100.

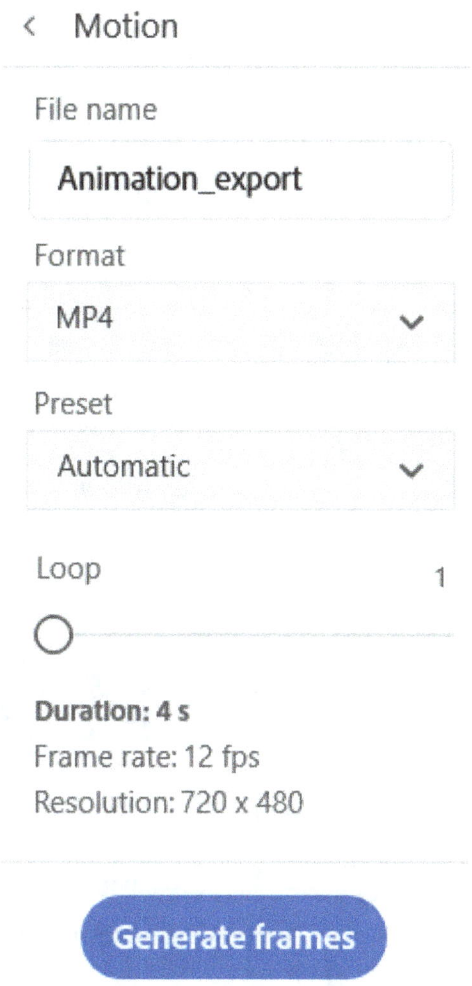

CHAPTER 8   BASIC ANIMATION IN FRESCO

Figure 8-100. *Share Motion options for MP4 files*

- Format: Choose one of the following formats from the list: MP4, GIF, or PNG sequence.

MP4 has a preset of Automatic (high resolution and larger file size) or Web ready (used to optimize the size and quality of the output for web displays). Then you can set how many times you want the file to loop, between 1 and 40 times since an MP4 cannot play forever. Refer to Figure 8-100.

GIF allows you to set whether the fill will have a transparent background or not. Earlier, however, in the Animation setting, you set Playback options for the animation to loop, boomerang, or only play once. However, be aware that when you export the animation, it will play as a loop when previewed. Refer to Figure 8-101.

627

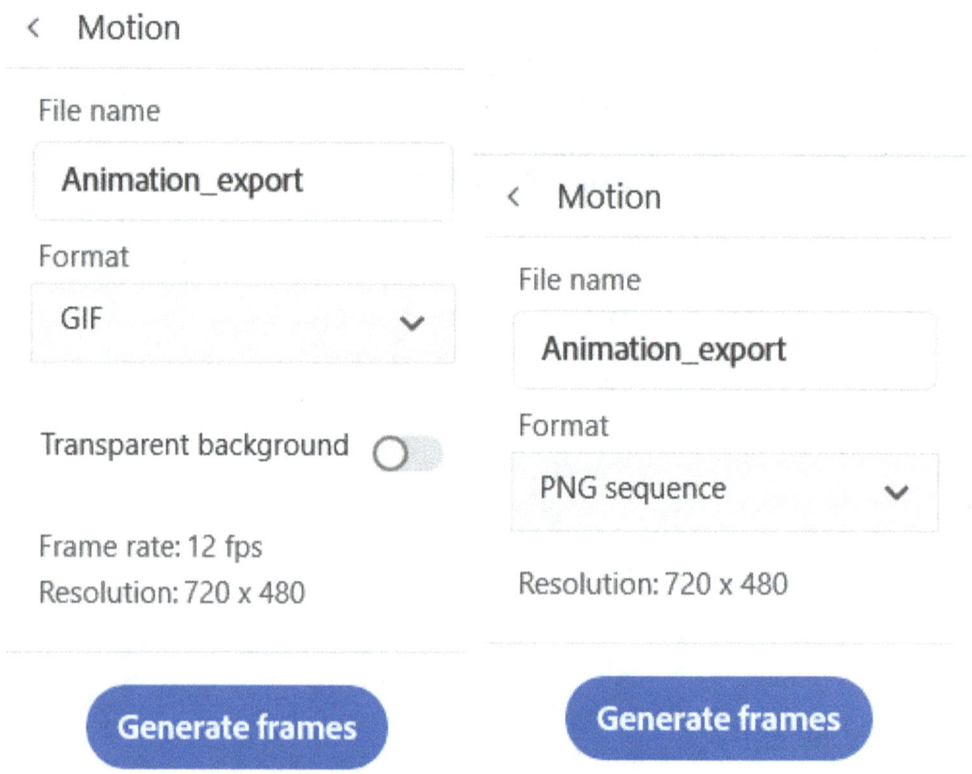

CHAPTER 8   BASIC ANIMATION IN FRESCO

Figure 8-101. Share Motion options for GIF and PNG sequence files

PNG sequence has no additional settings as it will be a collection of images stored as a PNG set. Be aware of this if it is a very lengthy animation. In my example, there are at least 48 images. Refer to Figure 8-101.

Each option will then list a summary such as the Duration, Frame rate, and Resolution which will vary for each file. These settings cannot be altered here, only in the original document outside of the Share Workspace when you alter settings for the animation or document size, as seen at the beginning of this chapter. Refer to Figure 8-100 and Figure 101.

When you have chosen your settings, you would then click the Generate frames button, and a Motion export preview is then generated which you can preview and play. Refer to Figure 8-102.

CHAPTER 8   BASIC ANIMATION IN FRESCO

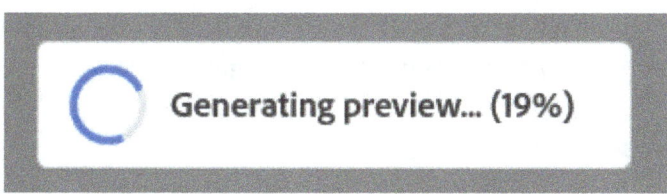

Figure 8-102. *Generating preview progress circle that appears while a preview animation is generated*

If all is correct, you would then click the Export button or Cancel button to exit and go back to adjust settings. Clicking Export allows you to save the file somewhere on your desktop so that you can use the file for a specific project or later share with others. This is what saving the file as an MP4 or GIF preview would look like. Refer to Figure 8-103.

Figure 8-103. *Generated preview is tested and the Export button is clicked*

629

CHAPTER 8   BASIC ANIMATION IN FRESCO

You would then find a location in a folder to save the file on your computer and click the Save button as seen with the MP4 file. Refer to Figure 8-104.

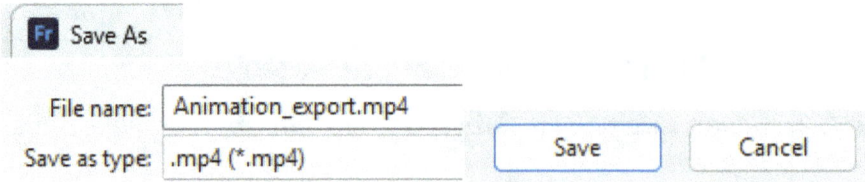

Figure 8-104. Save As dialog box for MP4 video files

Note that for the PNG sequence, when you click Export, this will put all the images into a (.zip) folder which you would need to double-click and extract the images from the folder. I would not recommend playing a preview of it in the Motion export area as this format takes quite a long time to play being many images. In this case, click Export right away rather than play the preview.

Here is how the files would appear in a folder. You can find these examples saved in my **Export_Files** folder. Refer to Figure 8-105.

Figure 8-105. Examples of exported files from Fresco

Once the export is complete, you can click the Done button to exit the Share workspace. Refer to Figure 8-106.

Figure 8-106. Exit the Share workspace after clicking Done

CHAPTER 8   BASIC ANIMATION IN FRESCO

Adjusting the Timing by Adding More Frames to Improve Motions

You may find that when you export the butterfly animation, it is not landing on the correct frame with its wings open. This is because there are only 10 frames, and we are working with 12 FPS so that the frame that the animation ends on is not the one we want. What I then did to correct this was, after exiting the Share workspace and reviewing my exported files, I then returned to my Fresco file and selected my butterfly Motion layer and frame 1. And then I duplicated frame 1 two more times so that I had a total of 12 frames. Refer to Figure 8-107.

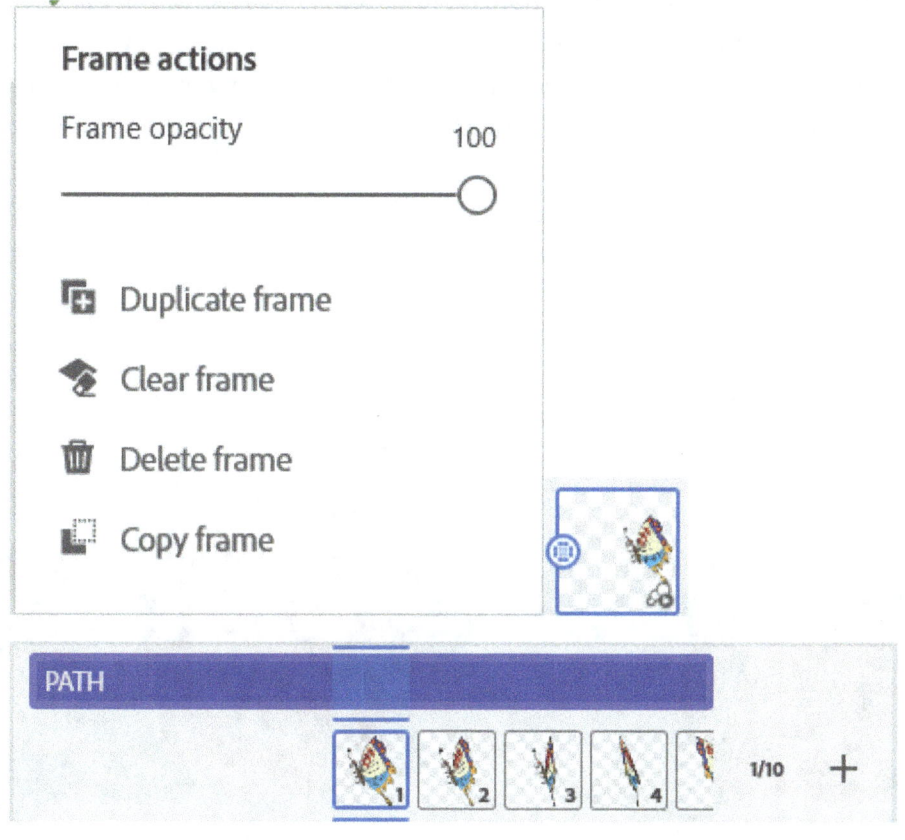

Figure 8-107. *Reviewing the Frame actions in the Timeline panel*

The original frame 1 is now frame 3 with two duplicates before it. Refer to Figure 8-108.

631

CHAPTER 8　BASIC ANIMATION IN FRESCO

Figure 8-108. *Adding more frames to the Timeline panel to correct the movement of the butterfly*

When I click Play all, the butterfly appears now to glide a bit more, before it lands on the leaf, but now you can see its feet and wings better. This maybe something you need to consider when an animation moves at 12 frames per second and the placement is crucial to where and when an object stops. If the butterfly had just flown out of the picture as the cars or clouds moved out of the scene in the other animation, then this would not have been important, and the frames could have remained at ten. Refer to Figure 8-109.

Figure 8-109. *Reviewing the movements of the butterfly with the Play all button*

632

CHAPTER 8 BASIC ANIMATION IN FRESCO

In this case, once I was happy with the placement, I then returned to the Publish & export Share workspace and exported and generated the frames for my motion files again with a slightly different file name for comparison. In this case, I added an _12 at the end so that I could review the differences. These are found in the **Export_Files** folder. Refer to Figure 8-110.

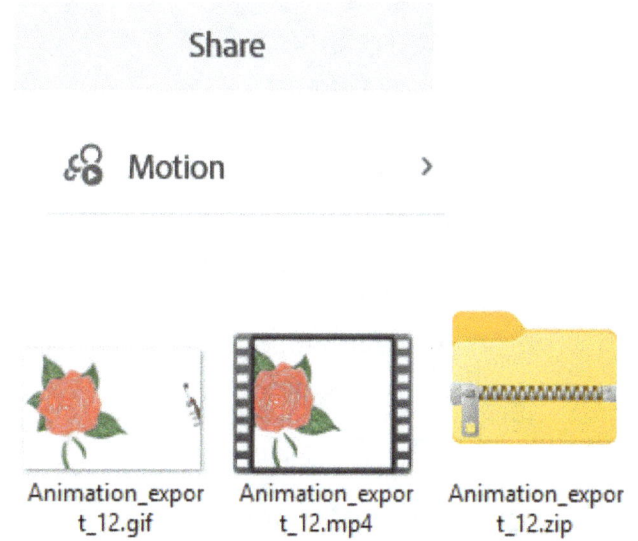

Figure 8-110. *Exporting new Motion files using the Share workspace*

You can also see the file **butterfly_frame_by_frame_Final_12.psd** if you need to compare.

You can see how this is all part of the animation process to get your animation to function as you intend.

Timelapse Settings

Another way to check your animation or create video before you share is also under Preview timelapse or Timelapse export in the Share workspace. However, this can take a bit more time before you see the preview result, but you can play the recording, export the file, and save the MP4 on your desktop. Click Cancel if you need to exit without exporting. Refer to Figure 8-111.

CHAPTER 8　BASIC ANIMATION IN FRESCO

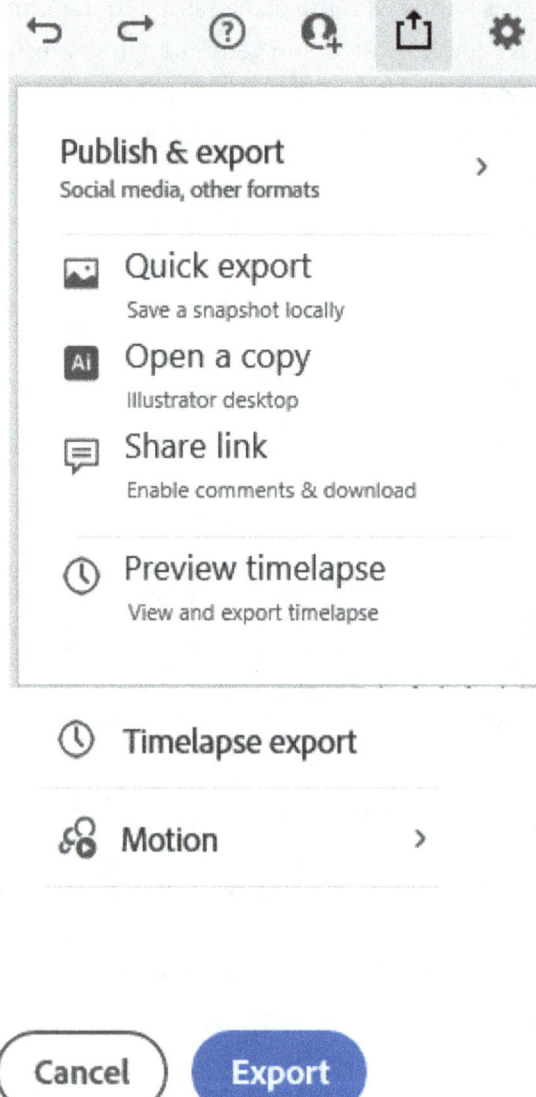

Figure 8-111. *Share panel and Share workspace from Timelapse export*

Tip Timelapse video settings can be found under the upper Settings gear icon ➤ App settings ➤ General ➤ Timelapse settings. You can adjust settings such as

Quality: Low, medium, or high

Dimensions: Original Fresco or High resolution

These settings will vary depending on the operating system and may require more diskspace based on the settings chosen. However, Fresco does not have the ability to regenerate the original art to a new resolution. Refer to Figure 8-112.

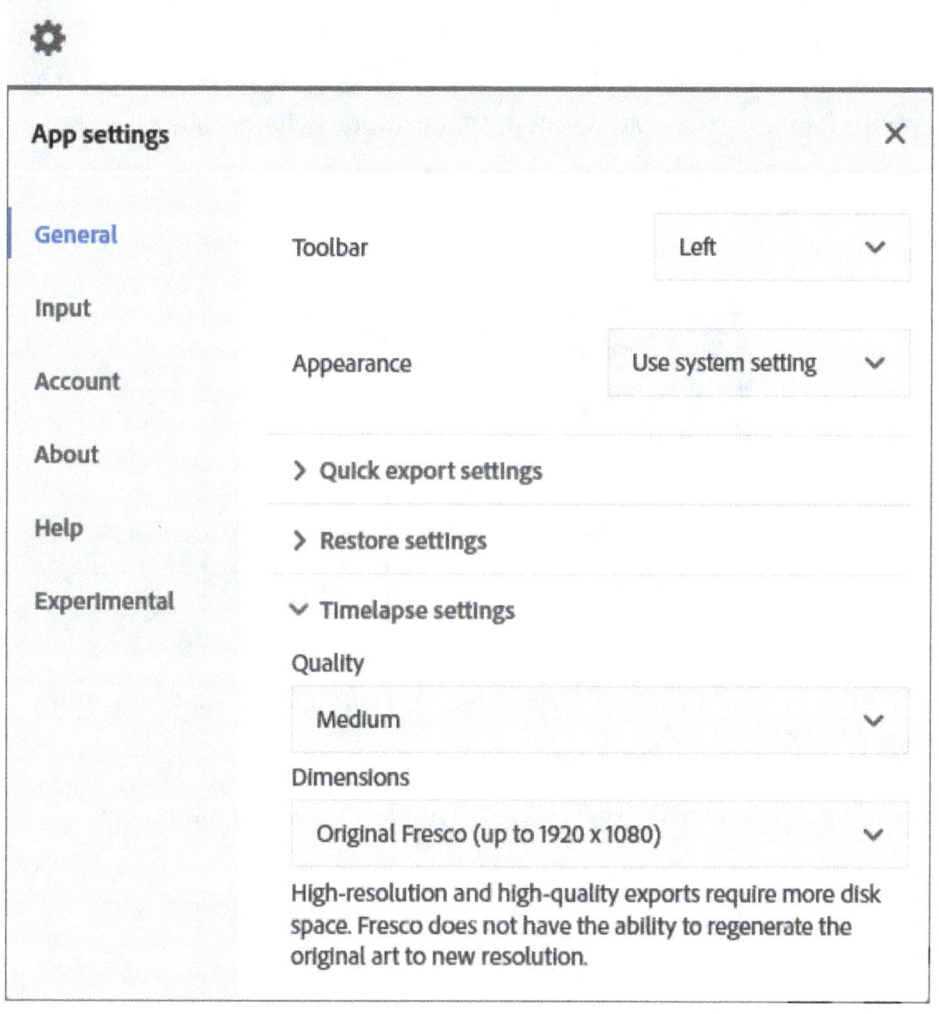

Figure 8-112. *App settings icon and dialog box for the Timelapse settings*

CHAPTER 8   BASIC ANIMATION IN FRESCO

More details can be found on this topic at this link:

https://helpx.adobe.com/fresco/using/publish-export-share.html

More details on Fresco animation can be found at the following link:

https://helpx.adobe.com/fresco/using/apply-motion-to-artwork.html

Possible New Drawing and Animation Features That Are to Come

Remember on your Fresco Home page to occasionally click the New and upcoming features View area under the What's coming tab. Earlier, I spoke about the addition of symmetry drawing in Chapter 4. However, for animation, motion GIFs will also have more options for transparent backgrounds in the future. Refer to Figure 8-113.

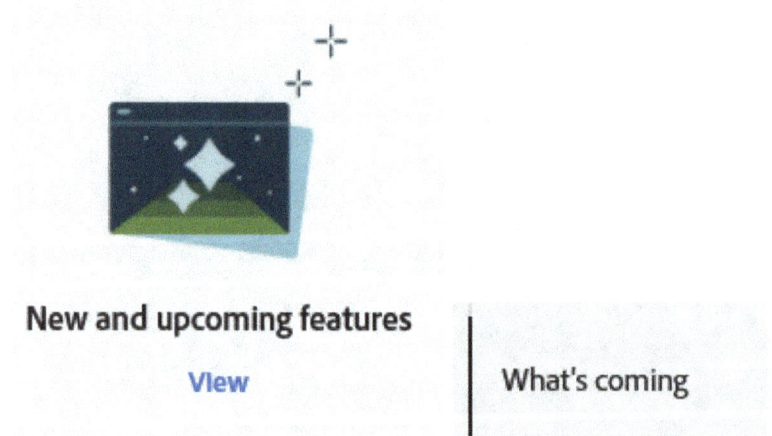

Figure 8-113. *From the Fresco Home page, you can always view new and upcoming features*

Fresco users can also make suggestions to Adobe as well, from this page.

CHAPTER 8　BASIC ANIMATION IN FRESCO

Animation Photoshop Tips

For those who are Photoshop users, you can open, for example, your recently created Fresco GIF animation in Photoshop and use Timeline panel if you need to adjust your looping again to a more precise time. Fresco appears to consider the Forever setting as 255 times. Refer to Figure 8-114.

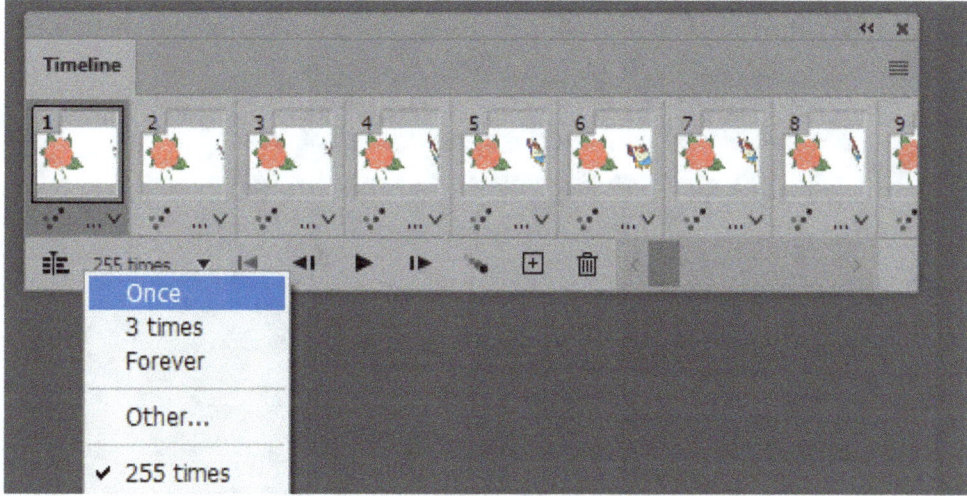

Figure 8-114. *Photoshop Timeline panel lets you alter your looping options after exported from Fresco*

Then, in Photoshop, if you need your GIF animations to have more transparent background options, you can find that setting in Photoshop under the following menu path after you have created or edited your GIF animation in Photoshop.

File ➤ Export ➤ Save for Web (Legacy). This allows you to enter the Save for Web dialog box and adjust the looping options as well. From here, you could then save a new copy with precise looping settings. Refer to Figure 8-115.

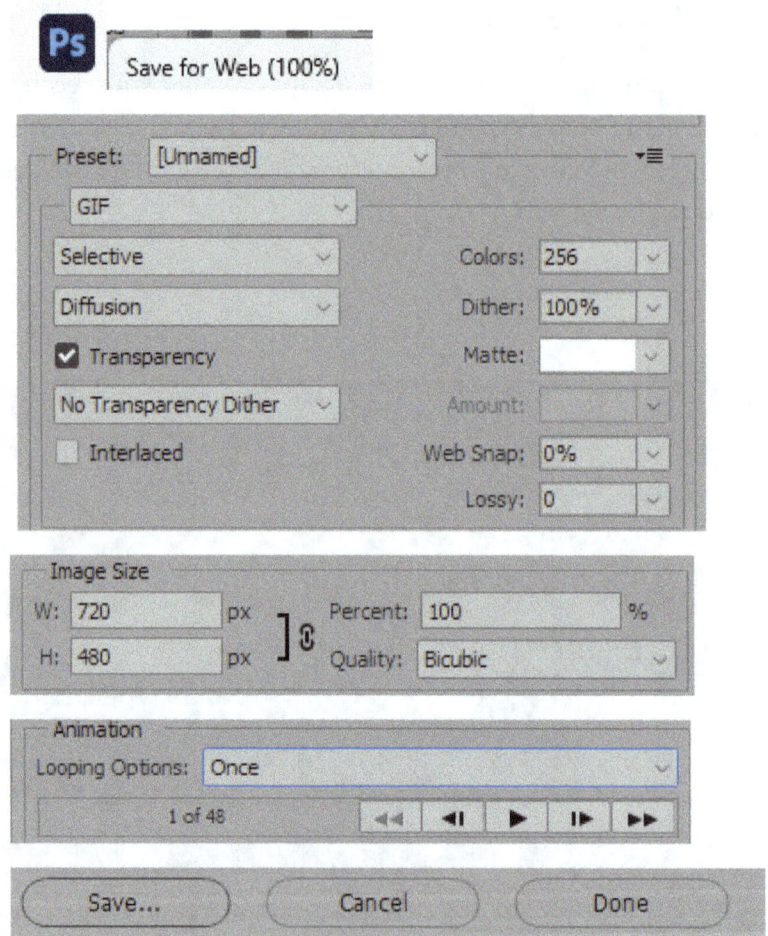

Figure 8-115. *Photoshop Save for Web dialog box with additional Transparency and Animation settings for GIF animations*

More details can be found here as the settings are the same for Photoshop and Adobe Animate: https://helpx.adobe.com/animate/using/export-for-web.html

For more details on Animate for GIF animations, you can refer to the link found in Chapter 9.

CHAPTER 8　BASIC ANIMATION IN FRESCO

Project Idea: Creating a Basic Animation

Sometimes a drawing from a previous chapter can inspire an idea for an animation. From the Fresco Home page, import and open my file **spider_animation_start.psd**. As I built the butterfly frame-by-frame animations in this chapter, I realized that I could adapt some of my drawings of the spider and web from Chapter 6, into a short animation. Refer to Figure 8-116.

Figure 8-116. *Spider animation example*

This project, like the racing car example earlier, has many layers that I copied and pasted to create the frames for the Motion layers. However, in this case, there are only about five Motion layers. As I did in the earlier animations, I had to copy each of the original images from Illustrator into Photoshop and save as a (.psd) file, and then once the file was opened in Fresco, I pasted a copy on each of those layers into separate frames onto one Motion layer.

What follows next is a breakdown of some of the steps I used to create the various Motion layers:

639

CHAPTER 8　BASIC ANIMATION IN FRESCO

- The spider as I discovered required 30 frames to complete the walk cycle. In the following figure, I'm just presenting a few of the layers here with the Motion layer; take a moment to look at the full amount in the Layer panel. As you hover over a layer, you will see they needed to be numbered to keep track of them, and then each layer hidden after the Layer content was pasted into a frame. Refer to Figure 8-117.

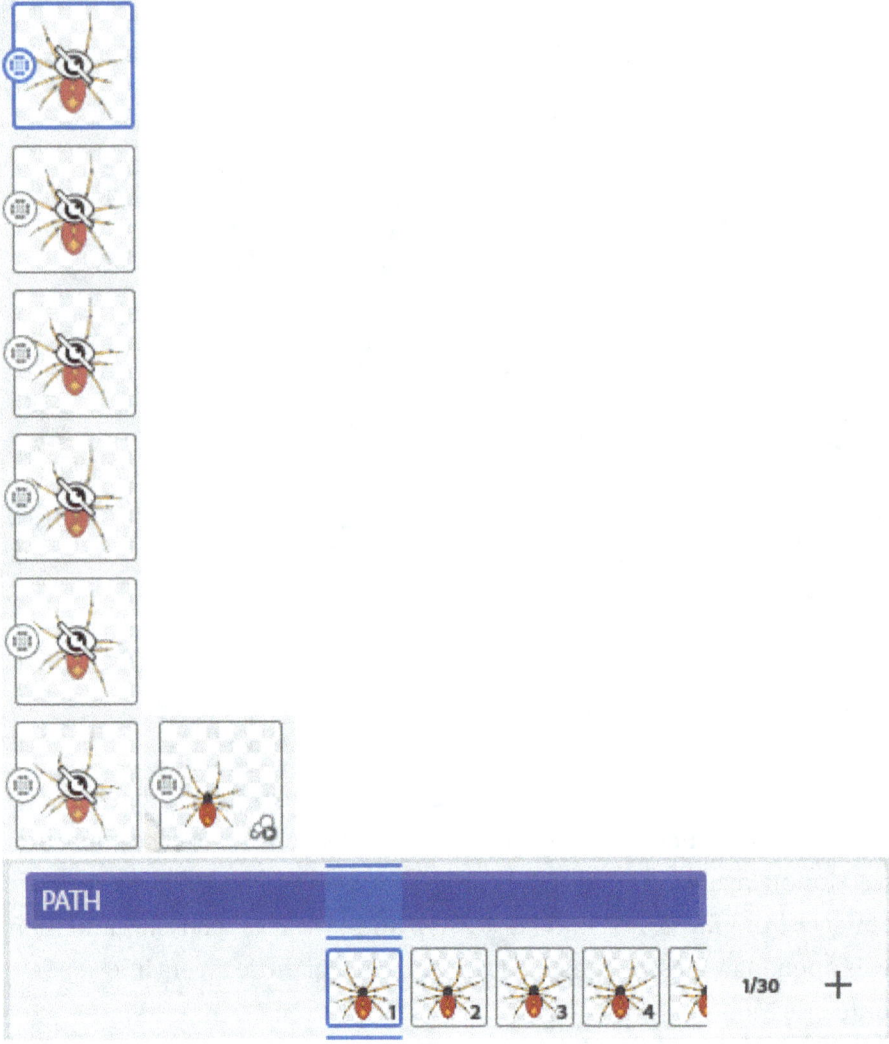

Figure 8-117. *Some of the spider layers that were used to create the Spider Motion Layer Frames*

Note To capture the spider's movements more accurately, I had to adapt my earlier illustrator drawing to make it less stylistic so that that spider would move in a more realistic way. Spider's legs are more in the upper part of the body, and they move in quite an independent and articulated way, and I had to watch a few videos online before I knew what I had to redraw. To understand animation better, it's important to study walking cycles. Other walking cycles you should study are the human body, various four-legged animals, like cats, dogs, and horses or other insects that you are interested in. Some walk cycles may take more or less frames to get a feeling of movement you want to recreate.

- The butterfly Motion layer has 12 frames created from the 6 layers. And you reviewed a similar Motion layer set in the earlier butterfly animation. Refer to Figure 8-118.

CHAPTER 8   BASIC ANIMATION IN FRESCO

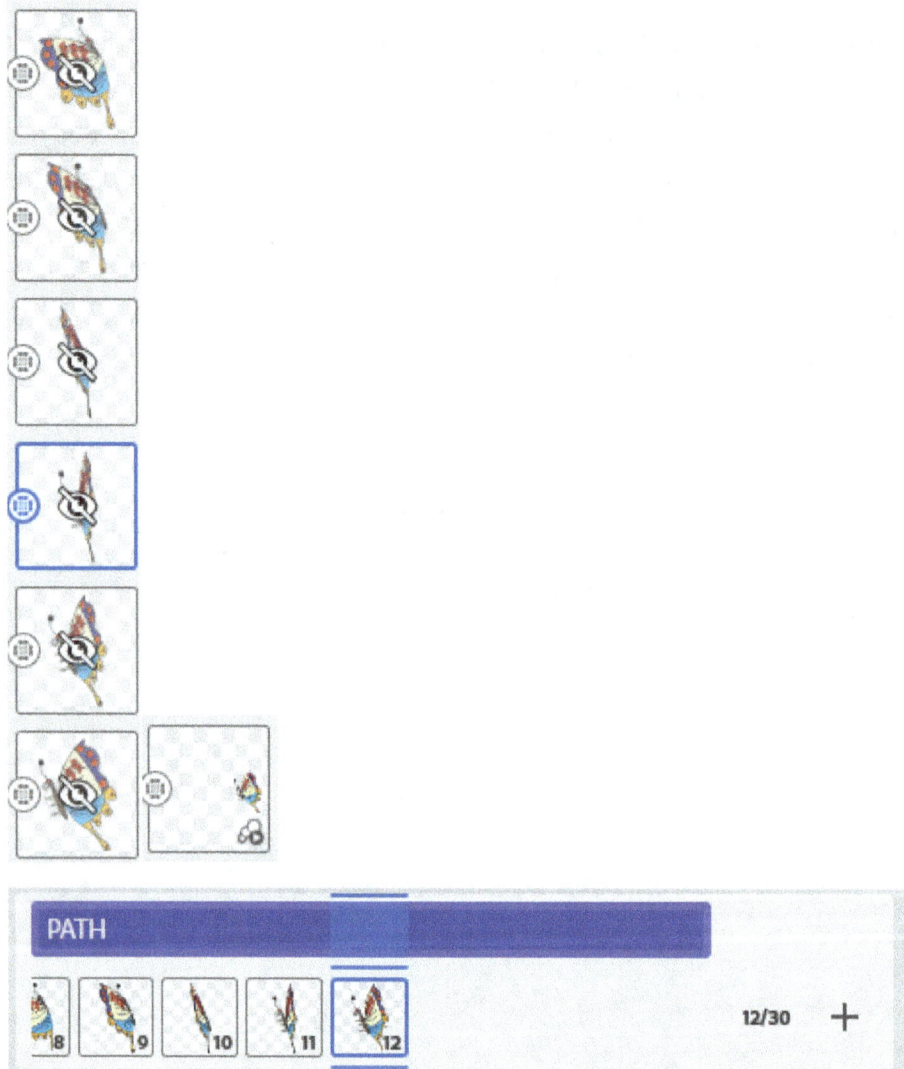

Figure 8-118. *Butterfly layers that were used to create the Butterfly Motion Layer Frames*

- The movement of the web Motion layer, which was created from 5 layers, but they were duplicated several times to create movements over 24 frames. Refer to Figure 8-119.

CHAPTER 8　BASIC ANIMATION IN FRESCO

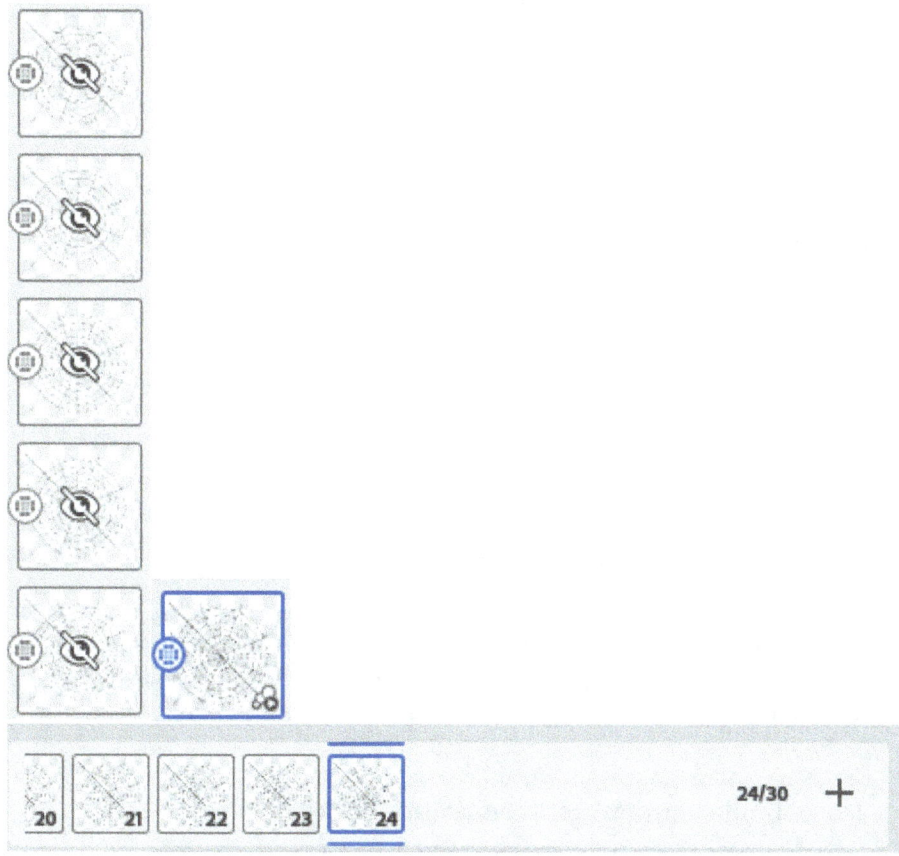

Figure 8-119. *Web layers that were used to create the Web Motion Layer Frames*

- The last two Motion layers that I created were frame-by-frame embellishment layers that I added for the spider. One is for when it touches the web and the other for eye shine. Refer to Figure 8-120.

643

CHAPTER 8   BASIC ANIMATION IN FRESCO

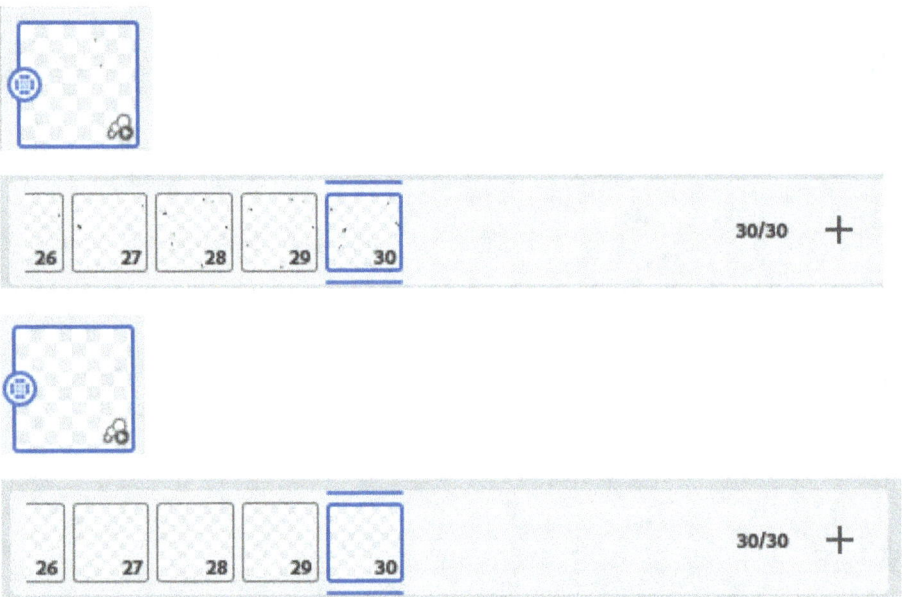

Figure 8-120. *Other Motion layers had had frames added for minor painting details on. The upper one shows the leg movements, and the lower example has white eye shine; both are 30 frames*

- The only other layer is the stationary iris flower which acts as an artistic anchor for the web. Refer to Figure 8-121.

Figure 8-121. *A stationary layer used in the animation is an iris flower*

I'll go into the details of the Motions layers in a moment.

In this example the butterfly, as we saw earlier in the chapter, flying onto the rose flower, this time lands on the web. While this is happening, the spider circles and moves onto the web close to the butterfly. And the web moves as the spider walks closer and then action stops. Refer to Figure 8-122.

CHAPTER 8 BASIC ANIMATION IN FRESCO

Figure 8-122. *The butterfly is captured by the spider at the end of the animation*

This is not meant to be a repetitive animation but rather a scene or video clip.

So, in this case, I set the resolution settings to HD settings 1920 by 1080 72 ppi so that it could be used for a video clip on the Web. Refer to Figure 8-123.

645

CHAPTER 8 BASIC ANIMATION IN FRESCO

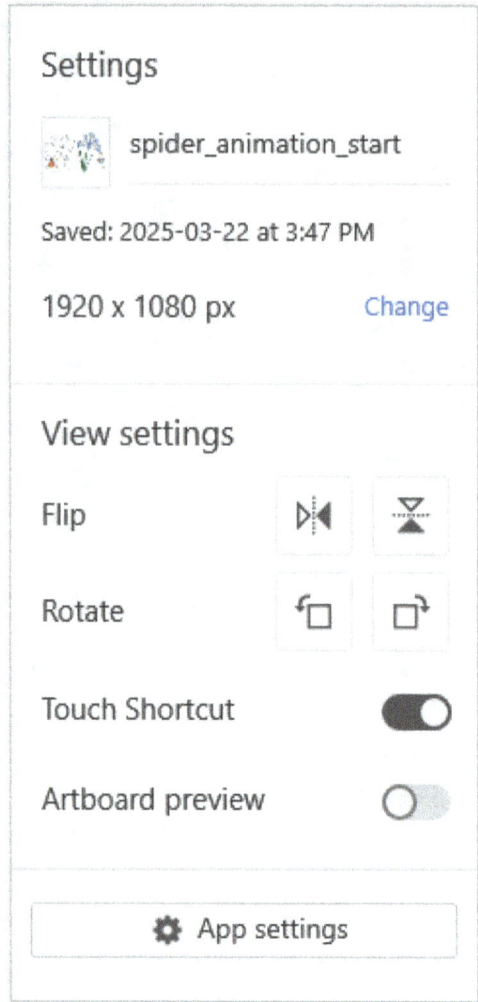

Figure 8-123. *Document settings for the spider animation*

Layer Motion Properties for Path Layers

The spider and the butterfly layers are the only two layers that have motion paths.

And you can study those settings of each in the Layer properties. For the butterfly, I reduced the frame speed to 30 rather than the default of 48. Refer to Figure 8-124.

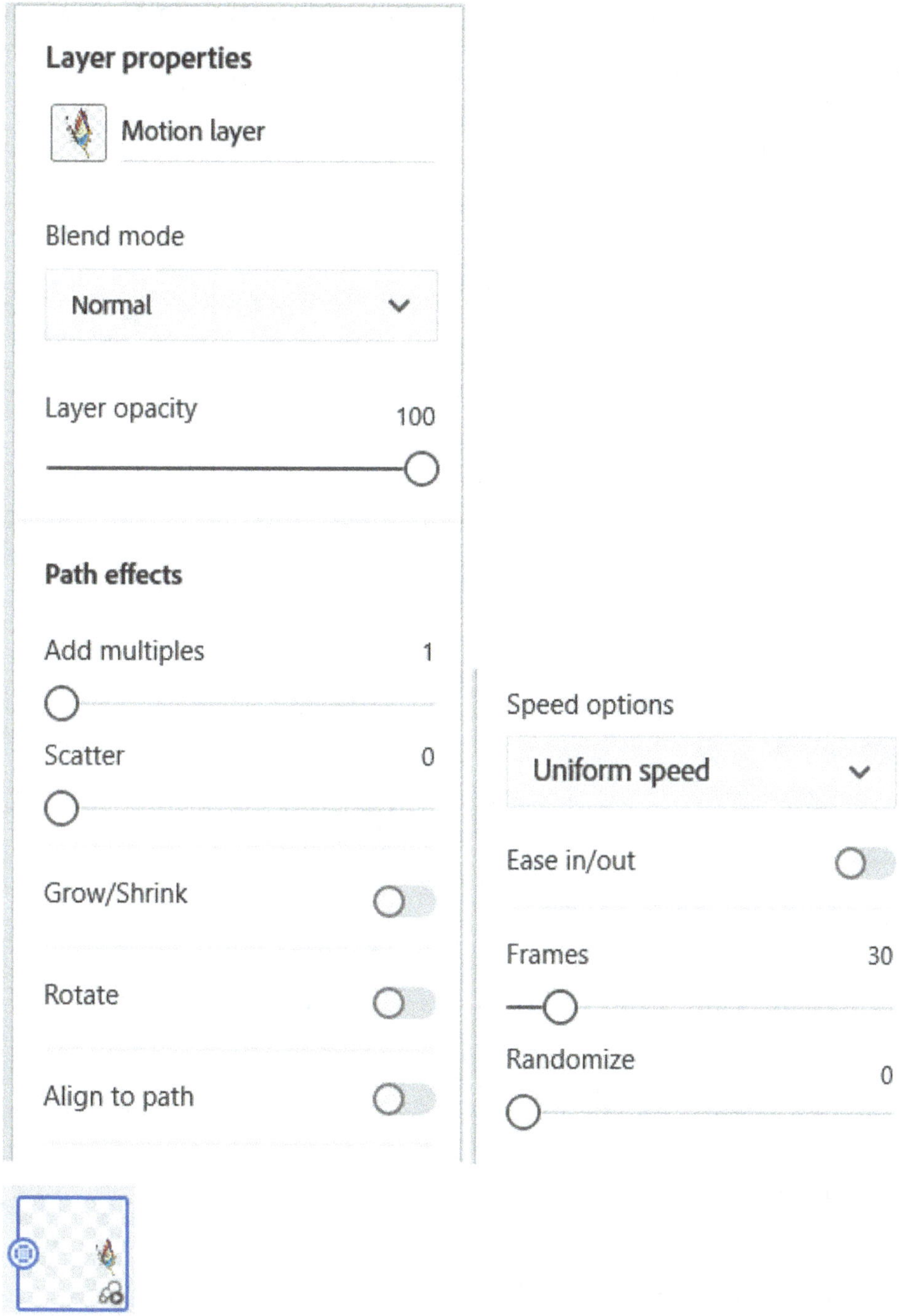

CHAPTER 8 BASIC ANIMATION IN FRESCO

Figure 8-124. *Layer properties and Path effects for the butterfly Motion layer*

CHAPTER 8 BASIC ANIMATION IN FRESCO

The spider had similar frame settings as the butterfly. However, in this case, it has the added feature of Align to path so that it moves more accurately on its set route. Refer to Figure 8-125.

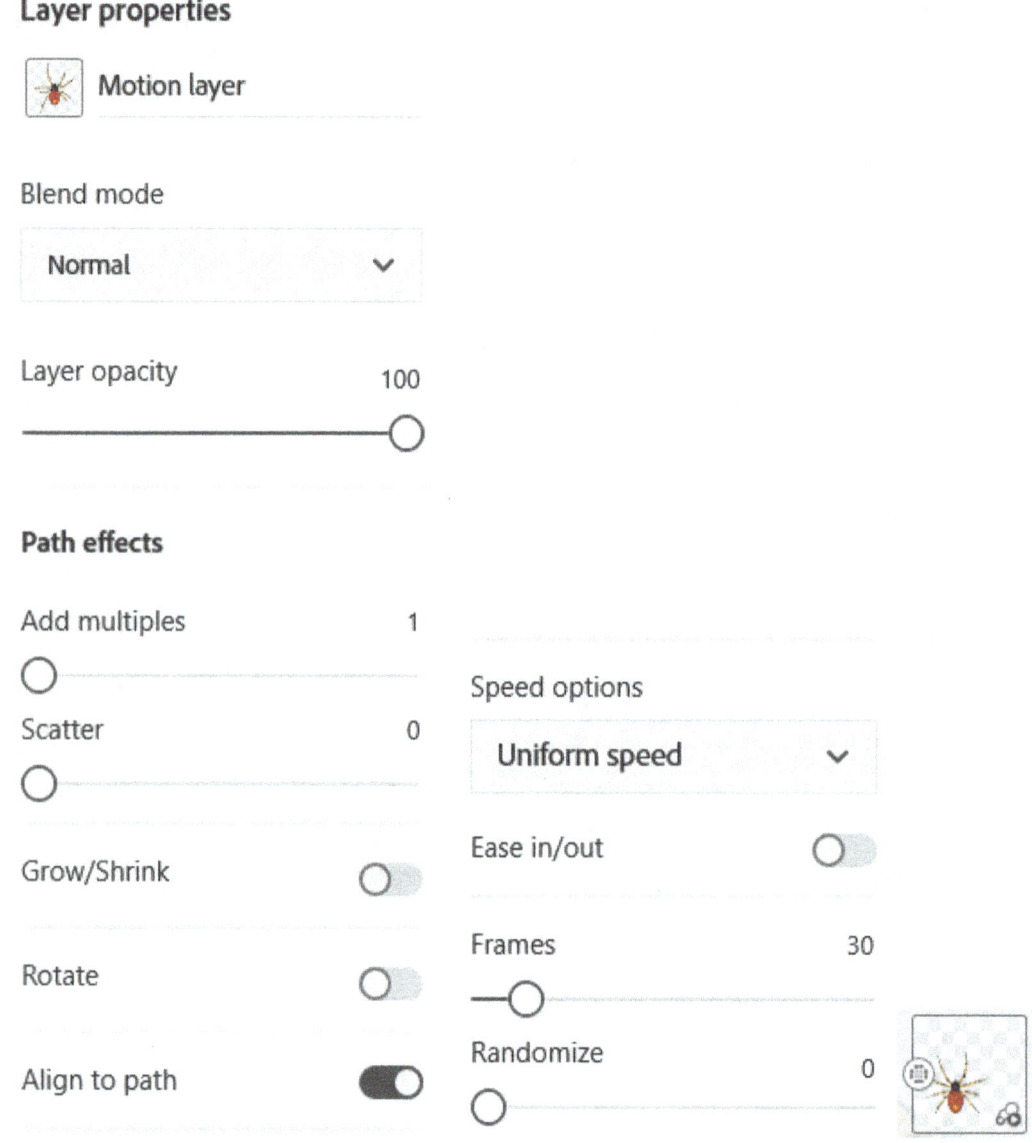

Figure 8-125. Layer properties and Path effects for the spider Motion layer

As noted, the web and the other spider details for movement and eye shine had no motion path attached to them. However, for one Motion layer above the web where the feet of the spider touch the web, I altered the layer properties' overall opacity to 82% and the Blend mode to Divide. Refer to Figure 8-126.

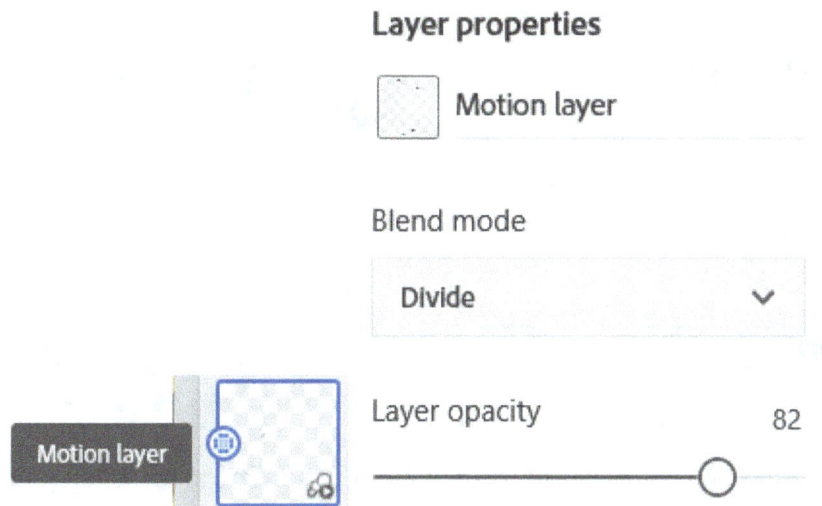

Figure 8-126. *Layer properties for the spider foot path layer*

I then painted on each frame with a Basic small Pixel brush (Hard round) in black so that it slightly lightened that area where the spider's tip of its foot touched. This effect is a result of choices in the Layer properties. Refer to Figure 8-127.

CHAPTER 8   BASIC ANIMATION IN FRESCO

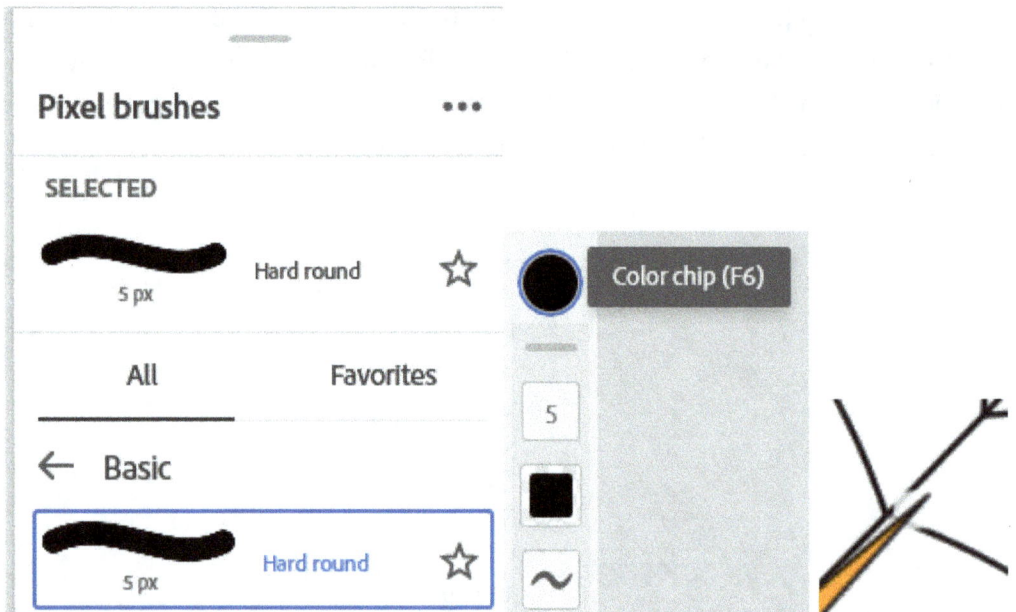

Figure 8-127. *Pixel brush for painting details of where the spider's tip of its foot touches*

To get this accurately when you paint each frame, you need to make sure that your settings for the Timeline panel are set to Motion settings and enabled Document timeline and Show paths as frames. Refer to Figure 8-128.

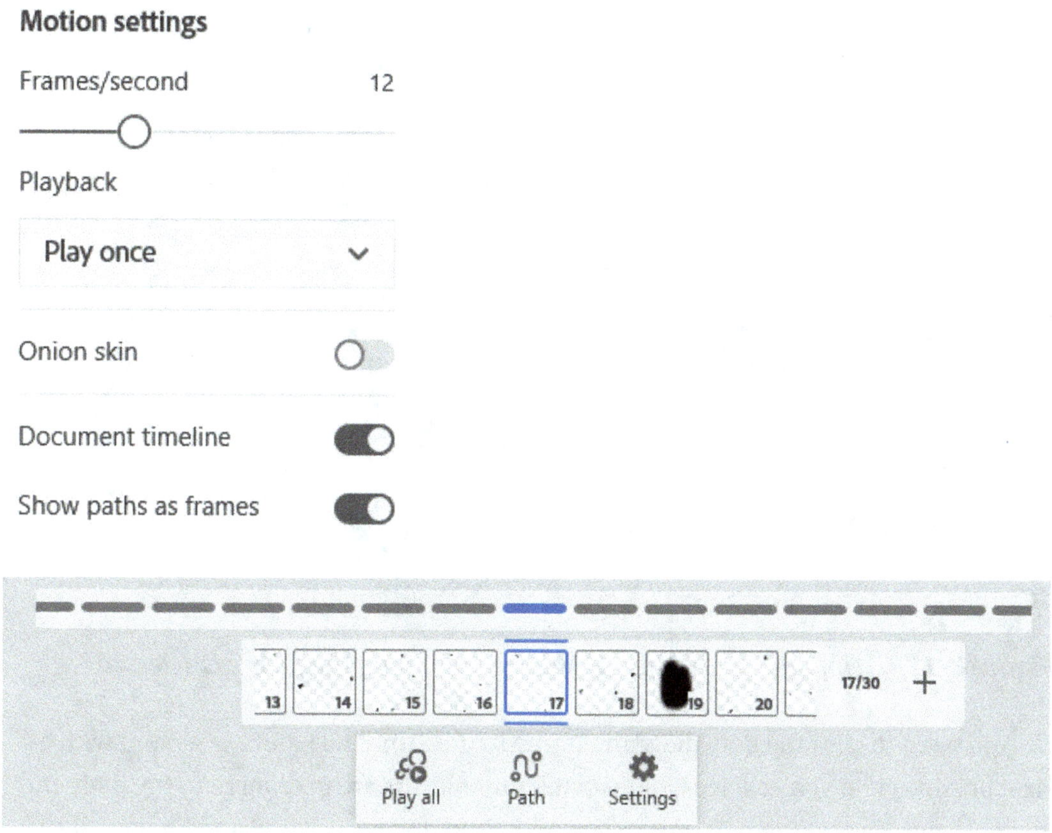

CHAPTER 8 BASIC ANIMATION IN FRESCO

Figure 8-128. *Adjust the Motion settings for painting on each frame in a Motion layer*

The reason for this is that if you just click on a frame, you will not see where it fits in with the other path movements of the spider. Refer to Figure 8-129.

CHAPTER 8   BASIC ANIMATION IN FRESCO

Figure 8-129. *How the animation displays when only the frame is selected*

You need to click the line above the frame in the Timeline before you paint with a Pixel brush so that you can see where all the other layers are in relation to the path and frame. In this case, we are looking at frame 17. Refer to Figure 8-128 and Figure 8-130.

CHAPTER 8　BASIC ANIMATION IN FRESCO

Figure 8-130. *How the animation displays when only the path as frames line is selected*

The same is true for the spider's eye shine on that Motion layer; each frame was painted with a Pixel brush of Basic (Hard round) small brush with white paint. This layer was placed above the Motion layer of the spider. Refer to Figure 8-131.

CHAPTER 8   BASIC ANIMATION IN FRESCO

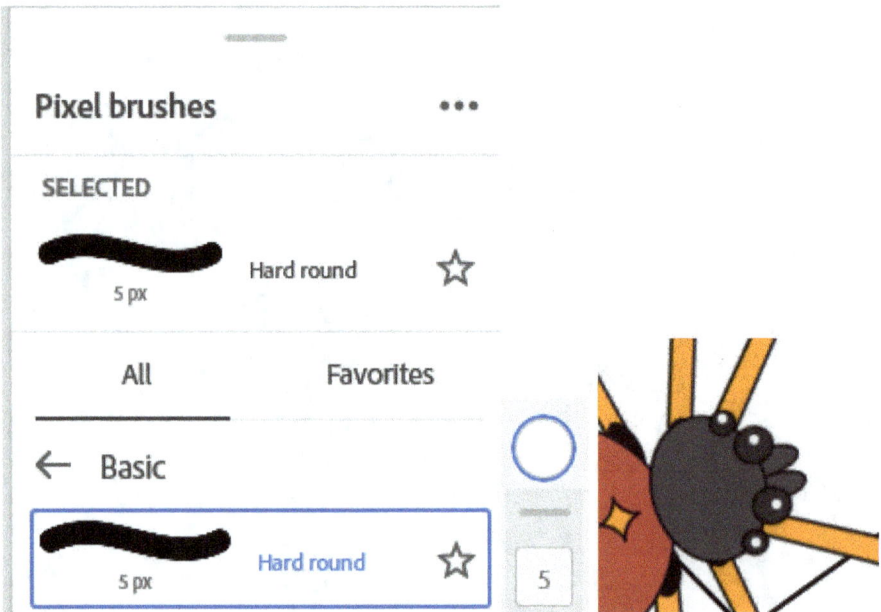

Figure 8-131.   Pixel brush for painting details such as the spider's eye shine

Once the animation was completed, I then went to the Share workspace under the Publish & export and, in the Motion settings, saved my file as MP4. However, this time, I set Loops to 2 so that it would play correctly to the end without cutting off unexpectedly. I clicked the Generate frames button, then the Export button, and saved the file in a folder, so that I could use the clip and edit it in other applications which I will mention in Chapter 9. Refer to Figure 8-132 and Figure 8-133.

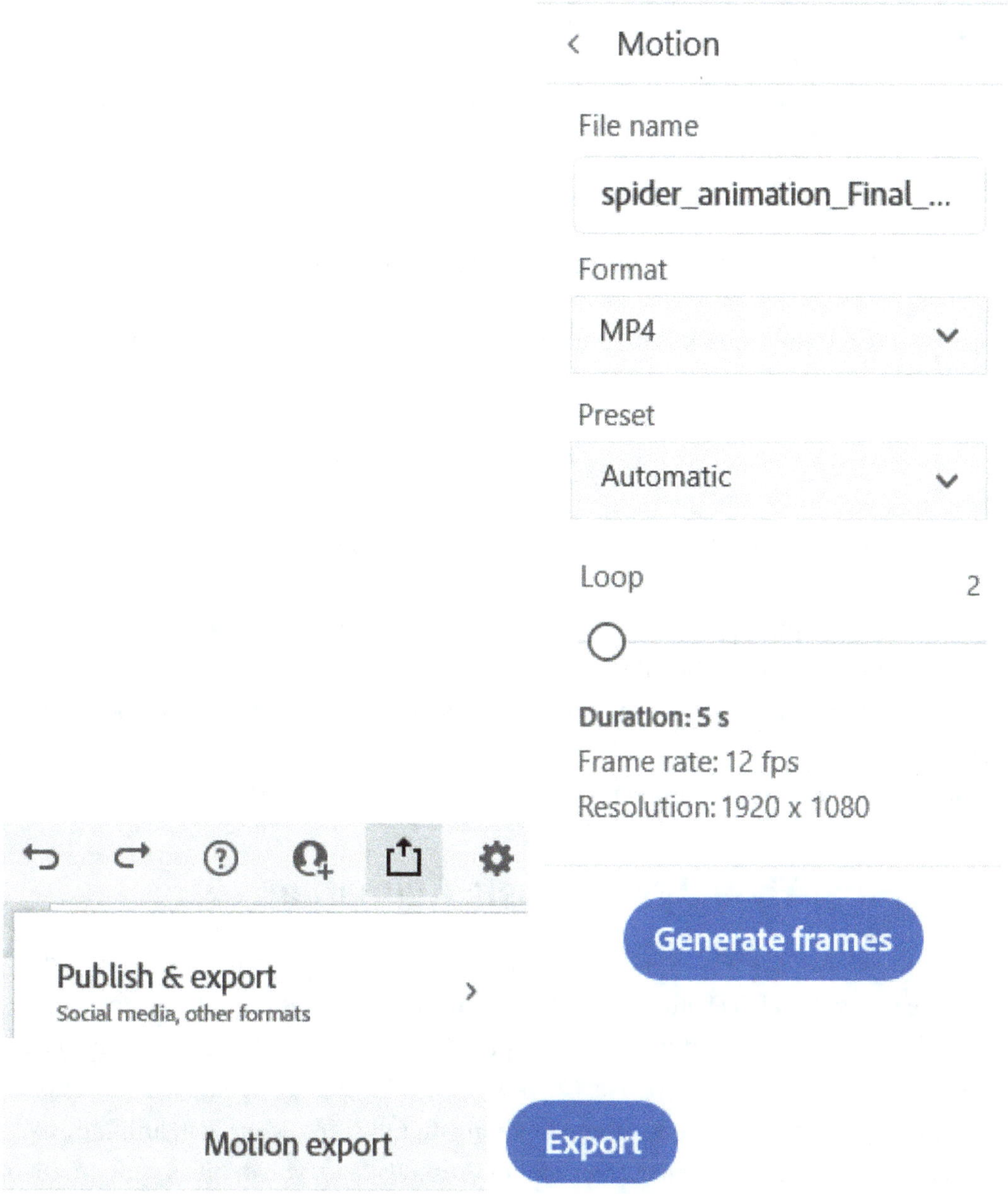

CHAPTER 8   BASIC ANIMATION IN FRESCO

Figure 8-132. *Publish & export settings for the MP4 video file*

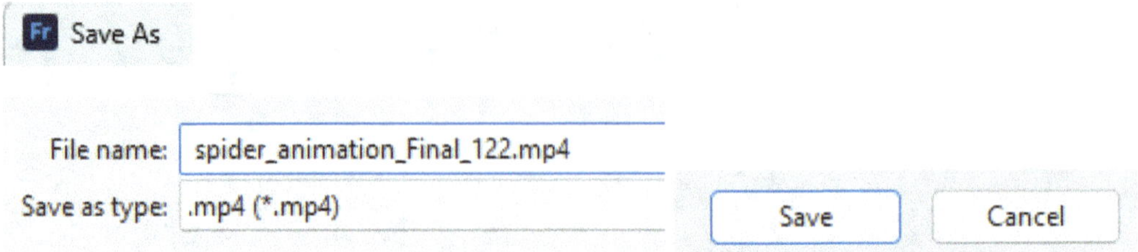

CHAPTER 8　BASIC ANIMATION IN FRESCO

Figure 8-133. *An example of saving the exported MP4 video file*

Then I clicked the Done button and exited the Share workspace. Refer to Figure 8-134.

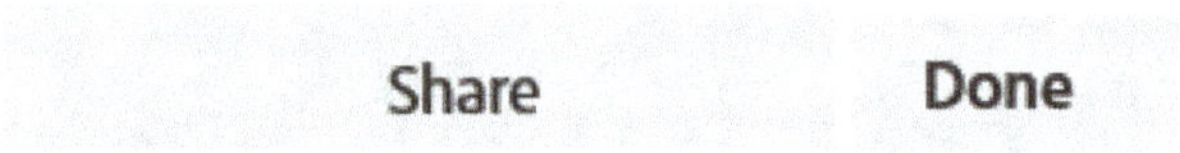

Figure 8-134. *Clicking the Done button to exit the Share workspace*

You can review the file found in the **Export_Files** folder **spider_animation_Final_122.mp4** along with the other exported examples in this chapter that I have stored in that folder as well. This includes the files **car_outdoor.gif** and **car_outdoor_masks.gif**.

You can then close any Photoshop or Fresco files you have open.

Fresco Final Thoughts on Basic Animation

I really enjoyed working with the Fresco animation tools within this workspace, and I encourage you to try all its features. However, one area that I feel could be improved is the ability to delay the timing in Timeline panel of certain frames before the next set of frames play as a type of long pause. Currently, with Fresco, it appears like all actions must happen at once as you may discover when you now build your own animations in this application. As mentioned, the point of Fresco is to let you express your creative side and not focus on precise timing. However, in cases where that is important, you can still use these files in other Adobe applications such as Photoshop or Animate as will be mentioned in the next chapter.

Summary

In this chapter, we reviewed some of the steps to creating basic animation using stationary Pixel layers and Motion layers. Then we learned how to export the animation in the correct format. Then, on your own, you reviewed an animation project which was then exported in a video format.

In the next chapter, we will look at reviewing how to export stationary graphic files and will consider some suggestions for later, using exported files with other Adobe applications.

CHAPTER 9

Exporting, Editing Files, and Using Them Later in Other Adobe Apps

In this concluding chapter, we will explore options for exporting files from Fresco for your project should you want to use various file formats offsite from the Creative Cloud or for your social media site. We will then review previously discussed Adobe applications and discover additional applications you can incorporate your exported Fresco files into.

> **Note** The project files for this chapter can be found in the Chapter 9 folder. Refer to the link in the introduction.

In this case, you may want to work with your own files or a previous file that you created for practice in this book. In this chapter, I am using the file **Seascape_final.psd** which is a copy from Chapter 5, to demonstrate. From the Home page, you can Import and open this file in Fresco if you want to follow along. Refer to Figure 9-1.

CHAPTER 9 EXPORTING, EDITING FILES, AND USING THEM LATER IN OTHER ADOBE APPS

Figure 9-1. *Import and open a file to practice with such as the seascape file*

Share: Publish and Export Settings

The Share icon is located in the upper right of the Title bar menu as we saw in Chapter 8. It offers a few great options for exporting our animation in the Share workspace. However, when you have non-motion graphics you need to download, then go again to the Publish & export (Social media, other formats) arrow to review a few more options. Refer to Figure 9-2.

CHAPTER 9   EXPORTING, EDITING FILES, AND USING THEM LATER IN OTHER ADOBE APPS

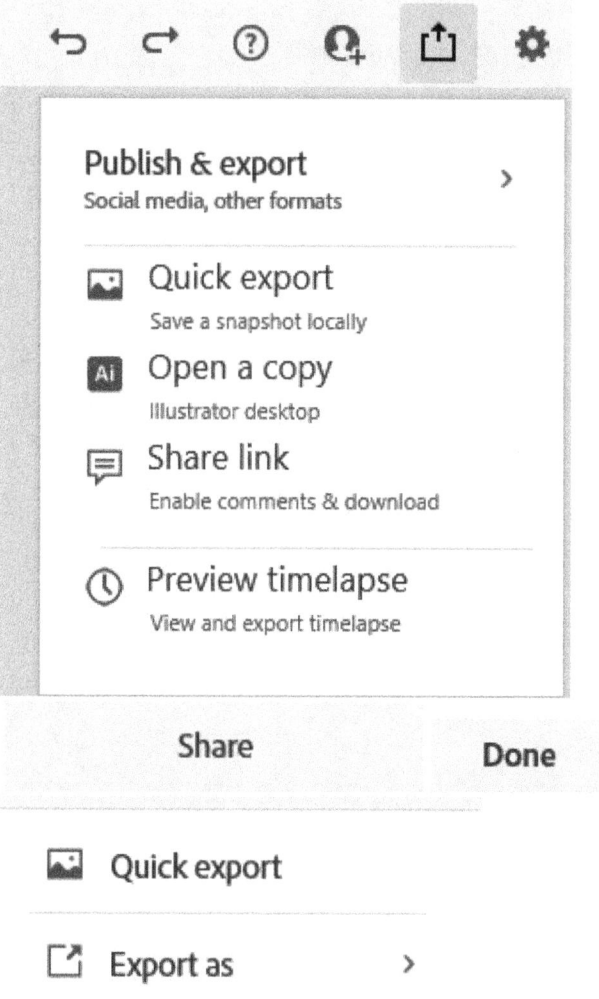

Figure 9-2. *Fresco options found in the Title bar menu for Share and the Share workspace settings*

In the Share workspace, there are two tabs we did not fully explore:

- Quick Export: This tab allows you to export your graphic as a JPG file. Refer to Figure 9-2. However, prior to entering the Share workspace, you can change this file under the Title bar Settings icon ➤ App settings ➤ General ➤ Quick export settings and choose a different file format from the drop-down menu. Refer to Figure 9-3.

CHAPTER 9   EXPORTING, EDITING FILES, AND USING THEM LATER IN OTHER ADOBE APPS

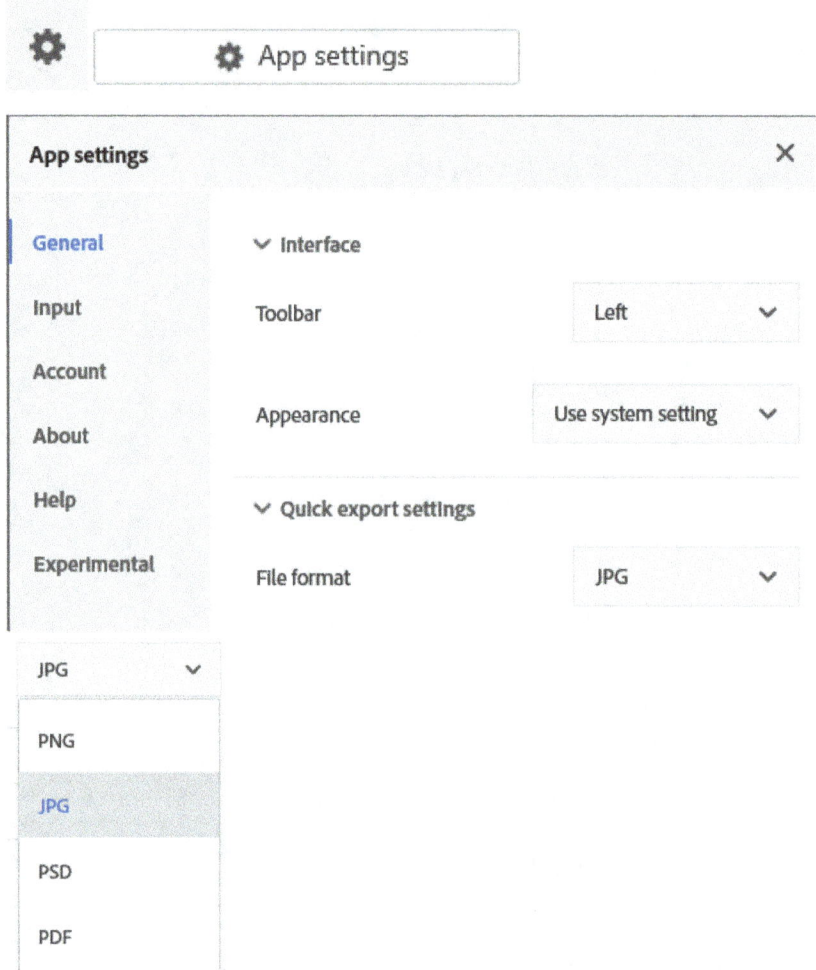

Figure 9-3. *Adjust your Quick export settings from the App settings dialog box and drop-down list*

Or, instead, you can access these same settings with more settings using the next Share option.

- Export As: You can give the file a new export name different from the original, and the four file options are available.

    - PNG: Use this file format when you want to add a graphic to your website which may have transparent and nontransparent areas.

662

- JPG: Can be set to a Quality of High, Medium, or Low. Use this format when you want to add images to your website that have a lot of detail or are more photographic-like. This format does not allow for transparent areas. Refer to Figure 9-4.

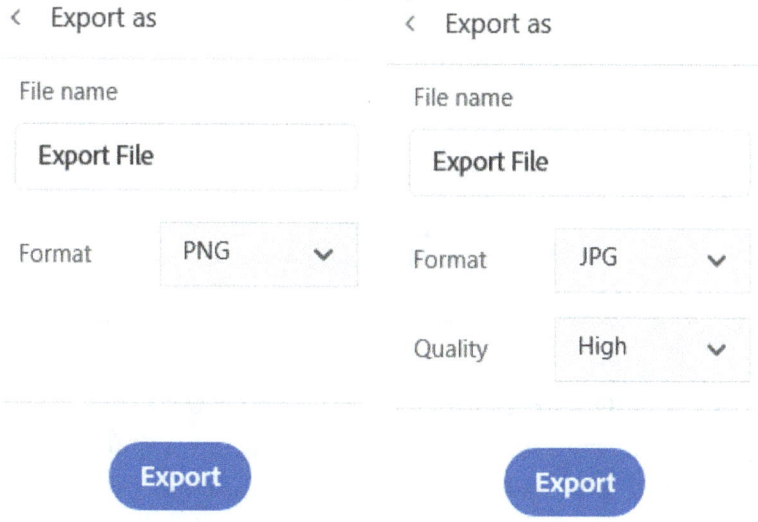

Figure 9-4. *Share workspace Export as settings for PNG and JPG formats*

- Photoshop PSD (.psd): This format is ideal for colorful details and layer preservation. We discussed the export of this option earlier in Chapter 7, and it is the best to use when you still have a lot more work to do within the file later in Photoshop. No additional settings are available.

- Portable Document Format PDF (.pdf): Is ideal if you need to email the documents to a client or collect in your folder for printing. No additional settings are available for this format. Refer to Figure 9-5.

CHAPTER 9 EXPORTING, EDITING FILES, AND USING THEM LATER IN OTHER ADOBE APPS

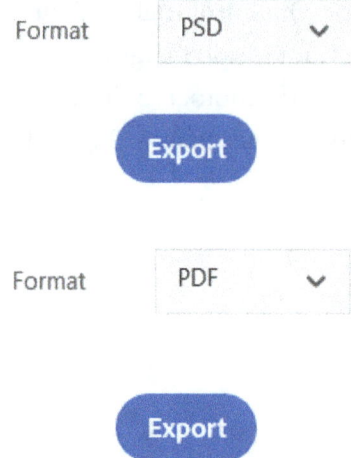

Figure 9-5. *Share workspace Export as settings for PSD and PDF formats*

After you click Export (see Figure 9-5), each file format option will take you to the Save As dialog box where you can locate the folder on your computer that you want to save the file into and click the Save button to compete the export. Refer to Figure 9-6.

Figure 9-6. *Fresco Save as dialog box options*

In my case, I exported my file as a .jpg on a high-quality setting, and then after clicking Save, Fresco informed me that the export was complete and saved in my chosen folder. Refer to the **Export_Files** folder and the file **Export File.jpg**. Refer to Figure 9-7.

664

CHAPTER 9   EXPORTING, EDITING FILES, AND USING THEM LATER IN OTHER ADOBE APPS

Export File.jpg

Figure 9-7. *Result of (.jpg) file that was exported to a folder*

Note   Remember, for more details on Timelapse export (Preview timelapse) and Motion, refer to Chapter 8. The option of Motion will not be available if there are no Motion layers in the file that is to be exported. Refer to Figure 9-8.

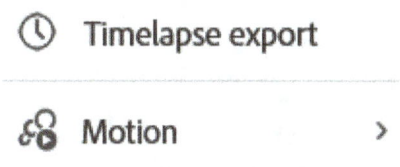

Figure 9-8. *Share workspace Timelapse export and Motion tabs*

Once you have finished working in the Share workspace, click the Done button to exit. Refer to Figure 9-2.

Pattern Options

On the desktop version in the Share workspace, you may not see the Option for Patterns as only the iPad version offers additional settings for creating Adobe Patterns using Fresco. You can learn more about that from the link at the end of this section.

However, as a workaround, you can alternatively create patterns in Photoshop from selected layers using its Capture app. Refer to Chapter 4 on the topic of Capture Shapes and the Creative Cloud Library via the plus icon (+) Add elements, and select the Extract from Image to access the dialog box. Refer to Figure 9-9.

665

CHAPTER 9   EXPORTING, EDITING FILES, AND USING THEM LATER IN OTHER ADOBE APPS

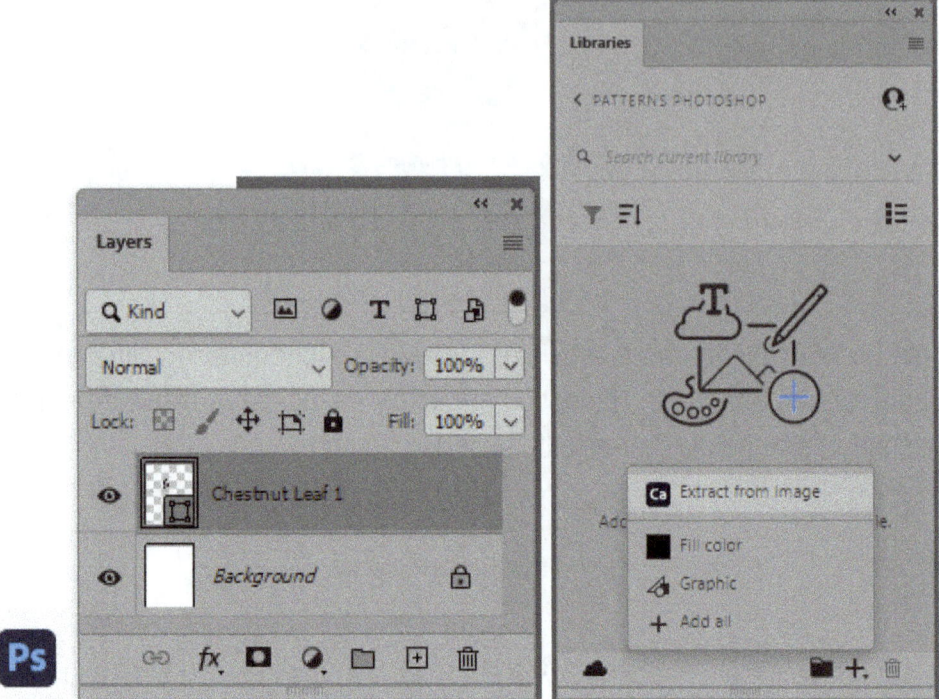

Figure 9-9. *Photoshop Layers panel and Libraries panel can be used to capture custom patterns*

In the dialog box, rather than selecting the Shapes tab, you can select the Patterns tab instead, to create Capture patterns with the various options of Pattern, Color Mode, Image Scale, and Rotation. Once done, click Save to CC Libraries to save your new pattern to a library; then click Close to exit. Refer to Figure 9-10.

CHAPTER 9　EXPORTING, EDITING FILES, AND USING THEM LATER IN OTHER ADOBE APPS

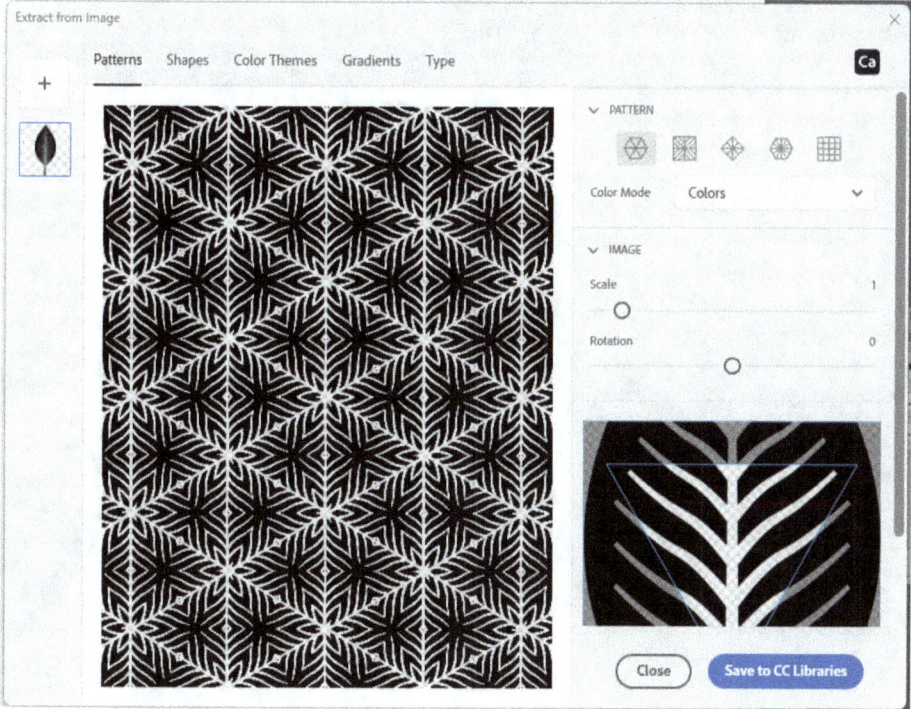

Figure 9-10. *Photoshop Capture Extract from Image dialog box used to create custom patterns*

Once the pattern is added to your library in the Libraries panel, then drag that pattern from the library into your Photoshop document. In the Layers panel, it will be saved as Pattern fill. Refer to Figure 9-11.

CHAPTER 9   EXPORTING, EDITING FILES, AND USING THEM LATER IN OTHER ADOBE APPS

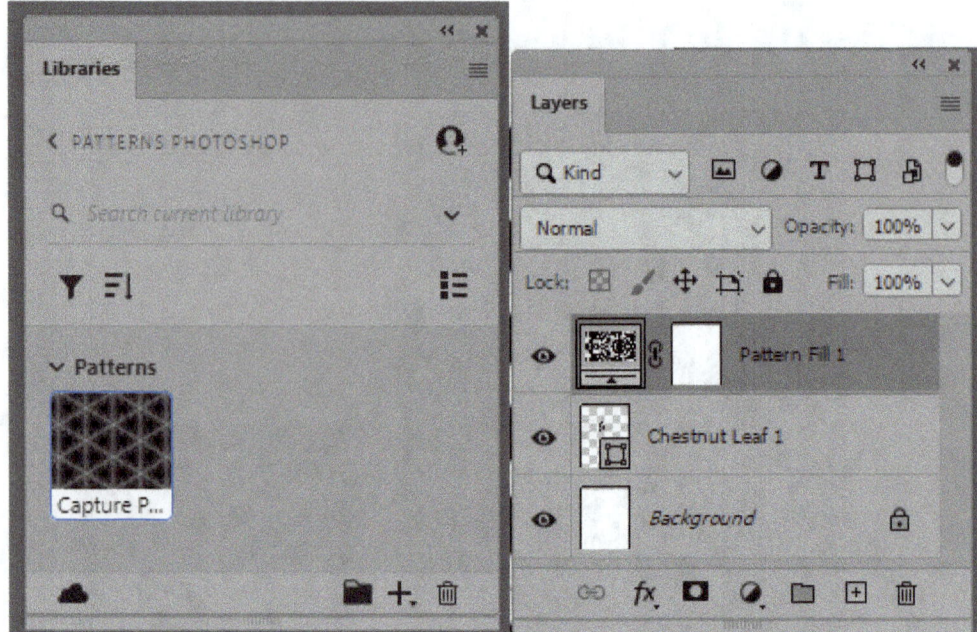

Figure 9-11. *Photoshop Libraries panel with a custom pattern added and it was added to the Layers panel*

Optionally, the pattern could be stored in Photoshop's Patterns panel, when the layer is selected and the option to create a new pattern is chosen from the panel. Once the pattern is named in the dialog box, it appears in the Patterns panel. Refer to Figure 9-12.

CHAPTER 9　EXPORTING, EDITING FILES, AND USING THEM LATER IN OTHER ADOBE APPS

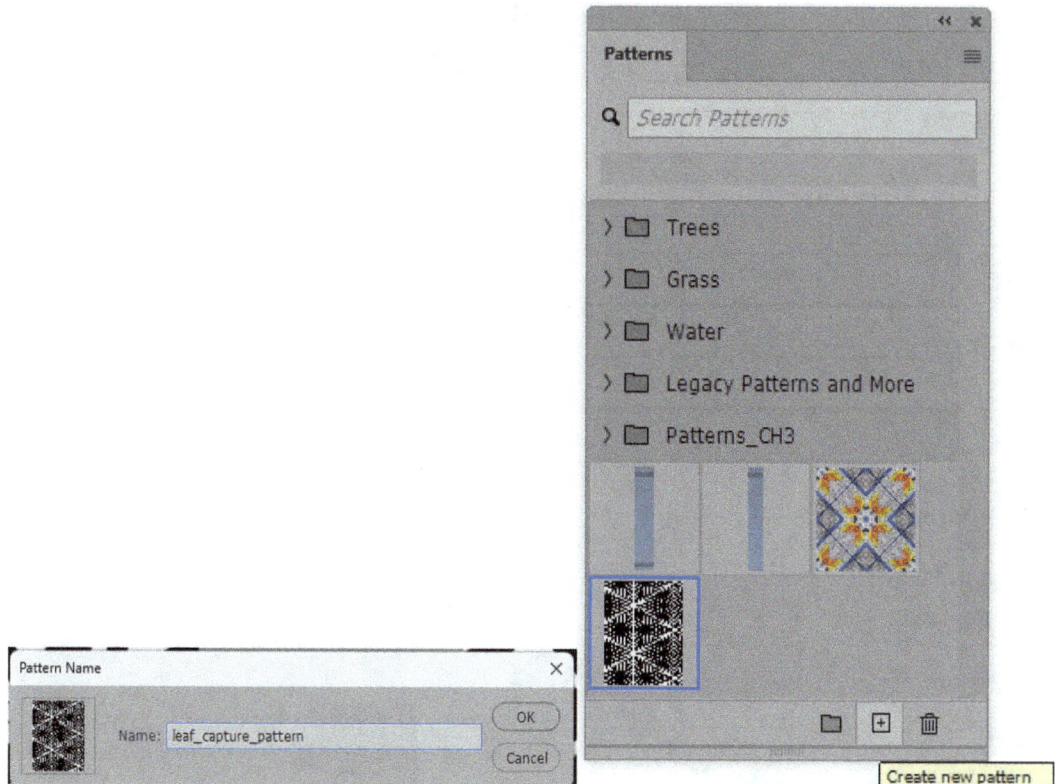

Figure 9-12. *In Photoshop a custom pattern selected from the Layers panel and added to your collection via the Patterns panel*

However, the layer could also be rasterized in Photoshop using the panel's menu and would be a Pixel layer and then later copied into Fresco for use as a background image layer or dragged back into the library, now as a graphic asset. Refer to Figure 9-13.

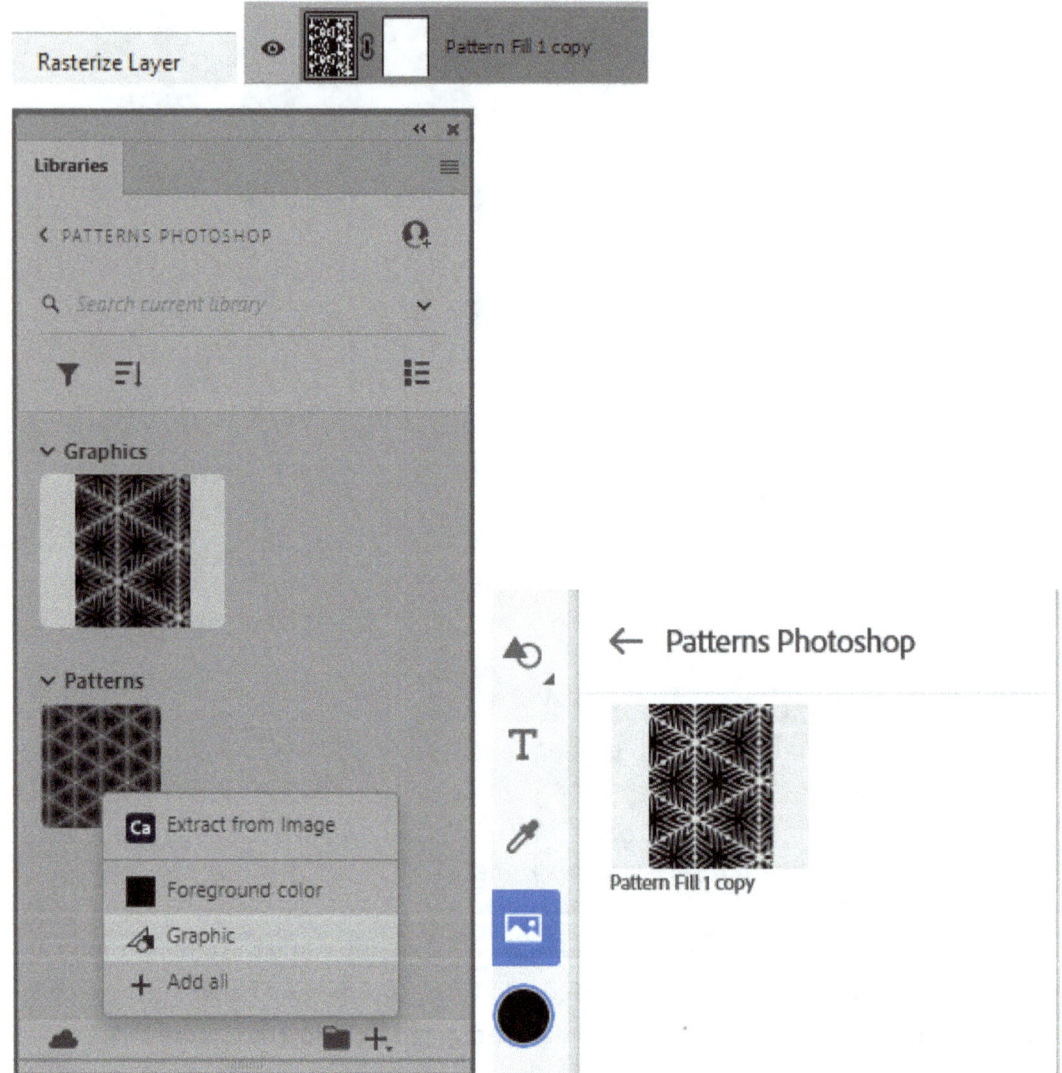

Figure 9-13. *A pattern layer can be rasterized and turned into a graphic asset and then added to the Libraries panel and placed into a document using Fresco Libraries*

Refer to Chapter 7 if you need to review how to change a Photoshop layer into a graphic asset for the Libraries panel for Fresco.

You can refer to my files **leaf_capture_pattern.psd** and the library file **Patterns Photoshop.cclibs** if you want to import it into the Photoshop Libraries panel.

CHAPTER 9   EXPORTING, EDITING FILES, AND USING THEM LATER IN OTHER ADOBE APPS

Additional Share Options

Now, we will review, in the Fresco Title bar, some of the additional Share options in the list that appear below the Publish & export options. Refer to Figure 9-14.

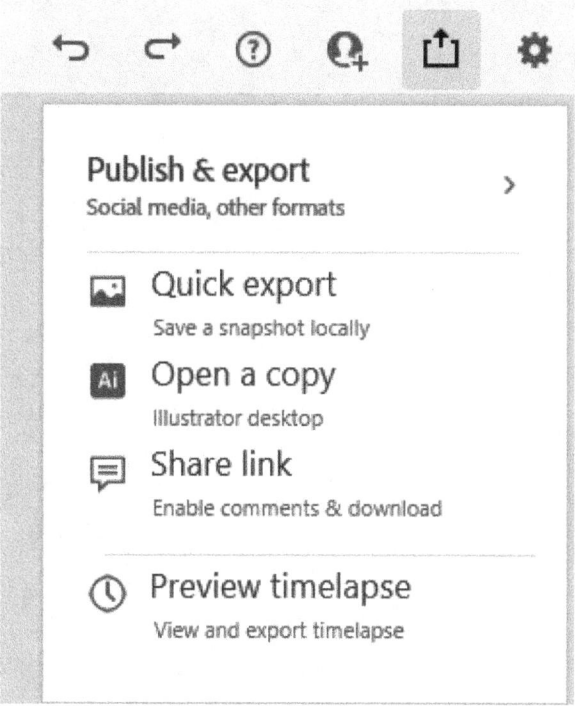

Figure 9-14. Fresco Share options list

- Quick Export: Save a snapshot locally. This option saves a copy of how your file currently appears in (.jpg) format. You can then quickly save the file on the computer for emailing or as a digital record of your progress. This setting is basically the same as Quick export found in the Publish & export (Share) workspace.

- Open a Copy for Illustrator Desktop: Once the file is sent to Illustrator, you will get a dialog box for Photoshop Import Options. I would recommend putting the setting to "Convert Layers to Objects Make editable where possible" rather than "Flatten Layers to a Single Image Preserves text appearance." Optionally, you can also enable Import Hidden Layers as well and click OK. In this example, I created a file

CHAPTER 9 EXPORTING, EDITING FILES, AND USING THEM LATER IN OTHER ADOBE APPS

that had a few Vector brush strokes to demonstrate what would occur. You can try this yourself if you create some Vector and Pixel layers in a new Fresco document. Refer to Figure 9-14 and Figure 9-15.

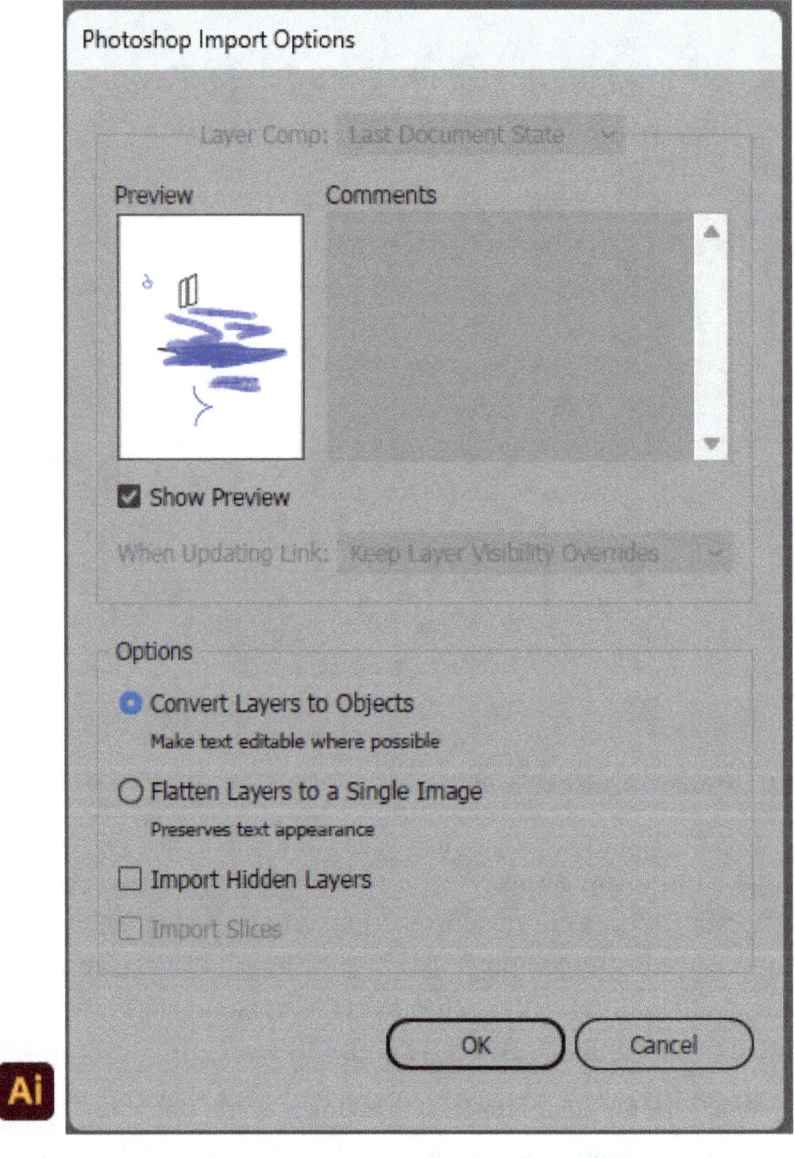

Figure 9-15. *Illustrator Photoshop Import Options dialog box upon the file being exported*

CHAPTER 9 EXPORTING, EDITING FILES, AND USING THEM LATER IN OTHER ADOBE APPS

In Illustrator, this will open the file as a (.psd) file. However, you can then choose File ➤ Save as and save a copy of this file as a (.ai) file to continue work on it in Illustrator. Refer to Figure 9-16.

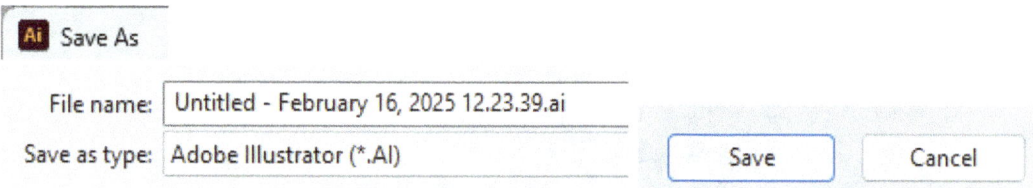

Figure 9-16. Illustrator Save As dialog box settings

Click OK to any Illustrator save settings and then consult Illustrator's Layers panel. Then on the artboard, use your Selection tool or Direct selection tool to select paths on layers. Refer to Figure 9-17.

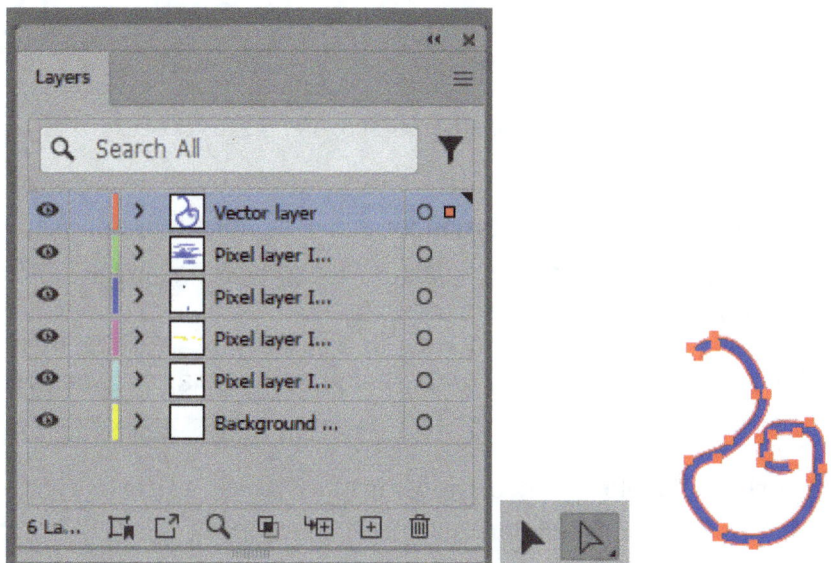

Figure 9-17. Illustrator Layers panel and Selection tools with a vector path selected with the Direct selection tool when clicking on the vector path on the artboard

For this file, Illustrator will only allow you to edit the Vector layer paths, not Pixel layers, as they will remain as an image as verified in the Control panel. Also, you cannot import the vector (.ai) file back into Fresco. Refer to Figure 9-18.

673

CHAPTER 9   EXPORTING, EDITING FILES, AND USING THEM LATER IN OTHER ADOBE APPS

Figure 9-18. *Illustrator's Control panel shows that the brush strokes on the Pixel layer when selected are an image and are not vector*

Refer to Chapter 7 for workarounds for adding Illustrator artwork to Fresco. Refer to this link for more details:

https://helpx.adobe.com/fresco/using/fresco-and-illustrator.html

Note   Though not part of the discussion for this book, for Illustrator users, see information on Image Trace which you can use for converting simple illustrations to Vector strokes and fills:

https://helpx.adobe.com/illustrator/using/image-trace.html

- Share Link: Enable comments and download to see "Invite In" section for more information. Refer to Figure 9-19.

Figure 9-19. *Fresco Share options list with Share link selected*

More details on the publish, export, and Share topic can be found at the following link:

https://helpx.adobe.com/fresco/using/publish-export-share.html

What Is "Invite In"?

In the Title bar, Invite In is found under the icon in the upper right and allows others to share the document with you. This would also allow options to comment and have access to the link that only invited people that you, the owner, have emailed. If you are working with a team or collaborators on a project this is great, but if you are working alone, you can ignore this icon and click the X icon to close the dialog box. Refer to Figure 9-20.

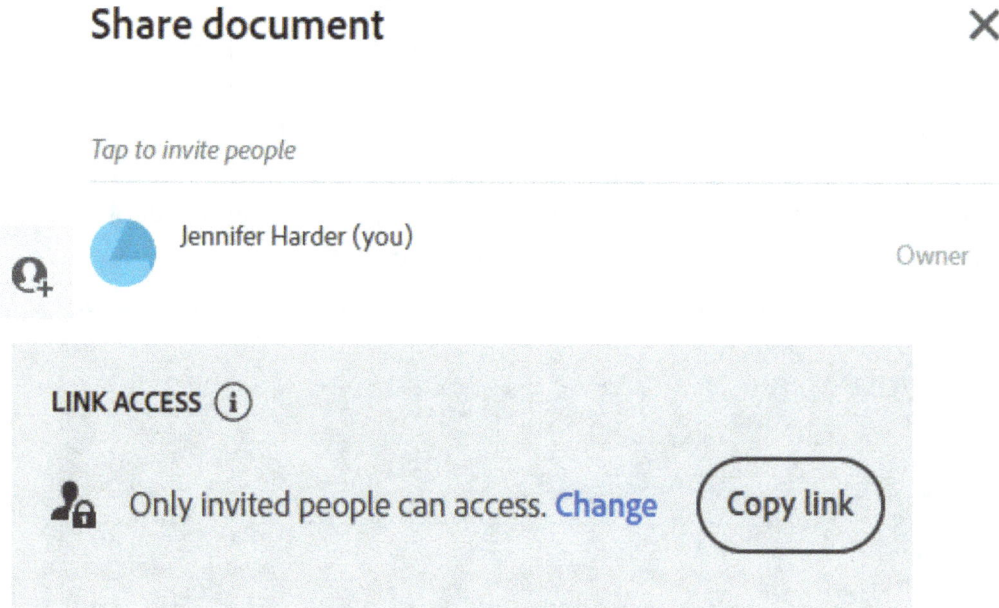

Figure 9-20. *Fresco Invite In and Share options*

Downloading from the Creative Cloud Desktop

Remember to review how to download any files from the Creative Cloud Desktop and Fresco, and refer to the notes in Chapters 7 and 8 before looking at this next section in Photoshop.

CHAPTER 9   EXPORTING, EDITING FILES, AND USING THEM LATER IN OTHER ADOBE APPS

Working in Photoshop with Your Fresco File

Fresco files, once downloaded after being exported as (.psd) files, can then be opened and edited in Photoshop. Here are a few things to review and remember when you do this. Refer to Figure 9-21.

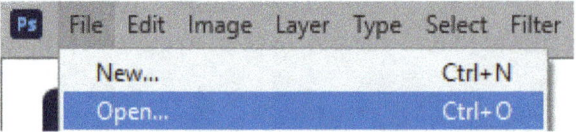

Figure 9-21. *Open a downloaded file Fresco (.psd) in Photoshop*

Upon opening the File from Photoshop Desktop, always create an Image ➤ Duplicate so that you do not edit the original by mistake in case you need to go back and reuse it for another project. Click OK. Later, you can File ➤ Save the duplicate (.psd) somewhere on your desktop in a folder. Refer to Figure 9-22.

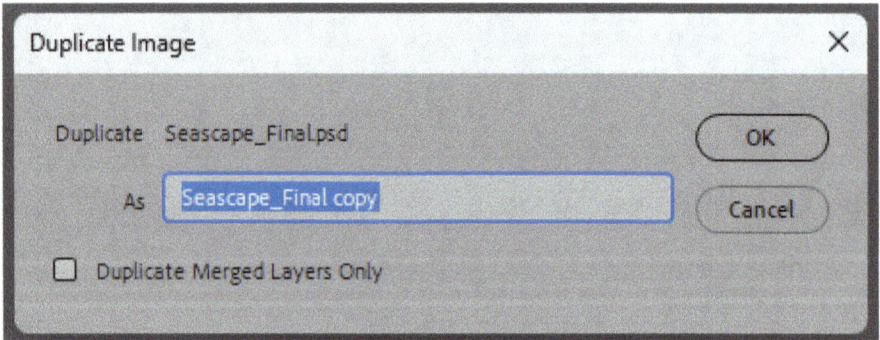

Figure 9-22. *Duplicate Image dialog box used to create copies of files*

When you open the file, you may get a few warnings, such as if a font is different than the one used in the Fresco application or if it needs to be updated. Click OK or in this case Update to any warning to continue if you plan to create a copy of the file. Refer to Figure 9-23.

CHAPTER 9   EXPORTING, EDITING FILES, AND USING THEM LATER IN OTHER ADOBE APPS

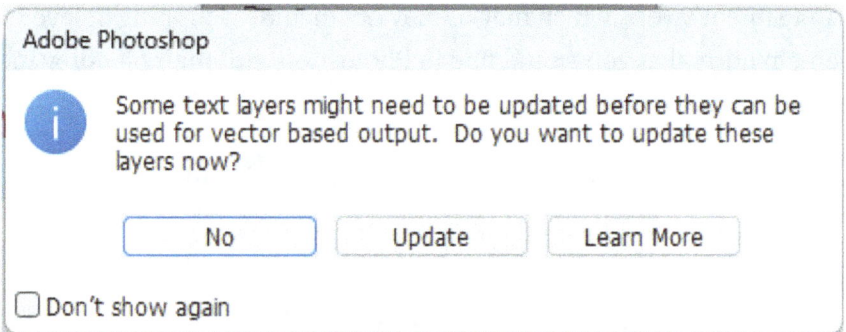

Figure 9-23. *Adobe Photoshop warning message in regard to text layers that may need an update*

Depending on the work done, some layers, created in Fresco, will have been turned into Embedded Smart Object layers. This is so that the details of those brushes can be preserved if scaled or transformed. Refer to Figure 9-24.

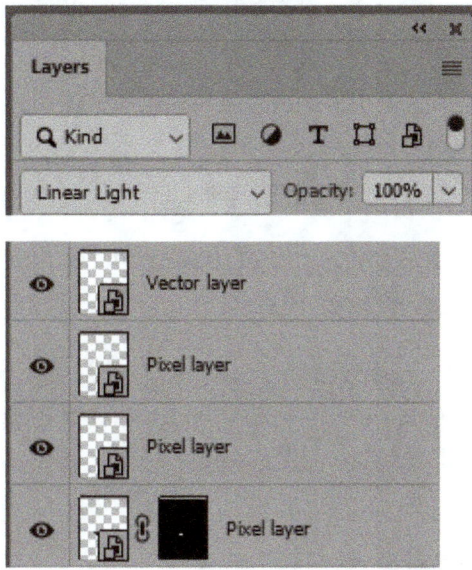

Figure 9-24. *Looking at the Layers panel to review different kinds of Smart Object layers*

Smart Object layers could be, for example, layers that were painted with Live brushes or Vector brushes, ones where a vector shape was used in conjunction with a layer mask. They could also be Motion layers that were created in Chapter 8. However, for other Pixel layers, or Adjustment layers, which may or may not include a clipping or layer mask, they will remain normal as you would find in Photoshop with their blending modes and opacities intact. Refer to Figure 9-25.

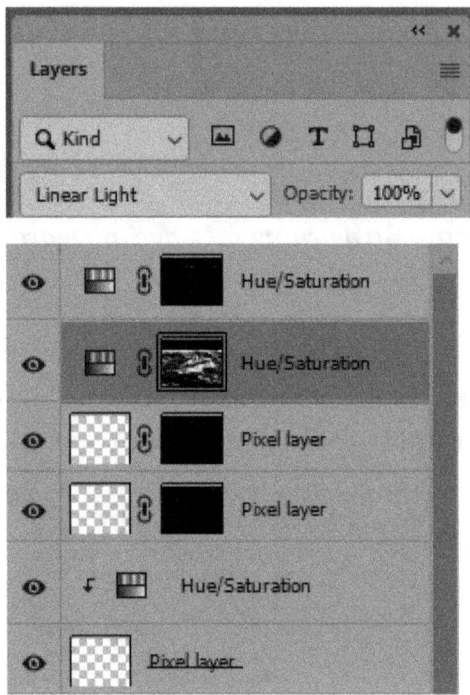

Figure 9-25. *Looking at the Layers panel to see different kinds of normal Pixel and Adjustment layers and their settings preserved*

However, if you do not intend to return the file to Fresco, you can always rasterize those Smart Object layers using the menu in the Layers panel if you intend to do some specific editing, but they will lose some scalability and quality as a result. Refer to Figure 9-26.

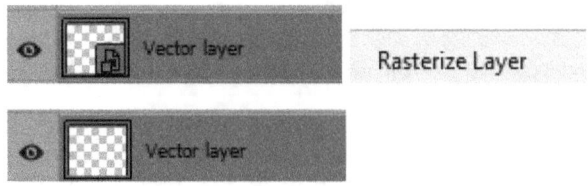

Figure 9-26. *In Photoshop converting a Vector Layer Smart Object layer to a Raster/Pixel layer*

If you do intend to work with the file again in Fresco, using Import and open, be aware that if you have altered some layers with new blend modes or Adjustment layers that are not supported by Fresco, this will cause those layers to become preserved Photoshop layers the next time you import and open the (.psd) file. As a result, you may not be able to complete some intended tasks, and you will get a warning message. Review Chapter 5 on layers for information on this topic.

Refer to this link for details on how to work between the applications Fresco and Photoshop and sync files:

```
https://helpx.adobe.com/fresco/using/fresco-and-photoshop.html
```

Recommended Exported File Formats to Use in Other Adobe Applications

Besides Photoshop and Illustrator, here I present a few other Adobe applications you may want to consider incorporating some of your exported Fresco files into after you have downloaded them or exported from the Creative Cloud Desktop.

Animate

After you have created the initial drawings, you could use Adobe Animate instead, for adding extra layers and frames for interactivity to your animations using its Timeline panel. Animate is a good alternative to Photoshop and Fresco if the animation is quite complex. Sounds or audio could also be added as well, using Animate. Recommended exported file formats that you could later import into an Animate library would be a (.jpg, .png, and .psd). These animations can also be exported as GIF or MP4. Refer to Figure 9-27.

CHAPTER 9 EXPORTING, EDITING FILES, AND USING THEM LATER IN OTHER ADOBE APPS

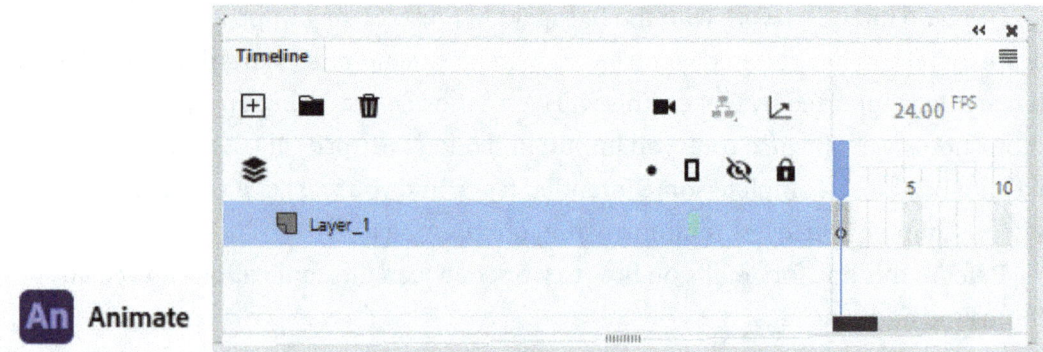

Figure 9-27. *Adobe Animate icon with the application's Timeline panel*

Refer to this link if you would like to learn more about Animate:

https://www.adobe.com/learn/animate

InDesign

For your final illustrations, once downloaded from the Creative Cloud Desktop or exported, you could incorporate them into an InDesign document (.indd) where you could continue to add more text, graphics, and later export the file as a PDF to create a booklet or other printed media. The recommended file format for working with high-resolution images in an InDesign document would be a (.psd) file and at least a resolution of 300 ppi. For web design-related work, you can alternatively use a high-quality (.jpg) file. Refer to Figure 9-28.

CHAPTER 9   EXPORTING, EDITING FILES, AND USING THEM LATER IN OTHER ADOBE APPS

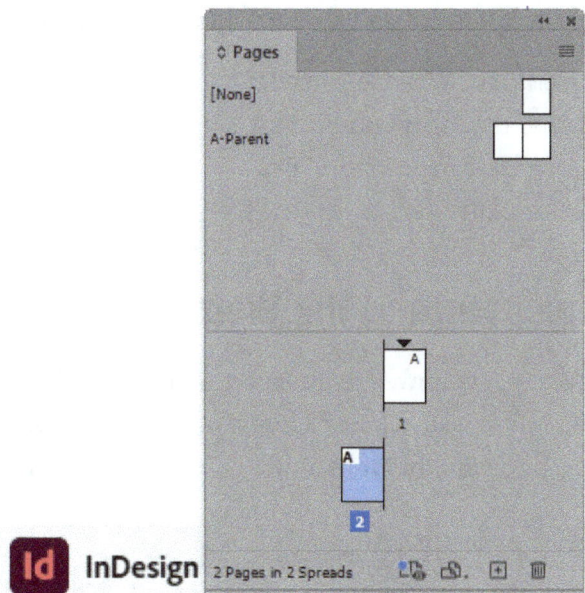

Figure 9-28. *Adobe InDesign icon with the application's Pages panel for booklet creation*

Refer to this link if you would like to learn more about InDesign:

https://www.adobe.com/learn/indesign

Video Applications

Sometimes, you want to create a video footage to tell your story which often requires painterly designs and artwork.

Exported images like (.jpg) and (.png) would be acceptable to incorporate into files that you may be creating with the Adobe applications of Media Encoder, Premiere Pro, Premiere Rush, and After Effects, for example, the PNG sequence, as mentioned in Chapter 8. With a Premiere Pro project, you could later add sound to your (.mp4) file as well as other video footage. Refer to Figure 9-29.

Figure 9-29. *Application icons for Media Encoder, Premiere Pro, Premiere Rush, and After Effects*

681

Refer to these links if you would like to learn more about those video applications:

https://www.adobe.com/learn/media-encoder
https://www.adobe.com/learn/premiere-rush
https://www.adobe.com/learn/premiere-pro
https://www.adobe.com/learn/after-effects

Adobe Dreamweaver and the Web

Use the application Adobe Dreamweaver to incorporate your still images and animations onto your own HTML web page designs. Example of file formats you could use for still images are (.jpg) and (.png) and for animation (.gif) or (.mp4). Refer to Figure 9-30.

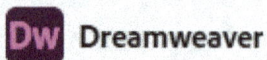

Figure 9-30. *Adobe Dreamweaver icon*

Refer to this link if you would like to learn more about Dreamweaver:

https://www.adobe.com/learn/dreamweaver

However, outside of Adobe, you can also add these same image or animation file formats to your social media or WordPress pages.

Getting Additional Inspiration from Behance

Behance is another online option from Adobe that is available for sharing your artwork and live streaming broadcasts of your files. Refer to Figure 9-31.

Figure 9-31. *Adobe Behance icon*

Note that you cannot directly connect to Behance in Fresco via the Windows desktop version. You can, however, export a copy of the document to the desktop. This can be done using one of the methods described in this chapter, and then use the Behance app to publish it through your Creative Cloud Desktop console. More details on this process can be found at the following links:

`https://helpx.adobe.com/fresco/using/publish-export-share.html`

`https://helpx.adobe.com/fresco/using/getting-started-with-user-interface.html#behance`

Refer to the following link if you need information on using content credentials:

`https://helpx.adobe.com/fresco/using/content-credentials-fresco.html`

With Fresco, we can see there are many possibilities even after you have completed your artwork.

Project: Saving an Exported File

In this final project, consider how you would expand upon one of your current projects in another application. Take one of your past document files, and then practice exporting it in one of the mentioned formats that we have reviewed in this chapter, using either the Share menu or Share workspace. For practice, export the file into the project folder **Export_Files** or a folder you have created.

File ➤ Save your work in any application you may have open.

You can now close the Fresco application.

Summary

In this chapter, we reviewed various ways to export still images and make them available for other applications that you may want to work with to further enhance your artwork. Then we completed this chapter with a project of saving one of your own Fresco files.

I hope that you have enjoyed working in the Fresco application and will continue using it to enhance your artistic creations.

Index

A

Accurate Layer Selections Using Photoshop's Selection Tools, 61
Adobe Animate, 520, 679, 680
Adobe applications
    Illustrator, 3, 5
    Photoshop, 2, 3, 5
Adobe Capture app, 270
Adobe Dreamweaver, 682
Adobe Fresco, 1
    applications, 8
    closing/exiting, 15
    cloud files, 4
    Creative Cloud app, 5, 6
    Creative Cloud Desktop, 12, 17, 18
    documents, 12
    home page, 11
    Home page, 14, 18
    icons, 14, 15
    installation, 8–10
    libraries, 4
    Mac and PC options, 9
    new blank file, 55, 56
    Photoshop and Illustrator, 7
    recent blank document, 30, 31
    resources, 7
    system requirements, 8
    tutorials, 13
    updates, 14
    Vertical Taskbar, 315
    workspace layout, 31, 32
Adobe InDesign, 521
Animation Photoshop tips, 637
Anti-alias, 240
Appearance/adjustment layer, 371
    brightness/contrast
        blend mode/layer opacity, 374, 375
        layer properties panel, 372
        Layer properties panel, 372
        sliders, 373
    clipping masks
        applying, 387
        color change, 387, 388
        layer properties, 388, 389
        uses, 386
        vertical taskbar, 389
    color balance
        blend mode, 383, 385
        layer opacity, 383, 385
        luminosity toggle, 383, 384
        properties, 381, 382
        sliders, 383, 384
        tone, 383, 384
    duplication, 385
    grouped/ungrouped layers, 385, 386
    Hue/Saturation
        blend mode, 380, 381
        color change, 388
        colorize toggle, 379, 380
        color range, 378, 379
        layer opacity, 380, 381
        lightness, 377
        options, 376, 377
        properties, 375, 376

INDEX

Appearance/adjustment layer (*cont.*)
    masks, 390, 391, 393, 394
    vertical taskbar, 371
Assign Profile dialog box, 507, 508

B

Behance, 682, 683
Blend mode, 280
Bloat tool, 220, 221
Brush creation in Photoshop
    add brush to library, 179, 180
    blank page, 167
    brush import limitation, 182–184
    Brush Settings panel and Brushes panel, 168
    Brush Tool and settings, 167, 168
    CC Library, 177–179
    create, 165
    create round brush, 169–174
    create shape brush, 175–177
    import and export libraries, 184–186
    new file, 166
Brushes, 67, 68
Brush tools, 66
    Angular and Filbert brushes, 68
    Eraser brushes (*see* Eraser brushes)
    Fan, Rake and Flat brushes, 68
    Live brushes (*see* Live brushes)
    main kinds, 67
    painting inside and outside of a boundary, 158–162
    pixel (*see* Pixel brushes)
    Round, Rigger, Liner and Stencil brushes, 69
    touch shortcuts, 162
    Vector brushes (*see* Vector brushes)

C

Capture patterns, 666
Capture ribbon brush, 187
Capture Shape, 519
Change Perspective Plane, 440
Charcoal, 76, 77
Circle drawing aid, 430–433
Cityscape drawing
    background solid color, 495
    Cityscape_Perspective_Final.psd, 497
    grid line, 484, 485
    grid perspective, 485
    perspective grid planes, 483
    Pixel brush Dry media Soft chalk, 496, 497
    Pixel layers, 483, 493
    round opacity brush, 495, 496
    Ruler drawing aid, 486
    Square drawing aid, 481, 487–491
    Stencil Edit Button, 484
    Vertical Taskbar Precision panel, 481
Clipping mask, 569
Color chip, 233, 258, 276–278, 286, 288–290, 295, 304, 309
Comics, 77, 78
Comments tool, 331, 332
Copy paths, 588
Create GIF animations with motion layers
    Add clipping masks/layer masks, animation, 609–617
    add frame-by-frame layer motion and frame actions
        add content to frames, other layers, 556–563
        editing the frames, 563–569
        frame actions, 556
        layer select, 554

motion layer properties (frame by frame), 576
Timeline panel, 555
transforming frames, 570–576
backup and hidden, 552
configure motion settings, 617–622
frame animation using motion path/path actions
    create path layer, 577–581
    edit and transform the path, 582–588
    example, Fresco document with multiple motion layers, 599–609
    path effects (layer properties), 588–599
    Photoshop layers, 577
    Vector path, 576
Layer panel, 553
Layers and Layer properties panels, 552
Pixel and Vector layers, 553
Pixel layer
    Contextual Task bar, 553, 554
    Timeline, 553, 554
play all and pause animation to adjust the frames, 622–624
separate layers, 552
Vertical Taskbar layers, 552
Create new document, animation
    Digital custom size create, Web, 546, 547
    Home page, 546
    import and open, 547
    layers, 550
    Magic wand tool, 549, 551
    Motion layers, 547
    Print tab, preset documents, 546
    settings, 548, 549

    stationary layers (Pixel and Vector), 547
Creative Cloud Desktop, 499, 538
    Delete folder, 539, 541
    Download, 541, 542
Creative Cloud Library, 254, 261, 293, 543
    Capture app, 511
    Fresco document, 513
    Fresco Library, 515
    Graphic assets, 513, 514
    graphics_start.psd, 509
    Image layer, 515
    Libraries list, 512
    Photoshop document, 509
    Photoshop's Layers panel, 510
    Photoshop's Libraries panel, 511
    Photoshop's Shapes panel, 510
    Place tool Libraries, 513
Cropping artwork, 616
Custom Shapes.csh, 268
CustomShapes.psd, 265

D

Delete paths, 588
Distort tool, 200–202
Document timeline, 620, 621
Download Creative Cloud Desktop
    Adobe Photoshop warning message, 677
    Duplicate Image, 676
    Fresco files, 676
    import and open, 679
    Pixel layers/Adjustment layers, 678
    Smart Object layers, 677, 678
Drawing aids
    adjusting settings, 440
    circle, 430–433

Drawing aids (*cont.*)
  cityscape drawing (*see* Cityscape drawing)
  drawing creatures, 470–480
  geometric tile pattern creation (*see* Geometric tile pattern creation)
  grid and perspective lines, 440–453
  polygon, 435, 437–439
  ruler, 426–430
  square, 433–435
  vertical taskbar selection, 426
Drawing creatures
  Circle drawing, 477
  Circle drawing aid, 474
  Illustrator and Photoshop, 470
  Pixel brush, 478
  Pixel brush Basic Hard, 471–473
  Pixel layer, 479
  rounded diamonds, 475
  Spider_web_Final.psd, 480
  Spider_web_start.psd, 470
Dry media, 78, 80

E

Ellipse Selection tool, 563, 564
Elliptical selection, 246, 308
Eraser brushes, 67, 141
  adjust size, flow and smoothing, 144
  artists use, example, 141
  brush settings
    brush flow, 145
    brush size, 144
    Painting inside settings, 145
    similar to Pixel/ Vector brushes, 145–151
    smoothing, 145
  Toolbar Fresco Vector eraser brushes, 142
  use Pixel brush, 143, 144
Eraser tool Pixel eraser, 534
Export as, 626, 662–664
Export_Files, 683
Extensive layer masking, 529
Eyedropper tool, 286–289, 304, 309

F

farm_barn_final.psd, 536
farm_barn_start.jpg, 527
Files
  Creative Cloud Desktop, 48, 49
  downloading/deleting, 50, 51
  Photoshop, 49, 50
  store, 50
  uploading, 52, 53, 55
Filter Gallery of Sketch > Stamp, 528
FlowerPainting.psd, 193
Frame opacity, 568
Frames per second (FPS), 618
Freestyle path, 579
Fresco application, 62
  blank document, 62
  Creative Cloud Desktop setting, 62
Fresco Collection.cclibs library, 506
Fresco document, review working with layers
  additional layers, 399
    adjustment layer, 409, 411
    adjustment layer, brightness/contrast, 418
    adjustment layer, Hue/Saturation, 416–419
    artwork, 420
    blend mode, 419, 420

INDEX

cancel multiselect/select single layer, 408
contextual task bar, 406
duplicate copies into Pixel layers, 406, 407
duplicate layer/conversion, 404, 405
extract from image option, 402
layer mask action, 414, 415
layer properties panel, 409, 410
layers panel, 421, 422
load as selection, 405
masking, 412, 413
mask modifications, 416
modifications, 400, 401
multiple layer action, 407, 408
Pixel brush, 405, 406
rectangle selection tool, 411, 412
SeaCreaturesFresco.cclibs, 401
shadow, 420
shape layer, 401
shapes, 399, 400
shapes tool panel, 402, 403
sliding mask, 413, 414
stamped shapes to vector layers, 399
transform tool, 403, 404
artwork, 395
file, import and open, 394
previous layers
adding layers, 396
hiding layers, 396, 397
layer opacity, 397, 398
Photoshop background layer, 396
Pixel layer, 396
vector brushes, 396
Fresco Flower Graphics, 510
Fresco Flower Graphics.cclibs file, 515
Fresco layer warning message, 300
Fresco Settings panel menu, 532
Fresco Toolbar brush options, 302

G

Geometric tile pattern creation
changing colors, 461, 462
Drawing_Aids_Final.psd, 458, 469
graph grid, 460
Layer action, 464–467
Pixel brush, 459, 460
Polygon hexagon, 462, 463
Precision panel, 469
Ruler drawing aid, 464
shapes, 458
undo and redo keys, 463
GIF, 625, 627
GIF animations, 546, 637, 638
Graph, 442
graphics_movenent.ai, 517
graphics_start.psd, 509
Grid and perspective lines
displaying grids, 442–444, 446
snapping, 441, 442
Grid/Precision tool, 224

H

Hand-drawn artwork, 61
HSB slider, 288, 290, 291, 309

I, J, K

Illustrator, 3
Illustrator swatches
and Libraries panels, 293
Illustrator tools, 190–193

INDEX

Image layer, 504, 532, 533
Image_placement.psd, 515
InDesign, 681
InDesign CC Libraries panel, 275, 296, 297
InDesign document (.indd), 680
Invert mask, 613
Invite In, 675

L

Layer actions, 336, 337, 557
    add layer, 338
    clear layer, 338
    convert to pixel layer, 348
    copy layer, 343
    create empty mask, 345
    cut layer, 343
    delete layer, 339
    duplicate layer, 343
    hide/show all other layer, 338
    hide/show layer, 338
    load as selection, 344, 345
    lock layer, 347
    lock transparency, 346, 347
    mask layer contents, 346
    merge down, 347
    paste from clipboard, 339
    paste layer, 343, 344
    select multiple, 339–341
    set as reference, 346, 355
    touch shortcut, 341, 342
Layer and frame actions, Paste motion panel, 588
Layer masks, 614
Layer motion properties, path layers, 646–656
Layer opacity, 280, 281, 535
Layer panel
    fish and cat, fish bowl, 317, 318
    Illustrator, 316, 317
    Photoshop, 316, 317
    Vertical Taskbar, 322
Layer properties, 607
Layer properties panel, 588
    blend mode, 324, 325, 327, 329
    layer opacity, 327–329
    naming selected layer, 323, 324
    text, 329, 330
    vertical taskbar, 322, 323
Layers, 317
    adding layer (vector/pixel), 333
    appearance/adjustment layer (*see* Appearance/adjustment layer)
    appearances layer, 335, 336
    background layer, 318
    blank layer, 319
    clip layer, 334, 335
    dragged up and down, 322
    grouping layers, 352, 353
    hand tool, 316
    image layer, 320
    information, 370
    Layer panel, 317
    layer visible, 333, 334
    more layer options and actions, 336
    motion layer, 320
    multiple layers, 351
    Photoshop layer, 321
    pixel layer, 319
    reference layer, 353
        add layer, 355
        fill tool, 355
        Illustrator/Photoshop, 354
        information, 357
        layer actions, 355
        release reference, 356

INDEX

undo button, 356
text layers, 320, 349, 350
uses, 315
vector layer, 319, 320
Legacy brushes, 175
Lettering, 83, 84
Library brushes, 92, 93
Liquify tool, 205
    Bloat tool, 220, 221
    Pucker tool, 217-219
    Push left tool, 222-224
    Reconstruct tool, 210-212
    Smooth tool, 212-214
    and sub-tools, 206
    in the Transform workspace, 207
    Twirl tool, 214-217
    use pixel layer, 206
    Warp tool, 208-210
Live brushes, 67, 535
    adjust water flow and paint mix, 124
    brush settings, 123-127
    categories, 120
    oil, 121
    painting inside settings, 124
    paint knife and painted on canvas, 122
    properties, settings and changing colors, 122-127
    settings and Toolbar, 123
    watercolor, 120, 121
Load last selection tool, 250
Loop/Boomerang, 619

M

Magic wand tool, 240-243
Markers, 84, 85
Mask
    actions, 366
    creation, 357
    cut/copy/paste, 367, 368
    delete mask, 366
    density, 364, 365
    enabled and linked, 362, 364
    flattens, 369
    invert, 368, 369
    on layers, 370
    pixel brush, 359, 360
    red overlay, 369
    reveal/hide layer, 358, 359
    Selection tool/Contextual Task bar, 357, 358
    select multiple, 367
    shape/touch shortcut tools, 360, 361
    sliding, 370
    text layers, 364
Masking, 357
Mixer brushes, 85, 86, 165
Mixer-like brushes, 164
Motion brush, 578-581
Motion layer, 580, 588, 601, 610, 612, 653
Motion layer properties (frame by frame), 576
Motion settings, 650, 651
Move and Transform tool, 190-193, 570-572, 582, 585
    bounding box handles, 196
    Distort tool, 200-202
    exit and enter the workspace, 204
    Flip vertically and horizontally, 197, 198
    Illustrator tool, 190-192
    import and open, 194
    Liquify in Photoshop (*see* Liquify tool)
    nudge arrow keys, 194, 195
    nudge keys, 198
    perspective graph, 226

INDEX

Move and Transform tool (*cont.*)
    Perspective tool, 202, 203
    Photoshop tool, 190, 191
    Precision panel, 225, 226
    Selection tool, 191
    Skew tool, 199, 200
    sub-tools, 190
    Symmetry Grid and tool, 227
    Touch shortcut circle, 195–197
    Transform workspace, 193
    Transform workspace Cancel button, 204
    transform workspace sub-tools, 224
    Vertical Taskbar, 224, 225, 279, 310
MP4, 625, 627
Multicolor, 87, 88, 99, 100
Multicolor Eyedropper, 287
Multicolor swatch, 290, 291, 309
Multiselecting layers, 570

N

New document
    background color, 26
    create document button/new document X, 28
    creation, 18, 19
    exiting, 29
    orientation, 25
    pixel size, 25, 26
    presets
        digital tab, 21, 22
        print tab, 22, 23
        recent tab, 19, 20
        saved tab, 20, 21
        save/rename, 27
    print document, 26
    unit of measurement, 23, 24
    width and height/keypad numbers, 24, 25

O

Oil paint, 121
Oilpaint round brush, 534
Onion Skin, 619, 620

P

Paint Bucket tool, 251–253
Painting, 88, 89
Paint selection tool, 243, 244
Paste Motion Paths, 588
Path effects (layer properties)
    add multiple objects, 589
    add multiples, 590
    add multiples and Scatter using the sliders, 591
    align to path, 595, 596
    disable, rotate, 594
    disable the grow/shrink, 592
    fade in/out, 595
    frame actions, 595
    grow/shrink: allows, 591, 592
    Layer properties panel, 588
    motion layer, 588
    Motion settings, 598
    Scatter, 590
    speed options, 596
        ease in/out, 597
        frames and randomize, 597
    Spin, 593, 594
    Sway, 592, 593
    Timeline Contextual Task bar, 588
Path layer, 577–581

INDEX

Paths, 576
Pattern options, Share workspace
    capture custom patterns
        Libraries panel, 666
        Photoshop Layers panel, 666
    iPad version, 665
    leaf_capture_pattern.psd, 670
    Libraries panel, 667, 668
    Patterns Photoshop.cclibs, 670
    Photoshop Capture Extract, 667
    Photoshop's Patterns panel, 668
    rasterized into graphic asset, 669, 670
Pen stylus, 47
Pen tool, 263, 264
Perspective, 443
Perspective grid
    Change Perspective Plane, 456, 457
    Contextual Task bar, 455
    creation, 454
    Grids toggle, 457
    Shapes tools, 455
Perspective settings
    Edit Vanishing Points Button, 449–451
    Grid color wheel panel, 453
    precision area, 452
    vanishing points
        1 point, 446, 447
        2 point, 447
        3 point, 448, 449
Perspective tool, 202, 203
Photoshop, 2, 3, 545
Photoshop and Illustrator, 292
Photoshop layers, 529, 530, 538
Photoshop Layers panel, 266, 267
Photoshop layers, preserved, 29, 30
Photoshop Libraries panel, 269, 273, 294, 296
    with menu open, 188

Photoshop PSD (.psd), 663
Photoshop shapes
    access via Toolbar and Shapes panel, 262
    add custom shapes, 267
    create group name folder, 268
    custom shapes, 266
    custom shape tool, 263
    edit and select shapes, 263
    Image dialog box Close and Save, 272
    Image dialog box erase tool, 271
    Image dialog box Shape settings, 272
    Layers panel menu, 266
    Libraries panel, 268, 270
    Libraries panel with Capture Shapes added, 273
    paste shape, 265
    Path Selection tool, 267
    Pen tool, 263, 264
    shape layer, 262
    Shapes tab, 271
    use Options bar panel, 265
Photoshop swatches
    and Libraries panels, 292
Photoshop tools, 190, 191, 193
Pixel brushes, 67, 69, 564, 649, 650, 654
    add brush feature, 93, 94
    All and Recents tabs and their options, 98
    App settings icon and dialog box, 75
    basic category selected, 72
    Basic Hard round brush selected, 72
    brushes menu
        basic, 75, 76
        charcoal, 76, 77
        comics, 77, 78
        dry media, 78
        FX, 80, 82

INDEX

Pixel brushes (*cont.*)
    ink, 82, 83
    lettering, 83, 84
    Library brushes, 92, 93
    marker, 84, 85
    mixer brushes, 85, 86
    multicolor, 87, 88
    painting, 88, 89
    rakes, 89, 90
    sketching, 90–92
Brush flow, 101
Brush settings, 104–106
    Angle, 106, 107
    Blend modes, 115, 116
    Brushes panel, 118
    brush size, 106
    Color dynamics, 113, 114
    hardness, 106
    Manage pixel brushes, 119
    Mixing, 112, 113
    Pressure dynamics, 109
    Scattering, 110, 111
    Shape dynamics, 107, 108
    spacing, 106
    Stylus pressure, 117, 118
    Transfer, 111, 112
    Velocity dynamics, 109, 110
Brush size and painting, 101
Brush Size Pixels, 100
category list and subcategory selected, 70
color chip and various settings, 95, 96
color wheel setting, 97
dry media and various brush strokes, 80
HSB and RGB sliders, 98
manage pixel brushes, 74
multicolor swatches, and themes, 99

    older brushes, 81
    Painting inside settings, 103, 104
    pastel artwork, crayons and holder, 79
    recent subcategory list, 70, 71
    Smoothing, 102, 103
    use eyedropper, 97
    use paint palette, 95
Pixel brush tool, 181, 622
Pixel layers, 612, 622
Pixel Library brushes, 164
Place tool, 297
    tool options and CC libraries, 298
Placing and importing options
    color profile and mode conversion, 507, 508
    copying and pasting image, 517–519, 521
    Creative Cloud Library, 509–515
    rasterizing illustrator, 521–524
    Toolbar panel, 501
        camera, 501
        files, 502–505
        libraries, 505, 506
Play all icon, the Contextual Task bar, 622
Playback, 619, 627
Play once, 619
PNG sequence, 625, 628, 630
1 Point perspective, 446, 447
2 Point perspective, 447
3 Point perspective, 449
Polygon drawing aid, 435–439
Polygon selection tool, 248–250
Portable Document Format PDF (.pdf), 663, 664
Power plan info message, 28, 29
Precision panel
    options, 443, 444

Precision perspective grid, 500
Precision tool, 330, 331
Project idea, create basic animation
    Fresco, 656
    Fresco animation tools, 656
    Fresco Home page, 639
    racing car example, 639
    Spider animation example, 639, 645
        butterfly layers, butterfly motion layer frames, 642
        layer motion properties, path layers, 646–656
        stationary layer, 644
        spider animation, document settings, 646
        spider layers, 640
        web layers, web motion layer frames, 643
Publish and Export
    GIF, 625
    motion settings, 626–630
    Motion settings, 654
    MP4, 625
    PNG sequence, 625
    settings, MP4 video file, 655
    Share icon, 625
    Share Motion options, GIF/PNG sequence files, 628
    Share workspace, 626
    timelapse settings, 633–635
    Timeline panel, add more frames to improve motions, 631–633
Pucker tool, 217–219
Push left tool, 222–224

Q

Quick Export, 626, 661, 662, 671

R

Rakes, 89, 90
Real-world artist tools, 60
Recents color tab, 290
Reconstruct tool, 210–212
Rectangle selection tool, 245, 246
Rectangular Marquee selection tool, 175
RGB color mode, 531
RGB slider, 288
Ruler drawing aid, 426–430, 601, 602

S

Scalable Vector Graphic (SVG), 261
Seascape_final.psd, 659
Selection tools, 191
    brushes and selections on single layer, 302–315
    Contextual Task bar, 233, 565
        anti-alias, 240
        deselect, 236
        erase, 235
        hide selection/show selection, 236, 237
        invert selection, 238, 239
        Marching ants/Selection overlay, 239
        mask, 235
        pop-up menu, 236
        transform, 234
        transform selection, 237, 238
    ellipse selection, 246–248
    key commands, 251
    Lasso selection, 229, 230, 232
    Load last selection, 250
    Magic wand, 240–243
    paint selection, 243, 244

Selection tools (*cont.*)
 Pixel Layer for selection creation, 227
 polygonal selection, 248–250
 rectangle selection, 245, 246
 tools icon, 227, 228
 Transform workspace, 234
 use stencils, 228
Shape tools, 253
 on canvas, 255
 with Contextual Task bar, 257–260
 custom shapes, 257
 discover new shapes, 257
 import SVG from Photoshop, 261
 Library shapes, 256
 and panel, 254, 256
 and panel access, 261
 Photoshop shapes (*see* Photoshop shapes)
 real stamp, 254
 work in Photoshop to create shapes, 261
 work with default shapes, 254–257
Share Link, 674
Share workspace, 626, 628, 633
 Additional Share Options
  Fresco Share options list, 671
  Open a Copy for Illustrator Desktop, 671–673
  Quick Export, 671
  Share Link, 674
 Export As settings
  JPG, 663
  .pdf, 663, 664
  PNG, 662, 663
  .psd, 663
 Export File.jpg, 664, 665
 Fresco Save as dialog box options, 664
 Motion tabs, 665

Pattern Options, 665–670
Quick Export settings, 661, 662
Timelapse export, 633, 634, 665
Show paths as frames, 621
Single color Eyedropper, 286
Sketching, 90–92
Skew tool, 199, 200
Smooth tool, 212–214
Smudge brushes, 67, 144, 151
 and Blur tools, 153
 brush flow strength, 154
 brush size, 154
 and options for Pixel brushes, 152
 scattering, 157
 settings panel, 155
 shape dynamics, 156
 similar to Pixel brushes, 154–158
 size, strength and smoothing, 153, 154
 smoothing, 154
 stylus pressure setting, 158
 tortillons and blending stumps, 151
 transfer, 157, 158
Snapping, 441, 442
Square drawing aid, 433–435
Stamp filter, 529
Symmetry Grid, 227

T, U

Text layers, 617
Text tool, 276
 Blend mode, 280
 color chip, 276
 create Vertical Type, 284, 285
 Hide and Show Keyboard options, 279
 Layer opacity, 280, 281
 Layer properties panel, 279, 280
 Style text, 278

Text alignment settings buttons, 284
Text caps settings buttons, 283
text color, use color chip, 277, 278
text from Text layer on canvas, 277
Text layer, 276
Text letter spacing settings, 283
Text line spacing settings, 282
Text option buttons, 284
Text properties, 281
Text size settings, 282
troubleshooting missing fonts, 286
Timelapse export, 626, 633, 634
Timelapse settings, 635
Timelapse video settings, 635
Timeline Contextual Task bar, 570, 574
Title bar menu, 32
    app settings button, 45, 46
    exiting file, 48
    full screen, 46
    help menu options, 35, 36
        browse tutorials, 36
        help resources, 40
        icons, 40
        keyboard shortcuts, 39
        primary touch shortcut circle and ring, 38, 39
        top shortcut map, 37, 38
        view gestures, 36, 37
    renaming file, 33
    saving file, 34
    settings menu
        canvas size, change, 41, 42
        options, 40, 41
        touch shortcut, 44
        transform workspace area, 42, 43
    undo/redo icons, 35
    zoom settings, 34
Toolbar panel, 63, 65
    disabled Touch shortcut and blank canvas, 63
    Photoshop *vs.* Illustrator *vs.* Fresco toolbar, 65
    Setting menu and App settings dialog box, 63, 64
    taskbar and active layers, 66
Touch screen devices, 47
Touch shortcut circle, 195-197, 200-202, 210, 215-219, 221, 223, 232, 243, 245, 247, 249, 252, 258
Transform layer/frame, 583
Transform options, 502
Transform Paths, 586
Transform tool selection, 234
Transform workspace, 504, 505, 527, 528, 558, 572-574, 584, 585, 587, 604, 616
Twirl tool, 214-217

V

Vector brushes, 67, 127, 578-581
    brush settings, 132
        brush size, 132
        Manage vector brushes, 139
        painting inside setting, 133
        shape and outline, 137
        similar to Pixel brushes, 133-135
        smoothing, 133
        Stylus pressure button, 138, 139
        tilt and rotation, 138
        velocity dynamics, 136
    style categories, 128
        Basic, 129
        Jitter, 129, 130
        Manga, 130
        Outline, 130, 131

INDEX

Vector brushes (*cont.*)
    Toolbar brushes and categories, 128
    Touch Shortcut map
        options, 140
    use secondary chip and color wheel,
        131, 132
Vector path, 576

vector_test.psd, 525
Video Applications, 681

W, X, Y, Z

Warp tool, 208–210
Watercolor paints, 120, 121

GPSR Compliance

The European Union's (EU) General Product Safety Regulation (GPSR) is a set of rules that requires consumer products to be safe and our obligations to ensure this.

If you have any concerns about our products, you can contact us on

ProductSafety@springernature.com

In case Publisher is established outside the EU, the EU authorized representative is:

Springer Nature Customer Service Center GmbH
Europaplatz 3
69115 Heidelberg, Germany